The Port Jews of Habsburg Trieste
Absolutist Politics and Enlightenment Culture

Stanford Studies in Jewish History and Culture
Edited by Aron Rodrigue and Steven J. Zipperstein

The Port Jews of Habsburg Trieste

Absolutist Politics and Enlightenment Culture

Lois C. Dubin

Stanford University Press
Stanford, California

Stanford University Press
Stanford, California
© 1999 by the Board of Trustees
of the Leland Stanford Junior University

CIP data appear at the end of the book

To my family

Acknowledgments

It is a pleasure to express my gratitude to those who have aided me in this study, and I ask the indulgence of anyone whose name I may have inadvertently omitted.

I began my research on the Jews of Trieste several years ago under the guidance of Yosef Hayim Yerushalmi and the late Isadore Twersky, who co-supervised my Harvard University doctoral dissertation. I consider it a privilege to have studied Jewish history and thought with them. I am grateful to each for his inspiring and unique model of scholarly excellence, and to both for the constancy of their demanding guidance. I also thank Yosef Hayim Yerushalmi for suggesting such a delightful intellectual home as Trieste and northern Italy.

As this work developed through dissertation to book, many people contributed in vital ways. I thank Howard Adelman, Israel Bartal, Robert Bonfil, Benjamin Braude, the late Robert Cohen, Stanley Elkins, David Fishman, Aron Rodrigue, and Michael Silber for their invaluable critical readings of the entire manuscript at different stages. I have also benefited from the insights and encouragement of David Myers, David Sorkin, and Steven Zipperstein. I deeply appreciate the gracious help and friendly support all have provided.

I am pleased to acknowledge the advice and assistance offered by several other colleagues and friends at different moments along the way: Orietta Altieri, Anna Botta, Ernest Benz, Paolo Bernardini, Robert Bufalini, Daniel Carpi, Tullia Catalan, Marina Cattaruzza, Giulio Cervani, Vittore Colorni, Ronald Coons, Bernard Cooperman, Lorenzo Cremonesi, Maddalena Del

Bianco Cotrozzi, Ugo Cova, Eva Faber, Richard Fish, Anna Foa, Carlo Gatti, Yosef Hacker, Dov HaKohen, Pier Cesare Ioly Zorattini, Yosef Kaplan, the late Jacob Katz, Erna Kelley, Jeremy King, Grete Klingenstein, Carol Herselle Krinsky, Miriam Levy, Klaus Lohrmann, Gadi Luzzatto Voghera, Giuseppe Minera, Claudia Prestel, Quentin Quesnell, Ada Rapaport-Albert, Elia Richetti, Marsha Rozenblit, David Ruderman, Renata Segre, Shlomo Simonsohn, Renato Spiegel, the late Mario Stock, Kenneth Stow, Franz Szabo, Ariel Toaff, Nikolaus Vielmetti, Klemens von Klemperer, Jeff Weintraub, James Weiss, and Nathan Wiesenfeld. I of course take responsibility for remaining errors and shortcomings.

I am indebted to the directors and staffs of the archives and libraries who so readily and graciously provided materials for my research: Archives Nationales, Paris; Archivio di Stato di Trieste; Biblioteca Civica, Trieste; the British Library; Central Archives for the History of the Jewish People, Jerusalem; Columbia University Libraries; La Comunità Israelitica di Trieste; Harvard College Library; Haus-, Hof-, und Staatsarchiv, and Hofkammerarchiv of the Österreichisches Staatsarchiv, Vienna; Hebrew Union College, Cincinnati; Hebrew Union College—Jewish Institute of Religion, New York; Centro di studi sull'Ebraismo Italiano, Jerusalem; Jewish National and University Library, Jerusalem; and Jewish Theological Seminary of America, New York.

I gratefully acknowledge those who helped fund my graduate studies and the subsequent research required for this book: the American Council of Learned Societies; Harvard University Center for Jewish Studies; Imperial Oil of Canada; Memorial Foundation for Jewish Culture; Quebec Government Ministry of Education; Social Sciences and Humanities Research Council of Canada; and Yad HaNadiv/Barecha Foundation. The Institute for Advanced Studies at the Hebrew University kindly granted me use of its facilities while I was a Yad HaNadiv Fellow in Jerusalem. At different stages of my work on this book, I was fortunate to serve on the faculties and enjoy the resources of Yale University, Hebrew College Boston, and Smith College. For many years now, I have benefited in manifold ways from my colleagues and friends at Smith College. I wish to thank the staff of the Interlibrary Loan department of Neilson Library, who worked prodigiously to obtain distant materials for me; and the Jean Picker Fellowships, the Setlow Family Fund in Jewish Studies, and the Committee on Faculty Compensation and Development, for their financial support.

I owe special thanks to my editors, Stacey Lynn and Sherry Wert, who skillfully and patiently guided this manuscript through copyediting to final production; and to Nicholas Read, who generously volunteered his artistic and map-making talents.

Finally, I scarcely have the words to express my gratitude to my family, whose love, faith, and patience have sustained me: my parents Shirley and Harry Dubin, my late in-laws Pearl and William Braude, my husband Benjamin Braude, and my children Rachel Sara and Naomi Ora. Having enriched and gladdened me beyond measure, my daughters have been part of this endeavor in more ways than they can imagine. Ben—my husband, colleague, and friend—knows that without him, this book would not be. To all three generations, I dedicate this book.

Contents

	Introduction	1
1	Foundations of the Free Port and the Jewish Community in the Eighteenth Century	10
2	Maria Theresa and the Legal Status of the Jews of Trieste: The Privileges of 1771	41
3	Joseph's Toleration Policy in Trieste, 1781–82	64
4	Civic Enlightenment as Cultural Policy: Language and the *Scuola Pia Normale sive Talmud Torà*	95
5	Trieste and the Haskalah	118
6	A Decade of Civil Toleration: New Rights and Duties in the 1780s	138
7	The Jewish Community: Public Order, Piety, and Authority	155
8	The Habsburg Marriage Reforms: Challenges to Religious-Communal Authority	174
9	Conclusion: Civil Inclusion of a Port Jewry in a Reforming Absolutist State	198
	Abbreviations	229
	Notes	231
	Bibliography	293
	Index	321

Illustrations follow page 154

The Port Jews of Habsburg Trieste
Absolutist Politics and Enlightenment Culture

MAP 1. Central Europe and the Adriatic in the late eighteenth century. Habsburg lands are shown in light gray. Map courtesy of Nicholas Read.

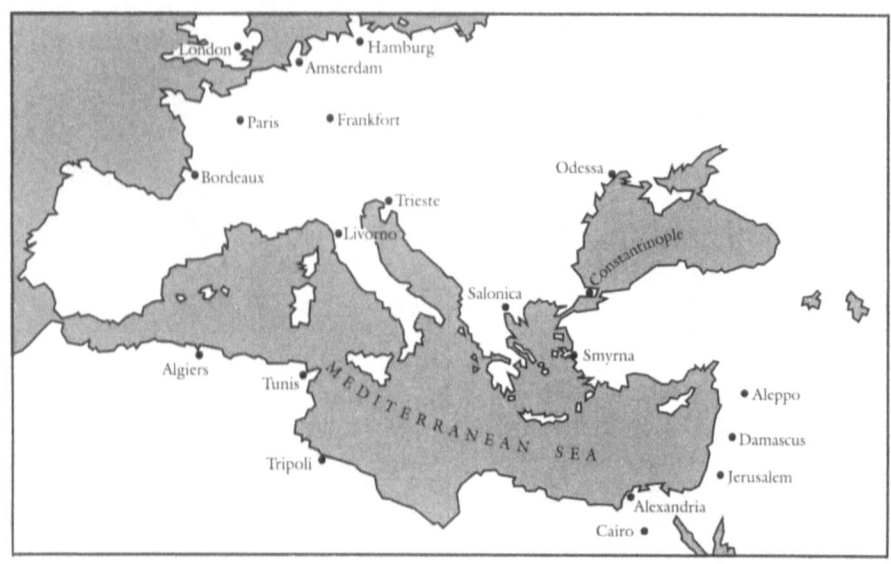

MAP 2. Europe and the Mediterranean Basin. Map courtesy of Nicholas Read.

Introduction

A Trieste composta in una sua strana unità,
c'era l'Austria, c'era Italia, c'era la Balcania,
c'era l'Oriente vicino.

Comprised in a strange unity of its own at Trieste,
there was Austria, there was Italy, there were the Balkans,
there was the Near East.
—Umberto Saba

The northern Adriatic city of Trieste has played many roles in recent centuries: free port of the Habsburg Monarchy and its outlet to the sea; economic rival and successor to Venice; major European commercial, shipping, and insurance center; the Italian southernmost outpost of *Mitteleuropa*; transmitter of literary modernism and psychoanalysis from the imperial metropolis Vienna to Italy; home of Italo Svevo and, for a time, James Joyce; object of Italian irredentist desires; flashpoint of nationalist tensions between Italians and Slavs; symbol of Cold War rivalry and the southern end of the Iron Curtain, immortalized in Winston Churchill's famous speech.[1] Situated on the frontiers of the Latin, German, and Slavic worlds, this dynamic city functioned from the late eighteenth century until the demise of the Austro-Hungarian Empire at the end of World War I as a transit point for, crossroads of, and mediator between central Europe in the north, Italy and the Adriatic in the south, and the Balkans and the Levant in the east. During its heyday, Trieste was a bustling hub for immigrants, a cosmopolitan center that attracted diverse non-Catholic religious-ethnic minorities: Jews, Greek and Serbian Orthodox, Protestants, and Armenians. Welcomed as individuals and as communities for the purpose of commercial development, in due course these minorities came to play prominent cultural and political roles as well.

Modern Trieste has been treated by Triestine, Italian, and Habsburg historians. The purpose of this book is to set this unusual Habsburg city within Jewish history: to investigate its Jewish community in the eighteenth century, the formative period for both the modern port city and its minority communities, and to see it as a case study of the changing roles of Jews in early modern and modern Europe. This study explores and analyzes the beginnings of the inclusion of Jews in the modern European civic realm: of the broad processes whereby Jews began to acquire civil and ultimately political rights, and the accompanying transformations of culture and identity out of which modern Judaism as a voluntaristic confession emerged. Simultaneously, it is a study from the local Triestine perspective, of the growth of the modern port city and of one of the important constituent elements in its diverse multi-ethnic commercial elite;[2] and from the Habsburg perspective, of mercantile and confessional politics in the age of absolutist state-building and the Enlightenment.

These subjects comprise many strange unities. First, there are the strange unities of place caused by Trieste's frontier location. In *Trieste: Un'identità di frontiera*, Angelo Ara and Claudio Magris highlight the indeterminate identity of the city, and the uncertainties and anxieties bred by the multiple identities of its inhabitants.[3] Multiplicity was fostered by the locations of Trieste itself, of Habsburg northern Italy, and of the monarchy as a whole. Habsburg northern Italy, the southernmost part of the monarchy's Hereditary Lands, was located "on the border between Germany (*Ashkenaz*) and Italy (*Italyah*)," as Elia Morpurgo, an eighteenth-century Jewish leader from nearby Gradisca, put it.[4] In the eighteenth century, Trieste was politically Habsburg, as it had been since 1382, but by location and culture it was more Italian. Writ large, the Habsburg Monarchy itself combined Germanic and Italian aspects, and was greatly influenced by reforming currents from both directions: cameralism and natural-law traditions from Germany, and Catholic reform from Italy. Thus, although this central European realm was often seen as a buffer between western and eastern Europe, it was also in fact a mediating point between north and south. This "multinational, multiconfessional, multicultural, and multiconstitutional" realm was a mediator between external regions, and within itself, between many diverse components.[5] Indeed, on the very frontier, Trieste embodied mediation of north and south, east and west, in an especially obvious and acute way. And like the monarchy as a whole, but in its own particular way, it embodied multiplicity and diversity.

In Jewish history, Italy has long occupied a central mediating position as a crossroad between different Jewries of Europe, the Mediterranean, the Near East, and North Africa.[6] In the eighteenth-century Free Port of Trieste, the cosmopolitan Jewish community had wide-ranging personal and commercial ties and broad cultural horizons. The original Ashkenazic Jews of Trieste were joined by Sefardim and by Levantine Jews. Of diverse origins, the immigrants came mostly from the Italian peninsula, but also from

Vienna, Prague, and Hamburg in the north, and the Balkans and the Ottoman Empire in the east. Though the dominant cultural tradition of Triestine Jewry was Italian, Habsburg rule forced the community's gaze also northward, eastward, and indeed southeastward, toward the predominantly Ashkenazic Jewries of Vienna, Bohemia, Moravia, Galicia, and Hungary.

Chronology and periodization provide another strange unity in the study of eighteenth-century Triestine Jewry. For it combines the characteristic features of two phases of Jewish history usually considered distinct: (1) the early modern period, from the late sixteenth through the seventeenth century, in which raison d'état and mercantilism were responsible for the admission of Jews into many areas from which they had previously been expelled or in which they had never lived at all;[7] and (2) the eighteenth century, in which Enlightenment ideologies and centralizing absolutist regimes began to integrate Jews within the human family and civic framework, and opened the way toward civil improvement, the end of separate corporate Jewish existence, and eventual equality.

Declared a free port by Charles VI in 1719, Trieste represents a late example of early modern European rulers' invitations to Jews (or sometimes crypto-Jews, known simply as Portuguese) along with other merchants to develop the commercial potentials of particular locales. Livorno is the best-known such case, but there were others, including Amsterdam, Bordeaux, Glückstadt, Hamburg, and London. Reputed Jewish commercial success in the Ottoman Empire was the catalyst for changing the image of the Jew in early modern Europe from medieval usurer to captain of international trade and valued economic asset.[8] Later in the eighteenth century, Trieste was receptive to the ideologies of Enlightenment and its Jewish variant, Haskalah, and, ruled directly from Vienna by means of novel institutions, it proved an especially fertile ground for the reforming zeal of Habsburg absolutism.[9]

Thus, eighteenth-century Trieste was on the cusp of the early modern mercantilist era and the transitional era of Enlightenment and absolutism in which Jewish hopes for civil equality first arose. The two trends were intertwined: the settlement of Jews for practical commercial motives, and the restructuring of Jewish life and aspirations according to new cultural and political prescriptions. Because of the simultaneity of mercantilist raison d'état with Enlightenment innovation and reforming absolutism, eighteenth-century Trieste affords insight into the relationship between the older concept of Jewish utility and the later ones of civil improvement, civil inclusion, and Jewish regeneration.

Accordingly, study of this particular port Jewry[10] in the eighteenth century allows us to examine the interplay of economic change, the absolutist state, and the Enlightenment in creating new opportunities for European

Jews and in spurring cultural adjustments. Each has been singled out by a leading twentieth-century Jewish historian as a major factor in the emergence of a new world for European Jews in the seventeenth and eighteenth centuries. Salo Baron emphasized the expanding economic opportunities for Jews, Shmuel Ettinger the intervention of the centralizing absolutist state, and Jacob Katz the effects of rationalist Enlightenment ideologies, both Gentile and Jewish.[11]

In the early modern period, the rise of capitalism and of international trade between the Old and New Worlds created new economic possibilities for Jews and new images of them. In Amsterdam, London, Bordeaux, Livorno, Hamburg, and the Dutch and British colonies in the New World, Sefardic merchants engaged in international wholesale trade were considered important contributors to these ports' vital activities. Whether openly or tacitly acknowledged as Jews or crypto-Jews, they were generally seen as not significantly different from other merchants in economic or cultural behavior.

In Trieste, the state itself was a prime agent throughout the drama of the free port, creating it by executive fiat, and inviting merchants and artisans of almost any nationality or religion to establish and develop it. Administratively, the free port was made directly dependent upon central institutions in Vienna. Its commercial raison d'être and its cosmopolitan mercantile class were designed and engineered by the absolutist state, which used the standard coin of the realm: general patents, which publicly announced intended programs, and privileges, which granted specific liberties and exemptions (or rights, in a later language) to particular groups or individuals. Patents and privileges provided the legal base for the unusual policy of promoting a religiously diverse reality in Trieste, a reality self-consciously recognized as exceptional by central policy-makers.

Yet while absolutist rulers always found it lucrative to deal in privileges—recipients normally paid dearly for them—they also found that a welter of varying particular privileges did not serve the cause of centralizing and strengthening the state. Thus, in the late eighteenth century, these rulers became increasingly reluctant to grant particular corporate privileges, and they gradually started to inch toward more general laws and forms of status. This process can be seen at work in Trieste. The status of the Jewish community of Trieste was forged by a series of privileges in the seventeenth and eighteenth centuries. Then, in 1781–82, the community faced the general policy of Toleration enunciated in Joseph II's edicts, which drew partly, as did many absolutist reform initiatives, upon the Enlightenment. Joseph's Toleration program represented for most Habsburg Jewries a new degree of civil acceptance and new opportunities, but also, at the same time, brought demands for wide-ranging changes in the patterns and structures of Jewish life. In Trieste, however, it was applied to a situation that had been ab initio structured by patent and privilege to be exceptional. Its application raised in acute form the question of the relationship between particular privileges and general laws.

The Enlightenment was, of course, a movement of high culture, forged by intellectuals who wrote treatises on a broad array of philosophical, cultural, social, and political subjects and who developed reason, nature, utility, and common humanity as key themes. Of the greatest significance for Jews were the ideas of humanity and the secular state: that the Jews shared—at least potentially—in a universally common humanity, though their many differences from others might temporarily obscure that fact, and that states ought to be seen in secular terms as civic commonwealths and ought to tolerate religious diversity. These two principles were indispensable for the civil inclusion of Jews in modern European states. But the promise of inclusion on the basis of rationalist universalist norms was not easily or smoothly realized. Necessary conditions were not in and of themselves sufficient. Trieste offers an unusual example in which to examine the working-out of these two important premises in a concrete setting.

Recent scholarship has treated most *philosophes*, *Aufklärer*, or *maskilim* (Jewish Enlighteners) as *engagés* who sought to implement their programs, and thus the Enlightenment has come to mean not only abstract ideas and values, but also the diffusion and practical influence of those ideas and values upon society and government. Thus, in this work, I consider the Enlightenment as both a cultural force and a political one: as a generally rationalist and critical climate of opinion, and as an important impetus to absolutist rulers' programs to modernize and reform their societies from above. There were many motives and forces influencing eighteenth-century reforming rulers; that the Enlightenment was among them is undeniable. Enlightenment working in tandem with practical state-building helped produce reforming absolutism.[12] Though the concept of enlightened absolutism has undergone many changes and has moved in and out of historiographical fashion, I consider it—as well as reforming absolutism—a useful term to designate the reforming efforts or regimes of eighteenth-century rulers who tried to improve the welfare of their subjects and rationalize their realms in accord with what they considered the intellectual and moral advances of their day. To many in his own time and later, the Habsburg monarch Joseph II exemplified enlightened absolutism.[13]

Study of the modern Jewish community of Trieste affords a fresh perspective on the decisive economic, political, and cultural processes that transformed Jews and Judaism in the seventeenth and eighteenth centuries. It also provides an unusual vantage point on two significant historical phenomena oft-discussed in Jewish history: Joseph II's Toleration edicts, and the Haskalah, or Jewish Enlightenment. These have seldom been approached by way of northern Italy, though indeed, the Jews of Trieste were more involved with both than is usually recognized.[14] By highlighting the interplay of Italian Jewish traditions and realities with central European policies and ideologies, the view from Trieste provides an example of Italian Jewry grappling with the challenges of modernity, a perspective that until recently has been generally missing in modern Jewish historiography.[15] Within Italian Jewish history itself, this work focuses upon the eighteenth century, which is often bypassed in favor of the Renaissance, the Risorgimento, or fascism.[16] One of the two places on the Italian peninsula with the most favorable status for Jews in the eighteenth century (Livorno in Tuscany was the other), Trieste grew in the course of the nineteenth century to become one of the largest Italian Jewish communities. Studying Triestine Jewry in the eighteenth century tells us something about Italian Jewish responses to modernity, and reveals—often by contrast—some of the distinctive features of the central European processes with which it was involved. Connected to the Ashkenazic experience yet distinct from it, the Italian experience also informs us about Mediterranean and Sefardic responses to modernity, another relatively neglected subject.[17]

One of the aims of this book is to show that the study of Triestine Jewry in the eighteenth century can help us better understand the broad cultural and political processes often conveniently called Haskalah and Emancipation, and in fact can help us contextualize these latter more precisely. It can free us from our familiar fixations upon Berlin and Haskalah when we consider cultural adaptation, and upon Paris and formal legal emancipation when we consider civil inclusion and political improvement. In different ways, the work of other scholars has implied decentering Berlin and Paris as commonly understood. For example, Azriel Shohet, Todd Endelman, Steven Zipperstein, and Steven Lowenstein have urged greater attention to nonideological cultural and social change. Baron long ago stressed that legal emancipation was not necessarily either the most secure road to Jewish rights and equality or the best instrument for measuring them. Shmuel Feiner and David Sorkin have called for greater care in delineating the specific contours of the Jewish Enlightenment, even in Germany.[18] What I am suggesting is that for understanding the changing situation and self-understanding of Jews in the seventeenth and eighteenth centuries, we need a tale not of two cities, Berlin and Paris, but one that includes a third city, Trieste, or perhaps a third and fourth city in tandem: Trieste and Vienna.

A look at Trieste-Vienna allows us to examine the process of change in a reforming absolutist state whose agenda included improving the lot of its Jewish subjects. Let us remember that the vast majority of European Jews lived under absolutist regimes well into the nineteenth century, and some, such as the Russian Jews, even into the twentieth. The French Revolution in general and its pronouncement of Jewish Emancipation in particular—equal rights and duties for Jewish citizens in a democratic state—have blinded us with their drama and clarity. They have thereby made it difficult for those following in its wake, including twentieth-century historians, to focus upon prerevolutionary eighteenth-century Europe, and to grasp the processes and potential for change affecting Jews in the absolutist-corporate-estates world of the ancien régime.

The status of Jews in absolutist states, such as the Habsburg Monarchy, Prussia, and Russia, and various efforts at change in the 1770s and 1780s have received some attention, but by and large, the assumption in Jewish historiography has been that the rulers of these states—Joseph II, Frederick the Great, and Catherine the Great—did either too little or too much. In other words, they either failed to change things sufficiently in order to improve the real living conditions of Jews, especially the poor, or they interfered too much with the formerly autonomous self-governing Jewish communities. Usually the efforts of these monarchs and regimes have been faulted for not bringing about a true equality for Jews, for leaving in place too many restrictions, for being too gradualist or unrealistic with regard to the problems of their Jewish populations, or for being motivated still by anti-Jewish prejudice mingled with a purely utilitarian, as opposed to humanitarian, conception of the Jews.[19] Yet it is anachronistic to fault these rulers for not ushering in the French Revolution. We, the late-twentieth-century heirs to the world created by that democratic upheaval, do have difficulty in imagining the world of the Old Regime, and in appreciating that people in the eighteenth century were not anticipating or waiting for the French Revolution and Jewish Emancipation to happen. Their aspirations and efforts should not be read backward from later developments, but rather as they unfolded in their own evolving contexts. In recent French historiography, the Old Regime has received much more nuanced treatment as the relationship between the Old Regime and the French Revolution has been probed anew, and a triumphalist teleological reading of the revolution has been dampened.[20] It is my contention that the same kind of process needs to take place in Jewish historiography: not a debunking of the French Revolution and its truly innovative granting of political emancipation and civic equality for Jews, but rather a reexamination of the dynamics of change—socioeconomic, cultural, but above all legal and political—within the Old Regime.

In general, there is no better place than the Habsburg Monarchy for observing eighteenth-century reforming absolutism in action. Joseph II (co-regent 1765–80; sole ruler 1780–90) followed in the footsteps of his mother

Maria Theresa (r. 1740–80) in many important ways, and pursued a truly radical, progressive, and ambitious plan of reform. Their determination to forge a unitary state that could compete against their thriving archrival Prussia produced a revolution from above that entailed a wide-ranging series of measures to transform the social, economic, religious, and educational fabric of their society, and to release the productive potential of all their subjects—including Jews. In the recent judgments of two Habsburg historians, H. Scott and Franz Szabo, "Maria Theresa and Joseph II presided over the most radical series of reforms anywhere in Europe,"[21] and "by the 1780s the Habsburg Monarchy had become the locus of the boldest and most ambitious innovations in Europe."[22] As Grete Klingenstein has argued, the monarchy is the place to examine evolutionary rather than revolutionary patterns of change: "Theorists of evolution, not of revolution, therefore may consider the Habsburg Monarchy their paradigm."[23]

For Jewish history in particular, the Habsburg Monarchy provides an important venue for the study of reforming absolutism. As a result of the late-eighteenth-century partitions of Poland, and especially the first one in 1772, which made Galicia a Habsburg province, the Habsburg Monarchy contained the largest Jewish population in Europe west of the Russian Empire, and this population comprised central and eastern European, northern and southern Jewries. When put on the map of eighteenth-century Jewish history, Vienna shows the centralizing interventionist tutelary absolutist state at work, and Trieste shows it operating in the fertile ground of a commercial port city whose new institutions it had fashioned and in which significant portions of the population, including Jews, were receptive to Vienna's designs. Though the Triestine Jewish experience of Enlightenment and reforming absolutism differed from that of other Habsburg Jewish communities, all of which were in fact quite diverse from one another, its example is critical for analyzing Habsburg reformist theory and practice with regard to the Jews. Eighteenth-century Trieste, like the Habsburg Monarchy in general, is crucial for the attempt to understand what civil improvement could mean in an absolutist corporatist polity proceeding in an evolutionary, rather than a revolutionary, fashion.[24] And because of its strange unities of place, Trieste provides an example that is both central European and Italian.

To study port Jews, absolutist politics, and the Enlightenment in eighteenth-century Trieste, I use a wide range of archival as well as literary sources. The most important archives are those of the Jewish community in Trieste (mostly in Italian), of the local Habsburg administration in Trieste (in Italian and German), and of the organs of the central administration in Vienna (primarily in German). Literary sources are mostly in Italian, Hebrew, and German. This range of material permits a study of Habsburg absolutism in action: the dynamics of interaction between center and periphery; the making of policy through consultation between the Crown and bureaucracy in Vienna with the local government in Trieste and, in turn, the interaction of the Jewish community and other local forces with the authorities in Trieste and Vienna; and the reception of policy by a group of subjects, the Jewish community of Trieste, and their concerted efforts to affect policy—in other words, their role as political agents as well as recipients of action from above.[25] All of these help provide a fuller picture of Habsburg absolutism, and of reforming absolutism and Jews in general. Given the fact that cosmopolitan diversity was structured in the port city from its inception, Trieste allows an unusual vantage point on the question of continuity or rupture between the reigns of Maria Theresa and Joseph, and especially on the question of religious toleration, an issue on which the two rulers are usually—and mostly correctly—depicted as diverging completely.

The realities of eighteenth-century Trieste—a port city, a mercantile class composed of privileged minority communities, a reforming absolutist state, a climate imbued with Enlightenment, a predominantly Italian Jewish cultural tradition—made for a distinctive mix. In Chapters One through Eight, I consider the foundations of the free port in the eighteenth century and its Jewish community, the economic role of Triestine Jewry, its legal status through Theresian privilege and the Josephinian Toleration policy, its cultural engagement with Jewish Enlightenment, and Jewish communal religious life and its relation to the absolutist state.

In the concluding Chapter Nine, this study provides new material for addressing more general questions about modern European Jewish history: In which conditions could the Enlightenment's rationalist universalist inclusion of Jews be realized? What kind of Jewry was receptive to the Haskalah? What paths other than ideological Haskalah led to Jewish acculturation to surroundings? How did Jews respond to the centralizing integrating programs of absolutist states? What kinds of liberty and equality could an absolutist corporate state allow Jews? Introducing the concept of port Jews in the exploration of these issues allows for reconsideration of Jewish politics and culture in Old Regime Europe, and thereby a new perspective on modern Jewish history generally.

CHAPTER ONE

Foundations of the Free Port and the Jewish Community in the Eighteenth Century

> In the shade of the caduceus of Mercury and of the trident of Neptune.
> —Charles-Albert Comte de Moré

Nestled on the Carso mountain range and spreading in an arc down to the Adriatic Sea, Trieste has historically fallen within the spheres of influence of both landlocked Vienna and maritime Venice. A meeting point of the Latin, German, and Slavic worlds, it has stood at a crossroads of central Europe and the Levant. But until the eighteenth century, Trieste was a small and sleepy town, its life dominated by local patriciate and clergy, and its three to five thousand inhabitants engaged in trading local products, such as salt, wine, oil, and fish. Its geographic potential was exploited only in the second half of the eighteenth century, when the Habsburg Adriatic freeports policy was effectively realized. The destruction of the city's old walls around 1750 symbolized the dramatic change of its horizons. By the last decades of the eighteenth century, Trieste's world had expanded to include the Italian peninsula, central Europe, the Balkans, the Levant, even the Far East and America. By that time, it had become a cosmopolitan city of some twenty-five to thirty thousand; the major Habsburg port, its "jewel"[1] on the Adriatic; and one of Europe's important commercial centers. It was this transformation that created the conditions for a flourishing Jewish community in Trieste from the mid-eighteenth until the early twentieth century.

The Habsburg Free Port on the Adriatic

Trieste became a Habsburg domain in the late fourteenth century, when it turned to Vienna for protection in order to resist domination by Venice.

Over the next few centuries, it was governed as a separate administrative unit and maintained a strong sense of itself as an autonomous commune. In the early years of Charles VI's reign (r. 1711–40), the Adriatic Sea, Trieste, and the entire Austrian and Croatian Littoral became significant in the light of Vienna's new vision of the monarchy as a major maritime commercial power. Also fueling this aim were the declining fortunes of Venice, the opening of commercial relations with the Ottoman Empire after the Treaty of Passarowitz (1718), which sealed Habsburg victories and gains in the Balkans, the Low Countries, and the Italian peninsula. The creation in 1717–18 of commerce councils in Inner Austria and Vienna reflected the new mercantilist orientation and the desire to forge the far-flung Habsburg possessions into an economically unified entity. Toward these ends, it would be necessary to stimulate domestic manufacturing; to build interconnected networks of manufacture, transportation, and export; and to develop an Adriatic port (or ports) to serve as an entry point for raw materials and as an outlet for the export of manufactured goods.[2]

In 1717, Charles VI challenged Venetian control of maritime commerce by unilaterally declaring freedom of navigation in the Adriatic. Now the idea of a free port in Trieste, first raised in the 1660s by the Oriental Trading Company, made sense.[3] Charles VI designated both Trieste and Fiume as "temporary free ports" with the Patent of March 18, 1719, and further elaborated the terms of that status with patents in November and December 1725. Essentially, normal tariffs would not apply on the import, export, and exchange of goods entering these ports by sea. Persons of "any nation, condition, and religion" were invited to settle and trade in these towns, and were promised immunity from crimes committed elsewhere and protection against attack or hindrance on sea and on land.[4] These were the essential principles, notwithstanding subsequent modification of their precise terms and the areas included within the free zones.

But more than sovereign fiat was needed to make the new Adriatic policy a success, and the poor backwater Trieste into a flourishing center of international commerce.[5] Transformation was slow. In Vienna, political will and experience had to be developed in order to translate commercial dreams into effective administrative and economic realities. During Maria Theresa's reign in particular, repeated efforts were made to reorganize the unwieldy administration of the monarchy and to create bureaucratic entities and channels fitting for an aspiring great power. Uncertainties at the center affected the implementation of the free-ports policy on the periphery. Despite Trieste's "felicitous location at the central point on the boundaries between Italy and Germany" and its qualification as a good "gateway from Germany," there were many false commercial starts and administrative experiments before Trieste, rather than the entire Littoral, became the prime focus of attention.[6] The institutional history of the entire Littoral, of the free ports, and of the city of Trieste, as well as the relations between these entities and other administrative bodies, is exceedingly complex. A few administrative facts emerge as salient.

In Trieste, Vienna sought to manage the free zone directly, independent of the municipal commune, which was enclosed by the old city walls. Developed outside those walls, the free port, its marketplace, and its merchants were excluded from local jurisdiction and subject to a new authority. Drawing upon the French Intendancy model, Vienna established a Commercial Intendancy—first for the entire Littoral, then centered and focused on Trieste. (The Intendancy existed in different forms from 1731 until 1776. In 1776, a governorship combining civil and military functions, on the model of Livorno, was instituted.) The name of the Commercial Intendancy proclaimed commercial interest as paramount. The purpose of this new institution was to bypass existing local bodies in order to report directly on commercial and economic matters to higher authorities. It was a short chain of command to Vienna. In 1748–52, the Intendancy, headquartered in Trieste, was raised to the status of a province, with no intermediary between it and Vienna. When other parts of the Littoral were subsequently separated from Trieste, the port city itself became the *Provincia Imperiale Commerciale*, a discrete administrative entity, an entire commercial province unto itself. Trieste was administered directly as an independent entity in the Hereditary Lands, its officials responsible to Vienna first through the Court Commerce Council (*Hofkommerzienrath*), and later through the Bohemian-Austrian Court Chancellery (*Böhmische-Österreichische Hofkanzlei*).

At first, the Intendancy had authority over only commercial and economic matters, but it was eventually invested with other civil and even military functions. In Trieste it came to assume virtually all the functions of the formerly autonomous Commune, whose power had eroded as the port and town had expanded. From the 1730s, a new modern quarter, the *Distretto Camerale*, was erected on the site of the old salt marshes, outside the city's walls. Its wide and straight streets set at right angles stood in stark contrast to the narrow and winding alleys of the old medieval town. Later renamed the *Borgo Teresiano*, this new section was the physical manifestation of the absolutist sovereign will at work in Trieste.[7] For it was the identifiable locus of the new mercantile activity, and its precincts and persons were excluded from the jurisdiction of the Commune, subject rather to the direct control of the new institutions established by and responsible to Vienna. When the city's old walls were destroyed and the old and new sections of Trieste amalgamated in 1749, the Commune no longer presided over an area of its own; though it continued to exist in name, it had in fact became a relic. The Intendancy and the new free-port city had in effect absorbed it. The neutralization of the local municipality and the absence of estates facilitated absolutist rule in Trieste.

In the first decades of the Adriatic free-ports policy, the obstacles to Trieste's development were not only administrative. Opposition came from Venice, hostile to new competition, and from the local Triestine patriciate, wary of mercantile enterprise and its disruptive potential, who, as early as 1732, pleaded, "How can commerce be a motive for departing from our own local laws and for a change in government?"[8] Fundamentally, physical and mercantile infrastructures were sorely lacking in Trieste: port facilities, transportation networks, and the human ingredient, experienced merchants and shipbuilders. Concrete steps were taken to address some of these problems. New piers, dockyards, warehouses, and quarantine areas were constructed, and better roads built to connect the city to its hinterland and the entire coastal area to the central European interior. Commerce itself was fostered by various measures: commercial treaties with the Ottomans and the Russians; the gradual removal of customs barriers between the various Habsburg provinces; codes of procedure to regulate mercantile courts, currency exchange, and navigation; improved facilities for credit, banking, and insurance. In 1754, the *Scuola matematica e nautica* was established in Trieste, and in 1755, the *Borsa dei Mercanti*, later called the *Borsa Mercantile*, the Mercantile Exchange, the corporation of wholesale merchants. The area of the free-port zone was steadily expanded from the original limited marketplace; in 1769 it was extended to include all of Trieste, old and new, and the immediate vicinity—all as a "free maritime city."

From an early date, Vienna recognized that the city's meager human resources had to be augmented. Shipbuilders, artisans, and merchants—all had to be enticed to come to Trieste, for there was no local merchant class. Political will at the center created the basis for a new mercantile class in Trieste, which in time ultimately became its new elite.[9] As early as 1719, utilitarian calculations outweighed religious scruples when Vienna rejected the advice of the Inner Austrian Commerce Commission to apply the usual restrictions on non-Catholic residence and economic activity in the free ports.[10] In the first patents, Charles VI invited merchants of "any religion or nationality" to Trieste. In the early years, some foreigners came to Trieste, especially Germans, English, French, and Dutch; but the privileged trading companies in which they were involved folded, and the authorities saw the need to attract others with commercial and artisanal experience.

In a lengthy report to Vienna in 1761, Giuseppe Pasquale Ricci, then the Commerce Councillor of the Intendancy and a leading official in Trieste throughout the late eighteenth century, noted the "insufficiency and inexperience of the native merchants" and argued forcefully for inviting foreign Greeks and Jews in particular in order to develop Triestine commerce. Ricci compared these two groups to the Huguenots, who in the previous century had contributed mightily to the economic development of German lands after their expulsion from France. But since, "in the present century, in which religious intolerance does not cause the interests of the state or of commerce to be sacrificed, emigrations of nations are rare," it would be necessary to attract merchants with privileges of settlement and freedom of commerce, to "welcome them, regard them and treat them with the same affection [as subjects]."[11] About Jews, his words echoed those of the earlier apologists Simone Luzzatto, Menasseh ben Israel, and John Toland:

Persecuted by almost all the nations, wandering through the old world and the new, [whether] dispersed or settled, the Jewish nation has accumulated great riches through commerce, and carries all of them with it. Since [the Jews] are able to own real property in few states . . . commerce is the only nourishment, the only profession, the only occupation of this nation which has been disqualified by all the nations from any other office. And its dispersion and settlement in all parts of the world have made it an experienced participant in all the world's commerce.[12]

Having no occasion for luxury, and mindful of widespread persecution, he continued, the Jews willingly expend their stored-up funds for personal protection. In Poland, where Jews serve the important function of trading in agricultural products, "they are oppressed, but in moderation. A greater moderation, united with free exercise of commerce, could transplant colonies to the Hereditary Lands."[13]

Views such as Ricci's prevailed, as the exceptional economic status of the Free Port of Trieste was mirrored in a population policy exceptional for the Habsburg Monarchy. The initial general statements welcoming all economically useful individuals became an explicit policy of toleration for religious and ethnic minorities, organized as intermediate corporate bodies within the city. Surprisingly, it was Maria Theresa, a monarch famous for her negative views and harsh treatment of non-Catholics, who created the institutional framework for a multireligious, polyethnic, cosmopolitan merchant class in Trieste. She permitted formal communal entities to be established, first by the Jews, then by the Greek Orthodox and the Armenian Uniates; her successors also recognized a second Eastern Orthodox group, the Serbians, as well as two Protestant ones, the Calvinists and the Lutherans.[14] Though these intermediate corporate bodies were subject to the state's civil and penal jurisdiction, they enjoyed a certain measure of self-government as well as rights of worship and education in their own schools. In time, their individual members were for the most part accorded the same civil and economic rights as Catholic merchants. Each community, called a *nazione* or *corpo nazionale*,[15] was charged by the authorities to admit only "economically useful" immigrants, not self-seeking "beggars" or "vagabonds." All around, it proved a bargain well-struck. Vienna found the manpower to turn mercantilist dreams into realities, and the minorities, often suffering ill treatment and persecution elsewhere, found in Trieste favorable conditions for secure settlement. As Ricci had envisaged, Jews and Greeks in particular flourished, and formed vital components of the city's new merchant class.

Indeed, Maria Theresa's reign was decisive for the growth of the port city, for it was then that the Habsburg Adriatic free-ports policy began to bear real fruit. A strong incentive for intensifying efforts to direct commerce southward toward the Adriatic and the Balkans was the loss of Silesia to Prussia, first in 1748 and then irrevocably at the conclusion of the Seven Years' War in 1763. The significant steps taken to foster commerce during Maria Theresa's reign earned her an unusual tribute in the eulogy composed by Elia Morpurgo, silk manufacturer and Jewish communal leader in nearby Gradisca. Describing her as the "woman of valor" of Proverbs 31, he explicated the wool, flax, and merchant ships of the Biblical text (31:13–14) in terms of Trieste's development: "What protection did she not grant the manufactured goods of Bohemia, Moravia, and Austria? If not for her, when would I ever have seen ships from the New World land at your shores?"[16] And he praised her commercial policies generally:

How much happiness did she not provide for her subjects? Open ports, roads made short, convenient, and easy, the flag at sea respected and secure, customs duties on transit lowered, manufacture increased and protected — in a word, commerce made flourishing and active, with benefit for her subjects, with profit for the Treasury . . . [to] the admiration of all peoples.[17]

Thus, implementation of the Adriatic free-ports policy radically transformed Trieste through the course of the eighteenth century, for it brought new quarters and facilities, a new commerce, new administrative institutions, and a new population.

Trieste's population grew significantly in the eighteenth century, increasing approximately five- or sixfold, with the greatest increase occurring after 1770. Population estimates for the beginning of the century range from 3,000 to 5,000. By mid-century, in 1758, there were 6,433 people, and by 1775, 10,664 in the city proper, and 15,784 counting both the city and the countryside immediately surrounding it. During the next twenty-five years, the total population doubled: around 1800, there were approximately 27,000 to 30,000 people, with some 20,000 to 24,400 in the city itself.[18]

Immigration had swelled the population of Trieste, and diversity was its watchword. Trieste's streets were a colorful mixture of peoples, languages, and costumes. Italians, Germans, French, English, Dutch, and newcomers from other Habsburg domains, the Balkans, and the Levant peopled the city, and the distinctive religious-ethnic groups—Jews, Greeks, Serbs, Armenians, and Protestants—comprised a significant element of the population. Though surely exaggerating, Antonio De' Giuliani, a noted writer on political economy and society, who returned to his native city after years of travel, estimated in 1809–10 that seven of every eight inhabitants were foreign-born.[19] Visitors were struck by the chaotic medley (*guazzabuglia*) that Trieste was. Some thought of north and south because of the mixture of Germans and Italians, while for others, "Turkish pantaloons" and "cries of 'Allah'" evoked the east.[20]

In the early years of the free port, visitors noted the tensions between the immigrants and the old inhabitants. The nobles and lower working classes especially were suspicious of the new merchants.[21] The new administration introduced by Vienna in order to implement its mercantile policy had greatly affected the city's social and cultural life. The influence of the patriciate declined as their base of power, the autonomous Commune, was eroded. Naturally, the old patrician and clerical elite resented the new forces at work in Trieste: state centralization and commerce, and the dynamic alliance of bureaucrats and merchants. While the tensions between the Commune and the new Habsburg free port did not dissipate, and nostalgia for the old subsequently lingered among certain circles, it was the free port—the city defined expressly by mercantile function—that set the tone for modern Trieste.

In the last decades of the eighteenth century, Trieste presented the spectacle of a cosmopolitan and dynamic city, undergoing feverish development. For example, in the 1760s the Venetian consul heard the sounds of masons and carpenters, a "fury of construction," everywhere.[22] Construction of the port and city, the movement of vessels and goods, the negotiations and speculations of ship captains, brokers, and merchants—all conveyed the impression of "a practical people always on the move and bustling," of "traffic . . . immense and continual."[23] International maritime commerce was becoming Trieste's lifeblood. From the late 1760s, Trieste began to compete seriously with Venice and Hamburg. In 1768, Venetian officials sounded the alarm about Trieste's recent growth as "distressing" and "fatal."[24] Whereas in 1761, the volume of goods shipped through Trieste was approximately 14,000 tons, by 1776 it rose to 65,865 tons, and by 1780 to approximately 82,000 tons. The great increase occurred in the years between 1760 and 1767, and by 1786, one-third of the monarchy's exports were passing through Trieste. The value of this traffic increased from approximately 4–5 million florins in 1750, to 6,888,467 florins in 1761, to approximately 15 million florins in 1780. In 1803, almost 75 million florins worth of goods passed through Trieste. The port specialized in transit commerce, first as a center of supply and exchange between central Europe and the Italian peninsula, and then between those areas and the eastern Mediterranean. It served as an important outlet for the industries of the interior Habsburg provinces, and also as a port of entry for overseas products, such as sugar and coffee. Some manufacturing and light industry, such as silk, soap, and liqueurs, developed in Trieste, but the pillar of its economy was international trade and its attendant activities, brokerage, finance, and insurance. The first steps toward Trieste's leading role in the insurance industry worldwide were taken in this period.[25]

By the end of the eighteenth century, Trieste's role as the major Habsburg port was assured. In his *Riflessioni politiche sopra il prospetta attuale della città di Trieste* published in 1785, De' Giuliani wrote of the factors which could make Trieste a great port; in his *Panorama politico della città di Trieste*, written in 1803–5, he shifted tenses from the future to the past and present, for the deed was accomplished, Trieste's success by then evident, "its destiny seems decided."[26] The Torinese Andrea Metrà put it succinctly in *Il mentore perfetto dei negozianti . . .* , his five-volume commercial geography written in the 1790s:

> Though Trieste does not conduct extensive trade in its own products, natural or manufactured, its traffic is nonetheless as great today as that of the most established European trading centers could be. . . . It has made its marketplace the most essential point of communication between the Levant and the west, Italy, Germany, and other realms of northern Europe. . . . This same city is a continuous trade fair, where one constantly finds all possible goods for sale.[27]

Trieste the entrepôt was becoming an emporium.

The transformation of Trieste was dramatic. After a lengthy absence from the city, De' Giuliani marveled at its tremendous growth. In 1803–5, he exclaimed: "Whoever knew this city thirty years ago would have trouble believing that in this short period of time the hard work of people otherwise deprived of special help could have created what one sees today."[28] The wide and regular streets of the new town, the recently built grand edifices housing commercial firms, and the neoclassical *Borsa* and theater all impressed visitors and conveyed its prosperity. In 1820, a Paduan visitor opined that the urban splendor of Triest seemed to have sprung up "as if by a charm, in a miraculous instant."[29]

The rise of the free port and the radical transformation of the city were the result of governmental policy formulated in Vienna and implemented in Trieste by officials and a diverse mercantile class. The new Trieste was quintessentially mercantile and cosmopolitan. Observers were struck by the apparent concord among the diverse merchants pursuing a common "aspiration" of profit under the aegis of the Habsburgs' "general tolerance."[30] The ethos of the new port city was captured by the French emigré Charles-

Albert Comte de Moré, who wrote around 1807 to his brother Joseph Labrosse, then a prospering commoner merchant in Trieste:

> The past is dead. . . . At the pinnacle of the new society there will shine no longer the noblemen of our ancient lineages, but [rather] the bankers, the industrialists, the shipowners, and the merchants, and those among us who have the will and know-how to become such. . . . And at Trieste true pioneers are all those who have gathered from the most diverse lands to remake their lives, and who become comrades here, through their common aspiration and iron will, in the steady work they carry out in the shade of the caduceus of Mercury and the trident of Neptune. The city you have chosen for your new undertakings is the most suitable and certain for your success; it is the Philadelphia of Europe, the city typical of pioneers of our old continent, the port where the shipwrecked find welcome and a promising new life. . . . "Consoler of the afflicted and refuge of sinners": for emigrants, that is Trieste.[31]

In fact, Trieste was an ark of refuge not only for French emigrés fleeing the revolutionary maelstrom, but for many others throughout the eighteenth and nineteenth centuries who sought security and livelihood on its shores. Modern Trieste offered a new and dynamic frontier to those prepared to seize the opportunities of international maritime commerce and to function in conditions of diversity and pluralism. The fraternity forged by commerce—a dream so beloved of Enlightenment *philosophes*[32]—seemed to find at least partial realization in this free port.

Jews in Trieste Before the Free Port

Our concern is the modern Jewish community of Trieste that arose as part and parcel of the eighteenth-century free port, but we must glance first at its prehistory. In the eighteenth and nineteenth centuries, some of the city's chroniclers and the Jews themselves considered the tenth century as the first date of Jewish settlement. But the thirteenth century is now generally accepted, for the first undisputed evidence of Jewish existence in Trieste dates from 1236. A document in the town's archives relates that the bishop borrowed the sum of 500 *marche* from the Jew David Daniele of Carinthia then residing in Trieste.[33] The transalpine origin and lending activity of this individual are paradigmatic of the Jews who lived in Trieste during the next few centuries. For the nucleus of the Triestine Jewish community was formed by Ashkenazic moneylenders like Solomon of Nuremberg, who, in 1414 and 1420, signed a contract with the town to reside there as its "public banker."[34]

In the sixteenth and seventeenth centuries, certain Jewish individuals and families, such as the Levis in 1556 and Ventura Parente in 1624, resided in Trieste on the basis of the privileges granted them by Holy Roman emperors in return for their services of "goods and blood" in time of war. These privileges promised sovereign protection and justice; unmolested practice of Judaism; the right of residence in any town where Jews already lived, including Vienna; unrestricted economic activities, including ownership of real property; the right of travel without distinguishing signs or special taxes; and immunity from any taxes not imposed on Christian merchants. These privileges and liberties were designated as those accorded other court Jews, Jewish merchant-financiers who prominently served central European courts in the seventeenth and early eighteenth centuries.[35] These privileges, issued by the Habsburg rulers and not dependent on local authorities, were valued highly by the Jews who held them. Eventually extended to the other Jews in Trieste, these privileges were invoked subsequently as the historic basis for many Jewish rights in Trieste.

The few Jews who lived in Trieste in the seventeenth century were mostly engaged in loan-banking, wholesale trade in textiles and foodstuffs, and army provisioning. A handful were known for their intellectual pursuits. One rabbi, Menahem Zion (Emanuel) Porto, attained fame as a scientific and mathematical scholar, and at least four Triestine Jews attended the University of Padua.[36]

Until the mid-seventeenth century, relations remained generally good between the Commune of Trieste and its few Jews. One exception was the accusation of Jewish responsibility for the outbreak of plague in 1601. In the second half of the century, however, expressions of hostility toward the Jews became frequent, with nobles and clerics charging them with economic excess and social and religious presumption. The litany recited by the Commune's leaders in 1675 was fairly typical:

Involving themselves with Christian women and retaining them as servants; occupying the loveliest houses, having their shops on the most convenient streets of the city; not wearing any sign to make them distinguishable from Christians. . . . They have enriched themselves greatly, usurped various properties that they now enjoy, [and] ruined the poor subjects of this city.[37]

The general economic decline of the city fueled resentment of the Jews, and the establishment of a *monte de pietà* (low-interest savings-and-loan association) in 1650 made them seem expendable. In addition, renewed fighting against the Turks in Hungary and near Vienna heightened distrust of non-Catholics, and the step taken in the capital in 1670, expulsion, seemed to some in Trieste an appropriate local solution. Others would settle for segregation of Jews in a ghetto.

The first order for the implementation of a ghetto did not actually come until 1693. Issued in Vienna on December 2, 1693, it was instituted in Trieste in 1697.[38] During those four years, there was much protest and wrangling among the Jews, the Commune, and Vienna, especially over the site of the proposed ghetto. The Jews' preference for the centrally located *Portizza di Riborgo* quarter prevailed. In 1697, the sixty to eighty Jews of Trieste, some ten to twelve families, moved into the thirteen houses of the *Riborgo*, which was bounded by three streets and three gates. Any enclosure would afford some protection against mob violence, which had occurred at least once during the years of bitter negotiations, but the Jews had pressed for this particular quarter because of its size and central location near one of the city's busiest commercial gates.[39] Indeed, Jewish economic activity in Trieste did remain viable. As their adversaries complained, the Jews continued as before to lend money, run shops, and own real estate outside the ghetto.[40] Generally, the regime of the Triestine ghetto was less harsh and more porous than in other Italian localities. Besides the crucial economic opportunities still permitted the Jews, there were no imposed conversionist sermons, they could keep their shops open on Sundays, and regulations concerning distinctive Jewish signs and Christian servants were gradually allowed to lapse. The effects of ghettoization were mitigated by the court Jew privileges of particular families and then most significantly by the Free Port Patents. The mercantile aims pursued by Vienna with absolutist means dictated that whatever the local sentiments, economically dynamic immigrants—Jews among them—be attracted to Trieste, and find a decent and prosperous existence in it. In fact, the ghetto and the Jewish community did not remain coterminous. Long before its formal abolition in the 1780s, many Jews received governmental permission to live outside the ghetto's walls.

The Burgeoning Jewish Community in the Free Port

The free port spurred the numerical and institutional transformation of the Jewish settlement in Trieste in the eighteenth century. At the end of the seventeenth century, as discussed above, some sixty to eighty Jews, ten to twelve households, lived in Trieste. A century later, there were some 1,250 Jews, at least 220 households, who comprised a formal corporate body, the *Università degli Ebrei in Trieste*.

Table 1 provides some of the available figures for the Jewish population of Trieste in the eighteenth and early nineteenth centuries. They show the tremendous and steady growth of the Jewish population of Trieste, which increased fivefold in the forty years from 1748 to 1788, approximately tenfold from 1748 to 1802, and more than twentyfold in the century preceding 1820. Through the eighteenth century, the Jewish population increased more rapidly than did the city's as a whole: its proportion of the total Triestine population grew from approximately 3 percent in 1735, to at least 5 percent in 1802, to more than 7 percent in 1818. During that period, the

TABLE 1
The Jewish Population of Trieste, 1735–1820

Date	Number of Jews	Number of households	Total population of Trieste
1735	103	—	3,865
1748	120	27	—
1758	221	—	6,433
1769	318	53	—
1775	404	—	10,664
1786	634	—	—
1788	730	154	—
1793	876	—	—
1798	1,082	—	—
1802	1,247	c. 220	20,333–24,603
1818	2,400	—	33,510
1820	2,300–2,400	c. 446	—

SOURCES: AST, C.R.S. Int. Comm., b. 78, f. 114, "Tabella delle Case stabilite e Foresti componenti gli Ebrei abitante in Trieste" (May 4, 1769); AST, C.R. Gov., b. 620, N. 3567 (June 17, 1786) (ad N. 3563); Dorsi 1989: 143 (Pittoni 1786 report); CAHJP, HM 2/5839, ff. 318–319r; Montanelli 1905: 103–4, 122, 124; Zoller 1924:6, 10–11, 24 (with 1788 figures corrected by Gatti 1991: 316–18); De Antonellis Martini 1968: 101, 112, 155; Cervani 1969: 36, 45–46; CAHJP, HM 2/5862, ff. 60r–66v, and AST, I.R. Gov., Atti Generali, b. 753, N. 10725, May 2, 1820 report.

Jews were in fact the largest single religious-ethnic minority in Trieste, comprising about one-half of all the non–Roman Catholics.[41]

The sustained growth of the Triestine Jewish population was due overwhelmingly to immigration. As the figures from 1776 demonstrate, at a time when the community's average annual increase was fourteen persons, natural increase alone accounted for only two persons.[42] In the census of 1748, two-thirds—eighteen out of twenty-seven heads of households—listed places of origin other than Trieste.[43]

The foreigners listed in the 1748 census were overwhelmingly Italian, from the neighboring areas of Gorizia-Gradisca, Friuli, and Istria, and the more distant Venice, Ferrara, and Ancona; the sole exception was one person from Hamburg. The census of 1775 showed the same Italian dominance.[44] Venice in particular was an important source of wealth and manpower: wealthy Venetians such as the Vivante and Treves families established branches of their businesses in Trieste, and many less-prosperous Jews—among them the family of Samuel David Luzzatto, the great nineteenth-century Judaic scholar—found refuge there after the expulsion of Jews from the Venetian countryside in 1777.[45] As the scope of Triestine trade broadened in the last decades of the eighteenth century, Jews from other parts of the Habsburg Monarchy (such as Vienna and Hungary) and from the eastern Mediterranean were increasingly drawn to Trieste.

Among the city's wealthy and prominent families were those of Joachim Hierschel from Hamburg, Philippo (Filippo) Kohen from Vienna, Memo Curiel from Greece, and the brothers Abram and Isach Camondo from Constantinople.[46]

Although the Jewish community of Trieste was diverse and became increasingly so, it remained largely of Italian origin, and its tone—like that of the city generally in that period—was set by the Italian elements. Immigrants learned Italian, the lingua franca of both daily life and commerce. Jews kept communal records in Italian, with but a few documents in Hebrew. When Joseph II tried to impose German as the language of administration and commerce in 1789, the *Borsa Mercantile* vigorously protested that this was impossible because the "local merchant body, composed for the most part of Italian, Greek, Jewish, and Armenian traders, conducts their business only in Italian."[47] Similarly, the Jews objected to Joseph's 1787 order that they take German names by stressing that most Jews were of Italian origin and knew only Italian.[48] German became increasingly the language of official communication with Vienna, but Italian was essential for those seeking to prosper in Trieste.

Growing numbers necessitated more formal organization and institutionalization as a community. Until the 1740s, the Jews of Trieste were loosely organized and conducted their affairs informally, referring to themselves simply as "li Hebrei di Trieste." They worshiped in a private home and owned land for a Jewish cemetery. In December 1746, the Jews of Trieste constituted themselves as a self-governing corporate body (*corpo d'Università*). The government-approved *Capi* (leaders, literally "heads"), Grassin Vita Levi and David Luzzatto, convened the Jewish notables—heads of the Morpurgo, Parente, Porto, Cusin, Treves, and Stella families, all engaged in banking, brokerage, and import-export trade—to vote on a statute for the community. Because the lack of "rules for self-governance and the collection of taxes" was leading to "much disorder and confusion," they wanted to institute "a sure and permanent means of self-government": formal written regulations "guided by Divine help" and decreed by governmental authorities to have the "force of inviolable Laws."[49]

The six-chapter Statute of 1746, drawn up by the Jews and approved by the government, provided for the typical tasks of Jewish communal self-government: collective decision-making, election of officers, management of worship and synagogue, record-keeping and collection of monies, discipline of members, and resolution of disputes. All tax-paying heads of families comprised the Assembly (*Radunanza*), and two *Capi* served as the executives. In general, the *Capi* were charged with managing all internal Jewish affairs (political, religious, or economic), maintaining good order, and representing the community in its dealings with external authorities and bodies. Their powers of discipline were backed by the arm of the state. The positions of scribe (*scrivano*), chancellor (*cancelliere*), rabbi (*rabbino*), cantor (*cantarino*), and beadle (*servente*) were also established.

Formal corporate organization seemed an attraction to immigrants: some Jews contemplating migration to Trieste inquired in advance about the status of the Jews and their community.[50] Through the second half of the eighteenth century, growing numbers necessitated new arrangements set forth in new statutes; new positions, such as tax assessor, treasurer, and syndic; new institutions, such as a school and a hospital; and a move from direct to indirect suffrage in 1762, when a deliberative and more powerful Small Council (*Consulta Ristretta, Riduzione Particolare,* or *vaad katan*) came into existence alongside the General Assembly (then *Riduzione Generale* or *kahal kelali*, later *Consulta Generale*).[51]

Around the same time that it was formally incorporated, in 1746, the community inaugurated a public house of worship and appointed an official rabbi. In the second half of the eighteenth century, the community employed four official rabbis, all of Italian origin: David Corinaldi (1746–49), Jacob Capriles (1750–65), Isach Formiggini (1766–88), and Raffael Nathan Tedesco (1788–1800).[52] Their position, in the tradition of the Italian communal rabbinate, represented a combination of the Ashkenazic *rosh yeshivah* (head of talmudic academy) and Sefardic *marbitz torah* (disseminator of Torah). Their duties were to teach (and supervise other teachers), preach, decide issues of Halakhah (Jewish law), occasionally mediate and arbitrate disputes, and generally serve as religious supervisors and moral authorities. Always subject to strong lay control, the religious authority of the rabbis was harnessed for administrative purposes, first by the lay leaders in the regulation of communal life and the discipline of individuals, and later increasingly by the government, as civil registrars.[53] By 1800, the community had four synagogues in which to worship, three public (the first two following the Ashkenazic rite, and the third the Sefardic) and one in a private home (also Sefardic).[54] The community supervised all ritual activities, including the provisioning of kosher meat and the ritual bath, and two confraternities, the *Fraterna Ghemilut Hazadìm, ò sia della Misericordia* (Society for Deeds of Loving-kindness), concerned with burial and poor relief, and the *Fraterna di Talmud Torà, ò sia Errudimento Religioso* (Society for Torah Study). How the Jewish community of Trieste in fact exercised authority and autonomy is a theme that runs throughout this study.

The Dynamics and Consequences of Rapid Growth

Immigration—the lifeblood of the community—was one of the important ongoing concerns of the *Capi*. They were charged by the governing authorities with controlling the influx of Jewish *forestieri* (foreigners) to Trieste. Like those of all free ports, the Triestine authorities in fact sought to both promote and control immigration. In 1732 they made clear the criteria for admission: "Nonprivileged Jews and other foreign Jews may be tolerated only if they can render an appreciable service to the public in commercial affairs, and inasmuch as the expected profit remains . . . in Trieste."[55] Repeatedly they admonished Jewish leaders to prevent the settlement or even the temporary sojourning of those with few resources or skills: the "poor, lazy, or scandalous," "vagabonds," and "wandering beggars." The government's usual economic and moral concerns were heightened at times of greatest influx, such as the 1750s, the decade of the most intensive Jewish immigration to Trieste, and the late 1770s, following the expulsion of Jews from the Venetian countryside, and at times of political turbulence, such as the 1790s.[56] Throughout the period, the authorities instructed the *Capi* to submit to the police regular and detailed records of all Jewish arrivals, and to distinguish between those worthy of residence permits and those who ought to be sent away immediately. In this respect, the absolutist government sought to involve the Jewish community in its own bureaucratic work.

Jewish leaders were in partial agreement with the government. They, too, sought "to combine the liberties accorded by the laws of the free port to every foreigner to settle here, with the interests regarding customs and economy that our community has in limiting and circumscribing such immigration."[57] Traditionally, European Jewish communities had controlled the right of settlement in their localities through devices such as the *herem ha-yishuv* (ban on settlement), lest too many Jews pursue too few economic opportunities in a limited area. Though scarcity of economic opportunity was not the problem in Trieste, still, the Jewish community wanted to restrict access in order to prevent inundation by the poor, by foreign beggars and vagabonds who "shed little honor on the nation"[58] and who, it was feared, would overburden the community and possibly endanger the standing of those already established in the city. Greater control of entry would also serve the cause of social and religious discipline within the community itself.

Thus, for reasons of self-interest, the Jewish community was prepared to comply with the governmental policy of immigration control. The *Capi* preferred to shoulder the responsibility rather than have the police make all decisions about Jewish residence and sojourns. In every communal statute, they reiterated their duties to superintend new arrivals; in the late 1770s, they appointed a specific deputy for Jewish foreigners and wayfarers.[59] Every resident was to notify these officials of the presence of foreign guests, and to obtain permits for temporary stays of a few days. Failure to comply would be punishable by fines. Through inquiries in former places of residence if necessary, the community was to obtain the vital information about such individuals: their means of support and their morals. "Wicked ways" and "scandalous conduct" were grounds for refusal of admission, or for expulsion. For example, when Salomon Parente applied to the Small Council in 1763–64 for a residence permit for a prospective employee, he vouched for him as a "punctilious observer of our Holy Torah."[60] The *Capi* would convey all pertinent information to the police with recommendations for the foreigner's stay or departure. In the 1750s, the early years of the community's formal existence, when the *Capi* may not yet have been entirely secure in their authority, they seemed somewhat reluctant to exercise this function too openly: in a letter to the chief of police in 1758, they proposed that they provide information on "lazy and scandalous" people in secret, since to do so in public might be dangerous "for those who must travel frequently on business."[61] But they seem to have grown into their role. In the late 1770s, when Jews from the Venetian countryside sought admittance, the *Capi* proposed that they themselves head the new commission that would screen newcomers, verify their means of support, and seek guarantees if necessary from prospective employers, in some cases Gentile as well as Jewish. The governor, however, preferred more direct control of the process and appointed the chief of police to head the commission.[62] In this instance, there were to be formal limitations to the integration of the Jewish community in the state's bureaucratic apparatus.

Lack of compliance was a frequent complaint of the *Capi* about other community members and, in turn, of the police about the *Capi*. Though Jewish leaders and the government both wanted to control the influx of newcomers to Trieste, there remained a gap in their perceptions of the problem. Pietro Antonio Pittoni, the long-serving chief of police, considered the Jews far too generous with their coreligionists in distress, and blamed their misplaced and exaggerated notions of piety: "What nation ever had more vagabonds in its midst than the Jews, who through their misdirected devotion and piety invite and welcome vagrant pilgrims on the occasions of their major festivals?"[63] The result, in his view, was "a multitude of idle and unemployed Jews who on the pretext of piety wander from one community to the next. Taking advantage of the superstitious piety of their brethren, they not only live at public expense but also collect abundant alms from the community."[64] He advocated immediate expulsion or even imprisonment of such strangers.

However, though they did not welcome the burdens of poor wayfarers, and indeed sought ways to reduce them, the Jews felt bound by religion, charity, and humanity to aid their coreligionists. The deputy in charge of poor foreigners and his assistant were responsible for providing them with food and shelter for a few days, as well as the means to continue their journeys away from the city. The community also took care of such people in their hospital, and formed an association to pay for the circumcisions of poor foreigners' sons. In 1780 they explained to the Venetian Jewish community that they had wanted to do more to help those expelled, but that the government's policy of strict control of admission had prevented them. In 1790, the *Capi* invoked the moral norm of "humanity" when they protested the proposal of the chief of police to fine them for their "overgenerosity": "We cannot be so inhumane as to deny temporary assistance and rest in our hospital to the poor who show up with children and women, and sometimes with sick people."[65]

Some Jews objected to the official policies for other reasons. For example, in 1762–63, Benedetto Vita Luzzatto urged the community to ease up and invite more Jewish families to settle in Trieste. He complained that the Jewish population of Trieste was too restricted, for during his ten years of residence he had failed to find a suitable marriage partner. Communal leaders found his petition "moving" but responded with "an evasive rescript." Fortunately, official action proved unnecessary, since life took its own course: a 1769 document shows Luzzatto as the head of a household with a wife and two children![66] There exists no detailed information on the marital status and age of immigrants to Trieste, though it can be assumed that many were young unmarried males.

Certainly the Jewish community's practices never met the government's aim of attracting only the rich and keeping out the poor. To control and pace immigration in a free port was ultimately a very difficult task, since both the city and its Jewish community depended upon newcomers.

One of the consequences of the Jewish community's rapid growth was the need for physical expansion. Although initially the three-street area of the *Riborgo* offered ample space, by the middle of the eighteenth century, especially with the rapid population increase betweeen 1748 and 1758, it was no longer adequate for Jewish needs. In the 1750s, the government became concerned as Jews moved outside the ghetto. It recognized the undeniable demographic realities, yet still sought to control the ongoing process of Jewish expansion beyond the ghetto. It therefore took two steps. First, the sovereign decree of August 15, 1753, granted wealthy Jews the right to request permission from the authorities to live outside the ghetto. Should they receive permission, they were to live only in buildings occupied wholly by Jews, not in mixed ones housing both Jews and Christians.[67] Second, in January 1755, the government offered the Jews an additional quarter of their own in the new part of the city, the *Borgo Teresiano*. This "new ghetto" never came into existence; in the words of a nineteenth-century Jewish chronicler, "The Jews did not take advantage of this authorization!"[68]

These two steps need to be considered together if sense is to be made of either one. The 1753 decree has been cited as evidence of the authorities' liberality insofar as they allowed a legal breach of ghetto walls, but the 1755 offer shows the limited terms they envisaged.

Thus the legal act of 1753 did not mark a new beginning but rather, like much legislation, was an acknowledgment of a fait accompli. Its purpose was not the creation of wholly new possibilities, but regulation of an ongoing process. The pressure of Jewish population growth was such that the authorities might hope to regulate and limit the expansion of Jewish residence, but they could not hope to halt it.

A number of steps were taken in the next few years that indicated the government's desire to assert more control: renovation of the ghetto gates in 1757 and repeated requests to the community for reports on its members' places of residences both inside and outside the ghetto.[69] For example, in 1758 the authorities specified that they wanted the names of people living outside the ghetto without permission. The *Capi* supplied this information, but asserted somewhat disingenuously that they did not know who "lives outside the Ghetto with authorization and who through abuse."[70] Though Trieste was indeed a rapidly growing city, it is extremely unlikely that they would not have known of the Jews present, given their small number at that time (around 220). In their response, they described their procedures for registering Jewish newcomers and provided samples of the documents used. They named twenty Jews living outside the ghetto, some in houses occupied solely by Jews, others in buildings shared by Christians and Jews. They also named seven recent arrivals staying in premises outside the ghetto whom they considered unworthy of residence permits. Thirteen of those dwelling outside the ghetto according to the 1758 list were still living in Trieste eleven years later.[71]

Two facts emerge from the foregoing. First, expansion beyond the Triestine ghetto was a gradual process, caused by the pressure of rapid population growth due above all to immigration. There was no one dramatic moment at which administrative fiat, revolutionary enthusiasm, or a conquering army breached the ghetto walls. Though initially ambivalent and hesitant, the governing authorities had permitted over decades an expanding ghetto. Second, we may not assume, as was often the case elsewhere, that Jews living outside the Jewish quarter were cut off from the life of the organized Jewish community. Jews who lived in the city, both inside and outside the ghetto, were subject to the community's disciplinary powers. Important communal officials lived outside, such as the beadle Vita Gattegno and the *Capi* Joachim Hierschel and the Luzzatto brothers.[72] These officials were an integral part of the community, not a defecting fringe.

What kind of atmosphere was created by the rapid growth and steady influx of newcomers to the newly constituted Jewish community of Trieste? We may assume a spirit of opportunity and promise, and an atmosphere of vitality, ferment, and instability often characteristic of such hubs and new frontiers. Newcomers could attain social advancement and communal prominence within a few years of their arrival. For instance, Anselmo Morschene presented his credentials for admission in 1767; only twelve years later, he became a *Capo* of the community.[73] The wealthy Vivantes of Venice assumed positions of leadership almost immediately upon their arrival in 1790. The ethos of freedom and opportunity was not frustrated by long-established, entrenched institutions and traditions, for the community had few. It seems to have been a relatively open and tolerant community. For example, Benedetto Frizzi, physician, man of letters, and devotee of Enlightenment, whose radical views caused him to be made unwelcome by the Jewish community of Mantua in the late 1780s, was received warmly when he settled in Trieste in 1790.[74] Still, it was a challenge for the community to establish authority while maintaining the advantages of the free port's promise of opportunity.

The Economic Activities of the Jews of Trieste

In official eyes, the function of the Triestine Jewish community, its very raison d'être, was to be "useful" in developing commerce in the free port. Accordingly, there were virtually no legal restrictions on the economic activities that Jews were allowed to pursue. In their invitations to productive foreigners, the Free Port Patents drew no distinctions between Gentiles and Jews. All the liberties conferred by those patents and by all earlier court Jew privileges were reiterated and extended to all Jews in Trieste by Maria Theresa in her Privilege of April 19, 1771. Essentially, they were permitted ownership of real and movable property and protection of it, and freedom to engage in commerce, manufacturing, and artisanry "on the same basis as other nations with respect to their persons, property, and taxes."[75] Exceptional economic activity brought further legal concessions: in 1768, the wealthiest and most commercially active Triestine Jews, including members of the *Borsa*, were exempted from the head toll (*Leibmaut*, or *Dazio corporale*) normally levied on Jews traveling in the Habsburg Monarchy.[76] The situation of Triestine Jews was so exceptional that they were scarcely affected by Joseph II's Toleration edicts that generally expanded the range of economic opportunities open to Habsburg Jews.

In the free port, the mainstay of the Triestine Jewish community became international commerce, finance, and related activities. Wholesalers traded variously in goods such as grains, tobacco, liqueurs and brandy, sugar, cloth, soap, and spices. Some specialized in trade with particular areas: the other parts of Italy, the Istrian and Dalmatian coasts, the Levant, and interior Habsburg German and Austrian lands from which they exported manufactured goods. Some Jews introduced trade with Roumania, Russia, and even Brazil. Several Jews specialized in shipping and forwarding, in brokerage, and in providing financial, credit, and banking services. Jews played a leading role in the insurance industry that began to organize in the 1760s, cofounding four of the city's first five firms and serving as partners with Gentiles. (A few Jews also were partners with non-Jews in commercial firms.) Some Jews engaged in light manufacturing of products such as pitch, silk, leather, cream of tartar, soap, candles, liqueur, and playing cards.[77]

Two precise occupational breakdowns show that in 1748, approximately 37 percent of the Jews earned a living from commerce and related activities, and that in 1820, approximately 47 percent did so. The exact figures are as follows.

The census of 1748 indicates a Jewish population of approximately 120 persons, and lists the occupations of nineteen of the twenty-seven heads of families. Ten were engaged in commerce and related activities (4 small-scale merchants, 1 larger-scale merchant, 1 head of a commercial firm, 1 agent, 2 brokers, 1 assistant/commercial traveler); one property-holder lived off the income of his own property, including rural property; six were salaried employees of the Jewish community (1 scribe, 1 rabbi, 2 teachers, 1 servant for the synagogue, and 1 undertaker); and two labored at unspecified kinds of work.[78]

The next exact breakdown of Jewish occupations was compiled by the Jewish community in 1820 for a report to the government (Table 2). At least 182 heads of families within the community (that is, nearly 41 percent) were connected with commerce and finance, counting the three categories of merchants, clerks, and shopkeepers. (Though the chief of police who received the report designated many of the laborers as resellers of goods, I do not include them since they were probably street peddlers.) The capital used to acquire property and to set up factories was derived initially from commerce; thus, if the twenty-eight property-holders and manufacturers are added, then the total of those whose incomes were tied to commerce rises to 47 percent. Teachers and other salaried employees of the community, including medical practitioners, who were paid in part by the community, were just over 10 percent. Artisans accounted for 9 percent, while the laborers and poor together comprised 33 percent.

From the government's perspective, the occupational distribution and economic profile of the Jewish community were respectable, and indeed praiseworthy on both economic and moral grounds. For example, one official reported in 1786: "Concerning the Jewish community of Trieste, it

TABLE 2
Occupations of Triestine Jews, 1820

Occupation	Number of heads of housholds
Merchants, property-holders, and free professions	137
Member of Executive Board of the *Borsa*	1
Member of the Council of the *Borsa*	3
Merchant, member of the *Borsa*	3
Insurance company	4
Wholesale merchant	11
Wholesale and retail merchant	22
Retail merchant	22
Authorized factory owner	4
Licensed broker for goods and services	12
Licensed broker for currency	10
Licensed broker for insurance and freight	1
Doctor	4
Surgeon	4
Midwife	3
Manufacturer of paint	1
Distiller of water	3
Other merchant	10
Property-holder	20
Clerk	65
Teacher/religious functionary	36
Shopkeeper	18
Artisan	40
Laborer	70
Poor	80
TOTAL	446

SOURCES: CAHJP, HM 2/5862, ff. 60r–66v; AST, I.R. Gov., Atti Generali, b. 753, N. 10725, report of May 2, 1820, "Stato delle Famiglie 446 circa in N.o di 2300 a 2400 anima circa."

is in any case well known that they mostly earn their livelihood respectably through trade and other decent occupations, and also that they distinguish themselves from other Jewish communities by virtue of the morality of their behavior."[79] In 1820, the chief of police commented thus upon the data submitted by the community:

In the aforementioned classes of merchants, property-holders, practitioners of the liberal arts, clerks, teachers, religious personnel, shopkeepers, and artisans, there seems to be relatively good morality and public behavior free of quarrels and complaints. The said classes show themselves to be sufficiently civilized in their mutual relations. Each of them is in a position to have and to earn a sufficient livelihood. But the last two classes of laborers and poor do not manage to obtain one, since they are for the most part foreigners, come in by chance seeking their fortune and deprived of the means of subsistence.[80]

This official deemed about one-third of the community—the laborers and poor together, whom the *Capi* had distinguished from each other—as failing to earn a living wage. Yet the overall profile was of a relatively prosperous community, with approximately two-thirds of the Jews of Trieste seen to be solid citizens making a decent living. To be sure, those deemed respectable by the chief of police ranged widely in wealth and status, from the high financier to the petty shopkeeper. And as Samuel David Luzzatto, son of the artisan Hezekiah, poignantly related in his autobiography, the lower ranks of the respectable might have but a tenuous hold on material well-being.[81]

At the other extreme were the wealthiest Jews, who ranked among the wealthiest merchants of Trieste. Joachim Hierschel, Grassin Vita Levi and son Marco Levi, their cousin Grassin Vita di Caliman Levi, Haim (Vita) Camondo and sons Abram and Isach, Memo and son David Curiel, Marco and Aron Parente, Philippo Kohen, and Leon and Aron Vivante were some of the most prominent. Several maintained households that included servants, private tutors, and scribes.[82] These wealthy notables tended to be involved in many different ventures at once; a person who listed his occupation as wholesale merchant or member of the Mercantile Exchange might also be a factory owner and a partner in an insurance firm. Two of the wealthiest, Joachim Hierschel and Marco Levi, held appointments as court agents. Hierschel was charged by the government with stimulating the export of Bohemian textiles through Trieste. Levi was granted a monopoly on the sale of tobacco, and in 1775 was one of the four prominent Triestine merchants consulted by the Intendancy when Vienna sought detailed information about actual conditions in the port city. Upon their deaths, Levi in 1786 and Hierschel in 1794, each earned the accolade "friend of humanity" for philanthropy and services to the city, and Levi's funeral was attended by hundreds of people, Jews and Gentiles, and was reported upon at length in the city's newspaper, *Osservatore Triestino*.[83] (Yet, as we shall see below, the prominent Levi gained considerable enmity as well as accolades.)

The wealthiest merchants dominated Jewish communal affairs. They served as *Capi* and directed institutions such as the school and the hospital. Some also had Jewish cultural interests. For example, Marco Levi headed the *Fraterna di Talmud Torà*, and during the visit of Hayyim Joseph David Azulai to Trieste in 1777, Levi impressed the great Talmudic scholar, as "very sharp." Levi was instrumental in organizing and in financing with a substantial bequest the new Jewish normal school in the 1780s. The insurance magnate Joseph Eliezer Morpurgo composed Hebrew poetry, translated Pope's *Essay on Man* into Hebrew, and wrote an entire Torah scroll.[84]

During the late eighteenth century, Jews played a recognizable role in the port city's development. In 1751, five of the city's twelve brokers were Jews.[85] A Jew was entrusted with recording and disseminating information about arriving and departing vessels before 1777, when the government began publishing these data.[86] Jews were members of the wholesale merchants' association from its inception in the 1740s.[87] In 1779–80, six of the forty-two members (that is, approximately 14 percent) of the *Borsa* were Jews, and in 1783, Jews were seven of the twenty-five members (that is, 28 percent) who voted for its executive board.[88] In 1797, Metrà's commercial geography listed Jews as heading approximately 14 percent of the city's commercial firms (21 of 147), with the percentage slightly higher—16.5 percent—in the three categories of larger-scale firms (8 of 55, that is, 15 percent, of *Borsa*-eligible authorized wholesalers; 11 of 51, that is, 22 percent of approved wholesalers; 1 of 15, that is, 7 percent of public wholesalers and retailers.)[89] As stated above, Jews were especially active in the city's burgeoning insurance industry.

Besides participating in the *Borsa*, Jews also contributed to the public discourse on the port and commerce in other ways. Samuel Vital, secretary of the Chamber of Insurance and member of the intellectual society *Arcadia Romano Sonziaca*, published a book on insurance; G. V. Bolaffio authored one on currency exchange. In the late 1790s, Vital also made proposals for the harbor's lighting and a new *Borsa* building. The *Borsa* deputies chose long-time member Abram Hierschel as one of the additional six to help them supervise the erection of the new neoclassical *Borsa*.[90] As will be discussed below, Grassin Vita di Caliman Levi had by the mid-1790s become the first Jew elected as a *Borsa* deputy.

Jews were a noticeable component of the city's commercial elite (though the Greeks dominated the Levant trade[91]), and the wealthiest Jews cast a high profile. In response to a Jewish petition in 1789 about a conflict between Jewish and Habsburg laws concerning the marriage of a man and his niece, Chief of Police Pittoni urged the governor to permit Jews to follow their own law; he argued that he did not want the rich Jews to leave the city or remove their fortunes from it.[92]

Jews and the 'Borsa' Leadership

Jews' commercial activities were valued, but their integration and prominence within the Triestine mercantile elite had not come without tension and resistance. In the 1750s, when the number of licensed brokers in the city was set at twelve, the seven Christian brokers complained that their five Jewish colleagues were too numerous, and competition with them too fierce.⁹³ The story of Jewish efforts, for some time unsuccessful, to reach the executive level of the *Borsa* well illustrates some of the strains.

When the wholesale merchant houses of Trieste joined together as a corporate body for the first time in 1744, they arranged their affairs "without distinction[s] of religion" and elected a Jew, Israel Levi, as secretary. In 1755 three Jews, Grassin Vita Levi, Iseppo Morpurgo, and David Luzzatto, were among those who formally constituted themselves as the *Borsa dei Mercanti* to serve both as a trade association and as the intermediary between the merchants and the government.⁹⁴ As an official channel of communication between the two, the *Borsa* was often consulted by the local governing officials as they deliberated policies and legislation on commercial matters. The *Borsa* played an increasingly significant political as well as economic role in the city, and eventually became a seat of local power. When it was first established in 1755, its scheduled meeting day was set on Saturday, but that was soon changed to Friday and then Wednesday in order to accommodate its Jewish members. However, as the 1779 reorganization of the *Borsa* showed, membership and an active role for Jewish merchants were one thing; full integration and positions of leadership were another.⁹⁵

The proposal for reorganization was made in April 1779 by the first governor of Trieste, Karl von Zinzendorf, who served in that position from 1776 to 1782, as one of his many appointments during a long and distinguished career as a Habsburg official.⁹⁶ He invoked the general goals of efficiency and promoting a greater sense of the common good among the *Borsa*'s members, in contradistinction to the all-too-prevalent spirit of purely private gain and factionalism. As an important change, he urged that the leadership of the *Borsa* be changed from a single director to an executive board of six deputies. Zinzendorf stipulated that neither Jews nor Greeks be eligible to vote for or serve as deputies—just as they had not previously been eligible for the position of director. He gave no specific reason for the exclusion of the Jews; for the Greeks, he stated that it need last only so long as they continued to enjoy the preferential tariff advantages of Ottoman subjects, for "impartial judgment concerning public affairs cannot be expected from a person holding a privilege."⁹⁷ (Further discussions of the exclusion of Jews made no reference to the Greeks.) At that time, Jews comprised six of the *Borsa*'s forty-two commercial houses (about 14 percent).

When the new plan was discussed by the entire *Borsa* on July 13, 1779, the Jewish firm of Grassin Vita Levi headed by Marco Levi suggested that the election of deputies "proceed with no distinction between the components of the Mercantile body." However, adhering to precedent, the majority of members preferred to follow the "rules adopted for the election of the [former] director of the *Borsa*."⁹⁸ Though exclusion of the Jews was in fact the issue, it was not explicitly mentioned. Whether or not the matter had been properly aired became later a point of contention between Trieste and Vienna.

Most of Zinzendorf's recommendations were incorporated in the sovereign resolutions issued in Vienna on August 28 and September 16, 1779. In some respects, however, these resolutions guaranteed a greater role for regular *Borsa* members, requiring that the governor consult and record the views of all members when responding to inquiries from Vienna. Furthermore, individual members could still present their views directly to the governor, see the protocols prepared by the deputies on matters involving their own businesses, and have the *Borsa* convened in general session if they deemed it necessary.[99] As far as the majority of *Borsa* members and the governor were concerned, these provisions afforded ample opportunity for the Jews to make their needs and views known.

At least some Jews disagreed, and one, the powerful Marco Levi—court factor since 1760 and a senior member of the *Borsa*—vehemently made his objections known to Zinzendorf.[100] In late December 1779, a petition to the governor in the name of the Jewish members of the *Borsa* asked for reconsideration of the exclusion of Jews from the managing board. Its first argument was the Jews' prior and potential service in building up commerce in Trieste. As good subjects, they had contributed considerably through advice and deeds, since "the Jewish nation . . . [is] by its nature accomplished in the theory and still more so in practice of commercial affairs."[101] Their exclusion from the board would harm not only the Jewish merchants, but indeed the cause of commerce generally in Trieste. On the contrary, permission to serve in this capacity would lead them to gratitude, obligation, and greater commercial efforts. The second argument was procedural, namely, that the issue of the Jews' exclusion had not been explicitly discussed by the *Borsa* when it had approved the reorganization plan in July 1779. An accompanying affidavit, dated December 27, 1779, contained the statement of eleven Christian *Borsa* members that they had not in fact intended to exclude the Jews.[102]

On December 31, 1779, Zinzendorf—clearly annoyed by what he saw as procedural irregularities and machinations—declared his refusal to reconsider the matter, stating that the Jews' request contravened prior practices in Trieste and the sovereign resolution from Vienna of August 1779. Now, appeal was made to the sovereign herself in January 1780. This petition, also in the name of the Jewish members of the Triestine *Borsa*, raised the rhetorical level when adding new arguments about equality and a free port:

Though never ambitious for any office or public task in the regulation of this body [the *Borsa*], [the Jewish merchant houses] have always been regarded without discrimination as being on an equal footing with the Christians, as the nature of a free port requires. . . . Motivated precisely by such equality, the Jewish merchants did not fail to present at every opportunity in the public sessions of the *Borsa* their theoretical and practical commercial reflections with the praiseworthy zeal and fervor of true subjects.[103]

Excluding Jews from the possibility of being *Borsa* deputies meant depriving them of a prior "equality of prerogative"—the right to give counsel—and depriving the *Borsa* of their very useful service. This exclusion was especially mortifying for Marco Levi, whose great contributions to commerce were singled out for special mention. If the exclusion were to be maintained, the petition asked at least for an honorary title, such as commercial councillor, for Levi. Otherwise, it was predicted, his shame and extreme anguish would lead to discouragement and incapacity to serve as in the past.

This petition created radically different impressions in Vienna and Trieste: the argument about equality in a free port found a receptive ear in Vienna, while in Trieste, the overriding sense was of Levi's arrogance.

In a private letter to Zinzendorf of January 22, 1780, Chancellor Heinrich Cajetan Blümegen (head of the Bohemian-Austrian Court Chancellery) expressed misgivings about the exclusion of the Jews and urged that Zinzendorf reconsider it. He stated that the exclusion had seemed regrettable even earlier and had only been approved on the assumption—now understood to be mistaken—that the matter had been explicitly and thoroughly discussed in Trieste. He continued:

In fact no well-founded reason presents itself why in a free seaport, in which there is otherwise no difference among the nations, Jewish merchant houses should practically be excluded from such a merchants' managing board, for which the practical knowledge and discernment of the aforesaid are just as good and useful as those of members of the other religions.[104]

From the perspective of Vienna, religious differences had no place in the business of the free port. The Jews ought to be considered eligible to be deputies of the *Borsa*, though not chairman, a position that carried along with it supervision of the Triestine normal schools and poor house. This change would further the interests of commerce and "avoid the hateful outcome of an unnecessary [and] perhaps prejudicial exclusion."[105]

Zinzendorf was taken aback by the chancellor's direct and strong support for the Jews' request. He required a few days' reflection and consultation with Chief of Police Pittoni in order to calm down and compose what seemed to them a measured response. Yet the length and heated tone of Zinzendorf's February 7, 1780, letter to Blümegen betrayed his annoyance and exasperation.[106] He told Blümegen that he would gladly implement the chancellor's suggestion and act with his own customary justice and impartiality if the chancellor had not been so seriously misled about the situation in Trieste. Zinzendorf unleashed a torrent of anger and a bill of indictment against Marco Levi; he held him responsible for the earlier petition, which he charged had not been sent through the usual channels, and for the pressure that produced the accompanying affidavit, whose contents were manifestly untrue. The salient facts were the following: the most important Christian *Borsa* members had told him repeatedly that their clear intention had been to keep Jews from being eligible for the new position of deputy just as they had been ineligible for the prior position of director, and furthermore, this exclusion did not deprive the Jews of any previously held prerogative. They would still participate in all general *Borsa* discussions and have many opportunities for expressing their concerns on all important matters. The request for the new prerogative came not from the Jewish community, but really from Marco Levi alone. Zinzendorf charged him with having instigated the petitions and with presenting them as if from all the other Jewish *Borsa* members. Zinzendorf may well have been right about this: certainly the petition to Vienna had focused markedly upon Marco Levi. To Zinzendorf, this petition represented the height of Levi's "insufferable pride, brazen despotism, and self-interested scheming."[107] Zinzendorf blamed Levi himself, his well-known chicanery, and his incessant boasting and self-aggrandizement for the continuing opposition of most Triestine merchants to granting a new prerogative to Jews. He took pains to stress that Levi's contribution to the growth of commerce in Trieste was nowhere near as substantial as Levi was wont to claim. As for the other Jewish *Borsa* merchants, Zinzendorf claimed to value them "on account of their knowledge and useful efforts as highly as any of the other Christian houses."[108] None had expressed to him the desire to be eligible to be *Borsa* deputies, but should they do so in the future, he would try to change the other merchants' minds on the matter. He could only do so, however, after a reasonable period of time, and only if Marco Levi would meanwhile behave himself appropriately and keep a low profile.

Blümegen sidestepped the anti–Marco Levi invective in his crisp answer of February 28, 1780, focusing instead on the political and structural issues. He reiterated that Vienna had wanted the general exclusion of Jews from the deputy board to be discussed explicitly and the opinions of all *Borsa* members to be clearly expressed. Most significantly, he presented a new interpretation of precedent in this case: the six new deputies were to function not like the former director of the *Borsa*, but rather like its former "tumultuous general assembly," in which the Jews had always participated; thus to allow Jews to become deputies would not constitute "a new privilege or greater influence . . . but rather [would] restore things to their former long-standing track."[109] Thus, Vienna had accepted the major arguments of the Jewish petitions: that equality of opportunity was appropriate in the free port, and that excluding Jews from the new managing board of the *Borsa* would in effect deprive them of a previously held right. Blümegen told Zinzendorf that he would rely upon him to come up with the most suitable way of implementing Jewish eligibility.

At first, Zinzendorf was unsure of how to respond. He wrote in his diary on March 3, 1780:

Ruminated a long time whether I ought to write to the chancellor in order to put to rest completely this ridiculous affair . . . made me understand that the Jews have always been represented, [and were] never [themselves] representatives, that if we want to go beyond prejudice, why not make them directors. It is unlikely that the [Jewish] community ever expected to be included on the deputy board.[110]

Ultimately, Zinzendorf himself was swayed. A few months later, in mid-June 1780, he instructed the *Borsa* to reconsider its earlier position. He was prompted in part by another Jewish petition of late May, this time signed by all the Jewish *Borsa* members, which stated—simply and humbly—their desire to be of service in this way.[111] Zinzendorf made no reference to his private correspondence of the earlier winter with the chancellor in Vienna, but rather tried to put the Jews' request in a new light. He explained that when the *Borsa* had been managed by only one director and vice-director, then all the remaining merchants were excluded from leadership positions. But now, when there was a collective leadership of six, and in fact fewer meetings of the *Borsa* as a whole, "the circumstance of being excluded by law from that honor" was rendered "more sensitive." Since the Jews were registered members of the *Borsa*, they should not be excluded from making themselves more useful to the association. He sought to allay fears of Jewish factionalism by stating that future elections would be carefully monitored. Besides, he argued,

The hatefulness of a legal exclusion was more likely to make them [factions] arise, while, on the contrary, the admission to the honor of representation of all the *Borsa* houses who contribute to the growth of commerce will be precisely the most efficacious means of extinguishing every spirit of faction and disunity so harmful to the common good of the marketplace.[112]

Zinzendorf urged the *Borsa* to allow its Jewish members to be eligible for its leadership positions, though still with certain limitations, namely, that only one Jew at a time serve as a deputy on the board of six, and that no Jew occupy the chairmanship.

The majority of Christian *Borsa* members did not accept Zinzendorf's new arguments. At their meeting on July 15, 1780, the vote went twenty to seven against his proposal. Denying having acted on "an erroneous principle of prejudice or unfounded animosity," the victorious opponents addressed the issues of practicality, precedent, and honor. Practically, Jews still had many avenues through which to make known their views, and would still be consulted on important matters equally with other merchants. The opponents did not accept the revised definition of precedent. Precedent dictated, they argued, that the Jews be excluded from the leadership positions of the *Borsa*, and moreover from that kind of honor, "since elsewhere in all our states as a general rule, the Jewish nation is generally not capable of real honor, nor would we know, to tell the truth, which new merits it would have earned by its own endeavors in Trieste in order to acquire a new prerogative of honor, which it has never enjoyed."[113] To three-quarters of the Christian *Borsa* members, the age-old prohibitions against Jews holding public positions of honor seemed valid. It is reasonable to assume that their negative feelings about Marco Levi—and Jews more generally—still played a significant role, for they closed their letter with a denunciation of the "illegal and crafty means" the Jewish nation had employed in this matter. These means, they charged, bespoke their merely self-interested spirit, which would be harmful in public deliberations. To put the charge in other words, the Jews' selfish clannishness made them unfit to exercise public authority. There the matter rested until the Toleration proposals of Joseph II contributed to a new climate of opinion in 1781.

The issue of the Jews' eligibility for the managing board of the *Borsa* revealed conflicting perspectives. The Jews considered themselves worthy candidates for the position of deputy by virtue of their ongoing commercial service, and argued against legally sanctioned exclusion and inferiority. The central authorities in Vienna took their views seriously and accepted their arguments about the appropriateness of equality in a free port. Vienna was expressly concerned not to increase Jewish influence and power,[114] but believed that allowing Jews to serve formally in leading positions would not substantially alter the status quo. In contrast, at the local level, most Christian merchants resisted this change. Distrust of Jews, or at least of one particularly powerful Jew, and competitiveness fueled their anxieties and self-protective exclusionary instincts. This was not the only time that the *Borsa* rejected initiatives from Vienna, and it fit into a larger pattern of the *Borsa*'s jealously guarding its own control over local affairs.[115] It is one illustration of the limitation of Vienna's absolutism by local forces.

As governor, Zinzendorf usually spoke for the interests of the central regime, but through much of the course of this affair, he stood by the local forces and represented their wishes. Pragmatic politics was surely one factor, since the Christian merchants of the *Borsa* well outnumbered the Jews. Yet there can be no doubt that Zinzendorf also shared the animus of many local merchants against Marco Levi. Though the economic principle of free trade may have been at stake when Zinzendorf opposed Levi's efforts to secure a monopoly on tobacco revenues,[116] it is clear that Zinzendorf disliked having to deal with this powerful and cantankerous personality. Zinzendorf both valued and resented Levi's connections with higher Habsburg authorities; once, for example, he complained that Levi had better connections than he in Vienna.[117]

But was it really Levi and his demands for himself that inspired all the dislike and mistrust? For Zinzendorf that may have been the case, but the majority of the Christian merchants also seemed opposed substantively to the rights he requested for the other Jewish merchants. The terms that Zinzendorf used to describe Levi's behavior—and that some merchants used more generally—bespoke long-standing negative stereotypes about Jews: scheming, devious, dishonest, self-interested, prone to forming factions. Zinzendorf even took recourse to the ever-suspect distinction between good and bad Jews. Would Levi have been considered so obnoxious if he had not been the member of a religious minority trying to claim new rights? These questions cannot be answered precisely. What is clear is that Zinzendorf first stayed in step with the majority opinion of the Christian *Borsa* members, and that then, after tempers had cooled and time had passed, he tried to implement the will of the central authorities. He was not opposed in principle to Jews serving as *Borsa* deputies. But given his extreme dislike of Marco Levi and his reading of the politics of the *Borsa*, he did not go to great lengths to overcome the opposition.

What the *Borsa* reorganization of 1779–80 shows are both the complicated dynamics of the relation between center and periphery, and the tensions accompanying the increasing Jewish presence in the leading circles of the city. Yet, a substantial minority of the voting *Borsa* members, one-quarter, was ready to have Jews formally exercise public power and authority; their only concern was how to handle a Saturday meeting if one should be deemed necessary during the term of a Jewish deputy. The episode shows that Jews were indeed becoming a more vital and central part of the Triestine economic elite, but that it was not always smooth sailing. Jewish commerce could be valued by those who wanted to build up the free port, but Jewish merchants could still be distrusted by their local competitors. It took some prodding from Vienna in 1781–82 to spur the merchants of Trieste to realize more fully the city's potential as the "Philadelphia of Europe," a city of "brotherly love." Yet, in terms of the total picture, this resistance was minor, and not enduring. Starting in the 1790s, Jews did become members of the *Borsa*'s executive board.

Economics and the Jewish Community

Proud of the Jews' manifest economic contribution to the burgeoning free port, communal leaders saw their economic responsibilities as threefold: (1) to control the influx of foreigners so as to maintain the profile of the community as a useful industrious group; (2) to regulate Jewish economic activities so as to maximize compliance with Jewish law;[118] and (3) to instill and foster in Jewish youth the mercantile values and work ethic of the free port.

Nothing better illustrates the marriage of economic and moral values within the Triestine Jewish ethos than a public performance by the Jewish schoolchildren in 1786 in the presence of communal leaders and honored guests, including the governor. They recited an ethical drama composed by Raffael Nathan Tedesco, then a teacher in the community school and assistant rabbi, entitled *Indagine di qual sia tra i morali mali il peggiore: Accademico garreggiamento scolastico* (Inquiry on which moral vice is the worst: Competitive scholastic recital). Idleness, the quintessential bourgeois sin, was decreed the worst moral failing, generating and subsuming all other vices as it harmed the self and society, nature and the universe.[119] Thus, Triestine Jews publicly proclaimed their sharing in the ethos of the new port city. Their active role in it was one of the pillars of Jewish communal existence and consciousness in Trieste in the eighteenth century.

CHAPTER TWO

Maria Theresa and the Legal Status of the Jews of Trieste: The Privileges of 1771

The modern Jewish community of Trieste owed its existence to the Habsburg Adriatic free-ports policy. And it was Maria Theresa—usually known as a zealous defender of the Catholic faith and firm opponent of extending religious and civil toleration to non-Catholics—who in fact created the institutional framework for the diverse religious-ethnic communities of Trieste. Allowing cosmopolitan diversity in Trieste was an important instance of her occasional divergence from Counter-Reformation ideals in order to pursue the absolutist goals of reform and state-building.

Generally Maria Theresa remained committed to the vision of the baroque *pietas austriaca*: the unity of crown, church, and nobility in a confessionally uniform state. As a Habsburg ruler, part of whose mission since the Counter-Reformation was to preserve or restore Catholicism, she saw herself responsible in an almost personal and maternalistic fashion for the spiritual welfare of her subjects. It would be extreme dereliction of her duty to expose Catholics to the dangers of heresy or Protestantism, or to fail to bring crypto-Protestants to the true faith. In 1777, during one of the many escalating clashes she had with her son and co-regent Joseph on these issues, Maria Theresa expressed her conviction that toleration of non-Catholics was tantamount to indifference to religious truth and salvation:

This general toleration that you tell me is one of your principles. . . . I shall continue to pray . . . that God will preserve you from this evil, which would be the greatest that the Monarchy has ever suffered. . . . You will be ruining your state, you will be the cause of so many souls being lost. What is the point of your possessing the true religion if you value and love it so little that you consider it unimportant to maintain it and strengthen it?[1]

Also that year, she wrote to Joseph: "Certainly no spirit of persecution; but still more, no indifference or systematic toleration: this is the policy I intend to follow so long as I live."[2] Among the means she variously advocated for dealing with non-Catholic Christians were conversion, forced religious instruction, harsh civil penalties, expulsion, and forced migration from the monarchy's central lands to Transylvania (where Habsburg rulers confirmed German Lutherans in their prior right of public religious worship at the time of conquest in the late seventeenth century).[3] Forced migration became preferable to expulsion as fear of contributing to the growth of foreign Protestant powers like Frederick's Prussia grew.

In the case of Jews, Maria Theresa was probably animated less by worry about religious temptation for Christians, and more by visceral aversion and hostility. Also in 1777, she wrote of the Jews: "I know of no worse plague in the State than this Nation, which brings people to beggary through swindling, usury, and moneylending, or exercising the lowest trades, which all other honest people abhor."[4] In 1778, she added: "I have repeatedly ordered to reduce the [number of] Jews, [and] in no way to increase them further on any pretext."[5] In Vienna itself, she tried to keep their numbers to an absolute minimum. To reside there, Jews had to pay a hefty annual toleration tax, and they were not allowed to appear in public before noon on Sundays and Christian holidays. She also tried expulsion—of the long-standing Prague Jewish community in 1745—but local and international pressure led her to rescind the order.

But Maria Theresa acted not only on her ideals of *pietas austriaca*. As recent scholarship has shown, she was a reforming absolutist monarch, intent on state-building and centralizing her Habsburg domains. The task was complicated by the fact that the essential tie holding all the different and heterogeneous regions together was dynastic. Considerable administrative, fiscal, judicial, and military reorganization was required to build even the rudiments of a unified Habsburg state. Toward that end, much effort was expended from the 1740s on, as competition with Prussia intensified. While few, if any, have ever accused Maria Theresa of being an enlightened as well as an absolute monarch, many of her closest advisors, including the powerful State Chancellor Wenzel Anton von Kaunitz-Rietberg, were influenced by the Enlightenment and other progressive eighteenth-century currents, such as cameralism and reform Catholicism.[6] Cameralism was a central European political philosophy that saw the state in secular terms as a unitary whole, and was concerned above all with administering it soundly to promote its economic and fiscal well-being. Reform Catholicism came in many varieties, but all tended to stress the role of individual conscience, the futility of force to fight religious heresy, and the need to limit papal authority. Enlightenment, Reform Catholicism, and cameralism were reflected in the Habsburg Monarchy in a wide-ranging program of ecclesiastical reform that fundamentally asserted state control over the Church, and over religion in general. Its measures included secularizing censorship and higher education, reducing the number of holy days, restricting monasteries, subjecting papal legislation to state veto, and taxing Church lands.[7]

However, toleration was precisely the one important religious issue over which Maria Theresa and her advisors most sharply disagreed. She was swayed sometimes by pragmatic political and economic considerations: for example, she was persuaded to recognize long-standing guarantees for Protestant worship in Hungary, to allow foreign Protestant craftsmen and diplomats to reside and worship privately in Vienna, and to tolerate tacitly Protestants in the Alpine mountains and in the Netherlands. Grete Klingenstein correctly points out that the confessional pattern during Maria Theresa's reign was not uniform, and indeed displayed varying shades of diversity.[8] But tacit toleration in a few cases was hardly acceptance of the principle of civil toleration. Until the end of her reign, religious conformity remained the norm for her, and toleration was to be granted, if necessary, only grudgingly and in exceptional circumstances.

Trieste, where mercantilist considerations had prevailed, was one such exception to the norm of religious uniformity both de facto and de jure. In Trieste—one of but a handful of places in the Hereditary Lands where Jews were even permitted residence—Jews were allowed to worship in public, and their community was formally recognized as a corporate entity in 1746. From 1752 the Greek Orthodox enjoyed similar rights. (Armenian Uniates were granted communal statutes in 1775, a testimony to ethnic diversity but less so to religious, since they were Catholic, albeit Eastern.) Protestant merchants and artisans of various nationalities had been welcome in Trieste from the early days of the free port, but they had the most difficulties securing religious rights. For some time they had enjoyed the right of domestic worship, but repeatedly, in 1775, 1776, and 1778, they requested the right of private worship in a church. Despite the arguments made on their behalf by Governor Zinzendorf—himself a Protestant until 1763—who stressed that it was better that they come to Trieste than go to rival Venice, their requests were opposed by the local Catholic clergy, court chancellery officials in Vienna, and Maria Theresa. It was finally Joseph's approval in 1778 that proved decisive. Triestine Protestants now gained the right of private worship in a chapel, but not the right of public worship in a church with a street entrance, bells, or tower. This significant step was taken during Maria Theresa's reign, but it was Joseph, not she, who was responsible for it.[9] She did, however, acquiesce. The extraordinary situation of the free port shows the limits to which Maria Theresa was prepared to go for pragmatic reasons, but it did not really signify a change in her ideology or principles.

Against this backdrop, the rest of this chapter will examine in detail the status Maria Theresa granted the Jews of Trieste. She approved the community's first corporate statute in 1746, but the privileges she signed in 1771 best reveal the terms of Theresian toleration for the Jews of Trieste.

The Theresian Diplomas of 1771

The status defined by Maria Theresa in April 1771 for the Jews of Trieste was issued in the form of sovereign diplomas, elaborately written on parchment and bound with velvet, bearing her signature and wax seal, and costing dearly: 1,000 gold ducats, or just over 4,500 florins, a sum almost equivalent to the Jewish community's annual budget. These beautiful specimens of ancien régime privilege are still in the Jewish community's possession today, carefully preserved in a locked safe. They were the result of an intensive process of negotiation and deliberation that involved the Jews of Trieste, the local Intendancy, Habsburg officials in Vienna, and even Maria Theresa herself. It was she personally who insisted on the high fee of 1,000 ducats when others deemed 500 sufficient.[10] Though the Jews of Trieste had tried to get the substantial fee lowered, they knew that all grants of privilege carried a price. The conferring or reconfirmation of private rights, exemptions, or status was an important revenue-raising device for all European monarchs in the seventeenth and eighteenth centuries, and especially for Maria Theresa in the aftermath of the Seven Years' War (1756–63). Of the essence of the absolutist-corporate society, privileges were always local and specific, defining the traditional rights or status granted to particular individuals or groups by favor of the ruler and in recognition of the special functions assigned the individual or group. They expressed a personal tie between sovereign and subject. There was a certain ambiguity as to whether privileges were supposed to be enduring, or subject to loss if not formally renewed. Payment for reconfirmation ensured revenue for the crown, and continued validity of the privilege's benefits for the recipients.[11]

The Theresian Privilege (*Privilegio*) of 1771 dealt primarily with the rights of Jewish individuals to live, work, and worship in Trieste, while the Statute (*Statuto*) of 1771 concerned the functioning of the Jewish community as a corporate entity. These two diplomas were essentially updated and adjusted confirmations of the three kinds of enactment that had previously defined the legal status of the Jews of Trieste. The Statute of 1771 built upon the previous statutes of the corporate Jewish community approved by the government in 1746, 1762, and 1766. The Privilege of 1771 was a modified melding and extension of two very different kinds of enactment: (1) the court Jew privileges granted to certain individual Jews in Trieste by Habsburg rulers in the sixteenth and seventeenth centuries, and (2) the Free Port Patents of 1719 and 1725, which invited merchants of "any nation, condition, and religion" to Trieste and thereby pertained to Jewish merchants—as to all other merchants engaged in international commerce—though Jews were not specifically mentioned. The Privilege of 1771 functioned both as a collective charter of protection (*Schutzbrief*),[12] outlining conditions of residence, protection, work, and worship, and as an open invitation to attract wealthy Jews to the free port. The Statute of 1771 contained the kinds of administrative regulation formulated in the ordinances (*takkanot*) of most autonomous Jewish communities.[13] Such ordinances, like those of all corporate bodies, were subject to governmental approval, but this statute, which functioned in effect as a governmental police ordinance (*Polizeiordnung*)—"police" in the broad sense of administration to provide orderly social existence—was issued with far greater governmental involvement and control than previously in Trieste.[14]

Though initially separate items on the agenda, the two diplomas became intertwined. Early in 1769, the Jews had been instructed to delegate a committee to work with local officials on revisions of their 1766 communal statutes, which were due to expire in 1771. Also in 1769, as a separate matter, they were told to request ratification within a year of the earlier privileges of residence and work.[15] When the Jews of Trieste learned of the high price they would have to pay for new communal statutes in the form of a sovereign diploma, they asked that their other privileges be included in it as well. Yet they later asked that the two documents be separated because of the differences between the two and their desire for greater flexibility in changing the Statute.[16] The documents were dated April 19, 1771, but only in 1775–76 were all the negotiations completed and did the Jews of Trieste finally pay for and take possession of them.[17] Both the process and the substance of the two Theresian diplomas of 1771 revealed the ever-increasing complexities of the relationship between the interventionist absolutist state and the Jewish community.

The Privilege of 1771

In its opening paragraphs, the Privilege of 1771 explicitly stated the prime concern driving governmental policy with regard to the Jews of Trieste, namely, the development of international trade:

We Maria Theresa. . . .
   The internal happiness of Our natural subjects always having been the principal

object of the concerns and actions of Our Regency; [and] Our being persuaded that external commerce contributes effectively to such happiness. . . . We have not spared care, effort, or funds in order to further the dual purpose of making commerce prosper especially in Trieste, and of *improving the condition* [emphasis mine] of merchants, subjects and foreigners, who have established themselves in that Port.

The Jewish Nation, especially suited to commerce, *invited* [emphasis mine] by the general Patents of Our Most August Parent and recognized with individual Privileges from His most glorious predecessors, arouses Our most merciful particular reflections, all the more since on the one hand the settlements of the Nation itself in Trieste already constitute a formal community, and [since] on the other, some of its Individuals who belong to the Mercantile Exchange (*Borsa mercantile*) contribute by means of work and counsel to the growth of Commerce and Navigation for the common benefit of the merchants and of the marketplace (*piazza*).

We therefore wish to give to the Jewish Community in Trieste in general, [and] to the Jewish Merchants of the Exchange in particular, a solemn demonstration of our Sovereign approval for the purpose of attracting more such families and individuals who would make themselves worthy of the City and State by establishing new commercial firms and by engaging in wholesale Trade.[18]

To further the development of the free port as a center of international trade, the Privilege promised valuable economic, religious, and judicial rights for all Jews "already settled or who will settle in Trieste." The Privilege confirmed the rights of the Jews of Trieste to enjoy security of life and property, both real and movable,[19] and to engage freely and equally in maritime and inland commerce, manufacturing, and artisanry. It also repeated the exemption of *Borsa* members and wealthy merchants from the head toll when traveling to Vienna and other cities (an exemption enjoyed also by the Sefardic Jews of Amsterdam and Livorno).[20] The Privilege guaranteed Jews the right to profess and practice their religious rites and ceremonies in public, for example in synagogue and cemetery, without "impediment or difficulty." Indeed, the local authorities were to be responsible for protection of the burial ground, and Jews were not to be pressured or forced to embrace another religion. The Privilege assured that Jews would not be required to discharge legal or financial obligations on their Sabbaths and festivals. They were granted access to the state's courts and tribunals on the same impartial basis as other subjects. This meant that they would not have to pay double fees, as was the case in some other places, such as Vienna and Moravia. The Privilege closed with explicit reconfirmation for all present and future Jews of Trieste of the rights granted by the Free Port Patents and by all subsequent sovereign resolutions issued in favor of the Jewish community of Trieste. All Triestine Jews—but especially the wealthy merchants who belonged to the *Borsa* and were trading in Austrian-made goods— could expect to enjoy "Sovereign Protection, Grace, and Munificence."[21]

The specific provisions of the Privilege, together with the facts that the

Jews of Trieste paid no regular toleration tax or protection fee,[22] wore no humiliating distinguishing signs,[23] and could—if wealthy—gain permission to live outside the ghetto, meant that their status was unusually favorable in the overall Habsburg context. This status was certainly an outgrowth of the seventeenth-century individual court Jew privileges and the early-eighteenth-century Free Port Patents, but its precise evolution from them is not clear. Both in the eighteenth century and in scholarly literature, there has been confusion: about the relation between these two sources of law, and about how and when precisely the earlier court Jew privileges were extended to the other Jews of Trieste. It is therefore difficult to determine to what extent this Theresian grant of privilege represented an extension of previously held liberties, or rather was a mere reconfirmation of them.

During negotiations over the diplomas in 1770–71, the Jews stated that they had not sought renewal of the individual privileges—granted by Ferdinand II to Ventura Parente in 1624, and reconfirmed by Ferdinand III in 1647 and again by Leopold I in 1696 for the communal heads Leone Levi and Caliman Parente—because they had thought that the Free Port Patents made that unnecessary. They based their argument on the 1696 privilege, which explicitly stated that it would apply not only to the Levi and Parente families and their descendants but also "generally to all the Jews of Trieste together with their wives, descendants, relatives and servants, to whomever was born there and will be born there."[24] In 1770–71, the Jews asked that the privilege now be extended beyond "all the families originating in Trieste" so as to be valid "indiscriminately for all the families settled" in Trieste.[25]

But views diverged as to what the 1696 privilege really meant. The Jews, supported by one local official, Valentinus Modesti, believed that Leopold's 1696 privilege had "not only confirmed [the earlier privilege], but also extended it to the whole community with the best consideration." Their claim was that the 1696 privilege had extended the earlier ones to cover all Jews *born* in Trieste; thus the issue now would be to extend them further to all Jews, including non-natives, *settled* in Trieste. Modesti urged that Vienna now renew all the privileges for all the Jews of Trieste and thereby "give comfort and joy to an entire community."[26] However, the official Intendancy report argued differently to the Court Commerce Council:

> It is surely not advisable to extend Ferdinand's privilege, which granted favor in very broad terms to two single families, to all the families born in Trieste without distinction. For too general a privilege would practically cease to be a privilege, or at least the distinction made in favor of the two named families would disappear.[27]

In other words, despite its explicit wording, Leopold's privilege of 1696 could not be understood already to have extended the earlier privileges to the collectivity. Superiors in Vienna upheld this view: Leopold's confirmation had pertained only to the two specific families and certainly not to all the Jews found in Trieste; had that been his intention, they argued, he would have said so explicitly in the privilege![28]

How were these divergences of opinion possible? Why was there such confusion? It is possible that the 1696 privilege extended the rights to all Jews who would be born in Trieste, but not necessarily to those who would settle in Trieste. The 1771 privilege would then represent a significant extension to the entire community, immigrants as well as natives. But the confusion about the meaning of the 1696 privilege suggests that it had not played a vital role in securing the status of the Jews of Trieste. Perhaps its precise terms had been forgotten, or some of its provisions seemed irrelevant, once the Free Port Patents were issued. For example, in the eighteenth century, how many Triestine Jews wished to avail themselves of a court Jew's right to reside and trade in Vienna, or to live anywhere that Jews were settled in the monarchy? What mattered to those in Trieste were the real opportunities available in Trieste itself. And there, of course, the situation had changed dramatically in the decades since 1696, when only ten to twelve Jewish families, some sixty to eighty people, had moved into the ghetto.[29] Even if Leopold had meant to extend the Levi and Parente privileges to all future Jews born in Trieste, he could not have envisaged the burgeoning free port and the Jewish community of 1770, composed of more than fifty families, between three and four hundred individuals. In that sense, most of the Habsburg officials were right: extension of the privileges from individual families to an entire community—one of a much larger size and charged with a different purpose in a vastly different social and economic reality—was extremely complicated and difficult to imagine.

Indeed, as their report indicated, Habsburg officials in Vienna found the old categories wanting. They decided to "improve the condition of [Jews as] merchants" (in the words of the 1771 Privilege[30]) by updating the older privileges and grafting them and the Free Port Patents together. The problem was how to reconfirm the old in a way that made sense. As they put it in their instructions to local Triestine officials in January 1771, "It would be completely unsuitable to declare the entire Jewish nation in Trieste as court Jews,"[31] which was what would be required if the earlier privilege of Ferdinand were simply extended. Similarly, they reasoned, the right to conduct wholesale and retail trade throughout the entire monarchy was the kind of privilege suitable for a particular person but not for an entire nation. Other provisions, such as those concerning residence in Vienna, credit transactions, and exemptions from future taxes, would be "senseless" if extended to the entire community, for then Jews would enjoy advantages by law greater than Christians. It would be sufficient, Vienna mandated, for the new Privilege to offer Jews simply the same protection as other subjects.

Accordingly, Triestine officials were told to draft a document that would extend the older privileges to the entire community in an appropriately updated fashion and that would uphold the Free Port Patents. Privileges usually opened with references to prior ones, but probably because it was not quite a reconfirmation, the final copy of the Theresian Privilege of 1771 omitted all such mention. Perhaps also as an expression of absolutism, this one started simply and baldly, "We Maria Theresa by the Grace of God Empress of the Romans." Those rights which could logically be granted to the entire Triestine Jewish community were so extended: for example, the rights pertaining to security of life and property, justice, trade, artisanry, religious freedom. But the Theresian Privilege of 1771 removed all references to court Jews and their customary liberties. There was to be no suggestion of an entire court Jew community. A community, no matter how favorable its status, could not enjoy special benefits over and above the majority of Christian subjects. Provisions that would have meant greater advantage if extended to the entire community had to be omitted or scaled down so as to offer parity with other subjects. Extension of the now-anachronistic court Jew privileges would have to proceed by way of dilution.

The notion of parity was expressed in a significant way in the changes made by Habsburg superiors to the draft of the Privilege drawn up in Trieste. In a number of instances (for example, with regard to duties on imports to the Austrian lands, access to Habsburg courts, and the free exercise of arts and manufacture), the conditions for Triestine Jews were declared equal to those of "Our other subjects" (*altri Nostri sudditi*). In one case, this phrase was added alongside "other nations." In another, the word "subjects" was substituted for "nations." The focus here was not only the Jewish community of Trieste in relation to the other religious-ethnic nations settled in Trieste, but parity of Jewish individuals qua individuals with all other Habsburg subjects, in other words, with Habsburg Catholics. In these respects, Triestine Jews were to be considered as Habsburg subjects like all others. To post–French Revolutionary ears accustomed to the rhetoric of equal rights for citizens, equal treatment for subjects may hardly sound inspiring or exalted. But parity with other subjects ought not to be underestimated when it is remembered that Jewish status in medieval and early modern Europe had often been that of temporary resident or resident alien.

It is also significant that Jews were being treated not only as members of their corporate group, but also in some respects as individuals—a trend discernible in other Habsburg enactments of the time.[32] This was part of the contribution of the Free Port Patents to the complex legal status of the Jews of Trieste. While eschewing the court Jew terminology, the Theresian Privilege of 1771 combined to some degree the exceptionality of those individual privileges for specific Jews with the generality of the Free Port Patents. Fittingly for this Jewish community "on the German-Italian frontier,"[33] its status was an outgrowth and amalgam of the central European court Jew tradition and the Mediterranean tradition of free-port invitations to individual merchants of diverse groups. Given the evolution of the city and of Habsburg legal-political sensibilities, the specifics of court Jew status gave way to free-port opportunities for individuals and communities. While the wealthiest Jews of Trieste and those most actively engaged in the export of goods from the Habsburg Hereditary Lands enjoyed the most favorable status, it is significant that they were not separated legally from the other Jews in the port city. In many central European Jewish communities, the wealthiest Jews, often those descended from original court Jews, successfully separated themselves from other Jews in order to gain more favorable rights. By contrast, in Trieste, the legacy of individual court Jew privileges and the Free Port Patents resulted in a favorable status for the entire Jewish community. Though the Theresian Privilege of 1771 modified and diluted the earlier privileges in order to update them, it did constitute a significant extension of favorable terms to all Jews in Trieste, at the time and for the future.

The Statute of 1771

The Theresian Statute of 1771 was a much longer and more detailed document than the Privilege. The preamble stated its purpose thus:

Order and regulation (*l'ordine e la polizia*) are those fundamental rocks upon which rests the happiness of all Societies, of all Communities who live together in civil assembly, and in order to put them on a stable and fixed footing among the ranks of the Jewish nation *tolerated* [emphasis mine] in OUR FREE PORT of Trieste, we have ordered OUR Intendant of the entire Littoral to examine the constitutions and customs currently in use, and to present a plan, according to which there can be granted and prescribed to the said community a secure and clear norm, to serve as a legislative guide, in order to maintain in the ghetto an uninterrupted harmony of the community, an exemplary order devoid of any Scandal, and finally an exact system of regulation (*Polizia*), without which no Society can be called perfect.[34]

Toward securing good order and administration, this statute reorganized the earlier communal statutes, and dealt in more detailed and formal bureaucratic language with communal leaders, the community at large, the Small Council, synagogues and associations, the rabbi and teachers, the treasurer, syndics, and secretaries, the beadles and servants, and the resolution of disputes.

In general, the Statute reaffirmed the authority of the *Capi* over all aspects of Jewish life, civil and religious, both inside and outside the ghetto, and their role as intermediaries between the government and the community. As before, the *Capi* were given the authority to arrest provisionally Jews who "dare[d] to commit any scandalous act, or [one] against the divine service in the synagogues," and then to turn to the communal council to decide the punishment and to the government to execute it. The Statute made an especially strong statement about the government's backing of the leaders of the community:

The government will uphold with all possible means the credit, respectability, and authority of the *Capi* in their office and their administration of it. Therefore they are instructed that, if they encounter any difficulty or impediment, personal or material, they can turn to the Intendancy's representative in matters of small importance, and in serious ones immediately to the government.[35]

Among their many duties, the *Capi* were supposed to monitor the probity and conduct of newcomers, Jews living outside the ghetto, and Christian servants in Jewish households, and to report regularly to the government.

One area in which the Statute accorded the *Capi* greater authority than before was the judicial sphere. According to earlier statutes, individuals were supposed to settle complaints against the community or its leaders by means of arbitration—a legal procedure recognized in Roman law and in systems derived from it—and not turn to the regular courts on pain of penalty.[36] But for the first time, the 1771 Statute accorded the *Capi* authority to decide certain civil disputes between individual Jews: in cases concerning persons or property, mercantile or maritime affairs, in which the claims did not exceed one hundred florins, and if the parties had failed to resolve their differences through amicable conciliation or voluntary arbitration. A Jew who brought such cases to the regular courts of the state would have to pay a fine of fifty florins to the communal treasury.[37] The community in the persons of the *Capi* was thus to serve as a court of first instance. The purpose was probably administrative efficiency, in order "not to bother the departments and courts of justice," in the words of the Statute. Officials of the Court Commerce Council cited Bohemia as the example to be followed. Indeed, this innovation in Trieste was consistent with Maria Theresa's policies of leaving intact long-standing Jewish judicial autonomy in both Bohemia and Galicia, and granting it to the Greek Orthodox community of Trieste in 1775.[38]

It seems that this innovation was also consonant with efforts of Jewish communal leaders in the mid-1760s to strengthen communal authority and disciplinary powers, and to have members settle more of their problems within the community. In December 1765, they decided to "treat [recalcitrant transgressors of communal regulations] with the rigors practiced in other communities," that is, to deny them religious and ritual services. They wanted their new rabbi to "exert his influence in case of any controversy between one Jew and another to reconcile them, and to induce them to submit themselves to the decision of Jewish arbiters, in order to avoid desecration of the [Divine] Name," that is, the resorting by Jews to Gentile courts.[39] In fact, the earliest extant set of records of judicial proceedings before Jewish authorities begins in the summer of 1766, when the noted halakhist Isach Formiggini arrived as the new rabbi of Trieste. But these efforts were only partly successful, to judge from the records, which show Jewish authorities dealing with only nine cases over the next fifteen years. These concerned personal quarrels, ritual transgressions, violations of synagogue decorum, and one paternity case, which the Criminal Court of the city asked the Jews to investigate.[40] In two particularly difficult cases of personal quarrels, Jewish leaders turned to governmental authorities for assistance.[41] Overall, if indeed only nine cases came before Jewish authorities in fifteen years, then judicial activity never became very intensive despite the 1771 Statute. Certainly for business affairs, and probably for other disputes as well, Jews continued to use the regular courts of the city.[42] The judicial authority accorded the Jewish leaders of Trieste by the Statute of 1771 was greater than that allowed during any other period, but it remained limited both in theory and in practice. Still, a significant element in the community complained a decade later about those judicial powers granted the *Capi*.[43]

The 1771 Statute charged the community with two other new responsibilities, both of which showed the widening range of the absolutist state's involvement in Jewish affairs and the ways by which it drew the community ever more tightly under its control. Both provisions were added by officials in Vienna to the draft submitted from Trieste.[44]

The first area of new responsibility was education. To the long article on the appointment and supervision of the rabbi and of public and private teachers, officials in Vienna added the following point: communal leaders should ensure that Jewish youth study not only Hebrew language and writing but also "the Italian and German languages current in the land."[45] Obviously the utility of Triestine Jews in the free port depended on their being fluent in the languages of the land and commerce. As stated above, Triestine Jews were quite accustomed to using Italian, though not German.

This seems to have been one of the first expressions of interest in Jewish education—specifically, the secular or civic education of Jews—by any European state.[46] The Habsburg Monarchy took the lead in establishing universal compulsory elementary education with the General School Ordinance (*Allgemeine Schulordnung*) of 1774 as part of its drive to make its subjects more productive and disciplined.[47] While systematic concern for

Jewish primary education would have to wait for Joseph II, the 1771 Statute shows that the matter was not entirely absent from official purview during Maria Theresa's reign. It is the first evidence of the tutelary state so familiar to Jews in central and eastern Europe in the eighteenth and nineteenth centuries, the state that saw itself as ultimately responsible for the practical and moral education of all its subjects. This clause in the 1771 Statute meant that Jewish education would no longer be considered purely an internal Jewish matter. Just as the education of Catholic youth was too important to be left to the Church, so, too, would the education of young Jews become a public matter of state concern. What was new for the Jewish community was the state's charge that Jewish education meet civic needs.

The Jewish community was given another duty that touched not only on morality but also on economics, namely, overseeing Jewish business ethics and practices. In a prominent location, in one of its closing paragraphs, the Statute made clear the essential logic of all the privileges granted to the Jews of Trieste in the eighteenth century. The Jews were warned to conduct all their commercial affairs honestly and in "good faith," and were put on notice that the local authorities would punish fraudulent practices in cases of bankruptcy and "wicked usury" according to the full rigor of the law. Moreover, "the behavior of the community [would] be subject to supreme legislative Vigilance on a regular basis," so that in cases of violations,

> it will be the formal duty of the said Tribunals to inform the Sovereign Court [in Vienna] through the Governor of Trieste of the specific contraventions case by case, in order that [the Sovereign Court] determine what considerations can and should necessarily be applied, as circumstances warrant, to the entire community tolerated so very mercifully in Trieste.[48]

The threat was transparent: disreputable business practices could undermine the position and raison d'être of the entire Jewish community of Trieste.

This stern admonition was the result of considerable deliberation among Habsburg officials in Trieste and Vienna. In January 1770, in the light of a recent problematic case of Jewish bankruptcy, Vienna instructed local officials to strengthen the penalties against Jews committing any irregularities when declaring bankruptcy. The question became whether to strengthen the general bankruptcy regulations, already considered quite severe, or to make special provisions for Jews. Local officials argued that general laws in principle had to apply equally to all, and that a harsher law pertaining to Jews alone and inserted in their new statute would be too "burdensome" and "painful." Therefore, they proposed to keep Jews within the framework of the general bankruptcy law, but to instruct the courts to punish Jewish violators always with the strictest penalty allowed by law. In other words, though Jews would be subject to the same law as all others, its provisions would be more harshly applied to them.[49]

However, the Court Commerce Council in Vienna, taking into account Maria Theresa's conviction that Jews in general were too prone to "fraud and trickery" and motivated by an excessive "desire for profit," decided to use the communal statutes to "instill a healthy fear" in the Jews. They wanted to "bind" the Triestine Jewish leaders, known to be possessed of a "praiseworthy zeal to contribute to the credit of the[ir] nation,"[50] to more active supervision of the business practices of their members. Therefore, the new Statute provided for all three: individual responsibility for Jews, who would be subject to the harshest possible penalties under the general law; a kind of collective responsibility for communal leaders; and governmental oversight both in Trieste and in Vienna. The collective responsibility imposed was more moral or political than financial, but the Statute left open just what the consequences of dishonest business practices by individual Jews would be for the community.

Thus the Theresian Statute of 1771 revealed that even as Habsburg officials valued Jewish international commerce, they were not entirely free of age-old mistrust of Jewish business ethics. Their sense was that they could not be too careful; it was only prudent to keep Jews—and themselves—on guard. Yet it is also significant that they were uncertain whether to treat Jews as individuals under the general laws or in their corporate group *en gros*. Their conservatism was evident in their choice of a corporative as well as an individual solution. What this provision also plainly showed was the absolutist effort to assert control over individuals' conduct through the multiple layers of community, local government, and central bureaucracy in Vienna.

The absolutist state showed its hand plainly in other places in the Statute. For the first time, it stipulated that a councillor of the Intendancy be present at communal elections, whereas earlier, notification of the results and a request for confirmation from the authorities was sufficient.[51] Though earlier statutes had required governmental approval, the new Statute was much more specific about Jewish religious and associational life: a government offical would have to approve any changes in the administrative or financial organization of the public synagogue, and the establishment of new synagogues in private homes or of new confraternities.[52]

Greater supervision of local and provincial bodies was part of the Habsburg effort to achieve administrative centralization and uniformity. Such bodies often resented this intervention as an invasive assault on their traditional autonomy.[53] It is clear that the Jews of Trieste, though not in possession of long-standing privileges of autonomy, were nonetheless wary on this score as well. Just a few years earlier, in 1767, the Jews had protested vigorously when, in response to a Jewish taxpayer's complaint, the authorities proposed attending the community's meetings at which taxes would be apportioned. They had argued that the divulgence of details about members' finances in the presence of an outsider would constitute "fetters too repugnant, which had no precedent in any community of our Nation, or in any Free Port," and that it would deter other Jews from establishing commercial enterprises in Trieste.[54] On that occasion, the government did decide to let the old system continue. Finances were probably the most sensitive issue, requiring the most discretion. By 1771, the Jews of Trieste claimed to be reconciled to regular governmental involvement in at least some of the community's business, and they cited as proof of their cooperation the presence of a governmental official at elections and at meetings in which organizational matters were discussed.[55]

Both the text of the 1771 Statute and the process by which it was produced bore the mark of absolutism. The draft sent from Trieste to Vienna in February 1770 opened with a statement about its genesis: it was the work of the four Jewish delegates and Intendancy Councillor Ricci, who had produced a draft based upon earlier statutes and then presented it for governmental and ultimately sovereign ratification. A similar statement had in fact opened the 1766 statutes. In Vienna, this entire preamble was crossed out and replaced with the simple, "We Maria Theresa, by the grace of God . . . ," with the lengthy list of her titles, followed by the paragraph about order and regulation quoted above. It continued with the statement that the sovereign had ordered the Intendancy to prepare a "legislative guide" that would be "granted and prescribed" to the Jewish community.[56] Though the paragraph went on to mention that the sovereign had considered the Jews' supplications before ratifying the 1771 Statute, still, the overall impression created by the preamble was certainly governmental dictate from above rather than voluntary consensual decision-making by the Jewish community.

The process itself had also made the point. Whereas in the past, the *Capi* and councils of the community had drawn up statutes and then submitted them to the government for ratification, this time the community had to struggle simply to see the February 1770 draft. When the Triestine Jews were told in June 1770 that they risked the loss of all former privileges if they did not pay for the issuance of the new statute in the form of a sovereign diploma, they had not yet seen it in draft form. When they asked to see it, they were denied permission by the committee of four Jews who had worked on the statute, who claimed to be following the Intendancy's orders. Later, however, one local official (again Modesti) professed amazement that the committee had not in fact shown the draft to the heads of the community, and claimed that the Intendancy had assumed that the approval of the four had signified approval by the broader community.[57] Though the draft was completed and sent to Vienna in February 1770, the Jewish community of Trieste did not see it until March 1771! Not surprisingly, until they finally saw the draft, the heads of the community were anxious that something detrimental to their status might have been included in the new statute.

During this interim period, communal leaders expressed their concern about the process in a lengthy memorandum submitted to the government in early September 1770. Basically, they felt that the process under way—that is, the exclusion of all the Jews except the four on the committee—violated the very purpose of communal regulations. Only if these regulations were to emanate from the community itself as "free and consensual decisions," and if all the community were to request their ratification by the sovereign, could they have effective force as the "laws of a well-regulated community," for "from universal agreement, greater observance would be assured." As a "civil body isolated from other [religious-ethnic] Nations," and like "all [lawful] subordinate political bodies (*corpi*)," the Jewish community in Trieste had previously enjoyed the "collegial" right, conforming to "reason of state," to formulate its own internal regulations; these then would of course be checked by the government to ensure their compatibility with the "felicity of the general state."[58] Now they feared what appeared to be a very different process.

Their closing signature on this petition indirectly signaled another of their concerns. They signed as "the community of the Jewish Nation settled (*stabilita*) in Trieste." When the Jewish leaders of Trieste chose to describe themselves in 1770 as "settled," they were repeating the wording of their 1766 statutes and, furthermore, reinforcing a point they had made earlier in their petition. In reviewing their prior individual and communal rights, their fidelity, and their contribution to the port and city in response to the invitations of Charles VI, they asserted that their community had "thereby rendered itself worthy of being considered as called and invited, rather than as tolerated."[59]

The prickliness of the Jews of Trieste with regard to the word "tolerated" was striking.[60] To them, toleration connoted mere sufferance rather than appreciation or recognized standing. Indeed, sufferance was the implication when the Jews of Vienna were always referred to as "tolerated" (*tolerierte*) and when Hungarian Jews were referred to as "only tolerated" in an official document in 1744,[61] and it was the fundamental assumption behind the "tax for toleration" that those Jewries had to pay. The Jews of Trieste were not subject to such a toleration tax, nor had they been called "tolerated" in any of their earlier communal statutes. As far as they were concerned, the word fit neither the prior legal expressions of their status nor the realities of Trieste.

The word "tolerated" was in fact inserted in the new statutes by Vienna earlier in 1770. The draft sent from Trieste had entitled the first article "the heads of the community," repeating the designation used in the 1766 statutes. But in Vienna, that phrase was crossed out and replaced by the wording "the heads of the community of Jews *tolerated* in Trieste" (emphasis mine). In two other prominent locations in the text of the new statutes, Vienna inserted the word "tolerated": in the preamble, to the "ranks of the Jewish nation tolerated in OUR FREE PORT of Trieste," and in the final clause of the last article warning about Jewish business ethics, to the "entire nation tolerated very mercifully in Trieste."[62] In all three cases, the word "tolerated" was used with regard to the Jewish collective entity, the formal community. Officials in Vienna may have wanted to stress the fact that the right to constitute the Jewish community as a legally recognized corporate entity was not to be taken for granted, and was indeed an act of toleration and grace on the part of the sovereign; after all, the wealthy but merely "tolerated" Ashkenazic Jews of Vienna did not enjoy the right of communal organization.[63]

When the Jewish leaders of Trieste referred to their community as "settled in Trieste," and as "called and invited, rather than tolerated," they had apparently not yet seen the text of the new statute, but they must have had some inkling that the new wording was in the works. Their assertion that "tolerated" was an inappropriate designation may at first glance appear prideful. But as much as pride, it may have indicated apprehension. It was a delicate point, one they could not really argue too forcefully. The final version of the Statute of 1771 did contain the word "tolerated" they so disliked in the three places to which it had been added. Interestingly, the Privilege of 1771, drafted a few months after the petition in which they indirectly voiced their dislike of the word, did not use the word at all.

The Jews of Trieste did, however, reiterate their concerns for autonomy and process when they expressed their views on the text of the statutes in March 1771. These were evident in their three requests: (1) that the Statute and the Privilege be made separate documents; (2) that the communal ordinances not be issued as an "inalterable Sovereign Diploma," but rather as "internal regulations" (*regolamenti interni*) that could be amended by the community in concert with the local government every five years as warranted by changing circumstances; and (3) that formally the name be changed from "statute" (*statuto*) to "internal regulations."[64] Local officials supported them in all these requests, as well as in their request for a reduction of the high fee. Intendancy Councillor Ricci thought the name change of little intrinsic significance, but added that *regolamento* "corresponded better to the Conventions of a particular society such as the Jewish Community," while *statuto* "properly belonged to the laws of an entire province, or at least of a city."[65] The Court Commerce Council in Vienna also acceded to all the Jews' requests.[66] But as noted above, Maria Theresa refused to lower the tax. She did, however, agree to the separation of the Statute from the Privilege, and accepted the principle of the changeability of the Statute, to which she referred in her notation as a "Regulation" (*Regulament*). Still, both documents were issued as sovereign diplomas, and the communal regulations could hardly be called "internal regulations" when issued in that form. However insignificant the name change seemed to some, for the Jews of Trieste it was linked to their desire that their communal regulations be recognized as internal consensual agreements, subsequently ratified by state authorities, rather than as laws dictated from on high. When the community underwent some reorganization in 1776–77, the Jews raised the issue again; this time, they succeeded in having their new "provisional plan of internal regulation" approved by the local governor simply as their "regulations" (*regole*).[67]

It took another five years from the time that the authorities in Vienna approved the texts for the two diplomas in April 1771 before the Jews of Trieste finally took possession of them. The great expense was surely one stumbling block; at one point the Jews claimed that their communal funds were exhausted, and eventually the money for the diplomas was taken from one individual's bequest.[68] The Jews also tried during that period to obtain stronger and more specific guarantees of their religious freedom than the Privilege provided. They argued that its statement against conversionist pressure—"that they [Jews] cannot be forced to embrace another religion"[69]—was too vague. It left open which rescripts on the subject were to be followed: the earlier ones of Charles VI and Maria Theresa (1739, 1740, 1744), which forbade all clandestine or forced baptisms of Jewish children, or Maria Theresa's own later rescripts (1765, 1768), which allowed such baptisms of children as young as seven if they were considered in mortal danger by Christian servants or if they were abandoned. The Jews of Trieste pleaded for the broader prohibition, a higher minimum age—fourteen—for legal baptism of Jewish children without parental consent, and an express guarantee of the return of illegally baptized children. They were especially alarmed about this issue because there had been a number of recent cases of clandestinely baptized Jewish children in different parts of the monarchy, and two of them in nearby Gradisca in 1768 and 1771.[70] How, they argued, could they calmly pursue commerce "without the security of our most precious substance, that is, our own children," and how could they encourage other Jews to settle in Trieste if their Privilege would lack the earlier guarantees? Given its "diversity of nations and of religions," the

Free Port of Trieste ought to have the same guarantees as the Tuscan Free Port of Livorno—where Maria Theresa's son, Grand Duke Peter Leopold, had set thirteen as the minimum age—or as Bordeaux.[71] Though Councillor Ricci supported these requests, they were turned down in Vienna, and the vague wording remained in the Privilege. The issue was of course a very sensitive one for the devoutly Catholic Maria Theresa. Vienna explained that it was important to "conserve the dominant religion in its honor and not expose it to the dangers of profanation"; besides, existing laws provided sufficient safeguards and penalties against most forced baptisms, and these laws were the same for the Jews tolerated in other Hereditary Lands as they were for the Jews of Trieste.[72] This meant that on this sensitive issue, Vienna had determined that Triestine Jews were not to be out of step; they were to enjoy no exceptional privileges.

In April 1776, the Jews of Trieste finally took possession of the two separate diplomas containing the Theresian Privilege and Statute of 1771. Despite its inadequacy in one respect, the Privilege was an important statement of the continuity of Jewish liberties in Trieste, as it explicitly made the entire community the beneficiary of the earlier individual privileges and Free Port Patents. The Jews probably accepted the Statute with greater reluctance. It is significant that they never undertook the expense of printing the 1771 Statute as they had the earlier one of 1766, or of publicizing it as a recruiting device.[73] Exactly when and how many of the 167 articles of the exhaustive 1771 Statute were actually implemented is not clear. In 1781, Governor Zinzendorf stated that it had been implemented for only three years, and that its many provisions were burdensome for both the community and the local government. Around the same time, the *Capi* referred to their earlier communal regulations (presumably the 1771 Statute and the 1777 provisional regulations) as "unobservable" and "unobserved," "useless and neglected," because of "changing times and circumstances, and their exceeding complexity."[74] Indeed, the next *Regolamento* of the Jewish community issued in 1783 was much shorter and less complex than the 1771 Statute.

An Exceptionally Favorable Status

No matter the degree of actual implementation of all the details of the Statute, the Statute and the Privilege of 1771 embodied the attitude and policy of the Habsburg state toward the Jews of Trieste. Essentially, these diplomas put all the Jews of Trieste on a firm footing by extending, albeit with modification, the earlier privileges of individual Jews to the entire community, and integrated the community more closely within the Habsburg administrative and political system. Whatever their shortcomings from the Jewish point of view, together they defined a very favorable status for the Jews of Trieste as individuals and as a corporate community. Triestine Jews could not fail to note the advantages of their status compared to their fellow Habsburg coreligionists. As a local Triestine official put it in 1768, one had only to contrast "the generous Liberties that they [Jews] enjoy here" to "the constraints and opprobrium that weigh them down and degrade them with misfortune in Prague and elsewhere."[75]

As mentioned above, unlike others, the Jews of Trieste had to pay no regular tax for toleration, nor did they pay double legal fees when using state courts. They did not have to wear any signs, badges, or beards in order to distinguish themselves from the rest of the population. The 1714 decree ordering Jews in Trieste to wear an orange string on the tops of their hats was allowed to lapse; already in 1729, Trieste was being cited as a place where Jews did not wear distinguishing signs. In Trieste, Jews were free to engage in virtually any kind of commerce or artisanry. They could own real estate, even outside the ghetto, and wealthy Jews had the right to live outside it. Wealthy Triestine merchants were exempted from the head toll and other restrictions in Vienna. Triestine Jews had the right to worship publicly, a right not enjoyed by Jews in Vienna, nor for that matter by Protestants in Trieste, who noted the difference when pressing their own case for more religious freedom in the late 1770s.[76]

Another Habsburg Jewry might have enjoyed one or another of these rights, and indeed, some communities had more extensive juridical powers, but no other enjoyed the Triestine combination of individual and communal rights: extensive economic opportunities, public freedom of religion, legal standing for the community, and freedom to grow, that is, a lack of limits on numbers of families or marriages. The population policy in effect in Trieste was designed to ensure the right kind of people for the community, but not to restrict its numbers, as was the purpose of laws governing Jews in Vienna, Bohemia, and even Gorizia-Gradisca. Even the other northern Italian communities of the monarchy in Gorizia-Gradisca and Lombardy, which were in several respects more advantaged than those of other Habsburg Jews, did not share all the favorable conditions of Triestine Jews.[77] In short, the Jews of Trieste had a privileged and exceptional status among the Jews of the Habsburg Monarchy.[78]

The small number of Jews in the Italian communities in the 1770s and 1780s—some 400–800 in Trieste, around 400 in Gorizia-Gradisca, and about 3,000 in Lombardy—helps explain the favorable conditions in these areas. During Maria Theresa's rule, there was little experimentation with the large Jewish communities in Bohemia and Moravia (population 50,000–70,000), in Hungary (around 80,000), and in Galicia after 1772 (about 200,000), where the demographic and socioeconomic realities were so different from the Italian Jewish communities.[79] But small numbers alone did not lead automatically to favorable status, as the special case of Vienna proves. Location on the periphery of the monarchy—far from the capital, where all issues concerning Jews were most sensitive—probably allowed greater flexibility in all the Italian domains. But the most important factors responsible for the exceptional status of Jews in Trieste were two others working in tandem: the purpose and the image of the modern Jewish community in the modern port city.

When the Jews of Trieste wrote to Vienna in 1770 that they deserved to be "considered as summoned and invited, rather than tolerated," they were highlighting a truly significant factor in their historical development and legal status. All Jews who could increase the commerce of the free port were welcome in Trieste. Their perceived economic utility made the Triestine community essentially a desired and invited Jewry settled in its locality for a specific economic purpose. Generally, the statuses of such invited Jewries differed radically from those of Jewries long resident in a place or acquired willy-nilly by a ruler along with a conquered piece of territory. In the late sixteenth and seventeenth centuries, whenever Jews (or Jews in the guise of New Christian Portuguese) were invited or tacitly allowed to settle in order to help develop a port city into a major commercial center—in places such as Livorno, Bordeaux, Amsterdam, and London—relatively favorable conditions were accorded them in order to attract and keep them.

The prime example is that of Tuscan Livorno, a free port from 1593, in which Sefardic Jews were offered extensive economic and civil rights, religious freedom (including protection from the Inquisition), and the opportunity to build a community with wide-ranging powers of self-government. There the Jewish community had broad juridical autonomy (both civil and penal), and the unique right to admit its members to local Tuscan citizenship.[80] In the late eighteenth century, its approximately 4,000 members still played a major role in Mediterranean and North African commerce, and enjoyed high economic and social standing in the city. As a free port and the Italian place with the most favorable status for Jews, Livorno's precedent set the standard for Trieste. With commercial and financial utility in a free port the very reason for its existence and the basis of its exceptional privileges and status, the Jewish community of Trieste represented a latter-day version of the earlier Tuscan experiment.

The comparison with Livorno is not one that the historian must strain to discern, for contemporaries in Vienna and Trieste were well aware of it. Giuseppe Pasquale Ricci, one of the most important Triestine officials in the second half of the eighteenth century, had come from Tuscany, and certain features of Triestine administration were directly copied from Livorno. In 1766, while the new Statute for the community was being drafted, the intendant of Trieste sought information from Livorno because he wanted "to order affairs according to the principles followed in other civilized mercantile centers."[81] In their correspondence with the government about the diplomas of 1771, the Jews of Trieste stated that their own privileges of residence, work, and worship had been based upon those granted to Jews in Livorno and Pisa. When they wanted a stronger prohibition against forced baptisms, not surprisingly, they cited Tuscan legislation.[82] Most importantly, officials in Vienna had a keen sense of the similarity between the Jewries of Trieste and Livorno, and often grouped them together when discussing exemptions from the usual restrictions on Jewish merchants visiting Vienna. The "eminent" Triestine merchants were explicitly said to "live in the style of the so-called Portuguese Jews of Amsterdam and Livorno."[83]

What distinguished all these Jews, the Sefardim and the Triestine Jews seen in effect as honorary Sefardim, was their engagement in international commerce in port cities and their cultural profile. From a mercantilist-cameralist outlook, wholesale and international trade were considered valuable occupations of manifest utility to the economy and state, in sharp contrast to petty commerce and moneylending. And the image of these Sefardic and northern Italian Jews was further enhanced because of the perceived links between economic utility, culture, and morality. Being useful was equated with being virtuous. So, too, were speaking the vernacular and functioning well in their respective economic and civic settings. In other words, economics, culture, manners, and morals were seen as all of a favorable piece when it came to the Jews of Trieste and Sefardic Jews in port cities.[84] Yet, this generally favorable view did not mean that all hesitations about Jewish business ethics were dispelled, even with regard to those engaged primarily in international or wholesale commerce. The discussions about fraudulent bankruptcies in the context of the 1771 Statute and about monopolistic practices in the context of the *Borsa* leadership showed that traditional stereotypes about Jewish economic behavior had not vanished, even when Triestine Jews were under consideration. Still, overall, the wealthy and useful merchants of Trieste were differentiated from other Jews, such as those of Lower Austria, whom the Court Chancellery considered prone to "smuggling and black marketeering."[85] The general principle was stated in 1778 Court Chancellery discussions of proposed new restrictions on Jews coming to Vienna: "For the Gorizian and Triestine Jews as foreigners, for the promotion of commerce, an exception to the general rule ought to be made."[86] The State Council agreed:

> The Triestine and Gorizian Jewish merchants, especially the former, have as do [the Jews] in Livorno their own particular privileges; they do not concern the government; and they hardly come here [to Vienna] except for important business opportunities. With respect to them here, various sovereign resolutions exist, and it mat-

ters to the state composed of useful people to follow these and not to impose new laws or oppressive measures on mercantile or manufacturing enterprises.[87]

For the most part, the Jews of Trieste were placed in a separate and exceptional category because the Habsburg authorities had decided that they had demonstrated their utility and ought to be encouraged to continue to do so. In the new framework of the free port, those Jews who came to help it prosper were considered, like the earlier court Jews, to have offered valuable services for which favor was due. By 1771, Habsburg bureaucrats considered individual court Jews anachronistic, and a court Jew community nonsensical. Since, in official eyes, the Jewish community was composed essentially of families who already possessed individual privileges and of free-port merchants, it was fitting to make its status an amalgam of the updated court Jew privileges and the Free Port Patents. The exceptionality inherent in each of those components was the basis for the exceptional status of the Triestine Jewish community among Habsburg Jewries.

Since Trieste was exceptional, it hardly violated Maria Theresa's stated principle of "no . . . systematic toleration." The case of the Jews of Trieste shows that in exceptional circumstances, she could envisage a status for Jews that went beyond mere sufferance to include corporate legal standing, relative religious freedom, extensive economic opportunities, and exemption from humiliating signs, taxes, and restrictions. Such measures, in different and varying forms to be sure, were the stuff of Joseph II's much-vaunted Toleration policy of the 1780s. Maria Theresa's actions and laws for the Jews of Trieste did provide a precedent for some of Joseph's later measures, but they constituted an exceptional precedent, not a program of civil toleration.[88]

CHAPTER THREE

Joseph's Toleration Policy in Trieste, 1781–82

The sarcophaghi of Maria Theresa and her son Joseph II in the basement crypt of the Capuchin church in Vienna reveal two very different sensibilities. Hers, every inch covered, adorned with swirling figures and images, seems the quintessence of baroque, while his, a stark and simple wooden box, seems the quintessence of the Enlightenment.[1] Yet, in recent historiography, their very real differences in sensibility, temperament, style and symbolism no longer obscure the similarities of many of their political goals and means. However much she cloaked herself justifiably as a traditionalist and he appeared determined to implement a "revolution from above," both rulers were absolutist state-builders, and there was considerable continuity between their reform efforts.[2] They both sought to strengthen the Habsburg Monarchy internally and externally through restructuring, centralizing, and increasing state control over many areas of economy, society, culture and religion.

Nonetheless, there is no doubt that, as sole ruler from 1780 to 1790, Joseph intensified and radicalized the measures taken by his mother. For good reasons, he, and not Maria Theresa, has been considered an archetypal enlightened absolutist ruler, or enlightened despot.[3] His personal sense of right and his zeal led him to pursue reforms with greater purpose, thoroughgoingness, and ideological awareness. His secular attitude toward the state and governance—seeing himself as the first servant of the state, which should promote the general welfare and whose interests all should promote—showed his affinity with the Enlightenment and modern conceptions of state.[4]

The issue of religion well illustrates both the continuity and the rupture between the two rulers.[5] Both, influenced by cameralism and reform Catholicism to varying degrees, increasingly exercised state supervision over Church activities and revenues. Joseph, however, certainly went further in asserting and establishing the principle of state control, in regulating religious institutions and practices, and in secularizing spheres such as marriage and the monasteries. In early 1782, it was reported that Joseph announced for the benefit of the pope, with whom his relations were steadily worsening, "My determination [in religious matters] is regulated by reason, equity, humanity, and religion"[6]—a formulation unimaginable for Maria Theresa.

Above all, religious toleration shows the genuine innovativeness of Joseph. Religious toleration involves a number of issues: conceptions of state, the proper relation between state-building and toleration of religious diversity, and attitudes toward particular religious minorities. Unlike his mother, Joseph saw the state as a purely civil entity. Accordingly, he placed greater emphasis upon usefulness to the whole of both subjects and the ruler. His side of the 1777 exchange with his mother made these premises clear:

For politically, differences of religion within a state are an evil only in so far as there is fanaticism, disunion, and party spirit. This vanishes automatically when all sectaries are treated with perfect impartiality. . . .

Temporal administrators! So long as the state is served, the laws of Nature and society observed, your Supreme Being in no way dishonoured but respected and adored, what ground have you for interference?[7]

Joseph never disputed the religious truth and supremacy of Catholicism, but he upheld "freedom of belief" and civil toleration as consonant with them:

God preserve me from thinking that it is a matter of indifference whether subjects become Protestants or remain Catholics. . . . I would give all I possess if all the Protestants of your states could become Catholics!

For me toleration means only that in purely temporal matters, I would, without taking account of religion, employ and allow to own lands, enter trades, and become citizens those who are competent and who would bring advantage and industry to the [Monarchy].[8]

For Joseph, the most important political calculus was that of utility. For pragmatic purposes, and on assumptions derived from Enlightenment rationalism and humanitarianism, he was prepared to view all subjects, even non-Catholics, through a utilitarian lens. The driving force behind many of his radical reforms was the conviction that irrespective of religious differences, all subjects—including clergy, religious orders, nobles, peasants, Jews—could be mobilized to become more useful to the state. In his "pastoral letter" in 1783, he instructed all his officials:

> I have reduced the conditions resulting from prejudices and old, deep-rooted habits by means of Enlightenment . . . I have tried to imbue every official of the state with the love I feel for the general weal and with zeal to serve it. . . . One should have no other purpose in one's actions save the utility and the good of the majority. . . . In all of them [the provinces of the monarchy] nationality and religion must make no difference, and as brothers in one Monarchy all should set to work equally in order to be useful to one another.[9]

From a combination of practical and idealistic motives, domestic and foreign considerations,[10] Joseph elevated toleration to a general principle of utility and rationality, and developed it systematically and dramatically. His premise that all potentially could be useful subjects of the Habsburg crown took concrete form in his Toleration Patent (or Edict) for Lutherans, Calvinists, and Greek Orthodox, issued on October 13, 1781, within a year of his mother's death and his accession to sole rulership. This, the first legislation of toleration by a Catholic monarch, opened with the rationale that "all violence to conscience is harmful" and the conviction "of the great benefit accruing to religion and to the State from a true Christian tolerance."[11] It offered these denominations religious, civil, and economic rights hitherto denied them. Most importantly, where numbers warranted, they gained permission to worship privately in their own chapels—but not in a church with chimes, bells, tower, or public entrance—and to have their own schools. They could have their own pastors and be judged in religious matters according to their own religious law. They were now allowed by dispensation to buy houses and real property, acquire rights of local burghers and master craftsmen, and take up academic or public-service posts.

In most places, the new Toleration legislation brought truly significant changes. But, when issued in Trieste on November 3, 1781, it was less innovative.[12] Still, the opportunities for public service were new. The rights of the Greek Orthodox were now held not only by privilege but also by a general monarchy-wide policy. The Protestants in Trieste were now emboldened to renew their request for public worship, which both the Greek Orthodox and the Jews enjoyed to a greater extent than they. Given those realities, the evident contribution of Protestant merchants to the port's commerce and the desirability of attracting more, Governor Zinzendorf supported their request to add a street entrance, bells, and tower to their existing structure. Officials in Vienna were divided. The Court Chancellery feared setting a precedent for non-Catholics elsewhere by going beyond the provisions of the general Toleration edicts. In contrast, important members of the State Council, including the dominant State Chancellor Kaunitz, a long-time supporter of toleration, reasoned differently: "No inference could be drawn from a free seaport open to all religions for any other place in the monarchy." The invitation of Protestants to Trieste and tacit permission for them to worship privately some sixty years earlier—"when one was so far removed from all principles of toleration"—had not served as an example for other places. As long as the Triestine Protestants' current request would not be allowed to "serve as an example or be considered as a contradiction of the [general] Toleration edict," Kaunitz was in favor of granting them the right to build a public church. Citing the rights already granted the Greek Orthodox in Trieste, the sovereign resolution of January 7, 1782, announced the favorable decision with express acknowledgment of the exceptionality of Trieste, explaining that it granted the request "only in consideration that Trieste is a free port, from which no example can be drawn for any other place."[13] By March, construction work on the Protestant church had begun and was reported beyond Trieste in the Venetian newspaper *Notizie del mondo*.[14]

Thus, both before and after the Toleration Patent, the situation for Christian minorities in Trieste was exceptional in the context of the monarchy as a whole. Although the patent was innovative for most parts of the monarchy, in Trieste itself it represented fundamental continuity between the policies of Maria Theresa and Joseph.

The main question of this chapter is whether the same can be said specifically with regard to the two monarchs' policies toward the Jews of Trieste. How was Joseph's new Toleration policy formulated for the Jews of Trieste in 1781–82? What were the similarities and the differences, the continuities and the ruptures, between the statuses granted by Theresian privilege and by Josephinian toleration?

Joseph's General Policy of Toleration for Jews

Joseph's extension of his Toleration policy to the Jews of the Habsburg Monarchy in a series of edicts starting in late 1781 was seen as radical, novel, and far-reaching by contemporaries and later observers, indeed as milestones in the history of Habsburg—and European—Jewry generally. Though early reports were exaggerated—some newspapers wrote in June 1781 that Joseph intended to grant Jews "the advantages of society like all other citizens"[15]— it was undeniable that Joseph's more modest plans did signal a new approach: the beginning of a systematic effort to integrate Jews into Habsburg civil society and the state. This was a novel legislative aim for a Christian European state.

A sense of deliverance, of relief that reason and light were finally being cast on the Jewish situation, was felt by some Jews. It was expressed at the time by the well-known Hebrew poet Hartwig Wessely (Naftali Herz Weisel), and captured later by the nineteenth-century Jewish historian Heinrich Graetz when he wrote that with "Joseph II of glorious memory," the "ignominy of a thousand years . . . was now partly removed."[16] Yet Graetz also captured the other dominant note in reactions to Joseph's Toleration edicts—the sense of unwanted intrusion in Jewish life—when he referred to their "sincere but forceful love of humanity."[17] In fact, in most places, Joseph's Toleration edicts represented inclusion and opportunity in some respects and intrusive encroachment on Jewish autonomy and culture in others. To both non-Catholic Christian minorities and the Jews, Josephinian toleration offered new recognition and benefits, but at the price of bureaucratic intervention and, of course, continued Catholic supremacy.[18] For Jews, Josephinian toleration also embodied the promise and the contradictions of the Enlightenment on the Jewish question.

Joseph's intentions for a new policy concerning Jews first found expression in his letter of May 13, 1781, to Court Chancellor Heinrich Cajetan Blümegen, written partly in his own handwriting. It is through a close analysis of this basic text that the logic and limits of his aims are best seen. His stated purpose was to "make the numerous members of the Jewish nation in the Hereditary Lands more useful to the state"—a variation of his general policy to mobilize all sectors of the population for maximum service. Very limited opportunities in employment and education were seen as the two main obstacles preventing Jews from fulfilling their potential for utility. Therefore, economic diversification and cultural transformation were the means by which the Jews were to be remade into productive subjects. In order to divert them from "their so characteristic usury and deceitful trade," the range of occupations legally open to them was to be widened and various civil and economic disabilities to be removed. Thus they would be encouraged to pursue agriculture, manual trades and crafts, fine arts, and manufacturing. The cultural barriers that isolated Jews from Christians were to be lowered by fundamental changes in language and education. After a grace period of two or three years, all Jewish contracts and documents would have to be written in the local language in order to be legally valid, and their own "national language" was to be confined to strictly religious purposes such as worship. Furthermore, Jews were to set up elementary schools in accord with the recently established system of state normal schools, or else attend the regular normal schools for Christian students. Thereby Jews would acquire the basics of German, arithmetic, and moral and civic training. In institutions of higher education, Jews would be able to pursue all studies except theology. Jews would be permitted to read books passed by the censor for the general reading public. Censorship of Jewish books would be facilitated by outlawing foreign books in favor of those published by the Hebrew press in Bohemia (though not mentioned, this would obviously bring economic benefits to a domestic enterprise). Finally, as a general palliative step, all distinguishing and humiliating signs previously forced upon Jews were to be eliminated.[19]

The precise circumstances in which Joseph's proposals originated are uncertain. What is known is that wealthy Jews in Vienna and Prague had made entreaties to have their status improved, and that Joseph was increasingly concerned about the masses of poor Jews in Galicia and the Bukovina, which had become Habsburg territories in the 1770s.[20] More important, however, than the genesis of the proposals were their content and purpose. Like the Edict of Toleration for the Protestants and Greek Orthodox, these proposals sought to regularize and standardize as much as possible the position of a non-Catholic minority within the monarchy. In these proposals, as in that edict, both humanitarian and pragmatic elements were intertwined. They were imbued with a cameralist view of the importance of useful subjects for the state; with the Enlightenment's rationalist assumption of the Jews' essential humanity, malleability, and potential utility; and with a gradualist approach to turning the Jews into ideal subjects.

The cameralist teaching that a wise state mobilizes all the productive capacities of all its subjects was reflected in the very opening of Joseph's May 13 letter: "To make the numerous members of the Jewish nation . . . more useful to the state." It is significant that Jews were included within the totality of subjects to be made useful. Where they already lived legally, they were now assumed to reside permanently, not temporarily and subject to expulsion. Joseph was trying to fashion a bureaucratic, interventionist, and tutelary state. Both economic and cultural regulation were within the purview of such a state, and often were linked. During the reigns of Maria Theresa and Joseph, many traditional restrictions on economic activities were removed, as in the cases of the serfs, guilds, and monasteries. A state seeking to mobilize its population had also to take charge of education in order to instill new civic and productive values in its subjects.[21]

Joseph's proposals were suffused with the conviction that Jews could be useful subjects and members of the civic realm, of the state viewed in secular terms. But major steps would be required: clearing away the oppressive limitations imposed by centuries of law and practice, and transforming the Jews themselves. This was the classic Enlightenment analysis that would inform the public debate on the Jews in the next decades, and that was articulated at much greater length the very same year by the Prussian bureaucrat

Christian Wilhelm von Dohm in his influential *On the Civil Improvement of the Jews* (*Ueber die buergerliche Verbesserung der Juden*): the Jews as they actually existed were undesirable, indeed unacceptable, but their underlying nature—like that of all human beings—was mutable and malleable. Their current undesirable condition was attributed to the oppression and restrictions from which they suffered. The proposed remedy was to remove the restrictions; the expected result was a change in Jewish character and behavior.[22] Though the proposals of Joseph II and Dohm differed in some important respects—for example, Dohm did foresee Jews in public service—their analyses rested on the same basic premises: both the civil conditions in which Jews lived and the Jews themselves required improvement (*Verbesserung*, the term made famous by Dohm). When Dohm in fact learned of Joseph's plans, he added an enthusiastic appendix about them to his own work.

Joseph's proposals were characterized by a gradualist, incrementalist approach. His program did not offer the Jews equality with other members of the state, but only ameliorative steps that would lead in the general direction of fuller integration in the Habsburg realm. These measures fell far short of complete civil and political equality—the defining characteristic of the Emancipation of the Jews in France in 1790–91. Of course, the context was very different, for Joseph was working within the framework of a corporate-absolutist state, whereas the revolutionaries in France destroyed precisely that in order to construct a new civic order of egalitarian citizens.

But even within the Habsburg context, the limited scope of Joseph's measures for the Jews is highlighted by contrasting them to the Edicts of Toleration for the Christian minorities. Possibilities of land ownership, burgher and craftsmen rights, and public-service posts were all offered to Christians, but not to Jews. The phrase "civil toleration" was used in the legislation for the Christians, but not for the Jews. The edicts for the Christians concentrated mostly on religious rights, with the addition of some civil rights; the edicts for the Jews focused primarily on economic opportunities and the moral and cultural transformation of the Jews themselves. Clearly their situations differed in actuality and in perception.

Redrafted as resolutions of the Court Chancellery of May 16, 1781,[23] Joseph's proposals were sent to local governing bodies, which were to submit their opinions and report on the suitability of the proposals for their particular areas. Considerable opposition was voiced not only by the Catholic clergy (some of whom had also opposed the edict for Christian minorities), but also by various state officials in Vienna and elsewhere. Many wanted assurances that these proposals would not affect the long-standing principle that the Jewish population was to be kept to a bare minimum in most of the Hereditary Lands. To calm those fears and to clarify his intentions, Joseph affirmed unequivocally on October 1, 1781, that he sought not to increase the area or extent of Jewish settlement, but only to render the already existing Jewish population more useful. Furthermore, he stated that the toleration tax on Jews would not be abolished—its revenue was needed—though it would be adjusted in accord with a family's means.[24] Retention of this tax was a good indication that Josephinian toleration, at least in its early stages, did not offer Habsburg Jews a totally new legal status, but rather maintained much of the old.

The widely differing responses elicited by his proposals convinced Joseph that his edicts on Jewish toleration would have to be issued separately from those for the Christians, and separately for each part of the monarchy, only after lengthy consultation with local authorities. The first edict of toleration for Jews was the court decree issued on October 19, 1781, intended for the "better education and enlightenment (*Bildung und Aufklärung*) of the Jews in Bohemia." Other edicts or patents followed for Silesia in December 1781, Lower Austria (including Vienna) in January 1782, Moravia in February 1782, Hungary in 1783, and Galicia in 1785 and 1789. For the northern Italian areas, patents were deemed unnecessary, so letters applying the proposals of May 1781 appropriately in each locality were sent to Lombardy in September 1781 (and reiterated in the December 1781 renewal of privileges), to Gorizia-Gradisca in November 1781, and to Trieste in December 1781. All followed the basic outline of Joseph's letter of May 1781, but there was change through the course of the decade. The earlier edicts in particular took account of local objections and were more circumscribed than the original May 1781 proposals, while the Galician patent of 1789 was the most far-reaching, citing as its aim to grant to Jews the same rights and obligations as other subjects. An amended version of this patent was then issued for Gorizia-Gradisca in 1790.[25]

In the Galician patent, the actual provisions did not fully realize the goal announced in the preamble. Still, such statements should not be ignored, for preambles often stated the rationale or long-term objective of a piece of legislation. Indeed, from the first steps of Josephinian Toleration, phrases were used that indicated the ultimate intent of civil inclusion. It should be recalled that newspapers in June 1781 reported that Joseph's aim was to grant Jews the same advantages as all other citizens. The orders of November 2, 1781, that accompanied the Bohemian edict told local officials to instruct their subjects "that the Jews are to be regarded like any other fellow human-beings" (*Nebenmenschen, confratelli*), and to warn Jews to "behave like decent citizens" (*zu dem Betragen eines rechtschaffenen Bürgers, di comportarsi come si conviene ad onesti, e bravi cittadini*) and to "show themselves worthy of His Majesty's favor" by "upright behavior as citizens of the world" (*Weltbürgers, cittadini onorati*).[26] The preambles to the edicts for Vienna-Lower Austria and Moravia issued early in 1782 contained similar language: all "subjects without distinction of nationality and religion should share in the public prosperity . . . and enjoy freedom according to the law" (*eine gesetzmässige Freyheit*). In their closing words, these edicts claimed "to place the Jewish nation on a virtually equal (*beynahe gleichsetzen*) level with adherents of other religious associations in respect to trade and employment of civil and domestic facilities."[27] To be acknowledged as fellow human beings, subjects, and citizens in a condition of near-equality was a step forward, a far cry from Maria Theresa's conception of the Jews as a plague in her domains.

Preambles and lofty declarations are of course not sufficient for interpreting the nature and the effects of the Toleration edicts. Such interpretation must also pay close attention to the local circumstances in which each piece of legislation was applied, for these often diverged from Vienna's view embodied in the edict. It has seldom been recognized that legislation drafted in Vienna might simply have been out of touch with a particular reality; for example, the edict for Bohemian Jews offered them crafts as a new field of endeavor, though in actual fact they had been working in legally recognized Jewish craft guilds for a long time.[28] Interpretation has often been skewed by the assumption of innovation, the presumption that provisions were necessarily novel rather than sometimes simply confirmatory of existing realities.[29] To be assessed correctly, each version of the Toleration edict must be studied within its specific local context: in terms of the realities of Jewish life, and the evolution of Jewish legal status.

In general, neither Joseph's original proposals nor the modified edicts could effect the desired major transformation in Jewish economic life, for they left intact too many of the very real impediments to Jewish occupational diversification.[30] To cite only two obvious examples, Jews were not about to start farming on land they could not own—the edict permitted Jews to work on the land for twenty years, but to buy land they would have to convert to Christianity—nor were Christian masters about to take on Jewish apprentices. Ultimately, the cultural provisions proved more significant. The cultural policies of Joseph's modernizing interventionist state, often in tandem with indigenous Jewish forces, obliged all Habsburg Jewries, even the most traditional, to embark on a course of ever-greater exposure to, and involvement with, the surrounding culture, society, and state. Though, in actual fact, the Toleration legislation fell far short of civil and political equality, and its transforming impact upon Jewish economic and social life was much less than expected, still, its importance was undeniable. The toleration of the Jews first enunciated in Joseph's letter of May 13, 1781, was systematically elaborated in a torrent of laws that flowed from Vienna in the 1780s addressing Jewish civil status, residence, education, and communal and religious life throughout the monarchy.

The Reception of Joseph's Toleration Proposals in Trieste: The Governor's First Responses, May–August 1781

As a separate administrative entity within the Hereditary Lands, Trieste was entitled to its own version of Joseph's proposals. To date, the tale of the application of Joseph's May 1781 policy of toleration to Triestine Jewry has not been told or analyzed in its entirety. Unfortunately, there has been confusion in the secondary literature. Some have erroneously assumed that the Jews of Trieste were subject to the legislation enacted for Jews elsewhere in the Hereditary Lands, notably the patent of January 2, 1782, for Lower Austria and Vienna. Others have mistakenly considered the Edict of Toleration of November 3, 1781, for the Christian minorities of Trieste, to have covered the Jews as well. One source of the confusion may be the fact that the Jews of Trieste did not in fact receive an *edict* of their own. Rather, they received a court resolution translated into a gubernatorial letter that, "in the name of His Majesty the Emperor," outlined the terms of their legal status. Dated December 19, 1781, it was issued locally in Trieste on January 16, 1782.[31] Use of materials from archives in both Trieste and Vienna allows reconstruction and analysis of the three-way negotiations between the Jewish community of Trieste, the local governor, and the central authorities in Vienna.

Toward the end of May 1781, the governor of Trieste, Karl von Zinzendorf, received the court resolution of May 16 (in German) that contained Joseph's May 13 proposals. On May 31, the governor conveyed them in writing (in Italian, as was customary) to Jewish community leaders and to the appropriate police and judicial authorities in Trieste.[32] When Zinzendorf presented the proposals in his Italian letter to Triestine Jewish leaders, he made some changes in phrasing, changes that appear to have been deliberate and purposeful. His rephrasing of the communication from Vienna was perhaps not at variance with Habsburg bureaucratic norms, according to which governors were supposed to make allowance for local conditions, though usually more in their reports to, rather than from, Vienna.[33] In this instance, the need for translation may have increased Zinzendorf's bureaucratic leeway. In any case, his omissions and additions were revealing of the realities of Jewish life in Trieste, his perception of those realities, and his strategy in dealing with the Jews. Some were obvious—for example, he omitted all mention of the abolition of humiliating distinguishing signs, since these had long before vanished from Trieste—but the other changes were more subtle, and require more analysis.

Whereas the preamble of the official version written by the Chancellery stated "making Jews more useful to the state" as its sole purpose, in his version Zinzendorf placed another aim first, namely, "improving (*migliorare*) the condition of the Jewish Nation residing in the most blessed Hereditary Provinces."[34] He thus maintained the utilitarian tone of Joseph's proposals, but tempered it somewhat by his invocation of the welfare of the Jews themselves, the improvement of their situation. Perhaps he was echoing the opening wording of their 1771 Privilege, which had spoken of "improving the condition of merchants, subjects, and foreigners, who have established themselves" in Trieste.[35] Zinzendorf's emphasis upon the improvement of the Jews' civil status—and not simply their own self-improvement—was evident in a letter he wrote a few months later to a fellow Habsburg bureaucrat, the governor of Fiume. Whereas officials in Vienna had referred to the "future improved education (*Bildung*) of Jewry," in his letter Zinzendorf crossed out *Bildung* and replaced it with *Schicksal*, meaning fate, in the sense of lot or condition, so that he now described the May proposals as referring to the "future improved condition of Jewry."[36] In the closing of his May 31 letter to Jewish communal leaders, he reiterated that the sole purpose of the sovereign's merciful proposals was "to benefit (*beneficare*) the individuals of the Jewish nation." For Joseph II and for Dohm, improvement referred both to the conditions in which Jews lived and to Jewish behavior, but for many who discussed these issues in the late eighteenth and early nineteenth centuries, Jewish self-improvement (often called regeneration) was paramount. Zinzendorf's emphasis upon *Schicksal* rather than *Bildung* was significant in this regard.

In fact, Zinzendorf did not believe that Triestine Jews needed to change much in order to comply with the cultural provisions of Joseph's proposals. When repeating the clause that gave Jews permission to attend the state's normal schools, Zinzendorf added that this was "the custom already introduced here." He was referring to the attendance of two Jewish students in the city's normal school. In 1776–77, the twelve-year-old Raffael Baruch (Benedetto) Segre—son of Vidal Benjamin Segre, a teacher and sometime assistant rabbi of the community—had enrolled in its third class, as the one Jew among forty-seven students.[37] The next year he was joined by another Jewish student.[38] On the requirement to introduce the local language in all contracts and documents within two to three years, Zinzendorf inquired whether it could be implemented more speedily, in fact immediately, since "all the Jews here know the language of the country."

In the text of the resolution sent from Vienna, the new occupations opened to Jews were presented explicitly as alternatives to their "so characteristic usury and deceitful trade."[39] But in his letter to Triestine Jewish leaders, Zinzendorf removed the phrase "so-characteristic" and added one significant word: "poor" (*poveri*). The beginning of this section thus read: "In order to provide to the poor Jews more means and ways by which they can procure their daily sustenance, and abandon the harmful practice of usury and fraudulent dealings."[40] The sting of the original phrase was removed because the qualifier "poor" functioned as both specification and exclusion: it linked usury and fraud to poor Jews alone, and implied that they—and not most Triestine Jews, certainly not their leaders—were the ones in need of the new economic opportunities.

The qualifier may have also subtly suggested the incongruity between Joseph's proposals and local Triestine realities and perceptions. As should be evident, the widened occupational opportunities envisaged by Joseph were not really innovations for the Jews of Trieste. The Privilege of 1771 had explicitly permitted them to pursue commerce, manufacturing, and artisanry on an equal basis with Christians. Indeed, they engaged in many types of commerce and, to a lesser extent, manufacturing. As for the arts and trades mentioned in the proposals, it seems doubtful that the legislation of 1781 really created many new opportunities for Jewish skilled and unskilled labor in Trieste.[41] The attempt to promote Jewish agriculture was particularly irrelevant in the "free maritime city and Port of Trieste." Moreover, the stipulations in the May resolution making a Jew's outright ownership of land contingent upon conversion to Christianity were less favorable that the rights of property ownership recently reconfirmed in the 1771 Privilege. In this particular respect, the new general policy of toleration appeared not only paltry, but even retrogressive for the Jews of Trieste.

Yet it was not only that Joseph's proposals of May 1781 offered to most Habsburg Jews less than what was already permitted to the Jews of Trieste. There was also a difference in kind. The underlying premise of Joseph's Toleration proposals was that state intervention was necessary to spur Jewish economic diversification precisely because most Habsburg Jews were considered woefully nonproductive at present. The hope was that dramatic economic and cultural transformation would enable the Jewish masses to qualify as useful and productive subjects in the future. The basic assumptions of those proposals simply did not fit the situation of the Jews of Trieste, for they, by contrast, were not considered a woefully nonproductive population. Their very existence as a community and their legal status were predicated upon their perceived contribution to the free-port economy. Of course, there were poor Jews in Trieste, despite the efforts to keep their number to a minimum. And concerns had been voiced, during the preparation of the 1771 Statute and the debates on the *Borsa* leadership in 1779–80, about the business practices and ethics of even the well-off merchant class of Triestine Jews. Still, the dominant profile and image of the community was that of a prosperous and dynamic group whose utility was a demonstrated fact, not an as-yet-unrealized hope for the future.

Thus, to the Jews, Governor Zinzendorf highlighted the positive aspects of the new proposals from Vienna, and hinted at his awareness of their limited application, perhaps even irrelevance, in Trieste. He couched the new initiative in a nuanced and diplomatic way in order to forestall insult and misgivings on the part of this economically dynamic, legally privileged, and sometimes prickly community, and to motivate them to further cooperation.

Zinzendorf's concern for the tactful presentation and positive reception of the May 13 proposals in Trieste was part of his overall endorsement of the new Toleration policy. As stated above, he had earlier supported the Protestants' efforts to gain greater rights in Trieste. He believed that the economically dynamic minorities ought to be kept satisfied lest they betake themselves elsewhere and contribute to Trieste's competitors, above all Venice. His rational, utilitarian, and tolerant approach to religious minorities had both personal and professional roots: this distinguished civil servant was himself a former Protestant who had converted to Catholicism only in 1763 for professional advancement. Through his extensive training and travels, he was well acquainted with the latest theories of political economy and the Enlightenment generally. Many years earlier, he had translated Josiah Tucker's work on the relation between economic welfare and religious toleration occasioned by the debates in England in the 1750s about naturalizing foreign Protestants and Jews.[42] Zinzendorf had been appointed the first governor of Trieste in 1776 because of his expertise in economics and finance, and the congeniality for him of its religious and ethnic diversity.

Therefore, when Zinzendorf received the Toleration proposals in May 1781, he treated them not merely as ideas about which he should express his opinion, but as instructions to be carried out immediately. In his two letters of May 31, 1781, to the Jewish leaders and to police chief Pittoni, his tone was matter-of-fact: those few provisions not yet in effect in Trieste were to be implemented as soon as possible. He instructed the *Capi* to convey the proposals to the community and to report to him about their effects after a convenient period of time.

Some months passed without any response from the Jews. On August 8, 1781, the Court Chancellery sent out reminders that Vienna was still awaiting reports on reactions to the May proposals.[43] Receiving the reminder in Trieste on August 16, Zinzendorf hastened to compose a reply the next day.[44] His very first inclination was to assert forthrightly that Jews enjoyed "almost all the privileges and equality with the rest of the people" (*Gleichheiten mit des übrigen Volks*). But then, even while composing his first draft, he changed his mind, and substituted the more specific and limited statement: "Here in Trieste the Jews already enjoy almost all the privileges and benefits (*Vorzüge und Begünstigungen*) so graciously accorded them in the May 16 decree," and "many of the ways of earning a living [mentioned there] are already divided between Jews and the other Triestine inhabitants."⁴⁵ Had he held fast to any of these formulations, the effect would have been striking: that the situation of the Jews of Trieste was so favorable that the May Toleration proposals had little new to offer them. But he thought better of stating things so baldly, and in the final draft of his report, he cautiously toned down these assertions, writing simply that the Jews had long enjoyed "the most essential prerogatives," especially since the 1647 privilege of Ferdinand III. Zinzendorf went on to specify:

> The Jews here are in no way subjected to humiliating and constraining laws that depress the spirit. On the contrary, Jews here have enjoyed the free public exercise of religion, which has not been permitted the Protestant merchants. Jewish merchant houses are like all the others incorporated in the so-called *Borse*, and six of them enjoy this privilege.

Other features of Triestine Jewish life to which he called attention were the absence of a marriage tax; the outright ownership of real property, including buildings, land, and manufacturing enterprises; and the "honor" brought to the Trieste marketplace by "upright" Jewish merchants, three of whom he cited by name.

Zinzendorf changed considerably the rest of his presentation about occupations. In his original draft, he had stated that many of the ways of earning a living listed in the May proposals were already open to Jews, that it depended upon their "good will, diligence, and skill" whether they turned to occupations such as transport, crafts, and cabinet-making, and that they would be assisted by the police administration if they wished to do so. But he presented the issue quite differently in the report he finally submitted. There he removed the general statement about previously existing opportunities, and replaced it with the announcement that he had indeed informed the Jews of the provisions of the May decree—which he then repeated in great detail and characterized as "His Majesty's beneficent law [which] opened up all those branches of useful industry." In his report, Zinzendorf predicted that if the Jews with their "good will, diligence, and skill" took advantage of the sovereign's mercy, then the "hitherto all-too-noticeable difference between them and the Christian subjects of the state would gradually disappear," as would the "hateful accusation" of their monopolistic suppression of general industry. (Was he alluding to the sentiments expressed in the *Borsa* business only a short time earlier, in 1779–80?) He added that he would require regular reports from the police on the number of Jews turning to agricultural day-labor or any of the other mentioned branches of work. Similarly, with regard to the language provision of the legislation, Zinzendorf revised his original draft: first he had stated emphatically how easy their implementation would be since virtually all Jews knew Italian well; now he wrote merely that he had informed the Jews of the language provisions. He did note that two Jewish children were already attending the city's normal school, and he expressed concern that operating a printing press of their own might be "too premature" for a community of somewhat more than 400 people, though this would be up to the Jews themselves to decide.

The overall effect of Zinzendorf's revisions was to minimize the difference between Joseph's proposals and the realities of Jewish life in Trieste. He provided much less information about the ways in which the Jews' situation anticipated—or even went beyond—the Josephinian proposals, and focused more upon the beneficence of the sovereign and the apparent novelty of his measures. Why raise all kinds of questions about the anomalies of Trieste? Taking the safer bureaucratic road, he stressed that he was doing his duty in passing on the proposals and requiring reports upon their implementation. Thus, Zinzendorf was careful and clever in drafting his report: to the Jews, he had indicated his awareness of the irrelevance and less generous terms of the Toleration proposals, while to his superiors, he conveyed his appreciation of the fundamental direction of the Toleration policy and his expectation of its salutary effects in Trieste. In other words, in each case, he adjusted his words to what he thought the recipient wanted to hear. His circumspect caution befit a bureaucrat concerned with career advancement, who had his eye on an eventual return to an important post in Vienna.

Overall, Zinzendorf blamed his delay in reporting to Vienna upon the Jews' failure to respond to two matters: (1) the effects of the May Toleration proposals, and (2) the orders they had received earlier in March to present their Privilege and Statute of 1771 for reconfirmation, along with suggestions for needed changes.[46] He added that one of their leaders had been absent from town on business, but that he would now press them to respond quickly. More substantively, he attributed their delay to the complexity of the 1771 Statute, which, he stated, needed drastic abridgment. In his report, he simply mentioned the two matters—the May Toleration proposals and the renewal of their 1771 privileges—alongside each other. The precise relation between them would later become an important issue for consideration.

On the Statute, as with other issues in the report, the rough drafts are most revealing of Zinzendorf's thinking. In this case, his first draft was the most succinct, stating simply that he would pass along the Jews' views as soon as he received them, together with his own comments. In his second (but not final) draft, he explained the problems he saw with the 1771 Statute. First, it reflected the earlier situation in Trieste, in which the religious-ethnic nations had been separated from one another in such a way that each constituted "a state within the state," thus overburdening the business of government unnecessarily with "the administration of so many political bodies." Second, the 1771 Statute "contained almost nothing but the general benefits that a sovereign normally denies to none of his faithful subjects, but for which the Jewish community had to pay one thousand ducats."[47] This remark reflected a certain impatience with corporations and privilege, the very structure of the Old Regime. Like many administrators and monarchs, Zinzendorf believed that corporations with their own privileges were inefficient, for they ran counter to the drive for uniformity of the centralizing state. More radically, he was suggesting that Jews should not have had to pay for privileges in order to receive their due as faithful subjects. But by his third and final draft, Zinzendorf obviously thought better of including these criticisms. Instead he wrote that the 1771 Statute should be shortened and simplified: its focus should be only the community's financial arrangements so as to provide for the upkeep of the synagogue in a fair and responsible fashion; otherwise, like all the nations living in Trieste, the Jews should remain dependent on the police and courts, that is, the city's administration.

Thus, only after much deliberation and with great circumspection did Zinzendorf file his report of August 17, 1781, to his superiors. The next day, he sternly warned Triestine Jewish leaders to respond within fifteen days about the May proposals and the renewal of their 1771 documents.[48] He demanded information on the effects of the Toleration proposals upon poor Jews, and on possible means for speedy implementation of the language provision. On August 18, he put one more item on the agenda: Would the Jewish leaders provide a stipend for the son of Vidal Benjamin Segre to continue his studies in the city's normal school? In his request for financial assistance, Segre had invoked the monarch's recent proposals. Governor Zinzendorf urged the *Capi* to cooperate in the effort to turn this young student into a "useful citizen."[49]

Jewish Responses and Requests, September–October 1781

The Jewish leaders of Trieste finally articulated their concerns in two petitions submitted to Governor Zinzendorf on September 27, 1781. Their basic purpose was to request the reconfirmation of their "liberties, benefits, and prerogatives" (*libertà, grazie e prerogativi*). The shorter petition was to be passed on to the sovereign; the much longer one addressed to the governor himself sought his endorsement and provided further historical and legal background on the particular issues. The central point of the Jewish leaders' petitions was that while they greatly appreciated the significance of Joseph's new proposals, they wanted to preserve all the privileges they had hitherto enjoyed. Their strategy—to combine the rhetoric of old and new—was evident in the very opening of their petition to Joseph II: "The individuals of the Jewish nation settled (*stabiliti*) in the city of Trieste enjoyed under the mild and most happy dominion of your very august predecessors three very important objects of notable toleration and singular beneficence."[50] With this sentence they described themselves as settled, highlighted their exceptional status, and acknowledged that it was due to special grace and toleration on the part of the Habsburg sovereigns; in other words, their status was due not to mere toleration, but rather to specially generous toleration. Throughout this petition, they staked their claim to continued exceptional treatment on the firmest ground possible, namely, the precedents of past privileges. And they postulated continuity between those and the goodwill of the sovereign now manifest in his Toleration proposals for all Habsburg Jews. The "three very important objects" upon which they focused were free and public practice of their religion, full ownership of real property, both urban and rural, and engagement in wholesale and retail commerce. They concentrated upon these three precisely because these were not addressed, or not favorably enough addressed, by the May proposals, and because their 1771 Privilege had provided them with far more extensive rights in these areas than were enjoyed by other Habsburg Jews.

The Triestine Jews asserted that the origins of these rights were so ancient as to be lost in the "obscurity of remote centuries." For each point, they established a chain of their privileges, both before and after the establishment of the free port, culminating in the Privilege issued by Maria Theresa in 1771. According to them, it added nothing substantially new, but was significant in that it "formed nevertheless an indelible title of the ancient possession of the said benefits and a gracious forecast of their continuation and uninterrupted enjoyment in the future." They emphasized their own deserving merit by citing their contribution to "the public happiness of Trieste and the state," that is, to the free port and to Habsburg commerce and industry more generally. Their registration in the *Borsa* from its inception was proof, they said, that their contribution was "equal to that of any other."

It was in their invocation of Joseph's proposals of May 1781 as the next link in their own chain of privileges that the Jewish leaders of Trieste rose to rhetorical heights. By opening to Jews throughout the monarchy vast fields of endeavor in the arts, professions, and trades, that "motuproprium rent in a flash the veil of prejudices of which some unfortunate Jewish individuals had often been the victims." It thereby signaled "the most happy and fortunate epoch for Jews, which will be written in our annals, which has penetrated our hearts, and [for] which we will instill sentiments of the most hearty gratitude in our children and grandchildren." Since the very essence of Joseph's May resolution was to increase the means by which Jews could contribute and show their worthiness to the state, it was, the *Capi* claimed, the most fitting principle upon which to base their own case for the continuation of their prior privileges.

In fact, what they proceeded to request really had little to do with the substance of Joseph's Toleration program. For indeed, they needed to address those issues on which the Toleration proposals were silent or less generous than the prerogatives they already enjoyed in Trieste. In the enthusiasm of new legislation for Jews whose situation differed radically from theirs, they hardly wanted their own long-standing and exceptional religious and economic rights to be forgotten. The Toleration proposals were a reminder, if they needed one, that they had something to lose.

Besides the three main issues, the Jewish leaders raised two other issues still troubling them from their 1770s negotiations for the Theresian diplomas. Again they requested stronger legal protection against clandestine baptisms of minors, warranted, they claimed, by their right of free exercise of religion, by justice, by several Church authorities, and indeed, by favorable sovereign resolutions of the 1730s–40s. They acknowledged that "enlightened people" did not engage in this practice; still, they wanted reconfirmation of the earlier favorable resolutions and guarantees of the return of abducted and clandestinely baptized children. Second, they returned to the subject of communal regulation. To safeguard some autonomy and loosen the tight absolutist embrace of the 1771 Statute, they asked for a local procedure: that the governor be authorized to approve plans that the community itself would determine appropriate by majority vote. While they repeatedly invoked the Privilege of 1771 as firm grounding for various liberties, in contrast they made no appeal to the Statute of 1771. The process and politics of it still rankled, and it was too complicated, or, in the words they used to the governor, "unobservable and unobserved," "useless and neglected."[51]

In their petition for Governor Zinzendorf himself, Jewish leaders appealed for his support in the name of his "humanity and justice."[52] On each point they went into much greater detail than in their official petition to the sovereign, supplying historical background from ancient to modern times, and citations from a wide range of legal and scholarly works in Latin and German, which Zinzendorf could draw upon in presenting their case. For example, they explained the widespread prohibitions against land-owning by Jews as the result of the feudal system, and consequently the legality of Jewish land-ownership in Trieste by the absence of the feudal system in that region. With regard to economic opportunities, they asserted that their rights to engage in commerce were consonant with Joseph's aim of removing impediments to Jews' earning an honest living. They stated the classic Enlightenment view propounded by Jews and their supporters that restrictive legislation — and not innate moral character — was to blame for any shortcomings or questionable business practices of the Jews. Joseph's wise and enlightened legislative changes would, they argued, lead to better behavior and better relations, that is, the elimination of prejudices and ill-feeling between Jews and Christians—all for the "happiness of the state, and of individuals."

The closing remarks of their petition to the sovereign were especially revealing of two of their fundamental concerns: parity and continuity. They asked for renewal of all their privileges so that they would be placed on a "perfect level with every other Nation settled and doing business in Trieste, [and] be able for our part to earn an honorable living, and show ourselves ever more worthy of the most merciful sovereign grace and protection." (They of course did not mention that with regard to public worship, their rights in fact surpassed those of the Protestants in Trieste.) They stressed that their request contained "nothing of novelty," for its aim was preservation of existing liberties. Failure to confirm their privileges—that is, denial of their equal footing with the other minorities in Trieste—would, they implied, constitute the real innovation. Indeed, as we have seen, the language of equality was hardly new in Trieste. During the *Borsa* negotiations in 1779, Jews claimed to "have always been regarded without discrimination as being on an equal footing with the Christians,"[53] and Zinzendorf himself had used the term "equality" in the rough draft of his August 1781 report. For the Jews of Trieste, their standard of comparison or reference point was not Jews elsewhere in the monarchy, but rather the other religious-ethnic minorities in Trieste—whose own situation was exceptional in the Habsburg context. The Jews of Trieste welcomed parity with their Gentile neighbors, but not with their Habsburg coreligionists in their current situation, no matter how much improved by Joseph's Toleration program.

In other words, the Toleration legislation represented for the Jews of Trieste—as did Emancipation for the Sefardic Jews of Bordeaux a decade later—the challenge of preserving their own privileged exceptionality.[54] Improvements in the status of their coreligionists were laudable, but the Triestine Jews did not want their own position to be adversely affected by any monarchy-wide adjustments. It was imperative to maintain what they already legally enjoyed. Toward that end, they were prepared to hail the effects of the Toleration resolution upon other Jews in the florid rhetoric of the day, but they were anxious that the genesis, history, and better provisions of their own privileges be acknowledged and preserved. Astutely, they used the harmonistic language of continuity in expressing their own desires, even as they praised the Toleration legislation as epoch-making. Yet almost in the same breath, they presented it as the complementary capstone of their old privileges. Since renewal of their Privilege and Statute of 1771 had become intertwined with Joseph's new program, they were determined to take advantage of the new dispensation—though it had little to offer them—and of the new climate of opinion in Vienna it betokened in order to press concerns of their own: improving, or at least maintaining, the favorable status quo in Trieste. Therefore, they spoke the language of the new Toleration; but it was the reality of privilege whose continuity they sought to ensure.

Governor Zinzendorf was well disposed to the Jews' claims and arguments, but before forwarding them to Vienna with his endorsement, he sought to tidy up some loose ends. On October 2, 1781, he requested from the *Capi* a brief draft of their proposed statutes and, again, an answer about the stipend for the Segre boy. He placed high stakes upon this second matter: if the *Capi* agreed to provide it, he would use that as an argument in their favor with Vienna, that is, as proof of their "efficacious zeal" to benefit from and cooperate with Joseph's intentions; if, on the contrary, they refused to supply the sum, Zinzendorf would cite that as evidence of their "inactivity and indolence."[55]

This veiled threat galvanized the *Capi* to action. In response to it, they addressed all of Zinzendorf's questions shortly thereafter. They had not yet drawn up a new statute, but they explained the few subjects they planned to include, such as leaders, elections, and taxes. Again they repeated their concerns for a more autonomous procedure: approval by the local governor should suffice, "since our desire is confined to a very simple Regulation, and we do not desire to form a totally separate nation with respect to regulations and principles." In addition, they appended two "Notes," in effect progress reports, which supplied some details of their compliance with the May proposals. The first note listed the names of ten or so Jews employed in the "arts," that is, trades such as upholstery, turnery, goldsmithing, distilling of liqueur, baking, and butchery. These in fact were all quite traditional occupations for Jews, and some of these people had been engaged in them well before the 1781 proposals. The second note listed the five Jews who had started to attend the normal school of the city—three more than Zinzendorf had mentioned in the summer. The Jewish leaders also reported the community's decision of late September to organize a special collection in order to provide young Segre with an annual stipend of sixty florins. In closing, they reiterated their confidence that time would make the effects of the May proposals "more brilliant and multiplied."[56]

Official Perspectives, October 1781–January 1782

In the early autumn of 1781, the Court Chancellery began discussing the reports received from the different lands about Joseph's May proposals. The gist of Zinzendorf's August report was understood to be that the Jews of Trieste already had a favorable constitution (*Verfassung*) or system; and that there, some of the sovereign's orders were already being carried out, and preparations had begun for the future implementation of the others. The Court Chancellery simply passed this information along to the State Council and awaited further instructions.[57] In the State Council, skepticism was voiced about the efficacy of forbidding foreign books in Trieste and Gorizia. Only one decision was then taken with regard to Trieste: to add permission for qualified Jews to earn doctoral degrees in law and medicine to the Triestine and Gorizian versions of the October 20 decree about normal schools for Jews. In their earlier report, Gorizian authorities had volunteered that such a step would arouse no opposition since Jews were already attending some Italian universities, most notably Padua. These comments on Italian precedent in fact led to the granting of this right elsewhere in the monarchy.[58]

During this period, Trieste was mentioned in the State Council in connection with two other subjects: the ghetto of Gorizia, and the head toll. Concerning the ghetto of Gorizia, Councillor Tobias Philipp Gebler, who had served in the Triestine administration in the mid-1750s, cited Trieste as an example to be emulated, and described it as a place "where matters have been on a reasonable footing for several years, almost as many Jews live in other places as in the old ghetto, and they have to some extent built splendid houses."[59] His colleagues decided, however, that the ghetto of Gorizia should be maintained, and that rich Jews could ask for permission to live outside it only on a case-by-case basis. State councillors also noted the complaints of wealthy Triestine Jewish merchants that they had been unjustly harassed by collectors of the head toll.[60] Discussion of all these topics served to highlight the unusual situation of the Jews of Trieste.

Meanwhile, in Trieste, Zinzendorf was preparing his extensive report to accompany the Jews' petition of late September. His lengthy letter of November 13, 1781, to Vienna was strongly supportive of the Jews' requests. In endorsing reconfirmation of their Privilege of 1771 and reporting on the implementation of the May proposals, he drew substantially from the materials supplied to him by the Jews and made bolder, clearer assertions about Triestine realities than he had in his earlier interim report.[61]

Zinzendorf began by acknowledging that some might think that the new Toleration policy for all the Jews of the Hereditary Lands, of which Trieste was a part, rendered a separate privilege for the Jews of Trieste superfluous. But, he argued, separate renewal of the Privilege of 1771 was still necessary because the long-held prerogatives it included were "still more numerous" than those contained in the May 16 decree. Now he was prepared to state without equivocation that the Jews of Trieste already enjoyed a superior status, and, he reasoned, "His Majesty's just and humanitarian purpose is too certain surely to deprive them of these more numerous prerogatives." Since rights explicitly guaranteed in their 1771 Privilege, such as land ownership and exemption from the head toll, were not covered by the May resolution, they required explicit reconfirmation in a separate privilege. Unlike the Jews, however, Zinzendorf believed that their religious and commercial rights were covered adequately by the new legislation.

His focus was land ownership, concerning which he tried to dispel the apparent contradiction between the prior rights of Triestine Jews and the May letter. Drawing upon the arguments in the Jews' petition of September 27, 1781, he explained at great length the local system of land tenure and agriculture, which were at variance with the vestiges of the feudal system existing elsewhere. In the region of Trieste, the relationship between landowner and tenant farmer was a contractual one between the individuals, involving no subjection, servitude, or permanent tie to the land—in other words, no feudal bond. Religion was not significant for this contract, since Catholics, Greek Orthodox, and Jews could and did own land. This local reality was not really in contradiction to Joseph's proposals, Zinzendorf argued, because their true spirit was to combat servitude and submission.

Zinzendorf fully supported the Jews' requests on the two issues still unresolved to their satisfaction since the negotiations over their 1771 diplomas: greater protection against clandestine baptism of minor children, and greater autonomy in determining communal regulations. Since such baptisms violated the Jews' religious rights and the principle of paternal authority, he urged that the earlier favorable sovereign resolutions on the subject be repeated. About communal regulations, he elaborated upon his earlier recommendation for drastic abridgment. He thought it completely unnecessary to bother the sovereign with the mundane details of communal administration. Instead of a statute valid for only five years, which would require review at regular intervals, he preferred a statute valid indefinitely to which changes could be made and approved in Trieste. He stated explicitly that despite the signature and seal of the empress, a "large part" of the Jewish community was dissatisfied with the Statute of 1771, especially with the judicial rights accorded the *Capi* in minor civil cases. He added that in any event, the Jews of Trieste were subject, as were the other religious-ethnic groups, to the local police and courts, that is, to the prevailing methods of civil and criminal law enforcement. He suggested that in their new regulations, the Jews acknowledge their willingness to comply with the recent decree of October 20, 1781, on normal-schooling for Jews.

Finally, Zinzendorf himself raised the outstanding issue of the *Borsa*. He now argued that Jewish eligibility for election as managing deputies was in conformity with Joseph's proposals of May 1781. Their eligibility should be declared by Vienna in a new statement of their privileges since their exclusion was originally stipulated in court decrees about the *Borsa*. Zinzendorf kept quiet about the events of 1780: Blümegen's support for Jewish eligibility, his private prodding to Zinzendorf for local implementation, and his own unsuccessful efforts to change the minds of *Borsa* opponents. Now, it was obvious to him that Joseph's new Toleration policy provided both a symbolic and a real opportunity to overcome local resistance, if it still existed. On this issue, action by the central authorities could improve and redress the Triestine Jewish situation.

The second purpose of Zinzendorf's report was to assess the implementation of the May 1781 proposals in Trieste. He now provided evidence for his earlier statement that much was already a reality in Trieste: he reported upon the Jews in manual trades and the normal school, as well as upon the commitment of the Jewish community to finance Segre's continued education in that school. As for Jewish agriculture, not yet a reality and not likely to become one, he expressed his skepticism with the laconic comment that only time would tell. As for the other cultural provisions, he informed Vienna that for a long time the Jews of Trieste had kept their records in the language of the country; the one exception was marriage and divorce documents, but the *Capi* had informed him of the steps taken to add Italian translations to those in the future.[62] Finally, Zinzendorf dissented from one aspect of the cultural policy stipulated in the May 16 proposals, namely, the forbidding of the importation of foreign books, for he agreed with the Jews that control of books was impossible in a free port. On this score, he passed on the interesting assurance profferred by the *Capi*: that most Jews had little free time for reading anyway, and those who did preferred "Romance-language (*welsche*) and German writings to their own books" (presumably in Hebrew).[63] He felt that a printing press of their own would be too costly.

Thus Zinzendorf assured Vienna that Joseph's proposals of May 1781 had found ready and fertile ground in Trieste, where much was already realized or was in the process of becoming so. For the important respects in which the proposals were incongruous with Triestine realities, Zinzendorf urged action in favor of the Jews of Trieste. It was his conviction that full application of the spirit of Joseph's Toleration program in Trieste required reconfirmation of the Jews' more advantageous privileges in a separate diploma and settlement of the *Borsa* question.

Vienna's response was not long in coming. By mid-December 1781, both the Court Chancellery and the State Council had reached a decision about the Jews' petition of September 27 and Zinzendorf's accompanying report of November 13, 1781.

In their December 6, 1781, discussion, the Court Chancellery proceeded from the fact that the Jews of Trieste had lived for a long time with "a completely favorable constitution," and from the consideration that above all, His Majesty's "generous intention is to take care to improve the fate of Jewry rather than to take away benefits already granted long ago."[64] Therefore, the Jews of Trieste should maintain their rights to ownership of real property and exemption from the head toll. Officials noted that the consequences were anyway not very serious, since in the first case, land tenure was not linked to the feudal system (they echoed Zinzendorf, who echoed the Jews), and in the second, Joseph had already decided on the future abolition of the head toll. As for eligibility for the *Borsa* board, they stated that they had already urged the governor of Trieste to implement it in early 1780, since "the practical knowledge and judgments of Jews can be exactly as good and useful as those of members of other religions." They were also willing to provide the Jews of Trieste with greater protection against clandestine baptisms. (Through the 1780s, in fact, Josephinian legislation for all Habsburg Jews did move in this general direction.[65])

These specifics all seemed rather straightforward. The more problematic question was in which form to present them to the Jews of Trieste, since it was argued that "the benefits recently granted so mercifully to the Jews of the Hereditary Lands did assume the character of a new legislative enactment (*Gesetzgebung*); thus it was deemed superfluous, indeed unseemly, to draw up in addition a privilege proper to the Jewry of Trieste."[66] The solution was to instruct the governor of Trieste to issue a decree to the Jews "in the name of His Majesty" conveying the dual message: the Jews of Trieste could enjoy all the "advantages and authorizations" (*Vortheile und Befugnisse*) now granted all the Jews of the Hereditary Lands, and beyond those, "all the other privileges and benefits" (*Vorzüge und Begünstigungen*, the words used by Zinzendorf in his first report) that they had long enjoyed by virtue of "sovereign concessions"—in other words, in substance, the best of both the new and the old. As Vienna had determined a decade earlier that the seventeenth-century privileges required a change in form in order to be appropriate in 1771, so did they determine that the 1771 privileges now required reissuance in a new form in 1781. Though a new formal privilege could not be granted, a positive response to almost all the specific substantive requests was possible.

To be mentioned specifically in the decree were the older three prerogatives—land ownership, exemption from the head toll, and protection against clandestine baptism—and the new one of eligibility for the *Borsa* managing board. The governor should state that the last was given with the confidence that the Jews would take pains to make themselves "ever more and more useful to the state." The Court Chancellery also recommended that they be instructed to draw up a simple new statute based on their earlier ones and to submit it to the governor for approval, but they maintained more centralist control than Zinzendorf had suggested, for they still made it subject to final approval in Vienna. Thus the absolutist embrace was to be loosened, but not undone. They repeated Zinzendorf's recommendations that Jews be subject to all general laws in matters of police and justice, and that control of foreign books in the free port would be impossible.

The thinking of the Court Chancellery was confirmed by the State Council discussion of December 13. There, concern was voiced about the sensibilities of Triestine Jews: Vienna placed a high priority on providing them with a feeling of security and maintaining their good disposition because of this eminent community's cultural development (*Bildung*), and especially its economic significance. However, the State Council added a qualification about the *Borsa* first suggested by Councillor Karl Friedrich Hatzfeld and supported by Joseph: that the right be clearly worded so as to mean that Jews "could" be elected as deputies, but not that they "always must" be. They did not wish to imply that the Jews "be considered completely equal to the Christian merchants."[67] In other words, there was to be no fixed Jewish seat on the Triestine *Borsa*, as on the London Stock Exchange or on the Livornese municipal council since 1778.[68] In effect, equality of opportunity was to be offered to individual Jewish merchants, but equality of results was not to be guaranteed to the corporate Jewish community.

The decisions of the Court Chancellery and State Council were embodied in the court resolution of December 19, 1781, sent to Zinzendorf.[69] Vienna refused to grant the Jews of Trieste a new privilege, but instead proferred a letter "in the name of His Majesty" to secure their long-held prerogatives and add an important new one. Significantly—and noted approvingly by Zinzendorf[70]—they did not have to pay for this letter in Joseph's name, as they had paid dearly for their Privilege from Maria Theresa only ten years earlier. The December 19 court resolution, then conveyed locally by gubernatorial decrees on January 16, 1782, to the Jewish community and to the *Borsa*, thus completed the first stage of the enactment in Trieste of Joseph's Toleration proposals.[71] Together with the October 20, 1781, decree on normal-schooling (enacted in Trieste on November 26, 1781, and to be discussed more fully below), the December 1781/January 1782 letter represented the version of the Toleration edict specific to the Jews of Trieste. In effect, the Jews of Trieste had all their privileges renewed in substance, though in a form different from that of the past. With the few additional changes made, the Jews of Trieste were to enjoy the best of both their former privileged status and the new general policy of Toleration.

Probably reflecting past difficulties and ongoing sensitivities, Zinzendorf approached the *Borsa* issue carefully in his January letters to both the

Jewish community and the *Borsa* board. To neither did he go into all the details and the qualification outlined in Vienna. Instead, he simply wrote that Jews should now be considered eligible for election and service as *Borsa* deputies. To the Jews, he added that this new measure of sovereign mercy should spur them to become "all the more useful and grateful as much to the state as to their fellow-citizens (*concittadini*)."[72] Gratitude—specifically to their fellows—was Zinzendorf's addition. He was reminding them that for their sake, they ought to pay heed to local forces as well as to the authorities in Vienna.

Indeed, though central authorities had earlier led the way on the *Borsa* issue, in other respects Zinzendorf now played a critical role on the local scene. There was a remarkable degree of congruence between his perspective and the Jews': that, at the least, it was desirable to maintain the favorable status quo. Zinzendorf's cooperation with Triestine Jewish leaders and his whole-hearted endorsement of Joseph's aims were striking. His adherence to Enlightenment principles and his utilitarian attitude toward the city's needs led him to approve the Toleration policy fully. In contrast, Joseph heard opposition from some other governmental appointees in Bohemia and Lombardy, in the latter even from the intendant who was generally one of his staunch supporters. In *Della influenza del ghetto nello stato*, published anonymously in 1782, Giovanni Battista Gherardo D'Arco forcefully charged Jews with immorality, misanthropy, and causing economic harm, and argued that Joseph's new policy was worthwhile precisely insofar as it aimed at the complete transformation of the Jews.[73] In other words, D'Arco stressed the self-improvement of the Jews, while Zinzendorf focused on the improvement of conditions for Jews. In Trieste, Zinzendorf and the Jews saw Joseph's program ultimately as confirming rather than transforming local realities.

Zinzendorf represented the consummate Josephinian bureaucrat: attentive to the needs of the locality and of the monarchy as a whole seen from Vienna. His long service at the center of the monarchy's administration both before and after his stint as governor of Trieste helped him take a perspective that transcended the merely local. There was an additional structural factor. In the Free Port and City of Trieste, the highest governing officials appointed by Vienna were neither traditional local leaders of patriciate or estate nor their representatives, for the political reorganization of Trieste had choked the power of the old patricians, and there had been no estates.[74] Thus Habsburg officials in Trieste did not generally try to safeguard the interests of a traditional local elite against Joseph's centralizing policies. Zinzendorf occasionally paid attention to the *Borsa*, representatives of the new elite of Trieste, but the opposition to Josephinian policies expressed by some clergymen in Trieste made little headway with him. In general, Zinzendorf's shepherding of the Toleration legislation between Vienna and Trieste showed the hand of an experienced, skilled, and diplomatic administrator.

Privilege and Toleration: The Continuity of Exceptionality

As discussed above, when first presented with the Toleration proposals by Zinzendorf in May 1781, Jewish leaders in Trieste strove to prevent any potentially undermining effect upon their own prior favorable status. But they also saw the general promise of Josephinian Toleration insofar as its basic thrust was to improve conditions for Jews. They readily resolved to implement the cultural requirements concerning language and normal-schooling. And Triestine Jews were clever in expressing a primary reaction of gratitude: appreciation for present favors and indeed for past ones, and the expectation of continued grace. The lavish rhetoric they used to praise the rescript was at least partly genuine. They could well recognize the merits of the new policy for other Jewries in the monarchy, especially for poor Jews, and they could appreciate its symbolic value. With his strong injection of secular utilitarianism, Joseph did seem to be transforming toleration from mere sufferance—his mother's conception—into a basis for civil standing and inclusion.[75] Though the status of Jews remained different from that of non-Catholic Christians and certainly of Catholics, still the rhetoric of "fellow citizens" and "near-equality"—though unmatched fully in reality—was unprecedented and significant, and it inspired optimism. A new, more favorable general policy toward Jews could perhaps benefit all, maybe even the Jews of Trieste themselves. Later sources claim that the Jews of Trieste greeted the May proposals with solemn prayers of thanksgiving.[76] And though their own responses and needs were mixed and required careful negotiation, it is indeed possible that Triestine Jews were shrewd enough to express the appropriate gratitude demonstrably in public. On the one hand, they were joyous for the sakes of their coreligionists; on the other, expressing gratitude was the best tactic for using the symbolism of the new turn of events to their own advantage.

By simultaneously expressing grateful enthusiasm for the new Toleration policy, and calling attention to their own anomalous situation, the Jews of Trieste succeeded not only in maintaining their prior status, but in actually going beyond it. Though the specifics of the Toleration legislation had little to offer them, they used its issuance to redress unresolved issues from the 1770s and to improve their own situation. A couple of years later, officials in Vienna made precisely that point when describing the Triestine situation to officials in Hungary: "His Majesty not only did not curtail their . . . [long] enjoyed liberties . . . , but on the contrary, certainly . . . extended them." And the example they cited was that "they now also could be elected as deputies of the merchants' *Borse* in Trieste, like the Christian merchants."[77]

Indeed, the right to serve as *Borsa* deputies was qualitatively different from any of their previous rights. As mentioned above in Chapter One, that position of economic power in Trieste of the 1780s was in fact a form of political influence, for the Mercantile Exchange was instrumental in determining a wide range of policies for the free port and the city. Previously, the wealthiest Jews of Trieste did have the opportunity to meet frequently with governing officials and to tender advice informally, but consultation was now to be partially institutionalized. Jewish eligibility as *Borsa* deputies, first stated in the Toleration letter of December 1781/January 1782, was confirmed in the new *Borsa* regulations of 1794, which stipulated that all its members, "of any community (*Nazione*) or religion," could vote for and be elected as deputies. The deputies were now the highest-ranking members, with no separate post of director above them. In fact, Jews participated in these elections from 1783, and in the 1790s, at least one Jew, Grassin Vita di Caliman Levi, served as deputy. When an additional executive body, the Council, was created by the new *Borsa* regulations of 1804, Jews held four of its forty seats.[78] Though different from the political right of a fixed Jewish seat on the Livornese municipal council, this political acknowledgment of Jewish economic integration was one of the most important results in Trieste of the issuance of the Toleration legislation. Economic rights verging on political power were a far cry from the occupational diversification outlined in Joseph's May 1781 proposals, and highlighted again the discrepancy between the realities of Trieste and those of most other Habsburg Jewries.

Yet as significant as this new *Borsa* right was, the Jews of Trieste had not gotten their privileges renewed as such. Why not? And what was the significance of the form in which Vienna conveyed their status in 1781? Why did Vienna choose a nonprivilege privilege for the Jews of Trieste: to renew the substance, but not the form, of their long-held privileges? What was the significance of Joseph's conferral of benefits being considered as a new legislative enactment (*Gesetzgebung*)? Why, in light of that, was a separate privilege for Triestine Jewry deemed "superfluous" and "unseemly"?

One reason was pragmatic. It might have diminished the impression made by Joseph's new proposals to publicize the fact that for Trieste, they were not entirely appropriate and required completion by a separate privilege. To issue such a privilege would highlight the special status and continued exceptionality of the Jews of Trieste; this more favorable exception might well show in sharper relief the limitations of the general Toleration policy. A gubernatorial letter "in the name of His Majesty" was a quiet diplomatic solution that conveyed without fanfare the substance, but not the old form, of continued privilege and exceptional status for the Jews of Trieste. Yet, outlined in a letter rather than a public patent, it would still set no example for the other Jewries of the monarchy.

However, the reluctance to issue a new privilege to the Jews of Trieste in fact reflected a deeper phenomenon: changing conceptions of law in the eighteenth-century Habsburg state. Starting in Maria Theresa's reign, especially among her advisors, and even more so during Joseph's reign, the assumptions of the natural law and Enlightenment traditions became influential in Vienna: that law should be uniform for all, clear, simple, public, and intelligible to all, and related to actual living conditions.[79] Toward this end, which also served cameralist and state-building purposes, legal education was reformed, and the standardization and codification of many branches of law begun. Whether for individuals or for corporations, privileges—by their nature specific and local—ran counter to the centralizing thrust of the absolutist state. In the Habsburg Monarchy, there was no outright and comprehensive attack on privilege, as on that famous August night of 1789 in France, but when opportunities presented themselves, the central authorities themselves chipped away at the multivariegated edifice of individual privileges. New privileges were not granted. And though many privileged corporate bodies were left standing, efforts were made to bring them under tighter control of the absolutist state.

The compromise developed for the Jews of Trieste reflected the fundamental tendency to diminish and weaken privileges: particular privileges as such were deemed no longer suitable once a general law had been enacted. Like other Jews, the Triestine Jews were subject to the new Toleration legislation, but of course only insofar as it was relevant to them. Where their situation required special attention above and beyond the legislation, for their sake and that of the free port, it was deemed appropriate for their prerogatives to be continued by letter, that is, by a means other than privilege.

Yet the legal situation was indeed murky. Though the Toleration edicts were considered new legislation, officials were unclear about their precise relation to already existing legislation, whether in the form of privileges or of ordinances and regulations. Joseph's advisors urged him to declare the Edicts of Toleration for Christians to be "revocable privileges," but he refused, indicating his desire that these be of a different nature. But he did not spell out precisely or theoretically what that nature was.[80] For the Jews, the nature of the new legislation and its relation to previous privileges and regulations was decided not *ab initio*, but rather *ex eventu*, through the course of events. In the fall of 1781, existing Jewish privileges were reconfirmed as such in Bohemia; yet they were not in Trieste in late 1781, in

Moravia in early 1782, nor in Gorizia-Gradisca in late 1782.[81] (The January 1782 edict for Vienna and Lower Austria stated that it repealed the earlier *Judenordnung* of 1754, but in fact, many earlier provisions concerning the terms of Jewish residence remained in effect.) Regarding privileges in particular, a certain process was at work: officials came gradually to the conclusion that it was neither necessary nor appropriate to renew old privileges once the new Toleration edicts were issued. And yet, the Toleration edicts hardly overturned or changed all existing regulations and ordinances about Jewish status. As incrementalist reforms, they left much intact, and did not bring into being a totally new legal reality.[82]

For the Jews of Trieste, these legal uncertainties raised particular anxieties, for their prior status—forged from individual and then communal privileges, and the Free Port Patents—was immeasurably valuable. They had something to lose if the general Toleration legislation were to supersede all previous privileges and equalize the situations of all Habsburg Jewries. Until they knew of Zinzendorf's support, they were not unjustified in feeling threatened by less advantageous proposals framed to meet conditions elsewhere. Indeed, in Gorizia, one writer proposed doing away with long-standing Jewish rights, including that of land ownership, on the basis of the more restrictive general Toleration proposals of 1781.[83] The Jews of Trieste were thus presented with the challenge of maintaining their own more favorable status quo. They succeeded in preserving their exceptionality, but not by privilege. The substance counted most, but the form probably caused some insecurity. Sovereign privileges and their currency of precedent were known commodities; the new Toleration was not. Were the new edicts as substantial? Did their general quality render them more or less secure than particular enactments or privileges, which had to be renewed, usually at great cost? What weight did a gubernatorial "letter in the name of His Majesty" carry for the future? In 1781–82, there were no real answers to these questions. The Jews of Trieste felt only that their old privileges rested on bedrock, and something was shifting. In the following decade, when Leopold and Francis acceded the throne in 1790 and 1792 respectively, the Jews of Trieste played it safe and asked for reconfirmation of their privileges and liberties. They were assured then that formal reconfirmation was "superfluous."[84] But in 1781–82 and the years immediately following, the Jews of Trieste could not know the longevity or full extent of Josephinian Toleration. A new kind of legislation brought a degree of uncertainty, apprehension, and insecurity, especially to a community that had enjoyed by privilege an exceptionally favorable status.

And yet, it is evident that the Jews of Trieste were buoyed by the invigorating new climate of opinion in Vienna. A tantalizing but, alas, incomplete reference to the Jewish mood of the times has come down to us.

Sometime in the early 1780s, when preparing a memorandum for submission to the governor, one of the Jewish leaders of Trieste, Aron Stella, exclaimed: "Times have changed. War is no longer waged with bow and arrow, but with rifle, musket, and cannon. That which formerly would have been reprehensible audacity merely to imagine, now would be foolish cowardice not to obtain."[85] In other words, the ceiling—what had formerly been beyond reach—had now become the floor—the minimum expected.

For the Jews of Trieste, there was fundamental continuity between Theresian privilege and Josephinian Toleration. The Toleration of 1781 was no ground-breaking innovation in Trieste. Though in a new form, Joseph reinforced the benefits conferred by his predecessors, and built upon the foundation of their prior privileges. The Free Port Patents and the Privilege of 1771 were more significant than the Toleration legislation of 1781–82 in determining their status. Yet the idea of Jews becoming "fellow citizens" made sense in Trieste precisely because the statuses of court Jews and port Jews had already been amalgamated.

Like the Protestants and Greek Orthodox of the city, the Jews of Trieste maintained their advantages vis-à-vis their coreligionists elsewhere in the Habsburg Monarchy. Though the new approach and legislation did narrow somewhat the gap between conditions in Trieste and those in other parts of the monarchy, still, Joseph's Toleration did not put other Habsburg Jewries on an equal footing with that of Trieste. Vienna decided in the early 1780s that Trieste could not serve as an example even for Gorizia-Gradisca and Mantua in northern Italy, because its circumstances as a free port were truly exceptional.[86] After the flurry of legislation in 1781–82, the Jews of Trieste enjoyed, as they had before, an unusual legal status among Habsburg Jewries.

CHAPTER FOUR

Civic Enlightenment as Cultural Policy: Language and the 'Scuola Pia Normale sive Talmud Torà'

The Josephinian Toleration legislation aimed to turn Habsburg Jews into useful, obedient, and civic-minded subjects. From the outset, its basic assumption was that bringing Jews into the civic and social order required their cultural transformation, with language and education to be the prime vehicles. With the sovereign resolutions of May and October 1781, the government sought to extend the recently established normal-school system of primary education to the Jews. One of the main tasks of the new Jewish normal schools would be to teach Jews German, the language of the state.

Habsburg authorities applied these policies in Trieste as elsewhere, but without the sense of urgency that the civil integration of Triestine Jews depended on for radical cultural transformation. In Trieste, there was no separate Jewish dialect isolating the Jews. The only issue became to what extent the Jews would adopt the state language, German, in addition to the vernacular Italian. Ultimately, Josephinian language policies reinforced the Italian identification of the Jews, while the entry of the state into the Jewish classroom led to the founding of a Jewish normal school, the *Scuola Pia Normale sive Talmud Torà*, an institution that, despite all vicissitudes, still exists today. The positive reaction of Triestine Jewry to the normal-school agenda decisively colored their view of the entire Josephinian program, and, as we shall see in Chapter Five, gained them a place on the map of Haskalah, Jewish Enlightenment, throughout Europe.

Language and Names

As discussed above, the cornerstone of Joseph's plan to reduce Jewish cultural isolation was Jewish proficiency in the local language and use of it, rather than Hebrew or Yiddish, in all records, contracts, and legal documents. (Similarly, Greek was forbidden in commercial records in favor of the more accessible German, Italian, and French.[1]) This kind of language legislation posed no problem for Jews in Trieste, where neither governmental concern with language nor the use by Jews of the local language were novelties. The Theresian Statute of 1771 contained the requirement that Jewish youngsters be taught Italian and German. Italian hardly had to be legislated, for Triestine Jews continued the traditional linguistic norms of Italian Jewry: facility with the local dialect and with written Italian. Jews in Italy generally spoke local Italian dialects and were taught to read and write Italian in Jewish schools. Though in some places their particular intonation and accent, as well as their use among themselves of words of Hebrew origin, resulted in local Italian-Jewish dialects, there was no significant linguistic barrier between Jews and Gentiles. Italian had long been used in sermons and in belles lettres (sometimes along with Hebrew), occasionally in rabbinic legal responsa, and increasingly in communal records.[2] In Trieste, the Jews conversed and conducted business in the local Italian vernacular, and kept the records of their own *Comunità Israelitica* in Italian. Only a few documents in the Triestine communal records, such as correspondence with other Jewish communities, were written in Hebrew. In 1781, Jewish leaders informed Zinzendorf that most Jews preferred Italian and German reading matter to that written in Hebrew.

The linguistic situation of Triestine Jewry, then, approximated the goal desired by Joseph for all Habsburg Jews. The one novelty due to Joseph's Toleration policy concerned marriage and divorce documents. In September 1781, the heads of the Jewish community informed its members that henceforth, these too must be written "in the Italian language customary in this city" in order for them to be considered as legal documents and their dowry and property provisions legally binding.[3] Since these would in all other respects continue to be written according to Jewish law, the Italian translation was to function as a supplement to, not a replacement of, the traditional Hebrew-Aramaic forms.

Concern with the languages used by Jews went hand in hand with Vienna's overall program of the mid- to late 1780s to standardize (that is, Germanize) the languages of administration, justice, education, and commerce throughout the realm. In Trieste itself, directives were issued from 1784 to 1787 to make German the language of judicial proceedings, legal documents, and many commercial transactions.[4] As elsewhere, these efforts provoked protest. When *Borsa* leaders objected in 1789, they stressed that the overwhelming majority of the merchants and brokers of Trieste—"Italians, Jews, Greeks, Armenians"—conducted business only in Italian and scarcely knew German: "The entire population of Trieste, except for some craftsmen and some official clerks, is Italian or [have] master[y] of the Italian language."[5] The same was true of most lawyers and officials. *Borsa* leaders argued that immediate Germanization would lead to grave disorders and chaos in the commercial life of the city. On the advice of local authorities, Vienna substantially modified the orders. (Eventually, the futility of the Germanization policy in some other areas was recognized by Joseph's successor Leopold, who rescinded many of the edicts in 1790.)

While Joseph's linguistic campaign was in force, in 1787, he ordered that by the beginning of 1788, all Habsburg Jews were to choose fixed surnames that were not merely designations of place of origin, and were to adopt German first names. They were also to start keeping all registers of births, deaths, marriages, and circumcisions in German.[6] The stated purpose of the legislation was to "avoid all the disorders" caused by the lack of fixed surnames among many traditional Jews in central and eastern Europe. Combating Jewish cultural isolation and integrating Jews more easily into the bureaucratic apparatus of the absolutist state converged with the aims of administrative standardization. For the Habsburg Monarchy, as for other modernizing absolutist states later, requiring legally binding surnames for Jews was often closely linked to mobilization through military conscription.

In September 1787, the decree about names was issued in Trieste, along with the accompanying list of permissible German or Christian versions of first names.[7] Once again, however, legislation from Vienna was ill-attuned to Italian Jewish realities, for Italian Jews had in fact long used family names. Accordingly, the Jews of Trieste informed the authorities that there, the issue was moot, since they already had fixed surnames. In Trieste itself, there is no evidence of any change in Jewish surnames.[8] As for first names, the Jews of Trieste—like the *Borsa* leaders—remonstrated specifically against Germanization. They also claimed legitimacy for their names by invoking the Bible and commonality with Christians:

Our community here [is] accustomed to the use of the Italian language, since the greatest part originates from Italy . . . and is instructed only in that language. . . . [Our] personal names . . . [are in] the aforementioned language . . . several of these are derived from the Sacred Scriptures, and others are used commonly by Christians. . . . To make changes in these would lead to confusion and disorder.[9]

The outcome is difficult to reconstruct. How the government responded to the Jews' claims is unknown. The Jewish community did compile a list of all Jews living in Trieste, which indicates that some Jews were to assume new names that conformed more to Biblical or common usage, for example, Judah instead of Leon, Mario instead of Majer, Ester instead of Stella. But since later documents show a number of people still using their former names, it is evident that formal compliance did not always lead to practical implementation.[10] And the pressure from the authorities obviously eased during Leopold's reign. In any case, the Jews in Trieste displayed a decided adherence to Italian rather than German. The Triestine Jewish protest against the adoption of German names was clearly based not upon allegiance to a Jewish tongue or a desire for insularity, but rather upon the Jews' customary use of Italian. Ironically, their protest against German and on behalf of Italian bespoke the kind of linguistic and cultural integration of Jews with the surrounding society that was the very goal of Joseph's policies. On the sensitive matter of personal names, the Jews of Trieste were more aligned with local society than with the state.

Elementary Education in Trieste and the Theresian School Reforms

For the Jews of Trieste, Joseph's educational program proved far less ambiguous and problematic than his linguistic policy. This program stemmed from the shared conviction of Maria Theresa and Joseph about the importance of education: both attached singular importance to the education of the young, considering the establishment of a state-controlled and compulsory system of elementary education a necessity for a strong state. For both, the reforming absolutist state had to be a tutelary one, preparing its young subjects for utility, civic duty, and public happiness.

In the 1760s and early 1770s, education and schools were formally declared a public political concern, the Court Education Commission (*Studienhofkommission*) was created, and the Jesuits were expelled. Reducing clerical power went hand in hand with promoting the cohesion of the state itself. In December 1774, Maria Theresa took the first step toward the establishment of a centralized, state-supervised, and compulsory system of elementary education, by issuing the General School Ordinance for German normal, upper primary, and lower primary schools in the Hereditary Lands (*Allgemeine Schulordnung*).[11] This law, fashioned in large part by the Protestant Johann Ignaz Felbiger, who had served in Prussia, outlined a uniform system of three levels of school: local primary schools (*Trivialschule*), upper primary schools (*Hauptschule*) in the larger towns of administrative districts, and normal schools (*Normalschule*), which would also include preparatory teacher-training, in provincial capitals. Government-appointed school commissions were to supervise the schools and to implement uniform curricula and pedagogic methods. Attendance of all boys and girls aged six to twelve was decreed compulsory, with exceptions only for those with approved private tutors. Religion, reading and writing, arithmetic, civics, and morality would be taught at all levels, while further instruction in language and various sciences would be added in the upper two. The decided emphasis of the program was practical and utilitarian. These Habsburg initiatives succeeded in establishing the most extensive system of elementary education in eighteenth-century Europe.

In Trieste, governmental authorities had already shown concern for educating the young. In 1761, they had provided for the establishment of regular classes in Christian doctrine and four elementary schools (*triviale*): two Italian, the second to teach Latin as well; one German; and one for girls alone. Also, private teachers, Jesuits, and some other religious orders—both male and female—ran their own classes, seventeen in total in 1772, teaching a total of 506 students subjects such as Italian, German, French, Latin, arithmetic, and Christian doctrine, variously in the different schools.[12] The Jesuits departed from the city in 1775 following papal condemnation of the order; in contrast, the Benedictine nuns of the San Cipriano convent, who had long taught the daughters of elite Triestine families, maintained a niche for themselves by adapting to the new normal-school system.[13]

The General School Ordinance was applied in Trieste in March 1775, and the government-sponsored German-language normal school opened in December of that year.[14] Reports submitted to the keenly interested Governor Zinzendorf mentioned language as the most significant cause of opposition to this new school. The Commune of Trieste, representing the old patriciate, set up two Italian public elementary schools, but the governor soon had them closed. By December 1776, he recognized the necessity of some instruction in the native tongues of the students, Italian and Slavic (Illyrian), and he made provisions for religion and grammar to be taught in those languages.[15] By March 1777, Zinzendorf himself was generally pleased with the academic progress of the normal-school students. After attending an examination at the school, he wrote in his diary that he was "surprised by the answers of the pupils, and charmed by the useful ideas taught to them in matters of morals, manners, arithmetic, and geometry."[16] Still, many parents continued to prefer private schools, which the government never succeeded in eliminating. In 1776–77, 200 students attended the normal school, while thirteen private teachers instructed 218. In 1782, 242 students (approximately 25 percent of the children between the ages of seven and eleven who lived in the new city) were enrolled in the normal school, while approximately 140 studied with private teachers and 102 received no instruction. In 1792, twenty-six private teachers were instructing 160 students.[17]

Jewish education in Trieste before the 1780s was conducted primarily by individual teachers, male and female, some of whom were designated as "public" and others as "private," probably private tutors in individual homes. Women had a well-defined role in many Italian Jewish communities as the teachers of the youngest children, aged approximately three to seven; they would teach Hebrew and the Bible, sometimes even Rashi's commentary on the Pentateuch and laws from Maimonides' *Mishneh Torah*, often in their own homes.[18] The census of 1748 listed three teachers in Trieste, one of whom was most likely the rabbi. One taught Hebrew language to the older boys, and a married couple instructed the younger children.[19] From 1752 on, a fixture on the local educational scene was Vidal (Yehiel) Benjamin Segre, who served as a teacher and sometime assistant rabbi for close to four decades (it was his son who later required a stipend to afford attendance at the normal school).[20] The communal rabbi continued to bear some responsibility for teaching youngsters until September 1757, when he was relieved of those duties because the "private teachers" were considered sufficient. However, he was to continue daily study sessions (*limmudim*) of rabbinic texts for advanced students and for adults who wished to attend.[21]

At some unknown date, a school, or at least regular classes under communal auspices, was established. The 1782 regulations drawn up for the new Jewish normal school described the earlier arrangements thus:

> Some Jewish families, established since most remote centuries in this city Trieste, founded a school (*scuola*), or *Talmud Torà*, for the instruction of their children in sacred studies and in Hebrew letters, with that method which was required by the small number of individuals and the circumstances of the times.[22]

Students were instructed in Hebrew, the Bible, *Aggadah* (by way of the collection *Ein Ya'akov*, called *Ein Yisrael*), Mishnah, Maimonides' *Mishneh Torah* ("R. Mose"), Italian, and arithmetic—all staples of the traditional Italian Jewish curriculum.[23] In the 1770s, the Jewish community itself played an increasingly active role in regulating the activities of the teachers, public and private. The Statute of 1771 outlined provisions for communal supervision and examination of teachers and students.[24]

As stated above, the Statute of 1771 also displayed for the first time governmental interest in Jewish education in Trieste, specifically in the teaching of Italian and German in the Jewish school. During Maria Theresa's reign, in 1776–77, the first tentative efforts were made to extend normal-schooling to Jews in Trieste and elsewhere. In Bohemia in 1776, the effort failed when Jews complained that their religious studies left no time for an added normal-school curriculum.[25] In Gorizia, the attempt succeeded for a six-month period in 1776, when a young Christian teacher instructed Jewish students in the normal-school curriculum of "German, reading, writing, arithmetic, orthography, eloquence, geography, history of the country, civility."²⁶ In Trieste, local authorities who were busying themselves with establishing the normal school took note of the experiment in Gorizia. In their November 1776 report on the new normal school, two prominent merchants and civic leaders, including the *Borsa* director Antonio Bellusco, advised Governor Zinzendorf:

Finally . . . some thought should be given to the public classes of the Jews, the Greeks, and the Armenians, who, except for religion and rites, are considered like the other citizens. In Gorizia, the [new] classes of the Jews are said to be already organized.²⁷

By that time, in fact, the Gorizian classes were no longer in existence. But in May 1777, Governor Zinzendorf ordered the Jews of Trieste similarly to engage a "normal teacher" for their children. There is no evidence of the Jewish response.²⁸ Nonetheless, during the period 1777 to 1781, there was some interest on the part of individual Jews in the city's new normal school. In March 1777, Marco Levi informed the governor of a Jew who wanted to "learn the method of the normal schools."²⁹ As mentioned above, Raffael Segre began to attend the third class of the normal school in 1776–77 in order to gain a "civilizing education."³⁰ But it was not until Joseph's educational initiative of 1781 that the Jewish community of Trieste began to organize its own classes on the normal-school model.

Joseph's Educational Initiative: Jewish Normal Schools

In the 1780s, Joseph continued his mother's efforts by establishing many new primary schools and by extending the system to the Jews, who were not hitherto included. The sovereign resolutions of May 16 and October 19, 1781, which sought to make the Jews "more useful to the state," provided for Jewish students to attend existing Christian normal schools, and for Jewish communities to set up their own Jewish normal schools. The existing provincial school commissions were to supervise the new Jewish schools, yet avoid interfering in Jewish religious practice or belief. Funds for the new Jewish schools were not apportioned from confiscated Jesuit monies, which had paid for the Christian normal schools, but were to come from the Jews themselves. Thus the absolutist state coopted Jewish education for the purposes of integration, but it did not pay its costs.

The October 1781 decree specified textbooks, teacher training, and the supervisory duties of the school commissions. These latter were to examine the Jewish pupils twice yearly, and compile in consultation with the

Jews themselves books that would teach "a philosophical morality." Texts for subjects such as reading, writing, mathematics, and geography were to be those used in the Christian normal schools, but with all material "offensive to their [Jewish] faith" expunged. The decree stressed the compulsory character of the new arrangements: all Jewish children were to attend new Jewish normal schools, or the existing Christian ones. Christian teachers were warned not to interfere with the Jewish religion lest they alienate Jewish parents. Qualified Jews were to be sent to state normal schools for teacher training.[31]

In Trieste, Governor Zinzendorf relayed both sets of instructions, those of May 1781 and of October 1781, to the heads of the Jewish community on May 31, 1781, and November 26, 1781, respectively.[32] He adjusted them to fit local realities but did not significantly alter them. The one notable difference between the general October resolution and the ones sent specifically from Vienna for Trieste, and for Gorizia-Gradisca, was the provision concerning Jews' eligibility to earn doctoral degrees in law and medicine. As stated above, because of their previous attendance at universities, these northern Italian Jews were the first Habsburg Jews to receive this authorization.

In conveying the October resolution about the establishment of a Jewish normal school, Zinzendorf placed particular stress upon the aim of moral education. To inculcate the "philosophical morality" that Vienna desired, that is, to "regulate behavior, according to a more sound philosophical morality and according to the duties of every man, without regard to differences of religion," Zinzendorf proffered an interesting suggestion: in compiling books on ethics, could the Jews not avail themselves of appropriate texts, such as those written by the "well-known [Moses] Mendelssohn in Berlin," or perhaps by some other Jewish author?[33] As we shall see in Chapter Five, that suggestion had momentous consequences, for it led directly to intensive and sustained contact between the Jews of Trieste and the Berlin circle of *maskilim*, Jewish devotees of the Enlightenment.

The Triestine Jewish Response: The 'Scuola Pia Normale sive Talmud Torà'

Among some Habsburg Jewries, the Josephinian entry into the Jewish classroom provoked real alarm and fear of encroachment on traditional Jewish ways. But in Trieste, the resolutions of May and October 1781 fell on fertile ground.[34] Initially they spurred increased attendance by Jews at the city's normal school, and subsequently, the restructuring of Jewish education in Trieste so as to accommodate the normal-school method within a Jewish institutional framework. These resolutions represented continuity of governmental attention to Jewish education and, more importantly, continuity of Jewish educational practice.

In the early autumn of 1781, Jewish leaders informed Zinzendorf that five Jews were now attending the city's normal school and that others were inclined to do so as well.[35] Exactly when these students joined the pioneering Raffael Segre is not known, but this document claims their attendance to be the "fruit and benefit" of the May proposals. The parents who thought it advantageous to send their children to the existing Christian normal school were by no means marginal members of the community. Vidal Benjamin Segre, who sent two sons, was a communal teacher and assistant rabbi, and the community itself, admittedly under governmental pressure, did agree to finance the next stage of one son's studies.[36] Studying in the Christian normal school did not necessarily exclude continuing Jewish education; that is, it supplemented but did not supplant Jewish studies. Two of the five students in question continued to pursue their Jewish studies that year, and in the placement examination held in April 1782 before the opening of the new Jewish school, they did so well that they comprised the upper class, to be taught by the rabbi.[37]

Though the Jewish community supported to a degree attendance of the city's normal school by Jewish children, it devoted itself primarily to setting up a normal school of its own under Jewish auspices. Efforts began in earnest toward the end of 1781. On December 16, 1781, the community delegated a committee of five prominent individuals to draft within fifteen days a provisional plan for a Jewish normal school.[38] By January 1, 1782, the task was completed, and in two sessions held on February 3 and March 20, 1782, the *Capi* and the community as a whole approved the plan. At the same time, three directors were chosen to supervise the new school along with Rabbi Formiggini: Grassin Vita di Caliman Levi, Isaia Norsa, and Jacob Vital, of whom the first two had worked on the provisional plan.[39] In the meantime, Zinzendorf had been reminding the community about the need for teacher training and for books of moral instruction, and in connection with the latter and at his suggestion, the secretary of the community, Joseph Galligo, wrote directly to Moses Mendelssohn in Berlin early in 1782, probably in late January or February.[40]

More important for the immediate establishment of the new school were the various administrative and logistical steps taken in the spring months of 1782. These included the appropriate class placement of the thirty-six pupils then studying with communal teachers, the engagement of the existing teachers for the new institution, and the organization of finances.[41] The site chosen for the new school was a building in the ghetto that also housed the community's offices, butchery, and public synagogue. An annual rental fee of approximately 113 florins would be paid the owner of the building, Isaac di Lucio Morpurgo.⁴² Funds were allocated for the purchase of books (50 florins annually), though initially community members were asked to lend appropriate texts to the school. The directors budgeted for two other minor annual expenses, 20 florins for prizes and 30 florins for the servant, or support staff, of the school.⁴³ But the greatest expenses were to be the salaries of the teachers, 250 florins annually for each teacher in the religious section, and 150 florins annually for the teacher of the normal-school curriculum.⁴⁴ The expenditures mentioned in the plan totaled 930 florins a year. To meet those costs, the directors proposed that parents of the thirty-six children of school age pay twenty-four florins a year (based upon a fee of two florins a month), for a total of 864 florins, and that the rest be obtained through voluntary donations from community members. Furthermore, though the intention was to make attendance at the new school compulsory, there still were parents who preferred private teachers. They, too, would be obliged to contribute to the maintenance of the school, a tax of one florin a month.⁴⁵

On May 3, 1782, following the recommendation of the inspector of schools, the governor approved the plan drawn up by the Jews for their new normal school, and it was published under governmental auspices as *Regole per la direzione della Scuola Pia Normale sive Talmud Torà dell'Università degli Ebrei di Trieste* (Regulations for the direction of the religious-normal school or Talmud Torah of the Jewish community of Trieste). On May 14, 1782 (1 Sivan 5542), the new institution was opened with much pomp and ceremony. Governmental officials attended the public festivities, at which many specially composed prayers and poems were recited.⁴⁶

The purpose that the directors outlined for the new school echoed that of Joseph's Toleration edicts. In the *Regole*, they stated that they saw their task as "reforming" and "broadening" the education already being offered the Jewish children of Trieste. They considered it of paramount importance to instill in the children a sense of gratitude to the sovereign for his "paternal love" and his encouraging Jews to earn their livelihood with "dignity and tranquility" in any art, profession, or trade. Through their studies in the new school, the pupils should acquire "obedience and respect for the Supreme God and for their sovereign, and with a sound moral philosophy become useful to themselves, to their families, and to society." Accordingly, their concerns included "as much . . . the studies of our religion, sacred worship, and [Hebrew] letters as those of sound morality and literature according to the method of the normal schools."⁴⁷

The poems recited at the school's opening repeated these and related themes: the mercy, graciousness, and wisdom of the monarch, which made him a worthy bearer of the Biblical name Joseph; the opportunity he was affording Jews to be educated, to earn a living in respectable and honorable ways, and to enjoy what was variously described as toleration, freedom, and equality; the common bonds linking all subjects and humanity; the felicitous coincidence of the opening of the school with the week of *Shavuot*, the season of the giving of the Torah; and the complementarity of the subjects that the monarch wanted taught and those which the Jews themselves considered important. The school directors expressed this last point thus: they had prepared an institution for the "teaching of religion and the law of the sovereign," that is, "the law of God, the law of nature, and the law of social ethics (*dat elohit, dat tiv'it, dat nimusit*)."[48] The mandate of their school was to teach both Torah and the normal-school curriculum. They had internalized the demand of civic education: they would promote civic and humanitarian values through their own religious teaching.

The *Scuola Pia Normale sive Talmud Torà* opened with three grades for religious studies, and one elementary class for normal-school studies; more advanced normal-school classes would be instituted later as the students progressed through the normal-school curriculum. There appears not to have been a one-to-one correspondence between grade and year; students might well spend more than one year at each level. The goal was compulsory attendance of all male children between the ages of five and fifteen. The initial student body seems to have numbered approximately thirty-five boys, that is, virtually all the pupils of the communal teachers who now took up posts in the new school. It was an important sign of continuity that the personnel of the new school were in fact the teachers already instructing the youth of the community. In the religious section, these were Vidal Benjamin Segre for the first class, Marco Mordecai Luzzatto for the second, and Rabbi Isach Formiggini for the third. Raffael Luzzatto was engaged to assist the others, particularly with the evening sessions of the third class, which were to be devoted to the study of books of ritual and moral instruction, and which were to be open to interested persons of any age; that is, they were to function also as a forum for ongoing adult study. Since the Jewish teachers, all residents of Trieste, were "Italian-born and ignorant of German," the teacher of the first class in the city's normal school was engaged for the normal class of the Jewish school and was allotted two hours a day to teach German. The directors' hope was that within two years, Jewish teachers would be able to take over this responsibility.[49]

All the teachers in the religious section were charged with one primary responsibility, namely, to

imprint on the heart of each pupil . . . with the greatest force of his zeal and spirit the fear of God, since without this strong impression all other labor would be futile. [They should] provide [students] with examples of their own devotion and submission in their character and work. The beginning of wisdom is fear of God [Ps. 111:10]. [They should] not fail to inspire them with the sentiments that nature teaches and that religion imposes, of love and charity for one's neighbor, those feelings of affection and piety [which] extend to all humankind as the fundamental base of all moral virtue.[50]

The language of Psalms—"fear of God," "beginning of wisdom"—meshed with the language of the Enlightenment—"nature," "affection . . . [for] all humankind"—as piety and humanitarianism were laid as the cornerstones of the *Scuola Pia Normale sive Talmud Torà*. No doubt this was precisely the kind of "sound moral philosophy" that the sovereign wanted taught in the new Jewish schools.

Prayer, both as a daily activity and as a subject of study, was an essential component of each class. The other subjects of the first class were the weekly readings of the Torah and Prophets, with the Aramaic translation of Onkelos, and with explanations in Italian or German for the more capable students; Psalms and Proverbs, especially those recited regularly in synagogue on Sabbaths and festivals, also with explanation in Italian or German; and the Mishnaic tractate *Pirkei Avot* (Ethics of the Fathers). On Sabbaths, the class also met in synagogue to worship and to recite chapters of Mishnah and Psalms; on those days, the Torah and books of religious-moral instruction would also be studied.

In the second class, students would proceed to the study of Hebrew grammar, using the text of Simone (Simhah) Calimani[51] or some other author; Mishnah, with the traditional commentaries of Obadiah Bertinoro and Yom Tov Lipmann Heller; Torah, with the traditional commentaries of Rashi, David Kimhi, and Abraham Ibn Ezra; *Aggadah* through *Ein Ya'akov*; Halakhah through Mishnah and Maimonides' *Mishneh Torah* or the *Shulhan Arukh*; Hebrew grammar and composition, in both prose and poetry; reading and writing in Italian; and arithmetic. On Sabbaths, synagogue readings were again Mishnah and Psalms, and attention was devoted to ethics or sermons.

In the third class, students would advance to the study of Talmud, and continue with Mishnah and commentaries, Halakhah through Joseph Karo's *Bet Yosef* or *Shulhan Arukh*, reading and writing in Hebrew and Italian, arithmetic, and works on ritual and ethics in the evenings. On Sabbaths, they would participate in "recitations of belles lettres" for the pleasure of all, or of "some sermon, panegyric, or poetry." In this way, the Triestine Jewish school was continuing the Italian Jewish tradition of the *accademia*, the public recital by students of ethical dramas or dialogues.[52] It was also expressing the appreciation of Hebrew literature, and poetry in particular, which was a noted feature of Italian Jewish culture and one cultivated by Triestine Jewry. No public event passed without the reciting of Hebrew poetry composed specifically for the occasion by members of the community. Appropriately, two works on poetry by Salomone Fiorentino and Samuel Romanelli were published in Trieste in the 1790s.[53]

Significantly, Italian language and arithmetic were designated as subjects for the "religious" classes. Because these had traditionally been taught in Italian Jewish schools, they took their familiar place, and teaching these subjects was well within the competence and experience of the community's Jewish teachers. For the Jews of Trieste, they were no innovation of the Josephinian normal-school system.

One other text not mentioned in the *Regole* was soon adopted in the curriculum of the *Scuola Pia Normale sive Talmud Torà*. When the *Regole* were drawn up early in 1782, the only text cited specifically for religious morality was *Pirkei Avot*. It was not yet clear which more recent texts imparting a philosophical and sound morality would be used; the letter from the community to Mendelssohn was part of the effort to resolve that question. However, help came from sources closer to home. Early in June 1782, the aged Rabbi Calimani of Venice sent a copy of his work *Esame ad un giovane israelita istruito nella sua religione* (Examination for a young Jew instructed in his religion) to Trieste, and, dedicating it to the directors of the new school, he offered it as an appropriate ethical text. Its ten chapters, or sessions of dialogue between teacher and student, covered a variety of topics such as God, revelation, the Written and Oral Laws, Sabbath and holidays, prayer, duties to God, duties to fellow human beings, sin and penitence, and the thirteen articles of faith. Calimani characterized it as

treating the duty of every person with regard to God, with regard to his neighbor, and with regard to himself. The work is geared to the understanding of all, and contains nothing novel, since religion is for all, and the divine commandments do not depend on novelty, just as they are not subject to defect.[54]

The catechismic form of presentation, while not new in Italy, was innovative for Ashkenazic Jews in central Europe, and their increasing use of this genre was an indication of the need they felt to repackage, systematize, and simplify their religious tradition in accord with changing norms. Unlike many of the Jewish catechisms that came into vogue in the following years, Calimani's *Esame* stressed the traditional theme of the importance of the Oral Law and observance of commandments.[55]

The normal-school teacher was allotted two late afternoon hours in which to teach the elementary class German reading, writing, and grammar according to the prescribed normal-school texts and tables. It was hoped that in the future, more advanced normal-school classes would cover the subjects taught in the Christian normal schools: Latin, morality, mathematics, physics, geography, history, architecture, and German language and letters. But, even in 1782, with its one elementary normal class, the *Talmud*

Torà of Trieste had transformed itself sufficiently so that it was called a *Scuola Normale*.

Yet in the *Talmud Torà*'s new incarnation as a normal school, it did not lose its primary focus. The *pia* classes outnumbered the *normale*, and most of the long (approximately eight-hour) school day was devoted to the *pia* curriculum. In general, the curriculum of the *Scuola Pia Normale sive Talmud Torà* of Trieste stood well within the traditions of Italian Jewish schooling. Though the school taught less Halakhah than those of some other communities (Mantua and Venice, for example), its curriculum displayed close affinity to theirs.[56]

Thus, the response of Triestine Jewry to Joseph's educational initiative of 1781 was overwhelmingly positive. The Jewish population readily accepted the principle of providing Jewish children with a normal-school education, and the community's central figures, Rabbi Formiggini and the lay leaders, cooperated in a sustained fashion to set up the new Jewish normal school. There were no forces of opposition. Neither Joseph's general Toleration policy nor its specific cultural and educational components were novel in Trieste.[57] Most significantly, the range of studies in the normal-school program was not innovative for these Italian Jews. In Trieste, the continuity between traditional Italian Jewish practice and the normal-school curriculum was symbolized by the continued service of the community's teachers in the new school, by the inclusion of Italian language and arithmetic within the "religious" section, and by the very name—*Scuola Pia Normale sive Talmud Torà*—of the new institution. The old *Talmud Torà* had expanded to include the new normal-school curriculum as an appendage or supplement to Judaic studies. As Hartwig Wessely the *maskil* and educational reformer noted, both the combination of curricula and the retention of the traditional name were highly unusual for modern Jewish schools in central Europe in the late eighteenth century.[58]

What was new about the Josephinian legislation of 1781 was that it represented a concerted effort to establish state supervision of Jewish schools and to introduce German as their language of instruction. In 1781, the emphasis upon German was surely new for the Jews of Trieste, and it is obvious that they, like many of the other residents of the city, were unable to comply immediately. Yet they never objected to it. No doubt they could see the benefits of teaching their children the language of the state. And, in a multicultural commercial center, knowing more than one language was always useful. In practice, however, though the German language became a subject of study in the new school, Italian remained its general language of instruction.

Besides resonating with Italian Jewish cultural traditions, the normal-school system met the practical needs of the Triestine Jewish community of merchants and entrepreneurs. Framed by international trade, their horizons were broad, cosmopolitan, and utilitarian. General education—that is, something beyond the realm of Jewish texts, practice, and tradition—was a necessity for the youngsters of Trieste, who were expected to be active participants in the commerce and life of the city. One of the spurs driving the Jewish community to set up its own normal school was the wish to offer the desired skills to Jewish students within a Jewish institution. Finally, there was a political motive as well: this community was eager to demonstrate publicly its appreciation of Joseph's policies. The *Scuola Pia Normale sive Talmud Torà* was intended to be a showcase of the entire community's dedication to Habsburg ideals of civic Enlightenment.

The Early History of the School

Soon after the school's opening in 1782, new teachers were hired for both the religious and the normal sections. In 1783, Raffael Nathan Tedesco of Verona (later the chief rabbi of Trieste) was first hired to teach the upper-level religious class and then to direct the religious section. In 1785, only one year after the target date mentioned in the *Regole* of 1782, the school increased its German normal classes to two and engaged the services of two Jewish instructors duly trained in the normal-school method. These were Herz Homberg, well-known associate of Mendelssohn and Wessely, who had most recently spent a couple of years teaching in the Jewish normal school of Gorizia, and the community's very own Raffael Baruch Segre.[59] (Homberg seems to have gotten on well in Trieste, in contrast to his experiences in the traditional Ashkenazic communities in central Europe and Galicia, where he became notorious as an overzealous radical.) Though Homberg remained in Trieste only a short time, until 1787, the other two appointments proved more long-lasting, with Tedesco serving as educator and then communal rabbi until his death in 1800, and Segre remaining on the school's staff for the next few decades. Thus the community's investment in young Segre back in 1781 had paid off. In the first twenty-five years of the school's existence, sometimes Jews taught the normal-school classes, sometimes Gentiles did so. It was with noticeable pride that in 1805, the directors proposed the appointment of one of the school's own graduates, citing this as proof of the school's success.[60]

However, in its early years, the school was also plagued with the usual growing pains: various sorts of "confusion," "disorders," and "irregularities"; the "wild" behavior of students during the hour of German-language instruction; the failure of some parents (of children attending both the public and private schools) to pay their monthly contributions; and the negligent conduct of some teachers and school employees.⁶¹ Two of the issues identified as problematic—finances, and the relation between public and private instruction—persisted as matters of concern for the school and the community. As indices of support for the school within the community, both deserve further attention.

Like all the Jewish normal schools established according to Josephinian mandate, the school in Trieste had to be financed by the Jewish community itself. The sources of funding outlined in the *Regole* of 1782, namely, fees paid by parents of school-age children and voluntary donations, proved insufficient. As accounts and reports from almost any year show, the school was beset by chronic deficits, and its directors were always searching for new sources of revenue. In April 1785, it was decided that the community would impose a school tax totaling 400 florins.⁶² As an economizing measure, the number of teachers was at the same time reduced to two. The following year, the directors of the school attempted to take over the lease for the slaughter and sale of kosher meat, with the proceeds to benefit the school, but the community balked at this request, and preferred that those already performing these vital functions continue to do so. Finally, in May 1786, with the intervention of governmental officials, agreement was reached: the General Council of the community would henceforth guarantee the school the sum of 1,240 florins a year, to be obtained from a monthly one-florin tax on parents of students, voluntary donations, contributions from the synagogues, interest on the bequest of 1,000 florins left the school by Marco Levi, and general taxes collected by the community. In September 1786, Vienna ratified the arrangement.⁶³ The sum stipulated would allow for two teachers in each section, the religious and the normal, and one assistant. Other revenues over the years came from individual bequests. However, the attempt to exact monetary penalties from parents who did not send their children either to the school or to approved private instructors seems to have failed.⁶⁴ The search for funds was constant, and at least once, in 1797–98, caused delay in the implementation of new regulations.⁶⁵ In 1803, the community instituted yet further taxes, on weddings and circumcisions, to benefit the school.⁶⁶

Most significant, however, is the fact that the community continued to pay regular lump sums to the school. By 1802, its payment had increased to 2,200 florins a year, the largest single outlay in its budget.⁶⁷ Despite all the difficulties, the *Scuola Pia Normale sive Talmud Torà* was able to function because of the steady financial commitment undertaken by the Triestine Jewish community. Over the years, communal leaders and members offered the school not only laudatory rhetoric, but also this most tangible means of support.

To consider further the place of the school in the community, it is necessary to examine the number of students who attended it. Unfortunately, such information is scanty, particularly from the years under consideration, 1782–1800. We know that the school opened in 1782 with approximately thirty-five male students. Its classes were only for boys; girls had to be instructed by private teachers. In 1786, a local governmental official regretfully estimated that barely one-half of the eligible school-age boys were attending both sections, the religious and the normal; according to him, the rest received either instruction in the classes run by private women teachers, or no instruction at all.[68] Had this official compared that attendance rate to the Christian normal school of Trieste or to the percentages of school-age children attending modern Jewish schools in some central European communities (approximately 40 percent in Prague, and 20 to 25 percent in Berlin and Frankfurt), he would not have despaired.[69] By 1797, an official report noted that Triestine Jewish boys were attending the school "with greater diligence," but it supplied no number, nor any indication whether this was a quantitative or qualitative judgment.[70]

We do not have figures for attendance in both the public and the private schools in any one year. The years 1807–8 provide the best rough basis of comparison. In 1807, some eighty boys attended the private classes taught by eleven teachers (six male and five female); in 1808, approximately fifty boys attended the three normal classes of the public school; some eighty-two girls attended private classes.[71] Thus, approximately 38 percent of the boys (that is, 23 percent of all the children) attending school went to the *Scuola Pia Normale*. In the next decade, the proportion remained around 33 percent of the boys in the community.[72] The rate of growth of the Jewish normal school between 1782 and 1820 compared favorably with the city's two Christian normal schools: enrollment at the former rose from 35 to 80 students, at the latter, from 242 to 364.[73]

Thus, by many measurements, the government's educational initiative was indeed a success among the Jews of Trieste. But numbers tell only part of the story. If possible, we must ascertain who went to the public school, and the relationship between the public and the private schools.

At the inception of the *Scuola Pia Normale* in 1782, the majority of its students came from middle-class or wealthy families. In the first years, about two-thirds of the sons who attended came from families whose heads paid taxes, sat on the Small Council, or served as *Capi*; approximately nineteen out of thirty fell into one or more of those three categories.[74] The heads of these families included some of the wealthiest members of the community, such as Grassin Vita di Caliman Levi and Philippo Kohen, as well as others of more modest means who still earned enough to rank among the taxpayers. Of those nineteen families, members of ten served as *Capi* of the community in the late 1770s and 1780s. The remaining one-third of the families (eleven out of thirty), who had no special distinction, were composed presumably of poorer members of the community, or communal functionaries who paid no taxes, or newcomers who were not yet on the tax rolls. In any case, at the outset, the *Scuola Pia Normale* of Trieste—unlike many other public Jewish schools, which were restricted to the poor alone—served both the wealthy and the not-so-wealthy. Significantly, its budgets did not provide meals and clothing for the students, as did those which served the poor in other communities.[75] Supported financially by the Triestine community, it was an institution that served all strata of the community.

Over time, the proportion of boys of the community attending the school decreased from approximately 50 percent to 33 percent, where it stabilized for many years. The school always had to compete against proliferating private classes, which remained an attractive option, presumably for those of greater financial means. As early as 1786, the local government noted that some graduates of the Jewish normal school were obtaining positions as private tutors.[76] In 1796, one school employee, Raffael Luzzatto, complained about the arrival in Trieste of too many new teachers who were conducting private classes.[77] Although the community supported the *Scuola Pia Normale*, the school directors were unsuccessful in their attempts to enforce compulsory attendance. Communal leaders had to tolerate and eventually sanction private instruction, which they sought increasingly to supervise rather than to eliminate. For example, they sought to oblige private teachers to use normal-school textbooks.[78] But perhaps the distinction between public and private ought not to be drawn too sharply. The private classes were in effect the system of education for all the girls of the community, since the *Scuola Pia Normale* was for boys alone. Furthermore, even for boys, they served in some sense as an adjunct to the public school, for (as in Mantua and some other Italian Jewish communities) it was in private classes called *depositori di creaturi* that the youngest children, aged three to six, received the required socialization and knowledge of Hebrew to enable them to proceed to the public school. Thus in Trieste, it was only the local primary (*Trivial*) classes for older children, aged six and up, that functioned as alternatives to the public school. The curricula of the private teachers varied, but most offered subjects such as Italian and arithmetic, and the most popular taught German as well as Hebrew and religion. Thus the vast majority of Triestine Jewish youngsters received general as well as Jewish instruction, whether in the *Scuola Pia Normale sive Talmud Torà* or in private classes.

During the last two decades of the eighteenth century, the school continued upon the path set out for it at its inception. We can chart its development by means of the *Regolamento per le Scuole Pie Normali degli Ebrei in*

Trieste, which was approved by the community and government in 1797, and published by the official press that same year.⁷⁹ In its title, the singular *scuola* had become the plural *scuole*, reflecting the increase in the number of classes. Throughout this period, the distinguishing features of the school remained its combination along parallel tracks of Jewish and normal studies—the *pia* and *normale* of its name—and the continuing emphasis upon the *pia* portion of the curriculum, with the *normale* never exceeding the two hours, or roughly one-quarter of the school day, allotted to it. But although the relationship between the different components of the school's curriculum did not change in the 1780s and 1790s, there were some shifts within the separate spheres.

For the *pia* section, the *Regolamento* of 1797 signaled change not so much in the subjects of study as in the order of study. Hebrew grammar and cursive writing, Italian writing, and explanation in Italian or German of the weekly Torah and Haftarah readings were introduced to all students in the first class rather than in the second, as had been the case according to the *Regole* of 1782. On the other hand, certain classic Jewish texts previously taught in earlier grades were, according to the *Regolamento* of 1797, now introduced only at the third level; these were Biblical commentaries (Rashi and Kimhi), Mishnah with *Tosafot Yom Tov*, *Mishneh Torah* with Karo's *Kesef Mishneh*, Karo's *Bet Yosef*, and *Shulhan Arukh*. Whereas in 1782, Talmud was supposed to be taught to all children in the third class, in 1797 it was designated only for its most "grown-up and discerning" pupils. That group of students would also study Psalms with Kimhi's commentary, and a text on science favored by central European *maskilim*, Barukh Lindau's *Reshit limmudim*. In the 1797 *Regolamento*, a greater emphasis upon books of religious-moral instruction was evident, with a variety of works prescribed: Calimani's catechism; Maimonides' *Sefer ha-ahavah*, with particular emphasis upon duties to the sovereign; Isaac Aboab's *Menorat ha-meor*; and Moses Hayyim Luzzatto's *Mesillat yesharim*.⁸⁰ Thus, by the end of the second decade of the school's existence, a certain dilution of the *pia* curriculum was evident.

During those decades, the normal part of the Triestine school also underwent some change. As stated above, the number of classes and teachers fluctuated, basically expanding beyond the initial one grade to two and sometimes three. In the 1797 *Regolamento*, German, Italian, arithmetic, and geography (taught according to the normal-school reader) were specified as the subjects of the normal classes. Italian (except for writing) and arithmetic had been transferred from the *pia* to the *normale* section. There is no evidence to suggest that this section implemented the range of subjects outlined optimistically in the 1782 *Regole*: Latin, physics, geometry, history, architecture, German letters. Thus it corresponded most closely to the first level in the Habsburg system, that is, the *Trivialschul*, or local primary school.[81] Later, in 1806, it was decided—not surprisingly in the Free Port of Trieste—to add commercial correspondence in Italian and German, and calculation of different rates of exchange, to the curriculum of the third normal class.[82]

The school paid much attention to one subject, morality, which actually straddled both realms, the religious and the normal. Considered an amalgam of religious teachings and civics, it was highly significant for the image of the school and the community in the eyes of watchful government officials. From the first, the central government had placed a premium upon cultural transformation and the inculcation of a "philosophical morality." In a March 1786 decree issued throughout the monarchy, it reiterated the need to counter the "very depraved morality of the Jews" through greater economic diversification and moral instruction in the Jewish schools.[83] To ensure Jewish attendance at normal schools, where the proper kind of moral instruction was supposedly available, it then decreed that henceforth, permission from the authorities for Jews to marry would be conditional upon proof of attendance at the new normal schools. Triestine officials promptly informed Vienna that this second decree was inapplicable in the free port city since Jews—like other Triestine residents—did not have to obtain permission from the state to marry. Trieste was again an exception. But local authorities said they would take note of the decree insofar as the intent was to encourage diligent school attendance.[84]

From the first days of planning their new school, the Jews of Trieste had taken seriously the government's preoccupation with morality. They had solicited advice from Mendelssohn, adopted Calimani's *Esame* as a textbook, stressed the teaching of "sound moral philosophy" as the school's mandate in their 1783 communal regulations, and included books of religious ethics, discourses, and sermons on religious ethics and morality in the regular program of the school.[85] That Jewish leaders and educators were keenly aware of the purpose to be served by a display of the students' progress in this subject is best illustrated by their public recital in March 1786 of Rabbi Tedesco's ethical drama on the various vices. As stated in Chapter One, this performance was attended by dignitaries of the city, and it was favorably reported in the official press, *Osservatore Triestino*, for its "rare eloquence" and for the literary distinction of Jews:

> This is not the first case in which the Jewish people have distinguished themselves in each of these genres. Even without reference to Mendelssohn in our time, we can with sacred and profane letters in hand cite those who have flourished in every age, and those who in our own days write works in every genre of literature.[86]

The school directors had the text of the drama published at their own expense because they felt that it would not only benefit the students, but also combat the "prejudice" of the "ignorant populace" that "morality is unusual and uncommon in Jewish schools." In the introduction, they made the additional point that every year students were supposed to perform such literary exercises in order to draw the "most sound [and] sturdy doctrines" from "the simplicity of noble natural morality" and the "purity of sacred Biblical sources."[87] In their public self-presentation, they were stressing the compatibility of the Enlightenment and their Jewish religious inheritance—construed primarily as Biblical rather than Talmudic.

The favorable report of that event in the official newspaper is not the only evidence that the school's efforts in the field of morality were appreciated by the government. The response penned by local officials to Vienna's decree of March 22, 1786, on the "depraved morality" of the Jews shows the nexus firmly etched in their minds between economic utility, Jewish morality, and successful schooling:

> Concerning the Jewish community of Trieste it is in any case well known that they mostly earn their livelihood respectably through trade and other decent occupations, and also that they distinguish themselves from other Jewish communities by virtue of the morality of their behavior. The main point therefore is that the appropriate continuation of their existing school institution be diligently maintained.[88]

In the official perspective, gainful employment was tantamount to moral rectitude. According to that criterion, the Jews of Trieste had for the most part proven themselves useful and moral. Thus, in official eyes, the *Scuola Pia Normale sive Talmud Torà* was refracted, as was so much else concerning the Jews of Trieste, through the lens of utility and exceptionality. As another report from Trieste to Vienna, dated May 14, 1786, put it:

> With respect to morality, it [this community], because of its efforts to be useful to the state with commercial activity and through other honest ways and modes of sustaining itself, does not deserve to be confused with the other, perhaps less ordered communities of its people.[89]

The school itself came in for special praise in another report submitted shortly thereafter on June 17, 1786. Local officials were pleased not only with the normal section, which had expanded the previous year, and its skilled teachers (especially Herz Homberg), but also with the religious section, whose task they considered so important because it touched upon morality, the dispelling of "noxious prejudices," and the spread of "Enlightenment."[90] They informed Vienna that the community was indeed fortunate to have Hebrew teachers who were distinguished by "their extensive reading, their philosophical studies, their pure ethical teaching, and their good writing style," who could present religious instruction in "wholly proper garb," that is, "so purified" that it combined "original Mosaic laws and fewer Talmudically based religious maxims" with "many good rules of conduct and civic duties."⁹¹ An additional source of satisfaction for the local government was the fact that all expenses of the school were borne by the community itself.

The *Scuola Pia Normale sive Talmud Torà* of Trieste was considered a success by local officials. Through their periodic inspections and attendance of public examinations, they arrived at a positive assessment of the normal, religious, moral, and civic instruction it offered its students. They wished only that a greater proportion of the community's male children would reap its benefits. In June 1786, they pointed to the practical results already in evidence, namely, the employment of some graduates as clerks in commercial firms or as private teachers in the homes of wealthy businessmen. These were in fact the classic opportunities for graduates of modernized Jewish schools and the frequent sources of employment for many *maskilim*, as well as the goal envisaged by government policy-makers. Thus, the school was seen within the context of the economic dynamism and utility of the Jewish community of Trieste, and in turn as a contributor to its continued economic well-being. Of course, though the government did not mention this explicitly, the ability of the community to support the school financially was itself a function of its prosperity. The government viewed that support, however unsteady it appeared at times, as proof of the commitment of the community to the school, to good education, to good citizenship, and to the new policies of Toleration and Enlightenment. In September 1786, Vienna issued a decree for Trieste that approved the new arrangements hammered out by the local Jewish community in the spring of that year, and that moreover formally and explicitly expressed the emperor's "Sovereign approval for the zealous and patriotic cooperation [of the Jewish Council of Trieste] in the establishment of such a pious and useful institution."⁹² Fine words were not all that emanated from Vienna: it seems that in the early years, Joseph also sent monetary subsidies to the school's teachers as a token of his appreciation.⁹³

Through the 1780s and 1790s, the government, both in Trieste and in Vienna, remained pleased with the *Scuola Pia Normale sive Talmud Torà*. In March 1787, a report appeared in *Osservatore Triestino* of the good impression that the recently conducted public examination of the pupils in normal studies had made upon Governor Pompeo di Brigido.⁹⁴ Herz Homberg, until then teacher in the Triestine school and soon to depart to assume a new post as inspector of the Jewish schools in Galicia, was praised for his pedagogic skills. Rather than provide his pupils with "superficial" knowledge and "useless occupation of their memories," he had given proof of having "lit up their intellects and formed their hearts."⁹⁵ When approval of the new *Regolamento* was under consideration in 1797, local officials again reported favorably on the aptitude of the teachers, the quality of instruction in the various subjects taught, the greater diligence of the students, and the "outstanding zeal of the school directors" in bringing the school "ever nearer" to "the desired result . . . of intended perfection."[96]

In compliance with the Josephinian educational initiative of 1781, then, the Jewish community of Trieste succeeded in establishing a school, the *Scuola Pia Normale sive Talmud Torà*, which, emerging from the traditions of Italian Jewish education, met its own needs and became a showcase for Habsburg visions of Jewish Enlightenment. The details notwithstanding, it was the very combination under one roof of Jewish and state curricula that earned the *Scuola Pia Normale sive Talmud Torà* of Trieste its distinction and fame. The readiness with which Triestine Jews responded to the Habsburg educational program was inspiring to Jewish modernizers elsewhere in Europe, who also wished to further the cause of reformed education and Enlightenment.

CHAPTER FIVE

Trieste and the Haskalah

The Josephinian educational initiative led to the establishment of Jewish normal schools not only in Trieste, but in other places as well: the first opened in Prague on May 2, 1782, with much fanfare, and others opened in Hungary during the next few years. But conditions in both places differed significantly from those in Trieste. Whereas in Trieste, both Jewish and state curricula were housed under one roof, in Prague, traditionalists led by Rabbi Ezekiel Landau permitted the establishment of a Jewish normal school only on the condition that they themselves maintain control of a separate and autonomous religious school; the reservations they had expressed about the initial normal-schooling proposals in the 1770s had not entirely dissipated. In Hungary, the new Jewish normal schools collapsed when Joseph's death in 1790 removed effective state coercion. Thus from its inception, the Triestine *Scuola Pia Normale sive Talmud Torà* was distinguished by the very combination of religious and normal studies, and Jewish educational reformers and governmental officials in Berlin, Prague, and Vienna hailed it as a model for emulation precisely for this reason. Mantua in the late 1780s was one community that did follow Trieste's lead in combining Jewish and normal-school curricula in one institution, but it did so in a much more limited fashion.[1]

Much of this chapter is based upon my earlier article, "Trieste and Berlin: The Italian Role in the Cultural Politics of the Haskalah," in Jacob Katz, ed., *Toward Modernity: The European Jewish Model*, © 1987 by the Leo Baeck Institute; all rights reserved. Reprinted by permission of Transaction Publishers.

Also noteworthy was the enthusiastic and sustained support the Triestine school enjoyed among the community's rabbinic and lay leadership. The special climate of opinion in Trieste is best illustrated by examination of the role that the Triestine Jewish community played in the educational and cultural controversies that swirled in central Europe in the 1780s, and its emergence as advocate of and model for the Haskalah, or Jewish Enlightenment.

Wessely's Appeal to Trieste

Though hardly identical, the positive responses of the Triestine and Prague Jewish communities to the Habsburg educational program stood out against the generally negative view of the new legislation held by most of the monarchy's Jews, who perceived it as threatening to their traditional way of life and culture. To prod them into realizing the benefits of Joseph's plans, Hartwig Wessely (Naftali Herz Weisel), a member of the Mendelssohnian enlightened circle in Berlin and a Biblical exegete, poet, and moralist, published a pamphlet in January or February 1782 entitled *Divrei shalom ve-emet* (Words of peace and truth). This manifesto contained both a hearty endorsement of the Josephinian educational reforms and a harsh indictment of traditional Ashkenazic education. For Judaic studies, it advocated a graded curriculum to proceed from Scripture to Mishnah to Talmud. But more startling and radical was its implied message that the "Torah of man" (*torat ha-adam*) should take priority over the "Torah of God" (*torat ha-elohim*), that is, the transmission of civic and vocational skills over religious tradition and values. Though he had previously been known as a pious man whose works had earned rabbinical approbations,[2] Wessely now depicted traditional Talmudists in contemptuous terms. Wessely was probably unaware of just how shocking some of his statements were, and although he had intended to soothe troubled Jewish spirits, he succeeded instead—however unwittingly—in arousing a storm of protest among rabbis in central and eastern Europe. Even Rabbi Ezekiel Landau of Prague, who supported the government's educational initiative, albeit gingerly, was alarmed and driven to public condemnation of *Divrei shalom ve-emet*. In the spring of 1782, Wessely was indeed in desperate straits as chilling rumors reached him of excoriating sermons and book-burnings in distant places, and, in Berlin itself, of threats of bans and expulsion.[3]

It was at that crucial moment that the letter from the Jewish community of Trieste written in late January or February 1782 reached Mendelssohn in Berlin. As mentioned above, this letter contained news of the community's plans to institute a Jewish normal school and its inquiries about textbooks for moral instruction. This turn to Mendelssohn proved especially timely for Wessely. Building upon this contact, Wessely ultimately enlisted the help of Triestine, and more generally Italian, Jewish leaders, in the struggle to clear his name and rebuild his reputation. He and his colleagues considered the subsequent intervention of Italian Jews crucial; as he later wrote of them, "From the depths I cried out, [and] they heard my voice."[4]

That initial link between Trieste and the Berlin *maskilim* was forged at the suggestion of Governor Zinzendorf. It was emblematic that a letter from Trieste to Berlin prompted by a Habsburg official led to the important contacts between Wessely and his Italian supporters. For Vienna was an important channel by which central European cultural currents reached Trieste. Prominent Triestine Jews, such as the court factors Marco Levi and Joachim Hierschel, had close ties with Vienna and the leading Jewish families there. These, the Honigs and Arnsteins, were themselves patrons of the Berlin Haskalah and functioned at times as intermediaries between Trieste and the *maskilim* of Berlin.[5] In turn, it was the Jews of Trieste and of nearby Gradisca and Gorizia who, by virtue of their location "on the German-Italian frontier" and of their dual identity as politically Habsburg and culturally Italian, served as conduits and mediators between the Jewries of Ashkenazic central Europe and of Italy.[6] Their role in the Haskalah controversies was another example of Trieste serving as the gateway between *Mitteleuropa* and Italy.

Trieste's contact with Mendelssohn and news of the projected *Scuola Pia Normale sive Talmud Torà* in early 1782 confirmed for Wessely his notion of Italian Jews as acculturated. In his first pamphlet, *Divrei shalom ve-emet,* written before the letter from Trieste arrived in Berlin, Wessely had praised Italian Jews as fluent speakers of the language of their surroundings: "The Jews who are in Italy speak the Italian language properly."[7] To his mind, they stood in sharp contrast to Ashkenazic Jews, who hardly spoke German. No doubt his contacts in Vienna had told him about the wealthy Jewish merchants of Trieste who traveled to the capital and who enjoyed better conditions and privileges than other Habsburg Jews. It is probable that the image of Italian Jews that Wessely entertained was based not only on an ideal and distant past, but also on concrete, contemporary realities.

In Wessely's second pamphlet, *Rav tuv le-vet Yisrael* (Abundant goodness to the House of Israel), published at the end of April 1782 and intended as both justification and modification of his first,[8] he continued to present Italian Jews in terms of the cultural and moral ideals of the Haskalah. Seeking to provide a model for other Jewries, he stressed the synthesis of Jewish and general culture characteristic of Italian Jews as he addressed Triestine Jews:

My words are unnecessary for you, you who from your youth have learned to speak the Italian and Spanish [sic] languages correctly, whose teachers are undoubtedly eloquent, and are able to translate Hebrew expressions into the language people understand, thereby explaining to their students the clear meaning of the Torah and Prophets. And your customs have always been wise, consistent with respect for living beings and peace among humankind. *In addition, trade in your lands is with the large states of Europe, Asia, and Africa, and you get to hear of the customs of areas distant from you* [emphasis mine]. All the communities of Israel in Italian lands have a similar advantage, and therefore many among you are experienced in civility, learned in rhetoric and poetry, and educated in ethical teachings based upon knowledge of the soul. Moreover, all these qualities are found among the Torah scholars in your midst, the distinguished rabbis and great luminaries who have brightened the universe with their wisdom and teaching. Through the generations, their compositions are filled with pleasantness, and their words are beautiful. Just as they include judgments and laws, so too do they include teachings of wisdom and civility.[9]

In brief, Wessely saw this port Jewry as a cultivated and enlightened Jewry. He believed that maritime commerce, the high level of Italian culture and civilization, and the Sefardic component of the Italian Jewish heritage had produced a Jewry that stood in sharp contrast to the insular, unworldly Ashkenazic Jewry. Now he hoped that the projected Triestine school, the very expression of Italian Jewish cultural values and of Habsburg civic norms, would serve as a model from which "the rest of our brethren the children of Israel . . . will learn . . . to walk on the path that you [Trieste] have trod."[10]

Why was Wessely so fulsome in his praise of Italian, and particularly Triestine, Jews in his second pamphlet? In fact, he was not only presenting them as a model for other Jewries; he was also grasping at them as a lifeline and trying to invoke their support. Flattery well served this end. Indeed, the desperate Wessely cast his second pamphlet as a response to a purported letter from Trieste to him endorsing his first pamphlet. The exact chronology is difficult to determine, since some of the letters are not extant, but it does not appear likely that he himself had heard directly from the Jewish community of Trieste or received their prior permission when he publicly claimed their support. In a letter of May 7, 1782 (23 Iyyar 5542), which Wessely addressed to the Jewish community of Trieste, and which Mendelssohn sent with his own letter and a copy of *Rav tuv le-vet Yisrael*, Wessely begged their indulgence for his taking this liberty:

Let it not appear improper to you, leaders and sages of Trieste, that we composed this epistle *as if (ke'ilu)* [emphasis mine] it were an answer to the precious letter we received from your distinguished hand, and that we turned to you concerning all the matters of which we spoke therein, for we thought it right to do so; and [it will be] an honor to you in the sight of all Israel because all eyes are upon me to see how I respond to the deeds of those rabbis [who condemn me].[11]

Still, it appears that Wessely had grounds for expecting a favorable response from Trieste. Correspondence between Trieste and Mendelssohn after the initial inquiry had both reinforced Wessely's positive image of Italian Jews and emboldened him. Mendelssohn had responded to Trieste by sending them information about his own works and Wessely's, and a copy of *Divrei shalom ve-emet* itself. And it seems that a second letter from Trieste was then dispatched to Mendelssohn that—according to a later account by Wessely—expressed thanks for the response, interest in more works by the two authors, and most importantly, approval of *Divrei shalom ve-emet*. It is unlikely that this second letter actually reached Mendelssohn before Wessely published his second epistle at the end of April 1782,[12] but in a certain sense, explicit endorsement and permission to cite that endorsement were immaterial to the frantic Wessely. Both his general impression of Italian Jews and the news of Trieste's ready compliance with the Josephinian normal-school program contributed to his belief that the Jews of Trieste would stand by him if called upon. As he put it suggestively in the opening lines of *Rav tuv le-vet Yisrael*: "Even before your letter reached us [i.e., Mendelssohn in Berlin], it was not hidden from us that our words would be pleasing in the eyes of intelligent people like you."[13] Moreover, Wessely's conviction was fueled by his growing sense of urgency, as he learned in early May 1782 ever more details of the rabbinic campaign against him.

Accordingly, in his letter to the Jewish community of Trieste of May 7, 1782, Wessely made an appeal for an open declaration of support.[14] He implored Triestine Jews to show him "mercy and truth." He asked them to distribute his two pamphlets to other Italian communities, such as Venice, Livorno, Mantua, Pisa, and Verona, and to canvass their "rabbis, judges, and sages" for a "friendly letter (*mikhtav shelomim*) to the House of Israel." He desperately sought written vindication of his name and approval for his "holy task" of "removing the veil of ignorance" from all Israel. Wessely saw Triestine leaders as ideally suited for the role because of their reputation and contacts with other Italian Jewish communities. And he considered Italian Jews in general the ideal arbiters for the Jewish world at large because he knew them to be "men of valor, great in Torah and crowned with worldly wisdom and manners" who could exercise broadminded judgment. In his appeal, Wessely employed flattery, promised merit, honor, and fame, and invoked the Jewish duties of mutual aid and unity. He even raised the specter of rescission of the new Toleration if Jews were uncooperative. Cleverly, he addressed Triestine Jews both as bystanders who had not needed his message and for whom it was not at all controversial, and as participants whose fate was at stake—for they were members of the entire House of Israel dwelling in the Habsburg house, *Casa d'Austria*. In his accompanying letter, Mendelssohn warmly commended Wessely and his cause.

Wessely was heartened by the expressions of goodwill he received from Habsburg northern Italy in May and June of 1782. Two encouraging letters reached Berlin: one addressed to Mendelssohn from Elia Morpurgo, the Gradiscan Jewish leader, dated May 8, 1782 (24 Iyyar 5542), and the second to Wessely from the Jewish community of Trieste written in late May and received by him in mid-June.[15]

In his letter, Morpurgo expressed his great admiration both for Mendelssohn and for the monarch "Joseph the righteous" (*Yosef ha-tzaddik*), and described two works of his own that he was sending to Mendelssohn. These were his eulogy for Maria Theresa, *Orazione funebre*, and the apologetic *Discorso* he had composed in praise of the May 1781 Toleration resolution and of Jewish worthiness of such policies.[16] Both in the concluding portion of the *Discorso* and in this letter, Morpurgo praised Wessely's *Divrei shalom ve-emet*, referring to it as a "book small in quantity and great in quality . . . sweet as honey," which gave "clear ideas . . . of the history of the Law of nature, and of that of the human heart."[17] To further Wessely's efforts to raise the cultural level of Ashkenazic Jewry, Morpurgo proposed publication of a German translation of his *Discorso*, and of a remedial reading program comprising medieval Sefardic poetic, philosophic, and ethical works, in order to "teach . . . language, rhetoric, and ethics all at once in the manner of the ancient Romans and Greeks."[18]

The letter from Trieste of late May 1782 informed Wessely of the progress of the new school, and more importantly for his immediate needs, of the approval in principle of *Divrei shalom ve-emet* by Rabbi Isach Formiggini. Accordingly, Triestine Jewish leaders urged Wessely to stand fast and continue his fight.[19] Also encouraging was their report of Elia Morpurgo's translation into Italian of Wessely's pamphlet. In fact, Morpurgo had wasted no time: he completed the translation in three days, and by the end of May was engaged in the final editing.[20]

The news from Trieste and Gradisca prompted Wessely to reiterate his earlier appeal. In his letter to Trieste of June 28, 1782 (16 Tammuz 5542),[21] he wrote glowingly of his impressions of the new school in Trieste, and bitterly about the ongoing conflicts over his book and efforts to reform Jewish education. He asked explicitly that Rabbi Formiggini put in writing his approval of *Divrei shalom ve-emet* and that Triestine leaders disseminate it among other Italian rabbis. Wessely planned eventually to publish the positive responses that he expected from Italian leaders. As in his previous letter, Wessely raised the stakes by alluding to the ever-delicate subject of the image and honor of the Jewish people in the eyes of the nations.

The Italian Campaign for Wessely and Haskalah

The entreaties of Trieste from Berlin yielded a rich result. An Italian campaign on behalf of Wessely was waged through the coordinated efforts of the Jewish community of Trieste and Elia Morpurgo of Gradisca, who corresponded with Wessely and Mendelssohn in Berlin, and dispatched letters of solicitation to rabbis in other communities in Italy and beyond, even to Constantinople.[22] The most prompt responses—the rabbinical judgments (*pesakim*), letters, and poems from Trieste, Ferrara, Venice, Ancona, Reggio, and Gorizia—formed the basis of Wessely's third epistle, *Ein mishpat* (Fountain of judgment), published in April 1784.[23] In addition, over the next few years, Morpurgo was spurred to great productivity: he wrote a rambling polemic in support of Wessely entitled "Iggeret ogeret ahavat ha-adam be-asher hu adam" (A treatise treating of love of man qua man), he had his *Discorso* and Italian translation of *Divrei shalom ve-emet* published, and he contributed to *Ha-Meassef* articles on education that combined Wesselian principles with Italian practice.[24] In association with the printers Tommasini and Coletti and with the *maskil* Homberg, Morpurgo tried to publish in Gorizia a journal devoted to Hebrew literature, rhetoric, and poetry, but there was insufficient support to bring the project to realization.[25]

The Italian campaign got off to a quick start. By the end of May 1782, even before Wessely's second letter of entreaty to Trieste, Morpurgo had written to his teacher Rabbi Israel Benjamin Bassan of Reggio.[26] By early July 1782, Morpurgo's "Iggeret" and the approving *pesak* of Rabbi Formiggini were ready for dispatch along with Wessely's two pamphlets. In his "Iggeret," Morpurgo cited the "honor and glory" of Wessely and "love for the righteous emperor" as his motivations for writing, and praised Wessely as being "full of the Lord's blessing, by virtue of knowledge of the sciences, precision of language, and acquaintance with the heart of man."[27] To argue for the necessity of Wessely's program, he analyzed the state of culture among Ashkenazic Jews—strong in Halakhah, midrash, and Kabbalah, but weak in areas now deemed important, Scripture, Hebrew language and letters (especially poetry), and the sciences—and he contrasted it to the illustrious cultural past of ancient, Sefardic, and Italian Jews. Morpurgo thought the times ripe for cultural improvement and greater participation in European culture because the "sun was appearing over the land and man was being recognized in his humanity"; in such a climate, governmental policies, the mighty efforts of Mendelssohn and Wessely, and the steadily growing contribution of Jews to general science and literature would all bear fruit.[28] To revive their rich cultural tradition would earn Jews honor in Gentile eyes; in contrast, to indulge in dissension could lead to disaster. Accordingly, Morpurgo closed with a prayer for peace. In his letter to Wessely of August 11, 1782 (1 Ellul 5542), Morpurgo reported his various activities, and tried to steel Wessely by comparing his trial of unjust persecution to those of Maimonides and Moses Hayyim Luzzatto.[29] Three days later, he continued the campaign by sending a letter to his teacher Rabbi Abraham Isaac Castello of Livorno.[30]

In the meantime, the missives from Trieste were prepared. Rabbi Formiggini's *pesak* of July 9, 1782 (27 Tammuz 5542) was accompanied by a letter of solicitation from the lay leaders of Trieste. His *pesak* is extant, but not their letter, though a later work contains an apparent paraphrase of it. To judge from this account, the letter echoed some of Wessely's themes, such as the need to fight the opponents of "all light, all progress," and the "responsibility" of Italian rabbis to rouse themselves from "pernicious immobility" to combat the "fatal spirit of obscurantism." But it also made a specific appeal to Italian Jewish cultural traditions: to aid Wessely in his struggle would help Italian Jews "recover their ancient valor, and become once again the great teachers of the Jewish world." For the message of the Italian legacy—Torah combined with worldly wisdom—was now urgently needed: "Rather than clash, religion and knowledge together embrace each other, so as to bring about in studies and in life the necessary and admirable harmony of civility and faith." The aim was to "nurture ardent religious observance and earnest zeal for civil progress"—the cardinal principle of Triestine Jewry in the time of Josephinian Toleration.[31]

In his written opinion, Formiggini framed the issue as the teaching of "Torah and also other sciences and disciplines (*hokhmot u-muskalot*)" to Jewish children "in order that they become exemplary in the eyes of the nations."[32] He praised both Wessely and Mendelssohn for advocating this truly commendable goal, and cited past Jewish worthies such as members of the Sanhedrin, the Mishnaic and Talmudic Sages, and Maimonides, who had exemplified the ideal combination of Torah with non-Torah Wisdom (*hokhmah*).[33] Because of the vehement arguments and actions of Wessely's detractors and their denial of this ideal, he charged them with "offering alien fire," a grave offense indeed.[34]

Yet, taking seriously the peacemaking role thrust upon him by Wessely and in a spirit of mediation, Formiggini judged all parties to the controversy well-intentioned and found merit on both sides. He favored the broader cultural horizons Wessely was trying to introduce among Ashkenazic Jews, but he shared the concern of his traditionalist opponents that Torah not lose pride of place. Thus he supported Wessely's threefold call for (1) an ordered Jewish curriculum to proceed from Scripture to Mishnah to Talmud, (2) recognition of the principle of division of labor in Jewish society (i.e., that not all are Talmudic scholars, and therefore such expertise should not be the only goal of Jewish education), and (3) inclusion of non-

Torah studies within the curriculum. But unlike Wessely, he stated unequivocally that those who specialize exclusively in Torah studies ought not to be disparaged, but rather on the contrary, valued as a "class of holy scholars" (*kat shel kedoshim*). And stressing that Torah study, which is intrinsically wide-ranging, difficult, and demanding, must always be primary (*ikkar*) and all other studies secondary (*tafel*), he disagreed with the precise details of Wessely's plan—above all, with his initial formulation that the "Torah of man" be taught before the "Torah of God." As Formiggini put it,

> Torah studies are the principle, since "from them the cornerstone, from them the support" [Zechariah 10:4] and the secure foundation for every edifice of knowledge and science. "Delve into [the Torah] again and again for all is contained within it" [Avot 5:22]. . . . In the first five years that our Sages designated [i.e., from ages five to ten, Avot 5:21], we ought not to confuse the children's minds with any other studies, "for their delight will be in the Torah of the Lord" [Psalms 1:2].[35]

Accordingly, Formiggini recommended that Scripture and Mishnah study be supplemented with Hebrew grammar, prayers, Proverbs, Job, and Psalms, religious ethics, and classic commentaries such as those of Rashi and Obadiah Bertinoro, while the study of Hebrew composition, the vernacular, and German, as well as arithmetic and any other subjects, be deferred until the age of ten and then relegated to but a minor portion of the day. (Broadly speaking, this was the program of the *Scuola Pia Normale sive Talmud Torà*.[36]) In sum, Rabbi Formiggini endorsed Wessely and his pamphlets, but he did so with reservations, and he considered his opponents not wholly deserving of blame.

Six other Italian rabbis joined Formiggini of Trieste in rendering favorable judgments of Wessely's two pamphlets. They were Samuel Yedidiah b. Eleazar Norzi (Norsa) of Ferrara; Simhah (Simone) b. Abraham Calimani, Abraham Hayyim b. Menahem Cracovia, and Abraham b. Isaac Pacifico, all of Venice; Hayyim Abraham Israel of Ancona; and Israel Benjamin Bassan of Reggio.[37] They were all respected leaders, advanced in years, men who occupied positions of responsibility as *dayyanim* (judges) and teachers. Some, such as Calimani and Bassan, were renowned among both Jews and Gentiles for their literary and scientific accomplishments. Their endorsements of Wessely ranged from the Venetians' enthusiastic one to Hayyim Abraham Israel's grudging one. Significantly, Israel was the only non-Italian respondent; born in Jerusalem, he settled in Italy only in his late fifties. During the course of 1783, all the responses were sent to Wessely along with some poems of praise, apparently by Morpurgo. In December 1783, Wessely acknowledged their receipt and promised to publish them. Wessely and Morpurgo seem to have hoped for still more positive responses; it was in January 1784 that Morpurgo, upon Wessely's suggestion, turned eastward to Rabbi Jacob Danon of Constantinople.[38] But when Wessely published *Ein mishpat* in 1784, apparently in the late spring or summer, it contained no additional responses. Nor did it include the one other extant *pesak*, namely, that of Rabbi Ishmael b. Abraham Kohen (Laudadio Sacerdote) of Modena, one of the most distinguished halakhists in Italy, whose strictures on Wessely's first pamphlet were severe, for he feared that Wessely's plan would make Torah "secondary" rather than "primary."[39]

Analysis of the written opinions of Wessely's Italian defenders is revealing of the state of the Italian Jewish cultural tradition in the late eighteenth century. And it was upon this potent cultural inheritance that the Jews of Trieste drew.

The Italian rabbis who responded to the solicitations from Trieste and Gradisca upheld Wessely's basic contention: that because Torah and non-Torah Wisdom are complementary, there is a legitimate and important place in Jewish education and culture for a wide range of linguistic, mathematical, moral, social, and physical sciences. They supported Wessely's demands for general studies, an ordered curriculum, and a division of labor because these were consonant with Italian Jewish educational practices. Italian Jewish schools had long included some general studies; graded instruction based upon the sequence of Scripture, Mishnah, Talmud; and implicit recognition of the corollary of division of labor, whereby advanced Talmud study was really the domain of specialists. Generally, Italian Jewish curricula were much less oriented to Halakhah than were Ashkenazic curricula: Hebrew grammar and Scripture, liturgy and ritual, ethics and Midrash were staples as important as Halakhah, and sometimes Talmud study itself was reserved for only the oldest and brightest pupils.[40]

So striking was the Italian endorsement of Wessely's *Divrei shalom ve-emet* and its general thrust that many then and subsequently did not notice that in fact that endorsement was qualified. Between the lines, the Italians' support expressed reservations. Formiggini and the other Italian rabbis were concerned that Torah remain primary; their overall message was that Torah ought to be supplemented, but never supplanted. And it was the problematic way in which Wessely had addressed this issue in *Divrei shalom ve-emet* that led to their misgivings.

Close reading of Wessely's first pamphlet and the Italian responses shows the measure of their distance from him. At the core of Wessely's first pamphlet lay the concept of the "Torah of man" (*torat ha-adam*). He defined the "Torah of man" as the very essence of humanity: the unwritten code of behavior and body of knowledge concerning man and the world that is accessible through human reason and empirical observation, and shared by all societies.[41] He contraposed it to the "Torah of God" known only by divine revelation, which prescribes laws and teachings for Jews alone. Significantly, he included even "fear of God," that is, piety or spirituality, in the "Torah of man," presumably on the assumption that the human capacity for belief in God is universal. The universalist and ethical dimensions of Wessely's "Torah of man" reflected Joseph II's emphasis on "sound morality," that is, universal and philosophic morality. In Wessely's schema of Jewish education, the universal "Torah of man" should precede the specifically Jewish "Torah of God"; hence instruction in civility, the vernacular, ethics, history and geography, and mathematics and natural sciences should precede Hebrew and Jewish texts. The novelty lay in Wessely's attempt to separate an autonomous realm of human culture from the Torah, his designation of it by the somewhat strange term *torat ha-adam*, and the radical dichotomy implied by his repeated juxtapositions of the two Torahs, human and divine. He asserted their complementarity, but the underlying logic was bifurcation of the two, and the priority of the human not only in time, but also in value. In his subsequent retractions, Wessely greatly reduced the scope and value of the "Torah of man," and collapsed the very structure of two independent and juxtaposed realms. Perhaps he was sincere in his protestations that he had not intended such radically novel implications, but they were grasped by others as the thrust of *Divrei shalom ve-emet* and the Haskalah's educational message.

Wessely's Italian champions did not in fact accept that novel juxtaposition and transvaluation. All followed Rabbi Formiggini of Trieste in registering their concern that Torah remain primary (*ikkar*) and other studies secondary (*tafel*). Most, like Formiggini, disagreed with Wessely's timetable for the introduction of non-Torah studies, stating that Italian practice was preferable. They shared the fear of Rabbi Ishmael Kohen that Wessely's changing the foundation of Jewish education from Torah to universal human culture meant upsetting the balance between core and periphery, "turning things upside down" with the inevitable consequence that "Torah will be forgotten in Israel."[42] And their conception of Torah did not match Wessely's initially circumscribed and dichotomous one. Following in the Maimonidean and Sefardic rationalist traditions, theirs was a harmonistic integrative conception of Torah and Wisdom, of religion and culture—in which God's Torah is the absolute value, the firm bedrock of education, and the all-embracing framework for every kind of knowledge.

Arguments from silence and by inference are sometimes problematic, but the Italians' reticence with regard to Wessely's very term *torat ha-adam* may suggest their discomfort. It is possible, of course, that they did not consciously reject his term after searching analysis. They may not have been aware of all its radical implications. But it is striking that they shied away from it, and used more familiar terms for the humanities and sciences, such as *hokhmah* (wisdom) or its variants *hokhmot u-muskalot* (the sciences and speculative disciplines) and *hokhmot hitzoniot* (external studies).[43] Those who used the term, the Venetians and Morpurgo—and, for that matter, the Triestine school directors on opening day in May 1782—did so in ways that implied no dichotomy or juxtaposition of two Torahs. Furthermore, Morpurgo specified the meaning of *torat ha-adam* as "ethics" or as one of its eighteenth-century subsets, the doctrines of tolerance and humanity. When he translated *Divrei shalom ve-emet* into Italian, Morpurgo hardly used the literal equivalent *la legge umana* (human law), preferring instead *la legge morale* (the moral law) and *la buona morale* (sound morality).[44] In any case, neither those who avoided the term nor those who modified its meaning can be considered exponents of Wessely's initially radical conception. (An interesting parallel was the failure of many Habsburg *Aufklärer* to accept, and sometimes even to grasp, the critical redefinition of *philosophe* as rationalist and anti-Christian put forward by the French Enlightenment.[45])

Thus, the outlook of the Italian rabbis was compatible with that of Wessely, but not identical to it. Their views converged, but the Italians maintained an independent and complicated stance toward Wessely and his message of Haskalah. They supported what struck them as familiar, while rejecting what struck them as novel. The result was a spirited but qualified defense. Yet for strategic and perhaps temperamental reasons, they did not emphasize their points of disagreement with Wessely. They preferred to minimize these so that they could better strengthen what they understood as his basic point: the complementarity of Torah and Wisdom, of Judaism and general culture. On this central issue, they stood steadfastly with Wessely.

Some of their arguments in support of Wessely's basic point were standard: precedents of polymath Sages from King Solomon through the Sanhedrin to medieval luminaries, explications of rabbinic texts concerning wisdom and morality, and the religious and halakhic utility of the sciences. In his "Iggeret," Morpurgo presented the argument of precedent most forcefully by reiterating the medieval claim that Jews were in fact the original masters of all the sciences, and that even Gentiles had acknowledged Jewish primacy.[46]

The Italians offered some less common arguments as well, ones that may have reflected in varying degrees their distinctive milieu. The Venetians argued the case for a wide range of studies through an analysis of individual and societal human needs that was imbued with eighteenth-century notions of the state of nature and of the explosion of knowledge. Norzi provided a kabbalistic variation on the theme of Wisdom and Torah when he stated, on the authority of earlier kabbalists such as Benjamin Kohen Vitale and Abraham Herrera, that the sciences and philosophy are compatible with "true Kabbalah"—a position long held in Italy.[47] The Venetians and

Morpurgo highlighted both music and poetry as necessary disciplines, thus reflecting the prominent roles of these arts in Italian Jewish culture.[48] One additional distinctive feature was revealed in Rabbi Bassan's disagreement with Wessely's strategy for introducing unfamiliar ideas and practices:

> Had it been possible in the early stages to advise Rabbi Naftali [Weisel], I would have humbly told him not to write or publish a word, not even half a word, but [rather] only through his own speech to lend support to implementation [of innovations] in practice. . . . Only persistence of habit in them enlightens, so that people come to see the truth.

His implication was that practice and experience persuade better than theory or ideology. Bassan was expressing the preference for pragmatic realism over ideological debate that was a point of pride with Italian Enlightenment figures generally, and a facet of the Italian temperament that became increasingly evident to both Italian and German Jews in their subsequent interaction.[49]

The argument most revealing of Italian Jewish culture was that which concerned the prophylactic teaching of non-Jewish Wisdom. The question for Italians was not whether, but how, non-Torah studies should be taught. What might in other quarters be construed as a dire threat was assumed as a reality, a fact of life by Norzi: Jews do pursue the arts and sciences willy-nilly; therefore exclusion of them is not a practical or desirable option. The only choice is between proper and improper exposure.

> If only the sages of Israel would assume their responsibilities [Numbers 7:2], and teach students those sciences that are called external (*hitzoniot*), then there would be no suspicion or questioning that they might cause confusion of mind or neglect of Torah, because they would show the straight path on which one cannot stumble . . . so that everyone who [wants to] approach the study of the sciences will not have to go knocking on the doors of people ignorant of the path of the Lord.[50]

Thus, it is not merely permissible to teach non-Torah Wisdom, it is indeed incumbent upon Jewish leaders to do so properly, for Jewish auspices obviate the need for recourse to less reliable teachers, such as skeptics, heretics, or Gentiles. As stated above, such a consideration may well have occurred to Jewish leaders of Trieste in 1781–82 when they rushed to establish a Jewish normal school. The underlying assumption of the prophylactic teaching of non-Jewish Wisdom was that non-Jewish culture in and of itself—if properly taught and integrated within a Jewish framework in which Torah remains paramount—need not be a threat to Jews or Judaism. These were themes that resonated through the Sefardic and Italian Jewish traditions. For example, Rabbi Bassan's concern that general studies be taught within a Jewish framework was similar to the Provenzalis' rationale for a Jewish university in the 1560s. And Morpurgo's use of non-Jewish culture to defend Judaism—his examples of how knowledge of Gentile cultures could enhance one's appreciation of Judaism—was reminiscent of Azariah de Rossi's approach.[51]

Thus the real question for Wessely's Italian defenders was method and parameters: how best to structure general studies in a Jewish curriculum. Legitimacy was not at issue; they argued that point for Wessely's opponents, not for themselves. With the exception of Hayyim Abraham Israel, all displayed familiarity and ease with such studies. For example, Morpurgo's references to Erasmus and Augustine, to cite just two of many, showed his broad knowledge of Western literature.[52] More significantly, even Wessely's critic Ishmael Kohen considered proper knowledge of European languages indispensable for Torah scholars. Furthermore, his own Hebrew compositions revealed his acquaintance with contemporary Italian literature and ancient Greek mythology: the Sirens, Ulysses, and Parnassus were characters in one of his cantatas. In contrast, it is worth recalling Wessely's own strictures on the use of mythology in Hebrew literature.[53]

Ease and familiarity with non-Jewish realms, what we might call acculturation, was the basic premise of the Italian responses. Morpurgo stated the mutual adaptation of peoples living in close proximity as a general social principle.[54] One contributing factor was surely demography, the small size and isolation of many Jewish communities. In Italy, ghetto walls never did eliminate contact between Jew and Gentile, or close Jews off from general intellectual and cultural trends. Older Jewish historiography assumed that such insularity was the effect of enclosure. But the recent interpretation of Robert Bonfil suggests rather that the security afforded by ghetto walls may well have enhanced the Jews' openness to outside currents.[55] Social adaptation was reflected in language and appearance. As mentioned above, there was no significant linguistic barrier between Jews and Gentiles. Early in the seventeenth century, Leone Modena considered vernacular sermons commonplace, and bemoaned the decline of Hebrew among Italian Jews.[56] He also called attention to males' uncovered heads and clean-shaven faces. These widespread practices were not dismissed by authorities as deviations. His own picture shows a full beard but no head covering, and pictures of a number of Italian rabbis of the seventeenth and eighteenth centuries, the distinguished halakhists Samson Morpurgo and Ishmael Kohen among them, show fashionable hairstyles and few beards.[57] In the 1780s, Morpurgo and Frizzi praised the order to open general normal schools to Jews precisely for the expected benefits of greater social interaction between Jews and Gentiles. In their words, this step would promote "a true human love among individuals of different nations," and "fraternal communication between Jews and others," "intermingling of minds" (*una compenetrazione d'animo*) and "mutual identification" (*una socievole medesimazione*).[58]

Italian Jewish acculturation was not simply a matter of social adaptation. It rested upon a positive evaluation of the high culture of Italian Gentiles. Long past Renaissance interaction, this fundamental appreciation continued to express itself in different ways: in the modicum of general studies always present in Jewish curricula, in the adoption of Italian literary forms in Hebrew literature, and in Jewish cultural norms that saw "Torah Wisdom" and "all branches of knowledge" as integrally linked.[59] This cultural ideal, reinforced to a degree by Sefardic legacies, was personified in the Italian tradition of the rabbi-poet-doctor. These were leaders such as Samson Morpurgo, Shabbetai Marini, and Isaac Lampronti, who were respected for their halakhic mastery, their university educations, and their literary prowess in both Hebrew and Italian, and often for their good relations with Gentile savants and authorities as well.[60] As David Ruderman has demonstrated, the graduation of hundreds of Jewish doctors from the University of Padua had a significant impact on Italian Jewish communities and culture in the early modern period.[61] Thus, late-eighteenth-century Italian supporters of Enlightenment were able to see cultural breadth as legitimate not merely in theoretical or distant historical terms, but concretely in terms of their own recent past and present. Supporters of Enlightenment found role models not only in medieval giants such as Maimonides and Ibn Ezra, but also in Italian Jews from the generations immediately preceding them, their own rabbis and teachers, such as those figures just mentioned and others: Calimani, Bassan, David Nieto, Israel Gedaliah Cases, Abraham Isaac Castello.[62] As Wessely's great Italian admirer Isaac Samuel Reggio put it in the early nineteenth century: "But without having recourse to the distant past, we have more recent examples in our Italy."[63]

Thus the ideal of cultural breadth had retained its legitimacy and currency among Italian Jews, and the Italians rose to Wessely's defense because they considered his program compatible with their own experience and values, and with important strands of their cultural traditions.

Another factor present to varying degrees was economic opportunity. Not only in Trieste but also in Ferrara, Venice, Ancona, Reggio, and Mantua, there were wealthy merchants who upheld the cause of modern education because they saw its economic and social utility and believed it would promote greater integration with Gentile society.[64]

But the Jews of Trieste had a special reason for leading the campaign of resistance against Wessely's opponents, for they were Habsburg subjects. Self-interest and political prudence dictated that they—as the vanguard—urge reluctant Jews elsewhere in the monarchy to comply with the government's new policies lest, as Wessely had warned, groundswells of opposition jeopardize the Jews' position. The Jews of Trieste responded readily to

Wessely's appeal in the spring and summer of 1782 because it presented them with the perfect opportunity to prove just how worthy they were of the terms that they had succeeded in renegotiating and having confirmed just months before. The campaign seemed the logical corollary of their establishment of the *Scuola Pia Normale sive Talmud Torà*. Thus the Trieste-led public campaign to vindicate Wessely served multiple purposes: aid for Wessely himself, propagation of a worldly cultural ideal among other Jews, reinforcement of desirable trends at home, and, like their new school, indubitable proof to Vienna of their allegiance to the progressive ideals of the day.

The Image of Italian Jews in Central Europe

Thus Zinzendorf's suggestion of late 1781 or early 1782 that the Jewish community of Trieste consult Mendelssohn had consequences far different than anyone had anticipated: rather than a textbook on moral instruction from Berlin, it yielded the Italian alliance with Wessely and the attempt to confer legitimacy on Haskalah in the Jewish world at large. These efforts raised the stature of Italian Jewry. For example, Mendelssohn praised the *pesak* of the Venetian rabbis as "very remarkable." More generally, the crucial role of Triestine and Italian Jews as Wessely's advocates gave rise to a positive, enlightened, and progressive image of Italian Jews among central European modernizers in the 1780s and 1790s.[65]

Other factors also contributed to this image. Reports in *Ha-Meassef* told of modern Jewish schools in Trieste and Mantua, and of these two communities' support for the Habsburg policy of military conscription.[66] *Maskilim* had personal contact with Italian Jews who spent time in Berlin or Vienna: the Triestine magnates Marco Levi and Joachim Hierschel; Giuseppe Moise Luzzatto, considered by Mendelssohn a "worthy and noble-minded friend" and lover of German philosophy; Samuel Romanelli, known as a "scoffer of commandments (*mezalzel be-mitzvot*)"; Elia Morpurgo's son Samuel, who attended university in Vienna. Some *maskilim*, such as Herz Homberg and Rabbi Saul Lewin-Berlin, formed their impressions during sojourns in northern Italy.[67]

The view of Italian Jews, both past and present, as culturally sophisticated and preeminent in Hebrew language and letters found expression in some of the literary endeavors of central European *maskilim*: in their biographies of Jews associated with Italy such as Joseph Delmedigo and Isaac Abarbanel, and in their publication of works by several Italian authors, among them Emanuel of Rome and Azariah de Rossi.[68] It is telling that when Isaac Satanov deplored the sorry state of Hebrew and called for its revival in his introduction to *Mishlei Asaf*, he employed an Italian pseudonym: "Joseph Luzzatto of Italy."⁶⁹

The broader cultural and social patterns of Italian Jewry also appealed to German modernizers. In his imaginary travelogue "Iggerot Meshullam ben Uriyyah ha-Eshtamoi," Isaac Euchel drew a portrait of Livornese Jews in which he emphasized peaceful coexistence with Gentiles unconstrained by ghetto walls, respected and productive economic activity, and Jewish adaptation to Gentile mores along with continued Jewish cultural creativity.⁷⁰ Some German *maskilim* went beyond culture and society to the sensitive realm of religion, imputing to Italian Jews a critical and flexible approach to religious tradition, law, and ritual. Interest in Azariah de Rossi's *Meor enayim*, Saul Lewin-Berlin's claim of Italian provenance for the manuscript of *Besamim Rosh* (the lenient responsa he forged), and the Florence Reform hoax of 1796, in which a synod of Italian rabbis was rumored to have sanctioned pork, Sabbath work, and other revolutionary changes—all showed how German radicals sought to further their own cause of religious reform by creating Italian Jews as a legitimizing spur and precedent.⁷¹ They also reveal how Italian support for Wessely and Haskalah could be misinterpreted as advocacy for any apparently progressive cause.

The support and legitimation that Italian Jews had provided Wessely at a critical moment, then, helped foster among German *maskilim* an image of Italian Jews as acculturated, enlightened, politically adroit, and religiously flexible. Italian Jewry thus emerged not only as an exponent of Haskalah ideals, but also as an embodiment of them. As a model, Italian Jewry was in fact as much a mirror as an independent entity for German *maskilim*, and the Italians served them not as initiators of new ideals, but rather as the justification and actualization of their own German-bred vision. This positive image of Italian Jewry—closely related to that of Sefardic Jewry, and itself an admixture of fact and fiction—offered central European *maskilim* inspiration and sustenance.⁷² They cast Triestine, and more generally Italian, Jewry as a staunch ally in their struggle to modernize Jewish society and Judaism.

The 'Scuola Pia Normale,' the Campaign, and Haskalah

The Triestine school was hailed by central European educational reformers as a model because of its unique combination of Jewish and state curricula. On this fundamental point, it met the prescription of Wessely and Berlin *maskilim*. But in fact, the *Scuola Pia Normale sive Talmud Torà* had emerged from Italian traditions and practices, and was not precisely the kind of school first envisaged by Wessely or established by *maskilim* in central Europe. It ought to be remembered that formulation of the school's plan preceded Trieste's consultation of Mendelssohn. The amount of attention the Triestine school paid to non-Judaic studies was far more limited than what was originally proposed by Wessely in his first epistle, *Divrei shalom ve-emet*. The school's students did not acquire knowledge of an extensive range of non-Judaic studies before proceeding to the study of Torah and Jewish tradition; the subjects they studied—arithmetic, Italian, German, and later geography—were fewer than the subjects outlined by Wessely, but more than what Rabbi Formiggini advised for students under the age of ten.[73] Thus, the Triestine school never effected the transvaluation that placed the "Torah of man" above the "Torah of God." As mentioned above, the normal-school part of the curriculum always remained but a fraction of the *pia*, no more than two of the school day's eight hours. This proportion—which was in accordance with Formiggini's recommendation—remained constant through the first few decades of the school's existence. These two hours, incidentally, were less than the four hours per day in summer and two per day in winter allotted to normal-school studies in traditionalist Prague in the 1780s.[74] The difference between the Triestine school and the schools opened by central European modernizers was even more marked, for in most of the latter, civic and vocational studies severely crowded Judaic studies. One exception was the school opened in Dessau in 1799, which also taught a combined curriculum of religious and general subjects, and enjoyed communal consensus and state support.[75] It was in view of the general trend that Wessely especially praised the *Scuola Pia Normale sive Talmud Torà* of Trieste for its scope and balance.

I have argued that both the Triestine school and the campaign for Wessely displayed independence from the Berlin program as well as convergence with it. Italian Jews were neither passive recipients nor imitators with regard to Wessely's message. Their support for him was in fact qualified, their implementation of his proposals partial. Yet in time, these qualifications, nuances, and differences became obscured. In later years, both Triestine Jews and distant observers focused upon the convergence between Trieste, Berlin, and Vienna. All became conflated: the Josephinian legislation, the campaign for Wessely, the *Scuola Pia Normale sive Talmud Torà*, and Wessely's appreciation and admiration for Trieste. The divergence of Italian prescription and practice from Berlin—expressed at the time only in muted fashion—faded from view.

Generally, as the stock of German Jewish culture rose in the late eighteenth and early nineteenth centuries, the Jewish community of Trieste became ever more proud of its association with Mendelssohn, Wessely, and the Haskalah. The famous son of Trieste, Samuel David Luzzatto, who attended the *Scuola Pia Normale* during its third decade of existence, described it as "Wesselian."[76] In the 1860s, the communal rabbi Professor Marco Tedeschi recounted how beneficial Wessely and the Triestine community had been to each other, and depicted with pride the important part played by the community in the "revival" of the "religion, morality, sacred and civic studies" among a "large portion of the Jews of Europe."[77] As discussed above, a Hebrew poem composed in 1886 for the celebration of the supposed centenary of the school's founding closely linked the roles of the Habsburg monarch and Wessely. But the ravages distance from the events had caused were revealed by the community's celebrating on the wrong date: it seemed unaware that the school had actually opened in 1782.

The conflation and the consequent emphasis upon the Berlin connection could easily lead to a misunderstanding of the nature of Jewish culture in late-eighteenth-century Trieste. The real support for Haskalah, the exaggerated sense of affinity with it, and the obscuring of divergence from it, might lead to the conclusion that what was happening in Trieste, and in Italy, was itself Haskalah, or else a trend greatly influenced by the Berlin Haskalah. But in fact, this was a case of convergence, not identity, and of mutually reinforcing but essentially independent trends. What Triestine involvement in the cultural politics of Haskalah and with the cultural policies of the enlightened absolutist government shows were the very different underpinnings and the very real distinctiveness of the Italian Jewish cultural tradition to which the Triestine community was heir.

In their *pesakim* and in their actions, the Italians had selected carefully from Berlin's wares: they had affirmed values and methods that seemed familiar, but had rejected those which struck them as radically new.[78] Their receptivity to Wessely's message of Haskalah was predicated on perceived familiarity, not novelty. Their reservations did not stem from a narrow or obscurantist view of Jewish culture—none appreciated European languages, and the arts, humanities, and sciences more than they—but rather from a different configuration of Judaism and general culture than that of the Haskalah. For Italian Jews, both Torah and general culture had long occupied legitimate and accustomed places; neither had to yield to make room for the other. It was on the basis of that configuration of Judaism and general culture, their tradition of acculturation, that Italians found Wessely's message paradoxically both familiar and unsettling. Their sense of continuity with their own cultural traditions and with those of medieval Sefardic Jewries allowed them to see themselves as allies in the task of Jewish cultural modernization, but at the same time, to distance themselves from its central European bearers. In the 1780s, they were unwilling to accept Berlin as an exclusive model for themselves because they had a sense of the differences in the cultural development of Ashkenazic and Italian Jews. As Samuel David Luzzatto expressed it a few decades later:

Italian Judaism was always pious (*ortodosso*) and always more or less enlightened. It did not have, like the Spanish, a period of domination by a foreign culture, and therefore by heterodoxy; nor did it ever have, like the northern [Ashkenazic], a period of coarseness and lack of all civilized culture.[79]

Over a long period, cultural boundaries between Jew and Gentile had been drawn differently in Italy than in Ashkenaz. Though Italian tradition had long accepted general culture as natural, and displayed certain tendencies critical of tradition itself, it had never deemed general culture of equal or greater worth than Judaism. To appreciate the value of general culture and to support educational reform in central Europe—and even to become models for central European modernizers—Italian Jews did not have to become *maskilim*. If by the Haskalah movement we mean a group of intellectuals who defined themselves as enlightened by virtue of their criticism of tradition and who called for significant, possibly radical, cultural remaking, then we may conclude that the sympathy that Triestine and Italian Jews displayed for the Berlin Haskalah was not in and of itself an instance of Haskalah. As an ideology, Haskalah was transportable, and as the case of Trieste shows, it could find an echo in far different circumstances than those in which it was first generated.[80] Despite the claims of earlier Jewish scholars, notably Salo Baron and Isaac Barzilay, I think it misleading to refer to the Italian Jewish culture of the sixteenth and seventeenth centuries as "Haskalah."[81] Not every instance of cultural openness to the non-Jewish world deserves to be equated with Haskalah. Italian Jewry was not just on a different timetable than was central European Jewry; it was on a different course. This was a course and a tradition that in Trieste of the 1780s allowed for a positive response to Habsburg cultural policies independent of the Berlin Haskalah, and, in turn, for a positive response to Wessely's appeal and an active role in the cultural politics of Haskalah. Yet in Trieste itself, both the ongoing Italian Jewish cultural tradition and governmental policy were more decisive than Haskalah in fashioning the Jewish cultural climate.

CHAPTER SIX

A Decade of Civil Toleration: New Rights and Duties in the 1780s

The Toleration edicts and letters of 1781–82 were only the opening salvo in Joseph's campaign to reform Jewish life within the Habsburg Monarchy. The decade of the 1780s was punctuated by his efforts to transform various aspects of Jewish society, culture, and behavior so as to mold the new Jewish subject useful to the state. The opening of one institution, the new *Scuola Pia Normale sive Talmud Torà*, and the abolition of another institution, the ghetto, were two highly visible effects of the Toleration policy in Trieste. Less tangibly, the Toleration program also affected communal administration, and caused some modifications of the rights and duties of Jewish subject-citizens.

The new *Regolamento interno religioso politico, ed economico* of 1783 was a drastically pared-down version of the 1771 Statute. Drawn up by Triestine Jews, these communal regulations were finally recognized—as the Jews had long wanted—as internal and consensual, that is, "as a plan of internal agreement . . . concerned with the economic administration, order, and internal regulation of our Community."[1] Not issued as an expensive diploma, the *Regolamento* was simply approved by the governor and sovereign at no cost. Reflecting Josephinian aims, it omitted regulations for the ghetto and for communal resolution of disputes. It thus ended the limited judicial autonomy granted by Maria Theresa and was consonant with the abrogation of all Jewish civil law and courts (along with other separate court systems) in the monarchy decreed in 1782–85.[2] And it expressed Joseph's keen interest in Jewish internalization of the norms of civic duty: Jewish leaders were charged with instilling "in hearts the sentiments of probity, in accord with the duties of man, and in conformity with the rules of sound moral philosophy," and fostering the "spirit of true patriotism."[3]

Civic duty and true patriotism were linked in the obligation of military conscription first imposed on most Habsburg Jews in 1788. Though the Free Port of Trieste was exempted from this duty, its Jewish leaders took this opportunity, as they had with the new educational policies, to voice their hearty endorsement of civil integration.

In one respect, Josephinian civil toleration touched on the religious sphere. As increasing symbolic weight was given to the humanitarian aspects of religious toleration, somewhat stronger guarantees of religious freedom were provided to Jews. The 1782 decree forbade clandestine baptism of Jewish children under the age of seven, but still permitted it for those between the ages of seven and fourteen if in mortal danger. The 1787 legislation was more significant, for it made baptism in such cases dependent on the permission of the civil authorities.[4] In other words, clerics were no longer to baptize a Jewish child without permission of either the parents or the state. There was still no guarantee of the return of clandestinely baptized children to their Jewish parents, but the state was declaring its supervisory interest and possibly restraining influence in this sensitive domain.

Formal Abolition of the Ghetto, 1785

The Josephinian aim of promoting civil integration and reducing Jewish segregation included lessening restrictions on Jewish mobility and residence.[5] For example, the Toleration edict for Vienna and Lower Austria stated explicitly that Jews would no longer have to live in houses assigned to them alone: "By the present Decree We hereby permit the existing restrictions with regard to definite Jewish houses to lapse and allow tolerated Jews to lease at their choice their own residences in the city as well as in the suburbs."[6] At the same time, however, the ghettos of Mantua, Gorizia, and Prague were left standing.

No provisions concerning place of residence were included in the Toleration letter to Trieste of December 19, 1781. In legal terms, Jewish residence in Trieste in the early to mid-1780s was still regulated by the sovereign resolution of 1753, which had permitted wealthy Jews to apply for the right to live outside the ghetto, though only in houses occupied wholly by Jews.[7]

The reality was somewhat different. Continuing pressures of population growth meant that what the 1753 law intended to be exceptional was in fact becoming the norm. Yet the civil authorities chose not to act upon repeated complaints that the regulations about separate buildings for Jews and about the nighttime closing of the ghetto were not being fully observed; for example, in 1772 they reasoned that the Jews had long been "tolerated and valued" (*geschäzet*) in Trieste and that Jewish leaders paid "the strictest attention to matters of good order (*Polizey*) and security."[8] As stated above, in December 1781, State Councillor Tobias Philipp Gebler noted that in Trieste, almost as many Jews lived outside the ghetto as inside.[9] Four years later, in the summer of 1785, the *Capi* estimated that nine-tenths of the Jews of Trieste were dwelling outside the ghetto—a situation that led the later public figure and historian Pietro Kandler to state that the "Ghetto itself [was] . . . a name, not a fact."[10] Though these were rough guesses and exaggerations to be sure, still, it is obvious that a significant proportion of Triestine Jews no longer lived inside the ghetto. In July 1785, Chief of Police Pittoni finally responded to the Catholic clergy's complaints and instructed Jews who were renting lodgings in buildings occupied by Christians to find new accommodations.[11] The *Capi* then requested a one-year grace period, claiming that such Jews had acted in good faith. But Pittoni considered that excuse a poor one, since the law was well known to all. Accordingly, he now turned to Governor Brigido for further instructions.

The eventual result of Pittoni's request was official permission for the Jews to live wherever they pleased in Trieste, even in buildings shared with Christians, and the formal abolition of the enclosed and locked ghetto itself. The process of aligning the old legislation of 1753 with both Josephinian principles and the realities of Trieste, and of arriving at an arrangement satisfactory to the authorities and to all the Jews, took a good half-year, from July 1785 to February 1786.

Initially, governmental officials came to a decision about freedom of residence for Triestine Jews rather easily. Within just a few days of Pittoni's report, Governor Brigido wrote to Vienna requesting a decision at the highest level. He explained that the ever-growing number of Jews in the city as well as the principles of the 1781–82 Toleration legislation rendered unsuitable the old law requiring an enclosed area and specific houses for Jews in Trieste. Moreover, no express Toleration edict had been issued for Triestine Jews precisely because of their prior enjoyment of better liberties and privileges. Pending a decision in Vienna, he instructed the other local authorities that no Jews were to be obliged to change their places of residence.[12] Officials in Vienna soon concurred. On August 4, 1785, the Court Chancellery issued the sovereign decree that stated explicitly that the new Toleration principles concerning residence should definitely be applied in Trieste without hesitation as elsewhere in the Hereditary Lands.[13] All Triestine Jews could thenceforth live among Christians legally.

But within the Triestine Jewish community itself, there was dissension about the ultimate implications for the formerly prescribed area of legal

Jewish residence, the ghetto. The *Capi* themselves had wasted no time. On August 19, 1785, only a few days after receiving notice of the sovereign decree and conveying it to the community, they had the locks removed from the main gates enclosing the ghetto.[14] However, opposition to this step came from an important quarter: the prominent and powerful Marco Levi, who certainly knew how to make his views known. His prime concern was physical security: the safety of his home and commercial warehouse. Failing to make his view prevail among his fellow Jews, he turned to the government, and succeeded in getting an order issued on August 23, 1785, that instructed the *Capi* to restore the locked gates to their former condition. The government also ordered the *Capi* to hold a general convocation of all community members to discuss this issue and to report back to the authorities.[15]

At the general meeting held on August 25, 1785, community members voted overwhelmingly in favor of the *Capi*'s proposal to destroy the locked gates: nineteen people in favor, two opposed, and four abstentions.[16] On August 30, 1785, Governor Brigido approved the abolition of the locked enclosure, citing the vote, the soundness of the arguments advanced, and the "general and particular Sovereign Principle of social Tolerance." But he nonetheless deemed it useful to leave the gates in place. If for reasons of physical security the community wanted to pay for the stationing of a military guard at the entrance to the ghetto, then the governor and local military commander would supply one.[17] (A similar request—for a nighttime guard patrol—had been made in Gorizia a few months earlier.[18])

Jewish reaction to this decree was mixed. The *Capi* considered it but a half-measure, while Marco Levi and some others thought it meritorious, for in their view, even unlocked gates might serve a useful purpose. Debates, attempts at reconciliation, and negotiations with the government continued. Marco Levi eventually withdrew his opposition to the majority's view and acceded to the plan for demolition of both the lock and the gates of the ghetto. On September 17, 1785, the governor approved the complete abolition of the ghetto gates, stipulating but one condition: that the destruction cause no harm to adjacent buildings.[19] Shortly thereafter, the gates were in fact destroyed, and a proclamation was issued in the community's two synagogues advising members of the changed halakhic status of the area. Since the streets of the formerly closed ghetto were now open, the area had become a public domain, *reshut ha-rabbim*, to which the prohibition against carrying goods on the Sabbath would henceforth apply.[20]

It appeared that a satisfactory resolution had been reached, but the controversy soon flared up again. Sometime in October or November 1785, Marco Levi began agitating anew for a military guard and for reconstruction of the ghetto gates. He argued that reassessment of the situation was warranted and his earlier fears justified: for only a fortnight after the demolition of the gates (and four times prior), his life and property were threatened by thieves attempting to force their way into his house. Upon investigation, the police determined that in fact there had been no attempted robbery, and that Levi's complaint was a false alarm due to a misunderstanding. As for security in general, the chief of police considered the open quarter more secure than the old closed ghetto, since it was now subject to the scrutiny of the regular half-hourly police patrols rather than the defense of an aged doorkeeper. To calm a prominent Triestine, the local authorities would be willing to supply special protection for the Levi home and warehouse, but since Levi refused to pay the costs of such protection, the governor considered frequent visits to the ghetto by the police in the course of their regular rounds to be quite sufficient.[21] The governor's view was upheld in the sovereign decree of February 9, 1786, and conveyed by the local authorities to the parties concerned—the Levi family and the police—on February 21, 1786.[22]

How Marco Levi himself would have greeted this news is unknown, for he had died but a short time earlier, on February 4, 1786, at the age of seventy-one.[23] In any case, the rest of the family, now headed by his cousin Grassin Vita di Caliman Levi, seem to have lodged no further protests about the demolition of the ghetto gates.

In legal terms, the decree of August 4, 1785, extended Maria Theresa's edict of 1753 by granting to all Jews without exception—and not only the wealthy—the right to live anywhere in Trieste. The removal of legal restrictions upon Jewish residence in Trieste in 1785 was merely a formality. Just as the 1753 legislation had been an attempt to control a process already well under way, namely, the moving of Jews outside the ghetto, so, too, did the legislation of 1785 merely sanction an existing reality, namely, the dwelling of a large proportion of Jews among Christians outside the ghetto, in the new part of the city, the *Borgo Teresiano*. The Catholic clergy was distressed by this process of integration, but governmental authorities in both Trieste and Vienna seemed hardly perturbed, especially after the Toleration policy affirmed the principle that residential segregation of Jews was no longer necessary. It seemed merely an oversight that this provision had not been explicitly applied to Trieste—an oversight due to the lack of a specific Toleration edict for Trieste.

Insofar as the 1785 decree ended restrictions on Jewish residence in Trieste, its practical effects were limited. Sanctioning an ongoing process, it did not effect a dramatic change in the pattern of Jewish residence. For example, in 1788, 86 Jewish households listed addresses inside the former ghetto and 128 outside, but almost all of the 128 were in the immediate vicinity of the former ghetto.[24] However, the second consequence of the decree—the abolition of the ninety-year-old locked ghetto—was highly symbolic. However natural and long overdue for most Triestine Jews and for civil authorities, removal of the ghetto gates was a visible sign of the new climate of opinion of the Josephinian era, and it was understood as release from the "restrictions," "ignominy," and "slavery" that Jews had suffered before the current age of "sound philosophy" and "humanity."[25] The *Capi*, most of the Jews, and the police chief considered the ghetto gates as the embodiment of humiliation and as vestiges of an uglier past, and consequently their destruction was seen as the tangible and logical expression of Joseph's policies of enlightenment and tolerance.

Marco Levi, the one outspoken opponent of the removal of the ghetto gates, viewed the matter quite differently. He disagreed about the symbolic meaning of those gates and their practical benefits or disadvantages. In his written presentations to the community and the government, he characterized the ghetto as a "privilege" and "benefit" (*favore*), even as a "right" (*ius*), whose worth had been manifest for eighty-nine years, and which he was not prepared to lose suddenly. Claiming that Jews had never before complained during the ghetto's existence, and that the decision to keep the gates locked or open had always been the Jews' own, he did not feel that the presence or absence of the gates now affected Jewish honor or status. Rather, what was at stake in his view was physical safety.[26] His concern for security was twofold: as an aged and ailing wealthy property owner, he was fearful of robbers, by whom he had been repeatedly victimized; and as a Jew, he recalled difficult moments in which ghetto locks, gates, and walls had afforded protection against mob violence. He alluded briefly to the rash of assaults upon ghettos in his own birthplace, Mantua, and other Italian towns some thirty years earlier, occasioned by the singing of the derisive anti-Semitic song "Gnora Luna." When the song had made its way to Trieste in those days, Marco Levi himself was one of those who petitioned the governor that it be banned, and in fact, no trouble occurred.[27] Thus Levi's own experience led him to counsel caution and to prefer the status quo to change.

Levi's personal knowledge of bad times for Jews in the past helped forge not only his fears, but also his views on strategy. For example, before the August 1785 decree, Levi had disagreed with the tactics of the *Capi* when they informed the authorities that Jews did indeed live among Christians, though that was still illegal. He preferred a more circumspect form of politics for the Jewish community. In a similarly prudent vein, Levi thought that leaving the front gates of the ghetto in place, whether locked or unlocked, might deter potential troublemakers of whatever stripe. To Levi, the gates of the ghetto were a familiar and comforting presence, a protection against unknown eventualities.

As was his wont, Levi riddled his arguments with petty personal charges.

Yet he raised one additional substantive issue: that of religion. He argued that the ghetto served to restrain those for whom religion was "almost tottering" (*quasi vacilante religione*), and to prevent the ever-increasing "disorders" due to "enlightened liberty, and depravity."[28] He provided no examples, but the nexus in his mind between ghetto, discipline, and religious observance on the one hand, and between liberty, licentiousness, and religious decline on the other, was clear.

Levi characterized the sources of his concerns as "caution . . . religion, and . . . politics."[29] He claimed to be prepared to let the seven-eighths of the community who lived outside the ghetto by "sovereign munificence" continue to do so and to enjoy "their enlightened liberty . . . in sacred peace," but similarly, he felt that they should permit his family to enjoy their "tranquility of mind, caution, [and] practice of religion."[30] Voicing concern about possibly adverse governmental reaction to Jewish dissension, he threatened to press the matter further through official channels if the community failed to take his views into account.

In Trieste, the views and desires of Marco Levi could not be brushed aside merely as those of one willful and cantankerous person. The words of this wealthy, prominent, well-connected, and determined communal leader carried weight with both fellow Jews and governmental officials. During the debates within the community in September 1785, Levi's powerful influence caused others to compromise and accept the continued presence of the gates he desired, even when they did not agree with him. They insisted, however, that the gates be left unlocked and that the keys be entrusted to the *Capi*, who alone would determine any possible reclosing.[31]

The majority of Triestine Jews, including property owners in the ghetto, argued in different terms than Levi about the symbolic and practical effects of the abolition of the ghetto. They saw the historical past and the present moment differently. They spoke for equal status with other groups in the city as well as equality among the Jews themselves, lest they be divided into two categories of "free" and "enclosed" Jews. Practically, they cited the economic interests of property owners in the ghetto, improved sanitation,[32] easier access through a central part of the city for all Triestine residents and especially for police and fire brigades, and the benefits of not relying upon the often arbitrary ghetto doorkeeper. Physical security would be enhanced, for the improved access and lighting of a public street would provide less refuge for evildoers than the dark, enclosed, unpatrolled ghetto. The chief of police himself agreed that the old arrangements offered no special protection against criminals, as Levi's own experience showed. As for a specifically Jewish concern for safety, the *Capi* dismissed Levi's fears, claiming that law and order prevailed under "this most fortunate sky," and that the experience of Triestine Jews living outside the ghetto had been calm and untroubled. They cited the experiences of many Jewish communities throughout Europe and the Ottoman Empire dwelling peaceably without the protection of ghetto walls; not surprisingly, they drew particular attention to the Jewish communities of Livorno and Amsterdam—to whom the Trieste community was often compared—whose elaborate synagogue buildings and sacred treasures might well have made inviting targets. The *Capi* also pointed to the experiences of the other religious minorities in Trieste, whose places of worship had come to no harm. In short, they felt that the climate of opinion in Trieste and the customary performance of their regular duties by the police would afford adequate protection for Jewish persons and property in the former ghetto and beyond. As the purpose of the ghetto had never been security, despite what Levi implied, but rather "discipline" and "custody" (in the Jews' words), and "humiliation" (in Chief of Police Pittoni's), its abolition could not endanger Jewish safety. The *Capi* stressed emphatically that destruction of the ghetto enclosure meant not a lapse in security, but rather the end of discrimination.[33]

The *Capi* also countered Levi's religious argument. They expressed surprise at his connection between Jewish residence outside the ghetto and irreligion, and at his invocation of the rabbi's support on this score. They noted that one of the community's synagogues, the one in the Camondo home, was situated outside the ghetto precinct, and that the community's assistant rabbi lived outside the ghetto. Indeed, the *Capi* claimed, most Triestine Jews, irrespective of residence inside or outside the ghetto, did "observe perfectly the rites of religion [sic]."[34] Furthermore, even if Levi's premise were correct, his religious scruples seemed to extend only to that one-tenth of the Jewish community who still lived in the ghetto, whereas the *Capi* had in mind the vast majority. Even the religious needs of those nine-tenths would be served by removal of the ghetto gates, for in inclement weather they would no longer have to stand outside the gates waiting upon the whims of the doorkeeper when they came to early morning synagogue services. Though they no doubt exaggerated the degree of piety and minimized the potential effects of geographic dispersal upon group cohesion and religious observance, the *Capi* did not consider a locked ghetto necessary to their maintenance. Given that the disciplinary powers of communal leaders had covered all Jews both inside and outside the ghetto, and that most Jews lived very close to the former ghetto, the *Capi* did not see abolition of the ghetto as a prelude to irreligion. With their proclamation of the changed halakhic status of the former ghetto on September 27, 1785, the *Capi* and rabbi signaled their intention that religious norms would not be relaxed.

To the general convocation of the community on August 25, 1785, the *Capi* also voiced a political argument. Might Levi's position not be misinterpreted as a "sign of arrogance"? Couldn't the Jews' attempt to gain special security arrangements for themselves be seen as impugning the ability of the police to maintain law and order? Moreover, might it not bespeak a Jewish desire for "a different destiny that is distinct from that of all the others" at a time when "sound philosophy and humanity no longer permit such separations and distinctions"?[35] Thus, the *Capi* were discomfited by the agitation for retention of the ghetto because it seemed unfitting in the Josephinian era and could be easily misconstrued as opposition to the Toleration policies. For them, security had to do not only with physical safety but also with the public image of the community.

The *Capi* were displaying sensitivity to the charge of Jewish separateness or clannishness, sometimes called misanthropy, which had been leveled at Jews in the classical and Christian eras and was regaining currency in certain Enlightenment circles.[36] They were sensitive on this score, even though no one in Trieste had publicly raised any version of that charge. Levi's own argument was hardly a principled ideological plea for Jewish separateness and against integration with the surrounding society. When he stated that the ghetto was an eighty-nine-year-old privilege and right, he was referring to physical security, not the right of Jews to lead a separate autonomous collective existence. But the *Capi* still felt that there was room for possible misinterpretation. And although there may have been no specific local cause for their anxiety, the *Capi* were aware of problems in the not-too-distant city of Mantua. Jewish separatism was a major theme of *Della influenza del ghetto nello stato*, the 1782 polemical work published by D'Arco, the Intendant of Lombardy, who argued that Jews mistrusted and hated all others because of Talmudic teachings, and desired desperately to remain separate from other religions and peoples. This book was combatted by Benedetto Frizzi, then a student in Lombardy, in his vigorous polemic *Difesa contro gli attacchi fatta alla Nazione Ebrea*, and by the Jews of Mantua, who sent a delegation to meet Joseph II during his short visit to Trieste in 1784 in order to protest the book and try to have its dissemination halted.[37] This incident was no doubt fresh in the minds of the *Capi* the following year, when the abolition of the ghetto was being debated, and it helps explain their sensitivity to the possible charge of Jewish separatism.

Because the charge had been made so recently, albeit elsewhere, the *Capi* took it seriously. The folly of the Jews of Trieste falling into the trap set by such accusations would be all the greater since most of them did not want the kind of "different destiny" provided by ghetto segregation. Thus the *Capi* saw the problem as one of image rather than of substance or genuine conviction. Their message to the rest of the community was that it would be especially bad politics for the Jews themselves to lend credence in any way to an essentially false charge and to convey such a problematic image.

Triestine Jewish leaders betrayed a certain anxiety in their concern with not appearing separatist and obstructionist of civil integration. Security to them was as much political and symbolic as physical. They did not want to appear to be repaying generous governmental policies with ingratitude, for they feared that might cast doubt upon their worthiness for future reforms and jeopardize the liberties already enjoyed. To avoid charges of ingratitude, disobedience, or unworthiness was one of their reflex reactions throughout the Josephinian decade. Efforts to retain favorable status could produce their own kind of insecurity and anxiety. Yet, with all Jewries subject to the integrating reforms of centralizing modernizing states in the late eighteenth and early nineteenth centuries, they shared the need to contend with the problematic image of Jewish clannishness. The political concerns of the Triestine *Capi* showed that the boundaries of civil integration and of permissible "separations and distinctions" were not clear to Jews or to anyone else; these were in flux, and it was precisely their definition or contestation that was at the crux of the process.

Marco Levi's views also raised issues that transcended the local Triestine situation. Jewish concerns for physical safety were voiced in Gorizia in 1785, when some requested special nighttime protection, and in Mantua following disturbances in the early 1790s, when Jews implored the new French administration in 1797 to delay the destruction of the ghetto (a year later, they felt more ready for that step, but still favored some kind of physical protection).[38] In a number of Italian cities in the late 1790s, physical destruction of the ghetto in a burst of revolutionary enthusiasm during French occupation brought not only the planting of trees of liberty, but also mob violence against Jews.[39] In Trieste, Marco Levi's fears for the physical security of Jews proved unfounded. By the time the porous Triestine ghetto was formally abolished, it was seen as an anachronism whose removal was long overdue. Precisely because it had been outgrown and then ended by a gradual and natural process rather than by the sudden actions of conquerors or revolutionaries, Triestine Jews were spared the mob violence that often occurred in the aftermath of its abolition in other Italian cities.

In Gorizia as well as in Trieste, the meaning of ghetto gates was debated in the 1780s: Did they guarantee physical security or betoken inferiority and humiliation? But Levi's reference to the ghetto as a benefit, privilege, and right suggests that he had found a deeper and more positive meaning in the ghetto than physical security and tranquility; he saw it as familiar and comforting. Levi was not the first Italian Jew to see something positive in the ghetto institution; others had, too, either as an alternative to the worse fate of expulsion, or as a means of fostering Jewish distinctiveness and sanctity through forced segregation. For example, in the sixteenth and seventeenth centuries, Jews in Verona held an annual celebration in commemoration of the establishment of the ghetto; Isaac Cardoso, the former New Christian who later lived openly as a Jew in Verona, saw ghetto separation as a sign of providence; and Jews in Rome referred to their ghetto as "our *ghet*" (bill of divorce), a sacred space that was exclusively theirs.[40] These examples bear out Robert Bonfil's emphasis upon the original function of a ghetto as providing Jews with a fixed location on the Italian urban landscape as opposed to the previous merely temporary residence outlined in a short-term *condotta* (contract).[41] The institution of ghettos starting in the sixteenth century certainly had provided an alternative to expulsion. When expulsion or temporary residence were the alternatives, the ghetto might be seen not merely as restrictive, but also as somehow positive. But by the late eighteenth century, when expulsion was no longer a real option, and the possibilities of civil integration and increasing parity with Gentiles beckoned, the function and meaning of the ghetto were necessarily changed. In the 1780s, Marco Levi's views were unusual, for most Jews could no longer see anything positive in ghetto existence.

In Trieste in 1785, the formal abolition of the ghetto was important symbolically, but less so practically. In effect, the old precinct was amplified, not abandoned. Jews who lived outside the old ghetto stayed relatively close to it, and that centrally located neighborhood long remained the heart of the organized Jewish community of Trieste, where Jews congregated, worshiped, studied, and bought their meat. For many, this recognizable Jewish neighborhood retained the designation "ghetto."[42] More than a century after the formal demise of the ghetto, Umberto Saba drew upon his mother's memories of it to evoke its color and intimacy, its narrow streets and crowded passageways, and the frenetic multilingual bargaining in its small shops; with poetic license, he stated that in 1860, the ghetto was "still in full flower."[43]

Military Conscription, 1788

One of the most important state-building steps taken by late-eighteenth-century modernizing regimes was the introduction of military conscription. Building a large army could serve multiple goals: foreign policy, social discipline and organization for the less economically productive members of society, civic cohesion, and centralization. When the new civic duty of military service was imposed on Jews, it became one of the most significant avenues of state intervention in Jewish life in the late eighteenth and nineteenth centuries. Generally, devotees of the Enlightenment, both Gentile and Jewish, saw military service as a logical step in the civil integration of Jews, indeed, as a quid pro quo, the surest way for Jews to demonstrate their worthiness for improvements in civil status.

The Habsburg Monarchy instituted military conscription in 1770. In principle, it was universal; in practice, certain geographic areas and certain social groups and occupations were exempted. The Littoral, including Trieste, was one area exempted, while the duchies of Gorizia-Gradisca were not.[44] In 1788, the Habsburg Monarchy became the first European state to conscript Jews into its army. The War Council felt generally pressed for increased manpower, but it was not eager to meet its needs with Jewish conscripts. It was the Court Chancellery and Joseph himself who initiated military service for Jews. They were motivated by the general aim of civil integration of the Jews, and particularly by a sense of the utility or socio-economic discipline of military service for the "idle" Galician Jews. Their first effort in 1785—to have Jews enter the supply and transport corps of the army—was unsuccessful, for the War Council refused. In February 1788, without consulting the War Council, Joseph decreed that Galician Jews should now be conscripted into the transport corps as drivers and into the artillery corps as auxiliaries. The new duty was extended to other Habsburg Jews in June–July 1788. In 1789, first Galician Jews and then all Habsburg Jews were permitted to volunteer for the infantry.[45]

Most Jewish communal leaders, fearful of the threat to Jewish religion and society as well as the more obvious one to life and limb, generally viewed the new policy of military conscription with alarm. Several Jewish communities sent delegations to Vienna and sought relief from the new obligation.[46] But all such efforts were in vain. Unease persisted, even when compliance was recognized as inevitable. When the Jewish community of Prague tearfully sent off twenty-five youths to the army on May 12, 1789, Rabbi Ezekiel Landau delivered a farewell address that bespoke the obvious misgivings even while praising duty and obedience to the state.[47]

Reactions of a different sort came from the two communities of Mantua and Trieste. In June 1788, when representatives of the Jewish communities of Alt-Ofen (O Buda) and Lvov were in Vienna preparing their entreaty to the authorities, they wrote to their Italian coreligionists for help and asked them to join in their protest. Probably because of the role the Italians had played in the earlier Haskalah controversies, these Hungarian and Galician Jews thought that the Italians possessed qualities that might be of use in this situation: linguistic and negotiating skills based upon their knowledge of the "ways of the world" and "manners of the royal court." In contrast, they depicted themselves as completely deficient in all of these, and hence in dire need of the assistance of their more acculturated and worldly-wise Italian coreligionists.[48]

This appeal yielded unexpected results: both Mantua and Trieste refused to protest the legislation. In their respective letters written in July 1788, they explained their views.[49] Although they, too, were concerned for the observance of Jewish law and traditions, they thought that religious duties need not necessarily be impaired by fulfillment of this new civic duty. They were prepared to assist their fellow Jews in explaining the issues to the Habsburg authorities, but they would not attack the basic policy of military conscription.

Their advocacy of conscription was not really an endorsement of military service in and of itself. Rather, theirs was a political argument. As the letter from Trieste put it, they saw the issue in the context of Joseph's overall Toleration policies, which they evaluated positively as efforts to "raise Israel's standard from the dust." They summarized these as greater economic and occupational opportunities for the Jews, continuing religious freedom, and the honor and unprecedented trust now being placed in Jews. They deemed it unwise to repay all this with ingratitude:

[Joseph] puts his trust in us, something that no monarch before him has thought to do, and his entire purpose is that we should love labor and hate idleness.

If so, "What shall we say and how shall we justify ourselves" [from Genesis 44:16, Joseph's brothers appearing before him in Egypt] before the compassionate king who shows mercy to us and to our children? . . . Should we appear ungrateful to one who has been so good to us, sons of the covenant, and who has placed his trust in us? Dare we arise and turn a good decree into a bad one, and bring, God forbid, disaster upon ourselves?[50]

They couched military service in terms of work and activity, the themes invoked so often in bustling mercantile Trieste. The monarch's benevolence and the general goodwill that Jews would gain for their readiness to serve in the Habsburg army were too precious to squander.

To strengthen the political rationale, the Jewish leaders of Trieste made religious arguments as well. They repeated traditional dicta that Jews should pray for the welfare of the city in which they dwell, and publicly sanctify the Divine Name. This latter often meant improving the image of Jews in the eyes of the nations; in this specific case, it meant obeying the monarch and serving society militarily. Furthermore, the Triestine Jews tried to allay the fears of their brethren about Halakhah. They acknowledged that soldiers would not be able to observe Jewish law punctiliously, but they found legitimizing precedent for this in the exemptions from halakhic duties that rabbinic sages had permitted Jewish soldiers in "camp," and even in "voluntary wars."[51] Their conclusion was that civic and religious duties could be reconciled. Therefore, the aim of their strategy was the facilitation of that outcome rather than repeal of the conscription order. They recommended that the Jews ask the "merciful emperor" to set up a commission of Habsburg officials, Jewish leaders, and rabbis, who would together draft instructions that would accommodate the needs of both Halakhah and the state. (Indeed, in the next few years, some efforts were made to allow Jewish soldiers to cook together and to be relieved of unnecessary work on the Jewish Sabbath.[52])

The letter from Trieste, longer than the Mantuan and fuller in exposition, was quickly and widely disseminated. In addition to the Hebrew original in *Ha-Meassef*, a German translation appeared in the next few months in a number of German and Austrian publications.[53] It soon became a celebrated response, understood as a hearty endorsement of the new civic duty. Modernizers in other communities were quick to seize upon it. Two years later, in 1790, a group of Jews in Prague cited the letter "of the rabbis [sic] of Trieste" as a precedent for their own favorable view of military conscription.[54]

A misconception arose because of the ambiguous signature of the letter and the heading then supplied by the editors of *Ha-Meassef*. The letter closed with the names of the "officials" (*meshartim*) of the Jewish community of Trieste: the *Capi* Moses Levi, Abraham b. Joseph Morpurgo, and Elia b. Moses Luzzatto, "signing also in the name of our distinguished rabbi and teacher." It is somewhat puzzling that no name then appears. But the rabbi of the community, Isach Formiggini, was then ill, and he died less than two weeks after this letter was written.[55] Though he may have been consulted, it is unlikely that he was involved in the drafting of the letter. Yet in *Ha-Meassef*, the "officials" no longer appeared as *meshartim*, but as *rabbanim*, a term that could indeed mean officials but more often meant rabbis. Thus later references often misleadingly depicted the letter from Trieste as a rabbinical opinion. In any case, the image of Italian Jews that had occasioned the appeal in the first place was reinforced by the renowned Triestine response on military conscription. Ever more did the Jews of Trieste gain a reputation as cooperative and willing partners in Habsburg schemes of reform.

However, contemporaries and many subsequent scholars failed to note that the situation of the Mantuan and Triestine Jews differed from that of their Habsburg coreligionists when they answered their appeals. These two communities had not received conscription orders for their sons.[56] The Mantuan community may well have expected that one was on the way. But in Trieste, no residents of the free port were subject to military conscription. Vienna had decided that the inhabitants of Trieste, the Jews among them, could better serve the realm through commercial rather than military exploits. As the Jews and local officials put it in 1795, "The Regulation on military conscription is not prescribed and is not in force for this city and its Territory."[57] Since the view from Trieste was expressed not in response to a governmental decree affecting their own sons, but rather as advice tendered to their coreligionists elsewhere, it was easier for them to depict military service in positive and lofty terms.

It would be a mistake, however, to conclude that Triestine Jews were insincere in stating that military conscription might yield civil benefits. Though unaffected directly in the 1780s, it was consistent for them to see this new civic duty within the overall context of reform and civil integration of Jews. Two decades later, during the Napoleonic wars, they were conscripted into the local militia of Trieste. Then, strongly motivated by local patriotism, they did serve. As the *Capi* put it in 1809: "The Jewish Community, forming an integral part of the population of this City, is also eager to bear this burden, and its individual members also aspire ardently to see themselves serving on an equal basis with other subjects of His Imperial Majesty."[58]

As for the many non-Triestine Jews serving in Habsburg battalions stationed sometimes in Trieste, the Jewish community did concern itself with their religious and material needs. They devoted a high proportion of their budget to supplying Jewish soldiers with kosher food, billeting them in Jewish homes, and providing them with medical care by Jewish doctors. In addition, they organized synagogue services for them on Jewish holidays.[59] Indeed, so concerned were they with the religious observance of Jewish soldiers that on occasion, as in November 1808, they complained to the local government about Jewish soldiers who publicly violated Halakhah, despite provisions made for its observance.[60] As they had proclaimed in 1788, the Jewish leaders of Trieste continued to believe that military duties and halakhic obligations generally could and ought to be reconciled.

Continued Exceptionality of Jewish Legal Status in Trieste

Joseph's final legislative enactment concerning the status of Habsburg Jews was the Toleration patent for Galicia issued in 1789. The culmination of his reforming efforts, it was the most far-reaching of all the Toleration edicts, claiming as its aim the imposition of the same rights and obligations on Jews as on other subjects. Toward that end, it repealed various limitations on Jewish population growth and marriages, permitted greater economic opportunities, and offered Jews the rights of membership and voting in local municipalities. At the same time, however, it did not cancel many of the onerous special Jewish taxes, and it severely regulated and curtailed the functions of Jewish communal and religious structures.[61]

As part of their attempt to make the patent for Galicia the basis for reordering Jewish life elsewhere in the monarchy, the central authorities in Vienna consulted officials in Trieste, Gorizia, and Gradisca about the suitability of the new patent for local conditions. In 1781–82, the Jewries of these areas had not received specific Toleration edicts of their own, but rather had been assured through official letters that the substance of their prior privileges remained in force, even as the new provisions were applied. In 1789, the exceptionality of Triestine Jewry was once again highlighted by the response of local authorities, who believed that the Galician patent could with modifications be applied to the Jewish communities of Gorizia and Gradisca, but that, in contrast, it was not at all suitable for Trieste. Governing officials and Jewish leaders in Trieste, and ultimately the authorities in Vienna, were agreed that the Jews of Trieste were well served by the Free Port patents and by the 1783 communal regulations, and that it was therefore best to leave things as they were.[62] Contrary to the claims of some scholars, the Jews of Trieste were not issued in 1789-90 a Toleration patent of their own based upon the Galician.[63]

Thus, at the end of Joseph's reign, the Jews of Trieste were still considered exceptional. Although throughout the decade they had been included in many of the monarchy-wide programs for Jews, their situation was nonetheless still recognized as significantly different from that of other Habsburg Jewries. This recognition could of course serve different ends: local authorities and the Jews of Trieste stressed exceptionality in order to preserve advantage, while officials elsewhere—in Mantua, for example, in 1784—asserted that conditions were so different in Trieste that they simply could not be used as a norm for their area.[64] The general Toleration policies of the 1780s notwithstanding, the sense persisted that the status of other Habsburg Jewries could not and ought not to be equated with that of the Jews of Trieste.

Joseph's successor, his brother Leopold, who ascended the throne in 1790, followed the Josephinian policy of increasing civil rights for individual Jews. The Jews of Trieste benefited from certain monarchy-wide regulations. For example, in 1790, the opportunity for Jews to earn advanced university degrees in civil law was reiterated, and extended to include the right to practice law among both Jews and Christians.[65] Also in 1790, the rights of Jewish prisoners to observe a modicum of Jewish law were recognized: overriding the protests of Police Minister Johann Anton Pergen, Leopold ordered that Jewish prisoners be supplied with kosher food and exempted from forced labor on Sabbaths and Jewish holidays. In Trieste in 1792, Governor Brigido invoked "the principles of humanity and equity" when he instructed the appropriate officials to enforce these provisions in the specific cases of two Jewish prisoners.[66]

The legal status of Jewish individuals and the Jewish community in Trieste were basically left intact by both Leopold and his successor Francis, who ascended the throne in 1792. When in 1792 the Jews of Trieste asked for reconfirmation of their long-standing privileges and liberties, they were assured that formal reconfirmation was "superfluous" because they were firmly grounded not only in the "general regulations and continuing laws of Toleration," but also in the "fundamental principles of Liberty of commerce adopted for this maritime city. . . . This Jewish community ought to remain tranquil in the peaceful enjoyment of the concessions granted it."[67] The Jews were in effect told that the substance of their earlier privileges was securely guaranteed by the more general Josephinian Toleration and Free Port patents.

When the Jews requested reconfirmation of their privileges in the 1790s, they were not taking for granted that the issuance of the Toleration edicts had settled Jewish status for once and for all. Renewal of their privileges now meant not the issuance of new separate formal documents, but rather, as in 1781–82, the written assurance from the sovereign that their substance was still in force. Thus, Triestine Jewish status remained what it had been: exceptionality within the framework of general toleration.

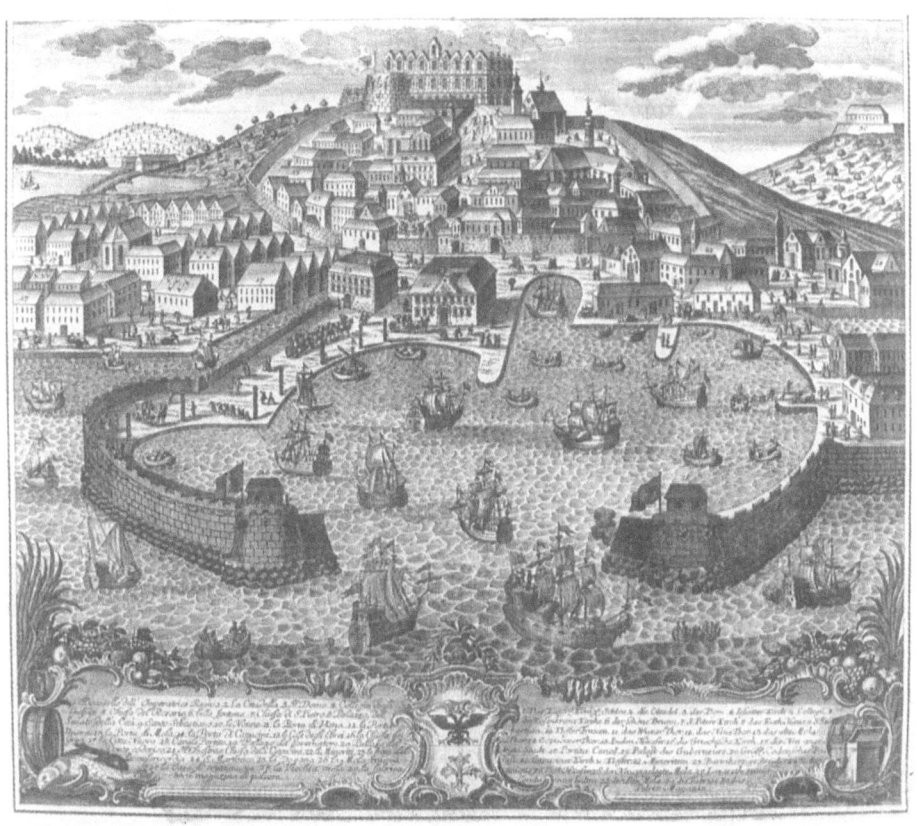

Albrecht Carlo Seutter, *Prospect of the Port and City of Trieste, before 1750*. Courtesy of Musei Civici di Storia ed Arte, Comune di Trieste.

General view of Trieste, c. 1800, from L. F. Cassas, *Voyage pittoresque et historique de l'Istrie et Dalmatie* (Paris, 1802). Courtesy of the Fine Arts Library, Harvard College Library.

View of the City and Port of Trieste, c. 1800, from L. F. Cassas, *Voyage pittoresque et historique de l'Istrie et Dalmatie* (Paris, 1802). Courtesy of the Fine Arts Library, Harvard College Library.

Governor Karl Graf von Zinzendorf und Pottendorf. Negative from the Bildarchiv of the Österreichische National Bibliothek, Vienna.

Benedetto Frizzi, 1817, from Giuseppe Caprin, *I nostri nonni* (Trieste, 1888). Courtesy of Harvard College Library.

Rabbi Raffaele Nathan Tedesco, from *La Porta Orientale*, 3 (1933). Courtesy of Harvard College Library.

Exterior of the building (on left) housing the Scuola Grande, synagogue no. 2. Santo Lucas drawing 1797. Courtesy of Musei Civici di Storia ed Arte, Comune di Trieste.

Interior of the Scuola Grande, synagogue no. 2, built 1797 (Camerini photograph, between 1927 and 1937, showing 1864 renovations, including installation of the large chandelier). Courtesy of Archivi Alinari/Camerini donation.

View of the Large Canal of Trieste, c. 1800, from L. F. Cassas, *Voyage pittoresque et historique de l'Istrie et Dalmatie* (Paris, 1802). Courtesy of the Fine Arts Library, Harvard College Library.

CHAPTER SEVEN

The Jewish Community: Public Order, Piety, and Authority

L'Università degli Ebrei was both a corporate *nazione* of Trieste, charged with civic responsibilities and answerable to the state, and a *kehillah kedoshah*, a holy community, in the usual Jewish terminology. The *Capi* and communal councils were responsible for both political and religious affairs, assisted in the latter by the official rabbi. As an intermediate corporate body, the Jewish community was doing the state's work when it policed Jewish behavior, served for a short time as a court of first instance, settled disputes through arbitration, taught civic morality, kept official population records, and collected funds from Jews for extraordinary wartime contributions.[1] The state was also served by the community's running of educational and social welfare institutions. Moreover, the community's supervision of Jewish religious life and enforcement of religious discipline fulfilled a purpose in the civic order. Both governmental and Jewish authorities shared the view that religion and politics were linked: good order depended on morality, which was derived ultimately from religion; thus, religious discipline could buttress social discipline.

Throughout the second half of the eighteenth century, the *Capi* and rabbi of Trieste retained the right to superintend the public observance of Jewish ritual law and to punish transgressors. The Josephinian edicts of 1783–85 abrogated Jewish law for civil matters, but upheld it for religious affairs. As the decree of August 25, 1783, put it: "In those matters then that refer to the Jewish religion, [Jews] ought to [be] judge[d] according to their [own] laws."[2] Though neater in theory than in practice, this distinction between civil and religious law left the *Capi* and the rabbi as the guardians of Jewish public piety. The state authorities usually backed up the *Capi*'s enforcement of Jewish law because they increasingly saw the Jewish community as a state agency, as part of the state apparatus designed to preserve public order and instill social discipline. Still, though the interests of state and community generally converged, their perspectives differed. While Jewish leaders welcomed the state's adding an external and powerful dimension of compulsion to their own religious-communal authority, they did not really see their *kehillah kedoshah* as a cog in the bureaucracy of the absolutist state.

Religious Leadership: The Rabbis

Always subject to strong lay control, the official rabbis of the Triestine Jewish community were expected to function as religious supervisors and officiants, moral authorities, teachers, preachers, halakhic decisors, mediators and arbitrators, pastors, and administrators, sometimes for the community and sometimes for the state. In the second half of the eighteenth century, all the rabbis of Trieste came from north-central Italy. The post itself did not confer the prestige of heading an institution of higher Jewish learning or leading a long-established community. Those rabbis who achieved fame beyond Trieste did so on the strength of their own individual accomplishments.

When the Jews of Trieste constituted themselves formally as a community in 1746, they defined the duties of the official rabbi as follows: to issue halakhic rulings ("*dare dinim*"), preach sermons twice a month, teach all boys under the age of ten, instruct adults twice daily in the synagogue, officiate at weddings, and minister to the sick and dying. He was also to resolve disputes in the synagogue concerning religious matters, and civil disputes between individuals and the lay leaders of the community.[3] The community's first appointment was unsuccessful: the scholar David Hayyim Corinaldi, son-in-law of the well-known Rabbi Isaac Pacifico of Venice, served only three quarrelsome years in Trieste. An outside mediator was required to settle the terms of his departure, and so disliked was Corinaldi that his name was sometimes omitted from later lists of Triestine rabbis.[4]

From 1750 until 1765, the community was served by Jacob b. Barukh Capriles, who hailed from nearby Venetian territory. His duties were generally similar to those of his predecessor. After two teachers arrived in Trieste in the late 1750s to teach the young boys, Capriles could concentrate upon adults. He was obliged to hold daily study sessions for adults, teaching Gemara in the mornings, Mishnah and commentaries in the evenings, and on winter evenings, also Torah in his home for the *Fraterna di Talmud Torà*. His contract of 1758–59 stipulated duties that were both religious and administrative: deciding Halakhah, preaching, and serving as communal secretary and treasurer.[5]

Following Capriles's death in May 1765, the community negotiated for several months with Menahem (Mandolin) Emanuel Navarra, communal rabbi in Verona since 1753, who held degrees in medicine and philosophy from the University of Padua. Active teacher, preacher, judge, and poet, he was in contact with important rabbis in Italy and beyond, most notably Ezekiel Landau of Prague. The contract under discussion with Triestine leaders in 1765 contained some new emphases that reflected Navarra's own experience and the changing expectations of the community: he was to serve as medical physician for the poor, and to exercise his influence to settle disputes among Triestine Jews, urging recourse to Jewish arbitrators rather than to Gentiles. His educational responsibilities included conducting adult study sessions four times daily and on the anniversaries of communal members' deaths, supervising the children's teachers, and instructing the community's poor boys as well as older students who wished to pursue higher studies. Though agreement was apparently reached, Navarra ultimately decided not to leave Verona for Trieste.[6]

The next choice worked out better: the distinguished sixty-six-year-old Isach b. Rabbi Moses Formiggini of Modena came to Trieste late in 1766, where he served as the community's official rabbi for twenty-two years, until his death in 1788. Scion of a prominent Modenese family who were court jewellers for the ducal house of Este for almost two centuries, son of a rabbi, he had already held rabbinical posts in his native Modena, Livorno, and Turin, in the latter as chief rabbi. Formiggini was one of the rabbinic scholars who wrote approbations for Isaac Lampronti's halakhic encyclopedia *Pahad Yitzhak*. Formiggini was held in high regard by his contemporary, the esteemed scholar Hayyim Joseph David Azulai, and was praised in Ghirondi and Neppi's nineteenth-century biographical dictionary as "both a genuine master of halakhic argumentation and a great decisor."[7] No doubt local pride was at play in the obituary in *Osservatore Triestino*, which acclaimed Formiggini as

> the most erudite Rabbi of Italy, such that there were none who dared oppose his teachings and theological decisions. From the most distant areas the scholars of the Nation joined in consulting the sage on the most abstruse questions of religious practice and theory.[8]

Yet Formiggini's literary remains are few: essentially a few halakhic rulings included in others' works, some still in manuscript. Widely known were his rulings on shaving during the intermediate days of festivals and on Wessely's educational reforms. His ruling on shaving, published in the third volume of the encyclopedia *Pahad Yitzhak*, upheld the traditional prohibition in direct rebuttal to Rabbi Ezekiel Landau's revolutionary permission for such shaving, which cited contemporary fashions. Without digressing on extra-halakhic subjects, Formiggini tended to concentrate on halakhic issues by examining the views of the classic authorities, and occasionally those of later scholars, among them Haham Zevi (Zevi Hirsch b. Jacob Ashkenazi) and Samuel b. Moses Kalai of Salonica. That Formiggini saw himself as a traditionalist was evident in his maintaining the prohibition on shaving, and in his castigating Landau for "contradicting the words of all the sages of Israel which are fixed in . . . truth and righteousness."[9] And his attempt to mediate between Wessely and his opponents showed him to be an Italian traditionalist, representing the Italian Jewish tradition's advocacy of both intellectual diversity and adherence to ritual law.

In Trieste itself, Formiggini provided the most active rabbinic leadership the community had yet known, helping to shape and stabilize its developing institutions. Shortly after his arrival, he was involved in drafting the communal statute of 1766. He was instrumental in strengthening the formal role of the community in settling disputes; indeed, the only period in which the Jews of Trieste had any formal authority for adjudicating minor civil matters as a court of first instance was during his tenure as rabbi. In 1776–77, Formiggini led the community in committing to writing its synagogal procedures and customs.[10] In 1781–82, he helped establish the new *Scuola Pia Normale sive Talmud Torà*.

None of Formiggini's contracts with the community are extant, but the communal statutes of 1766, 1771, and 1783 yield some information about the rabbinical post itself during his tenure. In 1766, the community institutionalized the signing of a written contract between community and rabbi. Around that time, the increased size of the community necessitated the creation of new posts—chancellor or secretary, and assistant rabbi—which released the official rabbi from certain administrative duties. Isach Luzzatto served as assistant rabbi for approximately four decades, until his death in 1806.[11]

Throughout the period, the rabbi's prime responsibility was as ritual and spiritual guardian, superintending the observance of religious rite and law by Jews in the synagogues, in confraternal associations, and in the community and city at large. The *Regolamento* of 1783 explained:

> It will . . . necessarily be the chief duty of our most excellent rabbi and his assistant to supervise with the greatest care and diligence, inculcating and promoting the correct practice of our dogma and rites, and redressing transgressions, suggesting at the same time to the *Capi*, that they go on to authorize the suitable correction.[12]

"Suggesting" was just the right word, for the rabbi was clearly subject to lay control. Though the Statute of 1771 stated that the rabbi's voice would be decisive in matters of "religion, or rite, or interdiction from sacred services," he was, like rabbis in most other communities, dependent upon the lay leaders to impose the punishments he recommended.[13] Indeed, it appears that the rabbi was not always present when the *Capi* took testimony from accused transgressors or determined the appropriate punishment. And not surprisingly, the *Capi* did not always impose the precise punishment urged by the rabbi. For example, in 1771, when David Gattegno was charged with having eaten nonkosher food in public, Formiggini urged that he be confined to his home for three days and undergo public humiliation in the synagogue—confess his sin and ask for forgiveness. But the *Capi* forced Gattegno only to sign declarations of contrition to be posted in the synagogues.[14] Thus, the rabbi had overall responsibility for the observance of Jewish law and his was the single most important voice in judging violations, but he was dependent for enforcement upon the lay leadership of the community. He could define observance and transgression, but he could not alone determine or execute punishment. In general, during Formiggini's term as rabbi, as during others' in Trieste, his main resource was moral suasion rather than formal judicial authority.

The statutes also outlined the rabbi's duties as public preacher and educator.[15] According to the Statute of 1771, he was supposed to examine the public teachers as part of the hiring process, monitor the conduct of the public and private teachers, and report regularly on the various classes and teachers. Before and after the founding of the *Scuola Pia Normale*, Rabbi Formiggini offered instruction. The *Regolamento* of 1783 made explicit the link between religion, education, and morality, and declared that all three intertwined were the proper object of the rabbi's concern. Moreover, it framed his responsibility for these last two areas in terms of the government's vital interest in the "sound education" of the young: since the new school was subject to government supervision, it was the duty of the rabbi and his assistant to superintend the school in such a way as to ensure its success, which was

> inseparable from that sound [and] instructive moral preaching that from time to time they ought to spread among the Nation in order to instill in [their] hearts the sentiments of probity, according to the duties of humanity and . . . the rules of sound moral philosophy, [which is] the guide of honest conduct and master of life.[16]

Thus the *Regolamento* of 1783 expressed the community's awareness of the state's growing interest in the rabbi as religious-moral educator and guide (or *geistlicher Beamte* [spiritual official], to use the early nineteenth-century German terminology). In the late eighteenth and early nineteenth centuries, the concern of modernizing European states for Jewish civic education led naturally to concern with rabbis, specifically with their qualifications and their communal roles. The state's paramount interest was in ensuring that rabbis be capable of instilling the proper civic-moral training and social discipline. Eventually in 1820, the Habsburg state made philosophical training mandatory for rabbis, the step that led to the founding of the first modern rabbinical seminary in Padua in the late 1820s.[17] But long before, in the late eighteenth century, the state began assigning civil tasks to rabbis. In the 1780s, the state made the rabbi's officiating at wedding ceremonies a requirement for a legal marriage, and in the early 1790s, it charged the communal rabbi with keeping the official population registers.[18] In both instances, the state was in effect making the rabbi a civil functionary or servant. The very beginning of this process is discernible in the *Regolamento* of 1783.

When Rabbi Isach Formiggini died in July 1788, the Jews of Trieste lost a distinguished communal leader. His funeral was attended by the entire Jewish community and many Gentiles. He was praised for his qualities of humility, piety, and forbearance in the face of personal tragedy, the untimely deaths of his son, daughter, and sons-in-law. The *Ghemilut Hazadìm* society compared him to Abraham and Job, while the obituary in *Osservatore Triestino* highlighted his "firm constancy and religious resignation, which characterize the true Philosopher and the deeply devout spirit."[19] When Capriles had died in 1765, Triestine Jewish leaders had notified only seven other communities; now in 1788, they sent word of their rabbi's death to twenty-five communities—in Italy, along the Dalmatian coast, and in central Europe—thus reflecting the greater stature of Rabbi Formiggini himself, and the growth and expanded horizons of the Jewish community of Trieste.

The community now found qualified personnel within its own midst: Isach Luzzatto and Vidal Benjamin Segre shared duties as assistant rabbis,[20] and Raffael Nathan b. Rabbi Isaac Tedesco (Ashkenazy), residing in Trieste since 1783, now became the community's rabbi. The Veronese native was related by marriage to Rabbi Formiggini and was a cousin of the communal leader Isaia Norsa. In Trieste, he had already served as teacher and director of the religious section of the *Scuola Pia Normale*, as rabbi of the community's second synagogue, and as coadjutor of Formiggini. He held the post of chief rabbi, *rabbino maggiore*, until his death in January 1800.[21]

Of Tedesco's early life, it is known that he was born around 1750, taught in Verona in the mid- to late 1770s, and received rabbinic ordination from his teacher, the scholar-poet Rabbi Israel Benjamin Bassan of Reggio, in 1780–81.[22] Instrumental in bringing the relatively young Tedesco to Trieste in 1783 was his student Joseph Eliezer Morpurgo, later to be an important Jewish communal leader, lover of Hebrew literature, and Triestine insurance magnate.[23]

Later accounts acclaimed Tedesco as a "worthy successor to Formiggini by virtue of his vast knowledge and dignified manner," and the period of his rabbinate as the "golden age" of Triestine Jewry.[24] During his tenure, the Jewish community virtually doubled in size and greatly expanded its religious institutions. Tedesco presided over the construction of the Sefardic "Synagogue no. 3" and the renovated Ashkenazic "Synagogue no. 2" in the same building, apparently playing an important role in smoothing initial tensions between the diverse Jewish groups, for his tombstone read:

> How good it is to dwell together
> two brothers in the home of goodness
> he brought forth peace, how great its virtue,
> between different rites.[25]

Indeed, peacemaking was stipulated as a duty in his 1793 contract; besides serving as religious judge, he was supposed to exercise his moral authority as "minister of peace" to mediate quarrels within families and the community.[26]

Tedesco earned praise first and foremost as a teacher and preacher. The poet Isaac Luzzatto called him "the first among teachers."[27] The later scholar Vittorio Castiglioni cited the Triestine chronicler Giuseppe Mainati paying tribute to him thus:

In this period Rabbi Raffael Nathan Tedesco, native of Verona, gave great luster to the Jewish Community. To his vast erudition in sacred literature [were] joined great oratorical talents, so that his sermons, by their depth of thought and purity of language, were always listened to with keenest interest.[28]

Ghirondi and Neppi also praised his oratorical skills:

With eloquent and winning words, he raised the banner of the Torah in his pleasing sermons full of wisdom, knowledge, and fear of God. And he sanctified the Name of Heaven among the nations since he was learned in different languages, to the degree that the Emperor and King Joseph II had considered him among the most distinguished preachers in all his realm.[29]

According to his 1793 contract, Tedesco not only superintended the *Scuola Pia Normale*, but also taught both youngsters and adults daily, offering one hour of moral instruction and a lesson on "Halakhah or other sacred study" mornings and evenings in the synagogue. He was also obliged to deliver sermons on eight specified days a year, such as the second day of *Rosh Hashanah* and *Shabbat Hagadol*, and on other occasions, such as funerals, as deemed necessary by the *Capi*.[30] Indeed, the literary works of Tedesco highlighted his activities as consummate teacher and preacher. As mentioned above, he composed the ethical drama *Indagine di qual sia tra i morali mali il peggiore: Accademico gareggiamento scolastico* for his students to recite in public in March 1786. In his discussion of the seven vices, Tedesco cited the Bible, *Pirkei Avot* (Ethics of the Fathers), and Greco-Roman history and literature (e.g., Sparta, Athens, Alexander the Great, Ovid, and Seneca). So pleased with the efforts of "the enlightened rabbi" and his students were the school directors Grassin Vita di Caliman Levi and David d'Isach Treves that they paid for publication of the drama by the government press.[31]

Tedesco's two elegies for the sovereigns Joseph and Leopold, published by the government press in 1790 and 1792 respectively, earned him renown among Gentiles as well as Jews. In these elegies, he lauded Joseph's "wise laws of tolerance in conformance with the spirit of right reason, and moreover with the laws of humanity and of God," and Leopold's "firm consolidation of the sacred Laws of Tolerance," which permitted all to enjoy "golden equality."[32] For Leopold, he used the Biblical verse, "Justice and Peace have kissed" (Psalms 85:11).

While chief rabbi in Trieste, Tedesco enjoyed a close relationship with the local bishop, Sigismond Hohenwart. Again citing Mainati, Castigioni wrote: "He [Tedesco] was a friend of Monsignor Hohenwart, bishop of Trieste, whom he would go especially to visit, thereby edifying the population with the good harmony and mutual esteem that reigned between the two venerable pastors."[33] Even after Hohenwart's departure from Trieste in 1794 to assume a higher post in Vienna, Tedesco sought his advice on how to handle some delicate negotiations with the central administration. Hohenwart's response displayed an unusual degree of tolerance and collegiality, for he advised Tedesco to stand on his right to "be considered like any other Parish Priest, Predicant, and Minister of Religion."[34]

In the early 1790s, the Jewish community formally gave the chief rabbi a consultative vote in the choice of officiants for the synagogues and school, and obliged him to submit his opinions in writing when requested by the *Capi* or Small Council. At that time, the state charged him to keep the civil registry of births and deaths, as well as to maintain responsibility for Jewish marriages and divorces.[35] Though not formally obliged to do so, the rabbi also translated Hebrew documents for the government.[36] Insofar as Tedesco was treated as a quasi–civil servant, and valued more for teaching and preaching than for halakhic decising, he represented the modern type of rabbi evolving in central and western Europe.

Tedesco tried once to turn the government's increasing involvement to his own advantage. In July 1792, a few months after confirmation of the communal statute that had declared the official rabbi's contract valid for five years as always, Tedesco took a highly unusual step: he appealed to the governor for "gracious and sovereign confirmation" of his position as rabbi in Trieste. He argued that it would benefit the Jewish community to have its rabbi "recognized also with public authority" and "his concerns and directions for morality and behavior" enjoy "greater, also external authority."[37] Governor Brigido solicited the opinion of the *Capi*, and upon their negative response, he rejected Tedesco's proposal, affirming that confirmation and dismissal of the rabbi were dependent upon the "free will" of the community, and that he would not now contravene their expressed will. Thus the local government refused this opportunity to get more involved in the community's pulpit.

Tedesco's career in Trieste, and indeed his very life, ended on a note of tragedy. Tedesco's authority in the community was said to be great, the proof being that his call for a communal day of fasting and prayer, with no reason given, was readily obeyed.[38] But in fact, a very radical challenge to his authority was presented by one of the lay leaders of the community in the late 1790s. The details of this incident will be discussed in Chapter Eight on their own terms. When Tedesco died in January 1800 at the relatively young age of fifty, rumors swirled that it was the pain of this challenge that caused his premature death. A lithograph of Tedesco inscribed after his death read:

> This is Nathan, the divine Orator, the strong
> Faithful Pastor, whose sincere Piety
> Was manifest in life and triumphant in death
> And he ended his days prematurely.[39]

Raffael Nathan Tedesco lived on in his community's memory as a distinguished, tragic, and beloved figure.

In the fourteen months that the community searched for a new rabbi, the schoolteacher Angelo (Mordecai) Isach Cologna of Mantua, resident in Trieste since 1798, and the long-serving Isach Luzzatto functioned as assistant rabbis. It was Cologna whom Samuel David Luzzatto credited with awakening his own love for the study of Hebrew grammar.[40] The community chose the esteemed halakhist and preacher Isach Raffael Finzi of Padua, but the seventy-two-year-old Finzi eventually declined the post for reasons of health.[41] The community next approached Abram Eliezer b. Rabbi Zevi Levi, the Jerusalem-born son of a distinguished Italian rabbinic family, who was living in Livorno.[42] Levi accepted, and served as chief rabbi of Trieste from 1802 until his death in 1825.

Levi's career in Trieste goes beyond the chronological limits of this study, but a brief sketch of him is in order since a number of late-eighteenth-century developments came to a head during his rabbinate. Born in Jerusalem in the 1750s, Levi studied as a very young boy with the distinguished Hayyim Joseph David Azulai. He served as an emissary for Safed and Jerusalem in both German and Italian communities and then settled in Livorno. There he acquired his knowledge of Italian, which he was said to have spoken with "rare grace" as a skilled preacher.[43] Though approximately the same age as his predecessor Tedesco, Levi cut quite a different figure: in contrast to Tedesco's clean-shaven face and fashionable Western garb and headgear, Levi continued to dress in Oriental robes throughout his tenure in Trieste. Samuel David Luzzatto, who studied Talmud with him for five years, depicted him on the one hand as "lacking in European culture," and on the other as "profound and very sharp in *pilpul* [halakhic argumentation], but it was a straightforward *pilpul*, never sophistical, as indeed his religiosity was austere but heartfelt."[44] This halakhist and dedicated teacher was indeed a traditionalist. In Trieste he helped establish the *Medrash Lecah tov* study society, and took his role as religious guardian seriously, trying, as we shall see below, to strengthen observance of Jewish law. Beyond Trieste, he enjoyed a considerable reputation, and when asked, he joined forces with—indeed, played a leading role among—other traditionalist rabbis in fighting the nascent Reform movement in the second decade of the nineteenth century. The well-known Hatam Sofer, himself on his way to becoming an architect of modern Ashkenazic Orthodoxy, hailed Levi as a *gaon* (genius). Some of Levi's halakhic and polemical correspondence with Italian, German, and Hungarian rabbis was published in others' works.[45]

Thus, from the mid-1760s to the mid-1820s, three relatively distinguished individuals—Formiggini, Tedesco, and Levi—occupied the rabbinate of the Triestine Jewish community. In the mold of traditional rabbis, Formiggini and Levi enjoyed stronger reputations as halakhists, whereas Tedesco was better-known for his gifts as orator and pedagogue and seemed to represent a more modern type of rabbi. It is perhaps ironic that although all three exerted themselves to guide Triestine Jews along the paths of Halakhah, it was Tedesco who, as we shall see below, emerged as a tragic figure for his efforts to uphold traditional Jewish marriage law in the face of internal and external challenges.

Communal Regulation: Public Piety and Transgression

In their regulation and discipline of public piety, Triestine Jewish authorities concerned themselves primarily with violations of ritual law regarding kosher food, and Sabbaths and festivals. They also took action against individuals who were disorderly in the synagogues or other communal institutions. They usually employed internal methods such as reprimands, fines, demands for public apologies and penitence, and denial of religious and communal services. In extreme cases, involving disobedience in the synagogue, the eating of food in a public inn on *Yom Kippur*, and unspecified acts of "religious transgression" causing "public scandal," they resorted to external measures: handing the wrongdoer over to the local police and civil authorities.[46] (Conversely, Jewish leaders sometimes interceded with the local authorities on behalf of individual Jews who had been apprehended for civil offenses, for example, asking that Jewish prisoners be released during Jewish holidays.[47]) Theoretically, the community's right to punish transgressors included imposing the ultimate sanction of excommunication, though there appears to be no instance of its use during this period.[48]

In practice, concern for observance of the dietary laws meant regulating the slaughter, inspection, and sale of kosher meat. From the time of its formal constitution in 1746, the community had an appointed *shohet* (ritual slaughterer).[49] When in 1749–50 it was unable to evaluate a candidate's qualifications for that post because there was no rabbi to examine him, the Jewish leaders sent the candidate to be evaluated by the Venetian rabbis.[50] When Hayyim Joseph David Azulai visited Trieste in January–February 1777, he had no hesitation about eating meals—specifically meat—in the homes of communal leaders. And, as we know from the account of his stay in Bordeaux in 1755, he did not refrain from expressing doubts about *kashrut* when he had them.[51] However, Samuel David Luzzatto reported that his father Hezekiah, who arrived in Trieste around the same time, so disapproved of the ways in which kosher meat was slaughtered and sold that he never ate beef, and only occasionally chicken, in Trieste.[52] Over the years, the community issued various ordinances, warnings, and reprimands in the attempt to ensure the monopoly and propriety of the ritual slaughterer, insisting that Jews buy their meat only from him, and that all his procedures be in order.[53]

Toward the end of the 1790s, "disorders" in the communal slaughterhouse and butchery seemed especially grave. Rabbi Tedesco issued specific instructions and warnings to the slaughterers in 1796 and again in 1798.[54] Upon his arrival in Trieste in December 1800, Rabbi Levi noted his predecessor's dissatisfaction and described the situation as one of "total lack of order in the communal slaughterhouse concerning the religious aspect, with regard to slaughtering, inspecting, purging, and watching."[55] Since responsibility for selling was then taken away from the slaughterer, it seems likely that a conflict of interest was now perceived between slaughtering and selling. A year or so later, Rabbi Levi became so exercised by the eating of unauthorized meat that he threatened to break his connection with the community unless the practice was halted.[56] It is difficult to know whether the practice really was becoming more widespread, or if Levi, the sternly traditional newcomer, was determined to combat existing shortcomings more effectively than his predecessor had. In any case, Levi did not act upon his threat.

Concerns about other foods, such as *matzot* (unleavened bread) for Passover and cheese, were voiced through the years,[57] but the issue that most consistently preoccupied communal leaders was the handling of food by Gentiles. In line with halakhic regulations, they repeatedly warned Jews not to let Gentile servants get for the household food whose *kashrut* they might compromise, such as cheese, fats, and especially meat. They warned Jews not to send their Gentile servants to get animals slaughtered or to pick up meat unless they were accompanied by a Jew, and they instructed the *shohet* not to do business with unaccompanied Gentile servants. But the frequent repetition of such instructions indicates that the Jews of Trieste continued to charge their Gentile servants with these marketing duties.[58] Indeed, in 1801 the authorities complained that some Gentile servants were getting meat for their Jewish employers from Gentile butchers, perhaps, they added, without their employers' knowledge.[59] At the same time, parents were warned not to send food to their children in school with Gentile servants unless its *kashrut* was clearly indicated and its packaging secure: both parents and teachers were urged to exercise vigilance so that the innocent children might not inadvertently eat forbidden foods.[60]

Other grounds for concern arose from the fact that Jews frequented Gentile eating-places near the ghetto, for recreation as well as for nourishment. In 1771, the community enacted a regulation prohibiting the eating of a particular kind of sweet that they declared to be nonkosher. In December of that year, Rabbi Formiggini informed the *Capi* and the Small Council in writing that David Gattegno had been observed publicly violating this communal ordinance. The lay leaders accepted Gattegno's plea of ignorance: he claimed that he was unaware of the ordinance and had thought the biscuits to be kosher, as they had been so considered in the past. As mentioned above, the Jewish leaders punished him less severely than the rabbi had urged.[61] But Gattegno was clearly not the only Jew in Trieste to disregard this ordinance. In 1784, it was reissued with explicit admission of the oblivion into which it had fallen. The Jews of Trieste were implored to "adopt immediately the old custom of abstaining from and not eating" these foods, and to eat only permissible ones, such as almonds.[62] It is difficult to know whether habits were really changing, or past behavior nostalgically idealized. One final example of the risks of Gentile establishments: in 1801, Jews were warned not to eat chickens or other animals they might win there as gambling spoils![63]

Communal authorities were concerned with public observance of Sabbaths, holidays, and fast days. In 1785, the *Capi* and Rabbi Formiggini informed the community of the halakhic implications for Sabbath observance of the abolition of the ghetto, and thereby signaled their intention that the end of the ghetto should not mean relaxation of religious norms. To allow carrying on the Sabbath, an *eruv* (symbolic encirclement) was set up, but in 1801 Rabbi Levi stated that it was insufficient because it applied only to those who lived inside the area of the former ghetto. He ordered that those who lived beyond that area should follow the others' example and set up their own *eruv*.[64] In 1790, the *Capi* requested from the local government that in accordance with the religious freedom they legally enjoyed, no Jew be summoned to court or other civil duties on Sabbaths and festivals.[65] Local officials did not accept the word of the pharmacist Samuel Coen Mondovi in 1797 when he claimed to have obtained an exemption from the usual prohibition against work on Sabbaths and festivals. The officials insisted on an affidavit from Rabbi Tedesco, who refused to provide one.[66] When Rabbi Tedesco reminded the community orally on *Shabbat Shuvah* (Sabbath of Repentance) of 1794 and then later in writing of the importance of proper Sabbath observance, he warned the busy Jewish merchants of Trieste specifically against discussing business, and sending or receiving merchandise.[67]

The community did punish people for public violations of the Sabbath and festivals. In 1790, the beadle had the police arrest two North African Jews who were seen in a public drinking-house on *Yom Kippur*.[68] The following year, three Jews were brought before the *Capi* after two other Jews reported to the rabbi that they had seen them playing billiards and exchanging money in a Gentile eating establishment on the Sabbath. After admitting their transgressions, the three were compelled to donate candles to the synagogue and money for the poor as penitence.[69] In 1791, just a couple of weeks after Rabbi Tedesco's reminder, Jacob Benjamin Levi of Bozzolo was chastised by the rabbi and the *Capi* for having written on the Sabbath, and was informed that he would be kept from synagogue services until further notice. When Levi then acknowledged his sin in writing and stated that he was ready to undergo any penance prescribed by the authorities, they decided to let him publicly request forgiveness in the synagogue and donate a candle.[70] In 1804, six youths, two of them apparently foreigners, were charged with riding in a carriage and frequenting a public inn on a festival, "public religious scandals" considered so severe that the *Capi* turned to the Gentile authorities to request appropriate punishment.[71]

The problem of Gentiles' working for Jews on the Sabbath came up frequently. In June 1784, Rabbi Formiggini had issued a proclamation instructing Triestine Jews that henceforth all contracts with Gentile workmen should contain written stipulations prohibiting their doing any construction work on Sabbaths and festivals.[72] What occasioned it was the case of Isach Morpurgo, who had raised the matter with his Gentile contractor only after they had signed a contract. The contractor refused at that point to stop work on those days, despite Morpurgo's offer of monetary compensation. Morpurgo then turned to Rabbi Formiggini and donated that money for pious works, in effect as a fine. Formiggini cast the opening of the proclamation thus: anyone seeing the work in progress on the Morpurgo property on Sabbaths and festivals should not be "scandalized" because of the special circumstances then explained. This phrasing and Morpurgo's turn to the rabbi suggest that Jewish opinion in Trieste in the mid-1780s would not have countenanced this kind of public desecration of the Sabbath. Yet, it is also possible that this reading of public opinion more reflected Formiggini's hopes than social reality. Just after the turn of the century and Rabbi Levi's arrival in Trieste, the issue was raised repeatedly. Levi delivered written warnings about the matter in 1802, 1804, 1806, and 1807, the last two times republishing Formiggini's proclamation. Obviously it was an ongoing problem, but some discipline was still exercised in the first years of the nineteenth century, as individuals were brought before communal authorities and fined for this violation.[73]

The later case of Moses Ventura of Correggio in 1815 is revealing of continuing norms and sensibilities, and of challenges to them. After having lived in Trieste but a short time, Ventura was observed eating nonkosher food in public, and also paying money in the post office on the Sabbath when collecting a letter for another Jew. What especially galled communal authorities, no doubt, was his response when reproved by his Jewish companions: "That's the way things are done here."[74] With these dismissive words, Ventura refused to acknowledge traditional norms or to accept the definition of his action as a transgression. He justified his action in terms of local habit. In fact, the other Jews with him at the time were dismayed by his behavior and reported it promptly to communal leaders. Because of Ventura's openly contemptuous attitude and in order to "put some brake upon others who may exist,"[75] they took a very grave view of the offense, and appealed to the civil authorities to expel Ventura. The civil authorities in turn upheld the right of the *Capi* to punish Ventura for his violation of a "religion [which is] tolerated and guaranteed by the paternal laws," but thought that a single commission of this sin, no matter how serious, was not sufficient to justify his expulsion.[76]

One other aspect of holiday observance—the prohibition against shaving during the intermediate days of festivals—shows changing habits and tactics of response. In October 1794, Rabbi Tedesco unearthed from the communal archives a copy of Formiggini's *pesak*, which upheld the traditional prohibition against Ezekiel Landau's opinion permitting it, and issued it publicly in the two synagogues. His stated purpose was to shore up the prohibition, which, he claimed, had always been observed in Trieste and in all Italian communities, and to impress upon the youth the gravity of transgression and its punishment, to be "cut off from everything holy."[77] For the benefit of the youth, he translated a portion of Formiggini's *pesak* into Italian. He stated that he did not doubt observance of the prohibition in Trieste, but intended solely to strengthen current practice. But he would not have issued the proclamation if he had not witnessed deviation from the norm and considered it important to restate the legal norm. Only two weeks later, a young man of the community was punished for shaving during *Sukkot*: he was forced to stay in his house on the Sabbath and holidays, confess his transgression and promise not to do it again, and undergo some other unspecified penance.[78] But that proclamation and that punishment were not sufficient to deter others. The tone was slightly different when Assistant Rabbi Angelo Isach Cologna and the *Capi* issued a similar proclamation in October 1800.[79] They warned that anyone who transgressed in this regard, whether knowingly or unknowingly, should stay away from the community's four synagogues on the three festival days from *Hoshanah Rabba* through *Simhat Torah* lest he cause public scandal and draw upon himself the justified censure and "vigorous" action of the community. They stated that the sanctity of the synagogue must be preserved by complete adherence to all divine prescriptions. Accordingly, they also instructed the leaders of the four synagogues not to permit entry to transgressors of this prohibition, for they wanted to avoid scandals and the setting of bad examples for others. Again in March 1801, just before Passover, the *Capi* and Rabbi Levi issued basically the same proclamation, with the same request that transgressors stay away from the synagogues.[80]

The proclamations of 1800 and 1801 show the efforts of communal leaders to maintain a religious norm that was being increasingly disregarded in practice. In effect, they were recognizing that more and more people were not observing the prohibition against shaving. Though they stated that transgressors would be punished—by appropriately "vigorous" action— that was not the thrust of their warning. They really were asking the transgressors to dissociate themselves voluntarily and temporarily from the law-abiding community so that the law-abiding community would not have to be troubled by them. This was a tacit admission that it would be difficult, if not futile, to punish all transgressors as they had that particular individual in 1794. It signaled a retreat in two senses: a retreat from supervising all public Triestine Jewish conduct according to Halakhah, and a retreat into the synagogue as the preserve of sanctity, as the place to stand firm because of its primary sacred purpose.

But it is important to note that the retreat was neither full nor hasty: Rabbi Levi did publicly grant permission to shave to Jewish members of the Municipal Council during the French occupations in 1805–6 and 1809, but with the express caveat that these circumstances and this allowance constituted an exception to the norm and should set no precedent whatsoever.[81] Apparently some people were upset by this departure from Rabbi Formiggini's ruling; the warning in the proclamations of 1800 and 1801 about "vigorous" action on the part of community members may not have been an idle one.

While the issue of shaving offers the clearest evidence of changing religious practice and attitudes in Trieste at the end of the eighteenth century, other pieces of allusive but fragmentary evidence are consistent with it. Considered chronologically, they suggest growing discomfort on the part of Jewish authorities with regard to the public observance of Jewish law.

In 1785, when the ghetto was formally abolished, Marco Levi had voiced the fear that religion was "almost tottering" because of ever-increasing "disorders," which he attributed to "enlightened liberty, and depravity."[82] In 1792, Rabbi Tedesco made his surprising request for governmental confirmation of his position so that his "concerns and directions for morality and behavior" would enjoy "greater, also external authority."[83] In 1795, Raffael Verona complained that grave "disorders" introduced in the synagogue threatened the very "maintenance of religion."[84] In the late 1790s, the community was faced with three cases—the pharmacist Coen Mondovi, and the Luzzatto-Pardo and Frizzi-Morschene marriages (to be discussed in detail in Chapter Eight)—in which individuals tried to gain sanction from the government for their own interpretations of Jewish law that ran counter to traditional norms. In February 1800, two foreign Jews, one from North Africa and the other from Prague, were described by Chief of Police Pittoni in a letter to the governor as leading "a scandalous way of life without professing true Religion, and even though Jews, not attending synagogues."[85] In September 1800, the community sent Stella Morpurgo back to her native Gradisca at their own expense because of unspecified "intolerable religious scandals."[86]

In 1801, the newly serving Rabbi Levi felt that people were not respecting his authority when he ruled against importing *matzot* because Triestine Jews would not know how the *matzot* had been made.[87] In March 1802, as mentioned above, he threatened to resign if stricter control were not exercised over meat-buying.[88] Two months later, he took the highly unusual step of appearing at a meeting of the Small Council in order to make an impassioned plea about the absolute necessity of religious fidelity and the gravity of the current situation:

How can we stand idly by while we see a few wretches scorn and trample upon [our religion]? . . .
    The danger has become extreme . . . our very existence . . . is at stake. . . .
    The shield of our people through its centuries-long existence . . . has been . . .

our constant determination to prevent the contamination of sound habits and to correct those individuals infected and contagious with danger and scandal, in order to stem evil and halt its spread. Nowadays we no longer declare that actions taken without regard for the deadly consequences of a momentary convenience . . . cause the distinction between the good and the wicked to be lost. . . .

Now are you surprised if these few miserable youths, raised and nurtured in the most profound ignorance of all the duties of social man, who constantly defame religion in public, not only with rebellious discourses but also with harmful deeds, are you surprised, I say, if they tempt the other youths, innocent and inexperienced?[89]

He urged the establishment of a committee to whom he would communicate the relevant information about the "eminent danger"; he hoped that it would propose the "necessary and indispensable measures" for the "preservation of religion and of good customs" and for "common salvation."[90] The *Capi* seemed to consider Levi's outburst not merely hyberbolic rabbinic hand-wringing, and they authorized him to set up a committee to address the matter.

In September 1802, communal leaders reiterated in detail the procedures to be followed in disciplining people, either foreigners or permanent residents, who might "show themselves profligate, and with scandal alter in the smallest way the exercise of religion . . . offending rite, dogma, and good morality."[91] They emphasized the link between Jewish religious observance and public morality. For example, when Rabbi Levi issued reminders about the upcoming fast of the tenth of Tevet in 1802 and 1803, he stressed the need to avoid "public religious scandals," stating that since the government was concerned with religious observance in general, dishonorable behavior in public eating-places would constitute violation both of "our holy religion" and of "the proper respect for public decency."[92] Wishing to remind Jews that the government stood behind the community's leaders in their efforts to enforce Jewish law, he employed the notion of public decency in order to convey the idea that there was a perceived connection between being an observant Jew and being a good subject. A Jew who publicly flaunted his disregard of religion would be suspect both to the community and to outside authorities as a disobedient law-breaker. Indeed, in January 1804, the *Capi* advised the community that the police had been authorized by governing officials to watch out for "scandals involving religion and public order."[93] In October 1804, communal leaders turned to the civil authorities for punishment of six youths whose behavior (unfortunately unspecified) had caused "public religious scandals."[94] Two months later, the *Capi* again appointed a committee at the rabbi's urging to consider "abuses introduced in our religion with public scandal."[95]

Many of the foregoing incidents and charges are too vague to permit either detailed analysis of the particulars or generalization about religious observance and authority. Methodological caution is in order for the use of all these sources. For example, statements by individuals—such as Marco Levi, or the *Capi*, who, by contrast, claimed they and Rabbi Formiggini believed that most Jews in Trieste did "observe perfectly the rites of religion"[96]—are not reliable indicators of the extent of observance, or of laxity, indifference, or rebelliousness within the community. Communal ordinances and specific instances of punishment of transgressors are also problematic. Communal warnings against a particular practice restate the halakhic norm, and repetition of the warning reveals its recurrent violation. But neither communal ordinances nor particular cases of transgression convey the frequency or valence of disobedience: did but a few individuals or a substantial proportion of the community deviate from the norms? Furthermore, earlier sources do not exist to permit a comparison of late-eighteenth-century violations with past behavior in order to determine innovation or continuity. Finally, the reports usually yield no information about the attitude of the transgressor, whether he acted for reasons of convenience or even sheer indifference, or rather believed in new values or ideologies that challenged the very system of halakhic regulation. This last point is critical for the evaluation of overall change or continuity of religious norm and practice. For inobservance or laxity was not necessarily a challenge to authority. Every Jewish community in every time and place has had its share of individuals who sometimes failed to observe Jewish law. That in and of itself hardly meant that such individuals were trying to upset the framework of traditional authority. The transgressor who acknowledged his sin and accepted his punishment had a familiar niche in traditional society.

The evidence shows that most problems dealt with by the Jewish leaders of Trieste in the second half of the eighteenth century were fairly standard ones encountered in most Jewish communities. Yet, despite the foregoing caveats, the accumulation of charges in the last years of the eighteenth and the first years of the nineteenth centuries suggests a sense of unease and crisis on the part of the communal and especially rabbinic leadership of Trieste. The difficulty lies in interpreting this mood and its causes. Was the behavior of Triestine Jews significantly changing? Or was it being evaluated according to new and stricter standards because of other changing circumstances? Was ritual laxity perceived as more dangerous when other economic, social, and civil barriers for Jews were lessening in Trieste, and when the 1790s generally brought revolutionary turmoil, ferment, and instability? Did the occupation of Trieste by French troops in March–May 1797 indirectly cause Jewish leaders to try to shore up established authority?[97] Was the alarm of Rabbi Abram Eliezer Levi simply that of a newcomer coming from different milieux, originally from the eastern Mediterranean and then Livorno? Or was it indicative of a growing gap between legal prescription and social-religious practice, between rabbinate and laity, which would come increasingly to characterize Italian Jewish communities in subsequent years? To what extent did the lay leaders of the community share his sense of urgency? Was their establishment of committees in response to his requests an indication of their concern and desire for remedial action, or was it a tactic to placate him?

At this stage, it is impossible to answer all these questions. But it seems fair to conclude that the sense of unease was not Levi's alone. Other communal authorities did seem genuinely concerned. The approach they took to the problem of shaving on intermediate days of festivals in 1800–1801 as opposed to the tack they took in 1794 shows a grudging recognition of change that they could not control. It seems that certain patterns of observance of Jewish law were weakening in late-eighteenth-century Trieste. Spurred partially by the dynamics of increasing economic, civil, and social integration in the free port, such changes occurred in Trieste without much ideological justification.[98] Yet, however uneasy about their authority with regard to public piety, Jewish leaders generally felt that they enjoyed governmental support for their efforts at religious discipline. As Chapter Eight will show, it took two "dangerous liaisons" in the late 1790s to show them not only the promise but also the peril of civil inclusion.

CHAPTER EIGHT

The Habsburg Marriage Reforms: Challenges to Religious-Communal Authority

The community's regulation of the public observance of Jewish law was challenged in the late 1790s in an unprecedented way. Though the legislation of the mid-1780s had theoretically left religious affairs within the hands of the community, and the government usually backed the community in enforcing religious discipline, the state and the Jewish community in the late 1790s locked horns over the very sensitive issue of marriage law. In the mid-1780s, the Habsburg state introduced a civil definition of marriage, a partial step toward the secularization of marriage law. In the late 1790s, certain Jews tried to take advantage of the new Habsburg marriage law in order to legitimize their own behavior, which was deviant according to the normative interpretations of Jewish law. The Triestine Jewish community was then caught in a bitter struggle with both the deviant individuals and the state authorities over the basic issue: to which sphere, civil or religious, did marriage really belong, and which of the two conflicting laws, Jewish or Habsburg, would prevail in these troublesome cases? It was on the sensitive issue of marriage that the Jewish community of Trieste tried to stand its ground on Jewish religious autonomy. The limits of cooperation between the *kehillah kedoshah*, the holy community, and the absolutist Habs-

---

This chapter draws substantially upon my article "Les Liaisons dangereuses: Mariage juif et état moderne à Trieste au XVIIIe siècle," in *Annales: Histoire, sciences sociales* 49, no. 5 (1994): 1139–70. © École des Hautes Études en Sciences Sociales, Paris, 1994. Reprinted with permission.

burg state were reached. The entry of the absolutist state into the realm of religion had at moments seemed promising to the Jewish community of Trieste; now the community became acutely aware of its perils. Like other Jewries in modern times—such as the French and Italian at the Napoleonic Sanhedrin in 1806–7—the Jews of Trieste were uneasy about the intrusion of the state in the domestic and communal realm of marriage and family law.[1] On the highly personal and symbolic issue of marriage, the Jewish community of Trieste resisted the state's efforts to redraw the lines between public and private, civil and religious spheres.

The Habsburg Marriage Patent

The 1783 Habsburg Marriage Patent (*Ehepatent*) and the Civil Code of 1786 introduced a civil definition of marriage and asserted secular jurisdiction over it. Marriage was to be a civil contract whose validity derived from the law of the land, and state courts were to be the only legal forum for resolving disputes about marriage. To be considered legally binding, a marriage required publicity: by prior banns, and the exchange of vows before clergy and witnesses in church. Parental—that is, paternal—consent was essential for minors, those under the age of twenty-four. No civil marriage ceremonies were instituted. Thus the law produced a hybrid: state control of marriage and the definition of marriage as civil, but with religious ceremonies and record-keeping by clergy.[2] As part of the state's efforts to integrate Jews into civil society, these marriage laws were soon applied to Habsburg Jews with obvious changes; for example, a rabbi was substituted for a priest. This application to Jews went hand in hand with the removal of civil matters from Jewish jurisdiction in 1782–85, with only religious matters left as the province of Jewish law.[3] From the state's point of view, Jewish marriage and divorce were now automatically subject to state law and jurisdiction. Yet official policy-makers claimed to respect the religious freedom of the Jews by leaving intact the "religious bond" of Jewish marriage, just as they had the "sacramental bond of Catholics."[4] This claim notwithstanding, civil jurisdiction over marriage did become highly problematic for some Catholic clergy and for Jews.[5]

State interest in defining valid Jewish marriages—and in separating civil from religious—was new and threatening for Habsburg Jews. Previously, the legally autonomous Jewish communities had superintended marriages according to Jewish religious law and custom. Now, despite the assertion of state control, Habsburg Jews continued to consider marriage and divorce as matters of their own still-valid religious law. Initially, Jewish leaders such as Rabbi Ezekiel Landau of Prague did not call attention to the fundamental conflict of laws and perspectives; they merely alerted Habsburg officials to particular instances of conflict between Jewish and state laws (e.g., the age of majority, twenty-four in Habsburg law, basically thirteen in Jewish law). Vienna ignored these warnings, asserting simply that Jews must be subject to the same laws as Christians.[6]

For the Jews of Trieste, the Marriage Patent seemed initially to pose no problems, just as the abrogation of Jewish juridical authority in civil matters had not perturbed them. They complied initially with the procedural requirements of the Marriage Patent: banns, rabbis, public ceremonies, and record-keeping. In 1786, lay leaders—Elia Moise Luzzatto among them—instructed Rabbi Isach Formiggini to observe the "prescribed formalities" so that Jewish marriages would be considered valid civil contracts.[7] In subsequent years, the Jewish community and the local government corresponded frequently about marriage. Their exchanges concerned the exact duties imposed upon the rabbi; the exemption of Triestine Jews from the 1786 decree that made Habsburg Jewish marriages conditional on normal-school attendance (they were exempt because residents of the free port city did not normally need state permission to marry);[8] and dispensations for marriages between relatives whose consanguinity violated civil but not Jewish law. Requesting such dispensations each time on an ad hoc basis proved complicated and irksome, even though Chief of Police Pittoni was usually cooperative. Concerning one such case in 1789, he stated to the governor that Jewish law did not prohibit the particular union between uncle and niece, and that he, Pittoni, was "convinced, that the spirit of true tolerance . . . [does not involve] impeding the tolerated religions [in the practice of] their own customs, their own ceremonies, their own rites."[9] In 1791, in response to Jewish entreaties, the sovereign Leopold relaxed most of the provisions concerning marriage between relatives. The same patent of February 18, 1791, also stipulated that civil confirmation was required to make a Jewish divorce legally valid.[10]

But eventually, in the late 1790s, the fundamental tensions surrounding the Habsburg Marriage Patent surfaced, brought to the fore by the dangerous liaisons of two Jewish couples in Trieste. In August of 1796, Jacob Pardo, a poor clerk in his early twenties, secretly married Corona Luzzatto, the teenage daughter of Elia Moise Luzzatto, a wealthy and influential Triestine merchant, then serving (as he had previously) as one of the *Capi* of the Jewish community. But their union was short-lived, for Corona's father objected. He protested that the customary Jewish ceremony—the groom's reciting the formulaic Hebrew words and placing a ring upon the bride's finger before two lay witnesses—had in this case violated the recently enacted Marriage Patent. Nearly two years later, Benedetto Frizzi, a middle-aged physician and proponent of the Enlightenment, sought to marry Relle (a.k.a. Rachel or Bella) Morschene, daughter of another wealthy merchant and communal leader. Though Jewish law forbade their union—since Frizzi was a *kohen*, a descendant of the ancient Israelite priests, and she a divorcée—the couple argued that it was sanctioned by the Marriage Patent. In both cases, the individuals tried to exploit for their own advantage the differences between Jewish and Habsburg marriage laws. The bitter power struggles concerning these liaisons involved the individuals, their families, the local Jewish community, and Habsburg officials in Trieste and Vienna.

The Luzzatto-Pardo Affair

When Jacob Pardo and Corona Luzzatto were married, the bride's father, Elia Moise Luzzatto, was outraged.[11] As a wealthy and prominent merchant, member of the Triestine *Borsa*, this communal leader was well able to direct his complaints to the city's authorities. He proved that this union violated the 1783 Marriage Patent, for the young couple, both minors, Jacob twenty or twenty-two, Corona only fifteen or sixteen years old, had proceeded without parental consent, banns, clergy, or synagogue. The irate father wanted Pardo, whom he branded a seducer, and his two friends who had served as the accomplices-witnesses to be punished, and the so-called marriage to be declared null and void. Other communal leaders, lay and rabbinic, felt differently. They acknowledged that the state-mandated procedures for marriages had not been followed, and that they would not have sanctioned such a ceremony in advance. But now, the deed done, its validity according to Jewish law could not be denied. Annulment could proceed, they argued, only according to the criteria of Jewish law, not by governmental fiat. They did investigate the possibilities allowed by Jewish law for finding the witnesses unfit and annulling the marriage, but after lengthy consultations with rabbis beyond Trieste, they determined that both the witnesses and the marriage were valid, and Jewish divorce the only possible means of dissolution.[12] However, though forced to step down as *Capo*,[13] Luzzatto *père* continued to demand annulment and would not countenance divorce.

At the police inquiry, Jacob Pardo claimed that he had not in fact seduced Corona Luzzatto, but rather that she had repeatedly declared her love for him during the past year and a half, and that together they had sought her father's approval for their marriage, with this ceremony as their ultimate pressure tactic. In a later deposition, Corona Luzzatto countered that she had always considered her father's consent vital and did not want to proceed without it, moreover that on the fateful day she, "more confused than persuaded," had not fully understood the significance of the Hebrew words of the ceremony, and had not considered them binding. Now she claimed to be no longer "forced or seduced," but rather to be speaking from her "own free and spontaneous desire for the love of truth, and for the peace of her very beloved parents."[14] However, some said that she wrote a love letter to Pardo even after her father had separated them.[15]

Investigations, charges and countercharges, remonstrations and entreaties continued for the next three years. From the outset, local Habsburg officials supported Luzzatto the father: they declared the "clandestine nuptial promise" to have constituted no legally binding marital tie. Because the young couple had violated "the laws [of the state], and the rights of parents," the authorities eventually banished the foreign-born Pardo and the two witnesses from Trieste, while leaving Corona Luzzatto's punishment to her father.[16] But the conflict between the father and the young couple quickly became a conflict between the father and the Jewish community, which then escalated into a confrontation between the state and the Jewish community, especially its rabbi, Raffael Nathan Tedesco. The crux of the matter was the correct understanding and adjudication of marriage, and the proper boundary between civil and religious spheres. Not surprisingly, Vienna ultimately decided in Luzzatto's favor by asserting unequivocally that Jewish marriage law could not overrule the civil law of the monarchy. It seemed that Luzzatto had triumphed: not only did Habsburg authorities declare the would-be marriage invalid and his daughter Corona free to marry another, but they compelled Rabbi Tedesco, on the threat of expulsion from Trieste, to do so as well, and furthermore, to state explicitly that religious scruples would not prevent his officiating at her future wedding. The only indignity spared Tedesco was that he was not forced, as Luzzatto had urged, to put in writing that he made this declaration with a clear conscience. Thus, in its conflict with the state, the Jewish community failed utterly to preserve its prior right of autonomous law and jurisdiction in matters of marriage and divorce.

But though the community was powerless against the state, it was in the end able to prevail over the recalcitrant father. Communal pressure made his stand against a Jewish divorce untenable: the next suitor—whom Luzzatto approved—became wary of marrying a woman of unclear status and bolted. By late 1799, Luzzatto buckled under the pressure, and he allowed his daughter to seek a Jewish writ of divorce (*get*) from the exiled Pardo.[17] It would seem that the immediate problem of Corona Luzzatto had been resolved to the satisfaction of both the state and the Jewish community. As for the two unfortunate lovers, perhaps even they found some happiness: within a few years, each was married to a new spouse, and Pardo was allowed to return to Trieste.[18]

Let us examine further the dynamics and arguments of this case. Corona

Luzzatto and Jacob Pardo were hardly the first young Jewish couple to elope, that is, to marry clandestinely without parental consent, and Elia Moise Luzzatto was hardly the first irate father to try to undo the deeds of impetuous youth. But in the past, such matters had usually been resolved within the parameters of the Jewish community and Jewish law: parents and Jewish authorities agreed that such marriages should not be allowed to stand, and that the safest way to dissolve them was to secure a writ of divorce for the woman. Even in cases where such marriages were actually declared null and void, a formal divorce was mandated in order to preclude any possible doubts about the eligibility of the woman for a future marriage and the legitimate status of her future children.[19] What was new in the Pardo-Luzzatto case was that the father, Elia Moise Luzzatto, refused to play by the old rules. He never explained his adamant opposition to the time-honored remedy of divorce for his daughter: perhaps he felt that divorce would stigmatize his daughter, or perhaps he was bothered by the restrictions in Jewish law that make divorcées ineligible for marriage with priestly descendants (no small matter, as we shall see in the Frizzi-Morschene case). In any event, the 1783 marriage legislation afforded him a different avenue: he could ignore the Jewish community and Halakhah through appeal to the state and civil law. As Triestine Jews were well aware, it was the deviant's refusal to play by the old rules and his forging an alliance with the state that forced the community into a new and difficult position.

At certain moments early in the controversy, Luzzatto appeared to cooperate with other Jewish leaders and to be "respectful of religious sensibilities,"[20] but only as long as he thought they could provide annulment by Jewish law. In most letters to the government, he expressed his basic animus toward other Triestine Jewish leaders and heaped invective upon them. He charged that they had "turned a family matter into an affair of the [Jewish] Nation,"[21] and that they were motivated by personal vindictiveness, not genuine concern for religious principle. He argued also in political terms: How could Jews suddenly claim that their sovereign privileges assured them of their own religious law, even in contradiction to the express civil law of the state? What the law of the land declares null and void must be so according to Jewish law, too, for "no religion in the state can have maxims contrary to the legislative power."[22] Luzzatto accused the Jewish community of political impropriety, and he used the charged slogan "state within a state" to describe what he perceived as the lamentable outcome of its unwarranted meddling in strictly political affairs.[23] All he wanted from the state, he claimed, was the protection of its very own civil law. Thus, when it suited him, Luzzatto claimed to be faithful to Jewish law; when it did not, he urged dispensing with it altogether, highlighting its conflict with state law. Though his support for state initiatives was consistent—he had earlier favored military conscription as a means of civil integration[24]—personal need now impelled him to formulate the rejection of rabbinic and halakhic authority as an ideological position.

Luzzatto's arguments in fact constituted a direct ideological challenge to Jewish law, to the Jewish community, and to the centuries-old tradition of Jewish religious autonomy. Earlier, Luzzatto had infuriated Rabbi Tedesco when he argued that the civil authorities would superintend the execution of the marriage legislation among "both the dominant religion and the tolerated communities." Tedesco was outraged that someone who had been an official communal *Capo* only a short time earlier would use such "intemperate language," especially "that humiliating appellation 'tolerated community,'" instead of the proper term "community [literally, nation] of subjects" (*suddita nazione*). Tedesco charged that Luzzatto was thereby disregarding the generous privileges that permitted Jews the exercise of their "communal and religious rights" (*diritti e nazionali e religiosi*) like the other communities (*nazioni*). Tedesco believed that "combining the divine laws with sovereign resolutions" was certainly a "noble objective," but that Luzzatto had a different agenda.[25]

Communal leaders based their case to Habsburg officials on three principles. The first two were theoretical and legal, namely, freedom of religion and the essential religious quality of marriage; the third was pragmatic, that is, the harm to be caused by violation of the first two. The Jewish leaders argued that their various privileges and statutes guaranteed them "complete and free exercise of their Religion and Rite, and equality with all other faithful subjects of His Majesty in their civil relations";[26] and they cited the 1783 rescript, which abrogated Jewish civil jurisdiction but explicitly left intact Jewish religious law. They further argued that precisely "divorce and marriage . . . the most essential objects of religion"[27] were matters of religious law, derived from divine precepts received at Sinai, and therefore not subject to arbitrary human decision or to civil law. This was the nub of the problem: where to draw the line between the civil and religious realms. The Jewish community felt that the state, by defining marriage as civil rather than religious, was now infringing upon the very freedom of religion it was supposed to guarantee. The Jewish leaders explained their earlier lack of protest with another legal point: namely, that "a general law can in no way contravene the special patents and generous Privileges granted to the [Jewish] Nation [in Trieste]."[28] Therefore, they had construed the 1783 marriage legislation not as a general abrogation of their own law, but only as an "outline [of] certain formalities . . . for example, the recording of marriages and such things . . . consonant with and indeed corroborating our sacred rite, but never in any way differing from it."[29] Finally, they predicted irreparable harm for both their own community and the city at large if they would no longer be permitted to observe Jewish laws of marriage and divorce: disharmony and disorder would reign in their own midst if "the ties of religion, which alone are those that unite them [the Jews] all and tightly bind them," were to be loosened, and their relations with Jews beyond Trieste would suffer, since the inability of Triestine Jews to observe their

> ritual and dogma as they are scrupulously observed by all Jews in the rest of the world . . . would cause . . . discouragement to the wealthy foreign houses that have established themselves recently in this free port and to those which might want to establish themselves in the future.[30]

These arguments reflected the Triestine Jews' fundamental identity as an immigrant mercantile community. With their far-flung families and connections, these Jews were acutely aware of potential problems if they were to be subject to laws of personal status different from those of other Jewries. Naturally, they couched their genuine concern for *kelal Israel*, the collective unity of Israel, in terms relevant to the authorities and their programs of expansion of the free port. Their claims also highlighted two genuinely perplexing aspects of the situation: the murkiness of the relation between general laws and specific privileges in the late eighteenth century, and the very distinction between the civil and religious realms, a distinction so alien to traditional Judaism, yet so essential to the modern state. Finally, their claims also showed their use of a time-honored strategy of Jewish accommodation to problematic innovative legislation: quiet partial compliance rather than outright challenge.[31] If indeed they had earlier seen a conflict between the new civil law and Jewish law, they may well have considered it prudent to leave it unstated, and to appear to implement the formal requirements of the new law while yet adhering to their own practices. But that made sense only as long as there was consensus within the community. It lost its viability as soon as an individual—especially one as prominent as Elia Moise Luzzatto—challenged Jewish law and communal practice by bringing the contradictions to the attention of the authorities.

Not surprisingly, the state found Luzzatto's presentation of the case convincing, since he enunciated the ideology of state absolutism. Officials both in Trieste and in Vienna never wavered from their initial determination that Jacob Pardo and Corona Luzzatto had contracted no legally binding marriage and that she was free to marry another man. Nonetheless, if formal dissolution were deemed desirable, annulment—not divorce—would suffice. Obviously, her father's insistence upon annulment rather than divorce struck a responsive chord in a Catholic state. State officials also concurred with him that violation of parental authority was a most serious offense, since that authority served "quiet, the order of families, the keeping of youth from temptation, morality, the security of private property, consequently the benefit of all of society, or of the state."³² Though initially somewhat confused by the conflicting claims of father and community, officials soon realized that nothing less than the universal applicability of state law was at stake in this case.³³

Still, the authorities were bothered by the complaints of Triestine Jewish leaders that their religious rights had been violated, and initially they made some effort to avoid giving religious offense. In the case of the Jewish uncle and niece in 1789, Pittoni had argued for the upholding of Jewish marriage law and custom in "the spirit of true [religious] tolerance."³⁴ Now in 1797, in order to "quiet the community,"³⁵ the government did solicit Rabbi Tedesco's view on the possibility of a solution satisfying both state law and Halakhah. They could accept Jewish religious law as long as it permitted a solution short of formal divorce. Though Tedesco did investigate the possibility of annulment according to Jewish law, he and the *Capi* always proclaimed the principle that Halakhah could not yield its pride of place, even to state law. As Tedesco continued to insist on divorce, local governmental officials resorted in late 1797 to a most interesting line of argument: they tried to convince the Jews that annulment would satisfy Jewish as well as civil law. They cited important Jewish legal sources—such as the Talmud, Maimonides, and Joseph Karo (*Shulhan Arukh*)—that seemed at variance with the position of Tedesco, and also cited practices in other Jewish communities, such as Mantua and Livorno, that required parental consent, public venue, and officiating clergy.³⁶ These examples showed, they argued, that the customs Tedesco upheld as inviolable were in fact merely disciplinary regulations, that is, human and mutable.

It is ironic that Habsburg authorities tried to persuade the Jews in religious terms, for they were thereby ignoring the new civil definition of marriage, and arguing—even if only tactically—as if marriage were indeed still a matter of religious law. It was the hybrid quality of the new marriage laws that led them into the thickets of halakhic argumentation, hardly the usual fare for Habsburg bureaucrats. Their smattering of knowledge about Jewish law and communal practice came obviously from Elia Moise Luzzatto, who, it seems, selectively summarized complex rabbinic discussions.³⁷ What he never conveyed, however, was the consistent conclusion that divorce was always the safest possible solution for a woman, even in communities in which norms of public marriage had been violated.

Habsburg officials became exasperated when their halakhic efforts failed to convince Rabbi Tedesco. Once the matter was starkly defined as the exclusive validity of Jewish law or state civil law, the authorities' position became clear and unshakable: they would not be swayed by economic or any other considerations. They reminded Triestine Jewish leaders that tolerated, protected communities owed obedience to the state, and warned them that they actually deserved punishment for their "rash expressions" about the inapplicability of a sovereign law.[38]

In fact, neither side could convince the other by argument or principle. It was the threat of his own expulsion in October 1798 that finally gained the grudging surrender of Rabbi Tedesco. In early 1799, he declared that he would officiate at the marriage of Corona Luzzatto to another man. It is interesting to note that he had consulted not only other rabbis, but also his old comrade Count Sigismond Hohenwart, former bishop of Trieste, who enjoyed very good contacts at court and was a few years later named archbishop of Vienna. The bishop proffered the rabbi moral support and tactical advice on how to cope with Luzzatto's demand for a declaration of clear conscience about the forthcoming marriage: not to cite texts in case other rabbis had expounded them differently, but rather to argue that he be considered like every other minister of religion, Catholic, Protestant, or Greek Orthodox, who was obliged to officiate at wedding ceremonies without revealing his innermost thoughts. That the chief rabbi of Trieste sought advice on this matter from the former bishop, in this case truly a colleague, suggests the existence of a neutral society in Trieste.[39]

It is important to try to gauge opinion about the Luzzatto-Pardo affair within the Jewish community itself. Throughout the long ordeal, Rabbi Tedesco enjoyed the strong backing of the community's other lay leaders. Among the community at large, Luzzatto enjoyed little support, though it seems that some people were inclined to share his view that Tedesco was being unnecessarily obdurate.[40] Still, a clear sense of public opinion did emerge in support of Tedesco and the mainstream halakhic view. Luzzatto tried to force a declaration of conscience from Tedesco in January 1799 because of widely circulating rumors in the community that although Tedesco had stated formally that he would perform a wedding ceremony for Corona Luzzatto without a prior Jewish divorce, he had also intimated his opinion that such a marriage would be valid only civilly, and not religiously. According to Luzzatto, people were repeating this so often that the new bridegroom for his daughter had withdrawn. It was Jewish public opinion that eventually forced Luzzatto to change his mind about divorce. Furthermore, according to oral traditions current in the community decades later, Luzzatto met a miserable fate—opprobrium, shame, poverty, and a "strange death"—whereas Rabbi Tedesco's premature death in January 1800 was attributed to his anguish and heartsickness over the entire affair. A lithograph bearing Tedesco's likeness made after his death described him as a "sacrifice" because of the Luzzatto-Pardo affair, a sacrifice that, it was hoped, would "atone for his people's day of trouble and blasphemy."[41] It is clear that the prevailing sentiment among Triestine Jews was that Luzzatto had gravely violated communal norms and offended communal values.

But communal leaders did not rest content with lamenting the sad fate of their respected rabbi: they sought to prevent a similar crisis from arising in the future. Both Rabbi Tedesco and his distinguished successor, Abram Eliezer Levi, corresponded with rabbinic authorities, Ashkenazic and Sefardic, in Italy and far beyond, in the effort to devise a halakhic solution to the now-vexing Habsburg Marriage Patent.[42] Early in 1805, Rabbi Abram Eliezer Levi and the *Capi* issued a communal ordinance, a *takkanah* or *Proclama*, prohibiting "clandestine marriages." Included in this prohibition were marriages outlawed by the Civil Code, such as those of minors without parental consent or soldiers without consent of a commanding officer, as well as some that violated Jewish law, for example, cases in which a woman's consent was obtained by physical force. The ordinance stated that all such marriage ceremonies would be automatically considered invalid and would require no divorce to undo them, and that all members of the community were taking upon themselves the obligation not to participate in such ceremonies on pain of excommunication. All Jews in Trieste were to instruct their children in the ordinance, which by its terms was to be publicly proclaimed in the synagogues year after year. (This was done at least as late as 1886.) The signators claimed that the authority for their proclamation was derived from "the Sacred Law of Moses, and the ever-revered traditions of our Teachers and Rabbis."[43] But this halakhic solution was itself problematic, since most rabbinic authorities had usually been reluctant to recognize in practice the right of a community to invalidate marriage by means of a prior communal ordinance and thereby to free a woman for remarriage without a writ of divorce.[44] Significantly, the Triestine *takkanah* satisfied the Sefardic authorities consulted, Rabbis Hayyim David Azulai and Hayyim Isaac Mussafia, but not the Ashkenazic Hatam Sofer.

In effect, the 1805 ordinance recast the provisions of Joseph's Marriage Patent as communal norms with the force of Jewish law behind it. It did so by setting the government's requirements within a valid halakhic category, preconditions to a marriage. Thus the proclamation represented acceptance, indeed internalization, of the civil law, which the Jews were powerless to block. By declaring such marriages invalid in advance and on the authority of Jewish law itself, Triestine Jewish leaders hoped to prevent the kind of bitter clash between Jewish law and the state's civil law that the Luzzatto-Pardo affair had caused. Yet, although the ordinance transparently showed the triumph of the state in matters of marriage law, it ought not to be seen solely as a gambit designed to satisfy the government. It also bespoke the genuine desire for halakhic continuity on the part of the communal leadership of Trieste.

The Frizzi-Morschene Affair

In the very midst of the Luzzatto-Pardo affair, the Triestine community faced another crisis over marriage. In July 1798, Benedetto (Ben Zion Rafael ha-Kohen) Frizzi—a forty-two-year-old physician, author, and devotee of the Enlightenment—and his beloved Relle (a.k.a. Rachel or Bella) Morschene—a woman in her late twenties, daughter of the former *Capo* Anselmo Morschene—requested permission from Habsburg authorities for a "purely civil marriage."[45] It should be recalled that the 1783 Marriage Patent had redefined marriage as a civil contract but had instituted no strictly civil marriage procedure. This older couple explained their predicament: they could not get married under "religious auspices" because Morschene was divorced from her first husband (Lucio Luzzatto, coincidentally the brother of Elia Moise Luzzatto), and Frizzi, a *kohen*, was prohibited by Jewish law from marrying a divorced—or, in their words, "repudiated"—woman. They claimed that their respect for Jewish religious sensibilities—"not wanting to offend religion"—left them no choice but to marry civilly, something that they asserted was permitted them in any case by Jewish law, and that, "taken for granted by all the laws of nature," could not offend "good custom and civil society."[46]

Local officials asked Jewish leaders whether the halakhic prohibition was a matter of "dogmatic law" or "only disciplinary custom." Rabbi Tedesco testified that any marriage of these two individuals would violate both dogma and custom, for it would contradict the divine precept in Leviticus 21:7. Accordingly, local authorities told Vienna in September 1798 that the couple's request could not be granted without "infringing upon the religious freedom guaranteed the Jews."[47] Frizzi pressed further: besides requesting a civil marriage, he also explained why he thought Jewish opposition to their union unfounded. He provided an alternative, indeed idiosyncratic, understanding of the problem based on what he claimed was the "true" or "pure" spirit of the Mosaic legislation, and he found justification for civil marriage itself in Jewish law.[48]

Focusing on the passive form in Leviticus 21:7—*gerushah* (*weggejagt* in Frizzi's German), a woman put away from her husband—and on the authority of scholars such as the seventeenth-century Biblical critic Richard Simon and the "immortal Montesquieu," Frizzi argued that Moses had in Leviticus 21:7 forbidden priests to marry repudiated women, and in Deuteronomy 24:1 outlined procedures for repudiation, but not for divorce.[49] Divorce, either by mutual agreement or by initiation of a woman, was thus a product of the later rabbis. The distinction was crucial: repudiation of a wife depended solely on the husband's will, while divorce involved the consent of both husband and wife.[50] On this view, Relle Morschene was divorced but not repudiated, since she had initiated her own divorce proceedings in the civil courts, and the Mosaic prohibition could not apply to her.

According to Frizzi's reading of Mosaic law, there was no impediment to his marrying Relle Morschene. Further, he posited the primacy of Mosaic law over any later elaborations, arguing that a later rabbinic teaching was invalid if it did not conform to the spirit of Mosaic legislation. He dismissed the later rabbis' inclusion of all divorced women within the prohibition directed to priests as "an [instance of] unpardonable ignorance, and the setting up of a defense against the true meaning of the law," and in the words of an official's paraphrase, as an effort to extend their influence and power. Frizzi urged that interpreters of the law not deviate from its "original purity and true spirit," that is, its Mosaic base, but rather adhere more closely to it, in order to avoid "blind devotion" and subservience to "arbitrary interpreters." To him, Triestine leaders were guilty of following "one-sided commentaries" rather than the "spirit of Mosaic law."[51] Frizzi also claimed that Jewish tradition itself provided precedents for civil marriage: in the examples of the Biblical Abraham, Jacob, and David, who had married without "rabbinic public formalities," and in the legal formulation of Maimonides that a man could marry a woman by means of a contract and without a ring.[52]

After a year had passed with no answer from Vienna, Frizzi and Morschene took their next step. Expecting eventual approval of a civil marriage, they signed a preliminary marriage contract before two witnesses on November 20, 1799, which called for effectuation within six months of governmental approval of the contract.[53] Although they intended this contract to be a purely civil document, they nonetheless included in it two statements of religious import, namely, their desires that it not be construed as contrary to Mosaic law and not impair Frizzi's status as a *kohen*.

Eventually Vienna responded favorably to the Frizzi-Morschene request. In March 1800, Triestine officials were instructed to "handle this petition according to Mosaic law."[54] Frizzi then submitted the preliminary contract to the authorities for approval and prompt action, while the *Capi* reiterated their unwavering opposition to the marriage. In October 1800, local authorities upheld Frizzi's arguments and brushed aside the objections of Jewish leaders, calling them "vague and unfounded [in their] contradiction" and not at all to the point, meaning presumably that the *Capi* had not responded to Frizzi's distinction between repudiation and divorce. The authorities adjudged the proposed marriage in compliance with both Mosaic and state laws: if no ring were given, the marriage would qualify as a civil marriage according to Jewish law as they, following Frizzi, understood it, and they saw no obstacle to fulfillment of all the formalities prescribed by the state's marriage law. If the rabbi refused to declare the banns and officiate, he should be obliged to comply with the sovereign orders. Accordingly, they declared the preliminary marriage contract valid and instructed the community to announce the forthcoming marriage.[55]

The Jewish community responded by temporizing and protesting. Angelo Isach Cologna, the teacher then serving as one of the community's two assistant rabbis while it awaited a successor to the deceased Rabbi Tedesco, explained immediately to the governor that he could not undertake the ordered action on his own authority, but needed to consult the lay leaders. After discussing the "painful and grave matter," they lodged a protest to the governor in order to "defend the rights of the community and of religion."[56] They argued that acceding to Frizzi's request and the government's order would mean that

religion would . . . suffer an affront and continual public desecration that could lead to infinitely grave consequences, making observance of religion and rites dependent not only on the Pentateuch and the decisions of the [ancient] Sanhedrin, but also on the sophistical distinctions and caprices of private individuals [which are] always inadmissible and insignificant in the face of dogmas and prescriptions [that have been] venerated and venerable since time immemorial.[57]

Thus their concerns were (1) improper interpretation of Jewish law, (2) excessive freedom of interpretation for individuals (what we might call "interpretive individualism"[58]), which would undermine rabbinic and communal authority, and (3) sanctity of the synagogue, if Frizzi retained his priestly status and exercised his priestly prerogatives in worship services. The Jewish leaders requested a one-month delay in order to prepare a more detailed presentation.

Their various protests bore bittersweet fruit: on November 8, 1800, the government informed the *Capi* that they could indeed postpone the matter until the arrival of a new rabbi, but that he then would be obliged to obey state orders and announce the marriage banns.[59] The *Capi* gratefully acknowledged the postponement, while reiterating their intention to explain further why the marriage was contrary to Mosaic law and the Jewish religion. They expressed the hope that the "governor would never permit the desires of an individual [man] and woman to lead to schism, and harm in the smallest point that Religion which the humanity of the monarch not only tolerates but wants conserved in all its rites."[60]

Once again, the government and the Jewish community were at odds because of the conflict between their respective marriage laws. Again the state insisted on its power to decide, and it appeared only a matter of time before the new rabbi would be subject to the same kind of pressure as

Rabbi Tedesco. But fate intervened: in early December the community learned that the aged Rabbi Finzi of Padua had decided not to come to Trieste after all.[61] In fact, the next incumbent did not take up the post until 1802, so Cologna's delaying tactic worked far longer than could have been expected. The news that Finzi was not coming must have thrown Frizzi and Morschene into despair: there would be no rabbi for the state to pressure.

From this point, the story is somewhat confused. What is clear, however, is that in mid-December 1800, the couple appeared before three Jewish arbiters—who, according to Jewish law, constituted a court—but it is not known who initiated this proceeding and for what precise purpose. Their appearance was voluntary, and signaled their agreement to consider the arbiters' decision as legally binding. The arbiters ruled that the two could not be married Jewishly, and that Frizzi should pay Morschene a considerable sum of damages. In early January 1801, Frizzi again asked the government to waive the requirement of formal marriage banns by the Jewish community. These would serve no purpose, he argued, for the government had already approved the marriage, the liberty of the parties to be married was well known, and besides, the announcement of marriages was a mere formality that had little to do with their "true substance," which was "always and forever dependent upon the sacred bond of Nature, and the free will of the contracting parties."[62] But sometime in January, a request was made—by Frizzi, Morschene, or both—that the decision of the arbiters be overruled by the civil authorities; those authorities then decided that only a higher court could overturn it. The case proceeded through the state court system, apparently with Frizzi as plaintiff and Morschene as defendant. Only at the end of January 1802 was the matter decided by a higher court: the arbiters' decision was now null because of Relle Morschene's "confession."[63]

Unfortunately, the court documents are incomplete, and do not explain either the payment of damages or the nature of Morschene's confession. But we can speculate about what happened. Morschene brought Frizzi before the arbiters in December 1800 in an attempt to force the issue and reach a resolution. She was fed up with his unfulfilled promises of marriage: though convinced of his own powers of persuasion, he had not in fact succeeded in getting any authority, civil or religious, to marry them. And both could well see that the Jewish community was effective in postponing and avoiding compliance with governmental dictate. Though not optimistic, perhaps she thought that the arbiters might reach a decision allowing the two to marry, or, failing that, at least force Frizzi to pay her damages for his broken marriage promise. In December 1800, she felt especially exasperated and desperate, not only because the prospective rabbi announced he was not coming to Trieste, but for her own very personal reason: pregnancy. The piecing together of various communal records reveals that Benedetto Frizzi had a daughter Anna, born in 1801, and that Relle (Rachele) Morschene had a daughter Nina, born on May 31, 1801.[64] Anna and Nina were no doubt one and the same. Morschene probably learned of her pregnancy in late 1800, and it was that knowledge which impelled her urgently to act. Matters had to be resolved once and for all. Why, then, was there a request the following month that the arbiters' decision be overturned? It did not serve the interest of either Morschene or Frizzi to leave on record that they accepted the arbiters' decision that no Jewish marriage could take place. Perhaps Frizzi convinced her that it was worthwhile to get the arbiters' decision overturned, that she need not worry about money and support, that he would stand by her whether or not they would succeed in getting married formally. It is not unreasonable to assume that during this trying period, Morschene may have experienced contradictory and changing feelings. She may well have been persuaded by Frizzi, and come round to regretting having turned to the arbiters in the first place. That would explain the request in January that the civil authorities disregard the arbiters' decision.

As for Morschene's confession, we do not know its content, but we do know its effect: it was sufficient to allow the authorities to disregard the couple's agreement to enter binding arbitration and to nullify the arbiters' decision. Morschene must have confessed to something that cast doubt on the validity of her earlier submission to arbitration.

Yet whatever the precise events at this stage, we do have some basis for figuring out the final outcome of the story. Morschene and Frizzi did resolve their differences and stay together. Marriage records of the Jewish community of Trieste show no trace of Frizzi or Morschene, and biographies of Frizzi never mention marriage or a wife. However, one letter of condolence sent to him at the time of his daughter's death did mention Signora Relle, and a population record from Trieste in 1830 lists him as married to a woman named Bella of approximately the same age as Relle Morschene (remember that Relle was also known as Rachele or Bella).[65] Frizzi and Morschene may not have gotten formally married because no religious or civil ceremony was available to them, but they probably considered themselves married according to natural law. This would be entirely consistent with Frizzi's dearly held values of natural law and rationalism. In any case, the two lovers lived several years together, first in Trieste and later in Frizzi's native Ostiano in Lombardy, and they died but four days apart in 1844.[66]

Thus, while Frizzi and Morschene failed to obtain what they really wanted—a formally sanctioned civil marriage—they apparently found their own solution. And the community succeeded again—this time with a bit of luck—in evading state dictates that would have required it to violate the authoritative interpretation of its religious law.

Now let us analyze further the perspectives of Frizzi and Morschene, the state, and the Jewish community. Benedetto Frizzi and Relle Morschene wanted to remain Jews even though Jewish law prohibited their marital union, and Frizzi wanted to maintain his status as a *kohen*. They claimed that it was respect for religious sensibilities that led them to request a "purely civil marriage." Perhaps they genuinely expected special civil arrangements to be made for them, but at the same time they probably hoped that failing that, the government would compel the Jewish authorities to marry them. Surely Frizzi and Morschene were emboldened by the actions of the government in the Luzzatto-Pardo case. It was important to justify their position in terms of Mosaic law in order to convince the Gentile authorities that there were no religious impediments to their marriage, however they would decide to proceed. Perhaps Frizzi hoped to convince even Jewish leaders.

In fact, the initial request of Frizzi and Morschene for the circumvention of Jewish law really became a request for its contravention. Their attempt ultimately became a challenge to the Jewish community's right to implement and indeed interpret its own law. For Frizzi not only misrepresented certain points of Jewish law; more fundamentally, he mounted an ideological challenge in a language of new values, namely, pure Mosaism and rationalism. Less notorious than that of Elia Moise Luzzatto, and couched in intellectual rather than political terms, Frizzi's challenge was nonetheless potentially more insidious and corrosive. Like the seventeenth-century Sefardic rationalists Uriel Da Costa and Spinoza, Frizzi bypassed the authoritative rabbinic chain of tradition in order to lodge authority solely in the Biblical text. Though to the uninformed, Frizzi's Mosaism might appear faithful to Judaism, it really marked a sharp break with normative Judaism, which postulated two revelations: the written law, and the oral law of rabbinic commentary to complete it. In contrast, Frizzi purported to understand the Biblical text on its own. His literal reading was buttressed by the critical rationalism of the Enlightenment, supposedly unencumbered by the weight of tradition. Frizzi's valuing his own reasoning and that of Enlightenment thinkers more highly than that of rabbinic authorities constituted an implicit attack on Jewish tradition.

Frizzi's Mosaism was not a tool newly forged in the heat of this particular battle, though his current predicament caused him to revise some details of his interpretation.[67] Earlier he had displayed great interest in Mosaic legislation, particularly in subjecting Biblical passages to rationalist criticism in the spirit of the Enlightenment.[68] Like many a contemporary central European *maskil*, Frizzi believed that Judaism the historical religion had to be evaluated according to rationalist criteria, and Jewish tradition modernized by means of Enlightenment philosophy. In the late 1780s, his writings had gotten him into trouble with Jewish authorities in Mantua—some branded him a "new Spinoza"—and he had been forced to leave Mantua for Trieste.[69]

Frizzi's Mosaism should be seen in the context of the Jewish Enlightenment's general interest in the Bible, of which Mendelssohn's translation-cum-commentary, the *Biur*, was the most notable example. Both the Haskalah's focus on Scripture and Frizzi's Mosaism can be seen as Jewish examples of the general classicist trend of the European Enlightenment, the leaping backward over centuries of medieval accretions to rediscover the purity of antiquity. For Jews, the pristine sources did not mean pagan antiquity, but rather the Bible.[70] The sense that Talmudic Judaism might be but an appendage to the real Judaism of the Bible later became one of the foundations of Reform Judaism. Frizzi did not state that as a general principle, but he did make that point with regard to laws concerning priestly marriage.

Frizzi never wanted to sever his ties to the Jewish religion or community. As a young man, though considered a heretic by some, Frizzi had described himself as a "true philosopher, and religious Jew at the same time."[71] Now, he expressed the desire to maintain his status as a *kohen*. In other words, he wanted the right to determine his own terms of belonging, to remain part of the community without accepting its traditional law as binding authority. Frizzi, like many other Jews in modern times, was able to act upon such desires primarily because state intervention eroded the legal autonomy of Jewish communities and transformed them ultimately into voluntary associations.

Vienna granted Frizzi and Morschene part, but not all, of what they wanted: Mosaic principles, but no strictly civil marriage. As in the early stages of the Luzzatto-Pardo case, officials believed—mistakenly—that Jewish law and state law could be reconciled. This time their mistake rested on their acceptance of Frizzi's arguments about Mosaism as the true Judaism. These arguments made sense to them because it was the Bible, after all, that Jews and Christians shared, and antirabbinism could appeal to officials who hoped to improve Jews by weaning them from the Talmudic tradition. But Mosaism was not the position of Triestine Jewish leaders, and once again, as in the Luzzatto-Pardo case, Habsburg authorities listened to a dissident individual rather than the community, confident that they could pressure the rabbi into compliance.

The leaders of the Jewish community of Trieste, meanwhile, never for a moment lent credence to Frizzi's claims. At one point Frizzi told the government that he had tried to explain his position to them, but that they had refused to consider his, in their view, "small-minded [arguments]."[72] Too much was at stake: Judaism as they knew it anchored in Halakhah and the rabbinic tradition, and their capacity as a body to enforce the authoritative interpretation of Jewish law and to discipline their members. As they said explicitly, the challenge was both religious and political.

It would be interesting to know just how much the Jewish public at large knew about this business—neither Frizzi nor Morschene was an obscure figure—and how people reacted to it. Alas, we have no information on Triestine Jewish social attitudes toward cohabitation, but apparently it was less of a problem than getting communal officials to perform a halakhically forbidden marriage. Certainly Relle Morschene was hardly the only Jewish woman in Trieste to conceive a child before or outside of marriage, as an 1803 communal ordinance prohibiting public celebration and honor for pregnant brides attests.[73] It is possible that with the passage of time, others did not know or care whether the two were legally married. We do know that Frizzi remained in Trieste another thirty long years after this episode, and served as doctor for two of the community's institutions, the hospital and the confraternity devoted to charitable deeds.[74] In his memoirs, the noted scholar Samuel David Luzzatto depicted Frizzi in the second and third decades of the nineteenth century as a kindly, erudite, and respected man.[75] At the least, we may state that in Trieste, unlike in Mantua, Frizzi was not ostracized by the Jewish community for his challenge to religious authority and attacks on Jewish tradition. Still, it appears that this community did tolerate in its midst someone who had posed a grave religious and political challenge to its norms. But perhaps the community exerted its influence upon Frizzi in another way. In 1815 Frizzi published the first volume of his *Petah enayim*, a multivolume commentary on the *aggadic* (nonlegal) portions of rabbinic literature. In this work, he engaged both in rationalist reinterpretation of the rabbis, and in vigorous defense of their intellectual and moral legacy. Might not this volte-face have been in part an act of *teshuvah* (repentance) by Frizzi, atonement for his Mosaism and antirabbinism of earlier days? Indeed, the community adopted this work as an official text in its public school.[76]

Marriage, Community, and the State

Two simultaneous struggles determined the outcome of the Luzzatto-Pardo and Morschene-Frizzi liaisons: the state versus the Jewish community, and the Jewish community versus deviant individuals. When the Habsburg state first asserted control over marriage with its 1783 Marriage Patent, Triestine Jews took a pragmatic procedural approach, and saw it as supplementing but not supplanting their own authority. They ignored the new civil definition of marriage and the fundamental conflict between civil and Jewish laws. But the second struggle, between specific individuals and the Jewish community, ended the viability of that strategy. Elia Moise Luzzatto, Relle Morschene, and Benedetto Frizzi refused to accept the authority of Jewish law when it thwarted their desires. In their struggles with the Jewish community, they now turned to the state, which had become an interested party and ally. As a result, the state's assertion of control over marriage assumed new significance, for its troubling aspects now had practical significance. What were the effects upon these dangerous liaisons and the Jewish community?

The outcomes of these episodes show no party able fully to realize its aims. The state came closest: it was clearly victorious on the plane of legal theory, for it had the power to declare the supremacy of civil law. The Jewish community could not block the state's entry into family law; it had to yield the exclusive authority of Halakhah and to acquiesce to state limits on its implementation. But ultimately, state law was not completely enforceable in this community when resisted by a determined leadership, and a customary morality anchored in religious law, public opinion, and traditional patterns of communal decision-making. Even the alliance of Jewish individuals with the state did not gain them what they wanted: Luzzatto *père* was forced to accept his daughter's marriage and divorce according to Jewish law, and Morschene and Frizzi seem never to have formalized their liaison.

In both episodes, the Jewish community of Trieste had to wage a battle on two fronts: against the state, and against the individuals who challenged its own religious-communal authority. Why did this community—used to being in the vanguard of Jewish support for Josephinian policies of toleration and civil integration of the Jews, and an ally of the government in developing the free port—fight the state tenaciously on the issue of marriage law? Why did the loss of control over marriage matter more to it than the loss of Jewish civil jurisdiction?

For Triestine Jews, state regulation of marriage was entirely unprecedented. As an immigrant community, part of a far-flung minority, they were of course alive to the dangers of special laws of personal status inconsistent with those of their coreligionists. But the deeper reasons for sensitivity had to do with the very meaning of marriage as a social institution. Determining who the legitimate members of society will be, who will form legally and socially recognized units for the purpose of procreation and transfer of property, marriage is a legal and symbolic act that defines the next generation of a society. To lose control over marriage law was to lose control over the vitals of collective identity. The Triestine Jewish community was especially reluctant to relinquish control over its individuals' rite of passage, marriage, at a time when it was undergoing its own collective rite of passage, integration into civil society.

The community fought hard to preserve what it could of religious, political, and social control over its own members. As the enlightened absolutist state brought new realms of Jewish life within its purview, the Jewish community—the traditional "holy community" (*kehillah kedoshah*) charged as a corporate body with both religious and political responsibilities—saw its own authority circumscribed, coopted, and ultimately constricted. State action weakened the ability of the Jewish community to superintend the behavior of its members and to punish violators of Halakhah and communal norms. Traditionally, the appeal by Jews to outside Gentile authorities had been sharply discouraged by Jewish communities, but the Marriage Patent and its implementation in the Luzzatto-Pardo and Frizzi-Morschene cases created a new structural alliance of deviants and outsiders. Precisely as it saw the rule of Halakhah contracted in both public law and private lives, the Jewish leadership of Trieste became all the more zealous in the struggle to retain its own rights. And indeed, though powerless against the state, the community could—with public opinion on its side—prevent the deviant individuals from achieving their goals. These individuals also failed to overturn established norms or to set new ones, as the ideologies they advanced—state absolutism, affective individualism, Mosaism, enlightened rationalism, and interpretative individualism—gained little support among other Jewish leaders or the rank and file.

The vigorous defense of Jewish law can be understood as symbolic or cultural resistance to state action. Yet in the process of defending its tradition, the community unwittingly renegotiated it. First, in its 1805 communal ordinance prohibiting clandestine marriages, the community internalized the state's law by reformulating it in the language of Halakhah. By using religious terms to express the alignment of Jewish law and communal practice with state law, the community was able to see the interests of "sovereign laws" as reinforcing "religion" and the "well-being of families."[77]

Second, internalization of the state's law brought with it willy-nilly a degree of secularization. Desacralization was at the heart of the Marriage Patent as it subjected marriage to civil control, defined it essentially as a contract rather than a sacrament, and created a civil-religious hybrid out of the religious institution it coopted.[78] Desacralization was evident in the 1805 communal ordinance insofar as it adopted a new stringent rule-oriented approach to marriage. Like Protestant and post-Tridentine Catholic marriage laws (both of which required publicity, whereas the former insisted also on parental approval), and the absolutist marriage laws that drew upon them, this ordinance specified procedures for marriages, set them forth clearly, and administered them with bureaucratic rigor. All marriages violating the rules were to be considered clandestine, and automatically null and void. This stood in sharp contrast to the traditional Jewish attitude, evident in the community's initial response to the Luzzatto-Pardo liaison, and the medieval Catholic attitude it resembled.[79] Religious authorities had tended to consider as valid even those marriages that violated specific communal rules or norms as long as they met the basic provisions of the law, which was regarded as ultimately divine: Catholics exchanging their vows freely, and Jews using proper words and a ring before two witnesses. Despite the violation of later human enactments, religious authorities could not be certain that the more basic divine law had not been satisfied. By contrast, the modern approach was to invest one's own human, rational, and enforceable rules with ultimate authority and hence to allow no exemptions. Marriage thus regulated was indeed more civil transaction than sacrament. Though couched in the language of Halakhah, the 1805 ordinance embodied the shift away from the traditional Jewish attitude, and represented a step toward the modern rationalization, bureaucratization, and desacralization of marriage.

What was the effect of the state's entry into the domain of marriage upon the concerned individuals? Luzzatto *père*, Frizzi, and Morschene believed that the Marriage Patent would afford them greater freedom of action in their struggle against Jewish law and community, for it theoretically removed marriage disputes from the informal processes of the community, and subjected them exclusively to state mechanisms of conflict resolution.[80] They welcomed the more amenable Josephinian law, or at least the possibilities it apparently created. But they failed to recognize the complex dynamics of community-state relations. Precisely because community and state were locked in a struggle over the conflict of Jewish and Habsburg laws, each exerted itself to be victorious. The deviant individuals became victims of the constraints operating from both sides, community and state; by turning to one, the individual could not escape the other.

What about free choice of marriage partner, touted by the Enlightenment? It was never invoked by the young lovers Corona Luzzatto and Jacob Pardo, both powerless minors, he poor, she female. In their case, parental control was actually strengthened by both state and community. The Jewish community only countered this control when it contradicted its own; the community had no trouble reasserting support for it once Jewish and Habsburg laws were reconciled through the communal ordinance of 1805. Thus individuals such as these were limited more than ever by the family-community-state pact[81] represented by the 1805 ordinance. In the Frizzi-Morschene case, state intervention in marriage law did seem to open more possibilities for the lovers. Older, more established, and independent, both members of the elite—she by wealth and birth, he by profession and intellectual renown—Morschene and Frizzi spoke the language of free choice and succeeded at least de facto in staying together as a couple. Taken together, these two cases demonstrate that individuals' choices were constrained by a number of factors that eventually reinforced one another: religious and civil laws, parental authority, public opinion, and social class.[82]

Of these, the most important was ultimately Jewish public opinion. For most Jews in late-eighteenth-century Trieste, the intimate realm of marriage still belonged to the Jewish public sphere, not the Habsburg public sphere, and when one married, one did so as a Jew, not as a Habsburg subject. Most Jews did not accept the transfer of marriage law from the Jewish community to the state for two reasons, one internal—the continued hold of Halakhah in matters of personal status—and the second external—the partial and incremental workings of the enlightened absolutist state.

While encroaching on new spheres, the enlightened absolutist Habsburg state did not assert radical control over them. Unlike the French revolutionaries, it did not create true civil marriage and divorce, but contented itself with a civil-religious mix.[83] Joseph II's Toleration program of the 1780s took significant steps toward integrating Jews into the Habsburg polity and society and creating the possibility of a civil identity for Jews. But in contrast to the emancipation proffered French Jews in 1790–91, the Habsburg process was partial and incremental: the enlightened absolutist state never struck the eventual bargain of emancipation—full integration and citizenship in exchange for relinquishment of communal autonomy—with its Jewish subjects. It was anticorporatist, but again, only to a degree. As its support of Luzzatto *père*, Frizzi, and Morschene showed, it readily interposed itself between individual subjects and corporate bodies, allying itself with the former against the latter. But its own state-building was not sufficiently extensive or thoroughgoing to do away with corporate bodies; at most, it succeeded in coopting and weakening them.

In the conflicts over Jewish marriage in late-eighteenth-century Trieste, the enlightened absolutist Habsburg state asserted civil control and, in theory, set the rules of the game. Communal leaders and most of the Jewish public were prepared to accept state involvement and possibly even state supervision, but only as a supplementary layer of authority, not as a substitute for Jewish control. The still-functioning intermediate corporate body, the Jewish community, while not able to prevent state action, could keep the state from effecting full and practical control, and the deviant individuals from making good their alliances with the state. Though civil integration of Jews was proceeding apace in Trieste, the enlightened absolutist state had not yet created the possibility of a civil identity for Jews encompassing enough to replace their religious and communal identity.

European Jewish communities were transformed in the crucible of enlightened absolutism. Loosened from their traditional moorings by state action, Jews as individuals and as communities were drawn increasingly into the civic realm and enmeshed in the surrounding state and society. During this transitional period, as Jewish communities were weakened and coopted by the state, they felt the pulls of both the new structural realities and the old ways of pre-emancipation corporate Jewish life. In their struggles, they simultaneously defended and redefined Jewish tradition.

CHAPTER NINE

Conclusion: Civil Inclusion of a Port Jewry in a Reforming Absolutist State

By the late eighteenth century, the Jewish community of Trieste had passed through its formative period to become a dynamic and thriving center. Its population had grown rapidly and prospered, and the community had succeeded in establishing itself as a formal corporate entity with self-governing institutions. Along with the other merchant *nazioni* in Trieste, it had a recognized role and place in the city's economic and civic order—an order constructed by the absolutist state to be exceptional and diverse. The transformation of this sleepy town into a cosmopolitan entrepôt was the result of the alliance between the Habsburg administration and the new traders of Trieste.[1] Habsburg officials on both the central and the local levels actively pursued this end, with figures such as Councillor Ricci, Governor Zinzendorf, and Chief of Police Pittoni keen to implement Enlightenment and reform in Trieste. The merchants who fueled the rise of the new port city benefited from more favorable privileges in Trieste than their coreligionists enjoyed elsewhere in the Habsburg Monarchy.

In the course of a century, the legal status of the Jews of Trieste passed through four distinct phases: (1) the Ashkenazic central European court Jew pattern of exceptional privileges for a few individuals; (2) the Sefardic Mediterranean port Jew pattern of privileges for Jewish merchants among others in the free port, which coexisted with the court Jew pattern; (3) exceptional Theresian privileges for the entire community, deriving from both court and port Jew statuses; and (4) Josephinian civil toleration. This civil toleration meant substantial parity for Jews as individuals and as a community with the other merchant *nazioni* of Trieste, and in many respects with all other subjects. For the Jews of Trieste, the lofty preambles of Joseph's edicts—"near-equality" for "Jewish fellow-citizens" based upon the productive contribution of Jews to the state—did not remain merely abstract formulas or slogans. They were translated into the concrete economic, civil, and religious rights of civil toleration—the status enjoyed by the other minority communities of Trieste. By the late eighteenth century, the Jews were well integrated and prominent in the new order of Trieste, achieving political expression in the *Borsa*, its most important institution.

Though the wealthiest members of the community belonged in effect to two corporate bodies, the Jewish community and the *Borsa*, it was significant that they enjoyed no distinct legal status separate from that of other Triestine Jews. The benefits gained because of utility and wealth accrued to the entire Jewish community in Trieste. The transition from a settlement of Jews in which a few individuals enjoyed the privileges of court Jews to a community of port Jewry was decisive. Port Jews subsumed court Jews: an open invitation to merchants with a minimum of restrictions imposed upon all those who came and formed a community prevailed over the central European pattern of restricted settlement and separate legal status for a wealthy elite. In that respect, eighteenth-century Trieste more resembled Livorno and Bordeaux than it did Vienna and Berlin.

Commerce, Utility, Virtue, and Diversity in the New Port City

In the modern port city of Trieste created by the initiative of the absolutist state, international maritime commerce, innovation, and structured diversity all worked together to make utility the coin of the realm and the entry ticket for the minority communities. As the raison d'être and lifeblood of Trieste, international maritime commerce set the city's rhythms and its cultural and moral tone. A wholly secular definition of virtue emerged: to contribute to maritime commerce meant to be useful, which in turn meant to be virtuous. Utility and virtue, commerce and morality, and, as we shall see below, culture were all linked tightly together.

Jews could—and did—meet the economic criterion of utility in Trieste. The existence of this Jewry in this port city was—like the existence of other port Jewries in places such as Livorno, Bordeaux, London, Amsterdam, and later Odessa—predicated on the perception of a Jewish aptitude for commerce that could stimulate trade and cause the city to flourish. Jews who came to trade in Trieste under the aegis of the Free Port Patents were by definition useful to society. It must be stressed that the assumption of utility adhered only to wholesale international commerce conducted by

Jews, since small-scale retail commerce or dealing in money was still tainted by the opprobrium of usury. As such ports thrived, all Jews had to do was to continue to demonstrate the utility that had first gained them settlement, pursue their normal business opportunities, and of course be obedient and loyal subjects. What was important about the perceived utility of a port Jewry was that it concerned the very vitals of a society built on maritime commerce: the Jews were valued for something considered fundamental to the general welfare. And their utility was already assumed and demonstrated; it was not a hope for the future, for improvement (*Verbesserung*) to be realized only through a dramatic transformation—be it economic, social, or cultural—of themselves or the society around them.

The image of Triestine Jews as economically useful was reinforced by demographics and culture. Few in number and relatively well-off, engaged in international commerce, wholesale brokerage, and related activities, Triestine Jews formed an elite community. Though there were poor Jews in Trieste, they did not comprise an impoverished mass leading a way of life that appeared distinct and alien from the majority population. Heirs to the Italian Jewish cultural tradition, the Jews of Trieste spoke the vernacular, used Italian as the language of business and communal affairs, and were at home with non-Jewish culture. That for pleasure they tended to read more in Romance languages than in Hebrew, and that a Triestine Jew supplied Governor Zinzendorf with Enlightenment reading material—these were signs of the acculturation requisite for utility. Their general deportment and behavior exemplified the kind of broad-minded mercantile mentality that Wessely had associated with Italian Jewry when he wrote, "Trade in your lands is with the large states of Europe, Asia, and Africa, and you get to hear of the customs of areas distant from you."[2] The authorities themselves considered the Jews of Trieste to conform to the expected cultural and social standards, and to stand in no need of radical transformation. Indeed, the receptivity of Triestine Jews to the cultural provisions of Joseph's Toleration program and to the related aspects of Wesselian-Mendelssohnian Haskalah seemed to provide proof positive that all that was required was continuity along familiar paths. Commerce and culture fused as secular virtue.

The newness of the port city of Trieste also contributed to enhancing the utility of the Jews and the other religious-ethnic minorities.[3] Because the absolutist state created a wholly new administrative structure for the port city, it could establish things as it saw fit, with relatively little interference or resistance from local elements who might not share the new vision. It could operate more freely in this environment than in jurisdictions in which it had to contend with existing estates, burghers, or guilds. Thus the central administration had more freedom of action in Trieste on the periphery of the monarchy than in Vienna, the monarchy's capital and sensitively symbolic nerve center. In Trieste, newness and administrative freedom also contributed to a certain dynamism and openness of spirit.

In Trieste, the central regime dictated that newcomers should be encouraged to come ply their trades and wares, and by fiat declared the conditions in which they could do so. It created a civic reality in which each diverse group was offered legal corporate standing. It was emblematic of the multicultural corporate reality of Trieste that the government almanac published in the 1780s contained "useful and pleasing notices for Roman Catholics, Lutherans, Calvinists, non-Uniate Greeks, Jews, Turks."[4] Though granted a measure of self-government, each corporation was subject ultimately to governmental oversight, and increasingly to absolutist involvement and cooptation into the state apparatus. Each *nazione* became in part a state agency. But as long as they fulfilled the common demands of good subjecthood, these *nazioni* were allowed to exist and function as separate entities.

The relation between commerce, morality, culture, diversity, and social interaction was elaborated by Chief of Police Pittoni in a report he submitted to the Court Chancellery in December 1786. A questionnaire from Vienna sent to local jurisdictions had specifically inquired about the population's mentality: Was it "sound, reasonable," or "dominated by base prejudices"?[5] Pittoni replied at length:

It has been a long time—since the declaration of the Free Port—that the populace has been composed of diverse nations and religions, who frequent this City and settle here. Since then the City has united these in business activities, which require knowledge and skills. This traffic in business and knowledge has made the City well-off and rich. The City has witnessed that the non-Catholic can be and is an honest man, that morality is the same, that he has learned the customs of the others, and felt their same needs. Since this brotherly sharing (*confrattellanza*) of knowledge, of customs, and of reciprocally useful needs has rendered the City not only tolerant, but friendly, it has rooted out from the mind an infinity of prejudices, such that compared to other provinces, Trieste can with reason call itself an enlightened populace (*un Popolo filosofo*).[6]

Novelty aided the cause of diversity. To participate in commerce and artisanry, the individual members of the *nazioni*, often newcomers to the city, did not have to wend their way through the old structures of commune and patriciate; they did not have to become burghers of the long-existing municipal Commune of Trieste. For the civil rights of the minority merchants derived from the Free Port Patents and the privileges granted by Vienna. For the Jews, as for the other merchants, citizenship in the municipal Commune was largely irrelevant for the enjoyment of economic rights.[7]

Local citizenship was also irrelevant for the political rights that mattered to this mercantile class. These had to do with the *Borsa*, the mercantile exchange that served not only their individual dealings and fortunes, but also their collective interests and standing as a corporate group. The most important political right for merchants was the right to self-governance in this corporate body. In the larger arena, the *Borsa* was the vehicle of political expression of the mercantile class of Trieste, and its representative to the local officials appointed by Vienna. The *Borsa*'s political business was with the Intendancy and then the governor, not with the old Commune. Part of the *Borsa* since its inception in the 1750s, the Jews from 1782 on could participate openly as political actors within it. Membership itself in the *Borsa* was significant, and not something to be taken for granted, even by a port Jewry. Whereas in London, ten percent of the seats for brokers on the Royal Exchange were set aside for Jews from the late seventeenth century, in Bordeaux, even as late as the 1780s, Jews were still pressing for admission to the Chamber of Commerce.[8]

The constellation in Trieste of port city, commercial utility, novelty, and structured diversity created a situation for Jews in the eighteenth century that highlights yet again points made long ago by Salo Baron: Jews often fared best in new centers, and in situations in which they were not the only minority; socioeconomic and cultural change were often more decisive than formal legal equality.[9] Raison d'état and mercantilism, the factors usually cited by scholars such as Baron, Shmuel Ettinger, and Jonathan Israel to highlight the singularity of the early modern period in European Jewish history, were crucial for the development of the Jewish community in the eighteenth-century Free Port of Trieste.[10] Trieste shows that those forces which had allowed for the reestablishment of Jewish settlement in western and central Europe in the sixteenth and seventeenth centuries were not exhausted by the eighteenth. Study of the Jews' entry into modern Europe and their acquisition of rights ought to start not with the late-eighteenth-century debates about Jewish status and character, but rather with the earlier process of their admission and settlement. Such analysis should distinguish the different dynamics obtaining in varied settings and different kinds of society.[11] The category of port Jewry can help make such distinctions.

Absolutism and Toleration

The port Jewry of Trieste was created by raison d'état and mercantilism of a particular stripe, that conceived and practiced by eighteenth-century reforming absolutism. The initial effects of Habsburg absolutism upon the minority *nazioni* in Trieste—the Jews, Protestants, Greek and Serbian Orthodox, and Armenians—were beneficial, for it created the framework for their distinct corporate existence within the port city. However, the relationship between the reforming absolutist state and these communities became more complex from mid-century on, as Vienna became increasingly intent on state-building and centralizing. The Theresian regime embarked on the process of subjecting these communities, like all corporations, to greater state purview and making them more integral parts of the state apparatus. The Josephinian regime greatly intensified this process, for its aim—civil integration of productive religious minorities, including Jewries—was far more radical.

The premises of Josephinian Toleration were different from those of Theresian sufferance. Maria Theresa's was a limited utilitarianism that for specific economic purposes was prepared to make exceptions to the prevailing political-religious ethos, that is, to carve out a few small spaces—such as Trieste—where pragmatism would contravene her general policies. Though Joseph Karniel and Grete Klingenstein have shown that more exceptions existed than are usually recognized, still, those instances did not constitute a general program. Joseph's civil toleration was intended as a norm, as a new framework, and not merely as sanction for isolated exceptions. Its basic assumption was that all subjects, including Christian minorities and Jews, could potentially be useful to the state if the right policies were implemented: civil restrictions removed, civil rights granted, civic morality and its basic tenet of productive service inculcated, and, in the case of the Jews especially, cultural transformation undertaken.

Overall, the Josephinian Edicts of Toleration offered regularization of status: room for the religious minorities within the state system and inclusion of them within the civil order. The Habsburg historian Robert Evans has suggested that the edicts be seen "as the final push toward a state church able to reconcile earlier divisions and to realize full confessionalization of the population under loose Catholic aegis." Confessionalization refers to the process of state recognition and cooptation of the various Christian denominations within the states of the Holy Roman Empire in the sixteenth and seventeenth centuries. This cooptation or integration served the state's interests of centralizing and social peace, and the religious minority's desire for legal standing. In turn, Evans has considered Joseph's policies toward the Jews in particular as "a kind of mercantilist confessionalization": freedom from previous disabilities and the grant of legal standing in exchange for service, primarily economic, to the state and a degree of willingness to be coopted by the state.[12]

Indeed, Triestine Jewry in the eighteenth century provides a prime example of "mercantilist confessionalization" at work. And it is is one of the rare examples on which to base the case for continuity of policies of religious toleration from Maria Theresa to Joseph. The case of Trieste does indeed support Grete Klingenstein's claim that even before Joseph's celebrated edicts, there was some toleration of religious diversity—even legally recognized—in the Habsburg Monarchy. Yet, although it set a precedent in some respects, the exceptionality of Trieste must be stressed. Theresian Trieste hardly constituted a program or norm of toleration. And throughout the Theresian and even Josephinian periods, when the status of religious minorities was regularized, the exceptionality of Trieste continued. Even in the 1780s, it was usually considered too exceptional for emulation elsewhere.

But for religious minorities throughout the Habsburg Monarchy, and indeed in all of Europe, the overall thrust of Josephinian civil toleration cannot be underestimated: the novelty of a systematic regularized status and a place in the social order for the minority confessions alongside the majority.[13] Civil standing and the beginnings of civil toleration were significant both for the Christian minorities and for the Jews. Even for the Jews, for whom civil toleration was more limited than for the Christian minorities, the significance of Joseph's edicts transcended mere economic utilitarianism.

For all the religious minorities, however, the civil toleration and integration proffered by the Josephinian absolutist state entailed centralization and greater state involvement in communal affairs. To release the full productive potential of the various sectors of society meant necessarily to rationalize and transform traditional social structures and mentalities. To be productive, subjects had to internalize the norms of the tutelary absolutist state and the basic tenet of its civic morality: the value of self-motivated and self-disciplined productivity in the service of all. This would constitute active subjecthood or citizenship in the absolutist state. As Franz Szabo has argued, Habsburg enlightened absolutism involved a "fundamental reshaping of society," and the "intent" on the part of the governing elite to promote the "liberation of individuals from the bonds that tied their ancestors"—so as to foster a greater identification with the whole.[14] Such liberation was especially glaring in the cases of the peasants and the clergy, but it was relevant also for the religious minorities. And it accounts for the duality of the Josephinian program with regard to most Habsburg Jewries: civil improvement and integration on the one hand, but intrusive encroachment on communal life and forced transformation of traditional ways on the other. In Heinrich Graetz's memorable words, Joseph's edicts displayed a combination of "sincere but forceful love of humanity." Notions of humanity and utility to the state were closely linked in Joseph's regularizing the civil status of the Jews and mobilizing their productive potential. And there is no denying that for most Habsburg Jewries, the price of intrusion and transformation seemed very high. In Jewish historiography, intrusion and transformation, usually branded as forced assimilation, have loomed larger than civil standing or betterment.[15]

Yet I would argue that the overall context should be kept in view when the far-reaching degree of absolutist state intrusion upon Jewish life is considered. And the eighteenth-century port Jewry of Trieste is an example that helps us to take more seriously the other side of the equation: to focus more specifically upon the goals of civil betterment and integration. For in Trieste, the thrust of the Josephinian program was not transformation but centralization. The absolutist state aimed for greater consistency in spheres such as language, education, and law, but the economic, social, and cultural realities of Triestine Jewish life—and the legal status through which these had long been reflected—were such that extensive Jewish transformation was not necessary. The transformative thrust of Josephinian Toleration was blunted and the goal of civil integration more plainly evident in Trieste. Precisely because the specifics of the initial Toleration legislation were not innovative, precisely because the ground had been otherwise prepared, precisely because the continuity between Theresian privilege and Josephinian Toleration was so great,[16] the Jews of Trieste were one Habsburg Jewry able to reap the benefits of the Josephinian program, so that civil toleration was significantly realized, and indeed formed the basis for civil, and ultimately civic, integration.

Under both Maria Theresa and Joseph, the centralizing absolutist state interfered with the internal life and governance of the Jewish community of Trieste. The Jews of Trieste did chafe at the tighter embrace of Theresian absolutism when it became involved with communal administration. Though they struggled for greater communal autonomy, for the most part they still considered the state favorably, since it guaranteed them a privileged status and opportunities for unlimited growth. Although during Joseph's reign the absolutist state withdrew from communal administration as such, it was far more thoroughgoing in its entry into other spheres, such as education, language, judiciary, and marriage law. Yet with extensive cultural, social, and economic transformation not on the agenda and the goal of civil integration apparently and increasingly realizable, the Jews of Trieste could view with favor the actions of the Josephinian absolutist state. In Trieste, there was a remarkable degree of congruence between the perspectives of the state and the Jews with regard to the desirability of the goal of civil integration, though that congruence was not without limits.

Initially in 1781–82, the Toleration legislation presented the Jews of Trieste with an unusual challenge: to maintain the substance of their prior, and more favorable, privileges. Once they succeeded in doing so, and in fact in acquiring new prerogatives, they responded readily and enthusiastically to most of the remaining Josephinian legislation through the 1780s. To them, the program meant civil integration, centralization, and continuity.

Specifically, in Trieste, the Josephinian program meant the end of the ghetto, the opening of the state-supervised *Scuola Pia Normale* erected upon the base of the old communal school, and entry into leadership positions in the civic institution most important to them, the *Borsa*. It also meant no longer paying for their status in the form of a privilege, though the full import of that was not immediately clear. Only in the case of the ghetto was some hesitancy evident on the part of one member of the community, the prominent Marco Levi. Most Jews considered the formal demise of the ghetto a salutary ending of discrimination. Yet the nervous communal response to this lone voice did show the pressure felt by the Jewish leadership of Trieste to demonstrate whenever possible their alignment with the Toleration program of civil integration. The increasing stress they placed upon civic morality in the *Scuola Pia Normale*, and their endorsement in principle of military conscription for Jews, were further indications of their keen awareness that greater civil opportunities necessarily involved greater civic duties. The community accepted greater state involvement in its tasks of educating, censoring, and keeping records of the population. The state's efforts to standardize systems of law, justice, and police were unobjectionable so long as the Jewish community retained control of religious law and communal discipline. (The two matters that caused the Jews of Trieste difficulty—mandated use of the German language and the partial secularization of marriage law—will be discussed below.)

Overall, the Triestine Jewish experience of Joseph's Toleration program stood in sharp contrast to those of the populous, more traditional Ashkenazic Jewries of central and eastern Europe, in which forced transformation and assimilation dominated. For the Jews of Trieste, the Toleration program of the enlightened absolutist state meant intervention, not encroachment; inclusion, not intrusion; centralization, not transformation; continuity, not rupture. Therefore, for the most part, it was not threatening but promising. It beckoned toward greater civil equality; it did not force assimilation to an alien culture and demand the destruction of traditional ways. Because of the special features that made Trieste what it was, the program was more positive and less dualistic than elsewhere.

Once they had secured their own status at the beginning of the decade and looked over the Alps, Triestine Jews could appreciate the broad aims of Joseph's Toleration program as leading toward greater civil integration of the Jews within the Habsburg realm. They felt that overall, the program removed the worst restrictions and humiliations affecting all Habsburg Jews, afforded more economic opportunities (and thereby greater potential productivity and honor), offered stronger guarantees of religious freedom, and granted the Jews fundamentally a more secure civil standing in the monarchy. Besides the practical steps toward civil improvement and inclusion, the

Jews of Trieste considered the symbolic and ideological dimensions of the Toleration program very important.[17] In poems composed for the opening ceremonies of the *Scuola Pia Normale* in 1782, Joseph was praised in Hebrew as a "righteous king" for fostering the "sweet union of men" and for "calling the sons of our people free men."[18] In his eulogies of Joseph and Leopold, Rabbi Tedesco heralded their promulgation of the "wise laws of tolerance" that established "golden equality," thereby setting new norms of religious freedom and mutual respect for the humanity inherent in all.[19] Samuel David Luzzatto, who grew up in Trieste in the first years of the nineteenth century, reflected local Jewish views of Joseph and Leopold when he described them years later as the "first to deal righteously and justly with the Jews," as the "first to recognize Jews as citizens."[20] Thus, from their initial insecurity about maintaining past privileges, the Jews of Trieste had decisively moved to a greater sense of optimism about civic integration based on the Enlightenment values of rationalism, humanity, and toleration.

But there were limits to the congruence of perspectives between Vienna, the local administration in Trieste, and the Jews of Trieste concerning civic integration. The state did not grant most Habsburg Jews the full measure of civil toleration accorded Christian minorities. It left intact many economic and civil restrictions. Though it provided a far greater degree of civic integration of Jews than before, and far more than is usually recognized in Jewish historiography, still, it did not fully create a "neutral polity"[21] in which religion was irrelevant to civil standing. In Trieste it came closer to that goal than it did elsewhere. Yet, even in Trieste, the state did not take over the financing of the *Scuola Pia Normale* as it did of all other normal schools. In marriage law, it created a secular-religious hybrid that left the rite of marriage in the hands of clerics and rabbis. And it left standing as a corporate body the Jewish community. The goal was greater civil integration of Jews as individuals while maintaining, albeit transformed, the corporate structures of society.

From the Triestine Jewish side, the divergence came on two matters pertaining to personal identity: the mandated use of German, especially for personal names, and the secularization of marriage law.

In Trieste, the call for assimilation to non-Jewish civic, cultural, and social norms was not in and of itself problematic. What was problematic was the specification that these be German rather than Italian. The Jews' defense of their use of Italian in fact bespoke their integration with their immediate local environment; and it reflected Trieste's position as an Italian outpost of the multinational monarchy.[22] On this issue, the Jews were closer to the local Triestine society than they were to the state.

The state's entry into the field of marriage law and the attempt to supplant Jewish law in this domain, considered quintessentially religious by the Jews, was the one instance when the Jews of Trieste experienced a sense of encroachment by the enlightened absolutist state on hallowed turf—the kind of encroachment that other Habsburg Jewries felt concerning other areas. It upset the implicit understanding with which Triestine Jews had reacted to and internalized the Toleration program: the distinction between civil and religious spheres.

All Jewish communities incorporated into the civic realms of modern states had to face squarely this question: Could Jews draw a boundary between the civil and the religious, the first the province of the state, and the second supposedly still the province of Judaism; and if so, where? For a religious tradition that had previously understood itself to be all-embracing and to have encompassed both spheres, this was an important and daunting task. It meant no less than defining, from the Jewish point of view, the entry terms upon which Jews could be expected to join and participate faithfully in the modern state, and the contraction of their religious civilization and way of life into a demarcated religious sphere. Jews could have a place in the new civic order if they defined Judaism as a religious faith, belief system, or set of ritual practices that were distinct from, and not opposed to, the civil sphere.

This distinction between the civil and the religious, with the religious ultimately subordinate to the civil, was articulated most sharply and dramatically by the Jewish representatives at the Napoleonic Assembly of Notables and Sanhedrin in 1806–7. These delegates faced the defining moment in the relationship between European Jews and the modern state when they were forced to formulate authoritative answers to twelve questions designed to test their readiness for the fraternity of French citizenship. In essence, they replied that Jews could willingly cede the civil sphere to the modern state as long as the religious sphere was left to the Jews and remained intact.[23] No other Jewry had to face quite the same test in the late eighteenth and nineteenth centuries. Yet, Joseph II's Toleration program in the Habsburg Monarchy raised essentially the same problem, though in a different and less acute form. There was no one moment of truth, no dramatic confrontation with imperial officials demanding answers from Jews in public assembly. Rather, the issue presented itself concretely in the course of the implementation of the different components of the Toleration policy.

On the whole, though the Jews of Trieste did not articulate it in the 1780s, their reactions to the Toleration program showed their implicit acceptance of the distinction between civil and religious spheres. Because their civil situation was so favorable, they had no trouble validating and legitimating that sphere. They were prepared to accept civic integration as long as what they considered to be strictly religious was left intact. In this, they resembled some of the more traditionalist Italian delegates to the French Sanhedrin, who wrote back home in relief that the French government had not really impaired the Jewish religion as such.[24] The Jews of Trieste were willing to accept the civil/religious distinction as valid if civil progress and Judaism were allowed to be compatible, with their religion left untouched. They did not consider the state's cultural policies or imposition of military conscription to violate Judaism as such. Generally, the Jews of Trieste had believed the interests of the Jewish religion to be well served by the new Toleration; they saw its fruits, for example, in stronger warnings against clandestine baptisms and in the provision of kosher food and Sabbath work exemptions for Jewish prisoners. In their letter of 1782 to other Italian communities urging support of Hartwig Wessely, they had stated their aim to be "to nurture ardent religious observance and earnest zeal for civil progress."[25] In other words, it was an article of their faith that the two were compatible, that Judaism could flourish along with civil improvement.

Only in the late 1790s, as a result of the "dangerous liaisons" that challenged their control of marriage laws, when they felt that the state was not respecting the religious side of the divide, did the Jews of Trieste actually articulate the religious/civil distinction for themselves. The real problem came for this Jewish community when individuals tried to use the theoretically redrawn boundaries between civil and religious inherent in Joseph's marriage reforms as a means to limit the Jewish community's enforcement of its own religious law. Had these individuals not pressed their apparent advantage in Habsburg marriage law, the clash may well have been averted. Had they not forced the issue, it might not have mattered if the Jews continued to consider marriage religious while the state called it civil.

The Jews of Trieste had arrived at an implicit understanding of the boundaries between the civil and the religious, and it was one that they had thought the government shared. But on this one issue, they found that they were mistaken. Ultimately, religious law, specifically on marriage and divorce, was the one area in which the Jews of Trieste saw both faces—the encroaching as well as the integrationist—of the centralizing absolutist state. On this issue, they did not welcome the state's drive toward "liberation of individuals from the bonds that tied their ancestors."[26] Only the controversial marriages of the late 1790s called into question their faith in the compatibility of Judaism and civil integration. Yet by finding a solution with the communal ordinance of 1805, they did manage to reestablish the communal-state-family pact. Ultimately, the marriage issue did not destroy Triestine Jewish faith in the Habsburg state, its toleration, or the goal of civil integration.

The Politics of Utility and Diversity: How to Translate the Enlightenment into Reality

Civil integration rested on the linchpin of utility or productive service, for as Joseph's proposals of May 1781 had put it, the goal was to make "the Jews more useful to the state." It is necessary to consider more broadly the meaning of utility in relation to the absolutist state, to morality, and to the Enlightenment.

Most Enlightenment thinkers considered tolerance of the religious Other a dictate of rationality and humanity, and a necessity for a modern secular state—in fact, the quintessence of enlightened political practice. On the basic assumption that all humans are bound together in one species of humanity by common rationality, they advocated freedom of conscience, religious toleration, and civil rights for all except those who endangered civil peace. As is well known, among many Enlightenment thinkers, the promise of rationalist universalist inclusion often fell short when it came to the Jews. Significant theoretical, practical, and emotional obstacles often blocked the realization of the promise of inclusion in humanity.[27] There is no need to rehearse the anti-Jewish diatribes of a Voltaire. The real issue is to highlight the basic problem and the basic dynamic at work: Jews in potential were to be included in humankind, but Jews in actuality were often considered not yet worthy of inclusion. In theory, Jews could be considered "men as well as we [Christians]" and "even more man than Jew" (in the famous words of Grégoire and Dohm),[28] but in reality, they were often considered too benighted, too corrupt, too different for immediate inclusion. Many European theorists and policy-makers agreed that the regeneration of the Jews' latent humanity required drastic transformation—of the Jews themselves, and also, in the view of Joseph II and Dohm, of the oppressive conditions and restrictions under which Jews lived.

Many *maskilim*, advocates of the Jewish Enlightenment, internalized the demand for Jewish self-improvement, and had it clearly in mind as they sought to prove Jewish worthiness and humanity by means of cultural renewal. Jews did not believe themselves to be less than human or human only in potential, but they knew there were those who thought this so. As even their advocate Grégoire put it, Jews had been long hated and "considered in a manner as intermedial beings between us [Christians] and the brutes" and had therefore "seldom [been] able to attain the dignity of the rest of mankind."[29] Thus, theoretical inclusion of the Jews among rational humankind or in the civic realm was a new and significant step taken by the Enlightenment. But the potentiality of it, its linkage to the demand for Jewish self-improvement, made the promise often conditional, qualified, and difficult to realize—and the whole process fraught with debilitating tension.

The usual bargain struck by late-eighteenth- and early-nineteenth-century regimes, enlightened absolutist and others, with their Jewish subjects was the following: the state would remove restrictions and grant rights to Jews in exchange for the Jews undergoing substantial transformation, variously called improvement, *Verbesserung*, *régénération*. It was understood as a quid pro quo. The only question was which would come first: the Jews proving themselves worthy or the state's granting of rights. Some, such as Dohm, Mendelssohn, and later Wilhelm von Humboldt, argued that humanity and prudence dictated first changing the objective conditions in which Jews lived, and that Jewish transformation would naturally follow in due course. But the majority, and even many Jews, placed priority on Jews' adapting to European ways as an essential first step, as proof of worthiness for civil inclusion. Generally in the Habsburg Monarchy, the process was to be simultaneous: removal of restrictions by the state and self-improvement by the Jews—all in the direction of greater civil inclusion.

The unusual situation of Triestine Jewry reveals a fundamentally different dynamic, and suggests conditions in which the theoretical abstract inclusion of Jews within humanity could be translated into concrete reality. In Trieste, the transaction was not rights in exchange for anticipated regeneration and future proof of humanity, but rather rights in exchange for already demonstrated utility and assumed humanity. As will be discussed below, utility, humanity, and morality were all closely linked. The mediator between theoretical inclusion and concrete reality was in fact utility.

In the case of the Triestine port Jewry (and of other port Jewries, often Sefardic, as in Bordeaux), their utility and adaptation to European ways were already taken as givens. They were not seen as "intermedial beings"—to use Grégoire's unfortunate but telling phrase—whose essential humanity needed to be regenerated. Their fitness for civil inclusion was already demonstrated by their economic utility and acculturation. Their humanity was not in question. I have seen no discourse of Jewish regeneration in late-eighteenth-century Trieste. Thus the exchange or transaction proceeded along different lines: civil rights were conditional not on Jews meeting a standard in the future, but rather on Jews continuing their past and present course—without dramatic transformation. For Habsburg rulers and local officials were mostly pleased with what they perceived as the industrious, moral, and cooperative Jewish community of Trieste. As Bishop Hohenwart wrote to Rabbi Tedesco in 1799: "The Sovereign [Francis] was generally content . . . with the [Jewish] nation in Trieste."[30]

Their long-standing economic utility and acculturation were the bases of the perception of Jewish productivity and humanity in Trieste. During

Joseph's reign, they also met the new civic requirements of utility: to serve the state as obedient, loyal, self-motivated, and productive subjects, imbibing and inculcating the "sound" universalist civic morality of the tutelary state. And their preference for Italian over German did not violate the other condition of Josephinian civic utility, speaking the language of their surroundings.

Of course, utility, productivity, and fitness for civil inclusion could not be proven once and for all. These still had to be demonstrated in an ongoing fashion—but that betokened continuation, not transformation. In whichever form the Jews enjoyed prerogatives, privileges, or rights, they still felt the need to show themselves ever worthy of the favors granted by the sovereign. The concern of Triestine Jews to do so was evident on a number of occasions, for example, when they established the *Scuola Pia Normale*, disassociated themselves from Marco Levi at the time of the abolition of the ghetto, and publicly supported military conscription. But I would argue that there was a fundamental difference between needing to prove something as yet unproven in order to gain rights for the first time, and continuing to show worthiness along well-laid-out paths in order to maintain rights already held. Continuation was not transformation. Transformation in order to prove civic fitness—the requirement for most central and eastern European Jewries—involved the anxiety of possibly never attaining the goal. Continuation—the far less frequent situation, which did exist for port Jewries or small wealthy elite communities—involved the anxiety of possibly losing privileges already enjoyed.

Thus, Trieste shows that demonstrated utility could mediate between theory and reality, between the ideal and the practical. It was one means by which the Enlightenment promise of universalist inclusion of Jews could be translated from potential to actuality. In this case, for all the reasons already discussed, Jews were assumed to be useful, human, and fit for civil inclusion. The reforming absolutist state did here implement in no small measure the Enlightenment ideals of toleration and humanity.

The moral dimension of utility has often been obscured in discussions of Josephinian Toleration because of the less-than-lofty sound of its key phrase, "being useful to the state." Some Jewish historians have chided Joseph for being too utilitarian and not sufficiently humanitarian. They have assumed that practical political motives could not be compatible with ideals or values. In fact, the dichotomy is false. Rulers did not have to choose to act exclusively for only one purpose. Also, the contents or effects of a ruler's policy often went far beyond the ruler's particular motives.[31] But more fundamentally, it must be recognized that in Joseph's eighteenth-century world of ideas, utility to society and the state was a way of expressing humanity. Utility functioned as a bridge between abstract humanity and actual society. To be civilly useful was to be virtuous. For Joseph, to give opportunities for useful service to all subjects without regard for religion or nation was to provide a path of inclusion—within the state and within humanity. Joseph's assertion—and demand—that Jews be useful was simultaneously utilitarian and humanitarian, and it represented a significant departure from his mother's conceptions.

Additionally, to serve usefully was to establish a sort of moral claim upon the sovereign and society. Zinzendorf expressed a notion closely akin to that when he wrote in a preliminary draft of his first report to Vienna about the 1781 Toleration proposals that the Theresian Statute of 1771 "contained almost nothing but the general favors that a sovereign normally denies to none of his faithful subjects, but for which the Jewish community had to pay one thousand ducats."[32] The implication was that faithful and useful service deserved favor, or fair treatment, in return from the sovereign. In sum, during Joseph's reign, utility was not only an economic concept, but also a civic concept and increasingly a moral one. Utility was an important way-station on the road to realization of Enlightenment ideals of humanity.

The case of Trieste reveals another factor that could play a key role in the translation of Enlightenment ideals into some measure of concrete reality, namely, diversity. The real question about the Enlightenment's inclusive ideals and the Jews was this: Though the Jews were said in theory to share in universal humanity, in reality were they comparable to anyone else, or were they *sui generis*? Could they in the present be included within a broader category such as humanity, subjects, or citizens? Enlightenment ideals stood a better chance of realization if there were a concrete referent group, a real social grouping, to whom the Jews could be seen as comparable. In the eighteenth-century Free Port of Trieste, the humanity of Jews was not just an abstract principle because the Jews were comparable to, and enjoyed parity with, the merchants of the other *nazioni*. Diversity in Trieste ensured that the Jews were not the only non-Catholic religious minority, nor the only people engaged in commerce. That the new port city was structured to contain diverse mercantile communities gave reality to both the Enlightenment ideals of rationalist universalism and the enlightened absolutist goals of civil integration.

Haskalah: Italian Jewish Continuities and Ambiguities

The positive response of Triestine Jewry, including its rabbinic and lay leadership, to Josephinian initiatives concerning Italian language and normal-schooling, and its related campaign on behalf of Wessely, demonstrated essential continuity with long-standing Italian cultural traditions. For the Jews of Trieste, tradition, Josephinian civil toleration, Enlightenment, and Haskalah all fit well together.

Some of the specifics of the normal-school program were novel in Trieste, but the basic principle that Jewish education not be restricted to Torah and Talmud was not. The new Triestine Jewish normal school was a natural outgrowth of the traditional Italian Talmud Torà, representing continuity, not deviation or rupture. A harmonious relation between old and new—claimed by Dinur as a hallmark of the Jewish community of Trieste[33]—was evident in the establishment of the *Scuola Pia Normale sive Talmud Torà*, and indeed in its very name. The normal school did not displace the Talmud Torà; the two coexisted under one roof, as parts of one institution. To become a normal school, the Talmud Torà expanded to absorb the new: it added a few subjects, and injected the curriculum with a dose of civic and Enlightenment morality. All the teachers of the Talmud Torà became staff members of the new school, and were joined for a three-year period by Herz Homberg, the associate of Mendelssohn who was notorious later in other Habsburg parts as a radical *maskil*. A school staff that included both Rabbi Formiggini and Homberg was surely evidence of old and new working together in Trieste.

What was unusual about Trieste was the support of the whole community for Enlightenment, as defined in the government's educational policies and in Wessely's message of Haskalah. In both cases, there was fundamental continuity between Italian Jewish cultural traditions and a positive attitude toward Enlightenment goals and doctrines. Because of the longer familiarity of the Italian Jewish tradition with an intellectual-cultural world beyond the strictly Jewish one, it was easier for Italian than for Ashkenazic Jews of central Europe to accommodate the new currents. The boundaries of tradition had always been more elastic for Italian Jews. Thus, as Baron put it, the Jewish community of Italy was able to "absorb the new movement [Enlightenment] without damage to its inner consistency."[34]

While Triestine, and Italian, Jews expressed their support for Wessely vigorously, their receptivity to Haskalah was not without qualification. They held reservations about its more radical tenets; specifically, they were reluctant to accept a transvaluation of Jewish and Gentile cultures. Thus, while they emerged as public defenders of Haskalah in the polemics of the day, their own cultural stance was not equivalent to it. The Italian Jewish cultural tradition converged with Haskalah. However, the two phenomena were not identical, but rather distinct and independent. One illustration: while the Jewish normal school in Trieste displayed similarities to German maskilic schools, it was in its context more traditional than those schools were in theirs. Italian Jews trod a different path to modernity than their central and eastern European cousins. The responses of the entire Jewish community of Trieste both to the normal-school program and to the Haskalah showed their sense of the compatibility of tradition and Enlightenment. That these two were not pitted as adversaries is one important measure of the difference between Italy and Ashkenaz.

Openness to modern currents combined with, and indeed stemming from, a rootedness in tradition—this characteristic Italian mix often perplexed contemporaries and later observers. Seizing upon the openness, Ashkenazic modernizers of the eighteenth and early nineteenth centuries often construed it as legitimation of radicalism.[35] Some historians have been sorely tempted to treat Italian Jews of the Renaissance and early modern periods as precursors of *maskilim* and modernity.[36] This is mistaken, for what the complicated Triestine and Italian response to Wessely in fact provides is not a mirror of Ashkenaz, but rather an example of a Jewry that, though not strictly speaking of Sefarad itself, could draw upon Sefardic rationalist legacies in its encounter with modern ideologies. Because of its frontier location, the Jewish community of Trieste became part of the history of Haskalah in central Europe, but by cultural inheritance and its own diverse composition, it belonged as well to the Mediterranean Sefardic world. Study of this community can help in the effort to place Sefardic, Mediterranean, and Middle Eastern Jewries within the purview of modern Jewish historians. And indeed, for analysis of those communities, the characteristic Triestine and Italian sense of continuity with tradition even while encountering and absorbing new currents is much more relevant than the *Kulturkampf* of Ashkenazic *maskilim*.

Cultural tradition was surely important in predisposing Triestine Jews to a positive response to Haskalah, but it was not the only factor. In this port city, as in Bordeaux, Amsterdam, London, and later Odessa, acculturation was not dependent on nor driven by ideology. Speaking the vernacular, being familiar with non-Jewish culture, behaving like other members of their respective socioeconomic group—these happened naturally in the diverse port setting. They were not spurred by a Haskalah movement nor by the designs of reformers, Jewish or Gentile, calling for fundamental transformation of Jewish life and behavior. Trieste illustrates the importance of socioeconomic conditions and dynamics, and, as scholars such as Todd Endelman, Steven Zipperstein, and Steven Lowenstein have argued, the need to distinguish between the processes of acculturation in general and the ideological movement of Haskalah in particular.[37]

The example of Trieste helps in the broader task of contextualizing Haskalah more precisely. If Haskalah is not simply identified with every kind of acculturation or openness to general culture, then Jewish historians can focus attention on questions such as the following: Who were its producers, and who its consumers? In which conditions was the Haskalah ideology generated? In which conditions was it received favorably and transmitted?[38] Trieste was surely an example of consumption, reception, and transmission, though not of production or generation. With its campaign for Wessely and its school, Trieste even became a model for central European *maskilim*. And yet, as I argued above, what was going on in Trieste converged with Haskalah, without really being an instance of Haskalah itself. The example of Trieste suggests that Jewish societies that did not need the Haskalah message of transformation because of their prior acculturation and ongoing socioeconomic realities were precisely those that could be most receptive to Haskalah. And it was precisely in such Jewish societies — which did not need articulated ideological programs of transformation from on high, whether from *maskilim* or from enlightened absolutist officials — that the rationalist universalist inclusive potential of Enlightenment ideals could be more easily realized.

Privileges and Equalities in an Absolutist-Corporate State: Legal Emancipation Reconsidered

Joseph's Toleration program was the most comprehensive and sustained legislative effort of a reforming absolutist monarch to improve the situation of his Jewish subjects. When the Napoleonic regime set out to reorganize and codify Jewish status in 1806–8 as part of its overall effort to regularize church-state relations, it considered Joseph's proposals of May 1781 "the most important legislative text" available.[39] It is interesting to note that even in France, and even after formal legal Emancipation, Joseph's measures were hardly consigned to the dustbin of history. Josephinian Toleration of the Jews deserves a more sustained and different kind of political analysis than it has so far received in Jewish historiography, both on its own intrinsic terms and for its continuing significance in the rest of Europe.

It is important to recognize that while the legal Emancipation granted French Jews in 1790–91 forever altered the aspirations of European Jews for equality, it did not immediately change all the political dynamics in which Jews were involved. Through much of the nineteenth century, most European Jews continued to live under absolutist rather than constitutional or democratic regimes. Furthermore, as dramatic as was formal legal equality in a democratic unitary state forged in revolution, it was not the only road to civil improvement and greater civic inclusion for Jews in the late eighteenth century. The dazzling light of Emancipation should not blind historians to other paths and significant steps toward civil equality: in overseas colonies in the Americas, where economic need and newness led to the improvement of Jewish status before continental Europe; in England and the United States, where equality never had to be legislated, since Jews were subject not to separate Jewry laws but to the same laws as everyone else, with occasional specific disabilities by virtue of not belonging to the established church; and in a few exceptional pockets of enlightened absolutist states in Europe.[40] It is anachronistic to condemn eighteenth-century attempts at reform in absolutist states because they failed to offer universal rights and equality in a democratic society; they could not, for such a society did not exist on continental Europe before the French Revolution. Thus, though it is clear enough what these states could *not* offer, it is still necessary to ask: What *could* they offer by way of civil improvement or civic inclusion for Jews?

Studying the status of Jews in late-eighteenth-century Trieste, composed of Theresian privilege repackaged in enhanced Josephinian Toleration, enables us to examine the questions: What kind of civil improvement was possible for Jews in a corporate-estates society of the Old Regime? If possessed of the will and situated in suitable circumstances, how far could an enlightened absolutist regime go in granting its Jewish subjects liberties (to use the proper eighteenth-century word)? What could equal (or even near-equal) subjecthood or citizenship mean in an eighteenth-century reforming absolutist state? To what kind of parity could Jews aspire in a corporate-estates society? The case of Trieste allows us a fresh vantage point from which to probe the Jewish policies and politics of the Old Regime, and thereby as well to contextualize better the seemingly ever-present concept of Emancipation. Trieste affords a fresh vantage point for two reasons: it has been little discussed in Jewish historiographical literature, and it was exceptional in its treatment of religious minorities in the eighteenth century.

As discussed above, in late-eighteenth-century Trieste, the Jews were not burghers of the local municipality, but they did enjoy substantial parity with the other members of the minority merchant communities. Members of these *nazioni* were not citizens of Trieste; hence, for example, they could not sit on its representative institution the *Consiglio di Patrizi* (Council of Patricians). But that world was irrelevant for the new mercantile class of Trieste. In their world, the world of the port, the marketplace, and the *Borsa*, the Jews had largely the same opportunities and obligations, the same rights and duties, as the other non-Catholic merchants and, in most respects, as the Catholic merchants. It should be remembered that the Jews' rights of public religious worship surpassed the Protestants' even when Joseph's Edict of Toleration was issued; only by special and exceptional dispensation were the Triestine Protestants then equalized in this respect to the Jews and Greek Orthodox. With regard to economic and civil rights, the Jews of Trieste suffered no particular disadvantages. As one celebrant expressed it in a Hebrew poem recited at the opening of the *Scuola Pia Normale*, the Jews were free (*benei horin*) to study, plant, and work as they pleased.[41] Like others in Trieste, Jews could live wherever they wanted, pursue various occupations, attend normal schools, and obtain doctoral degrees from universities; they were not subject to special communal or individual taxes, marriage restrictions, or civic military duties—in other words, to obligations or constraints that were unique to them. Much of this existed in Theresian times. One specific gain of Josephinian Toleration was the political right of Jewish *Borsa* merchants to elect and be elected to its executive body (though not to the top position of director). This political right, enjoyed by wealthy Jewish individuals, was an important measure of civil integration and near-parity. And its significance increased when, in 1804, the *Borsa* was formally invested with certain public political and economic responsibilities that had formerly belonged to state institutions.[42] A Jew could belong to both corporations at the same time: the Jewish community and the *Borsa*. Being Jewish was not an exclusive identity that separated a Jew from other aspects of Triestine economic and civic life.

The notion of parity or equality was used in a number of instances to describe the relation of Jewish status to that of the other minorities and merchants. In 1776, two wealthy Christian merchants, one of them *Borsa* Director Bellusco, reported to Governor Zinzendorf that normal-schooling should be extended to the "Jews, Greeks, and Armenians, who except for religion and rites, are *considered like* [emphasis mine] the other citizens."[43] When petitioning for eligibility for executive positions in the *Borsa* in 1779, Marco Levi argued that the Jews in other respects already enjoyed equality in Trieste.[44] On public occasions, Jews praised Joseph and Leopold for allowing them to enjoy "equality," even "golden equality," and Joseph specifically for "bringing *all to the same level* [emphasis mine] through the guidance of law and sound morality."[45] When the ghetto gates were formally opened in 1785, Jewish leaders, except for Marco Levi, compared their security situation to that of the other religious minorities in Trieste.[46] In their 1797 petitions about marriage law, Jewish leaders claimed that sovereign privileges had granted them "equality with all other faithful subjects of His Majesty in their civil relations."[47]

But Triestine Jews were not the only ones to use parity or equality to describe their status. So did Governor Zinzendorf in the preliminary draft of his first report to Vienna about Joseph's Toleration proposals in August 1781. And his wording is highly significant: "Here in Trieste the Jews already enjoy almost all the privileges and equality with the rest of the people."[48] It is difficult to translate precisely the plural word *Gleichheiten* that Zinzendorf used, for in English, we do not speak of equalities, but rather of equality. We can produce a plural if we add words: we can say "instances of equality" or "equal liberties." But in fact, the issue is not really one of language, but rather of politics—of late-eighteenth-century political theory and reality.

In the absolutist-corporate-estates society and polity of the Old Regime, equality as such could not in fact exist. Equality in the singular refers to an abstract universal concept: in the kind of modern democratic unitary state created in Revolutionary France, one could speak of equality, for equality meant equality with everyone, to all. Theoretically, every citizen was to stand in the same kind of unmediated relationship to the state, with no intermediary corporate bodies defining and determining the individual's status and life. Thus all citizens were to be equal to one another. But in a corporate-estates society, there was no one standard, no one measure of equality: subjecthood or citizenship was too much hedged and defined by intermediate corporate bodies and by different relations to the sovereign to ever become a true universal. It made sense only for individuals or groups to be equal to other individuals or groups in a similar station and a similar rank. And in an absolutist polity, it was ultimately the prerogative of the ruler to determine status by grants of privilege, which built realities on precedents and on personal grants of favor, not on abstract principles. Privileges always granted liberties or prerogatives or favors—the modern word "right" is not entirely appropriate—to specific individuals or groups. A privilege expressed and reaffirmed a quasi-personal relation between the sovereign and the faithful subject. By definition, privileges, essentially private laws, were particular, not universal. Privileges had to be multiple and plural, and they could grant equivalences or parities, but not equality or parity as such. The very concept of one privilege for all and universal equality for all would shatter the framework of an Old Regime state, and create, as it did in France, a totally different conception of society and state.

Thus, Zinzendorf's use of the plural *Gleichheiten* was fitting. By the late eighteenth century, the Jews of Trieste had gained substantially the same civil and economic rights as the other merchants and corporate *nazioni*. This near-parity was enhanced in political terms in 1782, when Jews became eligible to be *Borsa* deputies, and further in 1794, when deputy became synonymous with director; Jews were then eligible to serve in the very highest position of this important institution.[49] More work is needed comparing the statuses of the free-port merchants and the Commune citizens, and of the non-Catholic and Catholic merchants, in order to assess whether "equalities" constituted near- or complete parity. Nonetheless, it is clear that in late-eighteenth-century Trieste, the Jews were granted the economic, civil, and political rights that mattered to them. And their parity was not merely held by an abstract legal principle, but was anchored in the social and economic realities of their mercantile port city in which they, along with others, were playing a dynamic, vital, and valued role. The new corporate structures of the city, set up by absolutist rulers in order to promote commerce and diversity, allowed the Jews both independence and influence, and significant "equalities." A generation later, Triestine Chief of Police Ignazio de Capuano described the late-eighteenth-century situation thus: "[In] the formal privileges . . . with regard to the public rights of citizens, the . . . Jewish community is made equal in industry and commerce to the other inhabitants of this city."[50] When the French occupied Trieste twice in the 1790s and again in 1809–13, they judged Jewish status in Trieste to be sufficiently close to the Emancipation they were legislating elsewhere that their only innovation was to allow Jews into public service and to share in the political right to be elected to the municipal council, a right that was new for everyone.

Thus eighteenth-century Trieste was a place in Old Regime Europe in which the Jews enjoyed an extremely favorable status, one exceptional compared to that of most Habsburg and European Jews in the 1780s. And that status did not derive from equality granted by formal legal Emancipation. Trieste's example provides strong support for Baron's contentions that formal legal equality was not always the surest route nor the firmest base for Jewish rights, and that law often merely sanctioned existing economic and social realities. It also shows the importance of civil and economic rights (*privatbürgerliche Gleichberechtigung*), in addition to strictly political rights (*bürgerliche Gleichberechtigung*).[51] And it bears out his claim that historians ought not to bring an exclusively legalistic focus to the question of Jewish status in modern Europe.

Still the question remains: Given that the Jews enjoyed considerable "equalities" with the other merchants in Trieste, what was the nature of the legal source of their status? In 1782, Joseph confirmed Triestine Jewry's prior liberties, but in a new form: previously secured by sovereign privileges, these liberties now came disguised in an edict conveyed in a simple letter from the governor in the name of the monarch. What did this mean? And more generally, what kind of law was a Josephinian Toleration edict, what kind of right did it grant?

The Toleration edicts were no longer privileges. They were not paid for. They were not private grants of favor to specific individuals or groups. In fact, they were addressed not to the Jewish communities of the different parts of the monarchy, but rather to the general public, as patents or edicts. They thus defined and declared status in a public manner. Joseph never officially clarified the relationship of his Edicts of Toleration for non-Catholics to the fundamental law of the monarchy, but when important advisors such as Chancellor Blümegen urged him to state publicly that the edicts merely conferred privileges that could be revoked at the monarch's wish, Joseph refused.[52] There was considerable unclarity: Joseph left intact many provincial laws that denied the non-Catholics the rights mentioned in the edicts, yet the statements and general tone of the preambles suggest that he recognized the liberties granted as natural rights and intended them to be permanent. His officials ruled that alongside the Edicts of Toleration, Jewish communal privileges ought to be renewed in Bohemia, but not later in Moravia and Trieste. In the early 1790s, his successor Leopold suppressed the edict in Belgium, claiming that it was not part of the fundamental law of the monarchy; but he maintained the edicts elsewhere.[53]

The confusion was inherent in this transitional stage in the development of the state, law, and political theory in the enlightened absolutist Habsburg realm. The Toleration edicts did not grant privileges. They were meant to apply more generally and more uniformly than specific privileges. They breathed a new spirit of utility, service, and humanity into the secular civic realm, yet they did not grant rights according to abstract universal principles. The removal of restrictions and the opening of new opportunities to individuals belonging to religious minorities still came as grants of favor from the sovereign. Joseph's Toleration edicts offered something that was in between the old-style privileges that had long defined Jewish status, and the new-style abstract universal rights that first appeared with the French Revolution and formal legal Emancipation according to the principles of the Declaration of the Rights of Man and the Citizen.[54] Not privileges, not rights, but rather, I would suggest, sovereign dispensations. Though sovereign dispensations could refer to human rights or abstract principles, they were still offered at the discretion of the sovereign and were usually conditional upon some action or quality of the subject; after all, Joseph expected his subjects to be useful to the state. And dispensations, like privileges, might be time-bound and revocable. Reforming Habsburg absolutism was constructing a *Rechtsstaat* (unitary state of fundamental laws) for its subjects in the late eighteenth century,[55] but still within the framework of a corporate-estates society; it was not constructing a democratic unitary state whose citizens would enjoy universal rights based on natural law. In an enlightened absolutist polity, the sovereign could move toward equalities of subjects, but could not confer equality of citizenship in the modern sense. As an absolutist sovereign tried to do away with particularist privileges, he could grant regularized standing and specific measures of civil improvement by sovereign dispensation, but equal universal rights for all were not yet there to be given.

As it was generally, the lack of clarity of the new dispensation was a source of perplexity for the Jews of Trieste. Initially in 1781, it produced considerable insecurity. Everyone knew that the old coin of the realm was privilege, money, and favor, but they didn't know what the new coin of this changing realm was. They gradually came to see that it still operated on sovereign grace and favor in exchange for subjects' demonstrated worthiness and faithfulness. Though they could and did meet those terms, they felt somewhat insecure without their familiar privileges. What new status meant, and how secure it might be, was not known to the Jews of Trieste in the 1780s, just as it was not known to the first Jews presented with legal Emancipation: the Sefardim in Bordeaux and the Ashkenazim in Alsace-Lorraine in 1790–91, Dutch Jews in 1796, and some Italian Jews in the 1790s, who, like Marco Levi a decade earlier, were apprehensive when French troops brought down ghetto walls. Jewish insecurity in the face of new status was not uncommon.[56] In Trieste, the Jews took no chances: though Joseph had told them that the Toleration legislation rendered reconfirmation of their former privileges superfluous, they still asked his successors Leopold and Francis for renewal of those privileges.

How, then, finally to view the new dispensation in Trieste—Josephinian Toleration, which preserved and enhanced the substance of Theresian privilege—in light of the formal legal equality brought by the Emancipation of Jews in Revolutionary France? In Italian Jewish historiography, the term "first emancipation" has long been used for the period of French occupation from the 1790s to Napoleon's demise in 1813–14, during which French-style legal emancipation was imported and implemented in many places in Italy. The term "first emancipation" has also been applied by Renzo De Felice and Shlomo Simonsohn to the effects of Joseph's Toleration legislation in northern Italy.[57] In her study of civil society in nineteenth-century Trieste, Marina Cattaruzza wrote:

> From the founding of the emporium and the policy of religious toleration practiced by Maria Theresa, the Jewish community travelled in Trieste a route of political-civil emancipation about a century in advance of the other parts of the Empire, which brought it to an integration in urban society [that] remained unparalleled in the rest of the Habsburg possessions.[58]

All these scholars are correct in this respect: Joseph's dismantling of the worst instances of discrimination and his creation of new civil and economic opportunities for Jews was a step in the broad process of modern European history by which groups were emancipated from the traditional bonds and restrictions that hindered their activities and by which bourgeois societies were ultimately created.[59] Yet in Jewish historiography, given the dominant centrality of the concept of French-style legal Emancipation, it is necessary to be especially precise. Joseph's Toleration could, especially in optimal circumstances such as those in Trieste, offer *freedom from* restricting constraints. But it did not offer *freedom for* equal participation in a democratic state.[60] The latter is what "Emancipation" generally means in Jewish historiography. Given the very different dynamic, the different kind of right, and the different kinds of equalities dispensed by the absolutist

Habsburg sovereign, I would not use the term "Emancipation" for Josephinian Toleration.[61] It is sufficient to characterize it thus: by sovereign dispensation and as a result of long-standing economic and social realities, the Jews of Trieste enjoyed a very favorable status under the Old Regime, a status comparable to that of the other merchants in Trieste, and exceptional in terms of most Habsburg and European Jewish communities.[62] As yet, there is no convenient term to describe this transitional, anomalous status, other than perhaps "neutral polity," as Michael Silber has suggested, or "civil inclusion," as I propose.[63]

Jewish Civic Identity and Politics in an Enlightened Absolutist State

In the late eighteenth century, the Jews of Trieste felt that things were moving in the right direction: toward ever-greater civil inclusion and integration. Their initial uncertainties about the status of their valuable privileges gave way to appreciation of the benefits of Josephinian Toleration and a sense that they were indeed living in favorable times. However, this did not mean complacency: as their actions on a number of occasions showed, they knew that they could never provide too much proof of their utility and of their fidelity and commitment to Habsburg policies. Their identity was woven from at least three strands: they were Jews, merchants of the Free Port of Trieste, and Habsburg subjects. In general, these strands of identity seamlessly overlapped; one of the rare cases of conflict came over marriage laws in the late 1790s. It became apparent that although their Triestine and Habsburg identities were steadily growing, they had not displaced Jewish religious and communal identity. The relation between the civil and religious was not static, and the delicate balance of the 1790s would certainly change in the course of the nineteenth century.

What kind of collective political behavior did the Jews of Trieste display in the decades of Josephinian Toleration? What kind of politics did they practice?

A certain continuity was evident between their nervous assertions of pride in 1770—telling Theresian officials that surely they "rendered . . . [themselves] worthy of being considered as called and invited, rather than [merely as] tolerated"[64]—and their behavior in subsequent decades. Yet they became less hesitant in expressing their ever-keen desire to protect their privileged exceptionality and the gains of the Josephinian dispensation. Two reports in the local newspaper *Osservatore Triestino* from 1786 and 1787 were especially revealing of the symbolic public climate created in Trieste by the Toleration legislation, and of the Jewish approach to politics.

In August 1786, the newspaper's editor, Giuseppe De Coletti, wrote a spirited defense of Jews in response to an article in the Venetian paper *Gazzetta del mondo*. De Coletti believed that the Venetian article defamed Jews by wrongly imputing collective responsibility to them on the basis of improper behavior by some Jewish bankers in Graz. He wrote passionately:

> All of the human species form a universal society divided into different peoples . . . the crimes of one or a few do not ever become the crimes of all; to vilify a nation honored by Sovereigns is to act as if one were a King; to insult it [such a nation] when God preserves it is to go against the work of God; . . . to write a newspaper, a philosopher, not a theologian, is required.[65]

He went on to state that he could not ignore the "disgust" that this article occasioned in "men of wisdom" such as himself. The words were stirring and had the ring of conviction. De Coletti was practicing what we might call tutelary journalism: he was trying to inculcate in his reading public enlightened views about humanity, civil society, the Jews, and the press.

Half a year later, in the January 6, 1787, issue of *Osservatore Triestino*, an article appeared somewhat at variance with those lofty sentiments. It reported the well-attended Catholic baptism of a Jewish family, and the bishop's closing remarks that this occasion should serve for the "edification and glory of all faithful Christians, and also as an example and imitation for our erring brothers."[66] Jewish leaders were perturbed and incensed. Within two days, they prepared a long letter of protest to Governor Brigido that made the following points: The bishop's exhortation was contrary to the intentions of the gracious sovereign to permit religious freedom and to have his subjects develop "that fraternal love and union of sentiments" that "benefit a state." At a time when His Majesty was not only "graciously sympathetic" but indeed offered "golden protection against the hatred that perhaps still exists in less educated and coarser spirits," and tried to bring such people "to believe that the Jewish Nation is the same as any other with respect to being human," this article characterized the Jews as "wandering, dispersed in error." This was not only contrary to the sovereign will and enlightened principles, but also dangerous and possibly inciteful of the rabble.[67] The Jews asked for public redress in the newspaper to be accomplished in a manner deemed appropriate by the governor.

The public response came in the next issue of the paper, on January 13, 1787. In it, De Coletti apologized, explaining that he had received the article at the last moment just as the paper was going to press, and that he had inserted it without exercising his usual "preliminary critical judgment" or submitting it to governmental censorship. He expressed his "exceedingly great regret" and assured the public that he had had "no imaginable intention of offending anyone."[68]

Indeed, it is likely that the offending sentence would not have passed official censorship. Only some three weeks earlier, Chief of Police Pittoni had stressed in his report to the Court Chancellery

how much the laws of toleration are venerated in Trieste, and what scrupulous attention the civil government gives so that they are observed and so that the ecclesiastics proceed with prudence in such matters—inspiring in the populace sentiments of love and of harmonious union, in spite of errors of opinion that divide them, and keeping them far from superstition in the act of guiding them on the road to the true religion without ever arousing controversies.[69]

Toward that end, certain popular religious observances, such as processions in celebration of saints' days and of Holy Week, had been toned down or abolished in accord with sovereign ordinances. Pittoni took pride in the lack of opposition to these measures in Trieste, and believed it proved the philosophic—that is, tolerant and enlightened—tenor of Trieste. In January 1790, *Osservatore Triestino* published a warning in the name of Governor Brigido against clandestine baptism of Jewish minors, stressing their "diametrical opposition" to the sovereign laws concerning toleration and public order.[70] If the governor believed this warning necessary for the populace, then Pittoni's assessment was obviously overly rosy. But it also showed the commitment of the local government of Trieste to the realization of Toleration.

The Jews' protest about the exhortation to conversion in the 1786 newspaper article shows that they counted upon the government to uphold the norms of Josephinian Toleration. They took the rhetoric of toleration seriously and as a new public norm. This episode demonstrates not only that political correctness was alive and well in Trieste in the 1780s, but also how the Jews conducted themselves politically. Jewish leaders were acutely sensitive to how Jews were being portrayed in the news media of the developing public sphere. They still resorted to time-honored *shtadlanut*, behind-the-scenes intercession with governmental authorities. But they spoke in the discourse of the times and invoked the Enlightenment values of humanity and religious freedom. Yet they did not refer to these as abstract principles or universal natural rights. Rather, they appealed to the gracious protection and toleration of the sovereign as their source and guarantor. No episode better captures the mood of the period: the hopes engendered by Joseph's Toleration legislation, the conviction that successful appeal could be made in the name of new values and principles, and the prudence of private behind-the-scenes action. Like so much else in the age of reforming absolutism and enlightenment, Jewish politics in late-eighteenth-century Trieste also displayed a combination of old and new.

Reference Material

Abbreviations

ACIT	Archivio della Comunità Israelitica di Trieste
ADT	Archivio Diplomatico Comunale di Trieste, in BCT
AN	Archives Nationales, Paris
AST	Archivio di Stato di Trieste
AT	*Archeografo Triestino*
BCT	Biblioteca Civica di Trieste
CAHJP	Central Archives for the History of the Jewish People, Jerusalem
CI	*Il corriere Israelitico*
C.R. Gov.	Cesareo Regio Governo in Trieste, 1776–1809, in AST
C.R.S. Int. Comm.	Cesarea Regia Suprema Intendenza Commerciale per il Litorale in Trieste, 1748–76, in AST
HHSt	Haus-, Hof-, und Staatsarchiv, Österreichisches Staatsarchiv, Vienna
HKA	Hofkammerarchiv, Österreichisches Staatsarchiv, Vienna
HUC	Hebrew Union College, Cincinnati
HUC-JIR	Hebrew Union College–Jewish Institute of Religion, New York
I.R. Gov.	Imperial Regio Governo per il Litorale, 1814–50, in AST
JNUL	Jewish National and University Library, Jerusalem
JTS	Jewish Theological Seminary of America, New York
Komm. Lit.	Kommerz Littorale, 1749–1813, in HKA
MI	*Il Messaggero Israelitico*
PO	*La Porta Orientale*
RÉJ	*Revue des Études Juives*
RMI	*La Rassegna Mensile di Israel*

Notes

Introduction

1. On relations between Trieste and Venice over time, and their crossroads locations, see Salimbeni 1984. On literary modernism in twentieth-century Trieste, see the imaginative treatment of Svevo, Joyce, and Umberto Saba in Cary 1993.

2. For relevant works on Triestine history, see De Antonellis Martini 1968; Apih 1957; Cattaruzza 1995; Cervani and Buda 1973; Cova 1992; Faber 1995; Maternini Zotta 1983; Millo 1989; Tamaro [1924] 1976; and Tullia Catalan's forthcoming book, which I've not seen: *La ebraica di Trieste: Politica, società e cultura (1781–1914)*, Quaderni del Dipartimento di Storia dell'Università degli Studi di Trieste (Trieste, expected date of publication 1999). McCagg (1989: 164–71) may be consulted on the late nineteenth century, but is unreliable about language in Trieste for the eighteenth century. On the need for renewed attention to the era of Joseph II in Triestine historiography, see Salimbeni 1992.

3. Ara and Magris 1982.

4. Elia Morpurgo 1782b (unpublished): f. 32r. All translations are my own unless otherwise indicated.

5. Klingenstein 1990: 162. On the location and eclecticism of the Habsburg Monarchy, see Scott 1990: 24–25; and Klingenstein 1981: 94.

6. See Sonne 1960–61, on the effects of location upon Italian Jewry's exposure to and absorption of different Jewish cultures.

7. See Ettinger 1961 and Israel 1989. I follow Jonathan Israel's definition of mercantilism as a "political approach to socio-economic questions" that stressed the "deliberate pursuit of the economic interest of the state, irrespective of the claims of existing law, privilege, and tradition, as well as of religion," rather than as a

specific set of economic theories or policies (pp. 2–3). I agree with Israel that the early modern period in Jewish history deserves attention in its own right and not just as a precursor to the later process of political emancipation. However, I reject his use of Trieste to support a claim of Jewish urban decline in the eighteenth century (p. 238). He states that although Trieste eventually took over Venice's leading commercial role, the Jewish community had little to do with its rise; his evidence of the slow population growth of the Jewish community in Trieste between 1735 and 1748 is misleading, because the port as a whole did not really take off until the 1760s and 1770s, during which time the number of Jews rose dramatically. Rather, Trieste illustrates the same factors at work that Israel describes for the sixteenth- and seventeenth-century rise of European Jewry, but in Trieste they occurred in the eighteenth century, and then operating in tandem with the later forces of Enlightenment and absolutism. The example of Trieste does, however, accord with another thrust of Israel's work: that European Jewish history should be looked at bifocally with both Ashkenazim and Sefardim in view.

8. Braude 1991 and forthcoming. On various invitations and settlements, see Baron 1952–83, vols. 14–15; Cooperman 1976; Israel 1989; Ravid 1992.

9. On Trieste as a laboratory, political barometer, and symbol of eighteenth-century Habsburg reform, see Cervani 1961: 1, 3–6, 14–15; Romano 1981: 215; Salimbeni 1992; also Scott 1990: 22, 35, on the greater scope for absolutist rule in territories newly acquired or where new institutions were created.

10. I am indebted to David Sorkin for stimulating discussions that first raised the term "port Jewry" or "port Jews" to name this phenomenon and concept.

11. Baron 1964; 1937, 2: 164–90; and 1952–83: vols. 14–15; Ettinger 1961 and 1976; Katz 1993: 214–36, 251–53; and 1973.

12. I use the term "reforming absolutism" to stress the broad reform agenda and activity of absolutist regimes. These were not derived from, nor linked exclusively to, the Enlightenment. In choosing the word "reforming," I eschew the pejorative and teleological assumptions of Marxist historians who dismissed eighteenth-century absolutism as merely reformist, that is, as regressive or retardant; see Melton 1985: 390–91, for a succinct discussion of such views, and Birtsch 1996, for arguments in favor of the term "Reformabsolutismus." I consider the term "reforming absolutism" especially useful for Jewish historiography since it points to the broader dynamics of political, administrative, and social reform, and obviates the need to judge whether particular rulers or regimes held "enlightened" attitudes toward the Jews. For example, in the Jewish context, it is preferable to designate Maria Theresa as a reforming—rather than enlightened—absolutist monarch.

13. For insightful discussions of enlightened absolutism, see Scott 1990: intro., pp. 1–35; and Beales 1991; and on the Enlightenment in different settings, Porter and Teich 1981. For more on my own approach to the Enlightenment and the Haskalah, see Dubin 1997.

14. For northern Italian perspectives, see Altieri 1985; Bernardini 1996b; Del Bianco Cotrozzi 1983, 1989, 1991, 1993, 1995; Dinaburg 1949, 1950; Dubin 1987, 1991, and 1992; Ioly Zorattini 1984a; Vielmetti 1970–71, 12: 1–15.

15. On Italy as a lacuna and desideratum in Jewish historiography, see Hyman 1982: 312–13.

16. On the relative neglect of the eighteenth century, see Bernardini 1996a. Bernardini suggests that the last decades of the eighteenth century be included in the "long nineteenth century" by virtue of the Toleration reforms of the 1780s and the emancipation brought to some Italian Jewish communities by French soldiers in the 1790s. For some recent work on Italian Jews in the eighteenth century, see Allegra 1996; Bernardini 1996b; several articles in *Italia Judaica* 3 (1989), and Alatri and Grassi 1994; Luzzatto Voghera 1998. Unfortunately, Corrado Vivanti, ed., *Storia d'Italia*, Annali 11: *Gli ebrei in Italia*, vol. 2: *Dall' emancipazione a oggi* (Turin, 1997) was published too recently to be incorporated into my study. Generally scholars of eighteenth and nineteenth-century Italian Jewry focus more on political, social, and economic history than on cultural or religious history; two exceptions are Del Bianco Cotrozzi and Luzzatto Voghera.

17. For some examples of recent attention to modern Sefardic history, see Benbassa 1990; Benbassa and Rodrigue 1995; Goldberg 1996; Rodrigue 1990; Stillman 1995.

18. For example, Shohet 1960; Endelman 1979 and 1997; Zipperstein 1985; Lowenstein 1994; Baron 1928 and 1960; Feiner 1985 and 1995; Sorkin 1987, 1990a, 1992; and Sorkin and Feiner forthcoming.

19. Limitations and contradictions of absolutist policies stressed in Baumgart 1980; Dubnov 1971; Ettinger 1976: 750–63; Karniel 1985; Mahler 1971; Springer 1980. This book is not the place, but eventually an extensive comparison of Prussian and Habsburg absolutist policies toward the Jews is a desideratum. Indispensable starting-points for Prussia will be Selma Stern's voluminous work, *Der preussische Staat und die Juden*, 4 vols. in 8 (Tübingen, 1962–75), and Bodian 1984; and for the Habsburg Monarchy, Kestenberg-Gladstein 1969, the ongoing work of Michael Silber (e.g., 1985, 1987, 1988, 1989), and Bernardini 1996b.

20. E.g., Baker 1987; Schama 1989; Jones 1995.

21. Scott 1990: 25.

22. Szabo 1994: 5.

23. Klingenstein 1990: 157.

24. Silber 1988 and 1989.

25. On the importance of consultation, the bureaucracy, and subjects in the study of Habsburg absolutism, see respectively Klingenstein 1990: 157; Szabo 1994: 6–7; and Mueller 1994: esp. pp. 176–77.

Chapter One: Foundations of the Free Port and the Jewish Community in the Eighteenth Century

1. Valsecchi 1931, 1: 216.

2. Ingrao 1994a: 119–20, 137–42; Braude 1991: esp. pp. 333–38; Faber 1995: 37–78; Freudenberger 1978.

3. Bérenger 1975: 272.

4. Patents in Mainati 1817–18, 4: 90–109, 135–67, esp. 139, 142.

5. My account of the development of the free port in eighteenth-century Trieste draws upon Iacchia 1919, still of value for archival documents; G. Luzzatto 1953: 7–17; De Antonellis Martini 1968; Torbianelli Moscarda 1971; Babudieri 1981, 1983:

1–71, and 1990; Comune di Trieste 1981; Cova 1971 and 1992; Cervani 1961 and 1979; Faber 1995, especially for administrative history; and Caputo and Masiero 1988, with several graphic representations of the city's physical development. On Trieste in the eighteenth century more generally, see Tamaro [1924] 1976, vol. 2; F. Cusin 1930; and Apih 1957.

6. "Felicitous location" from Metrà 1793-97, 5: 326; and "gateway" quoted in Iacchia 1919: 131. On the original intention to develop the entire Littoral as a commercial area, see Faber 1995.

7. On the new Trieste as an expression of reforming absolutism, cf. Trampus 1996; and Salimbeni 1992: esp. 26–27, 32–34.

8. Iacchia 1919: 169. See also Negrelli 1970. On Venice, see Gasser 1997; and Salimbeni 1984.

9. Faber 1995: 212–13; Ara 1992a: 44–45; and especially Cattaruzza 1996, for a penetrating analysis of the formation of the new elite.

10. Iacchia 1919: 82–83.

11. Biagi 1986: 84–85. On Ricci (1721–91), who came from Tuscany to Trieste around 1750 and whose illustrious career in Trieste spanned some four decades, see ibid.: passim; De Incontrera 1969; and Faber 1995: 178–79, 246–55, and index entries.

12. Biagi 1986: 84.

13. Ibid.: 85.

14. De Antonellis Martini 1968; *Enciclopedia monografica* 1971–83, 3, pt. 2: 791–858; and Faber 1997. Kandler 1861 contains some of the minorities' communal statutes. Klingenstein 1993 discusses some other instances of Theresian toleration of religious minorities, though it should be noted that such toleration was mostly de facto, not de jure.

15. The word "nation" here does not have the later political connotations of nineteenth- and twentieth-century nationalism, but rather reflects medieval and early modern conceptions of "nation" as a group of individuals constituting a distinctive colony or community, originally resident aliens and typically devoted to commerce.

16. Elia Morpurgo 1781: 11–12.

17. Ibid.: 10.

18. Metrà 1793–97, 5: 329; Montanelli 1905: 122–24; Cervani 1969: 36, 45–46; De Antonellis Martini 1968: 112, 155; Cervani and Buda 1973: 53–55.

19. De' Giuliani 1969: 333.

20. Gasparini 1945: 404; Dollot 1961: 57; Trieste as chaotic medley (*guazzabuglia*) in G. De Brodmann, *Memorie politico-economiche della città e territorio di Trieste, Istria* . . . (Venice, 1821), quoted in Cervani 1969: 34–35. Cf. the later observations of Baron Philipp von Canstein, *Blicke in die Östlichen Alpen* (Berlin, 1837), quoted in Ciana 1959: 142–44; Yriarte 1875: 7–11.

21. Braun 1927–28: 228–29; Tucci 1980: 100. Cf. Iacchia 1919: 90–122, 166–80; Cusin 1930: 122–28; and Apih 1957: 50–62, 73–89, 202–5.

22. Observations of Venetian consul Marsan (1766), quoted in Tucci 1980: 95; cf. French General Desaix (1797), quoted in Gasparini 1945: 404.

23. Graneri 1784 report, quoted in Bulferetti 1944: 152, 156.

24. Report of the Magistrato de' V Savj alla Mercanzia (May 17, 1768), in *Per le*

auspicatissime 1879: esp. 12, 15. In contrast, Lord Stormont's 1765 report to London saw Trieste's great potential as still unrealized; see Dickson 1987, 1: 394-95.

25. Metrà 1793-97, 5: 336; Kaltenstadler 1969; F. Cusin 1931: 273, 287, 307; Cervani 1969: 46-47; Babudieri 1983: 80, 101, 125; 1990: 19-33; Ingrao 1994a: 167-68, 213-14.

26. De' Giuliani [1785] 1950; and *Panorama politico della città di Trieste*, in De' Giuliani 1969: 208.

27. Metrà 1793-97, 5: 336-37. The far-flung commerce and the growing fame of the free port were also celebrated in a Hebrew sonnet by Dr. Isaac Luzzatto, who lived in the Venetian San Daniele: I. Luzzatto 1944: sonnet no. 45, p. 49.

28. De' Giuliani, *Panorama politico della città di Trieste*, in 1969: 208.

29. Girolamo Polcastro, in De Tuoni 1921: 387; cf. Dollot 1959: 166-67; and Bevilacqua [1820] 1982: esp. 10-11, 38-46, 54-56.

30. De Incontrera 1960: 100-101; and Graneri in Bulferetti 1944: 151; cf. Dollot 1959: 166.

31. De Incontrera 1960: 99-101. Cf. Moré 1828: 221-22, 297-301. "Consoler of the afflicted" and "refuge of sinners" refer to Mary in the Catholic liturgy.

32. E.g., Voltaire's description of the London Exchange, in *Lettres philosophiques*, letter no. 6.

33. Cervani and Buda 1973: 3-5, 159; De Antonellis Martini 1968: 93-94. Milano (1963: 44) and Norlinghi (1858) mention earlier dates. On the early history of Jews in Trieste, see also Stock 1979; Kandler 1863; and Zoller 1913a and 1924: 32-35 (shorter version in his 1933b: 285-86).

34. Stock 1972, 1974a; and Paolin 1991.

35. On the privileges and excerpts from them, see Stock 1979: 12-22, 83-85; Zoller 1911a and 1911b; Wolf 1858; Edgardo Morpurgo 1909: 54-59; CAHJP, HM 5467a (1565, 1647); Norlinghi 1858: ff. 3-9; Cervani and Buda 1973: 5-6; Baron 1952-83, 14: 265-66. On court Jews, see Katz 1973: 15, 28-30, and the sources cited there; Israel 1989; Mann and Cohen 1996.

36. On occupations, see Cervani and Buda 1973: 88-89; and Paolin 1991. Porto, known among Jews and Gentiles, composed works on geography, astronomy, and mathematics: *Over la-sokher* (Venice, 1627); *Porto astronomico* (2 vols., Padua, 1636); *Breve della geographia* (1640, probably the *Introduzione alla geometria e trigonometria* mentioned by Norlinghi 1858: f. 6); and *Dipluranologia quo duo Scripturae miraculae de regressu solis tempore Hiskiae et ejus immobilitate tempore Josuae declarantur* (1643), composed originally in Italian, and then translated into Hebrew and Latin. On the university careers of Emanuel Porto, Aron Porto, Zaccaria Parente, and Dr. Jacob Levi, see Modena and Morpurgo 1967: 18, 41, 128-29.

37. "Humilissimo ricorso delli Giudici et Rettori della Città di Trieste, Contro l'hebrei della medema Città," to Leopold I (June 21, 1675), in CAHJP, HM 5467a. Other complaints are found in CAHJP, HM 5467a (1684, 1695), and AST, C.R.S. Int. Comm., b. 71, ff. 23-26 (1695). See also Norlinghi 1858: f. 4; Stock 1979: 24-34, 1974a, and 1974b; R. Curiel 1932: 446-72; and Paolin (1991), who places the question of the Jews within the larger context of political struggles between the Commune and the empire.

38. Most works state 1696 as the date of the ghetto's establishment, but al-

though the final decree from Vienna was issued in 1696, Jews did not enter the ghetto until sometime in 1697; R. Curiel 1932: 464–66.

39. On the ghetto itself, see Norlinghi 1858: f. 8; R. Curiel 1932: 453, 464, 471; Stock 1979: 31–32. For illustrations, see Milano 1967: 312–13; and S. Cusin 1978: 59–70. On the negotiations and violence, see R. Curiel 1932: 457; Stock 1979: 29; Apih 1957: 26, 30; Paolin 1991: 234–43. To the authorities in Vienna, the Jews described their anxiety in striking terms ("The Hungarians do not fear the Turk as much as we wretches do the aroused people of Trieste"), argued for the more desirable location, and asserted their rights as citizens and subjects ("We are citizens of Trieste, subjects of His Majesty"); AST, C.R.S. Int. Comm., b. 71, ff. 7–8. The matter of local Jewish citizenship requires further investigation.

40. Rossetti 1830: 296–97.

41. My calculations are based upon the sources cited in Table 1, and on Torbianella Moscarda 1971: 40.

42. AST, C.R. Gov., b. 83, N. 427, "Tabella de Nati, Morti, e Matrimonij seguiti nella Nazione Ebrea l'anno 1776."

43. Zoller 1924: 6; cf. 1735 list in ibid.: 4, from Montanelli 1905: 103–4.

44. Schiffrer 1937: 16; Gatti 1991: 313–14.

45. Boccato 1984; Ioly Zorattini 1984b; Cervani and Buda 1973: 108–13; S. D. Luzzatto 1878: 22–23, 28–31; Apih 1957: 57.

46. Cervani and Buda 1973: 90–110.

47. Apih 1951: 278–80; also Apih 1957: 129–31, 193–96. On changes in the Italian dialect of Trieste resulting from the great immigration to the free port, with the Venetian dialect replacing the local *ladino* or *tergestino*, see Tamaro [1924] 1976, 2: 184; and Zudini 1979.

48. Zoller 1913b, no. 2: 5–6, and Chapter Four below. Unlike McCagg (1989: 165–66), I see no evidence for German or Yiddish as spoken languages of Jews in Trieste in the eighteenth century. Only in the nineteenth century did a significant number of German-speaking immigrants come to Trieste, at which time German became an important language among Triestine Jews.

49. Statute of 1746, in Maternini Zotta 1983: 209–14; also in Cervani and Buda 1973: 159–66. More generally on communal organization, see De Antonellis Martini 1968: 101–25; Cervani and Buda 1973: 19–68; and Maternini Zotta 1983: 1–54.

50. De Antonellis Martini 1968: 101.

51. New statutes were issued and modified at relatively short intervals, in 1762, 1766, 1771, 1777, 1783, and 1792; see texts in Maternini Zotta 1983: 218–78 (the most complete of the published versions); Cervani and Buda 1973: 167–224; 1762 partially in AST, C.R.S. Int. Comm., b. 68, ff. 23r–26; *Statuti [1766]* ... 1767 in AST, C.R.S. Int. Comm., b. 78, ff. 207–20 (also microfilm in CAHJP, HM 5455).

52. On Isach b. Rabbi Moses Formiggini (1700–1788), see Ghirondi and Neppi 1853: 169–71; and Cervani and Buda 1973: 43. On Raffael b. Rabbi Isaac Tedesco (Ashkenazy) (c. 1750–1800), see Ghirondi and Neppi 1853: 274–76; and Cervani and Buda 1973: 43. For more on both of these important rabbis of Trieste, see Chapter Seven below.

53. Statute of 1746, ch. 1, in Maternini Zotta 1983: 211; Norlinghi 1858: ff. 21–22,

29, 31, 34, 36, 39, 51–53; CAHJP, HM 2/5847, f. 9 and HM 2/5857, ff. 15–17, 19; Statute of 1766, *Statuti [1766]* . . . , 4: 1, 6: 1–6, 15, 7: 1, in AST, C.R.S. Int. Comm., b. 78, ff. 214v–217v (also in CAHJP, HM 5455); Statute of 1771, 1: XXXVI–XXXVII and XL, 5: I and VIII–IX, XIII–XV, 8: XIV, and *Regolamento* of 1783, 5: 1–2, in Maternini Zotta 1983: 222–23, 229–31, 235, 243–44; and Richetti 1984. On the traditions of the Italian rabbinate, see Bonfil 1990: esp. 14–34, 143–57.

54. All were built in the Italian style: the Ark of the Law on the eastern wall, a reader's platform opposite on the western wall, seats running along the two long sides, and open space in the middle. "Synagogue no. 1," or *Scuola Piccola*, was opened around 1745–46; "Synagogue no. 2," or *Scuola Grande*, was opened in 1775 on the premises of a formerly private chapel, was twice enlarged, then was rededicated in 1798 as the community's official synagogue. The Sefardic "Synagogue no. 3" was opened in 1798 in the same building as "Synagogue no. 2." Sefardic services were also held in the Camondo home in the 1780s, and in the Vivante home in the 1790s; this *Scuola Vivante*, or *Scuola Sefardim*, became the public "Synagogue no. 4" in 1829. Despite their names and rites, each synagogue had both Ashkenazic and Sefardic members. Useful secondary works are Zoller 1911c, 1912d, 1913b, and 1913c; R. Curiel 1938; P. Nissim 1960; S. Cusin 1978; Krinsky 1985: 369–73; Cervani and Buda 1973: 37–41; Stock 1979: 76–82. Further primary material in Norlinghi 1858: ff. 19, 23–26; CAHJP, HM 2/5857, ff. 1, 39–42, and HM 5804a, ff. 34, 53v–55v, 60r; I. Formiggini 1777; *Seder* . . . 1798 in ADT; *Statuti [1766]* . . . 1767; Maternini Zotta 1983: 218–79; AST, C.R. Gov., b. 620, N. 5876/1966, 8319, 2732/1069, 3338 (1786–88), and b. 621, N. 746/1958, 2404/2812, and 681/1819 (1794–95); and ADT, 2D33, N. 3645 and 5408 (1798).

55. Zoller 1933a: 51 n. 2. My discussion of immigration policy is based primarily on documents from Norlinghi 1858; CAHJP, HM 2/5857; HM 2/5858, ff. 245–250 (Polizia ed affari politici); HM 5804a; AST, C.R. Gov., b. 83, b. 620, b. 621, b. 622; ADT, 2D33. Cf. De Antonellis Martini 1968: 107–9, 123–24.

56. E.g., AST, C.R. Gov., b. 549, Pittoni (Sept. 8, 1796); b. 550, N. 4267, Pittoni (Nov. 1, 1799); b. 622, N. 1480 (Apr. 10, 1802).

57. CAHJP, HM 2/5836, f. 498 (Aug. 16, 1801).

58. CAHJP, HM 2/5843, f. 53, N. 3012 (Nov. 28, 1807). Cf. CAHJP, HM 2/5837, f. 318 (Sept. 9, 1802); and AST, C.R. Gov., b. 622, N. 3917 (Aug. 26, 1806). On *herem ha-yishuv*, see Baron 1942, 2: 4–12.

59. See statutes in Maternini Zotta 1983: 210 (1746, ch. 1), 220–21, 225 (1771, art. 1: XXIII and 2: XIII), 243 (1783, ch. 4, art. 12), 254–55 (1792, ch. 4, art. I[g], X, and XI); also *Statuti [1766]* . . . 1767, 1: 10; and addition 8, in AST, C.R.S. Int. Comm., b. 78, ff. 210, 219v–220r, and in CAHJP, HM 5455. See also R. Curiel 1938: 254; and CAHJP, HM 5804a, f. 17, N. 88–89 (Feb. 4, 1778).

60. Norlinghi 1858: f. 46.

61. ADT, 2D33, *Capi* to Commission of Police, 1758 (cf. Comune di Trieste 1981: 120, N. 413).

62. R. Curiel 1938: 245; Cervani and Buda 1973: 111–13.

63. AST, b. 621, N. 1447, Pittoni to governor (July 13, 1795). One of the most important officials to implement Habsburg reform policies in Trieste, Pietro Anto-

nio Pittoni (1730–1807) served as police chief in Trieste from 1766 to 1801, and also as councillor of the governor, circle captain, and director of the theater. De Incontrera 1960: 151–52; Tamaro 1942–43; Pagnini 1978; and Dorsi 1989.

64. AST, b. 83, Pittoni to governor (n.d., apparently Apr. 1782); cf. R. Curiel 1938: 248.

65. AST, b. 620, *Capi* to governor (Mar. 10, 1790), with accompanying correspondence. On the association to pay for circumcisions, Norlinghi 1858: f. 44; CAHJP, HM 2/5857, f. 41 (Apr. 14, 1775), and HM 5804a, ff. 17, 34r, 50r–51v. On 1780 apology to Venice, CAHJP, HM 5804a, ff. 37v–38r, N. 198 (Nov. 15, 1780).

66. Petition and response, Norlinghi 1858: f. 46; 1769 record, AST, C.R.S. Int. Comm., b. 78, f. 114.

67. Cervani and Buda 1973: 14, 26, 171; Maternini Zotta 1983: 221 (1771 Statute, art. 1: XXIV, provides the correct date).

68. Norlinghi 1858: ff. 33–34, 1754–55. Cf. CAHJP, HM 2/5857 (Apr. 24, 1755); HKA, Komm. Lit., r. 502, f. 24 (1755) and f. 60 (1767 complaints); Curiel 1938: 244; Scussa and Kandler 1863: 208.

69. E.g., Norlinghi 1858: f. 35; also f. 32, on the government's effort to keep female Christian servants from staying in the ghetto overnight.

70. ADT, 2D33, *Capi* to police (1758).

71. AST, C.R.S. Int. Comm., b. 78, f. 114, "Tabella delle Case stabilite e Foresti componenti gli Ebrei abitanti in Trieste" (May 4, 1769).

72. ADT, 2D33, *Capi* to police (1758); Norlinghi 1858: f. 30. Communal regulation in *Statuti [1766]* ... 1767, 1: 10, addition 8, in AST, C.R.S. Int. Comm., b. 78, ff. 219v–220r (also in CAHJP, HM 5455); Statute of 1771, 1: XXIV, 2: XVI, 2: XVII, in Maternini Zotta 1983: 221, 225–26.

73. AST, C.R.S. Int. Comm., b. 78, ff. 48r–50r, 59; CAHJP, HM 5804a, f. 29.

74. On Frizzi's reception in Trieste, see Frizzi 1790: V; also AST, C.R. Gov., b. 842, the admission document that praised his "good moral conduct." On difficulties in Mantua, see S. D. Luzzatto 1873: 123–24; Simonsohn 1977: 711–12; and Bernardini 1996b: 323. On the openness of the community and Frizzi, see Dinaburg 1949: 251–52.

75. Maternini Zotta 1983: 215–17.

76. AST, C.R.S. Int. Comm., b. 78, ff. 89r–90v, 94, 106, 110, 116, 154–155; CAHJP, HM 2/5857, ff. 27–28, 46; 1771 privilege in Maternini Zotta 1983: 215–16; cf. Cervani and Buda 1973: 101.

77. On Jews' economic activities, see Metrà 1793–97, 5: 326–36, 356–58 (partially republished in Cervani 1969: 17–22); "Gl'Israeliti a Trieste" 1862–63: 10–11, 31–33; Cervani and Buda 1973: 87–128; Basilio 1914: 277–309; Babudieri 1983: 85–104; Braude 1991; D. Nissim 1970; AST, C.R. Gov., b. 83, N. 1831, "Nota delle Persone Impiegate nelle Arti" (1781), on Jewish artisans (also in CAHJP, HM 5467b, and Stock 1979: 40); Comune di Trieste 1981: 87–88, N. 318; *Centenario delle Assicurazioni Generali* 1931: 18, 22, 30; and Tucci 1980: 102–4.

78. Zoller 1924: 6–7.

79. AST, C.R. Gov., b. 620, N. 1998, Roth report of Apr. 8, 1786.

80. Capuano, May 26, 1820 comments, in AST, I.R. Gov., Atti Generali, b. 753, N. 10725; cf. Berengo 1987: 81–83, 86–87.

81. S. D. Luzzatto 1878: 39, 44, 50–58.
82. AST, C.R.S. Int. Comm., b. 78, f. 114, "Tabella" (1769); Zoller 1913a; CAHJP, HM 2/5838, f. 126r. A somewhat later example of Jewish wealth: in 1812, Filippo Hierschel's personal fortune was estimated at 80,000 florins, far and away the highest of the twenty-five members of the Municipal Council; AN, FIE 65 (Mar. 25–26, 1812).
83. Cervani and Buda 1973: 97–100; Norlinghi 1858: f. 41; HKA, Komm. Lit., r. 502, ff. 28–39, 533, on Levi; Faber 1995: 198–201; Pagnini 1978: 37, 67, 137, 162, for examples of Levi's frequent meetings with Governor Karl von Zinzendorf; *Osservatore Triestino*, no. 6, Feb. 11, 1786, p. 76, in De Incontrera 1953–63, 24 (1954): 77–78, and May 5, 1794, cited in ibid., 32 (1962): 161.
84. *Harif gadol*, in Azulai 1934: 88. Levi was one of the first heads of the new school; CAHJP, HM 5804a, f. 29, N. 145, and f. 38r, N. 199. On Joseph Eliezer (Giuseppe Lazzaro) Morpurgo (1759–1835), founder of the *Assicurazioni Generali* firm, see Dinaburg 1949: 252–53; "Biographien" 1840; and A. V. M[orpurgo] 1862–63.
85. Cervani and Buda 1973: 105.
86. Pagnini 1978: 160–61.
87. HKA, Komm. Lit., r. 617, f. 14v (June 30, 1754); Gasser 1971: 246.
88. Gasser 1971: 255; AST, C.R. Gov., b. 52, N. 977, contains names of the six: Grassin Vita Levi firm, headed by Marco Levi; Elia Tedesco and Co.; Isaac di Jacob Alpron; Fratelli Luzzatti qm David; Marco Bolaffio; and Moise David Luzzatto; and HKA, Komm. Lit., r. 617, 13. ex Januario 1784, ff. 414–15, on 1783 elections.
89. Metrà 1793–97, 5: 356–57; cf. Braude 1991: 346.
90. Samuel Vital, *Riflessioni sulle assicurazioni marittime e loro progressi in Trieste* (Trieste, 1797), and G. V. Bolaffio, *Speculazioni nei cambi della piazza di Trieste* (Trieste, 1806), cited in De Antonellis Martini 1968: 72, 80; *Arcadia Romano Sonziaca*, in BCT, R.P. Mss. 3-26/3, 3-26/5, 3-26/7; Mainati 1817–18, 5: 195. Other Jewish members of the society were Grassin (Gherson) di Moise Levi, Dr. Joel Kohen, Aron Vivante, and Alessandro Fano.
91. Braude 1991: 346–47.
92. AST, C.R. Gov., b. 620, N. 5324 (Aug. 5, 1789). In contrast, see Chapter Eight below.
93. Cervani and Buda 1973: 105.
94. HKA, Komm. Lit., r. 617, f. 14v, June 30, 1754; Gasser 1971: 246; Cervani and Buda 1973: 97.
95. Gasser 1971: 245–49, 253–58; also on the 1779 reorganization, see HKA, Komm. Lit., r. 617, and AST, C.R. Gov., b. 52. On the *Borsa*'s role in the city, see Cova 1992: 24–26; Negrelli 1970: 362; and Apih 1988: 12–13.
96. Zinzendorf (1739–1813) served in many high economic and political posts in the central Habsburg administration both before and after his stint in Trieste. He is a key figure for the study of the Enlightenment, reforming absolutism, and economic theory in the Habsburg Monarchy. His nearly sixty volumes of diaries provide abundant material on his own education, career, and theories; on the many places and people he observed in the course of his intelligence-gathering travels throughout Europe; and on the circles of high Habsburg officialdom. An

international research team directed by Grete Klingenstein of Karl-Franzens-Universität, in Graz, Austria, is currently preparing a multivolume edition and study of Zinzendorf's diaries. In the meantime, for Zinzendorf in Trieste, see De Incontrera 1960: 152; Pagnini 1978; Trampus 1990; Tamaro 1942–43; and the many entries in Faber 1995: index. On Zinzendorf more generally, see Klingenstein 1994; Trampus 1993; Liebel 1979: 365–67; and Beales 1985: 181–83, on his religious outlook.

97. HKA, Komm. Lit., r. 617, 9. ex Majo 1779, f. 300r, Zinzendorf report to Maria Theresa (Apr. 16, 1779).

98. Ibid., 20. ex Aug. 1779, ff. 334r–335r, protocol of the *Borsa* meeting of July 13, 1779.

99. Ibid., 20. ex Aug. 1779, f. 346; Gasser 1971: 254–55.

100. Unpublished Zinzendorf diary entries, Oct. 15, 1779, Dec. 6, 1779, Dec. 10, 1779; personal communication, Eva Faber, 1997.

101. HKA, Komm. Lit., r. 617, 17. ex Febr. 1780, f. 367v.

102. Ibid., 17. ex Febr. 1780, f. 371r–v.

103. Ibid., 17. ex Febr. 1780, f. 366.

104. Ibid., 16. ex Jan. 1780, ff. 349v and 351r, Blümegen to Zinzendorf, private letter (Jan. 22, 1780). Eva Faber tells me that such a position was unusual for Blümegen, who did not normally argue on behalf of religious minorities.

105. Ibid., 16. ex Jan. 1780, f. 351v.

106. Unpublished Zinzendorf diary entries, Feb. 3, 4, and 5, 1780, for his strong emotional reaction; personal communication, Eva Faber, 1997.

107. HKA, Komm. Lit., r. 617, 17. ex Febr. 1780, f. 376v, in letter of Zinzendorf to Blümegen (Feb. 7, 1780), ff. 361r–v, 374–376v; summary in Gasser 1971: 256–58. Unpublished Zinzendorf diary entries, Dec. 10, 30, and 31, 1779, Jan. 4, 1780, Feb. 3, 4, and 5, 1780, on his continuing annoyance with Levi; personal communication, Eva Faber, 1997.

108. HKA, Komm. Lit., r. 617, 17. ex Febr. 1780, ff. 374v–375r.

109. Ibid., 17. ex Febr. 1780, ff. 359r–360v, 378r–v.

110. Unpublished Zinzendorf diary entry, Mar. 3, 1780; Eva Faber tells me that the ellipsis is in the original (personal communications, 1997–98).

111. AST, C.R. Gov., b. 52, N. 977, Jewish *Borsa* members to Zinzendorf, n.d., pencilled notation "presented May 26, 1780."

112. Ibid., Zinzendorf to *Borsa* (June 15, 1780).

113. AST, C.R. Gov., b. 52, N. 1232, contains the protocol of the *Borsa* meeting of July 15, 1780, as well as a separate letter signed by several merchants who outlined the reasons for their vote.

114. HKA, Komm. Lit., r. 617, 17. ex Febr. 1780, f. 376r, Zinzendorf to Blümegen (Feb. 7, 1780), and f. 360v, Blümegen to Zinzendorf (Feb. 28, 1780).

115. Negrelli 1970: 343–65; cf. Apih 1951.

116. Liebel 1979; Klingenstein 1994.

117. Tamaro 1942–43: 326; Faber 1995: 199.

118. E.g., D. Nissim 1970; Richetti 1984: 58, 62–63; and examples brought below in Chapter Seven.

119. Tedesco 1786: esp. 53–65. *Osservatore Triestino* reported on the event in

no. 11, Mar. 18, 1786, pp. 144–45 (excerpts in De Incontrera 1953–63, 24 [1954]: 82–83). In it, Tedesco drew upon both Jewish literature (the Bible and the rabbinic *Pirkei Avot* [Ethics of the Fathers] and Greco-Roman history and literature.

Chapter Two: Maria Theresa and the Legal Status of the Jews of Trieste: The Privileges of 1771

1. Beales 1987: 468. On the baroque *pietas austriaca*, see Evans 1970.
2. Beales 1987: 468.
3. Klingenstein 1993: 6.
4. Pribram 1918, 1: 425–26; translation based on Dickson 1987, 1: 148 n. 26; and Lentin 1985: 152. On terms of Jewish residence in Vienna, see Pribram 1918: vol. 1 passim (with the fullest archival record); Lohrmann 1980; Karniel 1985: 109–18, 247–67; Wistrich 1990: 3–16.
5. Pribram 1918, 1: 428.
6. On this important figure, see Szabo's far-reaching study (Szabo 1994).
7. Klingenstein 1970 was key in establishing Maria Theresa's reform and state-building credentials. On state reorganization and ecclesiastical reform, see also Wangermann 1973: 56–88; Ingrao 1994a: 150–92; Szabo 1994: 209–47; Scott 1990: 160–67; and Beales 1987: 441–64. It is not my intention here to enter the debate on the definition and precise extent of Josephinism; what seems indisputable is that the essential component of state-led reform of the relationship between church and state, and between religion and society more generally, was indeed visible during Maria Theresa's reign. On the major historiographical approaches to Josephinism, see conveniently Beales 1987: 8, 439–79, esp. 439–41 and 479. Also useful are Blanning 1994: 27–55; Romano 1957; Garms-Cornides 1970; Szabo 1979; Dickson 1993.
8. In her important article "Modes of Religious Tolerance and Intolerance in Eighteenth-Century Habsburg Politics" (1993), Klingenstein draws upon the material assembled in Karniel 1985 in order to reconceptualize the issue of religious toleration in the Habsburg Monarchy in the eighteenth century. She argues that the usual view of intolerance until 1781 is wrong, since the monarchy was not really uniformly Catholic in the eighteenth century: "Toleration was practiced in various shades and modes before 1781. . . . Tolerance and intolerance coexisted side by side" (p. 2). The case of Trieste certainly supports these latter contentions, and is an important piece of evidence for de facto and indeed de jure toleration of non-Catholics, and for a degree of continuity between Maria Theresa and Joseph on the issue of religious toleration. However, I am not familiar enough with the other examples she cites to assess whether toleration in those cases was also de jure, as it was in Trieste. From the evidence presented, I don't see "fundamental changes that had already expanded denominational rights and liberties in the previous decades" (p. 15), and I do not consider the cases in which Maria Theresa permitted de facto residence to constitute her acceptance of the principle of toleration as such. I hesitate to overgeneralize from the case of Trieste precisely because I consider its free-port status to have made it exceptional. Cf. Blanning 1994: 88 n. 60, on this article.
9. O'Brien 1969: 19–20, 25. The religious settlement in the Holy Roman Empire after the Thirty Years' War defined three kinds of religious rights: (1) public wor-

ship—in churches with bells and spires—for the dominant religion only; (2) private worship—in a chapel or prayer house without bells or spires; (3) domestic worship—only in a family home, with the right to visit a church in a neighboring state.

10. Much material on the negotiations for the Privilege and the Statute is to be found in AST, C.R.S. Int. Comm., b. 78, and in HKA, Komm. Lit., r. 502. The community's annual budget is in AST, C.R.S. Int. Comm., b. 78, ff. 144r–145v (Sept. 19, 1769). On the form and fee of the diploma, see AST, C.R.S. Int. Comm., b. 78, ff. 156r–160v, sovereign rescript of May 14, 1770, and gubernatorial decree N. 770 (June 11, 1770); also HKA, Komm. Lit., r. 502, 34. ex Mayo 1770, ff. 80 and 167, 164v, and 44. ex Mayo 1770, ff. 168r–169v (Commerzien Hauptkasse, May 28, 1770). See Maria Theresa's insistence on the high fee in HKA, Komm. Lit., r. 502, 44. ex Aprili 1771, Apr. 8 protocol of the Court Commerce Council, f. 217v.

11. On privilege in the Habsburg realm, see Klingenstein 1993: 14; Spielman 1994: 110–18; and Koenigsberger 1991: 307; also on privilege elsewhere, specifically France, see Bossenga 1991.

12. This term was used later for the Privilege of 1771, though it appears nowhere in it. See, for example, HKA, Komm. Lit., r. 502, 70. ex Julio 1775, f. 322. See Kestenberg-Gladstein 1954–55, on the varieties of such protection charters.

13. The classic works on Jewish communal self-government are Baron 1942 and Finkelstein 1924.

14. On police ordinances in early modern Europe, see Raeff 1983.

15. On revision of the communal statutes (Apr.–June 1769), see AST, C.R.S. Int. Comm., b. 78, N. 834, ff. 112–116, 120–123, 126, 144, 169; CAHJP, HM 2/5857, f. 28; and HKA, Komm. Lit., r. 502, 27. ex Octobri 1770, ff. 178, 180. On presenting the privileges of residence and work (June–July 1769), see HKA, Komm. Lit., r. 502, 27. ex Octobri 1770, f. 184; AST, C.R.S. Int. Comm., b. 78, f. 170; CAHJP, HM 2/5857, f. 28.

16. HKA, Komm. Lit., r. 502, 27. ex Oct. 1770, ff. 173r–189, and AST, C.R.S. Int. Comm., b. 78, ff. 168–178, contain the Jews' request that the Privilege be included with the Statute. Their request in March 1771 that the two be issued as separate diplomas is in AST, C.R.S. Int. Comm., b. 78, ff. 231r–232r; also in HKA, Komm. Lit., r. 502, 70. ex Julio 1775, ff. 257r–v, 312r–313r; see also CAHJP, HM 2/5857, f. 32.

17. CAHJP, HM 2/5857, ff. 30–33, 40–41; AST, C.R.S. Int. Comm., b. 78, ff. 159–248, and b. 81, ff. 42r–43v, 50r–51r, 50r–61r; HKA, Komm. Lit., r. 502, 70. ex Julio 1775; R. Curiel 1938: 247; Wolf 1863: 76–78.

18. Maternini Zotta 1983: 215. I translate from the text of the Privilege there in App. B, pp. 215–17, which I've checked against the versions in HKA, Komm. Lit., r. 502, 15. ex Dec. 1781, ff. 441r–443v; AST, C.R.S. Int. Comm., b. 78, ff. 233r–238r; and CAHJP, HM 3145 (original in ACIT). Published texts also in Cervani and Buda 1973: 197–200; Stock 1979: 86–88; and Zoller 1914, 7: 4–5. For discussions of the Privilege, see Maternini Zotta 1983: 42–43; and Zoller 1914, 6: 5–6.

19. Jews in Trieste had had the right to own real property since the fifteenth century; see Cova 1984: esp. 123–27.

20. Pribram 1918, 1: 388–89, 425, 429, 431, 658; Mahler 1971: 235.

21. Maternini Zotta 1983: 217.

22. Neither discussions of Jewish status nor those of Jewish communal budgets

show any evidence of a special Jewish tax. The only long-standing collective tax burden I have seen mentioned—that Jews provided upkeep for some of the city's judges—had been abolished in 1759–60; Norlinghi 1858: f. 40; Stock 1979: 28. For toleration and protection taxes paid by Jews elsewhere in the Habsburg Monarchy, see Mahler 1971: 235–37, 246–50, 273; Silber 1985: 96–100; and G. Bolaffio 1957–58: 133, and Del Bianco Cotrozzi 1983: 136–37, specifically on nearby Gorizia and Gradisca.

23. Stock 1979: 35–36; De Antonellis Martini 1968: 95–96; Paolin 1991: 221. In the late sixteenth century, civic officials said that Jews did not have to wear a sign or badge in Trieste. In 1714, it was decreed that Jews in Trieste should wear an orange string on the tops of their hats, but even this rule was allowed to lapse. Already in 1729 Trieste was cited as a place—in contradistinction to Venice—where Jews did not wear distinguishing signs; CAHJP, IT/Go, B,I,2.

24. Privilege of 1696 in AST, C.R.S. Int. Comm., b. 78, N. 1571, f. 189; CAHJP, IT 1210; Mainati 1817–18, 4: 18–27; excerpts in Cervani and Buda 1973: 6. The 1624 privilege is in CAHJP, HM 5467a (original in ADT, 5A4); Mainati 1817–18, 4: 6–15; varying versions also in Wolf 1858 and Edgardo Morpurgo 1909: 54–59. Zoller 1911a and 1911b contain excerpts from the 1624 and 1647 privileges. The privilege of 1647 is also in AST, C.R.S. Int. Comm., b. 78, ff. 183r–188r, and in CAHJP, HM 5467a (original in ADT, 5A4).

25. AST, C.R.S. Int. Comm., b. 78, N. 1571, ff. 193r–194v, also ff. 221r–222v; also in HKA, Komm. Lit., r. 502, 43. ex Januario 1771, ff. 201r–204v.

26. AST, C.R.S. Int. Comm., b. 78, ff. 195r–202r. On Modesti, see Faber 1995: 154.

27. HKA, Komm. Lit., r. 502, 43. ex Januario 1771, ff. 201r–204v, Dec. 17, 1770, report; also in AST, C.R.S. Int. Comm., b. 78, ff. 191 and 203r–206v.

28. HKA, Komm. Lit., r. 502, 43. ex Januario 1771, ff. 198r–200v (Jan. 28, 1771); also in 44. ex Aprili 1771, ff. 214r–215r, and in AST, C.R.S. Int. Comm., b. 78, ff. 223r–224r and ff. 227–228r. The eighteenth-century disagreement is mirrored in different views of this legal history by contemporary scholars; for example, Paolin (1991: esp. 241–43) states that the privileges were not extended to the entire community until 1771, whereas Maternini Zotta (1983: 11; 1994: 246–47) considers them extended to the entire community as of 1696.

29. The relation between the opening of the ghetto and the confirmation of the Levi and Parente privileges in 1696 requires further investigation.

30. The theme of improvement (here *vantaggiare*, "to benefit or improve"; often *Verbesserung*) is an important element of late-eighteenth-century discourse about the Jews. Normally the word was used to imply that the Jews themselves had to undergo a process of self-improvement (often called "regeneration") in order to be worthy of membership in civil society. However, some important writers, most notably Christian Wilhelm von Dohm and Moses Mendelssohn, used improvement to refer not only to the Jews, but also to their civil status. Dohm's title, *Ueber die buergerliche Verbesserung der Juden* (Berlin, 1781), carried the dual meaning. It is significant that the Theresian Privilege for the Jews of Trieste used the concept to refer to the condition of merchants, i.e., their civil status.

31. HKA, Komm. Lit., r. 502, 43. ex Januario 1771, ff. 198r–200v (Jan. 28, 1771),

here f. 199r; also in 44. ex Aprili 1771, ff. 214r–215r, and in AST, C.R.S. Int. Comm., b. 78, ff. 223r–224r and ff. 227–228r.

32. On this trend, see Klingenstein 1981: 121–22; 1985: 213–14; 1993: 14; and Mueller 1994: 179.

33. Elia Morpurgo 1782b: f. 32r.

34. Maternini Zotta 1983: 218; I use this text of the Statute, ibid.: app. C, pp. 218–36. Another text, with some variations, in Cervani and Buda 1973: 167–96. For discussions of the Statute, see Maternini Zotta 1983: 29–42; Cervani and Buda 1973: 24–28; Stock 1979: 36–41. Here the meaning of "police" is the broader sense of administration and societal regulation, and not the modern and more narrow sense of crime control; Raeff 1983: 5.

35. Statute, art. 1: XXXIX, in Maternini Zotta 1983: 223. On provisional arrest, art. 1: XXXVIII, in ibid.: 222–23.

36. E.g., communal regulations of 1746, ch. 6, in Maternini Zotta 1983: 213 (cf. Norlinghi 1858: f. 20 [1745–46]); *Statuti [1766]* . . . 1767: ch. 7, art. 1, in AST, C.R.S. Int. Comm., b. 78, f. 217v (also in CAHJP, HM 5455). For example, arbiters from Gorizia were chosen in Isach di Jacob Alpron vs. The Community; AST, C.R.S. Int. Comm., b. 68, f. 28, and b. 78, ff. 2r, 4r–5v. On arbitration in Roman and Italian law, and the role of Jewish communities and courts within that system, see Bonfil 1990: ch. 5, esp. 220–23, 239–46.

37. Statute of 1771, art. 8, in Maternini Zotta 1983: 234–35.

38. Statute of 1771, art. 8, in Maternini Zotta 1983: 234, and HKA, Komm. Lit., r. 502, 34. ex Mayo 1770, ff. 158v–159r, N. 138, Court Commerce Council (Apr. 23, 1770). On Jewish judicial autonomy in Bohemia and Galicia, see Mahler 1971: 324; and Silber 1985: 109; on the Greeks in Trieste, see Stefani 1960: 149.

39. Norlinghi 1858: ff. 52–56. For other efforts, see also ff. 45, 47–49; Curiel 1938: 245; and Zoller 1913d: 12–13.

40. On the hiring and arrival of Formiggini, see CAHJP, HM 2/5857, ff. 15–16; Curiel 1938: 246. The file, which covers the years 1766 to 1825, is discussed in detail in Richetti 1984. In R. Curiel 1942, the contents of this file are listed in Cartella N. 55, Processi e Liti, 1667–1849, under the heading "A. Processi, liti, istruttorie ecc. dinnanzi agli organi della Comunità." Unfortunately, much of the material listed in this typescript catalogue compiled in 1942 has not survived. See also Cervani and Buda 1973: 66; De Antonellis Martini 1968: 101; Maternini Zotta 1983: 13.

41. Richetti 1984: cases 1 and 8. For more on the Morpurgo-Alpron case (1777–78), see AST, C.R. Gov., b. 83, Ad N. 169, and on the Morpurgo-Levi case (1781), N. 1441.

42. Paolin 1991: 219; and Pavonello 1982: 43–45, esp. 44 n. 1. Other examples of cases involving Jews in the city's courts (some involving Jews alone, and others involving charges brought against Jews—five between 1656 and 1697, two in 1762–63) are listed in R. Curiel 1942: Cartella N. 55, Processi e Liti, 1667–1849, under the heading "B. Processi davanti alle Autorità giudiziarie."

43. AST, C.R. Gov., b. 83, Ad N. 1659, 831, 934, Zinzendorf report (Nov. 13, 1781); HKA, Komm. Lit., r. 502, 15. ex Dec. 1781, ff. 437r–440v, 463r–476v.

44. The draft of the Statute drawn up by the Intendancy in Trieste along with the committee of four Jews was sent to Vienna in February 1770. The changes made

by the Court Commerce Council in Vienna in April 1770 are clearly evident on the draft copy in HKA, Komm. Lit., r. 502, 34. ex Majo 1770, ff. 87r–123r.

45. Statute of 1771, art. 5: XVII, in Maternini Zotta 1983: 231; HKA, Komm. Lit., r. 502, 34. ex Majo 1770, f. 113v.

46. Baden also showed early concern with Jewish education in 1775; Lewin 1908: 67. Wolf (1888: 74) claims that the regulations issued for the Jews of Moravia in 1754 also made reference to education, but I doubt that these concerned civic education for Jews.

47. See Melton 1988 for a wide-ranging cultural, political, and social analysis of the educational reforms.

48. Statute of 1771, art. 8: XVIII, in Maternini Zotta 1983: 235; HKA, Komm. Lit., r. 502, 34. ex Majo 1770, ff. 122r–123r. On continuing concern with usury, see Tucci 1978: 127–30.

49. AST, C.R.S. Int. Comm., b. 78, Ad N. 171, ff. 146r–148v, instructions from Vienna (Jan. 15, 1770) and Intendancy report (Feb. 19, 1770); also in HKA, Komm. Lit., r. 502, 34. ex Majo 1770, ff. 85r–86v, 138r–139r.

50. HKA, Komm. Lit., r. 502, 34. ex Majo 1770, report of Court Commerce Council to Maria Theresa (Apr. 23, 1770), ff. 82r–83v, 155r–165r, esp. ff. 161v–164r.

51. Statute of 1771, art. 1: II, in Maternini Zotta 1983: 219; *Statuti [1766]* . . . 1767, ch. 1: art. 5, in AST, C.R.S. Int. Comm., b. 78, f. 209v (also in CAHJP, HM 5455).

52. Statute of 1771, art. 4: III, XIII, XV, in Maternini Zotta 1983: 228–29.

53. For example, see the opposition of Lombard officials to the administrative reforms of the mid-1750s, which also involved royal delegates' supervision of elections and budgets, in Grab 1984: esp. 50–51.

54. AST, C.R.S. Int. Comm., b. 78, f. 52r, Ad N. 1671, Ricci to *Capi* (Dec. 15, 1767) (see also Cervani and Buda 1973: 23); ff. 79r–82r, *Capi* to Intendancy (n.d., apparently Mar. 9, 1768), and Ricci to *Capi*, Ad N. 486 (Mar. 29, 1768).

55. AST, C.R.S. Int. Comm., b. 78, f. 232r, *Capi* to Intendancy (n.d., submitted by mid-March 1771).

56. February 1770 draft in HKA, Komm. Lit., r. 502, 34. ex Majo 1770, f. 88. Printed version in Maternini Zotta 1983: 218. *Statuti [1766]* . . . 1767 in AST, C.R.S. Int. Comm., b. 78, f. 208r (also in CAHJP, HM 5455).

57. On Jewish complaints about not seeing the draft, see AST, C.R.S. Int. Comm., b. 78, f. 166 (June 24, 1770), and f. 169v, from 168r–172v, memorandum submitted by Jewish community (Aug. or early Sept. 1770); also in HKA, Komm. Lit., r. 502, 27. ex Oct. 1770, ff. 177r–187v. Modesti's dissenting opinion is in AST, C.R.S. Int. Comm., b. 78, ff. 196v–198r and 200v–201v.

58. AST, C.R.S. Int. Comm., b. 78, ff. 168r–172v; also in HKA, Komm. Lit., r. 502, 27. ex Oct. 1770, N. 1151, ff. 177r–v, 186r–188r. Cf. CAHJP, HM 2/5857, ff. 30–31: the community asked their well-connected court agent Joachim Hierschel to present their case directly in Vienna. They also followed the usual channel of submitting their memorandum to the local government for forwarding to Vienna; report of Sept. 7, 1770, from the Intendancy to Court Commerce Council, in AST, C.R.S. Int. Comm., b. 78, ff. 174r–175r, and HKA, Komm. Lit., r. 502, 27. ex Oct. 1770, ff. 175r–176r, 188v–189v.

59. AST, C.R.S. Int. Comm., b. 78, f. 168v; HKA, Komm. Lit., r. 502, f. 177r.

60. The only somewhat comparable example I have come across concerns the Jews of Shklov, a modernizing Belorussian mercantile center, in 1787: they told the empress Catherine that they didn't like being called by the derogatory and humiliating term *zhidy* ("Jews"), and asked that imperial documents henceforth use the more lofty Biblical term *evrei* ("Hebrews"); Fishman 1995: 80.

61. "The Jewish nation in Hungary is declared to be only tolerated," in Zoller 1914, 6: 5; Maternini Zotta 1983: 27 n. 50. Cf. Bernardini 1996b: 219.

62. HKA, Komm. Lit., r. 502, 34. ex Majo 1770, ff. 88r, 89r, 123r. For "tolerated" in the final version of the 1771 Statute, see Maternini Zotta 1983: 218, 235.

63. In contrast, the Sefardic Jews in Vienna, who were nominally Turkish subjects and who were admitted for purposes of furthering trade with the Levant, were allowed to form a community. However, the precise date of the formal constitution of the Sefardic community is not clear; Lohrmann (1980: 9) and Wistrich (1990: 9) date it in the late 1730s, but Karniel only in 1778 (1985: 116–18, 266–67).

64. *Capi* petition in AST, C.R.S. Int. Comm., b. 78, ff. 231r–232v in N. 334 (cf. CAHJP, HM 2/5857, f. 32); and HKA, Komm. Lit., r. 502, 70. ex Julio 1775, ff. 257, 312. The Jewish petition, quoted in part by Zoller (in 1914, 6: 5–6) and Maternini Zotta (1983: 29), and attributed to the period mid-March 1771, must have been written earlier, for it conforms to the mid-December 1770 document in AST, C.R.S. Int. Comm., b. 78, N. 1571, ff. 193r–194v, 221r–222v, in which the Jews asked that the privileges be included with the statutes in one diploma.

65. AST, C.R.S. Int. Comm., b. 78, N. 334, Ricci report (Mar. 12, 1771), ff. 239r–244v; also in HKA, Komm. Lit., r. 502, 70. ex Julio 1775, ff. 255–256, 314–317. The material in HKA makes it possible to date this undated document, which was quoted by both Cervani and Buda (1973: 30) and by De Antonellis Martini (1968: 113). Though the latter attributes the Jews' request for the name change to their "unitary Triestine consciousness," i.e., their sense of being a subordinate entity within the larger order in Trieste, I see it less as a sign of integration and more as a concern for maintaining some communal and local autonomy in decision-making.

66. HKA, Komm. Lit., r. 502, 44. ex April 1771, Court Commerce Council (Apr. 8, 1771), ff. 212r–213v, 217.

67. Reference to the "Regole" of 1777, approved by gubernatorial decree on Nov. 27, 1777, in AST, C.R. Gov., b. 83, N. 437 and N. 1659, governor to *Capi* (Sept. 12, 1781), and "Umilissima supplica . . . ," *Capi* to governor (Sept. 27, 1781) (also microfilm in CAHJP, HM 5467b); entitled "Primo memoriale del 27 settembre 1781" in Cervani and Buda 1973: 209 (with some errors).

68. R. Curiel 1938: 247.

69. Maternini Zotta 1983: 216.

70. On the entire issue, see AST, C.R.S. Int. Comm., b. 81, ff. 35r–43v, 50r–51r, 54r–55r, 60r–61v (Apr.–Dec. 1775); and HKA, Komm. Lit., r. 502, 70. ex Julio 1775, ff. 322r–354r, Intendancy report to Vienna (July 8, 1775). See also Wolf 1863: 76–78; Pribram 1918, 1: passim; Cervani and Buda 1973: 74–78; Stock 1979: 47–53; Karniel 1985: 296–305. AST, C.R. Gov., Atti amministrativi di Gorizia, 1754–83, b. 7, fasc. 57, has material on the 1768 Gradisca case.

71. Jews' petition submitted in July 1775, in HKA, Komm. Lit., r. 502, 70. ex Julio 1775, ff. 331r–332v, N. 1404.

72. AST, C.R.S. Int. Comm., b. 81, ff. 60r–61r.
73. Maternini Zotta 1983: 127; cf. Stock 1979: 40.
74. *Capi* report to governor (Sept. 27, 1781), in AST, C.R. Gov., b. 83, N. 1659 (also microfilm in CAHJP, HM 5467b, and "Primo memoriale . . . ," in Cervani and Buda 1973: 209). Zinzendorf report (Aug. 17, 1781), in HKA, Komm. Lit., r. 502, 40. ex Aug. 1781, Lit. ad N. 34. ex Oct. 1781, ff. 425r–427v; also in AST, C.R. Gov., b. 83, N. 1412.
75. AST, C.R.S. Int. Comm., b. 78, ff. 61r–64v, Commercial Councillor and Director of Buildings Fremaut (Jan. 1, 1768); on Fremaut, see Faber 1995: index.
76. The Jews in Vienna did not gain the right to build a public synagogue even with Joseph's Toleration edict in 1782. On cases in Moravia in which Jews were denied permission to build synagogues, see Karniel 1985: 120–25. On the Protestants in Trieste pointing to the more extensive religious rights enjoyed by Jews and Orthodox in the city, see Karniel, ibid.: 179.
77. E.g., Jews of Gorizia-Gradisca could own real property (Cova 1984). For a convenient summary of conditions in Gorizia-Gradisca, see Del Bianco Cotrozzi 1989: esp. 700–704. For more detailed expositions, see Del Bianco Cotrozzi 1983 and Altieri 1985. In Lombardy, the other northern Italian Habsburg possession, the venerable Mantuan Jewish community also enjoyed a relatively favorable status; in anticipation of Joseph's Toleration legislation, many economic and civil restrictions on Jews were removed, culminating in the 1779 Privilege. Short summaries are found in Roth 1946: 423; Simonsohn 1977: 148–49, 314–15, 813–18; Karniel 1985: 281–83. Karniel sees Kaunitz's Lombardy as a precedent and a kind of model for Joseph's Toleration legislation concerning the Jews. Recent more extensive treatments are Bernardini 1996b: esp. 4–5, 39–49, 334–35; and Mori 1994.
78. Maternini Zotta 1994: 246–48. On the status and situation of other Habsburg Jewries, see Mahler 1971: 233–35, 241–53, 268–74, 314–30; Karniel 1985: 103–26, 243–310; Silber 1985: 96–97, 109–14; much detail also in the older Scherer 1895; and in Mischler and Ulbrich 1906, 2: 950–90.
79. Estimates from Karniel 1985: 104; Friesel 1990: 34–35.
80. On Livorno, see R. Toaff 1989; Ravid 1992; and Cooperman 1976; on the eighteenth century, short summary in Milano 1963: 322–28. Though ruled by a Habsburg grand duke, Tuscany was a separate entity, and not part of the monarchy in the same sense as the other areas discussed. Comparison of the legal status and standing of the Jewish communities in Livorno and Trieste is desirable, but beyond the scope of this work.
81. AST, C.R.S. Int. Comm., b. 78, f. 14r, Schell to governor of Livorno (Nov. 15, 1766). On Livorno as a model for Triestine administration, see Faber 1995: 178–79, 222–29.
82. AST, C.R.S. Int. Comm., b. 78, f. 17o.
83. Pribram 1918, 1: 474; also p. 432. Habsburg rulers, like the French during the Revolution, considered Sefardic Jews more cultivated and worldly than Ashkenazic Jews.
84. Cf. Hartwig Wessely's praise of the connection between international mercantile activity and broad cultural horizons (also in Dubin 1987: 206): "Trade in your lands is with the large states of Europe, Asia, and Africa, and you get to hear of

the customs of areas distant from you. All the communities of Israel in Italian lands have a similar advantage"; Weisel (Wessely) [1782–85] 1826, 2: 26 (*Rav tuv*; translation in Dubin 1987: 206). The classic discussion of the Sefardic mystique among Jews is Schorsch 1994. On the linkage of Sefardic and Italian Jews common among German Jews in the late eighteenth and nineteenth centuries, see Dubin 1998.

85. 1776 Court Chancellery discussion, quoted in McCagg 1989: 263 n. 9.
86. Pribram 1918, 1: 431.
87. Ibid.: 432.
88. Thus I cannot agree with Beales that "historians . . . cannot find a shred of evidence for [Maria Theresa's] envisaging the measures of toleration for Protestants and Jews that were enacted during the 1780s," that "as for [Joseph's] toleration of Jews, that has no prehistory during the co-regency at all," and that "nothing at all was done about tolerating the Jews"; Beales 1987: 465, 473, 478. My argument is that Trieste certainly provides evidence of Theresian toleration, though, since it was exceptional by definition as a free port, it afforded no program for emulation elsewhere.

Chapter Three: Joseph's Toleration Policy in Trieste, 1781–82

1. I cannot resist a personal anecdote about my first visit to this site in 1989 with my husband and then two-year-old daughter Rachel. I was interested in seeing Leopold's sarcophagus as well, expecting it to resemble his brother's sarcophagus rather than his mother's. For some reason, it took a while before I found it, and my expectation was confirmed. The length of time it took us to find it, and the coldness of the crypt on that warm summer day, are forever etched in my memory, for my daughter kept referring to our long search for King Leocold!

2. The entire book Plashka and Klingenstein 1985 examines continuity and rupture between the two rulers on a wide range of economic, social, legal, and cultural issues. Klingenstein argued the case forcefully for continuity, first in *Staatsverwaltung* (1970); yet her essay "Riforma e crisi" (1981: 115–16) discusses differences as well as similarities (also Klingenstein 1985). The theme of continuity is central to Beales 1987, especially ch. 14, "Joseph and Josephism under Maria Theresa," pp. 439–79. Much of value is also found in Blanning 1970 and 1994; Scott 1990: 145–86; Ingrao 1994a: 150–209; and Szabo 1994. I think that both monarchs could be termed reforming absolutists.

3. The use of one or the other of these two terms depends on personal preference and changing historiographical fashions. For a recent discussion of the terms "absolutism" and "despotism," see Beales 1991 and the literature cited there. Beales gives sound reasons for his choice of "despotism" over "absolutism," but I prefer "enlightened absolutism" to "enlightened despotism" because of the political connotations, both structural and procedural, of the former, and the unavoidably negative moral connotations of the latter. I am no doubt influenced by the increasing currency of the word "absolutism" in English, evidenced, for example, in the three recent book titles of Melton (*Absolutism and the Eighteenth-Century Origins of Compulsory Schooling in Prussia and Austria*, 1988), Scott (*Enlightened Absolutism*, 1990), and Szabo (*Kaunitz and Enlightened Absolutism, 1753–1780*, 1994).

4. See Blanning 1994: 56–58; Klingenstein 1981: 116, 121; and Ogris 1981: 114–16, on Joseph's political philosophy. I agree with Blanning that raison d'état, or efficiency of the state, and Enlightenment are not to be seen in contradiction; though they were not identical, they were reinforcing. See Blanning 1994: 83: "Of course it would be absurd to suggest that the Enlightenment is a sufficient explanation of Joseph's regime, but it is no more sensible to suggest that it played no part beyond providing a rhetorical fig-leaf to conceal *raison d'état*"; see also Blanning 1970: 17–20. See Szabo 1994; and Beales 1987: 479 and n. 141, and the literature cited there, on the Austrian Enlightenment.

5. A concise summary of the religious reforms of the two monarchs can be found in Scott 1990: 160–72; relevant discussions also in Wangermann 1973: 74–88; Beales 1987: 441–64; Ingrao 1994a: 165–66, 170, 188–89; and Szabo 1994: 209–47. A wealth of documentation is to be found in Maass 1953, and much detail still in Mitrofanov 1910, 2: 666–801; valuable primary documents in translation in Macartney 1970: 96–105, 145–69; and Blanning 1970: 124–29, 138–46. On religious toleration in particular, O'Brien 1969; Karniel 1985; and Klingenstein 1993 are essential; discussions also in Beales 1987: 465–73; Blanning 1994: 72–75; Szabo 1994: 247–57; and Ingrao 1994a: 191–92.

6. The Venetian newspaper *Notizie del mondo*, quoted in Venturi 1991: 653.

7. Joseph to Maria Theresa, June 19, 1777, and n.d., June 1771, quoted in Beales 1987: 467–68.

8. Joseph to Maria Theresa, June 1777, July 20, 1777, quoted in ibid.: 467, 469.

9. Beales 1991: 12–13. The kind of equality praised by Joseph II was equal determination to serve the state and society.

10. Karniel (1985) posited a contradiction between practical and idealistic or humanitarian motives, and overstressed the foreign-policy considerations. See Scott 1990: 168, and Blanning 1994: 72–74, 88, for more balanced discussions of self-interest and principle.

11. Translation in Macartney 1970: 155–57; excerpts also now in Maclear 1995: 26–27. See further in O'Brien 1969: 22–29; Karniel 1985: 311–77, 550–64; Barton 1981a and 1981b, esp. 1981b: 152–202, on the different versions for different places; Maass 1953: 46–77, 272–80; Frank 1882.

12. See O'Brien 1969: 19–20, 25; De Antonellis Martini 1968: 85–88; Frank 1882: 90–91; Stefani 1960: 249–53. Contrary to the impression created in some accounts, this edict did not apply to the Jews of Trieste.

13. Frank 1882: 90–91; O'Brien 1969: 25.

14. Venturi 1991: 650.

15. Ibid.: 643.

16. H. Graetz [1853–76] 1900, 11: 68–69; 1967, 5: 357–58. Wessely expressed his enthusiasm in *Divrei shalom ve-emet* (Weisel [Wessely] [1782–85] 1826) and in his article in *Ha-Meassef* (1783–84: 161–65, 177–82).

17. H. Graetz [1853–76] 1900, 11: 68–69, "gewaltthätiger Art doch aufrichtiger Menschenliebe." The translation in H. Graetz 1967, 5: 357–58, "sincere if rather fierce philanthropy," is misleading given contemporary connotations of philanthropy. On intrusion, see, for example, Dubnov 1971: 336–39; Mahler 1971: e.g., pp. 229–33; and Ettinger 1976: 753–56, who does, however, refer to integrationist aims as well.

18. I am indebted to Evans's formulation "bureaucratic intervention and residual Catholic ascendancy," in his Introduction to Ingrao 1994b: 13.

19. Text of Joseph's letter of May 13, 1781, in Pribram 1918, 1: 440–42; also Karniel 1985: 547–49. Partial English translation in Padover 1967: 182–83; and in Blanning 1970: 142–44, along with a later ordinance of Nov. 2, 1781. For discussions, see Bernard 1968–69; Singer 1932: 1–10; Karniel 1985: 381–87; Mahler 1971: 229–32. Subsequent literature dates these proposals sometimes as May 13, 1781, the date of Joseph's letter, and sometimes as May 16, 1781, the date of the version prepared by the Court Chancellery for dispatch. The provisions concerning education were elaborated in subsequent decrees.

20. Singer 1932: 7–10; Karniel 1981: 206–8, and 1985: 380–87. According to Zinzendorf, Kaunitz himself took credit for the May proposals; unpublished Zinzendorf diary entry, Sept. 25, 1781 (Eva Faber, personal communication, 1997).

21. Melton 1988; Bazzoli 1986: 212–13, 218–25; Szabo 1994: 185–97.

22. Excerpt from Dohm in Mendes-Flohr and Reinharz 1995: 28–36; see also Liberles 1988, on Dohm. On the Enlightenment, see Hertzberg 1968: 7–11, 266–368; Katz 1973: 42–79; and Dubin 1997.

23. For the May 16, 1781, resolution, see HHSt, StK (Staatskanzlei), Notenwechsel mit der Hofkanzlei, no. 103, and HKA, Komm. Lit., r. 502, 28. ex Majo 1781, ff. 420r–421v.

24. Pribram 1918, 1: 476–77; Bernard 1968–69: 116. The name of the toleration tax was later changed to "cameral tax."

25. Pribram 1918, 1: 442–94; English translations of the patent for Lower Austria and Vienna (often assumed mistakenly to have been issued for all Habsburg Jews) in Mendes-Flohr and Reinharz 1995: 36–40, and the edict for Moravia in Iggers 1992: 48–52. Karniel's works (1981; 1982; 1985: 388–474) are the most comprehensive in scope; Singer's articles (1932, 1933, 1934) are still valuable for their archival material, much of which has been subsequently destroyed. See also general discussions in Mahler 1971: 229–32, 235–37, 253–58, 274–75, 330–33; Bernard 1968–69: 112–19; and Katz 1973: 161–66. For more detail and depth in particular areas, see specific local and regional studies, e.g., Lohrmann 1980; Hausler 1974; Kestenberg-Gladstein 1969; Bihl 1974; Silber 1985, 1988, 1989; Bernardini 1996b; Mori 1994; Del Bianco Cotrozzi 1989.

26. Singer 1933: 259–60; English in Blanning 1970: 144; Italian in contemporary documents in *Codice* 1787, 8: 48–49, and conveniently available in Samaja 1957: 303–4.

27. Preamble of Moravian edict translated in Iggers 1992: 48. The preamble to the Lower Austria-Vienna patent specified "subjects without distinction of nationality and religion, once they have been admitted and tolerated in Our States (*aufgenommen und geduldet*)"; Pribram 1918, 1: 494–500; and English translation in Mendes-Flohr and Reinharz 1995: 36–40. I quote the closing words from the Vienna patent.

28. Mahler 1971: 245.

29. Cf. Klingenstein 1993.

30. See Springer 1980, esp. pp. 251–58, for detailed exposition and analysis of some of the economic plans.

31. Some of the correct details emerge from the short but detailed Singer 1934, esp. 235–36). Singer examined material in the HHSt Staatsrat Akten, which no longer exists. See also Kohn 1919: 16–17. I have seen the related material in the Protocols of the Staatsrat. My account is based also upon material from the HKA, Komm. Lit., r. 502, and the local AST, C.R. Gov., b. 83. The resolution of Dec. 19, 1781, is in HKA, Komm. Lit., r. 502, 15. ex Xbri [Dec.] 1781, and AST, C.R. Gov., b. 83. The Jan. 16, 1782, gubernatorial decree from Zinzendorf to the Jewish community, and from Zinzendorf to the Deputazione di Borsa, are in AST, C.R. Gov., both Ad N. 359; also in Mainati 1817–18, 5: 13–14. Unfortunately, Karniel was confused on this point: contra 1985: 402–3, 530–32, the Jews of Trieste were not subject to the version of the 1790 Galician legislation applied to the Jews of Gorizia-Gradisca.

32. AST, C.R. Gov., b. 83, N. 934, contains the May 16 resolution (in German), presented May 28, 1781, and the letters to the other authorities in Trieste. CAHJP, HM 943, ff. 4r–6r, has a copy made in Trieste on June 8, 1781, of an Italian translation of the May 16 resolution. AST, C.R. Gov., b. 620, N. 1073, has another copy in Italian of Joseph's proposals dated May 16, but this copy appears to have been made later in 1786. There are some slight differences in wording between the two Italian versions. Zinzendorf's May 31 letter to the Jewish community is found in draft form in AST, C.R. Gov., b. 83, Ad N. 934 (printed with some omissions in De Antonellis Martini 1968: 118–19); a copy made from the original is in CAHJP, P17/1241.

33. Personal communications from Grete Klingenstein and Franz Szabo, 1997.

34. Zinzendorf letter to *Capi* (May 31, 1781), in AST, C.R. Gov., b. 83, Ad N. 934; CAHJP, P17/1241; and De Antonellis Martini 1968: 118–19.

35. Maternini Zotta 1983: 215.

36. HKA, Komm. Lit., r. 502, 12. ex Aug. 1781, f. 422r, instruction to various Länderstellen (Aug. 8, 1781); AST, C.R. Gov., b. 83, Ad N. 1712, Zinzendorf to governor of Fiume (Oct. 7, 1781).

37. AST, C.R. Gov., b. 126, Ad N. 1575. Segre (1764–1847) was probably the Jew interested in the normal-school method mentioned by Marco Levi to Zinzendorf in 1777; Pagnini 1978: 182. For an official report of Segre's achievements in the preparatory normal course, i.e., the teacher-training course, see AST, C.R. Gov., b. 622, N. 6377 (Nov. 1, 1784). Segre served the Triestine Jewish community for many years as a teacher of German, arithmetic, Italian, and Jewish studies. He was friendly with Herz Homberg, the radical *maskil* (advocate of Jewish Enlightenment), who himself taught for six years in Trieste in the mid-1780s, but Segre refused Homberg's offer to join him in Galicia. Segre was later to be the father-in-law of the renowned scholar Samuel David Luzzatto. For more on Segre's education and career, see S. D. Luzzatto 1878: 47–50; A. Luzzatto 1851: 16.

38. Zinzendorf report to Joseph II (Aug. 17, 1781), in AST, C.R. Gov., b. 83, Ad N. 1412, and HKA, Komm. Lit., r. 502, 40. ex August 1781, Lit. ad N. 34. ex Oct. 1781, f. 426r.

39. The phrase appears in the official German resolution from the Court Chancellery to Governor Zinzendorf of Trieste in AST, C.R. Gov., b. 83, N. 934; and also in a copy of the Italian translation made in Trieste on June 8, 1781, in CAHJP, HM 943 ("restino disviati dall'usure a Loro si proprie, e dal Fraudolento Traffico").

Interestingly, the Italian version found in AST, C.R. Gov., b. 620, N. 1073b, says simply "per levargli poi le usure, e frodi," without the words "si proprie," "so characteristic."

40. Zinzendorf letter to *Capi* (May 31, 1781), in AST, C.R. Gov., b. 83, Ad N. 934; CAHJP, P17/1241; and De Antonellis Martini 1968: 118–19.

41. Corporate and guild structures in Trieste were weaker and the exercise of artisanal trades freer than elsewhere. See *Enciclopedia monografica* 1971–83, 2: pt. 1, p. 123, and 3: pt. 1, pp. 267–68; Apih 1957: 41–42, 57–58.

42. Klingenstein 1994: esp. 183, 187–95. Zinzendorf translated Josiah Tucker, *Reflections on the Expediency of a Law for the Naturalisation of Foreign Protestants* (London 1751; photo reprint Farnborough, 1969).

43. HKA, Komm. Lit., r. 502, 12. ex Aug. 1781, f. 422r; AST, C.R. Gov., b. 83, N. 1412.

44. Zinzendorf report to Joseph II (Aug. 17, 1781), in AST, C.R. Gov., b. 83, Ad N. 1412, and HKA, Komm. Lit., r. 502, 40. ex August 1781. Lit. ad N. 34. ex Oct. 1781, ff. 425r–427v.

45. The original draft of Zinzendorf's report is in AST, C.R. Gov., b. 83, Ad N. 1412. The phrase *Gleichheiten mit des übrigen Volks* is difficult to read because it is crossed out with a thick line that goes horizontally through these words. I should emphasize that the amount of crossing out in this document is very great, more than I've seen in most other drafts of reports. There are whole paragraphs of the first draft crossed out and replaced with second and third formulations. Still, the rest of the paragraph in the first draft is easy to read because the vertical lines crossing it out do not cover up any of the words.

46. I've not seen those orders conveyed in the sovereign resolution of Jan. 27, 1781, nor in the gubernatorial decree of Mar. 14, 1781.

47. These paragraphs are written and crossed out on the last page of the draft of Zinzendorf's Aug. 17, 1781, report, in AST, C.R. Gov., b. 83. Even within the second draft, there were various changes of wording. "State within a state" was a classic line of anticorporatist critique in the eighteenth century. Zinzendorf himself had used it a few years earlier when criticizing the behavior of some of the *Borsa* members (not the Jews in that case). On its later use generally, see Katz 1971; and in Trieste by the Jewish leader Elia Moise Luzzatto at odds with the rest of the community, see Chapter Eight below.

48. AST, C.R. Gov., b. 83, Zinzendorf to *Capi* (Aug. 18, 1781).

49. AST, C.R. Gov., b. 83, Ad N. 1441, Zinzendorf to *Capi* (Aug. 21, 1781).

50. Petition to Joseph II, in HKA, Komm. Lit., r. 502, 15. ex Xbri [Dec.] 1781, ff. 458–61; also in AST, C.R. Gov., b. 83, N. 1659 (microfilm copy in CAHJP, HM 5467b). Petition to Zinzendorf also in AST, C.R. Gov., b. 83, N. 1659, and CAHJP, HM 5467b. Incomplete versions of both petitions in Cervani and Buda 1973: "Prima memoriale del 27 settembre 1781," pp. 201–10, is the petition to Zinzendorf; "Secondo memoriale del 27 settembre 1781," pp. 211–15, is the petition to Joseph II. I quote from the texts in AST. Unfortunately, we have no record of the discussions within the community that preceded these appeals to the authorities.

51. AST, C.R. Gov., b. 83, N. 1659, *Capi* to Zinzendorf (Sept. 27, 1781); also CAHJP, HM 5467b.

52. AST, C.R. Gov., b. 83, N. 1659 (Sept. 27, 1781); CAHJP, HM 5467b.
53. HKA, Komm. Lit., r. 617, 17. ex Febr. 1780, f. 366.
54. On the political strategies of the Jews of Bordeaux and their attitudes vis-à-vis their Ashkenazic coreligionists, see Malino 1978: 27–36, 45–53.
55. AST, C.R. Gov., b. 83, Zinzendorf to *Capi* (Oct. 2, 1781).
56. AST, C.R. Gov., b. 83, N. 1831, *Capi* to governor (undated), written sometime in Oct. 1781, after Zinzendorf's letter to them of Oct. 2 and before his report to Vienna of Nov. 13, 1781, with which he included copies of the two notes and the Sept. 19 decision by the *Capi* about Segre (HKA, Komm. Lit., r. 502, 15. ex Dec. 1781, ff. 467–71). The two lists appear also in CAHJP, HM 5467b, and the one containing the list of "artisans," also in Stock 1979: 40.
57. Singer 1934: 189, 234; Kohn 1919: 15–16. Kohn's date of Oct. 8, 1781 is correct (rather than Singer's of Aug. 8, 1781) because Zinzendorf only wrote his report to the Inner Austrian authorities on Aug. 17, 1781. The Oct. 8 date is confirmed by the State Council document I've seen in HHSt, StR (Staatsrat), Protocoll, vol. III, 1781, no. 2395, which refers to the Court Chancellery report. Zinzendorf's report of Aug. 17 was mistakenly referred to as being from Aug. 7, in the Oct. 20, 1781, decree on education issued specifically for Trieste in HKA, Komm. Lit., r. 502, 34. ex 8bri [Oct.] 1781, ff. 424, 429r, and AST, C.R. Gov., b. 83.
58. HHSt, StR (Staatsrat), Protocoll, vol. III, 1781, no. 2395; Pribram 1918, 1: 514, and HKA, Komm. Lit., r. 502, 34. ex 8bri [Oct.] 1781 (Oct. 20, 1781), ff. 424, 429r; Kohn 1919: 27; Singer 1934: 191, 235. On the role of Padua in forming a Jewish medical community in Italy and beyond, see Ruderman 1995: 100–117, and the sources cited there.
59. Singer 1934: 234. On Gebler's service in Trieste from 1754–56 as secretary of the Intendancy and director of the Chancellery, see Faber 1995: 158, 178, 247–49. For Gebler, as for Zinzendorf, Trieste was a way station on a distinguished career path that led to high office in Vienna.
60. Pribram 1918, 1: 474.
61. AST, C.R. Gov., b. 83, Ad N. 1659, 831, 934, Zinzendorf to Joseph II (Nov. 13, 1781); HKA, Komm. Lit., r. 502, 15. ex Xbri [Dec.] 1781, ff. 437r–440v, 463r–476v. Eva Faber tells me that his diary entries show him devoting considerable attention to this report (personal communication, 1997).
62. See CAHJP, HM 5804a, f. 41v, Proclama (Sept. 19, 1781).
63. AST, C.R. Gov., b. 83, Ad N. 1659, 831, 934, Zinzendorf report to Joseph II (Nov. 13, 1781): "They affirm that most of their coreligionists have little spare time to entertain themselves by reading, and that those few who do prefer Romance (*welsche*) and German writings to their own books (*ihren Nazional Büchern*)." Zinzendorf knew something about the reading habits of at least one Jew: Israel Coen gave him *Israel Vengée* (Paris, 1770), a work of seventeenth-century Jewish apologetics by Orobio de Castro that was translated and circulated by Enlightenment writers such as Voltaire and Holbach for its critique of Christianity; Pagnini 1978: 177; and Y. Kaplan 1989: 451–56. Zinzendorf noted his dissent from some of its arguments.
64. HKA, Komm. Lit., r. 502, 15. ex Xbri [Dec.] 1781, N. 953 (Dec. 6, 1781), ff. 457, 462r–466v; Kohn 1919: 16–17.

65. In 1782, clandestine baptism was forbidden for children under the age of seven, and for children between the ages of seven and fourteen except in cases of imminent death or parental consent; in 1787, permission of the civil authorities was required. Pribram 1918, 1: 516–17; and Cervani and Buda 1973: 78; but see Karniel 1985: 459–66, on continuing refusal to return clandestinely baptized children to Jewish parents.

66. HKA, Komm. Lit., r. 502, 15. ex Xbri [Dec.] 1781, N. 953 (Dec. 6, 1781), f. 464v.

67. Singer 1934: 235, which appears to be a close paraphrase of the State Council discussion of Dec. 13, 1781 (the actual records of that session no longer exist); the summary protocol contains the *Borsa* qualification: HHSt, StR (Staatsrat), Protocoll, vol. III, 1781, no. 2908; Kohn 1919: 16–17.

68. From 1697 until 1830, Jews were allowed exactly twelve seats out of 124 on the London Royal Exchange; Endelman 1979: 22. On Livorno, Roth 1946: 425. In Mantua a few years later, in 1786, Jews were admitted to the newly formed Chamber of Commerce, and two seats out of eight were reserved for Jews on the council that would adjudge controversies between merchants; Mori 1994: 229–30; and Bernardini 1996b: 200–203, 334–36.

69. HKA, Komm. Lit., r. 502, 15. ex Xbri [Dec.] 1781, ff. 430r–431v, and AST, C.R. Gov., b. 83.

70. Unpublished Zinzendorf diary, Jan. 11, 1782, where Zinzendorf notes that the new diploma "cost them almost nothing" (personal communication from Eva Faber, 1997).

71. AST, C.R. Gov., b. 83, Ad N. 359, Zinzendorf to the Jewish community, and Zinzendorf to the *Borsa* managing board (both Jan. 16, 1782); letter to the Jews printed in Mainati 1817–18, 5: 13–14.

72. AST, C.R. Gov., b. 83, Ad N. 359, Zinzendorf to the Jewish community (Jan. 16, 1782).

73. On Bohemia, see Singer 1933: 249–50; and Bernard 1968–69: 117. On D'Arco and the polemical exchanges between him and Benedetto Frizzi, see Bachi 1946–47: 66–68; Simonsohn 1977: 93–95; and now Luzzatto Voghera 1998: 39–50, and Bernardini 1996b: 59–80, which link D'Arco's views on Jews with his economic theories.

74. Macartney 1968: 23; Cervani 1961: 3–5, 9–11.

75. Cf. Ghisalberti 1992: 29–31; and Katz 1973: 161–66.

76. "Gl'Israeliti a Trieste" 1862–63: 11. This article states that thanksgiving services were held in the synagogues of Trieste, Gorizia, and Gradisca. However, the rest of the details that follow have to do with Gradisca and its leader, Elia Morpurgo, who praised Joseph's proposals in his *Discorso pronunziato da Elia Morpurgo Capo della nazione Ebrea di Gradisca: Nel partecipare a quella comunità la Clementissima Sovrana risoluzione 16. Maggio 1781* (Gorizia, 1782). Many discussions of the Toleration legislation in secondary literature have confused developments in Gradisca and Gorizia with those in Trieste. A second source is Tedeschi 1866: 16.

77. HKA, Komm. Lit., r. 502, 32. ex Januario 1784 (Jan. 26, 1784), f. 515.

78. *Istruzione* . . . 1794 [N. 2333], art. 7: LVI, and *Nuovo Regolamento di Borsa* . . . 1804, both in AST, Deputazione di Borsa, serie I, n. II, and cited by Cattaruzza

1996: 67–68. On elections, see for example HKA, Komm. Lit., r. 617, 13. ex Jan. 1784, ff. 414–415; and AST, C.R. Gov., b. 53, b. 167, b. 168, and b. 668. Grassin Vita di Caliman Levi appears as one of the six deputies serving in 1795 in Protocollo della Ces.a Reg.a Borsa in Trieste, 1795, f. 1, Jan. 13, 1795, but I've seen no other Jewish deputies in the election results from 1783, 1785–91, 1793–94, or 1796–1801. The four Jews on the 1805 *Borsa* Council were Philippo Kohen, Leon Vivante, Jacob Curiel, and David Abram qm Memo Curiel; AST, C.R. Gov., b. 668, session of Aug. 13, 1805. It is unlikely that these served in similar positions in the 1790s, as has sometimes been claimed.

79. Ogris 1981: esp. 147. See also Ogris 1988, and the still-valuable Voltelini 1910: esp. 90–102.

80. O'Brien 1969: 24; Stefani 1960: 250.

81. Katz 1973: 163–64, based on Singer 1933: 260, 295; Kohn 1919: 17; CAHJP, HM 5188, f. 191, no. 6, Consilio Capitaniale, Gorizia, 21 Xbre [Dec.] 1782, in which Trieste was the example cited for the solution of the best of old and new: "The Jewish nation of the Counties [Gorizia-Gradisca] is informed in the name of the Sovereign that besides the benefits recently accorded to it [by the Toleration resolution], it is to enjoy also all the other prerogatives that it tranquilly possesses on the strength of sovereign concession."

82. Much remains to be done on the legal status of the Toleration edicts. My sense is that more specialized work on the various areas of the monarchy, and especially on the bureaucrats' views and recommendations (such as Bernardini 1996b), will help clarify the political/legal theories and the historical realities.

83. CAHJP, It/Go, B,I,2, "Parere . . . 1782."

84. HKA, Komm. Lit., r. 502, 29. ex Martio 1792, ff. 626–638; AST, C. R. Gov., b. 621, Ad N. 298/568 (Apr. 7, 1792, decree).

85. Curiel 1938: 249. Though he provides no exact date for Stella's remark, he cites it from a communal register covering the period 1779 to 1783; from the context and the folio number he cites, 233ff., it is reasonable to assume that the statement is from the latter part of the four-year period.

86. Singer 1934: 234; on Mantua, CAHJP, HM 5188, f. 195, no. 26, chs. 5 and 7; and Bernardini 1996b: 54, on the denial of the Mantuan Jews' 1784 request that they be allowed—like the Jews of Trieste—unlimited rights to own real property.

Chapter Four: Civic Enlightenment as Cultural Policy: Language and the 'Scuola Pia Normale sive Talmud Torà'

1. *Osservatore Triestino*, no. 35, May 1, 1790, pp. 397–98, quoted in De Incontrera 1953–63, 29 (1959): 334. Since that article decried the "abuse" of continued use of Greek, there had obviously been earlier legislation concerning this matter.

2. Roth 1946: 222, 358–59, 475; Milano 1963: 571–76, 578; Della Torre on sermons and education in 1908, 2: 238–45, 334–39; Baron 1937, 2: 210–11, on Roman communal records. See more recently Bonfil 1976a, on the first Jewish sermons in Italian; 1992, on Jewish attitudes to Hebrew and Italian; and 1991: 239–41, for emphasis on the distinguishing features of Italian-Jewish dialects. Later, the value of Jewish linguistic integration was taken for granted by two Italian Jewish intellectu-

als, Benedetto Frizzi and Elia Morpurgo, who praised Joseph's Toleration legislation and its aim of civil integration: Frizzi [1784] 1977: 176–77; and Elia Morpurgo 1782a: 100–101.

3. CAHJP, HM 5804a, f. 41v, Proclama (Sept. 19, 1781).

4. Tamaro 1942–43: 147, about the 1784 effort to have contracts of sale of ecclesiastical property in German (Pittoni himself complained that he "was not strong enough" in German!). 1787 legislation about courts, judges, lawyers, and brokers reported in *Osservatore Triestino*, no. 18, May 5, 1787, p. 232; no. 20, May 19, 1787, pp. 251–52; and no. 22, June 2, 1787, p. 287, cited in De Incontrera 1953–63, 25 (1955): 166–67, 169, 252; De Antonellis Martini 1968: 121–22.

5. Apih 1951. On policy and protests elsewhere, see, for example, Macartney 1968: 123, 142–44; and Levy 1988.

6. For the Patent of July 23, 1787, and subsequent instructions, see Pribram 1918, 1: 582–85; BCT, ADT, 2D33, and 5A4, "Leggi per gli Ebrej emanate negli Stati Ereditarj Austriaci sotto diversi Regnanti, dal 1648 in poi sino inclusive 1803 (Traduzione dalla Collezione tedesca delle Leggi Politiche, Gradisca, 1804)" (Oct. 11, 1787) (microfilm in CAHJP, HM 5962).

7. AST, C.R. Gov., b. 620 (Sept. 1, 1787), N. 5609/1860. See also *Osservatore Triestino*, no. 36, Sept. 8, 1787, pp. 416–18, and no. 46, Nov. 17, 1787, p. 569, in De Incontrera 1953–63, 25 (1955): 424–25, 507; Zoller 1913b; and the summary in De Antonellis Martini 1968: 120–21.

8. On family names among Italian Jews, see Yoel 1944–45: 268; and Colorni 1989. Outside of Trieste, however, *Osservatore Triestino* reported that Elia Morpurgo of Gradisca replaced "Morpurgo," which indicated the family's far-off origin in Marburg, Stiria, with the new surname "Sarker"—from *sarkos*, *shohet*, "slaughterer"; thus he later referred to himself as "Sarker ex-Morpurgo"; *Osservatore Triestino*, no. 4, Jan. 12, 1788, p. 69, in De Incontrera 1953–63, 26 (1956): 135; and Del Bianco Cotrozzi 1989: 720–21. Morpurgo's zeal to support governmental initiatives was in this case unnecessary, since in fact the name "Morpurgo" was not problematic in the eyes of the authorities, and it remained a very common surname among the Jews of Trieste, Gorizia, and Gradisca.

9. Zoller 1913b, no. 2: 6. This episode disproves McCagg's contentions about Jewish language usage in eighteenth-century Trieste (1989: 165–67).

10. The Curiel catologue mentions both a "list of Hebrew names to change into the *German or Christian language*" and a list "of the persons, for whom names have already been changed" (R. Curiel 1942: Cartella N. 1, Leggi e decreti—Privilegi—1509–1890, no. 12). This latter must be the same as the Feb. 20, 1788, "Tabbela de Nazionali Ebrei dimoranti in Trieste Famiglie e Nomi de rispettivi Individui." One column lists "actual personal names" and a second "new names assumed." A complete copy was kindly sent to me by Carlo Gatti; it was reproduced partially in Zoller 1913b, no. 3: 5–6, and no. 4: 5–6. The entire matter requires further investigation: whether a significant number of Triestine Jews actually changed their names, and whether merely on paper or really in daily use. If the latter, then this would be evidence of the effect of Josephinian legislation in a highly personal and symbolic domain.

11. Above all, Melton 1988; also Wangermann 1978; convenient summary in In-

grao 1994a: 188–91. An English translation of much of the General School Ordinance of 1774 in Cubberley 1920: 474–79. The term "normal school" was used both for the method or system as a whole, and for the highest level of school within the system. On instructional methods, see Brotto et al. 1977: 143–52; and Peroni 1906: 90–101, 121–29. On education and educational reform in other European countries in the late eighteenth and nineteenth centuries, see Schmale and Dodde 1991; and Palmer 1985.

12. Tamaro [1924] 1976, 2: 178; De Rosa 1991: 15–17, 20–23.

13. Tremoli 1951: 65; Cova 1979: 297.

14. De Rosa 1991: 19–20, 24. For the opening date of Dec. 1775, see AST, C.R. Gov., b. 126, report of Feb. 5, 1777.

15. Pagnini 1978, on Zinzendorf's interest. On problems in 1776–77, see reports and decrees in AST, C.R. Gov., b. 126, N. 455, N. 644, N. 146, among others; also *Osservatore Triestino*, no. 70, Aug. 30, 1788, pp. 1467–69, in De Incontrera 1953–63, 27 (1957): 66–68; Apih 1957: 44–45, 49, 93–95, 107, 109, 128–30, 144–45 (report from a teacher in the school); and Tamaro [1924] 1976, 2: 178. On the early history of the school generally, De Rosa 1991: 24–40.

16. Pagnini 1978: 188.

17. AST, C.R. Gov., b. 126, N. 1575, Aug. 1776 table, and b. 127, Nov. 15, 1782, table; De Rosa 1991: 37 (with additional figures for other years); Apih 1957: 107. In 1786, there were 272 students in the normal school, and 112 girls in the lower primary school of the San Cipriano convent; Cova 1979: 305 and n. 33.

18. Assaf 1925–42, 2: V, and the references in the index to women teachers, esp. pp. 197–99, 228; Simonsohn 1977: 591, 593–94, 596. On the education and public roles of Italian Jewish women, see Adelman 1991a, 1991b, 1993.

19. Norlinghi 1858: f. 21; Zoller 1924: 6.

20. Vidal (Yehiel) Benjamin Segre (1733–92) mentioned the date of his arrival in a letter of Apr. 11, 1771, to the *Capi*, which is in the original file of documents discussed in Richetti 1984: case 4. Segre came from a family of rabbis in Vercelli, Piedmont. In Trieste, he served at different times as assistant to the cantor, scribe of the synagogue, teacher, and assistant rabbi. Norlinghi 1858: ff. 36–37; ACIT, N. 23, record of examination held on Apr. 28, 1782; S. D. Luzzatto 1878: 21, 48–49; CAHJP, HM 5804a, f. 120v, N. 592 (May 17, 1790) (community accorded him the title *ma-alat ha-haver*); A. Luzzatto 1851: 8; H. D. Bolaffio 1793: 71–72.

21. Norlinghi 1858: ff. 34, 36–37, 47; *Statuti [1766]* . . . 1767, in AST, C.R.S. Int. Comm., b. 78, f. 217r, ch. 6: art. 17 (also in CAHJP, HM 5455); CAHJP, HM 2/5857, f. 21 (Aug. 20, 1767); Statute of 1771, art. 4: XIV, in Maternini Zotta 1983: 229; CAHJP, HM 5804a, f. 29, N. 145 (Sept. 18, 1779), and f. 38r, N. 199 (early 1781). The voluntary association *Fraterna di Talmud Torà, ò sia Errudimento Religioso* sponsored adult study for some years, but it is not clear whether it also participated in organizing or financing education for the young; according to Cervani and Buda 1973: 44 and n. 15, it did exercise some control over the community's teachers. In Italy generally, such associations were sometimes involved with adult study, sometimes with providing funds for the education of poor youngsters, and sometimes with both activities; see Simonsohn 1977: 549; and Milano 1963: 504, 508.

22. *Regole per la Direzione della Scuola Pia Normale sive Talmud Torà dell' Univer-*

sità degli Ebrei di Trieste 1782: 3 (copies in CAHJP, HM 139, and HM 5188, f. 192, no. 5).

23. Information gleaned from the placement examination for the new Jewish normal school held on Apr. 28, 1782, in ACIT, N. 23. The 1771 Statute stated that Jewish youth were studying "scripture and Hebrew language"; art. 5: XVII, in Maternini Zotta 1983: 231. On Italian and arithmetic, see Castiglioni 1886: 7; and Cervani and Buda 1973: 45. On Italian Jewish curricula, see, e.g., *Entziklopedyah hinnukhit* 1964: 376–81, 406–9; Della Torre 1908, 2: 334–39; Assaf 1925–42, 2: 121–213; Simonsohn 1977: 590–99.

24. 1771 Statute, art. 5: XI–XVII, in Maternini Zotta 1983: 230–31.

25. Kieval 1987: 89.

26. CAHJP, IT/Go, VI,37 (Dec. 11, 1775), and rest of file. Zanei 1927: 16, 19, 23, 28, 38; and Lesizza 1988.

27. AST, C.R. Gov., b. 126, report of Ustia and Bellusco to Zinzendorf (Nov. 27, 1776).

28. CAHJP, HM 2/5857, f. 51, decree of May 10, 1777. The Greeks of Trieste were similarly instructed in March 1777; De Rosa 1991: 33–34.

29. Pagnini 1978: 182.

30. AST, C.R. Gov., b. 83, *Capi* to governor (Sept. 19, 1781), Note C accompanying N. 1831.

31. Oct. 1781 in Pribram 1918, 1: 513–14, 520–21; Italian translation in Zoller 1912a: 231. In December 1782, a similar warning was issued by Joseph in connection with the treatment of Jewish students in gymnasia and higher institutions of learning.

32. The May 1781 resolution in AST, C.R. Gov., b. 83, Ad N. 934 (partially in De Antonellis Martini 1968: 118–19; copy in CAHJP P17/1241). The version of the October resolution addressed specifically to Zinzendorf, and responding to his reports on local Triestine circumstances, in HKA, Komm. Lit., r. 502, 34. ex 8bri [Oct.] 1781, ff. 424, 429r, and AST, C.R. Gov., b. 83 (Oct. 20, 1781). Zinzendorf's letter to the *Capi* of Nov. 26, 1781, in AST, C.R. Gov., b. 83 and b. 620, and in CAHJP, HM 5187, f. 190, no. 33 (where it is incorrectly dated as Nov. 26, 1782); short summary in Stock 1973: 371.

33. CAHJP, HM 5187, f. 190, no. 33, Zinzendorf to *Capi* (Nov. 26, 1781).

34. See Chapter Five below. Developments in many of the other Habsburg Jewish communities, but not Trieste, support the contention in Melton (1988: 225): "Ethnic and religious minorities naturally viewed the reforms with a mixture of fear and suspicion."

35. AST, C.R. Gov., b. 83, N. 1831 and accompanying Note B: "Giovani Concorrenti alle Scuole Normali" (a copy of this note also in CAHJP, HM 5467b). The five students were Raffaele Sanson di Benjamin Sagre [Segre], Davide di Benjamin Sagre [Segre], Leon di Jacob Raffael Vita Levi, Jacob di Miriam Ben Porad, and Jacob di Vita Sachi.

36. However, according to S. D. Luzzatto (1878: 49), Segre was unable to fulfill his desire to go on to the Latin school because people were not as forthcoming with money as they had promised to be. But he did manage to complete the normal-

school training program for teachers; see his certificate in AST, C.R. Gov., b. 622, N. 6377 (Nov. 1, 1784).

37. ACIT, N. 23 (Apr. 28, 1782).

38. CAHJP, HM 5804a, f. 45v, N. 241; *Regole* 1782: 4; Sabbadini 1916: 6, 22. Committee members were Raffael Vita Pesaro, Beniamin Abendana, Menasse Morpurgo, Isaia Norsa, and Grassin Vita di Caliman Levi.

39. CAHJP, HM 5804a, f. 47r, N. 245; ACIT, N. 23; *Regole* 1782: 5 (ch. III) and 23.

40. It was after Zinzendorf's written reminder of Jan. 16, 1782, that Galligo wrote to Mendelssohn (AST, C.R. Gov., b. 83, Ad N. 359). Neither that letter from Galligo to Mendelssohn nor the response from Mendelssohn is extant, but in a second letter from Mendelssohn to Trieste dated 23 Iyyar 5542/May 7, 1782, Galligo refers to his letter to Trieste of one month earlier, i.e., early April; Mendelssohn 1972–84, 19: 281–82. It would therefore be reasonable to assume that Galligo had written by mid-March 1782. I think late January or February likely because Wessely later wrote that the first letter from Galligo reached Mendelssohn when *Divrei shalom ve-emet* was going to press, which, according to Alexander Altmann, occurred in January or February 1782; Weisel (Wessely) 1784: 7b–8b; and Altmann 1973: 477–78. Graetz's characterization of the interaction between the Jews of Trieste and Zinzendorf preceding Galligo's letter, namely, that they begged or entreated him to advise them how to obtain textbooks on religion and ethics, is clearly misleading; Graetz [1853–76] 1900, II: 87; and 1967, 5: 369.

41. ACIT, N. 23 (Mar. 25 and Apr. 28, 1782), and Raffael Luzzatto to directors (presented on Aug. 18, 1782, referring to Mar. 19, 1782); CAHJP, HM 5804a, f. 48r, N. 251 (Apr. 12, 1782); *Regole* 1782: 7–10, chs. X–XIII, XV, and pp. 14–20, chs. XXVII–XXXVI; Sabbadini 1916: 6–7.

42. R. Curiel 1938: 249; *Regole* 1782: 7, ch. VII; Cervani and Buda 1973: 46. The school remained on that site until 1798.

43. *Regole* 1782: 6, ch. IV; 10–11, chs. XVII–XVIII; 12, ch. XXI; 14, ch. XXVI.

44. Ibid.: 5, ch. II, and 6, ch. VI. These salaries compared favorably to the salaries of teachers in the Christian primary normal schools of Trieste: between 150–250 florins; *Osservatore Triestino*, no. 11, Mar. 18, 1786, p. 145, in De Incontrera 1953–63, 24 (1954): 83.

45. *Regole* 1782: 7–10, chs. X–XIII, XV; Sabbadini 1916: 7; Cervani and Buda 1973: 47–48.

46. Governmental approval in AST, C.R. Gov., b. 67, Ad N. 926=984 [sic] (May 3, 1782); and *Regole* 1782: 23. There has been much confusion in the secondary literature about the date of the school's opening. Castiglioni's very title displays the confusion—*L'istituto scolastico . . . 1786–1886 . . . primo centenario della fondazione . . .* 1886; he must have relied upon a poem stored prominently in the Archive of the Jewish Community of Trieste that was composed in 1886, supposedly in celebration of the 100th anniversary of the school's founding (Aron Romanini, "Mizmor" [1886], in ACIT). In 1786, the school did undergo some reorganization, primarily financial, and the document pertaining to governmental approval of that may have led to the confusion (Sept. 23, 1786, in Castiglioni 1886: 105). Sabbadini (1916) real-

ized that the school was functioning before 1786, but was unable to determine the opening date with certainty. The correct date of the schools's founding in 1782 emerges clearly from *Regole* 1782, and from a number of the poems and recitations prepared for the opening day's festivities, e.g., Colbi 1980: 187 and its Hebrew original (kindly sent to me by Nikolaus Vielmetti), and the poem by Joshua Barukh Pincherle in CAHJP, Ts, Varia, A2. For other poems composed in honor and then commemoration of the occasion, see CAHJP, Ts, Varia, A2; H. D. Bolaffio 1793: 52, 78; Weisel (Wessely) 1783–84: 161–65, 177–81; Raffael Nathan Tedesco in Sabbadini 1916: 2–3. The community planned to commemorate the opening day of the school with annual celebrations; *Regole* 1782: 10, ch. XVII; and *Regolamento per le Scuole Pie Normali degli Ebrei in Trieste* 1797: VII (name plural; see p. 113).

47. *Regole* 1782: 4.

48. Statement of the school directors published in Italian translation in Colbi 1980: 187–88; I quote and translate here from the Hebrew original.

49. *Regole* 1782: 7–8, ch. X (compulsory attendance); 5, ch. II, and 17–20, chs. XXXIV–XXXVI (*pia* classes); 6, ch. VI, and 20–21, chs. XXXVII–XXXVIII (*normale* class); 11, ch. XIX (evening session). On teachers, see ACIT, N. 23 (Mar. 25 and Apr. 28, 1782, and n.d., apparently Aug. 1782) (from normal-school teacher Giorgio [surname illegible] and response from school directors, Aug. 19, 1782); Sabbadini 1916: 6–7 (Mar. 19, 1782). According to Sabbadini, Raffael Luzzatto was also supposed to help during the normal-school instruction. On Marco Mordecai Luzzatto (1720–99), see S. D. Luzzatto 1878: 19–22, 29–30; Steinschneider 1879: 367; CAHJP, HM 5804a, f. 120v, N. 592 (May 17, 1790) (community accorded him title *ma'alat ha-haham*). Among his many works in manuscript, Marco Luzzatto compiled a Hebrew-Italian dictionary, and translated *Conciliador* of Menasseh ben Israel into Italian, the Ashkenazic liturgy into Italian, a number of polemics (e.g., *Fortalezza del Iudaismo* of Abraham Ger of Cordova) into Hebrew, and *Hizzuk emunah* of Isaac b. Abraham Troki into Italian.

50. *Regole* 1782: 14–15, ch. XXVII.

51. Simone (Simhah b. Abraham) Calimani, *Grammatica ebrea spiegata in lingua italiana con un breve trattato della poesia antica e moderna in essa lingua ebrea* (Venice, 1751; 2d ed., Pisa, 1815). On Calimani (1699–1784), a versatile Venetian rabbi, grammarian, poet, and playwright, see Ghirondi and Neppi 1853: 345–47; and Schirmann 1979, 2: 194–216. Calimani provides a good example of continuity between tradition and modernity among the Italian rabbinate. He was one of the Italian rabbis to support Wessely and his message of Haskalah. For the modernizer Benedetto Frizzi's consideration of Calimani as a praiseworthy model, see Frizzi 1791a.

52. *Regole* 1782: 20, ch. XXXVI. On *accademia* in Italian Jewish schools generally, see Schirmann 1979, 2: 74–80.

53. Fiorentino 1790; Romanelli 1799. On interest in Hebrew literature in the community generally, see Dinaburg 1949: 252–54; and Colbi 1978.

54. Calimani [1821] 1984: 4, dedicatory letter of Calimani to Grassin qm. [di] [Vita] Caliman Levi, Jacob Vita, Isaia Norsa, Amministratori e Direttori delle Pie Scuole Normali Israelitiche in Trieste (June 4, 1782). The word *catechismo*, which appears in the title of Calimani's third (1821) edition, was not present in the title of the

first edition. The exact dates of the first and second editions are not certain; they have been given variously as Venice 1782, Gorizia or Trieste 1783, Trieste 1784, Trieste 1785, and Trieste and Mantua 1786.

55. See Ruderman 1988b: 15, 18, and the sources cited there, on an early and unusual catechism, Abraham Yagel's *Lekah tov* (Venice, 1595). On later eighteenth- and nineteenth-century catechisms, see Petuchowski 1964.

56. On Mantua, see Simonsohn 1977: 592, 596–98; on Venice, see Assaf 1925–42, 2: 192–95; and Ioly Zorattini 1968. In these communities, certain texts were studied that were not mentioned in the *Regole* of Trieste, e.g., *Tosafot*, Alfasi, *Levush* on *Orah Hayyim*, *Hoshen Mishpat*. In Mantua, the need to prepare some pupils in ritual law and for sitting on the communal law court was explicitly stated. Thus when the Mantuan Jewish community reorganized its school under governmental supervision in 1789, it is not surprising that it claimed to have needs different from those of the Triestine community. Though the Mantuan Jewish community planned to comply with the government's directive to follow Trieste's example of two hours a day for normal-school studies, it felt that arrangements that would facilitate a "better cultivation of sacred studies" were in order. The proposal was to divide the two hours of normal-school studies, placing one hour before lunch and one after; the obvious effect would be to minimize the time and importance of normal-school studies. See CAHJP, HM 5194, f. 220, no. 5 (Nov. 5, 1789).

57. The lack of novelty of the basic approach also explained the readiness of Gorizian and Gradiscan Jews in the late 1770s and 1780s to incorporate normal-school studies within Jewish education; they tried various routes such as the hiring of a Gentile teacher, the attendance of Jewish children in the Christian normal school, and the reorganization of existing Jewish schools. G. Bolaffio 1957–58: 62; Lesizza 1988; Del Bianco Cotrozzi 1983: 121. The Gradiscan leader Elia Morpurgo enthusiastically endorsed Joseph's policy in his *Discorso* (1782a), and saw the issue of general education for Jews in the context of past Jewish contributions to states and civilizations in general—many of whom he proudly listed as representing Italian Jewish cultural traditions.

58. Weisel (Wessely) [1782–85] 1826, 4: 218 (*Rehovot*).

59. AST, C.R. Gov., b. 620, N. 3563, session of June 17, 1786. Homberg arrived in Gorizia in the autumn of 1782 and remained there until 1785; he taught in Trieste from 1785 to 1787. Some accounts state that he directed the Triestine school, but I have seen no supporting evidence; it is possible, however, that he was considered the more senior of the two normal-school teachers. On Homberg's sojourn in Italy, see Vielmetti 1984: 44–45; Fahn 1919: 23–24; S. D. Luzzatto 1878: 21, 47–49; Mendelssohn 1972–84, 13: 82–300 passim, correspondence between Oct. 1782 and Sept. 1785; *Osservatore Triestino*, no. 9, Mar. 3, 1787, p. 110, in De Incontrera 1953–63, 25 (1955): 74–75; and Lesizza 1988.

60. AST, C.R. Gov., b. 622, N. 6377 (June 24, 1805), school directors about Joseph Jacob Vita Tivoli.

61. Sabbadini 1916: 7–8; ACIT, N. 23, normal-school teacher's correspondence with school directors (Aug. 1782); CAHJP, HM 5804a, ff. 67v–69r, N. 351 and N. 357–358 (May 16 and June 20, 1784).

62. AST, C.R. Gov., b. 620, Ad N. 1073, 1074, Conto dell'attuale Stato delle Scuole Pie Normali, submitted in Feb. 1786; excerpt in Cervani and Buda 1973: 47–48.

63. AST, C.R. Gov., b. 620, N. 3563, protocol of May 14, 1786; N. 1339, ratification by Vienna (Sept. 8, 1786), conveyed to the community as 2952/5697 (Sept. 23, 1786) (another copy in ACIT, N. 23). It is this letter which Castiglioni (1886: 105) published as Document I, and which led him to think that the school opened only in 1786; ibid.: 7–8.

64. Such penalties were suggested in AST, C.R. Gov., b. 620, N. 1998, Roth report for session of Apr. 8, 1786 (944), and N. 3563 (June 17, 1786). Again in 1797, the directors of the school asked the government to stress the obligation of compulsory attendance of the Jewish public school, AST, C.R. Gov., b. 621, N. 1579 (June 26, 1797); report of governor to Vienna, b. 621, N. 1763 (Aug. 5, 1797), and court decree, b. 621, N. 2387 (Sept. 1, 1797).

65. AST, C.R. Gov., b. 621, N. 2035, correspondence of school directors and governor (May 16 and 26, 1798).

66. CAHJP, HM 2/5838, f. 45r (Jan. 23, 1803); reiterated in AST, C.R. Gov., b. 622, N. 1169 (Feb. 1808).

67. CAHJP, HM 2/5837, N. 83, f. 436r (Nov. 14, 1802), and f. 464 (Nov. 21, 1802). For other budgets and financial records of the school, see CAHJP, HM 2/5864, ff. 95r–98v, 133, 141, 149, and HM 2/5865, ff. 1–5, 8–9, 14, 20.

68. AST, C.R. Gov., b. 620, N. 1998, report of Apr. 8, 1786, and N. 3563, report of June 17, 1786 (cf. O'Brien 1969: 34).

69. On Trieste, see De Rosa 1991: 37. On Prague, Berlin, and Frankfurt, see Kieval 1987: 77, 97–98; more numbers in Eliav 1960: 173–76. It must be noted, however, that the comparison of percentages is necessarily imprecise, given the approximate population figures, and the lack of clarity in some cases, i.e., whether the figures and percentages refer to both boys and girls, or to boys alone.

70. AST, C.R. Gov., b. 621, N. 1763, session of Aug. 5, 1797.

71. For 1807, CAHJP, HM 2/5843, f. 13 (Aug. 30, 1807); for 1808, ACIT, H 18, Nov. 6, 1808 (which cites 50); and Castiglioni 1886: 17 (which cites 46).

72. CAHJP, HM 2/5846, ff. 174–175 (1814); CAHJP, HM 2/5847, ff. 257–258, 286–287, 297–303 (1815); HM 2/5848, ff. 1003, 1023, 1027 (1816); HM 2/5849, f. 564 (1817); Castiglioni 1886: 25 (1817).

73. AST, C.R. Gov., b. 127 (Nov. 15, 1782); Apih 1957: 132; AST, I.R. Gov., Atti Generali, b. 753, N. 10725, Chief of Police Capuano to governor (May 26, 1820).

74. The list of students is found in the record of the examination held on Apr. 28, 1782, in ACIT, N. 23; taxpayers in CAHJP, HM 5804a, f. 46v, N. 244 (Mar. 17, 1782), and f. 59v, N. 314 (Oct. 3, 1783); the 1783–84 Council is found in Stock 1979: 45, and *Regolamento . . . 1783 1784*: 15 (copies in AST, b. 219, and b. 621).

75. See, for example, Simonsohn 1977: 590, 593.

76. AST, C.R. Gov., b. 620, N. 3563 (June 17, 1786).

77. CAHJP, HM 2/5833, f. 320r (Jan. 1796).

78. AST, C.R. Gov., b. 621, N. 1597, school directors (June 26, 1797).

79. *Regolamento* 1797. It was approved by the Jewish community in Jan. 1797,

and by the governing authorities in Sept.–Oct. 1797. Copies of it are to be found in AST, C.R. Gov., b. 621, and in CAHJP, IT 544. This *Regolamento* remained in force for at least two decades.

80. *Regolamento* 1797: XVII, XXIV–XXVII. A report of an examination of older students, ages ten to fifteen, from 1816–17, shows the fundamental continuity of the curriculum—many of the same texts were still being studied; CAHJP, HM 2/5849, f. 538.

81. *Regolamento* 1797: XXVIII; *Regole* 1782: 21, ch. XXXVIII. See AST, C.R. Gov., b. 621, N. 2776 (Sept. 30, Oct. 5, and Oct. 14, 1797), on *Trivialschul* designation, since the school had only two teachers and classes for normal subjects.

82. AST, C.R. Gov., b. 622, N. 821, session of Apr. 22, 1806.

83. Decree of Mar. 22, 1786, in Pribram 1918, 1: 575–76; AST, C.R. Gov., b. 620, N. 1998, on its presentation and discussion in Trieste (Apr. 3 and Apr. 8, 1786).

84. Decree of Apr. 15, 1786, in Pribram 1918, 1: 576–77. Contra Apih (1957: 109), this decree was not ultimately applied in Trieste; see AST, C.R. Gov., b. 620, N. 2556, on the Apr. 28, 1786 presentation in Trieste and esp. the May 2, 1786 session with Councillor Roth's comments—"In this free trading-center . . . no marriage permission is sought . . . and the Jewish community in Trieste is also free from such a constraint"; see also N. 3107 (May 27, 1786) and N. 3563 (June 17, 1786). Later, starting in 1807, the Habsburg government did make Jewish marriages conditional upon ethics testing, eventually by means of Herz Homberg's catechism *Bne Zion*; Pribram 1918, 1: 153, 161–72; and Homberg 1815. The Jews of Trieste were subject to, and did comply with, this later requirement.

85. *Regolamento . . . 1783* 1784: ch. 5: art. 1, in Maternini Zotta 1983: 243–44; school programs, *Regole* 1782: 7, 11, 14–15, chs. VIII, XIX, XXVII, XXXIV–XXXVI, XXXVIII; and *Regolamento* 1797: II, IX, XVII, XXIV–XXVI; CAHJP, HM 2/5835, f. 211v (May 6, 1793), rabbi's contract, which stipulated that he give a daily one-hour lesson on morality in the school for the students and anyone else interested.

86. Tedesco 1786; *Osservatore Triestino*, no. 11, Mar. 18, 1786, pp. 144–45, in De Incontrera 1953–63, 24 (1954): 82–83; cf. Mainati 1817–18, 5: 34.

87. Tedesco 1786: intro., p. 3.

88. AST, C.R. Gov., b. 620, N. 1998 (Apr. 8, 1786).

89. AST, C.R. Gov., b. 620, N. 3563, protocol of May 14, 1786.

90. AST, C.R. Gov., b. 620, N. 3563 (June 17, 1786).

91. Ibid. The officials' preference for the supposedly pure Mosaic aspects of Judaism over the Talmudic was evident in this statement. Consistent with that was the attitude taken by the authorities in the Frizzi-Morschene marriage case a decade or so later, discussed in Chapter Eight below.

92. AST, C.R. Gov., b. 620, N. 5697, and ACIT, N. 23, for sovereign decree of Sept. 8, 1786, and local gubernatorial decree addressed to school directors (Sept. 23, 1786).

93. Stock 1979: 44–45; Wolf 1867: 9; Fahn 1919: 23–24.

94. Pompeo di Brigido (1729–1811), Triestine patrician and patron of the arts, succeeded Zinzendorf as governor of Trieste, serving from 1782 to 1803; De Incontrera 1960: 151–52.

95. *Osservatore Triestino*, no. 9, Mar. 3, 1787, p. 110, in De Incontrera 1953–63, 25: 74–75.

96. AST, C.R. Gov., b. 621, N. 1763 (Aug. 5, 1797).

Chapter Five: Trieste and the Haskalah

1. In Trieste and Mantua, the combination of curricula flowed naturally from the fact that Italian Jews had included general with Jewish education, but Mantua still required a greater concentration on traditional Jewish and halakhic subjects; CAHJP, HM 5193, f. 217; HM 5194, f. 220, no. 5 (Nov. 5, 1789); and Simonsohn 1977: 592–98. Praise for Trieste by Weisel (Wessely) [1782–85] 1826, 4: 218 (*Rehovot*); by headmaster of the Prague school Weiner, and by State Councillor Greiner in Vienna, cited in Silber 1988: 5 n. 8. On the new schools in Prague and Hungary generally, see Kestenberg-Gladstein 1969: 41–65; Kieval 1987: 89–92; and Silber 1987: 110–12.

2. Breuer forthcoming, on previously unnoticed continuities between Wessely's earlier and later work, and generally Breuer 1996, for an interpretation that stresses continuity of Jewish textual traditions in the Haskalah's approach to Scripture.

3. Subsequent editions of *Divrei shalom ve-emet* (Vienna, 1826, and Warsaw, 1886) contain Wessely's three later epistles: *Rav tuv le-vet Yisrael* (1782), *Ein mishpat* (1784), and *Rehovot* (1785). The first editions of these volumes are rare. I was able to obtain the first edition of the third, *Ein Mishpat* (Berlin 1784), which contains the Italian material and is most important for my analysis. For the other three volumes, I used one edition, Vienna 1826, for purposes of consistency. Henceforth references for the first, second, and fourth epistles are to the Vienna 1826 edition, while references for the third, *Ein mishpat*, are to the first edition (Berlin, 1784). In *Divrei*, Wessely explicitly granted the "Torah of man" priority only in time, but the implied message—even if not wholly intended by him—concerned value, and that was how it was generally understood. On his message and the controversy, see Katz 1973: 65–68, 124–28, 151; Eliav 1960: 39–51; Altmann 1973: 57–79, 142–60; Samet 1970: 233–57; Sorkin 1987: 54–62.

4. Weisel (Wessely) 1784: 46b, 4b, 7b–8b, and note on 40a–b; and the beginning of his fourth epistle, *Divrei* [1782–85] 1826, 4 (*Rehovot*). See also 1783–84: 158–60, for an announcement of *Ein mishpat*, the published collection of some of the Italian responses; also *Ha-Meassef* 7 (1794–97): 291 and *Ha-Meassef* 8 (1808–9): 266.

5. Rivkind 1929: 147, 151; Elia Morpurgo 1782a: 56–57, 74–75. On Vienna as a center for *maskilim* from the 1790s, see Fahn 1919 and 1937; Baron 1938; and Wolf [1876] 1974.

6. On frontier, Elia Morpurgo 1782b: f. 32r. See also Frizzi 1790–91, 1: preface, where his stated aim was to combine the "solidity" of German scholarship with the "grace" of Italian.

7. Weisel (Wessely) [1782–85] 1826, 2: 16–17; cf. 2: 26–27 (*Rav tuv*). He also praised Jews of England, France, the eastern Mediterranean, and Poland [sic] for their language skills.

8. *Mikhtav sheni . . . Rav tuv le-vet Yisrael* was dated 10 Iyyar 5542/Apr. 24, 1782.

For specific examples of modifications, see Weisel (Wessely) [1782–85] 1826, 2: 30–32, 43–45 (*Rav tuv*).

9. Weisel (Wessely) [1782–85] 1826, 2: 26 (*Rav tuv*); see also p. 55.

10. Ibid.: 25.

11. Wessely to the leaders of the Jewish community of Trieste, 23 Iyyar 5542/May 7, 1782, in Reggio 1833: 7. Most of the letter is published there (pp. 5–7); the remainder is in Rivkind 1929: 153 n. 2. Cf. Graetz's characterization of the second epistle *Rav tuv*—"supposedly (*angeblich*) addressed to the Trieste community" (translation and emphasis mine); Graetz [1853–76] 1900, 11: 90. Mendelssohn's accompanying letter to Joseph Galligo of Trieste (23 Iyyar 5542/May 7, 1782), in Mendelssohn 1972–84, 19: 281–82.

12. The second letter from Trieste is not extant. I am skeptical about its receipt in Berlin before publication of Wessely's *Rav tuv* because Mendelssohn made no reference to a second Triestine letter in his May 7 letter to Trieste. Furthermore, Wessely's account in the later *Ein mishpat* is vague and self-contradictory (Weisel [Wessely] 1784: 7b–8b).

13. Weisel (Wessely) [1782–85] 1826, 2: 25 (*Rav tuv*).

14. Reggio 1833: 5.

15. Morpurgo's letter in Rivkind 1929: 147–49; and Mendelssohn 1972–84, 14: 285–86. The letter from Trieste, not extant, was mentioned by Wessely in a subsequent letter to Trieste dated 16 Tammuz 5542/June 28, 1782, in Rivkind 1929: 150–55; he stated there that the communal secretary Galligo had written during the week of *Be-he'alotekha*, i.e., the last week of May, and that he had received the letter on 3 Tammuz 5542/June 15, 1782.

16. Elia Morpurgo 1781 and 1782a. On Morpurgo as an ardent supporter of Josephinian policies and of Enlightenment, see Tamani 1988; and Del Bianco Cotrozzi 1989: 715–25, and 1991: 50–52, which add considerable new material to Rivkind 1929, Vielmetti 1984, and Colbi 1980.

17. Rivkind 1929: 147; also Mendelssohn 1972–84, 14: 286.

18. Rivkind 1929: 148; also Mendelssohn 1972–84, 14: 286. Morpurgo mentioned works by Joseph Esobi, Shem Tov ben Joseph Falaquera, Nahmanides, Abraham Ibn Ezra, and Profiat Duran. See also Rivkind 1929: 141; Weisel (Wessely) 1783–84: 15, 31–32, 45–46; and Del Bianco Cotrozzi 1991: 45–50, on Morpurgo's desire to publish anthologies of poetry, ethics, history, and Halakhah. What he did manage to publish was a translation of Yedaiah Bedersi's *Behinat Olam*: Sarker Ex-Morpurgo 1796.

19. Rivkind 1929: esp. 151, 153. There appears to be a quote from that letter in Weisel (Wessely) 1784: 8, and a paraphrase in Tedeschi 1866: 19.

20. Morpurgo's translation of *Divrei* was published the following year: Elia Morpurgo 1783b. See also Elia Morpurgo 1782b: f. 14r; and Morpurgo's letter to Israel Benjamin Bassan of Reggio (17 Sivan 5542/May 30, 1782), in Rivkind 1929: 150.

21. Wessely to Trieste, in Rivkind 1929: 150–55.

22. Additional letters besides those already cited: Morpurgo to Wessely (1 Ellul 5542/Aug. 11, 1782), in Rivkind 1929: 155–56; Formiggini to Wessely (n.d., apparently summer 1783), in Weisel (Wessely) 1784: 42a–43a; Wessely to Morpurgo (18 Shevat 5546/Jan. 17, 1786), in Letteris 1862: 120–22. In this last letter, Wessely complained of

a hiatus in the correspondence from northern Italy, which he attributed to difficulties with mail and couriers. Extant letters of solicitation in Rivkind 1929, from Morpurgo to Israel Benjamin Bassan of Reggio (17 Sivan 5542/May 30, 1782); Morpurgo to Abraham Isaac Castello of Liverno (4 Ellul 5542/Aug. 14, 1782); and Morpurgo to Jacob Danon of Constantinople (28 Tevet 5544/Jan. 22, 1784). For a possible paraphrase of the letters sent by Triestine leaders, see Tedeschi 1866: 19–21.

23. Weisel (Wessely) 1784. Excerpts of *Ein mishpat* are in Assaf 1925–42, 2: 213–18. On the possibility of other Italian answers, see Rivkind 1929: 143, 145, 153 n. 3. Another rabbinic response, less positive (to be discussed below), was received from the noted Ishmael Kohen (Laudadio Sacerdote) (1785–96, 2: *Yoreh deah*, no. 107; also in Assaf 1925–42, 2: 219–21). As for the conspicuous absence of answers from Livorno and Mantua, we can only speculate about lost, late, or lukewarm answers, or failure to respond. In the introduction to his "Iggeret" (1782b), Morpurgo stated that he wrote it in further justification of Wessely because "some [rabbis] had turned a deaf ear" to his earlier letters; Elia Morpurgo 1782b: f. 13v. It seems that Morpurgo did not receive a positive response from his teacher Abraham Isaac Castello of Livorno; nonetheless, I do not think that Castello's poem against wealthy libertines and skeptics ought to be linked, as some have done, to *maskilim* and educational reforms, or construed as a negative answer to Morpurgo about Wessely (Castello's poem in Piperno 1846: 28a–29b, 78b–80b, 81b–82b; Assaf 1925–42, 2: 277; Ghirondi and Neppi 1853: 16–22). As for Mantua, was the death of Rabbi Jacob Saraval in April 1782 a factor in its silence?

24. He completed "Iggeret" by 20 Tammuz 5542/July 2, 1782. He began *Discorso* in 1781, completed it by May 8, 1782, and had it published shortly thereafter. He prepared *Traduzione . . . Discorsi . . . Weisel* in May 1782, and had it published in 1783. To *Ha-Meassef* he contributed "Divrei hokhmah u-musar" (written in 1783), published in *Ha-Meassef* 3 (1785–86): 131–37, 147–56, 164–76; and "Mikhtav me-Eliyyahu" (written in Feb. 1784), published in *Ha-Meassef* 3 (1785–86): 66–78 (fullest edition in Assaf 1925–42, 2: 222–33).

25. Elia Morpurgo 1783a; Weisel (Wessely) 1783–84: 15, 31–32, 45–46; Del Bianco Cotrozzi 1991: 48–50, also 45–46. The contents of the first issues were supposed to include Morpurgo's translations of Apocryphal works, medieval Hebrew poetry of Moses Ibn Ezra and Shem Tov Falaquera among others, and the *Minhat Yehudah* of the Karaite Yehudah Gibbor; works by Immanuel of Rome and David de Pomis were also under consideration.

26. Morpurgo to Bassan (17 Sivan 5542/May 30, 1782), in Rivkind 1929: 149–50.

27. Elia Morpurgo 1782b: ff. 13v–14r.

28. Ibid., f. 24. See also Elia Morpurgo 1782a: 57, 71, 95, and app., *Opere di celebri ebrei moderni*; 1783b: 13, note a; 1782b: ff. 22v, 23v; 1785–86b, also in Assaf 1925–42, 2: 223–34. Cf. Bassan in Weisel (Wessely) 1784: 41b; and Frizzi [1784] 1977: 81.

29. Rivkind 1929: 155–56.

30. Ibid.: 157–58.

31. Tedeschi 1866: 19–20. However, we cannot be certain whether this is paraphrase of the eighteenth-century document, or his imaginative reconstruction composed in the 1860s. *Pesak* of Formiggini dated 27 Tammuz 5542/July 9, 1782, in Weisel (Wessely) 1784: 9a–13a.

32. Ibid.

33. I use the terms "non-Torah Wisdom," "non-Torah studies," and "general studies" in order to avoid the term "secular studies," which I think prejudices the issue.

34. Offering "alien fire" was the sin that caused the death of Aaron's two sons, Nadab and Abihu; Lev. 10:1–2, Num. 3:4, 26:61.

35. Formiggini, in Weisel (Wessely) 1784: 12a.

36. There may have been divergence between Formiggini's recommendation to Wessely and the program of the Triestine school concerning the ages at which study of Hebrew composition, the vernacular, German, and arithmetic would commence. In the Triestine school, all of these subjects were designated for the second grade, but since the correlation between grade and age is uncertain, we cannot know whether children under the age of ten were learning them; by and large, however, these subjects did occupy only a minor portion of the day. One other difference was the deferral in the Triestine school of Mishnah until the second grade.

37. On Norzi (Norsa), see Ghirondi and Neppi 1853: 133, 277 (where he appears as Borgo [Borghi]); Simonsohn 1977: 459 n. 431. On Calimani, see Chapter Four above. On Cracovia, see Ghirondi and Neppi 1853: 42. On Pacifico, see ibid.: 33; and Simonsohn 1977: 460 n. 431. On Hayyim Abraham Israel, see Ghirondi and Neppi 1853: 115; Simonsohn 1977: 459 n. 431. On Bassan, see Ghirondi and Neppi 1853: 153; and Simonsohn 1977: 459 n. 431. Additional biobibliographical references in Dubin 1987: 218 n. 40. There were personal ties between the respondents and Trieste or Morpurgo: Norzi (Norsa) of Ferrara was the father of the Triestine school director, Isaia Norsa; Calimani of Venice had submitted his *Esame* for adoption as a text to the Triestine school directors; the leaders of the Ancona community were Morpurgos, relatives of Elia Morpurgo; and Elia Morpurgo had studied with Bassan.

38. Morpurgo to Danon (28 Tevet 5544/Jan. 22, 1784), in Rivkind 1929: 158–59, mentions Wessely's earlier letter to Morpurgo of Kislev 5544/Dec. 1783.

39. Kohen 1785–96, 2: *Yoreh deah*, no. 107; also in Assaf 1925–42, 2: 219–21.

40. Weisel (Wessely) 1784: 11, 23, 33, on curriculum and division of labor. On Italian Jewish educational practices, *Entziklopedyah hinnukhit* 1964, 4: 407–8, 410. On Talmud as a subject for advanced students in Mantua, see Simonsohn 1977: 598; but in Livorno, Ancona, and Modena, Halakhah was taught earlier and more intensively, a fact reflected in Israel's and Kohen's responses to Weisel's *Divrei*. See Bonfil 1990: 22–23, 28, 268, 284 n. 64, on the effects of the proscription of the Talmud in Italy.

41. Weisel (Wessely) [1782–85] 1826: ch. 1. The meaning of the term *torat ha-adam*, found in 2 Samuel 7:19, has perplexed commentators. Wessely's usage seems unlike previous ones.

42. Kohen 1785–96, 2: *Yoreh deah*, no. 107, using the phrase from *Baba Batra* 16a. In Weisel (Wessely) 1784, see Formiggini (pp. 10a–11a, 12), Norzi (p. 17), the Venetians (p. 33a), Israel (pp. 36b–37a).

43. In Weisel (Wessely) 1784, see Formiggini (pp. 10, 12), Norzi (p. 14), Israel (p. 36a). See also Galligo in H. D. Bolaffio 1793: 78a.

44. In Weisel (Wessely) 1784, see the Venetians (pp. 21, 34), and Triestine school

directors (p. 45); cf. Colbi 1980: 187–88. For Morpurgo, see 1782b: ff. 14v, 22v; letter to Mendelssohn, in Rivkind 1929: 158; 1785–86a: 168; 1785–86b, also in Assaf 1925–42, 2: 223, 229; 1783b: 6–12, 15–16. See also Elia Morpurgo 1785–86a: 75; and Assaf 1925–42, 2: 229–30, for Morpurgo's citation of the Italian use of the term *studia humanitatis* for studies such as German, arithmetic, grammar, history, and geography; he then revised it to *scuole normale* (normal classes). However, even *studia humanitatis* did not necessarily have dichotomous connotations (Kristeller 1961: 9–11, 74–75, 110–11).

45. Beales 1985: 169–73, 191.

46. Elia Morpurgo 1782b: ff. 17v–18r, with citation of the classic passage *Pesahim* 94b; and 1782a: esp. 36, 75–82. Cf. Maimonides, *Guide of the Perplexed*, I:71, and Judah Halevi, *Kuzari*, I:63, II:66.

47. Norzi in Weisel (Wessely) 1784: 14b. On Italian views that saw Kabbalah and science as compatible, see Idel 1992: 345–68, and especially Ruderman 1988b on Abraham Yagel. For debates on the question, see also Ruderman 1995: esp. chs. 4 and 7.

48. Venetians in Weisel (Wessely) 1784: 28a–29a; Elia Morpurgo 1782b: ff. 19v–20r (also in Rivkind 1929: 140); Elia Morpurgo 1785–86b, also in Assaf 1925–42, 2: 226. On Italian traditions of music and poetry, see Schirmann 1979, 2: 44–94 and 194–96, esp. n. 2; and Pagis 1976.

49. Bassan in Weisel (Wessely) 1784: 40b. Cf. Reggio 1830b: 3–4; and *Israelitische Annalen* 1 (1839): 79–80, 157. On the practical focus of Italian Enlightenment figures, see Cochrane 1961: 239, 248; Valsecchi 1931, 2, pt. 1: 119–21; and Chadwick 1981: 90.

50. Norzi, in Weisel (Wessely) 1784: 17a.

51. Neither Bassan nor Morpurgo referred to his predecessor. On the Provenzali plan, see Assaf 1925–42, 2: 115–20; and Simonsohn 1977: 583. In this connection, it is interesting to note that teaching Latin was the rabbi's duty in Ancona; see Di Segni 1971: 97–104. In Elia Morpurgo 1782a: 54–55 and 1785–86a: 174–76, Morpurgo suggested that knowledge of tales told by Gentiles in ancient times would make some Talmudic *aggadot* seem less strange; on Morpurgo's approach to Aggadah generally, see Dubin 1992. On Azariah, see, for example, Bonfil 1983: 23–48, esp. 38–43 nn. 81, 87.

52. Elia Morpurgo 1785–86b, also in Assaf 1925–42, 2: 225; 1782b: f. 18r; 1782a: 54.

53. On Ishmael Kohen, see Schirmann 1979, 2: 73–74; on Wessely, *Nahal habesor*, pp. 7–8, bound with *Ha-Meassef* 1 (1783–84).

54. Elia Morpurgo 1782b: ff. 14v–15r; see also 1785–86a: 167–69.

55. Bonfil 1991 and 1992.

56. L. Modena [1638] 1932–33: 383–84.

57. L. Modena [1638] 1932–33, I, 5: 312–13. For pictures, see Modena and Morpurgo in Roth 1946: 401–2, and Kohen in Cammeo 1911. See also Shabbetai Marini and Abraham Cohen in Benayahu 1978: 108, 140; Moses Gentili (Hefez) in *Encyclopedia Judaica* 1972, 7: 414; Abraham Reggio of Gorizia in Bolaffio 1957; Raffael Nathan Tedesco in Zoller 1933c. On the iconography of Jewish rabbinical portraits in the early modern and modern periods, see Richard I. Cohen 1998.

58. The first phrase comes from Elia Morpurgo 1782a: 96–97, and the last three from Frizzi [1784] 1977: 168.

59. On cultural norms, Formiggini and the Venetians in Weisel (Wessely) 1784: 11, 34; on belles lettres, Pagis 1976 and Schirmann 1979. On the impact of the Italian Renaissance upon Jews, see the classic works by Roth (1959) and Shulvass (1973), and Bonfil's critique of their harmonistic views, especially in his 1984 and 1991. For other recent views, see Ruderman 1981, 1988a, 1992; Lesley 1982 and Tirosch-Rothschild 1988 on humanism; Yerushalmi 1982: 53–75, esp. p. 60, on Renaissance historiography. Tirosch-Rothschild 1990 provides a convenient overview of the recent literature.

60. Benayahu 1978; Modena and Morpurgo 1967: 41, 55–57, 62–63; Ghirondi and Neppi 1853: 62–63, 131–37. For proud invocations of this tradition, see Elia Morpurgo 1782a: 85–90; and Reggio 1830a.

61. Ruderman 1995: esp. ch. 3.

62. See Elia Morpurgo 1782a; and Frizzi [1784] 1977: esp. 80–82; 1791a; and 1791b.

63. I. S. Reggio's anonymously published *Riflessioni* (1822: 4–5). Other expressions of Italian Jewish pride in Della Torre 1834: 34–35; and S. D. Luzzatto 1848–52, 1: 29.

64. E.g., G. Luzzatto 1950; Bachi 1946–47; Angelini 1973; Allegra 1996; Toaff 1981; Bernardini 1996b: 126–29.

65. Mendelssohn 1972–84, 13: 95. For more on the positive image of Italian Jews in this period, see Dubin 1987: 204–8 and 1998: 272–76 (and the sources cited there).

66. *Ha-Meassef* 1 (1783–84): 161–65, 177–81; and 5 (1788–89): 255–56, on schools; and 4 (1787–88): 386–88, on conscription.

67. Mendelssohn 1972–84, 13: 180, 186; Dinaburg 1949; Colorni 1983: 507–14; and Schirmann 1979, 2: 239–301, on Romanelli. On Samuel Morpurgo (later Philippe Sarchi), see Wessely to Elia Morpurgo (18 Shevat 5546/Jan. 17, 1786), in Letteris 1862: 122; and Del Bianco Cotrozzi 1993 (and the sources cited there). On Lewin-Berlin, see Samet 1968.

68. *Ha-Meassef* 1 (1783–84): 124–27, 140–44, on Delmedigo, and 38–42, 57–61, on Abarbanel; Steinschneider 1891; and for further examples, Dubin 1987: 207, and 222 (nn. 84 and 89).

69. Satanov 1789, 1: intro.; cf. *Ha-Meassef* 8 (1808–9): 233, 286–87.

70. *Ha-Meassef* 6 (1789–90): 171–76, 246–49.

71. Lewin-Berlin 1793: intro. On Florence, see *Ha-Meassef* 7 (1794–97): 271–73; Katz 1973: 136–37; and Dubin 1987: 207–8 and 1998: 273–74 (and the sources cited there).

72. For the tale of this image and its abrupt ending after the early Reform controversies of 1816–20, see Dubin 1998.

73. In the first chapter of *Divrei* ([1782–85] 1826), Wessely had also listed subjects such as civility, history, geometry, astronomy, and botany. Formiggini had counseled Wessely that no non-Torah studies should be introduced before the age of ten.

74. *Regole* 1782: 20–21, ch. XXXVII; and *Regolamento* 1797: V. The two-hour allotment remained in effect until 1820. On Prague, see Kieval 1987: 91.

75. Eliav 1960: 71–86, 172–76; Katz 1973: 124–31; Sorkin 1990b: 114–15, on Dessau; Feiner 1995: esp. 404, 410–13, on the Berlin *Freyschule* and Dessau.

76. S. D. Luzzatto 1878: 21. Cf. Roth 1946: 424; Milano 1963: 329; Colbi 1978: 71.
77. Tedeschi 1866: 15–16, and 9–23 more generally.
78. Cf. Candeloro 1956, 1: 74–75; and Cochrane 1961: 232–40, 247–48, on Italian receptivity to the Enlightenment. On the Enlightenment in Italy more generally, see, e.g., Venturi 1974 and Chadwick 1981.
79. S. D. Luzzatto 1848–52, 1: 29.
80. Katz 1987; and Sorkin and Feiner forthcoming, on transportability and receptivity in different settings.
81. Baron 1937, 2: 205–12; and Barzilay 1960. Barzilay noted parallels and differences between the earlier Italian and later Berlin movements, and concluded that the differences outweigh the similarities; still, he used the same term for the two.

Chapter Six: A Decade of Civil Toleration: New Rights and Duties in the 1780s

1. *Regolamento . . . 1783* 1784, in Maternini Zotta 1983: 237; entire text, pp. 237–45, 49–52. That version is fuller than the one in Cervani and Buda 1973: 216–24, 30–33, since it includes emendations made in Dec. 1783. AST, C.R. Gov., b. 219, N. 519 (Aug. 10, 1783), contains local officials' views on the community's draft.
2. Decrees of July 11, 1782, Aug. 25, 1783, and May 28, 1785, which abrogated Jewish jurisdiction for civil matters, but claimed to leave Jewish religious law valid (on complications stemming from this distinction, see Chapter Eight below). Pribram 1918, 1: 525; Colorni 1945: 354–59. For these decrees in Trieste, see AST, C.R. Gov., b. 621, Patente concernente i Tribunali per gli Ebrei (Aug. 25, 1783); and b. 219, N. 3127, session of June 11, 1785, and N. 3283, session of June 18, 1785; ADT, 14C 2/8, N. 78, Verordnung von dem Inner- und OberÖsterreichischen Appellazions-Gericht (June 3, 1785); on judicial administration generally in Trieste, see Pavonello 1982 and Faber 1995: 229–30. The Archives of the Jewish Community of Mantua, f. 198, no. 16 (a copy of which was kindly sent to me by Vittore Colorni) contains a letter from the Trieste Jewish community alerting the Mantua Jewish community to the new decrees, which would be of especial concern in Mantua because of the long-standing separate Jewish judicial system there. As mentioned above, some Triestine Jews had previously called for removing judicial rights from the *Capi*. More generally, on the abrogation of separate courts and the drive toward standardization of law as part of Habsburg centralization and state-building, see, for example, Voltelini 1910; Mitrofanov 1910, 2: 514–46; Ogris 1988; Szabo 1994: 180–83.
3. *Regolamento . . . 1783* 1784: ch. 5: arts. 1–2, in Maternini Zotta 1983: 244.
4. Pribram 1918, 1: 516–17; and Cervani and Buda 1973: 78.
5. This section is based on Dubin 1991, with some additions and changes. Short accounts of the end of the ghetto in Curiel 1938: 250–51; and De Antonellis Martini 1968: 119–20.
6. Jan. 2, 1782, edict, clause 18, in Mendes-Flohr and Reinharz 1995: 39; Pribram 1918, 1: 498. In 1785, Triestine officials also cited the edict for Silesia in this regard; AST, C.R. Gov., b. 219, N. 3819 (July 12, 1785).
7. Aug. 15, 1753; Cervani and Buda 1973: 14, 26, 171; and Maternini Zotta 1983: 221.

8. HKA, Komm. Lit., r. 502, 57. ex Jan. 1772, ff. 241r–242v; see ff. 24, 60, for earlier complaints.

9. Singer 1934: 234. For comparison, see Sciloni 1989 on Florence, where many Jews also lived outside the ghetto; though most of his evidence is from the nineteenth century, some pertains to the eighteenth century.

10. Scussa and Kandler 1863: 208; Kandler stated that only the poor lived in the ghetto. AST, C.R. Gov., b. 219, N. 4826, *Capi* and *Consultori* to governor (Aug. 23, 1785).

11. AST, C.R. Gov., b. 219, N. 3819, Pittoni to governor (July 6, 1785).

12. AST, C.R. Gov., b. 219, N. 3819 (July 12, 1785); also HKA, Komm. Lit., r. 502, 14. ex Aug. 1785, ff. 521r–526v.

13. AST, C.R. Gov., b. 219, N. 4612 (Aug. 4, 1785); HKA, Komm. Lit., r. 502, 14. ex Aug. 1785, ff. 521r–526v.

14. AST, C.R. Gov., b. 219, N. 4826, *Capi* and *Consultori* of the Jewish community to governor (Aug. 23, 1785).

15. Ibid., ref. Ricci n.d.

16. AST, C.R. Gov., b. 620, N. 1017; and b. 219, N. 4887, and N. 4934, *Capi* and *Consultori* to governor (Aug. 26, 1785), with additions (Aug. 29, 1785). See also b. 219, N. 4888, sons of Menasse Morpurgo and other owners of property in the ghetto to governor.

17. AST, C.R. Gov., b. 219, N. 4887, session and decree of Aug. 30, 1785 (copies of decree in b. 620, N. 1017, and ADT, 2D33).

18. G. Bolaffio 1957–58: 539–40; Del Bianco Cotrozzi 1989: 710. As late as 1810, there was still dissension within the Gorizian community about the demolition of the entry gates to the ghetto.

19. AST, C.R. Gov., b. 219, N. 5229 and N. 5230, session of Sept. 17, 1785. See also N. 5026, protocol of community meeting (Sept. 8, 1785) and *Capi* to governor (Sept. 9, 1785); and N. 5081/1763 (session of Sept. 10, 1785).

20. CAHJP, HM 5804a, f. 80r, N. 409, Proclama (Sept. 28, 1785). On the definition of public domain, see Maimonides, *Mishneh Torah*, Sabbath 14:1.

21. HKA, Komm. Lit., r. 502, 21. ex Nov. 1785; and AST, C.R. Gov., b. 219, N. 6902, session of Dec. 6, 1785; b. 620, N. 7471, Chief of Police Pittoni to governor (Dec. 24, 1785); b. 219, Ricci to Hofkanzlei (Dec. 31, 1785).

22. HKA, Komm. Lit., r. 502, 15. ex Feb. 1786, f. 534; AST, C.R. Gov., b. 620, N. 1017, session of Feb. 21, 1786.

23. *Osservatore Triestino*, no. 6, Feb. 11, 1786, p. 76, in De Incontrera 1953–63, 24 (1954): 77–78; Cervani and Buda 1973: 98.

24. Gatti 1991: 317–18.

25. AST, C.R. Gov., b. 219, N. 4826, *Capi* and *Consultori* to governor (Aug. 23, 1785); also b. 620, N. 1017, general convocation of Jewish community (Aug. 25, 1785). See also AST, C.R. Gov., b. 620, N. 7471, Pittoni to governor (Dec. 24, 1785).

26. AST, C.R. Gov., b. 620, N. 1017 (Aug. 25, 1785), Marco Levi to the general convocation of the community. On the ghetto as offering physical protection, cf. Sciloni 1989: 66, on eighteenth-century Florence.

27. On "Gnora Luna," see Roth 1946: 412–13; Simonsohn 1977: 88–91; and Bernardini 1996b: 25–27; on Trieste, see Norlinghi 1858: ff. 32–33.

28. AST, C.R. Gov., b. 620, N. 1017 (Aug. 25, 1785), Marco Levi to the general convocation of the community.

29. Ibid.

30. Ibid.

31. AST, C.R. Gov., b. 219, protocol of Jewish community meeting (Sept. 8, 1785), and *Capi* et al. to governor (Sept. 9, 1785).

32. On the detrimental effects of ghettos upon the health of Jews, see also Elia Morpurgo 1782a: 98; cf. Roth 1946: 420, 487.

33. AST, C.R. Gov., b. 219, *Capi* to governor, N. 4887 (Aug. 26, 1785), and N. 4934 (Aug. 29, 1785); b. 620, N. 7471, Pittoni to governor (Dec. 24, 1785).

34. AST, C.R. Gov., b. 219, N. 4887, *Capi* to governor (Aug. 26, 1785).

35. AST, C.R. Gov., b. 620, N. 1017, protocol of the general convocation of the community (Aug. 25, 1785).

36. Hertzberg 1968: 299–313.

37. Frizzi [1784] 1977; Colorni 1945: 352–53. The Mar. 9, 1784, letter from the two Mantuan deputies in Trieste is mentioned in CAHJP, P 17/1201, Mantua Repertorio, Tom. IV, Libri ebraici, f. 36.

38. On Mantua, Simonsohn 1977: 95–96; Bernardini 1996b: 152–53, 209–11, 326.

39. Roth 1946: 427–42; Milano 1963: 342–51; and De Felice 1955.

40. See Yerushalmi 1981: 387–88, on Cardoso, and on the Verona celebration (and his view of earlier interpretations of it in Roth 1924a and Sonne 1938); on Rome, see Stow 1992.

41. Bonfil 1992: esp. 407–10; 1991: 63–75.

42. Curiel 1938: 251. For an example of continued use of the term "ghetto," see AST, C.R. Gov., b. 621, N. 2240 (June 17, 1796).

43. Saba, "Il Ghetto di Trieste nel 1860" (1910–12), in Saba 1964, 1: 25–28; translation in Gilson 1993: 20–22.

44. Blanning 1994: 125–28; Szabo 1994: 293, and more generally, 278–95.

45. Schmidl 1989: 98–111, for the fullest account; also useful are Karniel 1985: 450–53; Wolf 1867–68: esp. 60–64; and Silber 1985 and 1988. Copies of the decrees in ADT, 5A4, "Leggi" (July 7, 1788) (microfilm in CAHJP, HM 5962), and CAHJP, IT/Go, II,39 (July 26, 1788). Other European countries followed suit in conscripting Jews, though none went to the extremes that Czarist Russia did under Nicholas I, where decades-long service was imposed upon young Jewish boys.

46. Trebitsch 1851: no. 59; CAHJP, P83 E8, XLI, ff. 39–41; G. Bolaffio 1957–58: 135–36. Even Elia Morpurgo of Gradisca—who saw military conscription within the overall context of civil improvement and integration, and praised its benefits especially for making the poor productive—nonetheless was well aware of the difficulties it posed for religious observance. He advocated separate regiments for Jews, and a synod of Jewish religious and lay leaders to determine the best way to reconcile civic and religious duties (cf. the letter from Jewish leaders of Trieste on military conscription, below). See Jare 1907, and *Schreiben eines Rabbi aus Gradiska* 1788, which was probably Morpurgo's work.

47. *Ha-Meassef*'s (1788–89): 252–55; and Kestenberg-Gladstein 1969: 70–73.

48. CAHJP, HM 5193, f. 216, no. 1 (12 Sivan 5548/June 17, 1788); see Simonsohn 1977: 475.

49. Responses from Mantua (11 Tammuz 5548/July 17, 1788), and from Trieste (25 Sivan 5548/July 1, 1788), in CAHJP, HM 5193, f. 216, no. 1. The letter from Trieste was reprinted in *Ha-Meassef* 4 (1787–88): 386–88. Partial English translation in Padover 1967: 184–85. Cf. other positive views of conscription of Jews in *Ha-Meassef* 4 (1787–88): 331–34; Dohm 1807: 127–43; Homberg 1783: 101–3.

50. CAHJP, HM 5193, f. 216, no. 1; *Ha-Meassef* 4 (1787–88): 387. Cf. *Schreiben eines Rabbi aus Gradiska* 1788: esp. 22–24.

51. For examples of such exemptions, see *Eruvin* 17 and *Sanhedrin* 20b; Maimonides, *Mishneh Torah*, Benedictions 6:3, Kings 6:11–13, Sabbath 2:23, 25.

52. Schmidl 1989: 107–9.

53. E.g., Geisler 1790: 66–70; *Die Vossische Zeitung*, no. 95, Aug. 17, 1788 (cited in Geiger 1889: 186); O. E. Kling, *Soll der Jude Soldat werden?* (Vienna, 1788), cited in Wolf 1862: 62.

54. Wolf 1862; Kestenberg-Gladstein 1969: 333–40, esp. 335 n. 14. In contrast, the answer from Trieste was criticized by Saul Ascher, the one Jewish advocate of Enlightenment who argued against military conscription of Jews given that they did not yet fully enjoy their liberties; Ascher 1788: 7, 36–37.

55. The community's letter was dated 25 Sivan 5548/July 1, 1788, and Rabbi Formiggini died on 8 Tammuz 5548, the evening of July 13, 1788.

56. The Galician letter was dated 12 Sivan 5548/June 18, 1788, the Triestine response 25 Sivan 5548/July 1, 1788, and the Mantuan response 11 Tammuz 5548/July 17, 1788. But the legislation extending conscription to Jews beyond Galicia was issued only on July 7, 1788, and received by local governing authorities in Trieste in the last week of July; CAHJP, IT/Go, II,39, copy of the sovereign rescript issued in Trieste (July 26, 1788); and Bernardini 1996b: 305, on Mantua. The legislation received in Trieste was actually for Gorizia-Gradisca, then administratively united with Trieste; it was not intended for the Jews of the Free Port of Trieste.

57. AST, C.R. Gov., b. 621, N. 2319, governor to *Capi* (July 25, 1795); also Pittoni to governor, Ad N. 1447 (July 13, 1795), and *Capi* to governor (June 25, 1795); Szabo 1994: 293.

58. CAHJP, HM 2/5844, ff. 160–161, *Capi* to governor (Apr. 14, 1809). See CAHJP, HM 2/5858, ff. 203–204, "Milizia provinciale"; HM 2/5847, ff. 202–204, 251, and HM 2/5849, ff. 332–333, 341, on the service of twenty-four Jews in the Triestine militia.

59. CAHJP, HM 2/5858, ff. 377–378, "Soldati ed affari militari." For further examples, see HM 2/5843, ff. 8r, 9r, 62v.

60. CAHJP, HM 2/5844, ff. 25–26 (Nov. 2, 1808). The question was participation in military exercises and functions on Sabbaths and Jewish holidays. Later the *Capi* requested and obtained the same exemption from the French occupiers of the city, CAHJP, HM 2/5844, ff. 226–228 (Oct. 18, Oct. 26, and Nov. 3, 1809).

61. Mahler 1971: 330–33; Karniel 1982; Del Bianco Cotrozzi 1989: 711–15. Silber (1989) sees the patent as particularly significant in that it "revealed the maximum extent which the ancien regime was willing and capable of integrating the Jews." In this regard, the Galician Patent ought to be compared to Leopold's toleration patent of Jan. 2, 1791, for the Jews of Mantua, which also contained significant innovations. For example, unlike previous charters, Leopold's set no termination

date, but rather offered toleration "forever," and aimed more generally at making the rights and duties of Jews equal to those of other subjects; Simonsohn 1977: 149, 818–27 (with text of patent); and Bernardini 1996b: 207–9.

62. Consultation in AST, C.R. Gov., b. 620, Court Chancellery to governor of Trieste (May 27, 1789), and Ricci (June 9, 1789), N. 3747/1391, session of June 13, 1789, and N. 7079/2589, session of Oct. 31, 1789.

63. Such claims have been made by Karniel (1981: 218, and 1985: 403 and n. 98) and Fubini (1974: 485). Confusion probably arose because the sovereign resolution of Jan. 21, 1790, which applied and modified the Galician patent for Gorizia and Gradisca, was addressed to the Governorship of Trieste, to which those areas were then administratively linked; see AST, C.R. Gov., b. 620, N. 1896/618 (Apr. 10, 1790), for correspondence and the German version; and CAHJP, IT/Go, III,14, for the Italian version. Cf. Del Bianco Cotrozzi 1989: 713, who independently reached the same conclusion.

64. CAHJP, HM 5188, f. 195, no. 26, chs. V and VII.

65. Pribram 1918, 2: 3–9; AST, C.R. Gov., b. 620, N. 7271 (Nov. 26, 1790). This law was both a specification (civil rather than canon law) and an extension (right to practice) of the earlier decrees of 1781–82 permitting Jews to pursue advanced studies in law and medicine.

66. Pribram 1918, 2: 1–2 (July 28 and Oct. 30, 1790); Bernard 1979: 116–17; AST, C.R. Gov., b. 620, N. 5195 (Aug. 13, 1790); Cervani and Buda 1973: 67. On the two cases in Trieste, AST, C.R. Gov., b. 621, N. 640/2574, session of July 7, 1792.

67. CAHJP, HM 5804a, N. 626, f. 128r (Jan. 23, 1791). Gubernatorial decree of Apr. 7, 1792, in AST, C.R. Gov., b. 621, Ad N. 298/568, session of Feb. 18, 1792; HKA, Komm. Lit., r. 502, 29. ex Martio 1792, ff. 626–638; ACIT, N. 23; close paraphrase in Mainati 1817–18, 5: 72–73, and in "Gli Israeliti a Trieste" 1853: 63–64.

Chapter Seven: The Jewish Community: Public Order, Piety, and Authority

1. On wartime contributions, see, e.g., CAHJP, HM 5804a, ff. 108–109, N. 547–549 (Jan. 12, Jan. 30, and Feb. 12, 1789).

2. Pribram 1918, 1: 525; Colorni 1945: 354–59; AST, C.R. Gov., b. 621, Patente concernente i Tribunali per gli Ebrei.

3. Norlinghi 1858: ff. 21–22; 1746 regulations, ch. 1, in Maternini Zotta 1983: 211.

4. On David Hayyim b. Rabbi Judah Moses Corinaldi, an accomplished but contentious rabbinic scholar, see Ghirondi and Neppi 1853: 74–75; Halevi 1875; Steinschneider 1879: 365, and 1900: 90. On Corinaldi in Trieste, Norlinghi 1858: ff. 27–28; R. Curiel 1938: 241–43; Cervani and Buda 1973: 42–43.

5. On his career in Trieste, see Norlinghi 1858: ff. 29, 31, 34, 36, 39, 50; CAHJP, HM 2/5847, f. 9 (Sept. 12, 1757), and f. 10 (June 1765); R. Curiel 1938: 246; Simonsohn 1977: 460; Vivian 1984: 39. It seems that Capriles lacked formal rabbinic ordination, though he functioned as the community's rabbi.

6. On Menahem Emanuel b. Isaac Navarra (Noveira), see Roth 1924b; Ghirondi and Neppi 1853: 243; Steinschneider 1877: 311. Contract in Norlinghi 1858: ff. 51–53.

7. On Isach b. Rabbi Moses Formiggini (1700–1788), see Ghirondi and Neppi

1853: 169–71; and Benayahu 1959: 550 n. 11. See also *Osservatore Triestino*, no. 58, July 19, 1788, pp. 1181–83, in De Incontrera 1953–63, 26 (1956): 475; Cervani and Buda 1973: 43; A. Luzzatto 1851: 7; Samson Morpurgo 1743: 1b–4a, for a rabbinical *pesak* of Formiggini; and Modenese rabbis' approbation in Isaac Lampronti's *Pahad Yitzhak* (1750–96). On Formiggini's appointment in Trieste, see CAHJP, HM 2/5857, ff. 15–17 (Mar. 16, July 6, and Oct. 6, 1766). On his family history, see Roth 1946: 376; and the family tree in A. F. Formiggini 1932.

8. *Osservatore Triestino*, cited in previous note; cf. Mainati 1817–18, 5: 39–40.

9. Lampronti 1750–96, 3: 107a–109b; also in HM 2/5833. In Lampronti, it appears along with Ezekiel Landau's decision under the heading "Omitted from its place in the laws of the intermediate days (*hol ha-moed*)." Landau's was first published in his collection *Noda bi-yehudah* (Prague, 1776), *Orah Hayyim*, no. 13. On this controversy and the issue generally, see Samet 1995.

10. On statutes, CAHJP, HM 2/5857, ff. 15–16 (June 21 and Aug. 3, 1766), and *Statuti [1766]* . . . 1767, in AST, C.R.S. Int. Comm., b. 78, f. 208r (also in CAHJP, HM 5455); I. Formiggini 1777.

11. *Statuti [1766]* . . . 1767, ch. 4: art. 1, in AST, C.R.S. Int. Comm., b. 78, f. 214v (also in CAHJP, HM 5455); Statute of 1771, art. 6, in Maternini Zotta 1983: 231–33; CAHJP, HM 2/5857, ff. 32–34 (Feb. 4 and Aug. 18, 1771). On Luzzatto, CAHJP, HM 5804a, f. 120, N. 592 (May 17, 1790); HM 2/5839, f. 308, N. 59 (July 1, 1804); HM 2/5841, f. 20r (Oct. 1805); HM 2/5842, ff. 1–2 (Sept. 1806).

12. *Regolamento . . . 1783* 1784: ch. 5: art. 1, in Maternini Zotta 1983: 243–44. See also Statutes of 1766, *Statuti [1766]* . . . 1767, in AST, C.R.S. Int. Comm., b. 78, ch. 6, ff. 215r–217r (also in CAHJP, HM 5455); Statute of 1771, art. 5: I and VIII, in Maternini Zotta 1983: 229–30; *Regolamento . . . 1783* 1784: ch. 5: art. 1–2, in Maternini Zotta 1983: 243–44.

13. Statute of 1771, art. 5: VIII–IX, in Maternini Zotta 1983: 230; and Statutes of 1766, *Statuti [1766]* . . . 1767, ch. 6: art. 1, in AST, C.R.S. Int. Comm., b. 78, f. 215v (also in CAJHP, HM 5455).

14. Richetti 1984: 57, case 2, and accompanying original documents (copies kindly given to me by Rabbi Elia Richetti): Formiggini to *Capi* and Council (Dec. 5, 1771), and decision of the *Capi* and Council (Dec. 8, 1771).

15. On preaching, see, for example, *Statuti [1766]* . . . 1767, ch. 6: art. 15, in AST, C.R.S. Int. Comm., b. 78, f. 216v (also in CAHJP, HM 5455). On education, see, for example, Statute of 1771, art. 5: XIII–XV, in Maternini Zotta 1983: 231; CAHJP, HM 2/5857, f. 19 (Nov. 6, 1766).

16. *Regolamento . . . 1783* 1784: ch. 5: art. 1, in Maternini Zotta 1983: 243–44.

17. On the development of the modern rabbinate, see Schorsch 1981 and Poppel 1983 on Germany; Schwarzfuchs 1993: 75–85 on France; Vielmetti 1970–71 and Del Bianco Cotrozzi 1995 on Padua.

18. CAHJP, HM 5804a, ff. 90v–91r, N. 463 (July 23, 1786), and 1792 *Regolamento*, ch. VIII: art. I, in Maternini Zotta 1983: 256.

19. *Osservatore Triestino*, no. 58, July 19, 1788, pp. 1181–83, in De Incontrera 1953–63, 26 (1956): 475; also Ghirondi and Neppi 1853: 169–71; and the elegiac poems in H. D. Bolaffio 1793: 63b–66a (also in Deinard 1959: 162–66).

20. CAHJP, HM 5804a, ff. 104v–105r, N. 528 and 530 (Sept. 24, 1788).

21. Tedesco was born around 1750 and died in the evening of 12 Tevet 5560/Jan. 8, 1800. On Tedesco's career in Trieste, see CAHJP, HM 5804a, f. 54r, N. 283 (Feb. 19, 1783); f. 54v, N. 288 (Apr. 3, 1783); f. 57r, N. 302 (Aug. 8, 1783); f. 120v, N. 592 (May 17, 1790); CAHJP, HM 2/6276 (Sept. 5, 1784); Sabbadini 1916; Ghirondi and Neppi 1853: 274–76; Steinschneider 1900: 83–84; Colbi 1978: 74; Zoller 1913–14: 143, and 1933c (with picture of Tedesco); I. Luzzatto 1944: sonnet 52, p. 56, and note on p. 145. On his relation as a nephew to Formiggini by way of marriage to Dolce Formiggini, R. Curiel 1942: Cartella N. 53, Pubblicazione e Stampe varie: A. Stampe Ebraico-triestine, item no. 1; AST, C.R. Gov., b. 621, N. 972, Protocollo Commissionale (Jan. 30, 1799); Cervani and Buda 1973: 43. On his relation to Norsa, CAHJP, HM 2/5834, N. 8 (Nov. 22, 1796). Tombstone inscription in A. Luzzatto 1851: 9, and elegy in Tivoli 1800 (also in Deinard 1915: 159), confirm the death date supplied by R. Curiel (1938: 251). Other elegiac poems by Rabbi Jacob Menahem Cracovia of Venice and Isaia Norsa and Zerah Samson Pincherle of Trieste were published in Trieste in 1800, and again in Deinard 1915: 152–59.

22. CAHJP, HM 5804a, f. 120v, N. 592 (May 17, 1790). When Tedesco showed this document to the Jewish community of Trieste in 1790, they accorded him the title *morenu ha-rav* ("our teacher the rabbi").

23. S. Formiggini 1867–68: 143. Morpurgo composed the poem inscribed on Tedesco's tombstone.

24. Castiglioni 1886: 11; Colbi 1978: 74.

25. A. Luzzatto 1851: 9.

26. CAHJP, HM 2/5835, ff. 211r and 212r, extract from Protocol (May 6, 1793).

27. I. Luzzatto 1944: sonnet 52, p. 56.

28. Castiglioni 1886: 11–12, and in "Gl'Israeliti a Trieste" 1862–63: 32.

29. Ghirondi and Neppi 1853: 274–76; cf. A. Luzzatto 1851: 9. Lelio Della Torre included Tedesco in his list of praiseworthy eighteenth-century Italian preachers (1908, 2: 243).

30. CAHJP, HM 2/5835, f. 211, extract of Protocol (May 6, 1793); Colbi 1978: 74.

31. Tedesco 1786: introduction, p. 3; cf. Mainati 1817–18, 5: 34.

32. Tedesco 1790: 5, and [1792]: 20, 22. For appreciations of his elegies, see Mainati 1817–18, 5: 50, 72; and H. D. Bolaffio 1793: 70.

33. Castiglioni 1886: 11, and "Gl'Israeliti a Trieste" 1862–63: 32. See also Zoller 1933c (and a shorter version, 1912c); and correspondence in Cervani and Buda 1973: 59–62. Hohenwart had a distinguished career and was close to the royal family; a few years later, he was appointed archbishop of Vienna.

34. Zoller 1933c: 21. In this case he meant that Tedesco should be allowed freedom of conscience, i.e., he should not have to reveal his innermost dissenting thoughts when performing a legal duty in compliance with state mandate. On this episode, see the section in Chapter Eight below, "The Luzzatto-Pardo Affair."

35. 1792 *Regolamento*, ch. VIII: art. I, in Maternini Zotta 1983: 256. The community did consult the rabbi about his concerns before they requested confirmation of the *Regolamento* from the government; CAHJP, HM 5804a, f. 128r, N. 626 (Jan. 23, 1791).

36. AST, C.R. Gov., b. 621, N. 4485, Pittoni to governor (Nov. 14, 1799).

37. AST, C.R. Gov., b. 621, N. 1527/2740, Tedesco to governor (n.d., apparently

early June 1792). His letter was received on June 13, 1792, and sent to the *Capi* on June 23, 1792, for comment within two weeks; the response of the *Capi* came on July 5, 1792, and the government's reply to Tedesco on July 21, 1792.

38. Castiglioni 1886: 13–14.

39. Zoller 1933c: 17–18.

40. CAHJP, HM 2/5835, f. 716r; and S. D. Luzzatto 1878: 46–47, 67–68. Cologna was the half-brother of the better-known Abraham Vita (Hai) de Cologna, vice-president of the Napoleonic Sanhedrin and president of the Central Consistory, later rabbi in Trieste from 1825 to 1832. Well versed in general subjects such as Latin and geometry, Angelo Isach Cologna taught Italian and Latin as well as Judaic studies in the *Scuole Pie Normali*. Cologna died in 1824; A. Luzzatto 1851: 10.

41. S. Formiggini 1867–68: 144; CAHJP, HM 2/5858, Oct. 22–Dec. 4, 1800 correspondence. On Finzi, see Ghirondi and Neppi 1853: 126–32. A few years later, however, Finzi made it to Paris, where he was elected vice-president of the Sanhedrin.

42. On Levi and his family, see Ghirondi and Neppi 1853: 268, 272; Yaari 1977: 122, 129, 176, 544, 580, 700–701; Benayahu 1986–87: 301–2; S. D. Luzzatto 1878: 47, 66–68; Castiglioni 1886: 36; Zoller 1912b. R. Curiel 1942: Cartella N. 53, A. Stampe ebraico-triestine, item no. 4, gives Levi's date of birth as 1758, but according to Benayahu (1959: 14), Levi was a very young student of Azulai during the latter's stay in Jerusalem from approximately 1757 to 1764; if he were born in 1758, he would have been a very young student indeed. It is more likely that Levi was born a few years before 1758. He died on 11 Kislev 5586/Nov. 21, 1825; A. Luzzatto 1851: 10.

43. Castiglioni 1886: 36.

44. S. D. Luzzatto 1878: 68, 47.

45. Michael Silber informs me that Halevi was one of the few contemporaries whom Hatam Sofer called a *gaon*. On Levi's role in the fight against Reform, see Dubin 1998, and the articles by Zoller (1919), Benayahu (1986–87), Samet (1990–91), and Luzzatto Voghera (1993) cited there.

46. For examples of internal punishments, see Norlinghi 1858: f. 38; and Richetti 1984: cases 2–4, 6, 9, 14, 17 (1771, 1772, 1776, 1791, 1802, 1808 [Richetti says 1805; date corrected on the basis of the original documents]). For resort to Gentile authorities, see AST, C.R. Gov., b. 620, N. 6336/2126 (1787); CAHJP, HM 5804a, f. 125r, N. 615 (Sept. 20, 1790) (in this case, the two foreign Jews who had been fed and sheltered at communal expense escaped punishment for their offenses by choosing to convert); CAHJP, HM 2/5837, ff. 297r–299r, no. 61 (July 26, 1802). See also CAHJP HM 2/5853, f. 77v, no. 18 (Oct. 29, 1804), and HM 2/5840, f. 185r (Dec. 30, 1804); and Richetti 1984: case 15.

47. R. Curiel 1942: Cartella N. 55, Processi e Liti, 1667–1849, under the heading "B. Processi davanti alle Autorità giudiziarie," nos. 41–42 (1782, 1800); Richetti 1984: case 16 (1806).

48. Only in 1807–8 did the Habsburg state limit the power of the Jewish authorities by decreeing that it was illegal to announce excommunication without prior governmental approval. In Trieste, the documents show the forwarding of these decrees by the *Capi* to Rabbi Levi, but no further comment or reaction; AST, C.R. Gov., b. 622, N. 6825 (Dec. 1 and Dec. 23, 1807), and N. 2998, sovereign decree of May 25, 1808, (promulgated in Trieste, June 14, 1808); and Pribram 1918,

2: 172–73. There was some precedent for this in Maria Theresa's 1776 *Judenordnung* for Galicia, which required that major excommunications be approved by civil authorities; Mahler 1971: 324; and more generally, Silber 1985: 109–14. In Prussia, the authority of Jewish leaders to impose excommunication bans or significant monetary fines was curtailed by Frederick II in 1750.

49. Norlinghi 1858: ff. 22, 27, 44; CAHJP, HM 2/5857, f. 17 (Oct. 5, 1766), and HM 5804a, f. 44r, N. 229 (Nov. 4, 1781); ACIT, N. 21 (Jan. 21, 1783, Jan. 29, 1787, and Jan. 30, 1789).

50. Norlinghi 1858: f. 27.

51. Azulai 1934: 87–88, on his favorable impression of Triestine Jewish hospitality; Hertzberg 1968: 160–61, on Bordeaux.

52. S. D. Luzzatto 1858–64, 2: 66. Theirs was a poor family; in part, piety may have been a respectable cloak for poverty.

53. For example, in 1765–66 the community announced that it would deny religious services to anyone who sold kosher meat clandestinely; Norlinghi 1858: ff. 55–56, also ff. 26, 37, 44; CAHJP, HM 5804a, f. 13v, N. 70 (eve of seventh day of Passover 5537/Apr. 27, 1777), f. 46r, N. 243 (Feb. 1, 1782), f. 90r, N. 459 (May 28, 1786), and f. 101v, N. 516 (Oct. 12, 1787); and Richetti 1984: 57–59, cases 3 and 6; CAHJP, HM 2/5833, f. 280, N. 20 (Jan. 1, 1796).

54. CAHJP, HM 2/5833, f. 280, N. 20 (Jan. 1, 1796), and HM 2/5835, f. 109, N. 23 (Jan. 21, 1798).

55. CAHJP, HM 2/5836, f. 147, rabbi to *Capi* (Dec. 9, 1800).

56. ACIT, N. 21 (Mar. 22, 1802).

57. E.g., CAHJP, HM 2/5833, f. 154v, N. 33 (Aug. 28, 1795), warning against the sale of imported foods that lacked attestation of *kashrut*, and f. 280, N. 20 (Jan. 1, 1796), reiteration with specific reference to the buying of cheese and goose fat from "adventurers." On cheese, see Richetti 1984: 58, case 4 (1772), and 62, case 14 (1802). On *matzot*, see Norlinghi 1858: f. 45, 1762–63; and ACIT, N. 22 (Feb. 21, 1782, and Feb. 1, 1789), for examples of contracts with individuals for manufacture and distribution; and CAHJP, HM 2/5833, N. 9–10 (Jan. 1795), and HM 2/5836, f. 290 (16 Shevat 5561/Feb. 13, 1801), for regulations prohibiting Gentile involvement in the baking process and importation.

58. CAHJP, HM 5804a: f. 13v, N. 70 (eve of seventh day of Passover/Apr. 27, 1777); f. 46r, N. 243 (Feb. 1, 1782); ff. 63v–64r, N. 337 (Feb. 1, 1784); and f. 101v, N. 516 (Oct. 12, 1787); CAHJP, HM 2/5833, f. 154v (Aug. 28, 1795), and f. 205r (Oct. 9, 1795); CAHJP, HM 2/5836, ff. 343r and 346r (Mar. 13 and Mar. 20, 1801). On the relevant halakhic regulations, see, for example, *Shulhan Arukh*, *Yoreh Deah*, 63:1, 112, 113, 115:2, 118, and Maimonides, *Mishneh Torah*, Forbidden Foods, 3:12–21, 7:1, 8:10 and 12; 13:10, 17:9–26.

59. CAHJP, HM 2/5836, f. 343r, N. 57 (Mar. 13, 1801).

60. Ibid., f. 346r, N. 60 (Mar. 20, 1801), on Gentile servants.

61. Richetti 1814: 57, case 2.

62. CAHJP, HM 5804A, f. 65r, N. 341 (*Shabbat Zakhor* 5544/early Mar. 1784).

63. CAHJP, HM 2/5836, f. 346r, N. 60 (Mar. 20, 1801); also in Richetti 1984: 60, case 9 (1791).

64. CAHJP, HM 2/5836, f. 346r, N. 60 (Mar. 20, 1801).

65. CAHJP, HM 5804a, f. 118v, N. 586 (Mar. 10, 1790). See 1771 Privilege, in Maternini Zotta 1983: 216.

66. D. Nissim 1970: 34–38.

67. CAHJP, HM 2/5833, f. 4r (Oct. 6, 1794). Of course, *Shabbat Shuvah* was an appropriate time for exhortations about sin and repentance, but his written warning does not read like the mere repetition of stock phrases.

68. CAHJP, HM 5804a, f. 125r, N. 615 (Sept. 20, 1790). The matter ended as far as the Jewish authorities were concerned when they learned that these two intended to convert to Christianity.

69. Richetti 1984: 60, case 9.

70. CAHJP, HM 2/5833, ff. 7r–10v, N. 2 (Oct. 18–20, 1794).

71. CAHJP, HM 2/5853, ff. 77v–78r, N. 18 (Oct. 29, 1804).

72. CAHJP, HM 2/5841, f. 170r; *Shulhan Arukh, Orah Hayyim*, 243–44; and Maimonides, *Mishneh Torah*, Sabbath, 6. On the issue generally, see Katz 1989.

73. For warnings, see CAHJP, HM 2/5837, f. 294r (June 1802); HM 2/5839, f. 242v, N. 50 (June 1, 1804); HM 2/5853, f. 56v, N. 50 (June 1804); HM 2/5841, ff. 170r–175r, N. 42 (Mar. 14–20, 1806); HM 2/5842, f. 168r, N. 40 (Mar. 1807). For fines, see CAHJP, HM 2/5837, f. 321r (Sept. 1802), and HM 2/5841, f. 189r, N. 45, Proclama (Mar. 20, 1806); and Richetti 1984: 63, case 17 (1808 [1805 in Richetti]).

74. Richetti 1984: 63, case 18 (Aug. 1815), and CAHJP, HM 2/5847, ff. 314r, 327r–328v, 340r (Aug. 13–30, 1815).

75. CAHJP, HM 2/5847, f. 314r (Aug. 17, 1815).

76. CAHJP, HM 2/5837, f. 340r, Imp. Reg. Direzione di Polizia to *Capi* (Aug. 30, 1815).

77. CAHJP, HM 2/5833, ff. 2r–5v (Oct. 6, 1794).

78. CAHJP, HM 2/5833, ff. 11r, N. 3 (Oct. 19, 1794).

79. CAHJP, HM 2/5836, ff. 8r (Oct. 2, 1800) and 30r (Oct. 6, 1800).

80. CAHJP, HM 2/5836, f. 366r, N. 66 (13 Nisan 5561/Mar. 27, 1801).

81. On 1805–6, see Samet 1995: 80–81, citing correspondence in manuscript between Levi and Rabbi Daniel Terni of Florence; on 1809, CAHJP, HM 2/5844, f. 152r, Proclama (Apr. 6, 1809).

82. AST, C.R. Gov., b. 620, N. 1017, Marco Levi to the general convocation of the community (Aug. 25, 1785).

83. AST, C.R. Gov., b. 621, N. 1527/2740, Tedesco to governor (n.d.; apparently early June 1792).

84. CAHJP, HM 2/5833, f. 170 (Sept. 6, 1795).

85. BCT, ADT, 13 F4/iv, Atti della Polizia Secreta, Pittoni to governor (Feb. 15, 1800).

86. CAHJP, HM 2/5836, f. 15r, N. 7 (Sept. 28, 1800).

87. CAHJP, HM 2/5836, f. 290 (16 Shevat 5561/Feb. 13, 1801).

88. ACIT, N. 21 (Mar. 22, 1802).

89. CAHJP, HM 2/5837, ff. 272r–274v (May 16, 1802).

90. Ibid.

91. CAHJP, HM 2/5837, f. 318, N. 64 (Sept. 9, 1802).

92. CAHJP, HM 2/5838, f. 11r, N. 7, Proclama (Dec. 31, 1802) and HM 2/5839, f. 75r, N. 14, Proclama (Dec. 23, 1803).

93. CAHJP, HM 2/5839, f. 94r, N. 21, Proclama (Jan. 13, 1804).
94. CAHJP, HM 2/5833, ff. 77v–78r, N. 18 (Oct. 29, 1804).
95. CAHJP, HM 2/5840, f. 185r (Dec. 30, 1804).
96. AST, C.R. Gov., b. 620, N. 1017, Marco Levi (Aug. 25, 1785), and b. 219, N. 4887, *Capi* to governor (Aug. 26, 1785).
97. Cervani 1984: 21–28; Scocchi 1951: 643–47. The French also occupied the city from November 1805 to March 1806, and from May 1809 to November 1812. Jews were reputed to be French supporters, and some were indeed Freemasons.
98. It would be interesting to know more about the individuals whom Pittoni claimed in 1800 were living "without professing true religion," and the youths whom Rabbi Levi in 1802 charged were slandering religion both by word and deed. Might they have been voicing new ideologies or values? On social integration, see Cervani and Buda 1973: 64, 137–38, 143–44, 146; Pagnini 1978: 74, 219; C. Curiel 1937: 389–90, 490–91. Social interaction between Jews and Gentiles in Trieste is a subject deserving of a study in itself; as an excellent start, see Cattaruzza 1995: 11–58, esp. pp. 43–50, on the Jews and the Casino Vecchio of Trieste in the early nineteenth century.

Chapter Eight: The Habsburg Marriage Reforms: Challenges to Religious-Communal Authority

1. The Sanhedrin, comprised of French and Italian Jews under French rule, ratified the supremacy of the state in marriage law, enacted in 1802 when Napoleon ordered rabbis to perform religious marriage ceremonies only after civil ones. See Tama 1807: 152–54, 290; Schwarzfuchs 1979: 67–71; Freimann [1945] 1964: 325–27; Graff 1985: 82–85, 92, and 183 n. 86. On the problem more generally in the modern period, see Freimann [1945] 1964: 310–79; Landman 1968: 137–43; Kohler 1915; and Simon 1915. On state interference with Jewish marriage law in other localities, see: for Brandenburg-Prussia, Baron 1942, 2: 210–11; and Katz 1973: 167; for Italy, Colorni 1945: 181–97, esp. 195–97; and Maternini Zotta 1994: 249–50, on the difficulties of legal unification and uniformity with regard to marriage; for England, Kochan 1990: 105–8; for Egypt, Zohar 1982: 125–43; and Stillman 1995: 41–43. For other treatments of marriage law and practices in the context of the broader issue of tradition and modernity, see Katz 1945: esp. 47–54, and abridged English versions 1959 and 1993: 112–24; Biale 1983; M. Kaplan 1991: 85–116; Cohen and Hyman 1986; Allegra 1996: 165–208.

2. On the *Ehepatent* of Jan. 16, 1783, see Macartney 1968: 120–21. For the Civil Code, see *Codice* 1787, 3: 98–119, esp. secs. 1, 3, 6, 29, 31, 35. On hybrid, cf. Ogris 1988: 48–49.

3. See Pribram 1918, 1: 525, on abolition of Jewish civil jurisdiction, and 528–48, on the 1785–86 application of the Marriage Patent to Jews. For Trieste specifically, see AST, C.R. Gov., b. 621 (Apr. 18, 1785), with N. 3682 (this copy incorrectly reads 1786), and b. 620, N. 3268, for a printed copy of the Patent of May 3, 1786. Summaries of Habsburg marriage legislation concerning Jews in Scherer 1895: 23; Cervani and Buda 1973: 60–63; Freimann [1945] 1964: 312–13; Graff 1985: 40–47.

4. Pribram 1918, 1: 530 and 543–44.

5. On clerical objections in Trieste, see Maass 1953: 182–83, and Tamaro 1929: 208; on responses elsewhere, Maass 1953: passim; Hasquin 1982; and Tosi 1990. Beales's contention that the introduction of civil marriage improved the legal position of non-Catholics does not hold for the Jews; Beales 1990: 45.

6. Pribram 1918, 1: 529 and 533; and Landau [1902–3] 1968: clause 6 on minors. Cf. Jare 1907 for Elia Morpurgo's concerns.

7. CAHJP, HM 5804a, ff. 90v–91r, N. 463 (July 23, 1786).

8. See AST, C.R. Gov., b. 620, N. 2556, esp. Councillor Roth's comments in May 2, 1786 session, on the inapplicability of the April 1786 decree in Trieste—"In this free trading-center . . . no marriage permission is sought . . . and the Jewish community in Trieste is also free from such a constraint." The documents that follow— N. 3107 (May 27, 1786) and N. 3563 (June 17, 1786)—also make it clear that this decree was not applied in Trieste. Triestine Jews did not have to seek permission from the civil authorities for ordinary marriages; only in exceptional cases (for example, involving relatives whose unions were allowed by Jewish law but not by Habsburg law) did Jews need to obtain authorization from the state. Consistent with the foregoing is that Jews in Trieste were also exempt from limits on the number of Jewish marriages; on such limits elsewhere in the monarchy, see Mahler 1971: 246, 250, 323. When the moral education requirement for marriage was pressed again in the early nineteenth century, then in the form of testing on Homberg's catechism (Homberg 1815), it was applied to, and implemented by, Triestine Jews.

9. AST, C.R. Gov., b. 620, N. 5324, Pittoni to governor (Aug. 5, 1789). See also AST, C.R. Gov., b. 620, N. 4580/2336, *Capi* to governor (July 24, 1786); Pribram 1918, 1: 590–91; and AST, C.R. Gov., b. 620, court decree 443 (Feb. 28, 1788), issued in Trieste, May 22, 1788; AST, C.R. Gov., b. 620, N. 2036 (Mar. 7–Apr. 4, 1789).

10. Pribram 1918, 2: 13–17, patent of Feb. 18, 1791, and the discussions leading to it; ADT, 5A4, "Leggi" (Feb. 18, 1791) (microfilm in CAHJP, HM 5962); AST, C. R. Gov., b. 621, N. 476/1316, Circolare (Mar. 19, 1791); Cervani and Buda 1973: 62–63.

11. Although the tale of the Luzzatto-Pardo case has been told before, the accounts are brief and without analysis: Spiegel 1933–34; Cervani and Buda 1973: 59–62; Zoller 1933c; Freimann [1945] 1964: 313–20; Graff 1985: 48–51. My account completes these with new sources: the voluminous archival record from Trieste (AST, C.R. Gov., b. 621 and b. 622; some in CAHJP, HM 2/5834) and Vienna (HKA, Komm. Lit., r. 502); and rabbinic responsa and correspondence in manuscript.

12. Rabbi Raffael Nathan Tedesco consulted with Eleazar Fleckeles of Prague, Ishmael Kohen of Modena, Abraham Jona of Venice, and the rabbis of Livorno, among others. See Fleckeles 1809, 1: no. 117; HUC, Laudadio Sacerdote [Ishmael Kohen] Collection 6/3.

13. Luzzatto had served many times as a member of the community's governing Small Council and also as *Capo*, one of its three official heads. He was in fact serving as *Capo* at the time of his daughter's marriage, but in the atmosphere of crisis that ensued ("very difficult present circumstances [requiring the] salvation of Jewish [*nazionali*] rights"), he was forced to step down and new elections were held. He did, however, retain his seat on the Small Council; CAHJP, HM 2/5833, N. 67, ff. 179, 581.

14. AST, C.R. Gov., b. 621, N. 3353, Inquisizione Politica contro Jacob Bardo[sic] e Corona figlia d'Ellia Moise Luzzatto (Aug. 31, 1796), and N. 3682 (Nov. 10, 1796).

15. HUC, Laudadio Sacerdote Collection 6/3, letter of Menahem (Emanuel) Samuel Poggibonsi to Ishmael Kohen (15 Sivan 5559/June 18, 1799).

16. AST, C.R. Gov., b. 621, N. 3352 (Oct. 8, 1796).

17. AST, C.R. Gov., b. 621, N. 972, Luzzatto to governor (Jan. 8, 1799); HUC, Laudadio Sacerdote Collection 6/3: III (5), letter of Abraham Jona to Ishmael Kohen (27 Ellul 5559/Sept. 27, 1799). See also Sofer 1865: *Even ha-ezer*, no. 108.

18. By December 1800, Corona Luzzatto was married to another, and in early 1801 Pardo's mother received permission for her son to return to Trieste; AST, C.R. Gov., b. 622, N. 5498 (Jan. 5, 1801), and N. 264/167 (Jan. 17, 1801); and C.R. Gov., Protocolli, protocollo 1290 de 1800 (Mar. 1, 1801). Pardo's will (June 10, 1817) and death records (d. Sept. 15, 1817) show that he married in late 1802; AST, Archivio notarile, serie Testamenti, b. 12, n. 1503; and AST, Giudizio Civico e Provinciale, Atti liberi, b. 442.

19. Katz 1959: 4–10.

20. AST, C.R. Gov., b. 621, N. 3682, Elia Moise Luzzatto to Governor Brigido (Nov. 15, 1796).

21. HKA, Komm. Lit., r. 502, f. 686r, Elia Moise Luzzatto to governor and emperor (Jan. 17, 1797).

22. AST, C.R. Gov., b. 621, N. 3682, Elia Moise Luzzatto to Governor Brigido (Nov. 15, 1796).

23. HKA, Komm. Lit., r. 502, f. 696v, Elia Moise Luzzatto to emperor (Jan. 17, 1797). On the development and meaning of "state within a state," see Katz 1971. Luzzatto's argument should be compared to modern broadened applications of the Talmudic principle *dina de-malkhuta dina*, the law of the land is the law; see Graff 1985.

24. He was one of the *Capi* who signed the 25 Sivan 5548/July 1, 1788 Triestine Jewish letter in favor of conscription; CAHJP, HM 5193, f. 216, no. 1; and *Ha-Meassef* 4 (1787–88): 386–88.

25. CAHJP, HM 2/5834, N. 8, session of 22 9bre [Nov. 22] 1796, Elia Moise Luzzatto to Rabbi Tedesco, and Tedesco's response to him approved by the *Capi*.

26. AST, C.R. Gov., b. 621, N. 1015 (Jan. 5, 1797). See also AST, C.R. Gov., b. 621, N. 2115 (Oct. 31, 1796), and N. 779 (Dec. 9, 1796).

27. AST, C.R. Gov., b. 621, N. 1015 (Jan. 5, 1797).

28. AST, C.R. Gov., b. 621, N. 779 (Dec. 9, 1796).

29. Ibid..

30. Ibid.; paraphrase in Spiegel 1933–34: 446.

31. Cf. Katz's description of traditionalist response in this period (1973: 156): "The rabbis did . . . try and avert infringement of their customs but, once legal steps had been taken by the authorities, they abided by the inevitable, and made their peace with it unless some way could be found to circumvent the law."

32. AST, b. 621, N. 3682 (Dec. 16, 1797), Triestine government report.

33. See especially AST, C.R. Gov., b. 621, reports from Trieste to Vienna, N. 4105 (Dec. 17, 1796) and N. 108 (Jan. 14, 1797) (N. 108 also in HKA, Komm. Lit.,

r. 502, ff. 709r–711v, 715r); and HKA, Komm. Lit., r. 502, decrees from Vienna, ff. 677r–678v (Feb. 16, 1797), 82/4 (also in AST, C.R. Gov., b. 621, N. 779 [Mar. 11, 1797]), and ff. 707r–708v, 714 (May 11, 1797) (also in AST, C.R. Gov., b. 621, N. 1015 [June 3, 1797]).

34. AST, C.R. Gov., b. 620, N. 5324, Chief of Police Pittoni to governor (Aug. 5, 1789).

35. Feb. 16, 1797, decree 82/4 from Vienna, in HKA, Komm. Lit., r. 502, ff. 677r–678v, and in AST, C.R. Gov., b. 621, N. 779 (Mar. 11, 1797).

36. AST, C.R. Gov., b. 621, N. 3682 (Dec. 16, 1797), Triestine government report to Court Chancellery. The government seemed unaware that in Trieste itself in July 1795 — one year before the ill-fated Luzzatto-Pardo marriage — community leaders had decided, "following the example of other places," to assert more control over marriage, namely, to require people to seek permission from the *Capi* and prove means of support before asking the rabbi to proclaim the banns; CAHJP, HM 2/5833, ff. 148–150 (July 26 and 31, 1795). Whether and how this procedure was implemented is unknown. It was not mentioned at all by any party to the Luzzatto-Pardo marriage controversy.

For regulations requiring public weddings in Italian Jewish communities in earlier periods, see Freimann [1945] 1964: 222–26; Finkelstein 1924: 300–309; Bonfil 1976b; A. Toaff 1989: 34–36; Green 1990–91; and Lampronti 1750–96, 10: 82a, "kiddushin be-asarah." On Sefardim, including the community of Livorno, see Y. Kaplan 1993; and Schwarzfuchs 1966: 356–59, and 1981. On Ashkenaz, see Cohen and Horowitz 1990: 229–31; and Hundert 1986.

37. The ever-resourceful Elia Moise Luzzatto had supplied them with material solicited from other rabbis. He did manage to get his hands on correspondence destined for Rabbi Tedesco that seemed to serve his own cause. Other Italian rabbis, in trying to find a way out of the predicament both for the young couple and for Tedesco, discussed a number of theoretical possibilities in their correspondence. Poggibonsi ventured the opinion that perhaps the state was acting within its prerogatives and Tedesco could legitimately marry Corona Luzzatto to another without a divorce, but he did not press this view in the face of Tedesco's adamant objections and other Italian rabbis' strong support of him. See HUC, Laudadio Sacerdote Collection 6/3: I, "anonymous rabbinic opinion"; III (3)b, letter of Emanuel Samuel Poggibonsi to Ishmael Kohen (24 Shevat 5559/Jan. 30, 1799); III (3)d, letter of Emanuel Samuel Poggibonsi (25 Tammuz 5559/July 28, 1799); III (4), letter of Abram Gur Arie Sacerdote (Aug. 24, 1799); III (6), letter of Jacob Nunes Vais to Ishmael Kohen (Sept. 6, 1799); and HUC-JIR, Ms. K. 94, f. 1, letter of Samuel Kohen.

38. AST, C.R. Gov., b. 621, N. 3126, session of Oct. 6, 1798, conveying court decree of Sept. 13, 1798.

39. On correspondence with Hohenwart, see Zoller 1912c and 1933c. On neutral and semi-neutral society, see Katz 1993 and 1973.

40. HUC, Laudadio Sacerdote Collection 6/3: letter of Menahem (Emanuel) Samuel Poggibonsi to Ishmael Kohen (15 Sivan 5559/June 18, 1799).

41. For perspectives on both Luzzatto and Tedesco, see Ghirondi and Neppi 1853: 276; and Castiglioni 1886: 11–12.

42. It was appropriate that this immigrant crossroads community turned to a

wide array of scholars, among them the distinguished rabbis Hayyim b. Joseph David Azulai of Livorno, Hayyim Isaac Mussafia of Spoleto, and the Hatam Sofer in Mattersdorf. See Freimann [1945] 1964: 313–20; Graff 1985: 48–51, and the sources cited there, most notably Sofer 1865: nos. 108–109; and also HUC, Laudadio Sacerdote Collection 6/3: IV and V (2), Abram Eliezer Levi, legal opinions (1 Av 5564/July 9, 1804, and 17 Ellul 5564/Aug. 24, 1804), and V (1), letter of Emanuel Samuel Poggibonsi (16 Ellul 5564/Aug. 23, 1804); and HUC-JIR, Ms. K. 94, ff. 2r–6v, legal opinion of Abram Eliezer Levi, and f. 7, legal opinions of Azulai and other Livornese rabbis.

43. CAHJP, HM 2/5840, ff. 184, 212, 223–24 (Dec. 30, 1804, and Jan. 20 and Feb. 7, 1805); Freimann [1945] 1964: 315–18; Castiglioni 1886: 12.

44. "Takkanot," in *Encyclopedia Judaica* 1972, 15: cols. 726–27; Elon 1973, 2: 686–711; Freimann [1945] 1964.

45. On Frizzi (1756–1844), see Robolotti 1878; Dinaburg 1949 and 1950; D. Nissim 1968; Cervani and Buda 1973: 131–34; Simonsohn 1977: 711–12; Dubin 1992; and Bernardini 1996b: 74–79, 323. Frizzi received an extensive Jewish and general education: he was the first Jew to study in Mantua's gymnasium and at the University of Pavia, where he studied medicine and philosophy. He was a prolific writer on subjects of medicine, natural philosophy, mathematics, music, and Biblical and rabbinic literature. Documents of the Frizzi-Morschene case refer to Relle, née Rachele, Morschene (1770–1844) sometimes as Bella. Her birth and death dates emerge from the death records of the Jewish community of Ostiano, Lombardy (copy kindly sent to me by Giuseppe Minera). In the 1788 list of Jews in Trieste she appears as the wife of Lucio Luzzatto; Zoller 1913b, 4: 5.

46. Petition in AST, C.R. Gov., b. 621, N. 3703 (July 16, 1798). The relevant prohibition is stated in Leviticus 21:7, "Neither shall they [the priests the sons of Aaron] take a woman put away from her husband, for he is holy to his God"; Maimonides, *Mishneh Torah*, Forbidden Intercourse, 17; *Shulhan Arukh, Even ha-ezer*, 6.

47. AST, C.R. Gov., b. 621, N. 3268, inquiry in gubernatorial decree (Aug. 6, 1798), and deposition of *Capi* and rabbi (Aug. 30, 1798); N. 3703, Triestine government report (Sept. 7, 1798).

48. AST, C.R. Gov., b. 621, Frizzi to emperor (Sept. 17, 1798).

49. Deut. 24:1: "When a man has taken a wife, and married her, and it come to pass that she find no favor in his eyes . . . , then let him write her a bill of divorce, and give it in her hand, and send her out of his house."

50. Though he didn't cite it explicitly, Frizzi was clearly drawing on Montesquieu's distinction between repudiation and divorce in *The Spirit of the Laws*, XVI:15. On the rabbis and divorce, Frizzi probably had in mind the tenth- or eleventh-century "enactment of Rabbenu Gershom," which made a woman's consent a necessary feature of a Jewish divorce; see Falk 1966: 113–43. In his letter, Frizzi justified both the Mosaic prohibition against repudiated women and what he called the rabbinic invention of divorce. He stated that the reason priests were prohibited from marrying repudiated women was the bad moral character of such women, who would bring dishonor to their husbands and consequently disrespect for the priesthood; in contrast, such danger was not posed by divorced women, because their character could not be presumed to be similarly flawed. The rabbis were,

in his view, clever to invent divorce because they had thereby reduced the "tyranny of men" among this "nation devoted to God."

51. AST, C.R. Gov., b. 621, Frizzi to emperor (Sept. 17, 1798); paraphrase in N. 2825, Councillor Capuano to governor (Oct. 6, 1798), and N. 4380/921, session of Oct. 11, 1800.

52. Biblical figures in AST, C.R. Gov., b. 621, Frizzi to emperor (Sept. 17, 1798). Frizzi on Maimonides (thinking no doubt of his *Mishneh Torah*, Marriage 3:3–4) in AST, C.R. Gov., b. 621, N. 2825, Councillor Capuano to governor (Oct. 6, 1800). Presumably Frizzi had in mind betrothal by *shetar*, i.e., writ or contract, one of the three methods of betrothal outlined by the rabbis in the Talmud, *Kiddushin* 2a, 9a.

53. AST, C.R. Gov., b. 621, with N. 2568 (Nov. 20, 1799).

54. AST, C.R. Gov., b. 621, N. 3974/470 (Mar. 20, 1800).

55. AST, C.R. Gov., b. 621, N. 2825, report of Oct. 6, 1800, and N. 4380, decision of Oct. 11, 1800.

56. AST, C.R. Gov., b. 621, 4643/972, in N. 4683, Cologna to governor (Oct. 24, 1800); CAHJP, HM 2/5836, N. 23, ff. 69r–71v (Oct. 26, 1800), and N. 24, f. 81 (Oct. 27, 1800).

57. AST, C.R. Gov., b. 621, N. 4717, *Capi* to governor (Oct. 29, 1800). One of the prerogatives of a *kohen* is to be called first to recite the blessing over the Torah when it is read in synagogue as part of the worship service.

58. I am adapting Lawrence Stone's term "affective individualism," which he used (1977) for the ideology of free choice of marriage partner based on romantic love. By "interpretative individualism," I mean the ideology of free choice of interpretation.

59. AST, C.R. Gov., b. 621, N. 4717, session of Nov. 8, 1800.

60. AST, C.R. Gov., *Capi* to governor (Nov. 20. 1800).

61. CAHJP, HM 2/5858 (Dec. 4, 1800), Finzi's negative response to the Triestine offer.

62. AST, C.R. Gov., b. 622, N. 257/52, Frizzi to governor (Jan. 2, 1801), for Frizzi's espousal of affective individualism. Cf. the advocacy of sentiment and free choice in marriage by French Enlightenment writers; for example, Traer 1980: 48–78 (esp. 70–78), 134–36, 192–97. On the ideology of romantic love and free choice among Jews, see Katz 1949, 1955, 1993; Biale 1983; and M. Kaplan 1991.

63. Unfortunately, the documents are very incomplete. I have found no documents recording the appearance before the arbiters on Dec. 17, 1800, or their decision on Dec. 24, 1800, nor any pertaining to the petition of Mar. 27, 1801, which set in motion the court case, which began officially on May 26, 1801. We learn of all of these only from the authorities' initial refusal to overturn the arbiters' decision, in AST, C.R. Gov., b. 622, N. 453/96, session of Jan. 31, 1801, and the eventual "Sentenza tra il D[ottor]e Benedetto Frizzi e tra Relle Morschene, Jan. 26, 1802," in AST, Giudizio Civico e Provinciale, 1767–1850, Atti Civili, b. 21, N. 101.

64. Anna Frizzi's marriage and death records in the Jewish Community of Trieste show her to have been Benedetto's daughter, born in 1801, and birth records show Rachele Morschene giving birth to Nina on May 5, 1801 (name of father not mentioned); copies of marriage record kindly sent to me by Vittore Colorni, Giuseppe Minera, and the Secretariat of the Jewish Community of Trieste; and per-

sonal communication from Carlo Gatti, 1992, on the birth and death records. The collection of condolences to Frizzi upon the death of his daughter refers to her as both Annetta Forti nata Frizzi (*Prose e poesie* 1821: title page) and as Nina (ibid.: 19); it also refers to Signora Relle (ibid.: 20). Also on Frizzi's daughter (there unnamed), see S. D. Luzzatto 1858–64, 7: 77.

65. Personal communication from Rabbi Elia Richetti, 1987, about the marriage registers, and from Carlo Gatti, 1992, for the information on the 1830 census; condolence letter in *Prose e poesie* 1821: 19. It is possible, though unlikely, that the two did get married elsewhere, in a place where the precise details of their statuses, as *kohen* and as divorcée, might not have been known. Had they succeeded in getting married elsewhere, Jewish law would have considered their prohibited marriage nonetheless valid after the fact.

66. Death records from Ostiano (copy kindly sent to me by Giuseppe Minera) show Benedetto Frizzi's death on May 30, 1844, and Rachele Morschene's death on June 3, 1844. This record does not indicate the marital status of either individual.

67. For his earlier views on priestly marriages and divorced women, see his *Dissertazione* (1787–90), vol. 2: *Dissertazione di Polizia Medica sul Pentateuco in riguardo alle leggi, e stato del matrimonio* (Pavia, 1788), pp. 40–42, where he had justified the prohibition against priestly marriage to "a woman who had had a divorce": it was not "reasonable" that a priest who must be wholly consecrated to divine service be embarrassed by such physical or moral imperfection. Ten years later, in his appeal to the emperor (AST, C.R. Gov., b. 621, Sept. 17, 1798), he justified the prohibition only for repudiated women, not divorced ones, and he denied that divorced ones were even included in the Biblical prohibition! Obviously the circumstances of Frizzi's personal life—this forty-two-year-old man had finally met the woman he wanted to marry—led him to advocate a position different from his earlier theoretical one. Had Triestine Jewish leaders been familiar with his 1788 work, they could have cited it against him.

68. Between 1787 and 1790, before his arrival in Trieste, he published a six-volume work entitled *Dissertazione di polizia medica sul Pentateuco* (Dissertation on public medical regulation in the Pentateuch), in which he applied medical, social, and philosophic perspectives to Biblical laws and teachings concerning subjects such as prohibited foods, marriage, early childhood, funeral and burial customs, cleanliness of public places, the priesthood and sacrifices, and agriculture: Benedetto Frizzi, *Dissertazione di polizia medica sopr'alcuni alimenti proibiti nel Pentateuco* (Pavia, 1787); *Dissertazione di polizia medica sul Pentateuco in riguardo alle leggi, e stato del matrimonio* (Pavia, 1788); *Dissertazione di polizia medica sul Pentateuco in riguardo alle leggi spettanti alla gravidanza, al parto, puerperio, all'educazione della fanciullezza, ed ai patemi di animo* (Pavia, 1788); *Dissertazione seconda di polizia medica sul Pentateuco in riguardo ai cibi proibite, e altre cose a essi relative* (Cremona, 1788); *Dissertazione di polizia medica sul Pentateuco sopra le leggi, e formalità ebraiche in istato di malattia, e ceremonie funebri, e sepolcrali* (Pavia, 1789); *Dissertazione di polizia medica sul Pentateuco in riguardo alle pulizie delle strade e case, formalità sacerdotali, e leggi di agricoltura* (Cremona, 1790).

69. Bonfil 1972: 189; S. D. Luzzatto 1873: 123 n. 1; and Simonsohn 1977: 711–12. Luzzatto reported that Frizzi was forced from Mantua because of the work on Jew-

ish customs that he began publishing in 1787. Given the date of publication, and the length of the work mentioned in the letters cited by Simonsohn, this can only be the *Dissertazione di polizia medica*.

70. On the Enlightenment's search for pagan antiquity, see Gay 1966–69, esp. vol. 1, subtitled *The Rise of Modern Paganism*.

71. CAHJP, HM 5191, f. 212, no. 31 (May 18, 1787); see also Simonsohn 1977: 711. In this 1787 letter, Frizzi stated that in one of his works—presumably *Dissertazione di polizia medica*—he had proposed some changes in "mere practice, but not in the spirit of religion, or rabbinic instructions." In fact, despite Frizzi's Mosaism, he did sometimes accord value also to rabbinic works. Even in his arguments about priestly and civil marriage, Frizzi referred to Maimonides' *Code*, and in some works, especially his later *Petah einayim* ([1815–25] 1878–81), he dealt extensively with rabbinic material.

72. AST, C.R. Gov., b. 621, N. 2568, Frizzi to governor (June 10, 1800).

73. CAHJP, HM 2/5838, ff. 43r, 54 (Jan. 23, 1803).

74. Nissim 1968: 280; and CAHJP, HM 2/6277 (Nov. 29, 1807).

75. S. D. Luzzatto 1878: 56–57; 1882–94, 1: 83; 1825: 131–34; 1858–64, 7: 77, and 9: 5.

76. Frizzi [1815–25] 1878–81; on this work, see Dinaburg 1949 and 1950; and Dubin 1992. On the work as a school text, see CAHJP, HM 2/5849, ff. 513, 523–30.

77. Opening paragraph of 1805 ordinance, CAHJP, HM 2/5840, f. 224r (Feb. 7, 1805). It is significant that in 1798, the community's lay leaders had rejected the idea of declaring in advance and on their own authority the nullity of marriages lacking parental approval (protocol of Oct. 18, 1798, Small Council meeting in AST, C.R. Gov., b. 621, N. 4994 [Feb. 28, 1799]). Rabbinic involvement and authority were critical to the ordinance they enacted in 1805.

78. Paradoxically for Jews, this process entailed clericalization, for the state made marriage conditional upon rabbinic participation, with the rabbi in effect now cleric and clerk, conducting and registering marriages for the state. The turning of rabbis into state functionaries was a widespread and significant development in modern Jewish history.

79. On medieval Christian theory and practice, see Duby 1978; Donahue 1983; Cohen and Horowitz 1990; Gottlieb 1980. On Protestant marriage law and the *Tametsi* decrees of the Council of Trent, see Ozment 1983: 25–48; Roper 1985: esp. 64–70 and 93–98; Traer 1980: 27–31; Flandrin 1979: 130–39. For a recent overview, see Gottlieb 1993: 68–88, 104–9.

80. In a variety of settings, legal anthropologists have shown the efforts of individuals to exploit the confusion caused by a state's move into a new area, one previously subject to local, partially autonomous groups and peripheral to state concerns. See Roberts 1983: esp. 5–6; and Castan 1983: esp. 258–60.

81. I am adapting the term "family-state pact," found in Hanley 1987; see also Hanley 1989. Cf. Traer 1980: 31–47.

82. Cf. the discussion of family formation in Wheaton's introduction to Wheaton and Hareven 1980: 9–12, which identifies five parties as consistently in conflict over marriage formation: the prospective husband and wife, their close kin, the Church (here the Jewish community), the state, and public opinion. Gender ap-

pears not to have been a critical factor in the Luzzatto-Pardo and Frizzi-Morschene cases, for in each one, the man and the woman were affected similarly by the state's assertion of control over marriage. Unfortunately, we have nothing written by the two women themselves.

83. On French revolutionary legislation, see Traer 1980: 79–165.

Chapter Nine: Conclusion: Civil Inclusion of a Port Jewry in a Reforming Absolutist State

1. On Jews' alliances with central state power in other settings, see Yerushalmi 1976, and Arendt 1951.
2. Weisel (Wessely) [1782–85] 1826, 2: 26 (*Rav tuv*).
3. Ara 1992a: 44–45.
4. *Osservatore Triestino*, no. 48, Dec. 2, 1786, p. 634, cited in De Incontrera 1953–63, 24 (1954): 569. Cf. Aron Rodrigue's observation on the Ottoman Empire, which is partially relevant to Trieste: "This was a world that recognized and accepted that groups did not necessarily have to share similarities to have a place in the overall arrangement" (Aron Rodrigue interview in Reynolds 1995: 82–83). To be sure, the Josephinian program aimed at more standardization than the Ottomans' did, yet in Trieste, it certainly did not aim at homogenization of the different *nazioni*.
5. Pittoni report of Dec. 21, 1786, in Dorsi 1989: 144.
6. Ibid. Cf. Pittoni's expression of satisfaction about the simplification of Holy Week, to him another sign of enlightenment in Trieste: "Notre évêque a fort simplifié l'idolatrie de la Semaine Sante. Ça lui fait honneur. Le choc qu'il a donné à la superstition n'a point fait de bruit. C'est une preuve que nous sommes philosophes." ("Our bishop has greatly reduced the idolatry of Holy Week. This does him honor. The blow that he struck at superstition has not caused any fuss. This proves that we are *philosophes*.") Pittoni's letter in French of Apr. 19, 1783, in Tamaro 1942–43: 93.
7. Cattaruzza 1996: esp. 58–59 (and sources cited in n. 7), 66–69, 72. According to Kandler (Cervani 1975: 195–212, esp. 203–4), neither foreigners nor members of the corporate *nazioni* had to be Habsburg subjects in order to enjoy the free port privileges. More extensive comparison of the rights of foreigners, naturalized subjects, and natives in Trieste is a desideratum. Cf. Maternini Zotta 1994, for juridical analyses of citizenship. On varying patterns of Jews' acquiring municipal citizenship rights, sometimes along with, sometimes separately from, state citizenship rights in different German states, see Toury 1977.
8. Malino 1978: 21, 29, 34.
9. E.g., Baron 1929; 1952–83, 9: v–vi, and 11: 199, 263, 281.
10. See Baron 1964; 1937, 2: 164–90; and 1952–83: vols. 14–15; Ettinger 1961 and 1976; and Israel 1989.
11. For examples of comparative historical study of Jewish societies, see Endelman 1997.
12. R.J.W. Evans, Introduction to Ingrao 1994b: 12–13. On confessionalization, see also the essays in that volume by Robert Bireley, S.J. (pp. 36–53) and Anton Schindling (pp. 54–70).

13. Ghisalberti 1992: esp. 30. Ghisalberti stresses the significance of confessionalization, which he calls "nationalization," though he also argues that in fact the Toleration edicts were not so removed from older restrictive conceptions.

14. Szabo 1994: 154–55; also pp. 180–97. See also Klingenstein 1981: 121. Szabo stresses that in the late-eighteenth-century Habsburg realm, public figures such as Kaunitz and Joseph von Sonnenfels were conceiving of subjects as citizens, not in the sense of active participation in legislating, but in the sense of identification with, and service for, the welfare of the commonwealth as a whole. On this view, the word "civic" would then be as appropriate as the word "civil" in phrases such as "civil integration" and "civil inclusion."

15. Graetz [1853–76] 1900, 11:68–69. On intrusion, see, for example, Dubnov 1971: 336–39; and Mahler 1971: 229–33. Important exceptions are the analyses of the Josephinian program as legal reforms in Katz 1973: 161–66; and Silber 1988 and 1989. Ettinger (1976: 753–56) does point to both integrationist and reformatory-restrictive tendencies.

16. In Mantua, too, Bernardini (1996b: 5, 48) finds significant continuity between Theresian privilege and Josephinian Toleration.

17. Cf. Del Bianco Cotrozzi 1989: 726.

18. H. D. Bolaffio 1793: 52; CAHJP, Ts, Varia, A2.

19. Tedesco 1790: 5; and 1792: 20, 22.

20. S. D. Luzzatto 1951: 43.

21. Michael Silber has extended Jacob Katz's concept of "neutral" or "semineutral" society from the social realm to the political with his use of the term "neutral polity"; Katz 1973 and 1993; and Silber 1988 and 1989.

22. For the problem of language in another Italian Habsburg possession, Tyrol, in the eighteenth century, see Levy 1988.

23. Schwarzfuchs 1979; Graff 1985: 71–94.

24. E.g., Rabbi Jacob Israel Carmi, in Balletti [1930] 1969: 22, 27–28, 76.

25. Tedeschi 1866: 19–20.

26. See Szabo 1994: 154.

27. Hertzberg (1968) first put forward the view that the Enlightenment was in fact the fount of modern secular antisemitism. This view has both gained many adherents and generated considerable controversy; see Dubin 1997: esp. 645–48, and the literature cited there. For two other recent discussions of Enlightenment universalism and the inclusion or exclusion of Jews in France, see Kates 1990 and Singham 1994.

28. Grégoire and Dohm respectively, in Mendes-Flohr and Reinharz 1995: 50, 38. See Sorkin 1992, on the relation between the new demand for regeneration and the old demand for religious conversion. On regeneration, see also Berkovitz 1989.

29. *Essai*, ch. 25, cited in Dubin 1997: 648.

30. Zoller 1933c: 21.

31. Scott 1990: intro., 16–18; Bazzoli 1986.

32. AST, C.R. Gov., b. 83, Ad N. 1412, Zinzendorf report (Aug. 17, 1781).

33. Dinaburg 1949: 251–54.

34. Baron 1942, 2: 359–60.

35. On misreadings of Italian traditionalism during the Haskalah and early Reform periods, see Dubin 1998.

36. Baron 1937, 2: 205–12; Barzilay 1960; and Roth 1959.

37. Endelman 1979 and 1997; Zipperstein 1985; and Lowenstein 1994.

38. For attention to such questions, see Feiner 1987 and 1995; Sorkin 1997; and Feiner forthcoming.

39. AN, F19 11004, "Notes prises sur les Ordonnances de l'Empereur d'Allemagne Joseph II." On the Consistorial organization of French Jewry, see Albert 1977; on Napoleon as an absolute ruler who consolidated the gains of the revolution in part by reconstructing intermediary corporate bodies of the ancien régime, see Malino 1978: 65–67.

40. E.g., Plantation Act of 1740, which permitted the naturalization of foreign-born Protestants and Jews in Britain's overseas colonies, in Mendes-Flohr and Reinharz 1995: 21–22; Baron 1960, and fuller treatment of American colonies in Baron 1971. See Cattaruzza 1996: 72 n. 57, for an interesting comparison of pre-1776 Intendancy Trieste to a colonial possession. The absolutist regimes of Catherine in White Russia and Peter Leopold in Tuscany also granted Jews new quasi-political rights: in White Russia in the 1770s–80s, Catherine proffered partial legal equality for Jewish merchants and municipal electoral rights (e.g. Ettinger 1976: 757; Mahler 1971: 370–77)—though such incorporation into the merchant class meant excorporation from the Jewish community—and in Livorno in 1778, Peter Leopold gave Jews a seat on the municipal council. While demographic, social, and economic realities made Russia quite different from Trieste and Livorno, which were more similar to each other, still, it is significant that absolutist rulers in various places were experimenting with granting some Jews some kinds of political rights in the 1770s–80s.

41. CAHJP, Ts, Varia, A2.

42. Cattaruzza 1996: 66–68. The question needs to be asked about the difference between the right for Jewish individuals to be elected, as in Trieste, and fixed seats for Jews as a collectivity, as in Livorno. In Trieste, a Jew was first elected to the managing board of the *Borsa* in the 1790s, and Jews served as municipal councillors during the third French occupation of 1809–13. The later *Borsa* regulations of 1851 did reserve for Jews one seat of the four-man executive board and two seats of the seven-man consulting board; Cattaruzza 1995: 44–45.

43. AST, C.R. Gov., b. 126, Ustia and Bellusco to Zinzendorf (Nov. 27, 1776).

44. HKA, Komm. Lit., r. 617, 17. ex Febr. 1780, f. 366.

45. Tedesco 1790: 12–13; and 1792: 22.

46. See above, Chapter Six; not surprisingly, they also compared their own situation to those of Jews in Livorno and Amsterdam.

47. AST, C.R. Gov., b. 621, N. 1015 (Jan. 5, 1797).

48. AST, C.R. Gov., b. 83, Ad N. 1412, Zinzendorf report (Aug. 17, 1781).

49. AST, Deputazione di Borsa, Istruzione . . . 1794; Cattaruzza 1996: 67–68, and n. 37. In practice, the political right to elect and be elected as *Borsa* deputies was exercised by only the very wealthy Jews, but qualifications of property and wealth limited the franchise in all European countries in the eighteenth and nineteenth centuries.

50. Capuano to governor, in AST, I.R. Gov., Atti Generali, b. 753, N. 10725 (May 26, 1820). By that point, of course, the French Revolution had granted Jews

emancipation, and made equality both a norm and a staple of discourse about Jewish status. When the Austrians returned in 1813, they removed democratic institutions, but they did not roll back any of the earlier rights enjoyed by Jews in Trieste. It was in that context that Capuano described the situation in Trieste during Habsburg rule.

51. Baron 1979, and 1960: 70. Though Baron says that the majority of Jews cared little for political franchise and public office because they were Orthodox, in Trieste that was not the reason.

52. O'Brien 1969: 24; cf. Stefani 1960: 250.

53. O'Brien 1969: 24.

54. On these two kinds of rights, and the continuum between them, see M. Graetz 1989: intro., pp. 9–64, and 1992: esp. 166–70; cf. Bernardini 1996b: 158, 209–10, 356–58.

55. Ogris 1981, 1985, and 1988; and Kocher 1983.

56. On insecurity in places beyond Trieste, see Hertzberg 1968: 325–27, 340–48; Malino 1978: 40–64; Baron 1960: 69–70, and 1979: 32–33; M. Graetz 1989: 29–49.

57. De Felice 1955 and Simonsohn 1989; also Del Bianco Cotrozzi 1989: 725–26; Luzzatto Voghera 1998: 34–35, with slight qualifications; and more generally on emancipation, D. Segre 1995.

58. Cattaruzza 1995: 43–44. Cf. Ara 1992a: 44; Maternini Zotta 1994: 243, 246–48; Bernardini 1996b: 356.

59. See Szabo 1994: 154–55; and Rürup 1986.

60. I am using Isaiah Berlin's famous distinction between negative freedom, i.e., freedom from something, and positive freedom, i.e., freedom for something, expounded in his *Two Concepts of Liberty* (1958).

61. Similarly, in his study of Mantuan Jewry, Paolo Bernardini compares, but does not conflate, the "advanced [degree of] toleration" sometimes offered by Habsburg reforming absolutism with the Emancipation brought by the French Revolution. He notes certain similarities in their effects, but also their radically different "philosophical-political principles"; Bernardini 1996b: 356; also 209–10, 351–52, 357–58. Bernardini and I have independently raised the same issue and arrive at similar conclusions in our respective works. However, I do not adopt his term *tolleranza avanzata* because of its possibly teleological connotations.

62. Triestine Jewry should be compared to other port Jewries, and especially to Livornese Jewry under the reforming absolutist regime of Grand Duke Peter Leopold.

63. Silber 1988 and 1989. If further analysis bears out the view that Habsburg subjects really ought to be called citizens, then the term might be amended to "civic inclusion."

64. AST, C.R.S. Int. Comm., b. 78, f. 168v; HKA, Komm. Lit., r. 502, 27. ex Oct. 1770, N. 1151, f. 177r.

65. *Osservatore Triestino*, no. 31, Aug. 5, 1786, pp. 414–15, cited in De Incontrera 1953–63, 24 (1954): 267.

66. *Osservatore Triestino*, no. 1, Jan. 6, 1787, pp. 4–5, cited in De Incontrera 1953–63, 25 (1955): 65.

67. CAHJP, HM 5804a, N. 492, ff. 95v–96r, *Capi* to Brigido (Jan. 8, 1787).

68. *Osservatore Triestino*, no. 2, Jan. 13, 1787, p. 20, cited in De Incontrera 1953–63, 25 (1955): 67.

69. Pittoni report (Dec. 21, 1786), in Dorsi 1989: 150.

70. *Osservatore Triestino*, no. 5, Jan. 16, 1790, p. 50, cited in De Incontrera 1953–63, 28 (1958): 474–75.

Bibliography

Unpublished Sources

Cincinnati, Ohio

Hebrew Union College.
  Laudadio Sacerdote [Ishmael Kohen] Collection.
    Responsa, novellae, decisions 6/3. Copy of decisions about the marriage in Trieste.

Jerusalem

Central Archives for the History of the Jewish People.
  N. M. Gelber. Private Archives.
    P83 E8.
  Gorizia, IT/Go.
    B,1,2
    II,39
    III,14
    VI,37.
  Mantua.
    HM 5186–HM 5188.
    HM 5191.
    HM 5193–HM 5194.
  Stern Collection.
    P17/1201.
    P17/1241.

Trieste.
   HM 139.
   HM 943.
   HM 3145.
   HM 5455.
   HM 5467a–b.
   HM 5804a.
   HM 5962.
   HM 2/5833–HM 2/5844.
   HM 2/5846–HM 2/5849.
   HM 2/5853.
   HM 2/5857–HM 2/5858.
   HM 2/5862.
   HM 2/5864–HM 2/5865.
   HM 2/6276–HM 2/6277.
   IT 535.
   IT 544.
   IT 1210.
   Ts, Varia, A2.

Jewish National and University Library.
   Formiggini, Isach b. Moses. 1777. "Minhagei battei ha-keneset ha-ashkenazim be-Trieste." 8° 2034. (Microfilm in The Jewish Theological Seminary of America, New York, Liturgy Collection, reel 22, no. 4417.)

Mantua

Archivio della Communità di Mantova.
   F. 198, no. 16.

New York

Hebrew Union College-Jewish Institute of Religion.
   Ms. K. 94.

Jewish Theological Seminary of America.
   Morpurgo, Elia. 1782b. "Iggeret ogeret ahavat ha-adam be-asher hu adam," "Devash ve-halav," ff. 13v–32r. Adler Ms. 2492, microfilm no. 3687.
   Norlinghi, Azriel Joseph. 1858. "Frammenti storici—Annali della Comunità israelitica di Trieste." Ms. microfilm no. 3923.

Paris

Archives Nationales.
   F1E 65. Personnel administratif. Les Provinces Illyriennes. 1810–14.
   F19 11004. Assemblée générale et Grand Sanhédrin. 1806–7.

Trieste

Archivio della Comunità Israelitica di Trieste.
> Curiel, Riccardo. 1942. "Archivio storico della Comunità Israelitica di Trieste: Catologo Generale." (Copy also in Central Archives for the History of the Jewish People, Jerusalem.)
> Romanini, Aron Matzliah b. Yirmeyah. 1886. "Mizmor le-todah le-yom hitkadesh hag be-edatenu Trieste yom meleat meah shanah li-yesodat bet Talmud Torah . . . 23 Ellul 5646 [1886] asher hudhah le-yom 16 Marheshvan 5646 [1886]."
> H 18. Libro di Protocolli delle Scuole Pie Normali. 1808–23.
> N. 21. Servizi rituali & Macellazione di Rito. 1783–1830.
> N. 22. Servizi rituali—Azzime. 1782–1908.
> N. 23. Istruzione—Scuole Pie Normali. 1782–1823.

Archivio di Stato di Trieste.
> *Archivio notarile.*
> Serie Testamenti, b. 12, no. 1503.
> *Cesarea Regia Suprema Intendenza Commerciale per il Litorale in Trieste. 1748–76.*
> B. 68. Juden. 1746.
> B. 71. Juden. 1694–97.
> B. 78. Judenschaft. 1766–72.
> B. 81. Judenschaft. 1772–76.
> *Cesareo Regio Governo di Trieste—Atti amministrativi di Gorizia, 1754–83.*
> B. 7, fasc. 57, Ebrei e Ghetto di Gradisca.
> *Cesareo Regio Governo in Trieste. 1776–1809.*
> B. 52. Borsa (Commercialwesen).
> B. 53. Borsa. 1780–83.
> B. 67. Servizio divino, religione, tolleranza. 1776–83.
> B. 83. Ebrei (Judensachen). 1776–83.
> B. 126. Scuole tedesche (Deutsche Schulen). 1776–77.
> B. 127. Scuole tedesche. 1777–83.
> B. 167. Affari commerciali (Commercialwesen). 1783–84.
> B. 168. Affari commerciali. 1785.
> B. 219. Ebrei. 1783–85.
> B. 549. Polizia. 1796–98.
> B. 550. Polizia. 1799.
> B. 620. Ebrei. 1786–90.
> B. 621. Ebrei. 1791–1800.
> B. 622. Ebrei. 1801–9.
> B. 668. Affari commerciali. 1786–1809.
> B. 842. Medikern.
> Protocolli. Protocollo 1290 de 1800.

Deputazione di Borsa, Serie I, n. II, Regolamenti di Borsa ecc., 1794–1855.
Istruzione per la Borsa mercantile di Trieste, e per la sua Deputazione, no. 2333, Aug. 2, 1794.

Giudizio Civico e Provinciale. 1767–1850.
Atti civili, b. 21. Sentenze 1801.
Atti liberi, b. 442. Ventilazioni ereditarie 1817.

Imperial Regio Governo per il Litorale. Atti generali. 1814–50.
B. 753. Affari del culto (V).

Protocolli della Cesarea Regia Borsa in Trieste.
Protocolli 1794–95.

Biblioteca Civica.
Archivio Diplomatico Comunale.
2D33. Ebrei.
5A4. Ebrei.
5A 3/4. Ebrei.
13F4. Atti della Polizia Secreta.
14C 2/8. Ebrei.
R.P. Ms. 3-26. Arcadia Romano Sonziaca in Trieste. 1796–1809.

Vienna

Haus-, Hof-, und Staatsarchiv. Österreichisches Staatsarchiv.
StK (Staatskanzlei). Notenwechsel mit der Hofkanzlei, no. 103.
StR (Staatsrat). Protocoll, vol. III. 1781.

Hofkammerarchiv. Österreichisches Staatsarchiv.
Kommerz. Littorale. 1749–1813.
R. 502. Akatholiken und Juden im Littorale. 1750–97.
R. 617. Handelstand im Littorale und Börse zu Triest. 1749–1810.

Books and Articles

Adelman, Howard E. 1991a. "Italian Jewish Women." In Judith R. Baskin, ed., *Jewish Women in Historical Perspective*, pp. 135–58. Detroit.

———. 1991b. "Rabbis and Reality: The Public Roles of Jewish Women in the Renaissance and Catholic Restoration." *Jewish History* 5: 27–40.

———. 1993. "The Educational and Literary Activities of Jewish Women in Italy during the Renaissance and the Catholic Restoration." In Daniel Carpi et al., eds., *Shlomo Simonsohn Jubilee Volume: Studies on the History of the Jews in the Middle Ages and Renaissance Period*, pp. 9–23. Tel Aviv.

Alatri, Paolo, and Silvia Grassi, eds. 1994. *La questione ebraica dall'illuminismo all'impero (1700–1815)*. Atti del Convegno della Società Italiana di Studi sul secolo 18, Rome, May 25–26, 1992. Perugia.

Albert, Phyllis Cohen. 1977. *The Modernization of French Jewry: Consistory and Community in the Nineteenth Century*. Hanover, N.H.

Allegra, Luciano. 1996. *Identità in bilico: Il ghetto ebraico di Torino nel Settecento.* Turin.
Altieri, Orietta. 1985. *La comunità ebraica di Gorizia: Caratteristiche demografiche, economiche e sociali (1778–1900).* Civiltà del Risorgimento, no. 26. Udine.
Altmann, Alexander. 1973. *Moses Mendelssohn: A Biographical Study.* Philadelphia and University, Ala.
Angelini, Werther. 1973. *Gli ebrei di Ferrara nel Settecento: I Coen e altri mercanti nel rapporto con le pubbliche autorità.* Urbino.
Apih, Elio, ed. 1951. "Una protesta della Borsa Mercantile di Trieste (1789)." *Scritti in onore di Camillo de Franceschi.* Centro studi per la storia del Risorgimento, 1. Supplement to *Annali Triestini* 21: 275–84.
———. 1957. *La società triestina nel secolo XVIII.* Trieste.
———, ed. 1988. *Trieste.* Rome and Bari.
Ara, Angelo. 1992a. "Gli ebrei di Trieste: Tra emancipazione e problema nazionale." In Sofia and Toscano 1992: 41–55.
———. 1992b. "The Jews in Trieste." In Max Engman, ed., in collaboration with Francis W. Carter, A. C. Hepburn, and Colin G. Pooley, *Ethnic Identity in Urban Europe*, pp. 221–39. Comparative Studies on Governments and Non-Dominant Ethnic Groups in Europe, 1850–1940, vol. 8. Dartmouth, N.H.
Ara, Angelo, and Claudio Magris. 1982. *Trieste: Un'identità di frontiera.* Turin.
Arendt, Hannah. 1951. *The Origins of Totalitarianism.* Part 1, *Antisemitism.* New York.
[Ascher, Saul.] 1788. *Bemerkungen über die bürgerliche Verbesserung der Juden veranlasst, bei der Frage: Soll der Jude Soldat werden?* N.p.
Assaf, Simhah, ed. 1925–42. *Mekorot le-toledot ha-hinnukh be-Yisrael.* 4 vols. Tel Aviv.
Azulai, Hayyim Joseph David. 1934. *Maagal tov ha-shalem.* Edited by Aaron Freimann. Jerusalem.
Babudieri, Fulvio. 1981. "Le attività economiche di Trieste nel periodo teresiano." *AT* 41: 53–67.
———. 1983. *Industrie, commerci e navigazione a Trieste e nella regione Giulia dall'inizio del Settecento ai primi anni del Novecento.* Milan.
———. 1990. "L'emporio marittimo di Trieste e sua evoluzione." *AT* 50: 19–47.
Bachi, R. B. 1946–47. "Sekirah al ha-kalkalah ha-yehudit be-Italyah erev tekufat Napoleon." *Zion* 12: 66–73.
Baker, Keith Michael, ed. 1987. *The French Revolution and the Creation of Modern Political Culture.* Vol. 1: *The Political Culture of the Old Regime.* Oxford.
Balletti, Andrea. [1930] 1969. *Gli Ebrei e gli Estense: Col l'aggiunta di Il Tempio Maggiore Israelitica e Lettere del Rabbino Maggiore Jacob Israele Carmi.* Bologna.
Baron, Salo W. 1928. "Ghetto and Emancipation: Shall We Revise the Traditional View?" *Menorah Journal* 14: 515–26.
———. 1929. "Nationalism and Intolerance." *Menorah Journal* 16: 405–15; 17: 148–58.
———. 1937. *A Social and Religious History of the Jews.* 1st ed. 3 vols. New York.
———. 1938. "Le-Toledot ha-haskalah ve-ha-hinnukh be-Vinah." In Isaac Silberschlag and Yohanan Twersky, eds., *Sefer Touroff*, pp. 167–83. Boston.
———. 1942. *The Jewish Community: Its History and Structure to the American Revolution.* 3 vols. Philadelphia.

———. 1952–83. *A Social and Religious History of the Jews*. 2d ed. 18 vols. New York.
———. 1960. "Newer Approaches to Jewish Emancipation." *Diogenes* 29: 56–81.
———. 1964. "Modern Capitalism and Jewish Fate." In *History and Jewish Historians: Essays and Addresses*, pp. 41–55. Philadelphia.
———. 1971. "The Emancipation Movement and American Jewry." In *Steeled by Adversity: Essays and Addresses on American Jewish Life*, edited by Jeannette Meisel Baron, pp. 80–105. Philadelphia.
———. 1979. "Civil Versus Political Emancipation." In Siegfried Stein and Raphael Loewe, eds., *Studies in Jewish Religious and Intellectual History Presented to Alexander Altmann on the Occasion of His Seventieth Birthday*, pp. 29–49. University, Ala.
Barton, Peter F., ed. 1981a. *Im Lichte der Toleranz: Aufsätze zur Toleranzgesetzgebung des 18. Jahrhunderts in den Reichen Joseph II., ihren Voraussetzungen und ihre Folgen*. Studien und Texte zur Kirchengeschichte und Geschichte, 2d ser., no. 9. Vienna.
———, ed. 1981b. *Im Zeichen der Toleranz: Aufsätze zur Toleranzgesetzgebung des 18. Jahrhunderts in den Reichen Joseph II, ihren Voraussetzungen und ihren Folgen*. Studien und Texte zur Kirchengeschichte und Geschichte, 2d ser., no. 8. Vienna.
Barzilay, Isaac E. 1960. "The Italian and Berlin Haskalah (Parallels and Differences)." *Proceedings of the American Academy for Jewish Research* 29: 17–54.
Basilio, Francesco. 1914. *Origine e sviluppo del nostro diritto marittimo*. Trieste.
Baumgart, Peter. 1980. "Die Stellung der jüdischen Minorität im Staat des Aufgeklärten Absolutismus: Das friderizianische Preussen und das josephinische Österreich im Vergleich." *Kairos*, n.s. 22: 226–45.
Bazzoli, Maurizio. 1986. *Il pensiero politico dell'assolutismo illuminato*. Pubblicazioni della Facoltà di lettere e filosofia dell'Università di Milano, no. 124. Sezione a cura dell'Istituto di storia medioevale e moderna, no. 8. Florence.
Beales, Derek. 1985. "Christians and 'Philosophes': The Case of the Austrian Enlightenment." In Derek Beales and Geoffrey Best, eds., *History, Society and the Churches: Essays in Honor of Owen Chadwick*, pp. 169–94. Cambridge.
———. 1987. *Joseph II*. Vol. 1: *In the Shadow of Maria Theresa, 1741–1780*. Cambridge.
———. 1990. "Social Forces and Enlightened Policies." In Scott 1990: 37–53.
———. 1991. "Was Joseph II an Enlightened Despot?" In Ritchie Roberston and Edward Timms, eds., *The Austrian Enlightenment and Its Aftermath*, pp. 1–21. Austrian Studies 2. Edinburgh.
Ben-Sasson, H. H., ed. 1976. *A History of the Jewish People*. Cambridge, Mass.
Benayahu, Meir. 1959. *Rabbi Hayyim Yosef David Azulai*. Jerusalem.
———. 1978. "Rabbi Avraham ha-Cohen me-Zante ve-lahakat ha-rofeim ha-meshorerim be-Padova." *Ha-Sifrut* 7: 108–40.
———. 1986–87. "Daat hakhmei Italyah al ha-neginah be-ugav bi-tefillah." *Asufot* 1: 265–318.
Benbassa, Esther. 1990. *Un Grand Rabbin sepharade en politique, 1892–1923*. Mensil-sur-l'Estrée.
Benbassa, Esther, and Aron Rodrigue. 1995. *The Sephardic Jews of the Balkans: The Judeo-Spanish Community, 15th to 20th Centuries*. Oxford and Cambridge, Mass.
Bérenger, Jean. 1975. *Finances et Absolutisme autrichien dans la seconde moitié du XVIIème siécle*. Vol. 1. Lille.

Berengo, Marino. 1987. "Gli Ebrei dell'Italia asburgica nell'età della Restaurazione." *Italia* 6: 62–103.
Berkovitz, Jay R. 1989. *The Shaping of Jewish Identity in Nineteenth-Century France.* Detroit.
Berlin, Isaiah. 1958. *Two Concepts of Liberty: An Inaugural Lecture Delivered Before the University of Oxford on 31 October 1958.* Oxford.
Bernard, Paul P. 1968–69. "Joseph II and the Jews: The Origins of the Toleration Patent of 1782." *Austrian History Yearbook* 4–5: 101–19.
———. 1979. *The Limits of Enlightenment: Joseph II and the Law.* Urbana, Ill.
Bernardini, Paolo. 1996a. "The Jews in Nineteenth-Century Italy: Towards a Reappraisal." *Journal of Modern Italian Studies* 1: 292–310.
———. 1996b. *La Sfida dell'uguaglianza: Gli ebrei a Mantova nell'età della rivoluzione francese.* Quaderni di Cheiron, no. 3. Rome.
Bevilacqua, Matteo di. [1820] 1982. *Descrizione della fedelissima imperiale regia città e portofranco di Trieste.* Trieste.
Biagi, Maria Grazia. 1986. *Giuseppe Pasquale Ricci funzionario Imperiale a Trieste (1751–1791): Prima risultati di una ricerca.* Studi storici e geografici, n.s., no. 1. Pisa.
Biale, David. 1983. "Love, Marriage and the Modernization of the Jews." In Marc Lee Raphael, ed., *Approaches to Modern Judaism*, pp. 1–17. Brown Judaic Studies, no. 49. Chico, Calif.
Bihl, Wolfdieter. 1974. "Zur Entstehungsgeschichte des josephinischen Patents für die Juden Ungarns vom 31. März 1783." In Heinrich Fichtenau and Erich Zöllner, eds., *Beiträge zur neueren Geschichte Österreichs*, pp. 282–98. Vienna, Cologne, and Graz.
"Biographien: Giuseppe Lazzaro Morpurgo." 1840. *Israelitische Annalen* 2: 105–6.
Birtsch, Günter. 1996. "Aufgeklärter Absolutismus oder Reformabsolutismus?" *Aufklärung* 9/1: 101–9.
Blanning, T.C.W. 1970. *Joseph II and Enlightened Despotism.* London.
———. 1994. *Joseph II.* Profiles in Power. London and New York.
Boccato, Carla. 1984. "Convergenze dell'imprenditoria ebraica veneziana sull'emporio di Trieste nella seconda metà del secolo XVIII." In Ioly Zorattini 1984a: 99–110.
Bodian, Miriam. 1984. "Ha-yazzamim ha-yehudim be-Berlin, ha-medinah ha-absolutistit ve-'shippur matzavam ha-ezrahi shel ha-Yehudim' be-mahatzit ha-sheniyyah shel ha-meah ha-18." *Zion* 49: 159–84.
Bolaffio, Giuseppe. 1957. "Abram Vita Reggio." *RMI* 23: 204–17.
———. 1957–58. "Sfogliando l'archivio della Comunità di Gorizia." *RMI* 23: 537–46, and 24: 30–40, 62–74, 133–41.
Bolaffio, Hezekiah David. 1793. *Ben zekunim.* Livorno.
Bonfil, Robert. 1972. "Shetem esreh iggerot me-et R. Eliyyahu b. R. Shelomo Rafael ha-Levi (De Veali)." *Sinai* 71: 163–90.
———. 1976a. "Ahat mi-derashotav ha-italkiot shel R. Mordekhai Dato." *Italia* 1: 1–32.
———. 1976b. "Kavvim li-demutam ha-hevratit ve-ha-ruhanit shel Yehudei ezor Venetzyah be-reshit ha-meah ha-16." *Zion* 41: 68–78.

―――. 1983. "Some Reflections on the Place of Azariah de Rossi's *Meor Enayim* in the Cultural Milieu of Italian Renaissance Jewry." In Bernard Dov Cooperman, ed., *Jewish Thought in the Sixteenth Century*, pp. 23–48. Cambridge, Mass.

―――. 1984. "The Historian's Perception of the Jews in the Italian Renaissance: Towards a Reappraisal." *RÉJ* 143: 59–82.

―――. 1990. *Rabbis and Jewish Communities in Renaissance Italy*. Littman Library of Jewish Civilization. Oxford.

―――. 1991. *Jewish Life in Renaissance Italy*. Translated by Anthony Oldcorn. Berkeley, Los Angeles, and London.

―――. 1992. "Change in the Cultural Patterns of a Jewish Society in Crisis: Italian Jewry at the Close of the Sixteenth Century." In Ruderman 1992: 401–25.

Bossenga, Gail. 1991. *The Politics of Privilege: Old Regime and Revolution in France*. Cambridge.

Braude, Benjamin. 1991. "The Jews of Trieste and the Levant Trade in the Eighteenth Century." In Todeschini and Ioly Zorattini 1991: 327–51.

―――. Forthcoming. "The Myth of the Sefardi Economic Superman." In Jeremy Adelman and Stephen Aron, eds., *Trading Cultures: The Worlds of Western Merchants*. Antwerp.

Braun, Giacomo. 1927–28. "Carlo VI e il commercio d'oltremare." *AT* 14: 193–242.

Breuer, Edward. 1996. *The Limits of Enlightenment: Jews, Germans, and the Eighteenth-Century Study of Scripture*. Cambridge, Mass.

―――. Forthcoming. "Wessely, Scripture, and Cultural Continuities." In Sorkin and Feiner forthcoming.

Brotto, Paola, Vanna Mazzucchelli, Costanza Rossi Ichino, and Emilio Venturini. 1977. *Problemi scolastici ed educativi nella Lombardia del primo Ottocento*. Vol. 1: *L'istruzione elementare*. Milan.

Bulferetti, Luigi. 1944. *L'assolutismo illuminato in Italia, 1700–1789*. Milan.

Calimani, Simone (Simhah). [1821] 1984. *Dialogo sull'ebraismo di Simone Calimani (1699–1784)*. Introduction by Riccardo Calimani. Venice. (Reprint of *Esame o sia Catechismo ad un giovane israelita istruito nella sua religione*, 3d rev. ed. [Verona, 1821].)

Cammeo, Giuseppe. 1911. *Per il centenario della morte di Rabbi Ismanhèl Coen Zedek*. . . . Udine.

Candeloro, Giorgio. 1956. *Storia dell'Italia moderna*. 3 vols. Milan.

Caprin, Giuseppe. [1888] 1973. *I nostri nonni*. Rev. ed. Trieste.

Caputo, Fulvio, and Roberto Masiero. 1988. *Trieste e l'Impero: La formazione di una città europea*. Venice.

Cary, Joseph. 1993. *A Ghost in Trieste*. Chicago and London.

Castan, Nicole. 1983. "The Arbitration of Disputes under the 'Ancien Régime.'" In John Bossy, ed., *Disputes and Settlements: Law and Human Relations in the West*, pp. 219–60. Cambridge.

Castiglioni, Vittorio. 1886. *L'istituto scolastico della comunità Israelitica di Trieste, 1786–1886*. Trieste.

Catalan, Tullia. Forthcoming. "La comunità ebraica di Trieste ed i suoi rapporti con il governo centrale austriaco e le autorità locali (1781–1918)." In *Österreichisches*

Italien—Italienisches Österreich. Proceedings of a conference held in Innsbruck, 1995.
Cattaruzza, Marina. 1995. *Trieste nell'Ottocento: Le trasformazioni di una società civile.* Civiltà del Risorgimento, no. 38. Udine.
———. 1996. "Cittadinanza e ceto mercantile a Trieste, 1749–1850." In Marina Cattaruzza, ed., *Trieste, Austria, Italia tra Settecento e Novecento: Studi in onore di Elio Apih*, pp. 57–84. Civiltà del Risorgimento, no. 52. Udine.
Il Centenario delle Assicurazioni Generali, 1831–1931. 1931. Trieste.
Cervani, Giulio. 1961. "Riformismo settecentesco nella provincia mercantile del Litorale (Trieste e Fiume)." *Fiume*, nos. 3–4 (July and Dec.): 1–34.
———. 1969. *La borghesia triestina nell'età del Risorgimento: Figure e problemi.* Civiltà del Risorgimento, no. 4. Udine.
———. 1975. *Nazionalità e stato di diritto per Trieste nel pensiero di Pietro Kandler: Gli inediti del procuratore civico.* Civiltà del Risorgimento, no. 7. Udine.
———. 1979. *Il Litorale austriaco dal Settecento alla 'Costituzione di dicembre' del 1867.* Udine.
———. 1984. "Gli Ebrei a Trieste nella seconda metà del Settecento." In Ioly Zorattini 1984a: 13–28.
Cervani, Giulio, and L. Buda. 1973. *La comunità israelitica di Trieste nel sec. XVIII.* Civiltà del Risorgimento, no. 5. Udine.
Chadwick, Owen. 1981. "The Italian Enlightenment." In Porter and Teich 1981: 90–105.
Ciana, Antonio, ed. 1959. "Trieste nel 1835 (Impressioni di un viaggiatore tedesco)." *PO* 29: 136–45.
Cochrane, Eric W. 1961. *Tradition and Enlightenment in the Tuscan Academies, 1690–1800.* Chicago.
Codice ossia collezione sistematica di tutte le leggi ed ordinanze emanate sotto il regno di Sua Maestà Imperiale Giuseppe II, tanto in affari secolari, quanto ecclesiastici.... 1787. Translated by Bartolommeo Borroni. Vol. 3. Milan.
Cohen, Esther, and Elliott Horowitz. 1990. "In Search of the Sacred: Jews, Christians, and Rituals of Marriage in the Later Middle Ages." *Journal of Medieval and Renaissance Studies* 20: 225–49.
Cohen, Richard I. 1998. *Jewish Icons: Art and Society in Modern Europe.* Berkeley, Los Angeles, London.
Cohen, Steven M., and Paula E. Hyman, eds. 1986. *The Jewish Family: Myths and Reality.* New York and London.
Colbi, Paolo S. 1970. "Note di storia ebraica a Trieste nei secoli XVIII e XIX." *RMI* 36: 59–73.
———. 1978. "Tekufat ha-zohar shel ha-sifrut ha-ivrit be-ir Trieste." *Sinai* 83: 70–79.
———. 1980. "Elia Morpurgo capo della nazione ebraica di Gradisca." *RMI* 46: 179–88.
Colorni, Vittore. 1945. *Legge ebraica e leggi locali.* Milan.
———. 1956. *Gli Ebrei nel sistema del diritto comune fino alla prima emancipazione.* Milan.
———. 1983. *Judaica Minora: Saggi sulla storia dell'ebraismo italiano dall'antichità al-*

l'età moderna. Pubblicazioni della Facoltà giuridica dell'Università di Ferrara, series 2a, no. 14. Milan.

———. 1989. "Cognomi ebraici italiani a base toponomastica straniera." In *Italia Judaica* 1989: 31–47.

Comune di Trieste. 1981. *Maria Teresa, Trieste e il porto*. Udine.

Cooperman, Bernard Dov. 1976. "Trade and Settlement: The Establishment and Early Development of the Jewish Communities in Leghorn and Pisa (1591–1626)." Ph.D. diss., Harvard University, Cambridge, Mass.

Cova, Ugo. 1971. *L'amministrazione austriaca a Trieste agli inizi dell'800*. Milan.

———. 1979. "I monasteri benedettini di San Cipriano a Trieste e di Santa Maria di Aquileia e le loro diverse sorti in epoca giuseppina." *AT* 39: 289–315.

———. 1984. "Un privilegio degli Ebrei delle Contee di Gorizia e Gradisca: Il godimento di diritti reali su beni immobili." *Mitteilungen des Österreichischen Staatsarchivs* 37: 120–48.

———. 1992. *Commercio e navigazione a Trieste e nella monarchia asburgica da Maria Teresa al 1915*. Civiltà del Risorgimento, no. 45. Udine.

Cubberley, Ellwood P. 1920. *Readings in the History of Education*. Boston.

Curiel, Carlo. 1937. *Il teatro S. Pietro di Trieste, 1690–1801*. Milan.

Curiel, Riccardo. 1932. "Le origini del ghetto di Trieste." *RMI* 6: 446–72.

———. 1938. "Gli ebrei di Trieste nel secolo XVIII." *RMI* 12: 239–55.

Cusin, Fabio. 1930. *Appunti alla storia di Trieste*. Trieste.

———. 1931. "Precedenti di concorrenza fra i porti del mare del Nord ed i porti dell'Adriatico: Saggio sul commercio del porto di Trieste nel secolo XVIII." *Annali della R. Università degli studi economici e commerciali di Trieste* 3: 263–328.

Cusin, Silvio. 1978. "Antiche sinagoghe triestine." In *Comunità religiose di Trieste: Contributi di conoscenza*, pp. 59–70. Istituto per l'Enciclopedia del Friuli Venezia Giulia. Udine.

[D'Arco, Giovanni Battista Gherardo.] 1782. *Della influenza del ghetto nello stato*. Venice.

De Antonellis Martini, Liana. 1968. *Portofranco e comunità etnico-religiose nella Trieste settecentesca*. Milan.

De Felice, Renzo. 1955. "Per una storia della problema ebraico in Italia alla fine del XVIII secolo e all'inizio del XIX: La prima emancipazione (1792–1814)." *Movimento operaio* 7: 681–727.

De' Giuliani, Antonio. [1785] 1950. *Riflessioni sul porto di Trieste*. Edited, with new introduction, by Giani Stuparich. Trieste. (Reprint of *Riflessioni politiche sopra il prospetto attuale della città di Trieste* [Vienna].)

———. 1969. *Scritti inediti*. Edited by Cesare Pagnini. Milan.

De Incontrera, Oscar, ed. 1953–63. "Vita triestina nel Settecento nelle cronache dell'*Osservatore Triestino*." *PO* 23–33.

———. 1960. *Trieste e l'America*. Trieste.

———. 1969. "Il Barone Pasquale de Ricci: Massimo artefice dell'emporio settecentesco." *PO* 5: 164–67.

De Rosa, Diana. 1991. *Libro di scorno, libro d'onore: La scuola elementare triestina durante l'amministrazione austriaca (1761–1918)*. Civiltà del Risorgimento, no. 43. Udine.

De Tuoni, Dario. 1921. "Un padovano a Trieste nel 1820: Dalle memorie del Conte Girolamo Polcastro." *AT* 9: 383–90.
Deinard, Ephraim, ed. 1915. *Shevilim bodedot*. Jerusalem.
Del Bianco Cotrozzi, Maddalena. 1983. *La comunità ebraica di Gradisca d'Isonzo*. Udine.
———. 1989. "Tolleranza giuseppina ed illuminismo ebraico: Il caso delle unite principesche contee di Gorizia e Gradisca." *Nuova rivista storica* 73: 689–726.
———. 1991. "Un incontro fra letterati alla fine del Settecento: Il carteggio di Elia Morpurgo con Giovanni Bernardo De Rossi." *Annali di storia Isontina* 4: 35–64.
———. 1993. "Samuel Morpurgo *alias* Francesco Filippo Sarchi, linguista e docente nella Vienna di fine Settecento." In Giulio Busi, ed., *We-Zo't le-Angelo: Raccolta di studi giudaica in memoria di Angelo Vivian*, pp. 199–231. Associazione Italiana per lo studio del Giudaismo, Testi e Studi, no. 11. Bologna.
———. 1995. *Il Collegio Rabbinico di Padova: Un'istituzione religiosa dell'ebraismo sulla via dell'Emancipazione*. Storia dell'Ebraismo in Italia, Studi e Testi, no. 17. Florence.
Della Torre, Lelio. 1834. *Cinque discorsi*. Padua.
———. 1908. *Scritti sparsi*. 2 vols. Padua.
Dickson, P.G.M. 1987. *Finance and Government under Maria Theresa, 1740–1780*. 2 vols. Oxford.
———. 1993. "Joseph II's Reshaping of the Austrian Church." *Historical Journal* 36: 89–114.
Dinaburg [Dinur], B. 1949. "B.Z. Rafael ha-Kohen Frizzi ve-sifro 'Petah einayim' (Li-demutah shel 'ha-haskalah' be-Italyah)." *Tarbiz* 20: 241–64.
———. 1950. "Ben Zion Refael Ha-Cohen Frizzi e la sua opera 'Pétach Enájm.' (Contributo alla storia dell'illuminismo ebraica in Italia)." *RMI* 16, nos. 6–8, *Scritti in onore di Riccardo Bachi*: 121–29.
Di Segni, Riccardo. 1971. "Due contratti di rabbini medici di Ancona del 1692 e 1752." *Annuario di Studi Ebraici* 1969–70, 1971–72. Rome.
Dohm, C. G. 1807. *Riforma politica degli ebrei*. Translated from the 1st German ed., 1781. Mantua.
Dollot, René, ed. 1959. "Trieste en 1807. Notes du Colonel Foy." *AT* 22: 163–68.
———. 1961. *Trieste et la France (1702–1958): Histoire d'un Consulat*. Paris.
Donahue, Jr., Charles. 1983. "The Canon Law on the Formation of Marriage and Social Practice in the Later Middle Ages." *Journal of Family History* 8: 144–58.
Dorsi, Pierpaolo. 1989. "'Libertà' e 'Legislazione': Il rapporto del Barone Pittoni sullo stato della Città di Trieste e del suo territorio (1786)." *Archeografo triestino* 49: 137–85.
Dubin, Lois C. 1987. "Trieste and Berlin: The Italian Role in the Cultural Politics of the Haskalah." In Katz 1987: 189–224.
———. 1991. "The Ending of the Ghetto of Trieste in the Late Eighteenth Century." In Todeschini and Ioly Zorattini 1991: 287–310.
———. 1992. "The Sages as *Philosophes*: Enlightenment and *Aggadah* in Northern Italy." In H. Blumberg, Benjamin Braude, Bernard H. Mehlman, Jerome S. Gurland, and Leslie Y. Gutterman, eds., *"Open Thou Mine Eyes . . . ": Essays in Ag-*

gadah and Judaica Presented to Rabbi William G. Braude and Dedicated to His Memory, pp. 61–77. Hoboken, N.J.

———. 1994. "*Les Liaisons Dangereuses*: Mariage juif et État moderne à Trieste au XVIIIe siècle." *Annales: Histoire, Sciences Sociales* 49, no. 5: 1139–70.

———. 1997. "The Social and Cultural Context: Eighteenth-Century Enlightenment." In Daniel H. Frank and Oliver Leaman, eds., *History of Jewish Philosophy*, pp. 636–59. Routledge History of World Philosophies, vol. 2. London and New York.

———. 1998. "The Rise and Fall of the Italian Jewish Model in Germany: From Haskalah to Reform, 1780–1820." In Elisheva Carlebach, John Efron, and David N. Myers, eds., *Jewish History and Jewish Memory: Essays in Honor of Yosef Hayim Yerushalmi*, pp. 271–95. Hanover, N.H.

Dubnov, Simon. 1971. *History of the Jews.* Vol. 4: *From Cromwell's Commonwealth to the Napoleonic Era.* Translated by Moshe Spiegel. New York.

Duby, Georges. 1978. *Medieval Marriage: Two Models from Twelfth-Century France.* Baltimore.

Eliav, Mordechai. 1960. *Ha-Hinnukh ha-yehudi be-Germanyah bi-yemei ha-haskalah ve-ha-emantzipatzyah.* Jerusalem.

Elon, Menahem. 1973. *Ha-Mishpat ha-ivri.* Jerusalem.

Enciclopedia monografica del Friuli Venezia Giulia. 1971–83. 4 vols. in 9 pts. Udine.

Endelman, Todd M. 1979. *The Jews of Georgian England, 1744–1830: Tradition and Change in a Liberal Society.* Philadelphia.

———, ed. 1997. *Comparing Jewish Societies.* The Comparative Studies in Society and History Book Series. Ann Arbor.

Entziklopedyah hinnukhit. 1964. Vol. 4. Jerusalem.

Ettinger, Shmuel. 1961. "The Beginnings of the Change in the Attitude of European Society Towards the Jews." *Scripta Hierosylmitana* 7: 193–219.

———. 1976. "The Modern Period." In Ben-Sasson 1976: 727–1096. Cambridge, Mass.

Evans, R.J.W. 1970. *The Making of the Habsburg Monarchy, 1550–1700: An Interpretation.* Oxford.

Faber, Eva. 1995. *Litorale Austriaco: Das österreichische und kroatische Küstenland, 1700–1780.* Schriftenreihe des Historischen Instituts, no. 5, Veröffentlichungen des Steiermärkischen Landesarchives, no. 20. Trondheim-Graz.

———. 1997. "Fremd- und Anderssein im 18. Jahrhundert. Eine Variation zum Thema am Beispiel von Triest." *Das achtzehnte Jahrhundert und Österreich. Jahrbuch der Österreichischen Gesellschaft zur Erforschung des achtzehnten Jahrhunderts* 12: 29–58.

Fahn, Reuven. 1919. *Tekufat ha-haskalah be-Vina.* Vienna and Brünn.

———. 1937. *Kitvei Reuven Fahn.* Vol. 2: *Pirkei haskalah.* Stanislav.

Falk, Z. W. 1966. *Jewish Matrimonial Law in the Middle Ages.* Oxford.

Feiner, Shmuel. 1987. "Yitzhak Euchel—Ha-'yazzam' shel tenuat ha-haskalah be-Germanyah." *Zion* 52: 427–69.

———. 1995. "Programmot hinnukhiyyot ve-idealim hevratiyyim: Bet ha-sefer 'Hinnukh nearim' be-Berlin, 1778–1825." *Zion* 60: 393–424.

Finkelstein, Louis. 1924. *Jewish Self-Government in the Middle Ages.* New York.

Fiorentino, Salomone. 1790. *Saggio di poesie*. Trieste.
Fishman, David E. 1995. *Russia's First Modern Jews: The Jews of Shklov*. London and New York.
Flandrin, Jean-Louis. 1979. *Families in Former Times: Kinship, Household and Sexuality*. Translated by Richard Southern. Cambridge.
Fleckeles, Eleazar. 1809. *Teshuvah me-ahavah*. Prague.
Formiggini, A. F. 1932? *Archivio della famiglia Formiggini*. Privately printed, date uncertain.
Formiggini, Saul. 1867–68. "La comunità israelitica di Trieste." *CI* 6: 141–45.
Frank, Gustav. 1882. *Das Toleranz-Patent Kaiser Joseph II: Urkundliche Geschichte seiner Entstehung und seiner Folgen*. Vienna.
Freimann, Abraham Hayyim. [1945] 1964. *Seder kiddushin ve-nessuin aharei hatimat ha-Talmud: Mehkar histori-dugmati be-dinei Yisrael*. Jerusalem.
Freudenberger, Herman. 1978. "Economic Progress During the Reign of Charles VI." In Jürgen Schneider, in association with Karl Erich Born et al., ed., *Wirtschaftskräfte und Wirtschaftswege*, vol. 2, *Wirtschaftskräfte in der europäischen Expansion: Festschrift für Hermann Kellenbenz*, pp. 624–44. [Stuttgart].
Friesel, Evyatar. 1990. *Atlas of Modern Jewish History*. New York and Oxford.
Frizzi, Benedetto. [1784] 1977. *Difesa contro gli attacchi fatti alla Nazione Ebrea nel libro intitolato Della influenza del ghetto nello stato*. Bologna.
———. 1787–90. *Dissertazione di polizia medica sul Pentateuco*. 6 vols. Pavia and Cremona.
———. 1790. *Elogio funebre di S.M.L'Augusto Giuseppe II. Imperatore*. Trieste.
———. 1790–91. *Giornale medico e letterario*. 4 vols. in 2. Trieste and Prague.
———. 1791a. *Elogio dei rabbini Simone Calimani e Giacobbe Saraval letto in un'accademia letteraria in casa del Signor Abram Camondo*. Pp. 37–70. Published with *Elogio del rabbino Abram Abenezra letto in un'accademia letteraria in casa del Signor Abram Camondo*. Trieste.
———. 1791b. *Elogio del rabbino Israele Beniamino Bassano capo dell'Università degli ebrei di Reggio*. N.p.
———. [Ben Zion Rafael ha-Kohen Frizzi.] [1815–25] 1878–81. *Petah enayim (Oculus Israelitici Populi)*. 2d ed. 7 vols. Livorno.
Fubini, Guido. 1974. *La condizione giuridica dell'ebraismo italiano: Dal periodo napoleonico alla Repubblica*. Florence.
Garms-Cornides, Elisabeth. 1970. "Giuseppismo e riformismo cattolico: Problemi sempre aperti nella storiografia austriaca." *Quaderni storici* 25: 759–72.
Gasparini, Lina, ed. 1945. "Trieste nel 1797, dalle memorie di viaggio del generale francese Desaix." *AT* 8–9: 391–414.
Gasser, Peter. 1971. "Triestiner Handel vor 1790: 'Corpo Mercantile,' die Anfänge der Handelsbörse und die Opposition Fiumes." *Mitteilungen des Österreichischen Staatsarchivs* 24: 245–79.
———. 1997. "Karl VI., Triest und die Venezianer." *Mitteilungen des Österreichischen Staatsarchivs*, Sonderband 3: Beiträge zur Österreichischen Wirtschafts- und Finanzgeschichte vom 17. bis zum 20. Jahrhundert, pp. 17–109.
Gatti, Carlo. 1991. "Gli ebrei a Trieste tra Settecento e Ottocento: Note demografiche." In Todeschini and Ioly Zorattini 1991: 311–26.

Gay, Peter. 1966–69. *The Enlightenment: An Interpretation.* 2 vols. New York.
Geiger, Ludwig. 1889. "Vor hundert Jahren: Mitteilungen aus der Geschichte der Juden Berlins." *Zeitschrift für die Geschichte der Juden in Deutschland* 3: 185–223.
Geisler, Adam Friedrich. 1790. *Skizzen aus dem Charakter und Handlungen Josephs des Zweiten.* Vol. 14. Halle.
Ghirondi, Mordecai Samuel, and Hananel Neppi. 1853. *Toledot gedolei Yisrael u-geonei Italyah . . . Zekher tzaddikim li-verakhah.* Trieste.
Ghisalberti, Carlo. 1992. "Stato nazionale e minoranze tra XIX e XX secolo." In Sofia and Toscano 1992: 27–39.
Gilson, Estelle, trans. 1993. *The Stories and Recollections of Umberto Saba.* Riverdale-on-Hudson.
Goldberg, Harvey E., ed. 1996. *Sephardi and Middle Eastern Jewries: History and Culture in the Modern Era.* Bloomington, Ind.
Gottlieb, Beatrice. 1980. "The Meaning of Clandestine Marriage." In Wheaton and Hareven 1980: 49–83.
———. 1993. *The Family in the Western World from the Black Death to the Industrial Age.* New York and Oxford.
Grab, Alexander. 1984. "Enlightened Despotism and State Building: The Case of Austrian Lombardy." *Austrian History Yearbook* 20: 43–72.
Graetz, Heinrich. [1853–76] 1900. *Geschichte der Juden von den ältesten Zeiten bis auf die Gegenwart.* 11 vols. 2d rev. ed. Edited by M. Brann. Leipzig.
———. 1967. *History of the Jews.* Vol. 5. Translated by Bella Löwy. Philadelphia.
Graetz, Michael. 1989. *Ha-Mahapekhah ha-tsorfatit ve-ha-Yehudim.* Jerusalem.
———. 1992. "Jewry in the Modern Period: The Role of the 'Rising Class' in the Politicization of Jews in Europe." In Jonathan Frankel and Steven J. Zipperstein, eds., *Assimilation and Community: The Jews in Nineteenth-Century Europe*, pp. 156–76. Cambridge.
Graff, Gil. 1985. *Separation of Church and State: Dina de-Malkhuta Dina in Jewish Law, 1750–1848.* University, Ala.
Green, Yosef. 1990–91. "Shaaruriyyat ha-kiddushin be-Alessandria (1579): Mekor nikhbad le-toldotehah shel ha-kehillah." *Asufot* 5: 267–308.
Halevi, Isaac Barukh. 1875. "Hosafot ve-hearot le-sefer toledot . . . Yitzhak Lampronti . . . ," in *Ha-Maggid* 19, no. 8 (Feb. 24): 69–70; and "Eleh toledot baal ha-maggid" and "Iggeret petuhah . . . ," in no. 22 (Jul. 8): 194–95.
Hanley, Sarah. 1987. "Family and State in Early Modern France: The Marriage Pact." In Marilyn J. Boxer and Jean H. Quataert, eds., *Connecting Spheres: Women in the Western World, 1500 to the Present*, pp. 53–63. New York and Oxford.
———. 1989. "Engendering the State: Family Formation and State Building in Early Modern France." *French Historical Studies* 16: 4–27.
Hasquin, Hervé. 1982. "La Tolérance et la question du mariage." In Roland Crahay, ed., *La Tolérance civile*, pp. 129–38. Colloque internationale, Mons, Sept. 2–4, 1981. Brussels.
Hausler, Wolfgang. 1974. *Das österreichische Judentum: Voraussetzungen und Geschichte.* Vienna and Munich.
Hertzberg, Arthur. 1968. *The French Enlightenment and the Jews.* New York, London, and Philadelphia.

Homberg, Herz. 1783. *Beurtheilung des Aufsatzes: Uiber die Verfassung der Juden und ihre Toleranz in den Oesterreichischen Staaten.* Gorizia.
———. 1815. *Bne Zion. Figli di Sion. Libro d'istruzione moral-religiosa per la gioventù della nazione israelitica.* Translated by Leon Vita Saraval. Trieste.
Hundert, Gershon David. 1986. "Approaches to the History of the Jewish Family in Early Modern Poland-Lithuania." In Cohen and Hyman 1986: 17–28.
Hyman, Paula E. 1982. "The History of European Jewry: Recent Trends in the Literature." *Journal of Modern History* 54: 303–19.
Iacchia, Irene. 1919. "I primordi di Trieste moderna all'epoca di Carlo VI: (Da documenti inediti negli archivi viennesi)." *AT* 8: 61–180.
Idel, Moshe. 1992. "Major Currents in Italian Kabbalah Between 1560 and 1660." In Ruderman 1992: 345–68.
Iggers, Wilma Abeles, ed. 1992. *The Jews of Bohemia and Moravia: A Historical Reader.* Detroit.
Ingrao, Charles. 1994a. *The Habsburg Monarchy, 1618–1815.* New Approaches to European History. Cambridge.
———, ed. 1994b. *State and Society in Early Modern Austria.* Introduction by R.J.W. Evans. West Lafayette, Ind.
Ioly Zorattini, Pier Cesare. 1968. "Fervore di educazione ebraica nelle comunità venete del '700." *RMI* 34: 582–91.
———, ed. 1984a. *Gli Ebrei a Gorizia e a Trieste tra 'Ancien Régime' ed Emancipazione.* Atti del Convegno di Gorizia, June 13, 1983. Udine.
———. 1984b. "L'emigrazione degli Ebrei dai territori della Repubblica di Venezia verso le Contee di Gorizia e Gradisca nel Settecento." In Ioly Zorattini 1984a: 111–18.
Israel, Jonathan. 1989. *European Jewry in the Age of Mercantilism, 1550–1750.* Rev. ed. Oxford.
"Gli Israeliti a Trieste." 1853. *Annuario Israelitico Italiano* 1: 238–42.
"Gl'Israeliti a Trieste." 1862–63. *CI* 1: 8–11, 30–32, 63–65, 125–28.
Italia Judaica. 1989. Vol. 3: *Gli ebrei in Italia dalla segregazione alla prima emancipazione.* Atti del III Convegno internazionale, Tel Aviv, June 15–20, 1986. Ministero per i Beni Culturali e Ambientali, Pubblicazioni degli Archivi di Stato, Saggi no. 11. Rome.
Jare, Giuseppe, ed. 1907. "Iggeret el benei amo me-et . . . Elia Morpurgo." *Ha'Olam* 1, no. 4 (Jan. 23): 37–38.
Jones, Peter M. 1995. *Reform and Revolution in France: The Politics of Transition, 1774–1791.* Cambridge.
Kaltenstadler, Wilhelm. 1969. "Der Österreichische Seehandel über Triest im 18. Jahrhundert." *Vierteljahrschrift für Sozial- und Wirtschaftsgeschichte* 55, no. 4 (Mar.): 381–500; 56, no. 1 (June): 1–104.
[Kandler, Pietro, ed.] 1861. *Raccolta delle leggi ordinanze e regolamenti speciali per Trieste.* Trieste.
Kaplan, Marion. 1991. *The Making of the Jewish Middle Class: Women, Family, and Identity in Imperial Germany.* New York and Oxford.
Kaplan, Yosef. 1989. *From Christianity to Judaism: The Story of Isaac Orobio de Castro.* Translated by Raphael Loewe. Littman Library of Jewish Civilization. Oxford.

———. 1994. "Famille, Mariage et Société: Les Mariages clandestins dans la Diaspora Sefarade Occidentale (XVII et XVIII siècles)." *XVIIe [Dix-septième] siècle* 46: 255–78.

Karniel, Joseph. 1981. "Zur Auswirkung der Toleranzpatente für die Juden in der Habsburgermonarchie im josephinischen Jahrzehnt." In Barton 1981b: 203–20.

———. 1982. "Das Toleranzpatent Kaiser Josephs II. für die Juden Galiziens und Lodomeriens." *Jahrbuch des Instituts Deutsche Geschichte* 11: 55–89.

———. 1985. *Die Toleranzpolitik Kaiser Josephs II*. Translated by Leo Koppel. Schriftenreihe des Instituts für Deutsche Geschichte Universität Tel Aviv, 9. Gerlingen.

Kates, Gary. 1990. "Jews into Frenchmen: Nationality and Representation in Revolutionary France." In Ferenc Fehér, ed., *The French Revolution and the Birth of Modernity*, pp. 103–16. Berkeley.

Katz, Jacob. 1945. "Nissuim ve-hayyei ishut be-motzaei yemei ha-beinayim." *Zion* 10: 21–54.

———. 1959. "Family, Kinship and Marriage among Ashkenazic Jews: The Sixteenth to Eighteenth Centuries." *Journal of Jewish Sociology* 1: 4–22.

———. 1971. "A State Within a State: The History of an Anti-Semitic Slogan." *Israel Academy of Sciences and Humanities, Proceedings* 4: 32–58.

———. 1973. *Out of the Ghetto: The Social Background of Jewish Emancipation, 1770–1870*. Cambridge, Mass..

———, ed. 1987. *Toward Modernity: The European Jewish Model*. New Brunswick, N.J., and London.

———. 1989. *The 'Shabbes Goy': A Study in Halakhic Flexibility*. Translated by Yoel Lerner. Philadelphia.

———. 1993. *Tradition and Crisis: Jewish Society at the End of the Middle Ages*. Translated and edited by Bernard Dov Cooperman. 2d ed. New York.

Kestenberg-Gladstein, Ruth. 1954–55. "Differences of Estate Within Pre-Emancipation Jewry: A Study in the Social Structure of Bohemian Provincial Jewry." *Journal for Jewish Studies* 5: 156–66; 6: 35–49.

———. 1969. *Neuere Geschichte der Juden in den böhmischen Ländern*. Vol. 1: *Das Zeitalter der Aufklärung, 1780–1830*. Schriftenreihe Wissenschaftlicher Abhandlungen des Leo Baeck Instituts 18/1. Tübingen.

Kieval, Hillel. 1987. "Caution's Progress: The Modernization of Jewish Life in Prague, 1780–1830." In Katz 1987: 71–105.

Klingenstein, Grete. 1970. *Staatsverwaltung und kirchliche Autorität in 18. Jahrhunderte: Das Problem des Zensur in den theresianischen Reform*. Vienna.

———. 1981. "Riforma e crisi: La monarchia austriaca sotto Maria Teresa e Giuseppe II: Tentativo di un'interpretazione." In Pierangelo Schiera, ed., *La dinamica statale austriaca nel XVIII e XIX secolo: Strutture e tendenze di storia costituzionale prima e dopo Maria Teresa*, pp. 93–125. Annali dell'Istituto storico italo germanico 7. Bologna.

———. 1985. "Les États autrichiennes." In B. Köpeczi, A. Soboul, É. H. Balázs, and D. Kosáry, eds., *L'Absolutisme éclairé*, pp. 201–16. Budapest and Paris.

———. 1990. "Revisions of Enlightened Absolutism: 'The Austrian Monarchy Is Like No Other.'" *Historical Journal* 33: 155–67.

———. 1993. "Modes of Religious Tolerance and Intolerance in Eighteenth-Century Habsburg Politics." *Austrian History Yearbook* 24: 1–16.

———. 1994. "Between Mercantilism and Physiocracy: Stages, Modes, and Functions of Economic Theory in the Habsburg Monarchy, 1748–63." In Ingrao 1994b: 181–214.

Kochan, Lionel. 1990. *Jews, Idols and Messiahs: The Challenge from History*. Oxford and Cambridge, Mass.

Kocher, Gernot. 1983. "Rechtsverständnis und Rechtsreformen im aufgeklärten Absolutismus Österreiches." In Zöllner 1983: 54–70.

Koenigsberger, H. G. 1991. "Epilogue: Central and Western Europe." In R.J.W. Evans and T. V. Thomas, eds., *Crown, Church and Estates: Central European Politics in the Sixteenth and Seventeenth Centuries*, pp. 300–310. London.

Kohen, Ishmael [Laudadio Sacerdote]. 1785–96. *Sheelot u-teshuvot Zera emet*. 3 vols. Livorno and Reggio.

Kohler, Kaufman. 1915. "The Harmonization of the Jewish and Civil Laws of Marriage and Divorce." *Yearbook of the Central Conference of American Rabbis*: 335–78.

Kohn, Helene. 1919. "Beiträge zur Geschichte der Juden in Österreich unter Kaiser Joseph II." Ph.D. diss., Wiener Universität.

Krinsky, Carol Herselle. 1985. *Synagogues of Europe: Architecture, History, Meaning*. Cambridge, Mass. and London.

Kristeller, Paul Oskar. 1961. *Renaissance Thought*. New York.

Lampronti, Yitzhak. [1750–96] 1874. *Pahad Yitzhak*. Vols. 1–3. [Lyck.]

Landau, Ezekiel. [1902–3] 1968. *Hukkei ha-ishut al pi dat Moshe ve-ha-Talmud*.... Translated by Z. V. Shenblum. Jerusalem. [Issued with Yekutiel Aryeh Kamelhar, *Mofet ha-dor*.]

Landman, Leo. 1968. *Jewish Law in the Diaspora: Confrontation and Accommodation*. Philadelphia.

Lentin, A. 1985. *Enlightened Absolutism (1760–1790): A Documentary Sourcebook*. Newcastle-upon-Tyne.

Lesizza, Chiara. 1988. "Scuola e cultura ebraiche a Gorizia nel XVIII secolo: Istanze tradizionali e fermenti di rinnovamento." *Studi Goriziani* 63: 51–73.

Lesley, Arthur M. 1982. "Hebrew Humanism in Italy." *Prooftexts* 2: 163–77.

Letteris, Meir. 1862. *Mikhtevei ivrit*. 7th rev. ed. Vienna.

Levy, Miriam J. 1988. *Governance and Grievance: Habsburg Policy and Italian Tyrol in the Eighteenth Century*. West Lafayette, Ind.

Lewin, Adolf. 1908. "Die Vorarbeiten für badische Judengesetzgebung in den Edikten 1807–1809." *Monatsschrift für Geschichte und Wissenschaft des Judentums* 52: 66–99, 226–34, 344–71, 473–96.

[Lewin-Berlin, Saul.] 1793. *Sefer sheelot u-teshuvot Besamim rosh*. Berlin.

Liberles, Robert. 1988. "Dohm's Treatise on the Jews: A Defence of the Enlightenment." *Yearbook of the Leo Baeck Institute* 33: 29–42.

Liebel, Helen P. 1979. "Free Trade and Protectionism under Maria Theresa and Joseph II." *Canadian Journal of History/Annales canadiennes d'histoire* 14: 355–73.

Lohrmann, Klaus. 1980. "Das österreichische Judentum zur Zeit Maria Theresias und Joseph II." *Studia Judaica Austriaca* 7: 5–29.

Lowenstein, Steven M. 1994. *The Berlin Jewish Community: Enlightenment, Family and Crisis, 1770–1830.* New York and Oxford.

Luzzatto, Aron, ed. 1851. *Gal avanim.* Trieste.

Luzzatto, Gino. 1950. "Sulla condizione economica degli ebrei veneziani nel secolo XVIII." *RMI* 16, nos. 7–8 (*Scritti in onore di Riccardo Bachi*): 161–72.

———. 1953. "Il portofranco di Trieste e la politica mercantilistica austriaca nel '700." *Problemi del Risorgimento triestino.* Centro studi per la storia del Risorgimento, no. 2, published as supplement to *Annali Triestini* 23: 7–17.

Luzzatto, Isaac. 1944. *Toledot Yitzhak.* Edited by D. J. Eckert and M. Wilensky. Tel Aviv.

Luzzatto, Samuel David. 1825. *Kinnor naim.* Vol. 1. Vienna.

———. 1848–52. *Il Giudaismo illustrato nella sua teorica, nella sua storia e nella sua letteratura.* 2 vols. Padua.

———. 1858–64. "Toledot Shadal." *Ha-Maggid* 2–8.

———. 1873. *Kinnor naim.* Vol. 2. Warsaw.

———. 1878. *Autobiografia di S. D. Luzzatto preceduta da Alcune notizie storico-letterarie sulla famiglia Luzzatto a datare dal secolo decimosesto.* Padua.

———. 1882–94. *Iggerot Shadal.* Edited by Eisig Graeber. 9 pts. in 2 vols. Przemysl and Cracow.

———. 1951. *Pirkei hayyim.* Edited by Moses Shulvass. New York.

Luzzatto Voghera, Gadi. 1993. "Cenni storici per una ricostruzione del dibattito sulla riforma religiosa nell'Italia ebraica." *RMI* 60: 47–70.

———. 1998. *Il prezzo dell'eguaglianza: Il dibattito sull'emancipazione degli ebrei in Italia (1781–1848).* Milan.

Maass, Ferdinand. 1953. *Der Josephinismus.* Vol. 2: *Entfaltung und Krise des Josephinismus 1770–1790.* Vienna.

Macartney, C. A. 1968. *The Habsburg Empire 1790–1918.* London.

———, ed. 1970. *The Habsburg and Hohenzollern Dynasties in the Seventeenth and Eighteenth Centuries.* London and Melbourne.

McCagg, Jr., William O. 1989. *A History of Habsburg Jews, 1670–1918.* Bloomington and Indianapolis, Ind.

Maclear, J. F. 1995. *Church and State in the Modern Age: A Documentary History.* New York and Oxford.

Mahler, Raphael. 1971. *A History of Modern Jewry, 1780–1815.* New York.

Mainati, Giuseppe. 1817–18. *Croniche ossia Memorie storiche sacro-profane di Trieste.* 6 vols. Venice.

Malino, Frances. 1978. *The Sephardic Jews of Bordeaux: Assimilation and Emancipation in Revolutionary and Napoleonic France.* University, Ala.

Mann, Vivian B., and Richard I. Cohen, eds. 1996. *From Court Jews to the Rothschilds: Art, Patronage and Power, 1600–1800.* Munich and New York.

Maternini Zotta, Maria Fausta. 1983. *L'ente comunitario ebraico: La legislazione negli ultimi due secoli.* Milan.

———. 1994. "La condizione giuridica delle comunità ebraiche italiane nel secolo XVIII." In Alatri and Grassi 1994: 235–50.

Ha-Meassef. 1–10 (1783–1811).

Melton, James Van Horn. 1985. "Absolutism and 'Modernity' in Early Modern Central Europe." *German Studies Review* 33: 383–98.

———. 1988. *Absolutism and the Eighteenth-Century Origins of Compulsory Schooling in Prussia and Austria.* Cambridge.

Mendelssohn, Moses. 1972–84. *Gesammelte Schriften: Jubiläumsausgabe.* Edited by Alexander Altmann. 27 vols. in 36. Stuttgart.

Mendes-Flohr, Paul R., and Jehuda Reinharz, eds. 1995. *The Jew in the Modern World: A Documentary History.* 2d ed. New York and Oxford.

Metrà, Andrea. 1793–97. *Il mentore perfetto dei negozianti.* . . . 5 vols. Trieste.

Milano, Attilio. 1963. *Storia degli ebrei in Italia.* Turin.

———. 1967. "Immagini del passato ebraica, IX: Trieste." *RMI* 33: 312–13.

Millo, Anna. 1989. *L'elite del potere a Trieste: Una biografia collettiva, 1891–1938.* Milan.

Mischler, Ernst, and Josef Ulbrich, eds. 1906. *Österrichisches Staatswörterbuch: Handbuch des gesamten österreichischen öffentlichen Rechtes.* 2d ed. 4 vols. Vienna.

Mitrofanov, Paul von. 1910. *Joseph II: Seine politische und kulturelle Tätigkeit.* Translated by V. von Demelič. 2 vols. Vienna and Leipzig.

Modena, Abdelkader, and Edgardo Morpurgo. 1967. *Medici e chirurghi ebrei dottorati e licenziati nell'Università di Padova dal 1617 al 1816.* Edited by A. Luzzatto, L. Munster, and V. Colorni. Bologna.

Modena, Leone. [1638] 1932–33. *Historia de riti Hebraici. RMI* 7: 293–325, 383–93, 493–509, 558–77.

Montanelli, Pietro. 1905. *Il movimento storico della popolazione di Trieste.* Trieste.

Moré, Charles-Albert Comte de. 1828. *Mémoires.* . . . Paris.

Mori, Simona. 1994. "Lo stato e gli ebrei mantovani nell'età delle riforme." In Alatri and Grassi 1994: 209–34.

M[orpurgo], A. V. 1862–63. "Biografia: Giuseppe Lazzaro Morpurgo." *CI* 1: 309–11.

Morpurgo, Edgardo. 1909. *La famiglia Morpurgo di Gradisca sull'Isonzo, 1585–1885.* Padua.

Morpurgo, Elia. 1781. *Orazione funebre in occasione della morte dell'Eroina della Germania S.S.C.R.A.M. Maria Teresa Imperadrice, e Regina ec. ec.* . . . Gorizia.

———. 1782a. *Discorso pronunziato da Elia Morpurgo Capo della nazione Ebrea di Gradisca nel partecipare a quella comunità la Clementissima Sovrana risoluzione 16. maggio 1781.* Gorizia.

———. 1783a. *Nachricht an die Liebhaber der hebräischen Literatur.* Gorizia.

———. 1783b. *Traduzione di Elia Morpurgo de' Discorsi ebraici di tolleranza e felicità diretta da Naftali Herz Weisel agli ebrei dimoranti ne' domini dell'Augustissimo Imperadore Giuseppe II, il Giusto.* Gorizia.

———. 1785–86a. "Divrei hokhmah u-musar." *Ha-Meassef* 3: 131–37, 147–56, 164–76.

———. 1785–86b. "Mikhtav me-Eliyyahu." *Ha-Meassef* 3: 66–78.

Morpurgo, Samson. 1743. *Shemesh tzedakah.* Venice.

Mueller, Christine L. 1994. "Enlightened Absolutism." *Austrian History Yearbook* 25: 159–83.

Negrelli, Giorgio. 1970. "Dal municipalismo all'irredentismo: Appunti per una storia dell'idea autonomistica a Trieste." *Rassegna storica del Risorgimento* 57: 347–416.

Nissim, Daniele. 1968. "Modernità di vedute in un nostro illuminista: Benedetto Frizzi e le sui opere." *RMI* 34: 279–91.

———. 1970. "Le peripezie di un farmacista ebreo a Trieste nel Settecento." *RMI* 36: 31–38.
Nissim, Paolo. 1960. "Intorno alle vecchie sinagoghe di Trieste e a due cantiche di Ischeq e S. D. Luzzatto (con cinque illustrazioni)." *RMI* 26: 329–34.
Nuovo Regolamento di Borsa Mercantile in Trieste: Sovranamente approvato in virtù del Decreto dell'Eccelsa Ces. Reg. Camera Aulica emanato il dì 2. Luglio 1804. 1804. Trieste.
O'Brien, Charles H. 1969. "Ideas of Religious Toleration at the Time of Joseph II: A Study of the Enlightenment among Catholics in Austria." *Transactions of the American Philosophical Society*, n.s., no. 59, pt. 7.
Ogris, Werner. 1981. "Joseph II: Staats- und Rechtsreformen." In Barton 1981b: 109–51.
———. 1985. "Zwischen Absolutismus und Rechtsstaat." In Plaschka and Klingenstein 1985, 1: 365–75.
———. 1988. "Aufklärung, Naturrecht und Rechtsreform in der Habsburgermonarchie." *Aufklärung* 3/2: 29–51.
Ozment, Steven. 1983. *When Fathers Ruled: Family Life in Reformation Europe.* Cambridge, Mass., and London.
Padover, Saul K. 1967. *The Revolutionary Emperor: Joseph II of Austria.* 2d rev. ed. London.
Pagis, Dan. 1976. *Hiddush u-masoret be-shirat ha-hol ha-ivrit: Sefarad ve-Italyah.* Jerusalem.
Pagnini, Cesare, ed. 1978. "Il periodo triestino del diario inedito del Conte Carlo de Zinzendorf Primo Governatore di Trieste (1776–1777)." *AT* 38.
Palmer, R. R. 1985. *The Improvement of Humanity: Education and the French Revolution.* Princeton.
Paolin, Giovanna. 1991. "Alcune considerazioni sugli ebrei triestini tra XVI e XVII secolo." In Todeschini and Ioly Zorattini 1991: 215–57.
Pavonello, Roberto. 1982. *L'amministrazione giudiziaria a Trieste da Leopoldo I a Maria Teresa.* Vol. 1: *L'età anteriore al portofranco.* Trieste.
Per le auspicatissime nozze del nobile Sig. Dottore Adelchi Avv. Guaita con la nobile Contessa Caterina Gozzi. 1879. Venice.
Peroni, Baldo. 1906. *Le prime scuole elementari governative a Milano, 1773–1796.* Rome and Milan.
Petuchowski, Jakob J. 1964. "Manuals and Catechisms of the Jewish Religion in the Early Period of Emancipation." In Alexander Altmann, ed., *Studies in Nineteenth-Century Jewish Intellectual History*, pp. 47–63. Cambridge, Mass.
Piperno, Abraham Barukh. 1846. *Kol ugav.* Livorno.
Plaschka, Richard, and Grete Klingenstein, eds. 1985. *Österreich im Europa der Aufklärung: Kontinuität und Zäsur in Europa zur Zeit Maria Theresias und Josephs II.* Internationales Symposion in Wien, October 20–23, 1980. 2 vols. Vienna.
Poppel, Stephen M. 1983. "The Politics of Religious Leadership—The Rabbinate in Nineteenth-Century Hamburg." *Yearbook of the Leo Baeck Institute* 28: 439–69.
Porter, Roy, and Mikuláš Teich, eds. 1981. *The Enlightenment in National Context.* Cambridge.

Pribram, A. F., ed. 1918. *Urkunden und Akten zur Geschichte der Juden in Wien.* 2 vols. Vienna and Leipzig.
Prose e poesie in occasione della morte immatura della Signora Annetta Forti nata Frizzi unica figlia del D. Benedetto Frizzi seguita nel giorno XVII. Aprile anno corrente. 1821. Trieste.
Raeff, Marc. 1983. *The Well-Ordered Police State: Social and Institutional Change Through Law in the Germanies and Russia, 1600–1800.* New Haven and London.
Ravid, Benjamin. 1992. "A Tale of Three Cities and Their Raison d'Etat: Ancona, Venice, Livorno, and the Competition for Jewish Merchants in the Sixteenth Century." In Alisa Meyuhas Ginio, ed., *Jews, Christians, and Muslims in the Mediterranean World after 1491*, pp. 138–62. London.
[Reggio, Isaac Samuel.] 1822. *Riflessioni d'un Israelita del Regno Illirico sopra un Articolo del Decreto di S.M.I.R.A. in date 4 Febbrajo 1820 . . . futuri rabbini. . . .* Published anonymously. Venice.
———. 1830a. "Devarim ahadim: Bet limmud ha-rabbanim be-ir Padova." *Bikkurei ha-ittim . . .* 5591 11: 5–10.
———. 1830b. "Petihat. . . ." *Bikkurei ha-ittim . . .* 5591 11: 3–4.
———, ed. 1833. "Mikhtav aleph." *Kerem Hemed* 1: 5–7.
Regolamento interno ad uso della Università degli ebrei in Trieste, Clementissimamente approvate e confermato con Aulico Rescritto di Sua Sacra Apostolica Maestà, segnato il dì 15 Marzo, ed intimato alla medesima con venerato Decreto di questo Eccelso Governo, in data 7 aprile 1792. 1792. Trieste.
Regolamento interno religioso, politico, ed economico ad uso della Università degli Ebrei in Trieste, Clementissimamente approvate e confermato con Aulico Rescritto di Sua S.C.R.Ap Maestà, segnato il dì 28 agosto, ed intimato alla medesima con venerato decreto di questo eccelso governo in data 16 settembre 1783. 1784. Trieste.
Regolamento per le Scuole Pie Normali degli Ebrei in Trieste. 1797. Trieste.
Regole per la direzione della Scuola Pia Normale sive Talmud Torà dell'Università degli Ebrei di Trieste. 1782. Gorizia.
Reynolds, Nancy. 1995. "Difference and Tolerance in the Ottoman Empire: Interview with Aron Rodrigue." *Stanford Humanities Review* 5, no. 1: 81–90.
Richetti, Elia. 1984. "Attività del tribunale rabbinico a Trieste." In Ioly Zorattini 1984a: 51–70.
Rivkind, Isaac. 1929. "Elia Morpurgo mesayyeo shel Weisel be-milhemet ha-haskalah le-or teudot hadashot. . . . " In *Studies in Jewish Bibliography and Related Subjects in Memory of Abraham Solomon Freidus*, pp. 138–59 (Heb.). New York.
Roberts, Simon. 1983. "The Study of Dispute: Anthropological Perspectives." In John Bossy, ed., *Disputes and Settlements: Law and Human Relations in the West*, pp. 1–24. Cambridge.
Robolotti, L. 1878. *Commemorazione del Dottor Benedetto Frizzi di Ostiano.* Cremona.
Rodrigue, Aron. 1990. *French Jews, Turkish Jews: The Alliance Israélite Universelle and the Politics of Jewish Schooling in Turkey, 1860–1925.* Bloomington, Ind.
Romanelli, Samuel. 1799. *Grammatica ragionata italiana ed ebraica: Con trattato, ed esempj di poesia.* Trieste.

Romano, Salvatore Francesco. 1957. "Studi su Giuseppe II e il 'Giuseppinismo.'" *Rivista storica Italiana* 69: 110–27.

———. 1981. *La monarchia degli Absburgo d'Austria dalla riforma protestante all'austromarxismo*. Civiltà del Risorgimento, no. 10. Trieste.

Roper, Lyndal. 1985. "'Going to Church and Street': Weddings in Reformation Augsburg." *Past and Present* 106: 62–101.

Rossetti, Domenico. 1830. "Trieste al tempo di Giuseppe I." *AT* 2: 258–318.

Roth, Cecil. 1924a. "La Fête de l'institution du ghetto: Une célébration particulière à Vérone." *RÉJ* 79: 163–69.

———. 1924b. "Rabbi Menahem Navarra: His Life and Times, 1717–1777." *Jewish Quarterly Review* 15: 427–66.

———. 1946. *The History of the Jews of Italy*. New York.

———. 1959. *The Jews in the Renaissance*. Philadelphia.

Ruderman, David B. 1981. *The World of a Renaissance Jew: The Life and Thought of Abraham ben Mordecai Farissol*. Cincinnati.

———. 1988a. "The Italian Renaissance and Jewish Thought." In A. Rabil, Jr., ed., *Renaissance Humanism: Foundations, Forms, and Legacy*, 1: 382–433. Philadelphia.

———. 1988b. *Kabbalah, Magic, and Science: The Cultural Universe of a Sixteenth-Century Jewish Physician*. Cambridge, Mass. and London.

———, ed. 1992. *Essential Papers on Jewish Culture in Renaissance and Baroque Italy*. New York and London.

———. 1995. *Jewish Thought and Scientific Discovery in Early Modern Europe*. New Haven and London.

Rürup, Reinhard. 1986. "The Tortuous and Thorny Path to Legal Equality: 'Jews Laws' and Emancipatory Legislation in Germany from the Late Eighteenth Century." *Yearbook of the Leo Baeck Institute* 31: 3–33.

Saba, Umberto. 1964. *Opere di Umberto Saba*. 2 vols. Edited by Linuccia Saba. Milan.

Sabbadini, Salvatore. 1916. *I primi passi della scuola ebraica triestina: Per nozze Levi-Morpurgo XXXI December MCMXVI*. Trieste.

Salimbeni, Fulvio. 1984. "Trieste tra Venezia e Vienna." *AT* 44: 47–72.

———. 1992. "Variazioni storiografiche e culturali su una città 'nuova': Trieste tra Sette e Ottocento." *AT* 52: 21–36.

Samaja, Nino. 1957. "La situazione degli ebrei nel periodo del Risorgimento." *RMI* 23: 298–309, 359–70, 412–21.

Samet, Moses Shraga. 1968. "R. Shaul Berlin u-khetavav." *Kiryat Sefer* 43: 429–41.

———. 1970. "M. Mendelssohn, N. H. Weisel ve-rabbanei doram." In Akiba Gilboa and Bustenay Oded, eds., *Mehkarim be-toledot am Yisrael ve-eretz Yisrael*, vol. 1, *Le-zekher Tsevi Avneri*, pp. 233–57. Haifa.

———. 1990–91. "Ha-Shinuyyim be-sidrei bet-ha-keneset: Emdat ha-rabbanim keneged 'ha-mehadshim' ha-reformim." *Asufot* 5: 345–404.

———. 1995. "Maamar al hitgalhut be-hol ha-moed." In Meir Benayahu, ed., *Tiglahat be-holo shel moed*, pp. 55–105. Jerusalem.

Sarker Ex-Morpurgo, Elia [Elia Morpurgo]. 1796. *Esame del Mondo*. Trieste.

Satanov, Isaac. 1789. *Mishlei Asaf*. Berlin.

Schama, Simon. 1989. *Citizens: A Chronicle of the French Revolution*. New York.

Scherer, J. G. 1895. *Übersicht der Judengesetzgebung in Österreich vom 10. Jahrhunderte bis auf die Gegenwart*. Vienna.
Schiffrer, Carlo. 1937. *Le origini dell'Irredentismo triestino (1813–1860)*. Udine.
Schirmann, Hayyim. 1979. *Le-Toledot ha-shirah ve-ha-dramah ha-ivrit*. 2 vols. Jerusalem.
Schmale, Wolfgang, and Nan L. Dodde, eds. 1991. *Revolution des Wissens? Europa und seine Schulen im Zeitalter der Aufklärung (1750–1825): Ein Handbuch zur europäischen Schulgeschichte*. Bochum.
Schmidl, Erwin A. 1989. *Juden in der k.(u.)k. Armee 1788–1918 / Jews in the Habsburg Armed Forces*. Studia Judaica Austriaca 11. Eisenstadt.
Schorsch, Ismar. 1981. "Emancipation and the Crisis of Religious Authority: The Emergence of the Modern Rabbinate." In Werner E. Mosse, Arnold Paucker, and Reinhard Rürup, eds., *Revolution and Evolution: 1848 in German-Jewish History*, pp. 205–47. Tübingen.
———. 1994. "The Myth of Sephardic Supremacy." In *From Text to Context: The Turn to History in Modern Judaism*, pp. 71–92. Hanover and London.
Schrieben eines Rabbi aus Gradiska zur Entscheidung, dass die jüdische Religion dem Kriegsdienste nicht im mindesten widerspreche. 1788. Vienna.
Schwarzfuchs, Simon. 1966. "Les Juifs de Bayonne au XVIIIe siècle." *RÉJ* 125: 353–64.
———. 1979. *Napoleon, the Jews and the Sanhedrin*. London.
———. 1981. *Le Registre des déliberations de la Nation Juive Portugaise de Bordeaux (1711–1787)*. Paris.
———. 1993. *A Concise History of the Rabbinate*. Oxford and Cambridge, Mass.
Sciloni, Gaio. 1989. "Noterelle sul 'Fuorighetto': Un aspetto della vita degli ebrei di Firenze nell'ultimo periodo della loro reclusione nel ghetto." *Italia* 8, nos. 1–2: 63–77.
Scocchi, Angelo. 1951. "Gli Ebrei di Trieste nel Risorgimento italiano." *Rassegna storica del Risorgimento* 38: 631–63.
Scott, H., ed. 1990. *Enlightened Absolutism*. London.
Scussa, V., and P. Kandler. 1863. *Storia cronografica di Trieste dalla sua origine sino all'anno 1695 al 1848*. Edited by F. Cameroni. Trieste.
Seder hannukat ha-bayit . . . [and] Traduzione italiana dell'inno ebraico da cantarsi all'occasione della consacrazione della Publica Scuola di orazione. . . . 1798. Trieste.
Segre, Dan V. 1995. "The Emancipation of Jews in Italy." In Pierre Birnbaum and Ira Katznelson, eds., *Paths of Emancipation: Jews, States, and Citizenship*, pp. 206–37. Princeton.
Shohet, Azriel. 1960. *Im hillufei tekufot: Reshit ha-haskalah be-yahadut Germanyah*. Jerusalem.
Shulvass, Moses A. 1973. *The Jews in the World of the Renaissance*. Leiden.
Silber, Michael. 1985. "Shorshei ha-pillug be-yahadut Hungaryah: Terumot tarbutiot ve-hevratiyyot me-yemei Yosef ha-sheni ad erev mahapekhat 1848." (Roots of the schism in Hungarian Jewry: Cultural and social change fom the reign of Joseph II until the eve of the 1848 revolution.) Ph.D. diss., Hebrew University.
———. 1987. "The Historical Experience of German Jewry and Its Impact on Haskalah and Reform in Hungary." In Katz 1987: 107–57.

———. 1988. "Enlightened Absolutism and Traditional Jewish Society: Tradition in Crisis? State Schools, Military Conscription and the Emergence of a Neutral Polity in the Reign of Joseph II." Paper presented at Tradition and Crisis Revisited: Jewish Society and Thought on the Threshhold of Modernity, conference held at Harvard University, Cambridge, Mass., October 11–12.

———. 1989. "Jewish Equality Before Egalité? The Policy of Joseph II Towards the Jews, 1781–1790." Paper presented at the Tenth World Congress of Jewish Studies, Jerusalem, August 16–24.

Simon, Abram. 1915. "The Harmonization of Jewish and Civil Laws of Marriage and Divorce." *Yearbook of the Central Conference of American Rabbis*: 379–402.

Simonsohn, Shlomo. 1977. *History of the Jews in the Duchy of Mantua*. Jerusalem.

———. 1989. "Some Reactions of Italian Jewry to the 'First Emancipation' and the Enlightenment" (Hebrew). In *Italia Judaica* 1989: 47–68 (Hebrew section), 225–26 (English abstract).

Singer, Ludwig. 1932. "Zur Geschichte und Bedeutung des Toleranzpatentes vom 2. Jänner 1782." *B'nai B'rith Mitteilungen für Österreich* 32: 1–20.

———. 1933. "Zur Geschichte der Toleranzpatente in den Sudentenländern." *Jahrbuch der Gesellschaft für Geschichte der Juden in der Čechoslovakischen Republik* 5: 231–311.

———. 1934. "Neue Beiträge zur Geschichte der Toleranzpatente Josefs II." *B'nai B'rith Mitteilungen für Österreich* 34: 186–91, 233–37.

Singham, Shanti Marie. 1994. "Betwixt Cattle and Men: Jews, Blacks, and Women, and the Declaration of the Rights of Man." In Dale Van Kley, ed., *The French Idea of Freedom: The Old Regime and the Declaration of Rights of 1789*, pp. 114–53. Stanford.

Sofer, Moses (Hatam Sofer). 1865. *Sheelot u-teshuvot Hatam Sofer*. Pressburg.

Sofia, Francesca, and Mario Toscano, eds. 1992. *Stato nazionale ed emancipazione ebraica*. Atti del Convegno "Stato nazionale, società civile e minoranze religiose: L'emancipazione degli ebrei in Francia, Germania e Italia tra rigenerazione morale e intolleranza," Rome, October 23–25, 1991. Rome.

Sonne, Isaiah. 1938. "Avnei binyan le-toledot ha-Yehudim be-Verona." *Zion* 3: 123–67.

———. 1960–61. *Ha-Yahadut ha-italkit: Demutah u-mekomah be-toledot am Yisrael*. Jerusalem.

Sorkin, David. 1987. *The Transformation of German Jewry, 1780–1840*. New York.

———. 1990a. "Emancipation and Assimilation: Two Concepts and Their Application to German-Jewish History." *Yearbook of the Leo Baeck Institute* 35: 17–33.

———. 1990b. "Preacher, Teacher, Publicist: Joseph Wolf and the Ideology of Emancipation." In Frances Malino and David Sorkin, eds., *From East and West: Jews in a Changing Europe 1750–1870*, pp. 107–25. Oxford.

———. 1992. "Jews, the Enlightenment and Religious Toleration—Some Reflections." *Yearbook of the Leo Baeck Institute* 37: 3–16.

———. 1997. "Enlightenment and Emancipation: German Jewry's Formative Age in Comparative Perspective." In Endelman 1997: 89–112.

Sorkin, David, and Shmuel Feiner, eds. Forthcoming. *New Perspectives on the Haskalah*.

Spiegel, Guido. 1933–34. "Un matrimonio contestato." *RMI* 8: 444–47.

Spielman, John P. "Status as Commodity: The Habsburg Economy of Privilege." In Ingrao 1994b: 110–18.
Springer, Arnold. 1980. "Enlightened Absolutism and Jewish Reform: Prussia, Austria, and Russia." *California Slavic Studies* 9: 237–67.
Statuti e regolamenti dell'Universita' Ebrei, in Trieste [1766]. 1767. Trieste.
Stefani, Giuseppe. 1960. *I Greci a Trieste nel Settecento*. Trieste.
Steinschneider, M. 1877–78. "Letteratura italiana dei giudei." *Il Vessillo Israelitico* 25: 309–11.
———. 1879. "Letteratura Giudaica Italiana: Opere inedite del secolo XVIII." *Il vessillo Israelitico* 27: 365–68.
———. 1891. "Hebräische Drucke in Deutschland (Berlin 1762–1800)." *Zeitschrift für die Geschichte der Juden in Deutschland* 5: 154–86.
———. 1900. "Die italienische Litteratur der Juden." *Monatsschrift fuer Geschichte und Wissenschaft des Judenthums* 44: 80–91.
Stillman, Norman A. 1995. *Sephardi Religious Responses to Modernity*. Luxembourg.
Stock, Mario. 1972. "Salomon zudio da Norimberga, publico imprestador a Trieste." *RMI* 38 (*Scritti in memoria di Paolo Nissim*): 197–210.
———. 1973. "Giuseppe II d'Austria e l'emancipazione ebraica." *RMI* 39: 369–72.
———. 1974a. "Le relazioni fra banchieri ebrei e il Comune di Trieste nei secoli XVI–XVIII." *RMI* 40: 502–7.
———. 1974b. "Il Seicento: Epoca di transizione per gli ebrei triestini." *RMI* 40: 548–50.
———. 1979. *Nel segno di Geremia: Storia della comunità israelitica di Trieste dal 1200*. Udine.
Stone, Lawrence. 1977. *The Family, Sex and Marriage in England, 1500–1800*. London.
Stow, Kenneth R. 1992. "Sanctity and the Construction of Space: The Roman Ghetto as Sacred Space." In Menachem Mor, ed., *Jewish Assimilation, Acculturation and Accommodation: Past Traditions, Current Issues and Future Prospects*, Proceedings of the Second Annual Symposium of the Philip M. and Ethel Klutznick Chair in Jewish Civilization, September 24–25, 1989. Studies in Jewish Civilization, 2. Lanham, Md.
Szabo, Franz A. J. 1979. "Intorno alle origini del giuseppinismo: Motivi economico-sociali e aspetti ideologici." *Società e storia* 4: 155–74.
———. 1994. *Kaunitz and Enlightened Absolutism, 1753–1780*. Cambridge.
Tama, M. Diogene, ed. 1807. *Transactions of the Parisian Sanhedrim [sic]*. . . . Translated by F. D. Kirwan. London.
Tamani, Giuliano. 1988. "L'emancipazione ebraica secondo Elia Morpurgo da Gradisca." *Annali de Ca' Foscari* 27 (Serie Orientale no. 19): 5–20.
Tamaro, Attilio. [1924] 1976. *Storia di Trieste*. 2 vols. Trieste.
———. 1929. "Documenti di storia triestina nel secolo XVIII." Part 5: "Aneddotti sulla situazione religiosa e morale." *Atti e memorie della società istriana di archeologia e storia patria* 41: 207–26.
———. 1942–43. "Fine del Settecento a Trieste: Lettere del Barone P. A. Pittoni (1782–1801)." *AT* 5–6: 3–430.
Tedeschi, Marco. 1866. *Due discorsi in morte del Professore Samuel David Luzzatto*. Trieste.

Tedesco, Raffael Nathan. 1786. *Indagine di qual sia tra i morali mali il peggiore: Accademico garreggiamento scolastico*. Trieste.

———. 1790. *Per le solenni Esequie dell'Augustissimo Imperadore Re de' Romani Giuseppe II. Celebrate nella Scuola grande degli Ebrei di Trieste il dì 25. Marzo 1790: Orazione*. Trieste.

———. [1792.] *Per la morte de Leopoldo II. Cesare, Re, Padre, Pacifico ecc. ecc. ecc. Orazione di Raffaele Natan Tedesco: Rabbino della Nazione Ebrea di Trieste, nella Scuola grande la sera del dì 6 Nissan 5552, 29 Marzo 1792*. Trieste.

Tirosch-Rothschild, Hava. 1988. "In Defense of Jewish Humanism." *Jewish History* 3: 31–57.

———. 1990. "Jewish Culture in Renaissance Italy—A Methodological Survey." *Italia* 9, nos. 1–2: 63–96.

Tivoli, Isaac Hayyim. 1800. "Al ha-lekah Raffael Natan Ashkenazy [Tedesco]." Trieste.

Toaff, Ariel. 1981. "Gli ebrei d'Italia nell'età moderna." Unpublished manuscript.

———. 1989. *Il vino e la carne: Una comunità ebraica nel Medioevo*. Bologna.

Toaff, Renzo. 1989. "La Nazione Ebrea di Livorno dal 1591 al 1715: Nascita e sviluppo di una comunità di mercanti." In Ariel Toaff and Simon Schwarzfuchs, eds., *The Mediterranean and the Jews: Banking, Finance and International Trade (XVI–XVIII Centuries)*, pp. 271–90. Ramat-Gan.

Todeschini, Giacomo, and Pier Cesare Ioly Zorattini, eds. 1991. *Il mondo ebraico: Gli ebrei tra Italia nord-orientale e Impero asburgico dal Medioevo all'Età contemporanea*. Collezione Biblioteca, no. 90. Pordenone.

Torbianelli Moscarda, Dea. 1971. *Vicende giuridico-amministrative a Trieste da Carlo VI a Leopoldo II*. Milan.

Tosi, Claudio. 1990. "Giuseppinismo e legislazione matrimoniale in Lombardia: In Costituzione del 1784." *Critica storica* 27: 235–301.

Toury, Jacob. 1977. "Types of Jewish Municipal Rights in German Townships: The Problem of Local Emancipation." *Yearbook of the Leo Baeck Institute* 22: 55–80.

Traer, James F. 1980. *Marriage and the Family in Eighteenth-Century France*. Ithaca, N.Y., and London.

Trampus, Antonio. 1990. "Economia e stato delle riforme del Litorale Austriaco del diario del Conte Zinzendorf (1771)." *AT* 50: 67–106.

———. 1993. "Karl von Zinzendorf: Tra Maria Teresa e Giuseppe II." *Quaderni giuliani di storia* 14: 45–55.

———. 1996. "Die Gründung einer neuen Stadt: Aufbruchsstimmung im Triest des 18. Jahrhunderts." *Das achtzehnte Jahrhundert und Österreich*. Jahrbuch der Österreichischen Gesellschaft zur Erforschung des achtzehnten Jahrhunderts 11: 47–55.

Trebitsch, Abraham. 1851. *Korot ha-ittim*. Lemberg.

Tremoli, P. 1951. "Intorni alla cultura classica nella Trieste dell'Ottocento." *Scritti in onore di Camillo de Franceschi*. Centro studi per la storia del Risorgimento, 1. Supplement to *Annali Triestini* 21: 63–152.

Tribel, Antonio. 1884–85. "Gli Ebrei di Trieste." *CI* 23: 126–28, 147–49.

Tucci, Ugo. 1978. "Die Triester Kaufmannschaft im 18. Jahrhundert: Ihre Ausrichtung, ihre Gutachten." In Paul W. Roth, ed., *Beiträge zur Handels- und Verkehrs-*

geschichte, pp. 121–32. Grazer Forschungen zur Wirtschafts- und Sozialgeschichte 3. Graz.

———. 1980. "Una descrizione di Trieste a metà del Settecento." *Quaderni giuliani di storia* 1, no. 2: 95–113.

Valsecchi, Franco. 1931. *L'Assolutismo illuminato in Austria e in Lombardia*. 2 vols. Bologna.

Venturi, Franco. 1972. *Italy and the Enlightenment: Studies in a Cosmopolitan Century*. Edited with introduction by Stuart Woolf. Translated by Susan Corsi. New York.

———. 1991. *The End of the Old Regime in Europe, 1776–1789*. Vol. 2: *Republican Patriotism and the Empires of the East*. Translated by R. Burr Litchfield. Princeton.

Vielmetti, Nikolaus. 1970–71. "Die Gründungsgeschichte des Collegio Rabbinico in Padua." *Kairos* 12: 1–30; 13: 40–66.

———. 1984. "Elia Morpurgo di Gradisca protagonista dell'Illuminismo ebraico." In Ioly Zorattini 1984a: 41–46.

Vivian, Angelo. 1984. "Il cimitero ebraico di San Daniele del Friuli: Studio preliminare." In *Judaica Forojuliensia: Studi e ricerche sull'Ebraismo del Friuli-Venezia Giulia*, 1: 37–80. Biblioteca Utinese testi e studi no. 3. Udine.

Voltelini, Hans von. 1910. "Die naturrechtlichen Lehren und die Reformen des 18. Jahrhunderts." *Istorische Zeitschrift* 105: 65–104.

Wangermann, Ernst. 1973. *The Austrian Achievement, 1700–1800*. London and New York.

———. 1978. *Aufklärung und staatsbürgerliche Erziehung: Gottfried van Swieten als Reformator des österreichischen Unterrichtswesens, 1781–1791*. Vienna.

Weisel, Naftali Herz (Hartwig Wessely). [1782–85] 1826. *Divrei shalom ve-emet*. 4 vols. in one. Vienna.

———. 1783–84. "Li-khevod ha-kesar Yosefus ha-sheni. . . ." *Ha-Meassef* 1: 161–65, 177–81.

———. 1784. *Mikhtav shelishi . . . Divrei shalom ve-emet . . . Ein mishpat*. Berlin.

Wheaton, Robert, and Tamara K. Hareven, eds. 1980. *Family and Sexuality in French History*. Philadelphia.

Wistrich, Robert S. 1990. *The Jews of Vienna in the Age of Franz Joseph*. Oxford.

Wolf, Gerson. 1858. "Zur Geschichte der Juden." *Monatsschrift für die Geschichte und Wissenschaft des Judentums* 7: 368–71.

———. 1862. "Die Militärpflicht der Juden." *Ben Chananja* 5: 61–63.

———. 1863. *Judentaufen in Oesterreich*. Vienna.

———. 1867. *Zur Geschichte des Unterrichtes der israelitischen Jugend in Wien*. Vienna.

———. 1867–68. "Wie wurden die Juden in Oesterreich militärpflichtig?" *Wiener Jahrbuch für Israeliten . . .* 5628: 34–66.

———. [1876] 1974. *Geschichte der Juden in Wien (1156–1876)*. Vienna.

———. 1888. *Aus der Zeit der Kaiserin Maria Theresia*. Vienna.

Yaari, Abraham. 1977. *Sheluhei eretz Yisrael*. Jerusalem.

Yerushalmi, Yosef Hayim. 1976. *The Lisbon Massacre of 1506 and the Royal Image in the Shebet Yehudah*. Hebrew Union College Annual Supplements, no. 1. Cincinnati.

———. 1981. *From Spanish Court to Italian Ghetto: Isaac Cardoso, A Study in Seventeenth-Century Marranism and Jewish Apologetics*. New York.

———. 1982. *Zakhor: Jewish History and Jewish Memory*. Philadelphia and Seattle.
Yoel, Yissahar. 1944–45. "Ketubbot me-Italyah be-ginzei bet ha-sefarim." *Kiryat Sefer* 22: 266–304.
Yriarte, Carlo. 1875. *Trieste e l'Istria*. 2d ed. Milan.
Zanei, Giuseppe. 1927. "Brevi notizie sulle condizione dell'istruzione elementare del goriziano nel 1775." *Studi Goriziani* 5: 5–120.
Zipperstein, Steven J. 1985. *The Jews of Odessa: A Cultural History, 1794–1881*. Stanford.
Zohar, Zvi. 1982. *Halakhah u-modernizatzyah: Darkhei heanut hakhmei Mitzrayim le-etgarei ha-modernizatzyah, 1822–1882*. Jerusalem.
Zoller, Israel. 1911a. "Ancora sui privilegi concessi ad Ebrei triestini nel secolo XVII." *CI* 50: 134.
———. 1911b. "Due privilegi concessi ad Ebrei triestini nel sec. XVII." *CI* 50: 86–87.
———. 1911c. "La scuola Vivante a Trieste." *Il Vessillo Israelitico* 59: 592–96.
———. 1912a. "L'Istituto Scolastico della Comunità Israelitica di Trieste negli anni 1803–1808." *CI* 50: 208–11, 230–33.
———. 1912b. "Il maestro di S. D. Luzzatto Dr. Abram Eliezer Levi e la questione della riforma del culto in Italia." *Rivista Israelitica* 9: 37–48.
———. 1912c. "Monsignor Conte Hohenwart ed il rabbino R. N. Tedesco." *CI* 51: 42–44.
———. 1912d. "Un tempio Israelitico a Trieste nella seconda metà del Settecento." *CI* 51: 135–37.
———. 1913a. "Il Codice Diplomatica Istriano quale fonte per la storia degli Ebrei nell'Istria." *CI* 51: 197–99.
———. 1913b. "La coscrizione degli Ebrei di Trieste nel 1788." *MI*, no. 2 (Sept.–Oct.): 5–6; no. 3 (Oct.–Nov.): 5–6; no. 4 (Nov.–Dec.): 5–6.
———. 1913c. "L'età d'oro nella storia della Comunità Israelitica di Trieste." *CI* 52: 141–43.
———. 1913d. "Le origini dei primi due Oratori pubblici di Trieste." *CI* 52: 11–14, 29–32.
1914. "Maria Teresa e gli Ebrei." *MI*, no. 6 (Feb.): 5–6; no. 7 (Mar.): 4–5; no. 8 (Apr.): 4–5; no. 9 (May): 4–5.
———. 1919. *Gli inizii della riforma sinagogale e l'ebraismo italiano, 1818–1820*. Trieste.
———. 1924. *La Comunità israelitica di Trieste: Studio di demografia storica*. Ferrara.
———. 1933a. "Notes sur la famille Luzzatto après son expulsion de S. Daniele." *RÉJ* 94: 50–56.
———. 1933b. "Il periodo triestino della vita di Samuel David Luzzatto." *RMI* 8: 285–99.
———. 1933c. "Il Principe arcivescovo Sigismondo Hohenwart ed il suo atteggiamento verso l'ebraismo." *PO* 3: 16–23.
Zöllner, Erich, ed. 1983. *Österreich im Zeitalter des aufgeklärten Absolutismus*. Vienna.
Zudini, Diomiro. 1979. "Elementi di storia linguistica giuliana." In *Enciclopedia monografica del Friuli Venezia Giulia* 1971–83: vol. 3, pt. 2, pp. 1019–34. Udine.

Index

In this index an "f" after a number indicates a separate reference on the next page, and an "ff" indicates separate references on the next two pages. A continuous discussion over two or more pages is indicated by a span of page numbers, e.g., "57–59." *Passim* is used for a cluster of references in close but not consecutive sequence.

Abarbanel, Isaac, 133
Aboab, Isaac, 113
Absolutism: Joseph II and Maria Theresa as absolutist state-builders, 64; privileges and equalities in absolutist-corporate state, 216–23; in Statute of 1771, 54–55. *See also* Enlightened absolutism; Reforming absolutism
Acculturation: decentering Berlin and Haskalah regarding, 6, 9; of Italian Jews, 131–32, 136–37, 200, 215
Adriatic Sea: Charles VI declares freedom of navigation on, 11; Habsburg free-ports policy, 11, 15, 41; map, *xv*
Agriculture, 72, 75, 86
Allgemeine Schulordnung of 1774, 52, 98–99
Alpron, Isaac di Jacob, 239n88
Alsace-Lorraine, 222
Alt-Ofen, 149
Amsterdam: head toll exemption in, 46; Jewish merchants in, 3f, 61; Triestine Jews compared with, 62, 145, 199

Ancona, 132, 267n37
Annulment, 177, 179, 181f
Apprentices, 72
Ara, Angelo, 2
Arcadia Romano Sonziaca, 32, 239n90
Armenian Uniates, 14, 43, 218
Ascher, Saul, 273n54
Ashkenazi, Zevi Hirsch b. Jacob, 158
Ashkenazic Jews: German as spoken by, 120; Habsburg rulers contrasting Sefardic Jews and, 247n83; Homberg in communities of, 109; and Italian Jews, 6, 214f; Levi consulting on marriage with, 184; Morpurgo on state of culture of, 124; in Triestine Jewish community, 18, 23, 237n54; Triestine Jews transmitting ideas of to Italy, 120; in Vienna, 57; Wessely on insularity of, 121
Assembly, 22
Assembly of Notables (Napoleonic), 208
Assimilation, forced, 204, 206
Azulai, Hayyim Joseph David: on Formiggini, 157; and kosher meat in

Trieste, 165; Abram Eliezer Levi as student of, 164, 277n42; on Marco Levi, 31; in Luzzatto-Pardo affair, 184, 284n42

Bankruptcy, 53–54, 62
Baptism of Jewish children: Brigido warning against, 225; in Joseph II's Toleration proposals, 81, 85, 87, 209, 254n65; legislation of 1787 on, 139, 254n65; in Privilege of 1771, 58–59; Tuscan legislation on, 62
Baron, Salo W., 4, 6, 202, 214, 220, 291n51
Barzilay, Isaac E., 270n81
Bassan, Israel Benjamin, 124, 126, 130, 132, 160
Beales, Derek, 248n88
Bellusco, Antonio, 101, 218
Benedictine nuns, 99
Berlin: decentering regarding Haskalah, 6; Jewish schools in, 111; Jews of Trieste in contact with, 102, 133; Triestine Jewry compared with that of, 199
Berlin, Isaiah, 291n60
Bernardini, Paolo, 233n16, 289n16, 291n61
Bertinoro, Obadiah, 106, 126
Bet Yosef (Karo), 106, 113
Birtsch, Günter, 232n12
Biur (Mendelssohn), 191
Blanning, T. C. W., 249n4
Blümegen, Heinrich Cajetan, 35–37, 68, 86, 220
Bne Zion (Homberg), 263n84
Bohemia: Hebrew press in, 69; Jewish privileges reconfirmed in, 92; judicial autonomy in, 51; normal schooling for Jews in, 100; restricting number of Jews in, 60; Toleration policy in, 71f, 89, 221
Bohemian-Austrian Court Chancellery (*Böhmische-Österreichische Hofkanzlei*): Blümegen as head of, 35; on military conscription of Jews, 149; on Protestant worship in Trieste, 66–67; on reports on May 1781 proposals, 83–84, 86–88; Trieste administered by, 12; Trieste ghetto abolished by, 140
Bolaffio, G. V., 32
Bolaffio, Marco, 239n88
Bonfil, Robert, 131, 148
Books, prohibition of foreign, 69, 84, 86
Bordeaux: Azulai on, 165; baptism of Jewish children in, 59; Emancipation in, 82, 222; Jewish merchants in, 3f, 61, 199, 202, 211; Trieste compared with, 199
Borgo Teresiano, 12, 26–27, 142
Borsa dei Mercanti (*Borsa Mercantile*; Mercantile Exchange): Council of, 91, 255n78; establishment of, 13, 33; Jews in, 32f, 77, 199, 202, 239n88; Jews in leadership of, 32–39, 85–89, 91, 218, 290n42; Joseph II's language policy opposed by, 22, 97; new building of, 32; political rights derived from, 201–2; reorganization of 1779–80, 33–39
Braude, Benjamin, 232n8
Brazil, 29
Breuer, Edward, 264n2
Brigido, Pompeo di: on abolition of the ghetto, 140f; on baptism of Jewish children, 225; as governor of Trieste, 263n94; on *Scuola Pia Normale sive Talmud Torà*, 116; on Tedesco's proposal on the rabbinate, 163; on treatment of Jewish prisoners, 153
Bukovina, 69
Business ethics and practices, 53–54, 62, 74–75, 82

Calimani, Simhah (Simone) b. Abraham, 260n51; *Esame ad un giovane israelita istruito nella sua religione*, 106f, 113f, 260n54, 267n37; as role model for Enlightenment supporters, 132; on Wessely, 126
Calvinists, 14, 66
Cameralism, 2, 42f, 62, 65, 69, 92
Camondo, Abram, 22, 31
Camondo, Haim (Vita), 31
Camondo, Isach, 22, 31
Capi: in abolition of the ghetto, 141, 143–47; children at *Scuola Pia Normale sive Talmud Torà*, 111; clandestine marriages prohibited by, 184, 194–95; Frizzi-Morschene marriage opposed by, 186f; functions of, 22–23, 51; in Gattegno case, 159, 166; immigration as concern of, 23–26; Jewish law enforced by, 155–56, 159; on Jews living outside the ghetto, 27, 140; on military conscription of Jews, 152; on Sabbath observance, 166–67; on shaving during festivals, 169; Statute of 1771 on, 51–52; on Tedesco's proposal on

the rabbinate, 163; and Toleration proposal of May 1781, 76, 83; watching out for scandals, 171; wealthy merchants serving as, 31
Capriles, Jacob b. Barukh, 23, 156–57, 160, 274n5
Capuano, Ignazio de, 220
Cardoso, Isaac, 147–48
Cases, Israel Gedaliah, 132
Castello, Abraham Isaac, 125, 132, 266n23
Castiglioni, Vittorio, 161f, 259n46
Castro, Orobio de, 253n63
Catechisms, 107, 261n55
Catherine the Great, 7, 246n60, 290n40
Catholicism, reform, 2, 42–43, 65
Cattaruzza, Marina, 222
Censorship, 69
Centralization, 8, 12, 203–9
Chamber of Insurance, 32
Charles VI: on baptism of Jewish children, 58; maritime commercial ambitions of, 11; merchants invited to Trieste by, 13, 56; Trieste made free port by, 3
Cheese, 166
Civil equality, *see* Equality
Civil improvement: in discourse about Jews, 48, 70, 73–74, 89, 210–11, 243n30; Enlightenment ideology and absolutist centralization in, 3; as evolutionary, 8; as Joseph II's intention, 87, 204, 216, 221; rights granted in exchange for, 211
Civil inclusion, 198–225; decentering Paris regarding, 6; defined, 223; and Joseph II's Toleration policy, 67–68, 71–72, 90; mercantilism and raison d'etat in, 2–3, 62, 202; rationalist universalist norms in, 5
Civil marriage: as contract rather than sacrament, 194; in France, 280n1; in Frizzi-Morschene affair, 185–92; Habsburgs introducing, 174f; and Luzzatto-Pardo affair, 180
Civil toleration: centralization entailed by, 204; Enlightenment ideologies and absolutist centralization in, 3; and Haskalah, 214; Joseph II on, 65; Maria Theresa as opposed to, 41f, 63; new rights and duties in 1780s, 138–54; as a norm, 203; parity for Jews as consequence of, 198–99; reforming absolutism and, 202–9; term as not used for Jews, 70. *See also* Toleration edicts
Clandestine baptism, *see* Baptism of Jewish children
Coen, Israel, 253n63
Coen Mondovi, Samuel, 167, 170
Cohabitation, 192
Cologna, Abraham Vita (Hai) de, 277n40
Cologna, Angelo (Mordecai) Isach, 163, 169, 187f, 277n40
Commerce: *Borgo Teresiano* as center of, 12; fostering of Trieste's, 13; fraternity as forged by, 18; Habsburg maritime ambitions, 11; Jewish aptitude for, 199; Jews in, 28–29, 62; in Privilege of 1771, 46; Ricci on commercial potential of Jews, 14; *Scuola Pia Normale sive Talmud Torà* courses in, 114; in Triestine Jews' petitions on May 1781 proposals, 80f; Triestine rhythm set by, 199. *See also* Merchants
Commercial Intendancy, 12
Communal records, 22, 96f, 160, 162
Communal regulation, Jewish, *see* Jewish communal regulation
Commune of Trieste: elementary schools set up by, 99; free port as outside jurisdiction of, 12; as irrelevant to merchants, 201f; patriciate's power declining with erosion of, 16; relations with Jews, 19–20
Confessionalization, 203
Consanguinity, 32, 176, 282
Consiglio de Patrizi, 217
Consulta Generale, 23
Consulta Ristretta, 23, 50
Conversion to Christianity: for land ownership, 72, 75; pressures for, 20, 46, 58–59; Triestine Jews' reaction to, 224–25. *See also* Baptism of Jewish children
Corinaldi, David Hayyim b. Rabbi Judah Moses, 23, 156, 274n4
Corpo nazionale (nazione), 14, 201, 217, 288n7
Corporations: absolutist state bringing under control, 92, 203; in Habsburg enactments, 49; Jews of Trieste organizing as, 22–23; modern democracies eliminating, 219; *nazione*, 14, 201, 217, 288n7; privileges and equalities in absolutist-corporate state, 216–23; Zinzendorf on, 78–79.

See also Jewish community of Trieste as formal organization
Counter-Reformation, 41
Court Chancellery, *see* Bohemian-Austrian Court Chancellery
Court Commerce Council, 12, 47, 51, 58, 62
Court Education Commission, 98
Court Jew privileges: as anachronistic by 1771, 63; port Jew status amalgamated with, 94, 198f; and Privilege of 1771, 45, 47–50 *passim*; in sixteenth and seventeenth centuries, 19, 47
Cracovia, Abraham Hayyim b. Menachem, 126
Cracovia, Jacob Menahem, 276n21
Crafts, 70, 72, 77
Crypto-Jews, 3f, 61
Curiel, David Abram qm Memo, 31, 255n78
Curiel, Jacob, 255n78
Curiel, Memo, 22, 31
Cusin family, 22
Customs barriers, 13

Da Costa, Uriel, 190
Daniele, David, 18
Danon, Jacob, 127
D'Arco, Giovanni Battista Gherardo, 89, 146, 254n73
Dazio corporale, 28, 46, 60, 85, 87
Declaration of the Rights of Man and the Citizen, 221
De Coletti, Giuseppe, 223–24
De Felice, Renzo, 222
De' Giuliani, Antonio, 16f
Del Bianco Cotrozzi, Maddalena, 233n16
Della influenza del ghetto nello stato (D'Arco), 89, 146
Delmedigo, Joseph, 133
Desacralization, 194
Dessau, 135
Dietary laws, *see* Kosher food
Difesa contro gli attacchi fatta alla Nazione Ebrea (Frizzi), 146
Dinaburg (Dinur), B., 214
Discorso (Morpurgo), 123f, 254n76, 261n57
Dispensations, sovereign, 221–22, 223
Dissertazione di polizia medica sul Pentateuco (Frizzi), 286n67, 286n68, 287n71
Distinguishing signs for Jews, 20, 47, 60, 63, 73, 79, 243n23

Distretto Camerale, 12, 26–27, 142
Diversity, 2, 5, 15–18, 58, 199, 201f, 204, 213, 215
Divorce: in Frizzi-Morschene affair, 185–86; in Luzzatto-Pardo affair, 177–83; state jurisdiction over, 175, 176
Divrei shalom ve-emet (Wessely), 119f, 122ff, 127–31, 264n3
Dohm, Christian Wilhelm von, 70, 210f, 243n30

Economic utility, *see* Utility
Education: General School Ordinance, 52, 98–99; in Josephinian program, 205; rabbi's role in, 159; Statute of 1771 on, 52–53; in Toleration edict for Jews, 68–69; Torah and non-Torah studies in Jewish, 119, 125–31. *See also* Elementary education; Higher education
Ein mishpat (Wessely), 124, 127, 264n3
Elementary education: curriculum, 99; *depositori di creaturi*, 112; Joseph II's reforms, 53, 101–2, 108; Maria Theresa's reforms, 98–101; private schools, 99–100, 104, 111f. *See also* Normal schools
Elopement, 179
Emancipation: Baron on, 6, 202, 220; contextualizing, 6; decentering Paris regarding, 6; Joseph II's Toleration policy contrasted with French, 7, 70, 82, 196, 216–23
Emanuel of Rome, 133
Endelman, Todd, 6, 215
England, 217
Enlightened absolutism: encroaching on marriage, 194, 196; and enlightened despotism, 248n3; Joseph II as exemplifying, 5, 64–65; and Maria Theresa, 42, 232n12
Enlightenment, the, 5; antisemitism in, 210, 289n27; classicist trend of, 191; as cultural and political force, 5; Habsburg officials influenced by, 42f; on the Jews, 69–70, 81–82, 210–13; Joseph II's affinity with, 65, 249n4; and reforming absolutism, 232n12; on religious toleration, 210; and *Scuola Pia Normale sive Talmud Torà*, 117; Trieste as receptive to, 3, 198, 214. *See also* Haskalah
Equality: in *Borsa* leadership debate, 34–35, 37; civil toleration providing for Jews,

198–99; Enlightenment ideologies and absolutist centralization in, 3; in Joseph II's Toleration, 7, 70–2, 82, 90, 196, 206, 216–23; Privilege of 1771 on parity with other subjects, 46, 49, 75; Triestine Jewish leaders claiming, 180; in Zinzendorf's report on May 1781 proposals, 76–77, 218–19
Eruv, 167
Esame ad un giovane israelita istruito nella sua religione (Calimani), 106f, 113f, 260n54, 267n37
Ethics, *see* Morality
Ettinger, Shmuel, 4, 202
Euchel, Isaac, 134
Evans, R. J. W., 203, 250n18
Excommunication, 165, 277n48

Fano, Alessandro, 239n90
Feiner, Shmuel, 6
Felbiger, Johann Ignaz, 98
Ferdinand II, 47
Ferdinand III, 47, 77
Ferrara, 132
Festivals: communal regulation of, 164, 166–70; Privilege of 1771 on, 46; shaving on intermediate days of, 157–58, 168–70, 173
Finzi, Isach Raffael, 163, 188, 277n41
Fiume, 11
Fleckeles, Eleazar, 281n12
Florence, 271n9
Florence Reform hoax of 1796, 134
Forced assimilation, 204, 206
Forced migration, 42
Foreign books, prohibition of, 69, 84, 86
Formiggini, Isach b. Rabbi Moses, 157–60; death of, 160; in Gattegno case, 159, 166; and Habsburg Marriage Patent, 176; as halakhist, 157, 164; and letter on military conscription, 151; as rabbi in Trieste, 23, 52, 158, 244n40; on Sabbath observance, 166–68; as *Scuola Pia Normale sive Talmud Torà* supervisor, 103, 108, 158; on shaving during festivals, 157–58, 169f; as teacher, 105; as traditionalist, 158; and Wessely, 123, 124, 125–26, 128
Francis II, 93, 153, 211
Frankfurt, 111
Fraterna di Talmud Torà, ò sia Errudimento Religiosa (Society for Torah Study), 23, 31, 157, 239n84, 257n21
Fraterna Ghemilut Hazadìm, ò sia della Misericordia (Society for Deeds of Loving-kindness), 23, 160
Frederick the Great, 7
Free Port Patents: as drawing no distinction between Gentiles and Jews, 28; ghettoization mitigated by, 20; and Privilege of 1771, 45–50 *passim*; and Statute of 1771, 59; Toleration legislation compared with, 94, 153f; Trieste made free port by, 3, 11
French Revolution, 7, 70, 196, 219, 222, 290n50
Frizzi, Anna (Nina), 189, 285n64
Frizzi, Benedetto (Ben Zion Rafael ha-Kohen): and D'Arco, 146, 254n73; death of, 189, 286n66; *Difesa contro gli attacchi fatta alla Nazione Ebrea*, 146; *Dissertazione di polizia medica sul Pentateuco*, 286n67, 286n68, 287n71; education and writings of, 284n45; on Joseph II's Toleration legislation, 256n2; as *kohen*, 177, 185f, 190f; in Mantua, 28, 192, 286n69; marriage to Relle Morschene, 170, 176–77, 185–97; Mosaism of, 185–86, 190–91, 284n50, 287n71; as the "new Spinoza," 191; on normal-schooling for Jews, 131; *Petah einayim*, 192, 287n71; reception in Trieste, 28, 238n74

Galicia: Habsburgs acquire, 8; Homberg in, 109, 116; Jewish juridical autonomy in, 51; Jews of, 8, 60; military conscription of Jews in, 149; poor Jews in, 69; Toleration edicts for, 71, 152–53, 273n61
Galligo, Joseph, 103, 259n40
Gattegno, David, 159, 166
Gattegno, Vita (Caliman), 27
Gazzetta del mondo, 224
Gebler, Tobias Philipp, 140, 253n59
General Assembly, 23
General School Ordinance of 1774, 52, 98–99
German language: Jews of Trieste and, 236n48; Joseph II's policy on, 22, 96–97, 207; schools teaching, 52, 95, 99, 108, 112; in *Scuola Pia Normale sive Talmud Torà*, 105, 107, 109, 113; Statute of 1771 on, 96

Ghetto of Trieste: abolition of, 20, 139–48, 206, 218; establishment of, 19–20, 235n38; halakhic implications of abolition, 141, 166–67; Jews living beyond, 20, 26–27, 47, 60, 84, 140; regime of, 20
Ghirondi, Mordecai Samuel, 157, 161
Ghisalberti, Carlo, 289n13
"Gnora Luna," 143
Gorizia: ghetto of, 139; Homberg in, 109, 261n59; land ownership by Jews in, 93; Morpurgo's Hebrew literature journal project, 124; nighttime patrol in, 141, 147; normal schooling for Jews in, 84, 100–101; thanksgiving for Toleration edicts, 254n76; and Toleration edict for Galicia, 152–53
Gorizia-Gradisca: Jews as eligible for doctoral degree in, 102; military conscription in, 149, 273n56; real property ownership by Jews in, 247n77; reconfirmation of privileges in, 93; restricting numbers of Jews, 60; Toleration proposals for, 71; Trieste as example for, 94, 255n81
Gradisca, 58, 152–53, 254n76
Graetz, Heinrich, 68, 204, 249n17, 259n40, 265n11
Greek Orthodoxy, 14, 43, 51, 66f, 94, 217
Greeks, 32, 33, 218
Grégoire, Henri, 210f

Habsburg Monarchy: as buffer between western and eastern Europe, 2; changing conception of law in, 92; ecclesiastical reform in, 43; education policy, 52–53, 98–102; Ferdinand II, 47; Ferdinand III, 47, 77; Francis II, 93, 153; free-ports policy, 11, 15, 41; Galicia acquired by, 8; Germanic and Italian aspects in, 2; Leopold I, 47–48; map, xv; maritime commercial ambitions, 11; Marriage Patent, 175–77, 192–97; military conscription instituted by, 149; privileges granted to Jews in Trieste, 18–19; reforming absolutism in, 7–8; religious toleration in, 241n8; Trieste acquired by, 10. *See also* Charles VI; Joseph II; Leopold II; Maria Theresa
Haham Zevi (Zevi Hirsch b. Jacob Ashkenazi), 158
Halakhah: in Calimani's catechism, 107; *Capi* in enforcement of, 155–56; communal regulation of public piety, 164–73; *eruv*, 167; in Frizzi-Morschene affair, 185–92; and Habsburg marriage reform, 174, 175–76, 193–96; in Luzzatto-Pardo affair, 177–84; and military conscription, 150–51, 152; rabbis in enforcement of, 156–59, 161f, 164; in *Scuola Pia Normale sive Talmud Torà* curriculum, 106, 108. *See also* Festivals; Kosher food; Sabbath observance
Hamburg, 3f, 16
Haskalah: on the Bible, 191; contextualizing, 6, 215–16; decentering Berlin regarding, 6; Frizzi as *maskil*, 190–91; internalizing need for Jewish self-improvement, 210; Italian campaign for, 124–33; Italian Jewish acculturation compared with, 136–37; Jews of Trieste and the, 118–37, 213–16; Jews of Trieste in contact with Berlin, 102; maskilim on Italian Jews, 133–34; Trieste as receptive to, 3. *See also* Enlightenment, the
Hatam Sofer, 164, 184, 277n45, 284n42
Hatzfeld, Karl Friedrich, 88
Hauptschule, 98
Head toll, 28, 46, 60, 85, 87
Hebrew language: Bohemian press for, 69; among Italian Jews, 131, 133–34; Jews of Trieste using, 22, 96; schools teaching, 52, 100, 112; at *Scuola Pia Normale sive Talmud Torà*, 106–7, 113
Heller, Yom Tov Lipmann, 106
Herem ha-yishuv, 24
Herrera, Abraham, 129
Hertzberg, Arthur, 289n27
Hierschel, Abram, 32
Hierschel, Filippo, 239n82
Hierschel, Joachim, 22, 27, 31, 120, 133, 245n58
Higher education: doctoral degrees permitted to Jews, 84, 101, 132, 153; Jews admitted to, 69; University of Padua, 19, 84, 132, 157
Hofkommerzienrath, 12, 47, 51, 58, 62
Hohenwart, Sigismond, 162, 183, 211, 276n33
Homberg, Herz: *Bne Zion*, 263n84; in Italy, 133, 261n59; and Morpurgo's proposed Hebrew journal, 124; as *Scuola Pia Normale sive Talmud Torà* teacher, 109, 115f, 214; and Segre, 251n37

Huguenots, 14
Humanity: Enlightenment view of, 5, 210; of Jews, 69, 213; morality and utility linked to, 211–13; rights exchanged for assumed humanity of Jews of Trieste, 211–12
Humboldt, Wilhelm von, 211
Hungary, 43, 60, 71, 118, 149

Ibn Ezra, Abraham, 106, 132
"Iggeret" (Morpurgo), 124, 129, 266n23
Indagine di qual sia tra i morali mali il peggiori: Accademico garreggiamento scolastico (Tedesco), 40, 114, 162, 240n119
Inner Austrian Commerce Commission, 13
Insurance industry, 17, 29, 32
Israel, Hayyim Abraham, 126, 131
Israel, Jonathan, 202, 231n7
Israel Vengée (Castro), 253n63
Italian Jews: acculturation of, 131–32, 136–37, 200, 215; and Ashkenazic Jews, 6, 214f; Central European view of, 133–34; "first emancipation" for, 222; Haskalah as continuous with traditions of, 213–16; and Sefardic Jews, 6, 215, 285n84; Wessely on, 120, 122, 200. *See also* Jews of Trieste
Italian language: Jews of Trieste using, 22, 77, 96–97, 99, 200, 207, 212, 236n47; schools teaching, 52, 112; at *Scuola Pia Normale sive Talmud Torà*, 107f, 113; Wessely on Italian Jews speaking, 120
Italy: Ancona, 132, 267n37; as crossroad between different Jewries, 2; Ferrara, 132; Lombardy, 60, 71, 89, 247n77; map, *xv*; Modena, 267n40; Pisa, 63, 122; Reggio, 132; Rome, 148; Tuscany, 61f, 247n80; Verona, 122, 147–48. *See also* Italian Jews; Livorno; Mantua; Trieste; Venice

Jesuits, 98, 99
Jewish communal regulation: Habsburg marriage reforms as challenge to, 174–97; of public piety, 164–73; rabbis in, 23; *Regolamento interno religioso politico, ed economico* of 1783, 138–39, 158ff; in Triestine Jews' petitions on May 1781 Toleration proposals, 81; Zinzendorf on, 85. *See also* Jewish community of Trieste as formal organization

Jewish community of Trieste as formal organization: elections, 22, 54; establishment of, 22–23; juridical autonomy, 32, 51–52, 61, 138, 175, 270n2; self-perception as civil-religious entity, 56–58, 155f, 174–75; size at end of eighteenth century, 20; as state agency, 156; under Statute of 1746, 22–23, 43f; under Statute of 1771, 50–53; as *Università degli Ebrei* in Trieste, 20, 155. *See also* Capi; Jewish communal regulation
Jewish law, *see* Halakhah
Jews: changing role in early modern Europe, 2–3; civil and religious distinguished by, 208–9; commercial aptitude of, 199; doctoral degrees permitted to, 84, 101, 132, 153; Enlightenment antisemitism, 210, 289n27; Enlightenment's significance for, 5; Enlightenment view of, 69, 81–82, 210–13; as faring best in new centers, 202; of Galicia, 8, 60, 69, 149, 152–53, 273n61; "improvement" in discourse about, 48, 70, 74, 89, 210–11, 243n30; invited Jews, 61; Italy as crossroad between different Jewries, 2; *Judenordnung* of 1754, 93; *Judenordnung* of 1776, 278n48; Maria Theresa on, 42, 72; military conscription of, 139, 148–52; normal-schooling for, 84, 100–102; Portuguese Jews, 3, 61f; raison d'état and mercantilism in inclusion of, 3; Ricci on commercial potential of, 14; right of settlement controlled by, 24; separateness of, 146–47; stereotypes about, 39; Toleration edict for, 67–72; Toleration's effect on, 4–5, 95. *See also* Ashkenazic Jews; Italian Jews; Jews of Trieste; Port Jews; Sefardic Jews
Jews of Trieste: in *Borsa* leadership, 32–39, 85–89, 91, 218, 290n42; census of 1748, 29; census of 1820, 29, *30*; central European ideas transmitted to Italy by, 120; civic identity and politics of, 223–25; confraternities of, 23; court resolution of December 19, 1781, 88; distinguishing signs or badges for, 20, 47, 60, 63, 73, 79, 243n23; economic activities of, 28–32; economic responsibilities of leadership of, 40, 53–54; as an elite, 200; exceptionally favorable status of, 59–63, 90–94,

152–54, 204, 220; first evidence of, 18, 235n33; before the free port, 18–20; Frizzi-Morschene affair, 170, 176–77, 185–97; gratitude expressed for Toleration, 90, 254n76; on Habsburg Marriage Patent, 176–77, 281n8; and the Haskalah, 118–37, 213–16; as honorary Sefardim, 62; immigration in growth of, 2–3, 15–16, 21–26; Italian origin of most, 22; languages used by, 96–97, 200; legal status of, 41–63, 198–99, 220; Luzzatto-Pardo affair, 170, 176, 177–84, 192–97; on military conscription of Jews, 149–52; names, 97–98; official response to petitions on May 1781 proposals, 83–90; petitions regarding Toleration proposals of May 1781, 79–83; population growth, 20–21, 21, 28–32, 232n7; privileges in 16th and 17th centuries, 18,–19, 47–48; Privilege of 1771, 45–50; privileges and equalities for, 216–23; rabbis of, 23, 156–64; rights in exchange for utility of, 211–13; and Statute of 1771, 50–59; synagogues of, 23, 161, 237n54; Theresian diplomas of 1771, 44–45; on "tolerated" versus "invited," 56–57, 61, 223; violence against, 20, 236n39; wealthy and prominent families, 22, 31; Wessely's appeal to, 119–23; Zinzendorf on May 1781 proposals, 73–79. *See also* Ghetto of Trieste; Jewish community of Trieste as formal organization; *Scuola Pia Normale sive Talmud Torà*

Jona, Abraham, 281n12

Joseph II: as absolutist state-builder, 64; changing conception of law in reign of, 92; continuity of policies with Maria Theresa's, 8, 65, 203–4, 205, 94, 241n8, 248n2; educational initiative, 53, 101–2, 108; enlightened absolutism of, 5, 64–65; German language policy, 22, 96–97, 207; Jewish historiographical views of, 7, 68, 249n16, 249n17, 289n15; and Maria Theresa on religious toleration, 41–42, 241n8; on military conscription for Jews, 149; Protestant worship approved by, 43; reforming absolutism of, 7–8; on religious toleration, 65–66; Tedesco's elegy on, 162, 207; Toleration policy of, 64–94; utilitarianism of, 65–66, 68–69, 89. *See also* Toleration edicts

Judenordnung of 1754, 93
Judenordnung of 1776, 278n48
Juridical autonomy, 32, 51–52, 61, 138, 175, 270n2

Kabbalah, 124, 129
Kahal kelali, 23
Kalai, Samuel b. Moses, 158
Kandler, Pietro, 140, 288n7
Karniel, Joseph, 203, 247n77, 249n10, 251n31
Karo, Joseph, 106, 113, 182
Kashrut, *see* Kosher food
Katz, Jacob, 4, 282n31, 289n21
Kaunitz-Rietberg, Wenzel Anton von, 42, 67, 247n77, 250n20
Kehillah kedoshah, 155f, 174, 194
Kesef Mishneh (Karo), 113
Kimhi, David, 106, 113
Klingenstein, Grete: on confessional pattern under Maria Theresa, 43; on continuity of Maria Theresa and Joseph II, 203, 241n8, 248n2; on Habsburg Monarchy as evolutionary paradigm, 8; on Maria Theresa as reformer, 241n7; and Zinzendorf's diaries, 240n96
Kohen, Ishmael b. Abraham, 127f, 131, 281n12
Kohen, Joel, 239n90
Kohen, Philippo (Filippo), 22, 31, 111, 255n78
Kosher food: communal regulation of, 23, 164, 165–66; Gattegno case, 159, 166; for Jewish prisoners, 153, 209; Levi on ritual slaughter in Trieste, 165–66, 170–71; for soldiers, 152; Ventura case, 168

Labrosse, Joseph, 18
Lampronti, Isaac, 132, 157, 275n9
Landau, Ezekiel: on Habsburg Marriage Patent, 175–76; on military conscription of Jews, 149; on normal school in Prague, 118; on shaving during festivals, 158, 168, 275n9; on Wessely's *Divrei shalom ve-emet*, 119
Land ownership: conversion to Christianity required for Jewish, 72, 75; by Gorizia Jews, 93; Joseph II offering to Christians but not Jews, 70; by Triestine Jews, 77, 80f, 85, 87. *See also* Real property ownership
Language, 96–97; European languages for

Index 329

Torah scholars, 131; in Josephinian program, 205; in schools, 99; in Toleration edict for Jews, 68, 74, 77. *See also* German language; Hebrew language; Italian language
Law: changing conception of in eighteenth century, 92; civil, 92, 153, 178–79; natural, 2, 105, 189, 221
Law, Jewish, *see* Halakhah
Leibmaut, 28, 46, 60, 85, 87
Lekah tov (Yagel), 261n55
Leopold I, 47–48
Leopold II: civil rights for Jews extended by, 153; Jews asking reconfirmation of privileges from, 93; on marriage between relatives, 176; Tedesco's elegy for, 162, 207; Toleration edict in Belgium rescinded by, 97, 221; toleration patent for Mantua, 273n61
Levi, Abram Eliezer b. Rabbi Zevi, 163–64; alarm over behavior in Trieste, 172–73, 280n98; clandestine marriages prohibited by, 184; on the eruv, 167; on Gentiles working for Jews on the Sabbath, 168; Orthodoxy of, 164, 277n45; on ritual slaughter in Trieste, 165–66, 170–71; on shaving during festivals, 169; as student of Azulai, 163–64, 277n42
Levi, Grassin (Gherson) di Moise, 239n90
Levi, Grassin Vita, 22, 31, 33
Levi, Grassin Vita di Caliman: becomes head of Levi family, 142; as Borsa deputy, 32, 91, 255n78; and *Scuola Pia Normale sive Talmud Torà*, 103, 111; on Tedesco's ethical drama, 162; wealth of, 31
Levi, Israel, 33
Levi, Jacob Benjamin, 167
Levi, Leone, 47
Levi, Marco: as *Borsa* member, 239n88; and *Borsa* reorganization, 33–36, 38f, 218; as court agent, 31; death of, 142; ghetto abolition opposed by, 141–48, 206, 218; Jewish educational activities, 31, 110, 239n84; on religion as "almost tottering," 144, 170; and Segre, 101; Viennese ties of, 120, 133; wealth of, 31
Levi, Moise, 151
Levi family, 18
Lewin-Berlin, Saul, 133f
Lindau, Barukh, 113

Livorno: conversion regulation in, 59; Euchel on Jews of, 134; favorable status of Jews in, 6, 61–62; ghetto walls as absent in, 145; head toll exemption for Jews in, 46; Jewish education in, 267n40; Jewish merchants in, 3f, 199; Jewish seat on municipal council, 88, 91, 290n42; marriage practices in, 182; Peter Leopold, 59, 290n40, 291n62; Triestine governorship modeled on, 12, 61–62, 199; Wessely appeals to Jews of, 122
Lombardy, 60, 71, 89, 247n77
London, 3, 4, 61, 199
London Stock Exchange, 88, 202, 254n68
Lowenstein, Steven, 6, 215
Lower Austria: housing restrictions abolished, 139; Jewish business practices in, 62; Toleration edict for, 71, 73, 93, 250n27
Lutherans, 14, 42, 66
Luzzatti, Fratelli qm David, 239n88
Luzzatto, Benedetto Vita, 26
Luzzatto, Corona: marriage to Jacob Pardo, 170, 176, 177–84, 192–97; marriage to second man, 178, 183, 282n18
Luzzatto, David, 22
Luzzatto, Elia Moise: as *Capo*, 177, 281n13; daughter's marriage to Pardo, 176, 177–84, 193, 195, 283n37; and Habsburg Marriage Patent, 176; and letter on military conscription, 151; on state within a state, 179, 252n47, 282n23
Luzzatto, Giuseppe Moise, 133
Luzzatto, Hezekiah, 31, 165
Luzzatto, Isaac, 161, 235n27
Luzzatto, Isach, 158, 160, 163
Luzzatto, Lucio, 185
Luzzatto, Marco Mordecai, 105, 260n49
Luzzatto, Moise David, 239n88
Luzzatto, Moses Hayyim, 113, 125
Luzzatto, Raffael, 105, 112, 260n49
Luzzatto, Samuel David: on Cologna, 163; family comes to Trieste, 21; on Frizzi, 192; on Italian and Ashkenazic Jews, 136–37; on Joseph II and Leopold II, 207; on kosher meat in Trieste, 165; on Rabbi Levi, 164; on poor Jews, 31; on *Scuola Pia Normale sive Talmud Torà*, 135–36; and Raffael Segre, 251n37, 258n36
Luzzatto, Simone, 14

Luzzatto Voghera, Gadi, 233n16
Lvov, 149

Magris, Claudio, 2
Maimonides, Moses: on marriage, 182, 186; *Mishneh Torah*, 100, 106, 113, 284n50, 285n52; as model for Morpurgo and Formiggini, 125; as role model for Enlightenment, 132; in *Scuola Pia Normale sive Talmud Torà* curriculum, 106, 113; *Sefer ha-ahavah*, 113; women teaching from, 100
Mainati, Giuseppe, 161f
Mantua: Frizzi in, 28, 192, 286n69; ghetto of, 139; Jewish school curriculum in, 108, 118, 132, 261n56, 264n1, 267n40; Jewish separatism charged in, 146; Jews in Chamber of Commerce, 254n68; Jews' status in, 247n77; marriage practices in, 182; and military conscription of Jews, 149–51; real property ownership by Jews, 255n86; and *Regolamento interno religioso politico, ed economico*, 270n2; Toleration patent for, 273n61; Trieste as not serving as example for, 94, 153; violence against Jews in, 143, 147; Wessely appeals to Jews of, 122
Manufacturing, 17, 29, 46, 75, 77
Maria Theresa: as absolutist state-builder, 64; administrative reorganization by, 11; on baptism of Jewish children, 58; changing conception of law in reign of, 92; confessional pattern in reign of, 43; continuity of policies with Joseph II's, 8, 65, 94, 203–4, 205, 241n8, 248n2; diplomas of 1771, 44–45; education reforms, 98–101; on Jews, 42, 72; *pietas austriaca* ideal of, 41, 42; Privilege of 1771, 28, 45–50; as reforming not enlightened absolutist, 42, 232n12; religious toleration for merchants, 14–15, 234n14; religious toleration opposed by, 41–44, 63, 241n8, 248n88; Statute of 1771, 50–59
Marini, Shabbetai, 132
Marriage, 174–97; consanguinity dispensations, 32, 176, 282; Frizzi-Morschene affair, 170, 176–77, 185–92; Habsburg Marriage Patent, 175–77, 192–97; limits on number of Jewish, 60, 281n8; Napoleon's laws on, 175, 280n1; normal-school attendance as requirement for, 114, 176, 263n84; Pardo-Luzzatto affair, 170, 176, 177–84; parties involved in, 287n82; a rabbi as required for, 160, 287n78; as social institution, 193–94; state and community contesting, 192–97, 205, 207–9, 283n36; Triestine Jews prohibit clandestine, 184, 194–95. *See also* Civil marriage
Marriage tax, 77
Maskilim, *see* Haskalah
Maternini Zotta, Maria Fausta, 243n28
Matzot, 166, 170
Meassef, Ha-, 124, 133, 151
Medrash Lecah tov study society, 164
Melton, James Van Horn, 232n12
Menassah ben Israel, 14
Mendelssohn, Moses: *Biur*, 191; Formiggini on, 125; on improvement for Jews, 211, 243n30; Morpurgo's letter to, 123; response to letter from Trieste, 121–22; Triestine Jews writing to, 103, 107, 119–20, 259n40; Zinzendorf and, 102, 133
Menorat ha-meor (Aboab), 113
Mentore perfetto dei negozianti, Il (Metrà), 17
Mercantile Exchange, *see* Borsa dei Mercanti
Mercantilism: defined, 231n7; in Habsburg policy, 11; and Jewish inclusion, 3, 62, 202; mercantilist confessionalization, 203
Merchants: bureaucrats allying with, 16; the Commune as irrelevant to Triestine, 201f; concord among diverse, 17–18; favorable status of Triestine, 198; Maria Theresa's religious toleration policy for, 14–15, 234n14; suspicions regarding, 16; Trieste creating class of, 13–14. *See also* Borsa dei Mercanti
Mesillat yesharim (Luzzatto), 113
Metrà, Andrea, 17, 32
Military conscription, 139, 148–52
Mishneh Torah (Maimonides), 100, 106, 113, 284n50, 285n52
Modena, 267n40
Modena, Leone, 131
Modesti, Valentinus, 47, 55
Monte de pietà, 19
Montesquieu, 185, 284n50
Morality: business ethics and practices, 53–54, 62, 74–75, 82; economic utility

linked to, 40, 62, 115, 212–13; humanity as linked to, 211; as rabbinical concern, 159–60; schools teaching, 99, 102; in *Scuola Pia Normale sive Talmud Torà* curriculum, 104–7, 114–15, 206; in Wessely's theory of education, 128
Moravia, 60, 71, 93, 221, 247n76
Moré, Charles-Albert Comte de, 10, 17–18
Morpurgo, Abraham b. Joseph, 151
Morpurgo, Elia: *Discorso*, 123f, 254n76, 261n57; on education for Jews, 261n57; on Habsburg Northern Italy's location, 2; Hebrew literature journal project, 124, 266n25; "Iggeret," 124, 129, 266n23; on Joseph II's Toleration proposals, 254n76, 256n2; on Maria Theresa, 15; on military conscription of Jews, 272n46; name change of, 256n8; publishing program of, 123, 265n18; and Wessely, 123–30 *passim*; Wessely's *Divrei* translated by, 123f, 265n20
Morpurgo, Isaac di Lucio, 104
Morpurgo, Isach, 167–68
Morpurgo, Iseppo, 33
Morpurgo, Joseph Eliezer (Giuseppe Lazzaro), 31, 161, 239n84
Morpurgo, Samson, 131f
Morpurgo, Samuel, 133
Morpurgo, Stella, 170
Morpurgo family, 22, 267n37
Morschene, Anselmo, 28, 185
Morschene, Relle (Rachel; Bella): birth and death dates of, 284n45; confession of, 188f; death of, 189, 286n66; as divorced, 185–86; marriage to Benedetto Frizzi, 170, 176–77, 185–97; as mother of Anna, 189, 285n64; pregnancy of, 189
Mussafia, Hayyim Isaac, 184, 284n42

Names: changing of Jewish, 98, 256n8, 256n10; Joseph II's 1787 order on, 22, 97–98
Napoleon, 175, 216, 208f, 280n1
Napoleonic Wars, 152
Natural law, 2, 189, 221
Navarra, Menahem (Mandolin) Emanuel, 157
Nazione, 14, 201, 217, 288n7
Neppi, Hananel, 157, 161
Neutral polity, 217, 223, 289n21

Neutral society, 183, 283n39
New Christians, 3f, 61
Nieto, David, 132
Normal schools (*Normalschule*): General School Ordinance on, 98; for Jews, 84, 100–102; private schools competing with, 99–100; regulations of 1782 for, 100; term's meaning, 257n11; in Toleration edict for Jews, 68–69, 74; Triestine Jews attending, 74, 78f, 83, 86, 101, 103, 251n37. *See also Scuola Pia Normale sive Talmud Torà*
Norsa, Isaia, 103, 160, 267n37, 276n21
Norzi (Norsa), Samuel Yedidiah b. Eleazar, 126, 129f, 267n37
Notizie del mondo, 67

O Buda, 149
Occupations: agriculture, 72, 75, 86; crafts, 70, 72, 77; of free port Jews, 29–30, 30; impediments to diversification of Jewish, 72; insurance industry, 17, 29, 32; manufacturing, 17, 29, 75, 77; public-service posts, 70; in Toleration edict for Jews, 74–75, 77, 83; of Triestine Jews before the free port, 19, 235n36. *See also* Merchants
Odessa, 199, 215
On the Civil Improvement of the Jews (Dohm), 70
Oriental Trading Company, 11
Orthodox Judaism, 164
Osservatore Triestino: on Formiggini, 157, 160; on Marco Levi's funeral, 31; on Morpurgo's name change, 256n8; on *Scuola Pia Normale sive Talmud Torà*, 116; on Tedesco's ethical drama, 114, 240n119; on Toleration climate, 223–25
Ottoman Empire, 3, 11, 13, 19
Ownership, *see* Land ownership; Real property ownership

Pacifico, Abraham b. Isaac, 126
Pacifico, Isaac, 156
Padua, University of, 19, 84, 132, 157
Panorama politico della città di Trieste (De' Giuliani), 17
Paolin, Giovanna, 243n28
Pardo, Jacob: banishment of, 178, 282n18; marriage to Corona Luzzatto, 170, 176, 177–84, 192–97

Parente, Aron, 31
Parente, Caliman, 47
Parente, Marco, 31
Parente, Salomon, 25
Parente, Ventura, 18, 47
Parente family, 22
Parity, *see* Equality
Passarowitz, Treaty of, 11
Patents, 4; Habsburg Marriage Patent, 175–77. *See also* Free Port Patents; Privileges
Patriciate: *Consiglio de Patrizi*, 217; influence as declining, 16, 89; as wary of merchants, 13, 16
Pergen, Johann Anton, 153
Petah einayim (Frizzi), 192, 287n71
Peter Leopold, 59, 290n40, 291n62
Pietas austriaca, 41, 42
Pincherle, Zerah Samson, 276n21
Pirkei Avot, 106f, 162, 241n119
Pisa, 63, 122
Pittoni, Pietro Antonio, 237n63; and *Borsa* leadership debate, 35; on consanguinity dispensations, 32, 176, 182; on foreign Jews living scandalously, 25, 170, 280n98; and German language, 256n4; on the ghetto as a humiliation, 143, 145; on Jews living outside the ghetto, 140; on mentality of Trieste, 201, 225, 288n6; and Toleration proposals of May 1781, 76
Plantation Act of 1740, 290n40
Poggibonsi, Emanuel Samuel, 283n37
Polizeiordnung, 44
Portizza di Riborgo quarter, 20, 26
Port Jews: as invited, 61; on mercantile exchanges, 202; and new opportunities for European Jews, 3–4; status amalgamated with that of court Jews in Trieste, 94, 198f; utility of, 199–200, 211. *See also* Jews of Trieste
Porto, Menahem Zion (Emanuel), 19
Porto family, 22
Portuguese Jews, 3, 61f
Prague: attempted expulsion of Jews of, 42; ghetto of, 139; military conscription of Jews in, 149, 151; modern education in, 111, 118, 135; wealthy Jews seeking improvement in status, 69
Private schools, 99–100, 104, 111f
Privilege of 1771, 44–50; as dated April 19, 45; earlier privileges reiterated in, 28; reconfirmation of, 78, 84, 87; Statute of 1771 compared with, 44–45, 57–58; Toleration edict for Jews compared with, 75, 80, 94
Privileges, 4; as costly, 44; as diminishing and weakening, 92–93; evolution in Trieste, 198–99; Jewish desire to maintain, 82–84, 93; as local and specific, 44; relation to general law, 87–88, 91–93, 180–81, 221–22; in 16th- and 17th-century Trieste, 18–19, 47–48; Toleration edicts compared with, 220–21. *See also* Court Jew privileges; Privilege of 1771
Protestants: Calvinists, 14, 66; in Habsburg lands, 43; Lutherans, 14, 42, 66; Maria Theresa on, 41–42; in Trieste, 43, 60, 66–67, 76, 94, 217
Provenzalis, 130
Prussia: Frederick the Great, 7; Habsburgs attempting to compete with, 8, 42; Jewish excommunication in, 278n48; Silesia taken by, 15
Public piety: communal regulation of, 164–73. *See also* Festivals; Kosher food; Sabbath observance
Public-service posts, 70

Rabbis: as civil functionaries, 160, 162; marriages requiring, 160, 175, 287n78; philosophical training mandated for, 160; Statute of 1771 on authority of, 159; of Trieste community, 23, 156–64. *See also by name*
Radunanza, 22
Raison d'état, 3, 202, 249n4
Rashi, 100, 106, 113, 126
Rav tuv le-vet Yisrael (Wessely), 120–21, 122, 264n3, 265n11
Real property ownership, 28, 46, 60, 77, 80f, 85, 87. *See also* Land ownership
Reform Catholicism, 2, 42–43, 65
Reforming absolutism: in action, 6–9; and civil toleration, 202–9; in Habsburg Monarchy, 7–8; of Maria Theresa, 42; *Rechtsstaat* constructed by, 221; term's utility, 5, 232n12; Trieste as fertile ground for, 3, 232n9
Reform Judaism, 134, 164, 191
Régénération, *see* Civil improvement
Reggio, 132

Reggio, Isaac Samuel, 132
Regolamento interno religioso politico, ed economico (1783), 138–39, 158ff
Regolamento per le Scuole Pie Normali degli Ebrei in Trieste, 112–13, 116, 262n79
Regole per la Direzione della Scuola Pia Normale sive Talmud Torà dell'Università degli Ebrei de Trieste, 104
Rehovot (Wessely), 264n3
Religious toleration: civil toleration and, 139; Enlightenment thinkers on, 210; in Habsburg Monarchy, 241n8; before Joseph II, 204; Joseph II on, 65–66; Maria Theresa as opposed to, 41–44, 63, 241n8, 248n88; for merchants under Maria Theresa, 14–15, 234n14; after Thirty Years' War, 241n9. *See also* Toleration edicts
Repudiation of a wife, 185–86, 284n50
Reshit limmudim (Lindau), 113
Ricci, Giuseppe Pasquale, 13–14, 55–62 *passim*, 234n11
Riduzione Generale, 23
Riduzione Particolare, 23, 50
Riflessioni politiche sopra il prospetta attuale della città di Trieste (De' Giuliani), 17
Rodrigue, Aron, 288n4
Romanelli, Samuel, 133
Romania, 29
Rome, 148
Rossi, Azariah de, 133f
Ruderman, David, 132
Russia: Catherine the Great, 7, 246n60, 290n40; Habsburgs establish commercial relations with, 13; Jews in trade with, 29; Odessa, 199, 215

Saba, Umberto, 1, 148
Sabbadini, Salvatore, 259n46
Sabbath observance: and abolition of the ghetto, 141; communal regulation of, 164, 166–68; Gentiles working for Jews on, 167–68; by prisoners, 153, 209; Privilege of 1771 on, 46; by soldiers, 151
Sanhedrin (Napoleonic), 175, 208f, 280n1
Satanov, Isaac, 133–34
Schutzbrief, 45
Scott, H., 8
Scuola matematica e nautica, 13

Scuola Pia Normale sive Talmud Torà, 102–17; curriculum of, 105–9, 113–14, 135; early history of, 109–17; enrollment at, 111; –establishment of, 95, 103; family background of pupils, 111–12; financing of, 104, 110, 207; Formiggini in establishment of, 108, 158; and Formiggini's response to Wessely, 126, 267n36; morality taught in, 104, 114–15, 206; name change, 112–13; normal and religious studies combined in, 108, 117f, 134, 214; official approval of, 115–17; opening date of, 104, 259n46; site of, 103–4; teachers, 105, 109; and Wessely's program, 108, 134–36
Scuole Pie Normali, see *Scuola Pia Normale sive Talmud Torà*
Secularization, 194
Sefardic Jews: cultural legacy of, 132; Emancipation in Bordeaux, 82, 222; Habsburg rulers contrasting Ashkenazic Jews and, 247n83; in international commerce, 62; and Italian Jews, 6, 215, 285n84; Levi consulting on marriage with, 184; in Livorno, 61; Morpurgo contrasts Ashkenazic Jews with, 124; in Triestine Jewish community, 23, 237n54; in Vienna, 246n63
Sefer ha-ahavah (Maimonides), 113
Segre, Raffael Baruch (Benedetto): as normal-school pupil, 74, 79, 83, 86, 101, 103, 251n37, 258n36; as normal-school teacher, 109, 251n37
Segre, Vidal (Yehiel) Benjamin: as assistant rabbi, 100, 103, 160, 257n20; son as normal-school student, 74, 79, 100, 103; as teacher, 100, 103, 105, 257n20
Serbians, 14
Shaving on intermediate days of festivals, 157–58, 168–70, 173
Shklov (Belorussia), 246n60
Shohet, Azriel, 6
Shulhan Arukh, 106, 113, 182
Silber, Michael, 223, 273n61, 277n45, 289n21
Silesia, 15, 71
Simon, Richard, 185
Simonsohn, Shlomo, 222
Singer, Ludwig, 251n31
Small Council, 23, 50
Sofer, Moses (Hatam Sofer), 164, 184, 277n45, 284n42

Solomon of Nuremberg, 18
Sorkin, David, 6, 232n10
Sovereign dispensations, 221–22, 223
Spinoza, Baruch, 190f
State, tutelary, 8, 53, 69, 98, 204, 212. *See also* Absolutism
State Council (Staatsrat), 84, 86, 88
"State within a state," 78, 179, 252n47, 282n23
Statute of 1746, 22–23, 43f
Statute of 1771, 50–59; as dated April 19, 45; draft of, 244n44; education provisions, 100; language provision, 96; Privilege of 1771 compared with, 44–45, 57–58; on rabbi's authority, 159; reconfirmation of, 78; and *Regolamento interno religioso politico, ed economico*, 138; in Triestine Jews' petitions on May 1781 Toleration proposals, 81; Zinzendorf on, 59, 78–79, 213
Stella, Aron, 94, 255n85
Stella family, 22
Stone, Lawrence, 285n58
Stormont, Lord, 235n24
Studienhofkommission, 98
Synagogues, 23, 54, 161, 237n54
Szabo, Franz, 8, 204, 289n14

Taxes: head toll, 28, 46, 60, 85, 87; marriage tax, 77; for *Scuola Pia Normale sive Talmud Torà*, 104, 110; toleration tax, 42, 47, 56, 60, 71, 242n22
Tedeschi, Marco, 136
Tedesco, Raffael Nathan b. Rabbi Isaac, 160–63; death of, 163, 183, 276n21; elegies on Joseph II and Leopold II, 162, 207; on Frizzi-Morschene marriage, 185; on governmental confirmation of rabbis, 162–63, 170; *Indagine di qual sia tra i morali mali il peggiori*, 40, 114, 162, 240n119; on kosher meat in Trieste, 165; literary works of, 161–62; in Luzzatto-Pardo affair, 163, 178, 180, 182–84, 281n12, 283n37; as rabbi of Trieste, 23; on Sabbath observance, 167; on shaving during festivals, 168–69; as teacher and preacher, 161, 164; as teacher at *Scuola Pia Normale sive Talmud Torà*, 109, 161
Toland, John, 14
Toleration edicts: court resolution of December 19, 1781, 88; Emancipation compared with, 7, 70, 82, 196, 216–23; for Galician Jews, 71, 152–53, 273n61; and Jewish worship in Vienna, 247n76; for Jews, 67–72; Jews affected by, 4–5, 95; for Lower Austria, 71, 73, 93, 250n27; for Lutherans, Calvinists, and Greek Orthodox, 66–67; Maria Theresa's policy contrasted with, 63; moral dimension of utility in, 212–13; official responses to reports on May 1781 proposals, 83–90; as opening salvo of Joseph II's policy, 138; premises of, 203; privileges compared with, 220–21; and Triestine exceptionality, 90–94, 152–54; Triestine Jews' petitions on May 1781 proposals, 79–83; for Vienna, 71, 73, 93, 250n27; Zinzendorf as supporting, 89; Zinzendorf on May 1781 proposals, 73–79, 84–86, 218–19
Toleration tax, 42, 47, 56, 60, 71, 242n22
Torah: Formiggini on study of, 125–26; *Fraterna di Talmud Torà, ò sia Errudimento Religiosa*, 23, 31, 157, 239n84, 257n21; Italian rabbis on study of, 127–31; in *Scuola Pia Normale sive Talmud Torà* curriculum, 106; Wessely on study of, 119, 127–31
Transylvania, 42
Treves, David d'Isach, 162
Treves family, 21f
Trieste: becomes Habsburg domain, 10; centralizing absolutist state in, 8, 12; commerce setting tone of, 199; Commercial Intendancy headquartered in, 12; competing with Venice and Hamburg, 16; before the eighteenth century, 10; elementary education in, 98–101; as free port, 3, 10–18; French occupations of, 172, 220, 280n97; geographical location of, 2, 10f; human resources of, 13; immigration to, 15–16; infrastructure of, 13; insurance industry in, 17, 29, 32; manufacturing in, 17; merchants attracted to, 13–14; multiplicity and diversity in, 2; newness of the port, 200–201; obstacles to development in, 13; old city walls destroyed, 10, 12; as Philadelphia of Europe, 39; as politically Habsburg but culturally Italian, 2, 120; population growth in eighteenth century, 15; Protes-

tants in, 43, 60, 66–67, 76, 94, 217; as *Provincia Imperiale Commerciale*, 12; as receptive to Enlightenment and Haskalah, 3, 198; roles of, 1; the state as prime agent in, 4; transit commerce as specialty of, 16–17. *See also* Commune of Trieste; Jews of Trieste; Patriciate
Trivialschule, 98, 112, 113
Tucker, Josiah, 76
Turks, *see* Ottoman Empire
Tuscany, 61f, 247n80
Tutelary state, 8, 53, 69, 98, 204, 212. *See also* Absolutism

Ueber die buergerliche Verbesserung der Juden (Dohm), 70
United States, 217
Università degli Ebrei in Trieste, 20, 155. *See also* Jewish community of Trieste as formal organization
University of Padua, 19, 84, 132, 157
Usury, 53, 74–75
Utility: civil integration linked to, 210–13; of Jews in port cities, 28, 63, 75, 199–200; Joseph II's utilitarianism, 65–66, 68–69, 75, 89; Maria Theresa's utilitarianism, 203; morality linked to, 40, 62, 115, 211–13

Vaad katan, 23, 50
Venice: Charles VI's navigation policy as challenging, 11; *Gazzetta del mondo*, 224; Jewish school curriculum in, 108, 132; Jews emigrating to Trieste from, 21; Jews expelled from countryside of, 21, 24ff; Trieste as rival and successor to, 1, 232n7; Trieste as within sphere of influence of, 10; Trieste beginning to compete with, 13, 16; Wessely appeals to Jews of, 122
Ventura, Moses, 168
Verbesserung, *see* Civil improvement
Verona, 122, 147–48
Verona, Raffael, 170
Vienna: central European culture reaching Trieste via, 120; centralizing absolutist state in, 8; housing restrictions abolished, 139; Jewish privileges in, 19; Jews of, 42, 56f, 60, 69, 246n63, 247n76; Protestant worship in, 43; Toleration edict for, 71, 73, 93, 250n27; and Trieste, 10, 199
Vital, Jacob, 103
Vital, Samuel, 32
Vitale, Benjamin Kohen, 129
Vivante, Aron, 31, 239n90
Vivante, Leon, 31, 255n78
Vivante family, 21, 28
Voltaire, 210

Wessely, Hartwig (Naftali Herz Weisel): appeal to Trieste, 119–23; *Divrei shalom ve-emet*, 119f, 122ff, 127–31, 264n3; *Ein mishpat*, 124, 127, 264n3; on Galligo letter to Mendelssohn, 259n40; Italian campaign for, 124–33, 213–14; on Italian Jews, 120, 122, 200; on Joseph II's Toleration policy, 68; *Rav tuv le-vet Yisrael*, 120–21, 122, 264n3, 265n11; *Rehovot*, 264n3; and *Scuola Pia Normale sive Talmud Torà*, 108, 134–36; on trade and culture, 247n84
Wheaton, Robert, 287n82
Wolf, Gerson, 245n46
Women: pregnant brides, 192; private education for girls, 111f; repudiation of a wife, 185–86, 284n50; as teachers of Judaica to young children, 100; Triestine school for, 99

Yagel, Abraham, 261n55
Yiddish, 236n48

Zinzendorf, Karl von: in *Borsa* leadership dispute, 33–39, 85–86, 88–89; as consummate Josephinian bureaucrat, 89–90; diaries of, 239n96; and education, 99, 101ff; as governor of Trieste, 33, 89; on Kaunitz and the Toleration edict for Jews, 250n20; on Protestants in Trieste, 43, 66, 76; on Statute of 1771, 59, 78–79, 213; Toleration policy supported by, 89; and Toleration proposals of May 1781, 73–79, 84–86, 218–19; on Triestine Jews contacting Mendelssohn, 102, 133; and Triestine Jews' petitions on May 1781 proposals, 79, 81, 83
Zipperstein, Steven, 6, 215

Library of Congress Cataloging-in-Publication Data

Dubin, Lois C.
The port Jews of Hapsburg Trieste : absolutist politics and enlightenment culture /
   Lois C. Dubin.
      p.   cm. — (Stanford studies in Jewish history and culture)
   Includes bibliographical references and index.
   ISBN 978-0-8047-7603-5 (pbk)
      1. Jews—Italy—Trieste—History—18th century.   2. Jews—Legal status,
laws, etc.—Italy—Trieste—History—18th century.   3. Haskalah—Italy—Trieste.
4. Trieste (Italy)—Ethnic relations.   I. Title.   II. Series.
DS135.I85T735   1999
945'.393004924—dc21   98-43111

Original printing 1999

The authorized representative in the EU for product safety and compliance is:
Mare Nostrum Group
B.V Doelen 72
4831 GR Breda
The Netherlands